music directory

CANADA

FIFTH EDITION

National Library of Canada Cataloguing Data
Music Directory Canada

'83-
Bi-annual.
ISSN 0820-0416
ISBN 0-9691272-5-I
1. Music--Canada--Directories.
ML21.C3M87 780'.25'71 C83-030994-2

Publisher: Jim Norris
Editors: Andrew Charron, Richard Allen
Research: Andrew Charron, Julian Kanarek
Cover and Interior Design: Christopher Offen for Whitney Graphics
Production: Scott Lonergan, Darren Macartney, Donna Barber, Colleen Donohue, Lori Pengelley, Robyn Lisa Burn, Ed Velasquez, Katherine Whitney
Advertising Sales: Jim Norris, Melinda Donohoe, Jeff Stiles
Printed in Canada by Gagne Printing Ltd., Louisville, PQ.
Published by CM Books, a division of Norris-Whitney Communications Inc., 3284 Yonge St., Toronto, Ontario M4N 3M7 (416) 485-1049

CONTENTS

FOREWORD

This fifth edition of *Music Directory Canada* is our biggest ever. Nearly a year of research, mailing, telephoning, editing and production was required to make this edition twenty percent bigger, more comprehensive and more informative than the last. The result of offering the most complete music reference guide in Canada was well worth the effort.

The sources of information for the directory were wide and varied. Numerous companies, organizations, associations, publishers, and individuals generously provided the means by which we contacted many of the 5000-plus entries listed in this book.

The wording in each entry is for the most part that of the individual who submitted the information. All listings are free of charge and in no way constitute a recommendation, approval or endorsement by the publisher.

The directory is organized in two major sections. The first comprises fifty-three categories of companies, individuals and services, and the second, an appendix, consists of six categories of historical, bibliographical and classified information which serve as a "yellow pages" of the Canadian music industry.

The categories of each section are listed alphabetically. Within each category, entries are listed in a variety of ways. In the first section, entries are arranged alphabetically within each category and within each province, as the case may be (each province would also then be listed alphabetically, eg. *Booking Agencies*). Two categories, *Night Clubs* and *Radio Stations*, are divided into provinces and also municipalities. The categories of the second section are arranged as follows: *Award Winners* are listed first by ceremony (eg. Junos) and then by award (eg. Best Band); *Artists Contacts* are listed alphabetically, and *Schedule of Events* chronologically; *Selected Discography* is arranged alphabetically, first by the name of the group or artist and then by the title of the recording; each book title of the *Suggested Reading* section is listed alphabetically under each heading (eg. Instructional, Technical, etc.), and a directory of all respective publishers follows in a separate subsection; finally, *Two Decades of Canadian Chart Toppers* gives a chronological listing of the top Canadian albums and singles from 1970 to 1989.

Two new categories have been added to the Directory. The first, *Music Services*, includes a variety of companies that provide such new services as special touring arrangements, market information and referrals. The second, *Ticket Agencies*, lists not only the major networks but also single-location offices which serve a number of halls and venues on a municipal basis.

The Canadian music industry is one of rapid growth and change, and *Music Directory Canada* seeks to reflect this state and answer to the needs of the many musicians and businesses who perpetuate that growth. We therefore try to be as representative of Canada's musical spectrum as possible in the interest of meeting these responsibilities. If you, your company, artist, event or organization were not listed in this year's edition and would like to be listed in the next one, please send your name, address and a brief description of your activities to our office.

We would like to send out our sincere and warm thanks to all those who generously shared their time, knowledge and information resources in helping to make *Music Directory Canada* a continuing success.

Andrew Charron
Richard Allen
editors

ACOUSTIC CONSULTANTS

Acouscience Inc.
83 Trenton
Montreal, PQ H3P 1Z1
(514) 733-2988
Services Provided: Architectural acoustics and noise control.
Specialization: Studio design.

Acoustical Services Canada
212 Fern
Toronto, ON M6R 1K4
(416) 530-4423
Services Provided: Architectural and environmental acoustics, TDS analysis, studio design.

Acoutherm Insulation Ltd.
19 Passmore Ave., Unit 18
Scarborough, ON M1V 4T5
FAX (416) 299-7783
Services Provided: Manufacturing of acoustical materials for recording studios.

ARCOS Acoustical Consulting Ltd.
1400 Kensington Rd. N.W., Suite L400
Calgary, AB T2N 3P9
(403) 283-1191
Services Provided: Consulting services in architectural acoustics and sound control. Acoustical design of theatres, recording studios and rehearsal rooms. Also, noise and vibration isolation, acoustical measurements and improvements to existing spaces and facilities.

9

Barron, Kennedy, Lyzun & Associates Ltd.

145 W. 17 St., Suite 250
N. Vancouver, BC V7M 3G4
FAX (604) 988-7457
Services Provided: Room acoustics and extraneous noise isolation for control rooms, performance and rehearsal spaces, and recording and broadcast studios. Also, electro-acoustic and sound system design and on-site noise surveys and feasibility studies.
Comments: Longest-established and largest acoustical consultants in Western Canada. Has amassed considerable experience in design of live performance, broadcast and recording facilities.

Bota Consulting Ltd.

174 Colonnade Rd., Suite 22
Nepean, ON K2G 7J5
(613) 226-2262
FAX (613) 226-5420
Services Provided: Consultation, research and development plus hardware sales and servicing.
Comments: Teleconferencing service bureau.

DSE Production Equipment and Services Ltd.

P.O. Box 8043, Stn. F
Calgary, AB T2J 2V2
(403) 287-2496
Services Provided: Speaker systems for concert halls, recording studios, churches and theatres.
Specialization: TEF analysis.

Danaudio Inc.

33 Mayer St., Suite 318
Ste. Therese, PQ J7E 4T3
(514) 430-1994
Services Provided: Electro-acoustic consulting and engineering.
Specialization: Studio design, treatment, isolation, plus equipment installation and repair.
Clients: Marko Studios, Cinar Films, Bell Canada.

Digital Ears

24 Erindale Ave.
Toronto, ON M4K 1R9
(416) 463-5830
Services Provided: Custom audio equipment design, installation and repair.
Specialization: Design and installation of quality microphone pre-amps, parametric equalizers, power amps and monitor speakers.
Clients: Umbrella Sound, Doug Koch Cinematography Inc., Michael Philips.

Doyle Custom Enclosures

52 Budworth Dr.
West Hill, ON M1E 3H8
(416) 755-9101
Services Provided: Selection and design of public address systems, studio monitoring, stage monitoring and DJ installations.

Enertek

112 Forge Rd. S.E.
Calgary, AB T2H 0S8
(403) 253-1031
FAX (403) 252-5362
Services Provided: Professional A/V services.
Specialization: Sales, service, design and installation of professional audio, video, lighting, CCTV, lasers, paging systems and controllers. Rentals available.
Comments: Clients include nightclubs, arenas, cultural centres, studios, restaurants, family amusement centres, theatres, and engineered homes.

GERR Electro-Acoustics Ltd.

363 Adelaide St. E.
Toronto, ON M5A 1N3
(416) 868-0528
FAX (416) 868-6419
Services Provided: Assistance in the designing of recording studios and theatres.

Group One Acoustics

1538 Sherway Dr.
Cooksville, ON L4X 1C4
(416) 896-0988
Services Provided: Acoustic consultation and design.
Specialization: Architectural acoustics for public buildings, studios, theatres and broadcast facilities.

HFP Acoustical Consultants Ltd.

10201 Southport Rd. S.W., Suite 1140
Calgary, AB T2W 4X9
(403) 259-3600
FAX (403) 259-4190
Services Provided: Acoustic designs for practice rooms, radio stations, TV stations and recording studios.
Specialization: Acoustics and noise control.

JDB Sound Acoustics Inc.

63 Lockerbie Ave.
Weston, ON M9N 3A3
(416) 241-4240
Services Provided: Acoustical enhancement.
Specialization: Living rooms, control rooms and churches.

Kay Consultants

3065 Matis
Montreal, PQ H4R 1A4
(514) 332-2106

Labbe Interiors Ltd.

11508-119 St. N.W.
Edmonton, AB T5G 2X7
(403) 454-6585
FAX (403) 452-1959
Services Provided: Acoustic consultation for ceilings and wall panels.

Long Audio Consultants

P.O. Box 323, Stn. K
Toronto, ON M4P 2G7
(416) 489-5242

Mecart

110 de Rotterdam
St. Augustin, PQ G3A 1T3
(418) 878-3584
FAX (418) 878-4877
Services Provided: Noise control.
Specialization: Insulation for modular and pre-assembled buildings.

Neil Muncy Associates Ltd.

109 Fieldwood Dr.
Scarborough, ON M1V 3G3
(416) 293-3835

P. Mundie and Associates Ltd.

160-3300 boul. Cavendish
Montreal, PQ H4B 2M8
(514) 488-9581
FAX (514) 488-9066
Services Provided: Architectural acoustics; architectural and mechanical noise control; electronic systems.
Specialization: Radio, TV and recording studios; film projection theatres, exhibit systems.

Night Life Music Services

Heffley Creek, P.O. Box 1
Kamloops, BC V0E 1Z0
(604) 578-7956
Services Provided: Public address facilities and mobile music services.
Specialization: Conventions.

Donald Olynyk

8403-87 St., Suite 201
Edmonton, AB T6C 3G8
(403) 465-4125
Services Provided: Acoustical consulting.
Specialization: Architectural acoustics and noise control.

Ontario Acoustic Supply

139 Bentworth Ave.
Toronto, ON M6A 1P6
(416) 787-0271
FAX (416) 787-9788
Services Provided: Supplier of ceiling tiles and wall panels.

Pacific Sound and Signal

2851 Simpson Rd., Suite 100
Richmond, BC V6X 2R2
(604) 270-6010
FAX (604) 270-0841
Services Provided: Installation of sound systems and manufacturing of loudspeakers.
Specialization: Home A/V systems.

Pilchner Associates Acoustical Planners and Contractors

66 Beech Ave., Unit 10
Toronto, ON M4E 3H4
(416) 698-4023
Services Provided: Complete turnkey services available for the design and implementation of recording studios and broadcast facilities.
Specialization: Development of all technical drawings and specifications; project management, acoustic evaluation and renovation of existing facilities, design and installation of all electroacoustic systems, quantity surveying and construction.
Clients: Command Post, Fanshawe College, North Hero.

Gert A. Rutters

Main P.O. Box 5110 .
Vancouver, BC V6B 4A9
(604) 731-8850
Services Provided: Sound design, production supervision, quality control.
Specialization: Theatrical and industrial installations, touring and permanent.
Recent Clients: Vancouver Playhouse and the North Vancouver Centennial Auditorium.

Silentec Ltd.

785 Plymouth, Suite 304
Montreal, PQ H4P 1B2
FAX (514) 731-1282
Services Provided: Designing and building of recording studios, concert halls and conservatories.
Specialization: All aspects of sound and vibration control related to building structures.

Tacet Engineering Ltd.

111 Ava Rd.
Toronto, ON M6C 1W2
(416) 782-0298
FAX (416) 785-9880
Services Provided: Architectural acoustics plus designing of performance and recording rooms.

Philip Tiddings, P.Eng.

16 Wilkins Ave.
Toronto, ON M5A 3C3
(416) 867-3978
Services Provided: Audio systems designer and project manager.

Valcoustics Canada Ltd.

30 Wertheim Ct., Unit 25
Richmond Hill, ON L4B 1B9
(416) 764-5223
FAX (416) 764-6813
Services Provided: Architectural acoustics, sound system specifications and noise and vibration control.
Specialization: Valcoustics has been providing consulting services for theatres, cinemas and broadcast studios for over 30 years.
Clients: IMAX Systems, Douglas Cardinal, Safdi.

Vibron

1720 Meyerside Dr.
Mississauga, ON L5T 1A3
(416) 670-4922
FAX (416) 670-1698
Services Provided: Architectural acoustics, noise and vibration control, environmental and plant noise.

ARTWORK AND GRAPHICS

ART-TEC Records & Tapes
(Graphic Art Division)
323 Talbot St., 2nd Floor
St. Thomas, ON N5P 1B5
(519) 633-6518
FAX (519) 633-6518
Services Provided: Logo and album cover design and typesetting. Computer graphics with full colour scanning and separations.
Specialization: Record, CD and cassette cover design.
Comments: Don Baker, Toronto representative (416) 924-2386; Tony Mariano, Southwestern Ontario representative (519) 676-8939.

d'Anjou et Poirier Inc.
P.O. Box 5418, Stn. B
Montreal, PQ H3B 4P1
(514) 731-3397
Services Provided: Design, illustration and photography for posters and record jackets.
Clients: Kebec Disc, Spec d'ici, Falco.
Comments: Won the 1982 Felix award for Best Record Cover.

Apple Communication Corporation
7321 Victoria Park, Unit 10
Markham, ON L3R 2Z8
(416) 940-0662
FAX (416) 447-5550
Services Provided: Graphic design, copywriting, typesetting, photography and photostats.
Specialization: Graphic design, typesetting and copywriting.
Clients: TD Bank, Honeywell Ltd., Hunt Canada International.
Comments: Print brokers.

Art Effects
1028 Hamilton St., Suite 403
Vancouver, BC V6B 2R9
(604) 681-7739
Services Provided: Design and illustration for posters, ads, logos, and album covers.
Specialization: Airbrush illustration and creative design.
Clients: Bruce Allen Talent, Lou Bair Management, Axis Mime Theatre.

Berkeley Studios Ltd.
155 Withrow Ave.
Toronto, ON M4K 1C8
(416) 465-6825
Services Provided: Consulting, design, public relations, finished art and printing.
Clients: CBS Records, Norstar Entertainment, CBS Fox Video.

Biserka Photografix
25 Liberty St., Suite 102
Toronto, ON M6K 1A6
(416) 537-7790
Services Provided: Photo sessions on location or in studio. Also provides graphic layout.
Specialization: Can design and do graphic work for album covers and posters. Specialization in airbrushing for backgrounds and colouring B&W photos.
Clients: *Canadian Composer, Music Scene, Vital Sines.*

Heather Brown Design
201 Madison Ave., 2nd Floor
Toronto, ON M5R 2S6
(416) 967-9131
Services Provided: Art direction, illustration and design.
Comments: Five-time Juno nominee for Dalbello, Luba, Strange Advance and Robotman. Also album jackets for Helix.

Jerry Brown Designs Ltd.
123 York St.
Fredericton, NB E3B 3N6
(506) 454-3626
FAX (506) 458-2617
Services Provided: Logos, promotional packages including posters, record covers, programs, buttons, pins and stationery.

Bureau One Communications Ltd.
10336-121 St.
Edmonton, AB T5N 1K8
(403) 482-7466
FAX (403) 482-6064
Services Provided: Advertising, public relations and graphic design.

Cochrane & Cassidy Design Ltd.
12760 Bathgate Way, Suite 2
Richmond, BC V6V 1Z4
(604) 276-0838
FAX (604) 276-0551
Services Provided: Graphic design, photo-mechanical art techniques and illustration.
Specialization: Design.

Coventry Design Studio
31 Ingersoll Cr.
Regina, SK S4T 5Y9
(306) 949-5409
Services Provided: Complete commercial artwork and graphic design service.
Specialization: Finished illustration.

Creative Thinkers
1220 W. 6 Ave., Suite 101
Vancouver, BC V6H 1A5
(604) 736-9796
FAX (604) 731-5870
Services Provided: Creative graphic design and marketing consultation.
Specialization: Printed imagery.
Clients: VU13 Vancouver, ATV Halifax, North Shore Studios.

Dimension Display
66 King St., Suite 300
Winnipeg, MB R3B 1H6
(204) 943-7551
Services Provided: Exhibits and displays, corporate identity.
Specialization: Local representative for laser companies.
Comments: A one-stop creative house for designing and presenting the image of a musician, entertainer or actor. Also involved in cross-promotions with corporate sponsorships and merchandising.

Disada Productions
5788 Notre-Dame-de-Grace Ave.
Montreal, PQ H4A 1M4
(514) 489-0527
Services Provided: Film and video production, conception and consultation, plus art graphics.
Specialization: Film animation.
Clients: Polydor, Bell Canada, Government of Canada.

Pierre Dostie Designers
185 rue Sherbrooke e.
Montreal, PQ H2X 1C7
(514) 287-1735
FAX (514) 288-7337
Services Provided: Posters, brochures, pamphlets, annual reports.

Dragonfly Promotions
3303 Coldstream
Vernon, BC V1C 1Y1
(604) 545-7283
FAX (604) 545-2631
Services Provided: Graphic artwork for promotional items.

Dreamsource Communications Inc.
50 West Beaver Creek Rd.
Richmond Hill, ON L4B 1G5
(416) 886-9480
FAX (416) 764-6237
Services Provided: Illustration, logo design, air-brushing and marker renderings.

Eklipse Art & Design Inc.
99 Queen St. E., Suite 500
Toronto, ON M5C 1S1
(416) 864-0811
FAX (416) 864-0276
Services Provided: A graphic design studio dealing with major advertising firms.
Specialization: Logos.

Farrace & Farrace Art & Design
22 Norfield Cr.
Rexdale, ON M9W 1X6
(416) 741-7639
Services Provided: Design artwork from concept to complete printed product.
Specialization: Album jackets, posters, brochures and promotional materials.
Clients: The Agency, 20/20 Management, Arnyard Studios.
Comments: Farrace & Farrace has been dealing in music promotion since 1980.

Fourway Graphics Ltd.
58 Queen St., P.O. Box 200
Kingston, ON K7L 4V8
(613) 546-5526
Services Provided: Art design, colour separations, final film or plates for printing, photography, record jackets and posters.

GSM Design Inc.
317 Place d'Youville
Montreal, PQ H2Y 2B5
(514) 288-4233
FAX (514) 288-3820
Services Provided: Graphic design and visual communications for museums and exhibitions.

Galactic Graphica
17 Paradise Rd. S., Unit 2
Hamilton, ON L8S 1S1
(416) 572-7474
Services Provided: CD, cassette and album artwork. All types of band and artist promotions.
Clients: Roto-Noto Records, Lynne and the Rebels, Michael Terry.

Galbraith Reproductions Inc.
201 Dufferin St.
Toronto, ON M6K 1Y9
(416) 531-6913
Services Provided: Reproduction of B&W and colour photos in quantity.

Georgia Straight
1235 W. Pender St.
Vancouver, BC V6E 2V6
(604) 681-2000
FAX (604) 681-0272
Services Provided: Layout, paste-up and illustration for posters, albums and newsletters.

Garnet Giesbrecht
575 Adelaide St. W., Suite 1109
Toronto, ON M6J 3R8
(416) 869-3793
Services Provided: Artwork and graphic design.
Clients: NOW magazine.

Graphic Design Associates
1697 Brunswick St.
Halifax, NS B3J 2G3
(902) 423-6306
FAX (902) 429-9382
Services Provided: Art Direction, design and mechanical artwork for LPs, cassettes, CDs and posters.
Specialization: Hand lettering, photo manipulation and computer imaging.
Clients: Dave MacIsaac, Susan Dibbin, McGinty.

Graphics Factory Inc.
43 Glen Rd.
Hamilton, ON L8S 3M6
(416) 527-5280
FAX (416) 527-2588
Services Provided: Typesetting, graphic design and production of camera-ready art. Experience with album jackets, liners, disc labels, logo design, brochures and publication advertising.
Comments: In-house process camera work, typesetting and assembly illustration. Also, co-ordination of colour separation work and film printing services.

Gregory Gregory Inc.
1081 River Rd.
Ottawa, ON K1K 3V9
(613) 741-4027
FAX (613) 744-0168
Services Provided: Two- and three-dimensional graphic design production.

Here's How Productions
181 Carlaw Ave., Suite 216
Toronto, ON M4M 2S1
(416) 469-8320
FAX (416) 469-0020
Services Provided: Advertising, print work.
Clients: Master's Workshop.

High Touch Communications Inc.
4480 Cote-de-Liesse
Montreal, PQ H4N 2R3
(514) 739-2461
FAX (514) 739-6121
Services Provided: Graphic artwork.

Image Ade Inc.
3855 boul. Decarie
Montreal, PQ H4A 3J6
(514) 481-0291
FAX (514) 481-6864
Services Provided: Design and photography.
Clients: PolyGram, Aquarius Records, Justin Time Records.

Infinity Graphics Ltd.
744 Dundas St. E.
Toronto, ON M5A 2C3
(416) 363-3251
FAX (416) 363-0658
Services Provided: Cassette packaging design.
Clients: Virgin Records.

JCO Communications Inc.
4091 Pheasant Run
Mississauga, ON L5L 2C2
(416) 820-6400
FAX (416) 820-9512
Services Provided: Artwork and graphic design services for the entertainment industry.
Specialization: Artwork for nightclubs, the record industry and for special events.
Clients: Vicom '90, Curzons Sporting Club, Hot Spots Network
Comments: Publishes *Hot Spots Magazine* in Toronto, Los Angeles and Atlanta. Produce nightclub reports on CHUM-FM and MAJIC 102 Buffalo.
Branch:
P.O. Box 6942
Beverly Hills, CA
90212-6942

Kerr Graphics
179 John St., 6th Floor
Toronto, ON M5T 1X4
(416) 599-5788
Services Provided: Record jacket and magazine covers.

Lawrence & Associates Ltd.
43 Powell St., Suite 303
Vancouver, BC V6A 1E9
(604) 684-0966
Services Provided: Art, graphics, photography and creative promotion.

Andre Lim Design
3060 E. 19 Ave.
Vancouver, BC V5M 2S9
(604) 434-6019
Services Provided: Commercial and advertising design services including consultation, illustration, art direction, photography and photographic direction.
Comments: Worldwide assignments.

Matrix Design Studios
67 Mowat Ave., Suite 344
Toronto, ON M6K 3E3
(416) 537-2845
Services Provided: Designs for logos, record and cassette jackets, and point of purchase displays. Also design and manufacturing of custom T-shirts, sweats and stationery.
Clients: Attic Records, Intrepid Records, CINRAM.
Comments: Covers for Lee Aaron, National Velvet, Spitfire Band, ABBA, Honeymoon Suite.

Multimedia Design Group Inc.
16 Beechwood, Suite 202
Ottawa, ON K1L 8L9
(613) 749-6663
FAX (613) 749-9449
Services Provided: Graphic design, advertising and public relations.
Specialization: Logos, print advertising, press releases and promotional events.

Dennis Nagy Graphic Design
40 Powell St., Suite 401
Vancouver, BC V6A 1E7
(604) 685-2641
FAX (604) 685-4143
Services Provided: Graphic design in all areas.
Specialization: Brochures, logos, pamphlets and direct mail.
Clients: Vancouver Symphony, Knowledge Network, Vancouver Cantata Singers.

Nova Design
222 Osborne, Suite 6
Winnipeg, MB R3L 1Z3
(204) 477-1404
FAX (204) 477-4068
Services Provided: Advertising, consulting and graphic design.

Nubar Graphics
59 Comstock Rd.
Scarborough, ON M1L 2G6
(416) 752-6161
Services Provided: Film, printing and system retouching.

O'Mara & Ryan Ltd.
2897 Bellevue Ave.
West Vancouver, BC V7V 1E7
(604) 926-9155
FAX (604) 926-9152
Services Provided: Complete marketing services including photography, graphic design and art direction. Firm also provides music video production and direction.
Specialization: Concepts for creative marketing in the music industry.
Clients: A&M Records, MCA Records, Bruce Allen Talent, S.L. Feldman & Associates.

John Ortner Photography and Design
53 Regal Rd.
Toronto, ON M6H 2J6
(416) 656-6919
Services Provided: Photography, design and creative concepts. Full design work to finished product.
Specialization: Creative photography.
Clients: Rus Lee, S.P.I. Productions, *Metropolis* magazine.
Comments: Will work hand-in-hand with the art director to build a concept and creative image.

Peak Productions
P.O. Box 433
Westport, ON K0G 1X0
(613) 273-2818
Services Provided: Complete album and cassette packaging and design service. Artist publicity and promotion, graphics and photography.

Pinpoint Design Studio
430 King St. W., Suite 107
Toronto, ON M5V 1L5
(416) 979-5800
FAX (416) 979-8574
Services Provided: Artwork for ads, brochures and corporate identity programs. Also designs for logos, books and stationery. Additional services include packaging designs, logos, and designs for books and stationery.

Plum Studios Inc.
70 Villarboit Cr., Unit 7
Concord, ON L4K 4C7
(416) 660-2491
FAX (416) 660-2492
Services Provided: Album design, graphics and photography.

Pro Motion
P.O. Box 5663, Stn. L
Edmonton, AB T6L 4G1
(403) 437-4803
Contact: Al MacKechnie.

Promart

740A William
Montreal, PQ H3C 1P1
(514) 954-1308
FAX (514) 954-1309
Services Provided: Merchandising and
promotional concepts, plus graphic design and
production of visual communications.
Specialization: Large format images including
indoor/outdoor banners, backlit signage and
posters. Promart also designs point of purchase
promotional materials and advertising specialties.
Clients: Panda International, Cirque Chinois,
Montreal International Jazz Festival, CBS
Disques.
Comments: Promart is an integrated, one-stop
production facility.

Raeber Graphics Inc.

88 DeBates St.
Winnipeg, MB
(204) 661-2865
FAX (204) 663-9368
Services Provided: Design, layout and
production.

Reactor Art & Design

51 Camden St.
Toronto, ON M5V 1V2
(416) 362-4245
FAX (416) 362-1913
Services Provided: Illustration and design.

riff raff

28 Burgess Ave.
Toronto, ON M4E 1W7
(416) 691-6534
FAX (416) 691-9769
Services Provided: Graphic arts including
advertising, packaging, biographies and posters.
Specialization: Two-colour advertising with fast
turnaround.
Clients: Virgin Canada, CBS Music Products
Inc., Alert Music.
Comments: 10 years in the Canadian music
industry.

Rock Design

P.O. Box 1056, Stn. B
Montreal, PQ H3B 3K5
(514) 933-5950
FAX (514) 933-5951
Services Provided: Comprehensive services
for two- and three-dimensional design of printed
material, exhibitions and architectural graphics, as
well as complete visual identity programs. Rock
Design also offers historic period illustrations and
visual references from, among others, the following fields: music, medicine, natural sciences,
technology, cartography, topography, trades and
daily life.

Rudnicki-Murphy Advertising Inc.

1498 Lower Water St.
Halifax, NS
(902) 421-1500
FAX (902) 425-5719
Services Provided: Professional graphic de-
sign and advertising.

Silver Quill Graphics Ltd.

318 Homer St., Suite 801
Vancouver, BC V6B 2V3
(604) 685-5832
Services Provided: Custom logos and graphic
design.
Specialization: Promo kits, albums and
posters.
Clients: Grescoe Communications, Industrial
Revolution, Environmental News Service (ENS).

Skerret Communications Ltd.

165 Portland St.
Dartmouth, NS B2Y 1J2
(902) 463-8822
FAX (902) 464-7980

Sound Path Productions Ltd.

1100 Invicta Dr., Unit 20
Oakville, ON L6H 2K9
(416) 842-1743
FAX (416) 849-3886
Services Provided: Complete graphic design
and layout of corporate logos, brochures, album
jackets and promotional literature.
Specialization: Custom packages for all needs.

Specktrom Graphics

207 West Hastings St., Suite 206
Vancouver, BC V6B 1H7
(604) 681-3029
FAX (604) 683-5357
Services Provided: Computer graphics and
artwork for tickets, flyers, posters and laminated
passes.
Clients: Club Soda, Twilight Zone, Sagacity
Publishing.

The Stanford Group

1681 Bayview Ave., Suite 101
Toronto, ON M4G 3C1
(416) 483-9341
FAX (416) 483-9434
Services Provided: Graphic design to camera-ready art, film and printing.
Specialization: LP, cassette and CD design plus video jackets and ads.
Clients: Sabian Cymbals, Quality Special Products.
Comments: Paul Weldon, art director.

Stirling Ward Photographic Design

1020 Hamilton St.
Vancouver, BC V6B 2R9
(604) 687-3554
FAX (604) 683-8145
Services Provided: Photographic illustrations.

Studio 3

10107-115 St., Suite 203
Edmonton, AB T5K 1T3
(403) 482-3333
FAX (403) 488-3966
Services Provided: Promotional materials plus record jacket and poster designs.

Topix Computer Graphics and Animation Inc.

217 Richmond St. W.
Toronto, ON M5V 1W2
(416) 971-7711
FAX (416) 971-6188
Services Provided: On-line/off-line, video special effects and two- and three-dimensional animation.
Specialization: Producing computer graphics and animation for TV.
Clients: CBC, Vickers & Benson, Sears Canada.
Comments: Largest computer graphics and animation house in Canada.

Tri-Colour Studios

779 Prince St., P.O. Box 1703
Truro, NS B2N 1G7
(902) 893-4442
FAX (902) 893-4442 (days only)
Services Provided: Desk-top publishing, graphic design and paste-up.
Specialization: Computer publishing.
Clients: Greco Pizza Restaurant, Bridgestone.
Comments: Five years in computer publishing. Complete audio and video broadcast studio production. Training in computer publishing.

Ullrich, Schade and Associates Ltd.
1445 W. Georgia St., Suite 400
Vancouver, BC V6G 2T3
(604) 669-1180
Services Provided: Complete design, photography, illustration and production of album covers, as well as promotional packages for recording artists and new releases of albums.

Whitney Graphics
3284 Yonge St.
Toronto, ON M4N 3M7
(416) 485-8292
FAX (416) 485-8924
Services Provided: Start-to-Finish graphic design. Complete in-house production facility, including illustration, copywriting, and photography.
Specialization: Magazines, CDs & cassettes, posters, logos, catalogs, media kits, direct mailers and print advertising.
Clients: *Canadian Musician* magazine, Canadian Music Centre, Roland/Rhodes Canada, Music Industries Association of Canada (MIAC).

Windmill Printers Ltd.
1350 Clark Dr.
Vancouver, BC V5L 3K8
(604) 254-8448
Services Provided: Printing.
Specialization: Posters and stationery.

Zed Graphic Communications Inc.
2110 Bonin St.
Montreal, PQ H4M 1A3
(514) 331-2419
FAX (514) 331-7757
Services Provided: Logo, ad, brochure, album cover and poster designs.

Zeppelin Graphics Inc.
620 King St. W.
Toronto, ON
(416) 364-4146
FAX (416) 364-5398
Services Provided: Creation and production of posters for film theatres.

ASSOCIATIONS

Alberta Choral Federation
10136-100 St., Suite 608
Edmonton, AB T5J 0P1
(403) 428-1096
Date Established: 1972.
Aims and Objectives: To promote choral singing throughout Alberta. The Federation sponsors choral festivals and promotes research and composition in the field of choral music.
Membership Criteria: Payment of dues.
Number of Members: 638.
Membership Fees: $25 individual, $30 institutional, $10 student.
Membership Benefits: Newsletter, discounts and a choral lending library.

Alberta Recording Industry Association
9738-51 Ave., Suite 202
Edmonton, AB T6E 0A6
(403) 437-1362
Aims and Objectives: To promote Alberta talent, and to educate by means of workshops, seminars and competitions.
Membership Fees: $20 individual, $100 corporate.
Comments: The association's aim is to foster Canadian content in the music industry.

Algoma Arts Festival Association
P.O. Box 536
Sault Ste. Marie, ON P6A 5M6
(705) 949-0822
Date Established: 1972.
Aims and Objectives: To promote interest in, and study of, the arts (music in particular).
Number of Members: 350.
Membership Fees: By donation.
Membership Benefits: Income tax receipt, advance notice of performances and pre-box office selection of seats.
Comments: Annual presentation of the Algoma Fall Festival, September/October.

Alliance of Canadian Cinema, Television and Radio Artists (ACTRA)
2239 Yonge St.
Toronto, ON M4S 2B5
(416) 489-1311
FAX (416) 489-1435
Date Established: 1963.
Aims and Objectives: To represent performers and writers in film and broadcasting in negotiation of collective agreements, and to make representations to the government concerning cultural industries.
Membership Criteria: Probationary membership granted on first engagement; full membership after a set number of professional engagements.
Number of Members: 12,235.
Mandate: Negotiating of minimum fees and conditions; administering an insurance and retirement savings plan, contributed to by the producers; and lobbying for a greater number of Canadian productions.

ASSOCIATIONS

Alliance for Canadian New Music Projects

20 St. Joseph St.
Toronto, ON M4Y 1J9
(416) 963-5937
Date Established: 1967, incorporated 1978.
Aims and Objectives: To encourage music students to study, enjoy and perform the music of their own time and country. The alliance sponsors Contemporary Showcase, a biennial non-competitive festival of adjudications, workshops and concerts.
Membership Criteria: Teachers, performers and others interested in promoting the goals of the ACNMP.
Number of Members: 50.
Membership Fees: Free.
Membership Benefits: Members enjoy an alliance with an organization that has gained a high profile across the country.
Comments: The Contemporary Showcase syllabus, which includes graded music in 28 different disciplines, is available on request.

Alliance des Chorales du Quebec

4545 ave. Pierre-de-Coubertin
P.O. Box 1000, Stn. M
Montreal, PQ H1V 3R2
(514) 252-3020
FAX (514) 251-8038
Date Established: 1975.
Aims and Objectives: Development of choral music and representaion of choirs in the province of Quebec.
Membership Criteria: Choirs having a minimum of four singers.
Number of Members: 132 choirs.
Membership Fees: $25 individual, $195 corporate.
Membership Benefits: Newsletter every two months, discounts on music scores purchased through the alliance and participation in special music events.

American Federation of Musicians of the United States and Canada (A.F. of M.)

75 The Donway West, Suite 1010
Don Mills, ON M3C 2E9
(416) 391-5161
FAX (416) 391-5165
Date Established: 1896.
Aims and Objectives: To unite all local unions of musicians and, regardless of race, creed or national origin, the individual musicians who form such local unions of the A.F. of M. into one grand organization for the purpose of general protection and advancement of their interests. The federation seeks to enforce good faith and fair dealing as well as consistency with union federation principles.
Membership Criteria: Must be a musician.
Number of Members: Approximately 30,000 in Canada.
Membership Fees: Varies from local to local.
Locals:
Belleville Federation of Musicians
Local 357
R.R. 1 Carrying Place
Belleville, ON K0K 1L0
(613) 962-5880
(613) 477-2003
Contact: Mr. Norman Post, secretary.

Brantford Musicians' Association
Local 467
105 Wellington St.
Brantford, ON N3T 2M1
(519) 752-7973
Contact: Mr. George Rose, secretary.

Brockville Musicians' Association
Local 384
P.O. Box 398
Brockville, ON K6V 5V6
(613) 342-5181
(613) 342-5032 Emergency
(613) 342-8276 Emergency-President
Contact: Mr. Richard Crotty, secretary.

Calgary Musicians' Association
Local 547
630-8 Ave. S.W., Suite 703
Calgary, AB T2P 1G6
(403) 264-6610 or 261-0783
(403) 247-2650 Emergency.
Contact: Mr. Ray Petch, secretary.

Cape Breton Musicians' Association
Local 355
226 Charlotte St., P.O. Box 1812
Sydney, NS B1P 6W4
(902) 539-8631
(902) 564-4676 Emergency.
Contact: Mr. Ivan Melanson, secretary.

Chatham Federation of Musicians
Local 582
P.O. Box 521
Chatham, ON N7M 5K6
(519) 354-6307
Contact: Mr. Bill Mankiss, secretary.

Cornwall Musicians' Guild
Local 800
2012 Pitt St., P.O. Box 11
Cornwall, ON K6H 5R9
(613) 933-2377
(613) 933-0357
Contact: Mr. Bradley Lewis, secretary.

Edmonton Musicians' Association
Local 390
10026-105 St., Room 202
Edmonton, AB
(403) 422-2449 or 424-9924
(403) 454-3053 Emergency.
Contact: Mr. Eddy Bayens, secretary.

Halifax Atlantic Federation of Musicians
Local 571
6307 Chebucto Rd.
Halifax, NS B3L 1K9
(902) 422-6492,3,4
(902) 422-1451 Emergency (page 479).
(902) 868-2284 Emergency.
Contact: Mr. Peter J. Power, President

Hamilton Musicians' Guild
Local 293
20 Jackson St. W., Suite 408
Hamilton, ON L8P 1L2
(416) 525-4040
Contact: Mr. James Begg, secretary.

Huntsville Musicians' Association
Local 682
P.O. Box 1977
Huntsville, ON P0A 1K0
(705) 789-8108
Contact: Mr. Steve Michell, secretary.

Kingston Musicians' Union
Local 518
181-1/2 Division St.
Kingston, ON K7K 3Y9
(613) 542-3732
(613) 546-2090
Contact: Mr. Richard Baldwin.

Kitchener Central Ontario Musicians' Association
Local 226
125 Union St. E.
Waterloo, ON N2J 4E5
(519) 744-4891
Contact: Mr. Doug Janke, secretary.

London Musicians' Association
Local 279
1069 Wellington Rd. S., Suite 105
London, ON N6E 2H6
(519) 685-5888
Contact: Mr. Ron Shadbolt, secretary.

Newfoundland-Labrador Musicians' Association
Local 820
P.O. Box 1876, Stn. C
St. John's, NF A1C 5R4
(709) 739-7103
Contact: Mr. John Barela, President

Niagara Falls Musicians' Association
Local 298
6881 Lundy's Lane
Niagara Falls, ON L2G 1V7
(416) 357-4642
Contact: Mrs. Leah Ann Kinghorn, secretary.

North Bay Musicians' Association
Local 458
P.O. Box 1371
North Bay, ON P1B 8K5
(705) 474-8458
(705) 472-0943
Contact: Mr. Norm Mauro, secretary.

Ottawa-Hull District Federation of Musicians
Local 180
485 Bank St.
Ottawa, ON K2P 1Z2
(613) 235-3253
Contact: Mr. Robert Langley, secretary.

Peterborough Federation of Musicians
Local 191
P.O. Box 1935
Peterborough, ON K9J 7X7
(705) 743-3309
(705) 292-8151 Emergency.
Contact: Mr. Steve Stretten, secretary.

Quebec Musicians' Guild
Local 406
1000 St. Antoine St. W., Suite 615
Montreal, PQ H3C 3R7
(514) 876-1100
FAX (514) 876-1106
Contact: Mr. Claude Landry, secretary.

Regina Musicians' Association
Local 446
2835-13th Ave., Suite B
Regina, SK S4T 1N6
(306) 352-1337
Contact: Mr. Brian Dojack, secretary.

Sarnia Musicians' Association
Local 628
851 Ratlaw Dr.
Sarnia, ON N7V 2W9
(519) 542-9304
(519) 542-1872
Contact: Mr. Norman Stewart, secretary.

Saskatoon Musicians' Association
Local 553
2310 Preston Ave.
Saskatoon, SK S7J 2E9
(306) 477-2506
(306) 382-3170
Contact: Mr. Michael Millar, secretary.

Sault Ste. Marie Musicians' Association
Local 276
285 Wilson St.
Sault Ste. Marie, ON P6B 2K6
(705) 254-2210
Contact: Mr. Paul Leclair, secretary.

St. Catharines Musicians' Association
Local 299
187-1/2 Church St.
St. Catharines, ON L2R 3E8
(416) 688-0273
Contact: Mr. Stephen Boyuk, secretary.

St. John New Brunswick Musicians' Association
Local 815
82 Germain St., 2nd Floor, Suite 6
Saint John, NB E2L 2E7
(506) 652-6620
Contact: Bernadette Hedar, secretary.

St. Thomas Federation of Musicians
Local 633
6 Sinclair Ave.
St. Thomas, ON N5R 3A8
(519) 633-3730
Contact: Mr. Richard Butterwick, secretary.

Stratford Musicians' Association
Local 418
P.O. Box 329
St. Marys, ON N0M 2V0
(519) 284-1288
(519) 284-3255
(519) 271-1362
Contact: Mr. Ronald Coulthard, secretary.

Sudbury Federation of Musicians
Local 290
1453 Laurentian Village
Sudbury, ON P3E 2M5
(705) 522-6439
Contact: Mr. Doug Dandeno, secretary.

Thunder Bay Musicians' Association
Local 591
P.O. Box 1053, Stn. F
Thunder Bay, ON P7E 4Y1
(807) 622-1062
Contact: Mr. Ernie Slongo, secretary.

Timmins Musicians' Association
Local 817
67 Pine St. S.
Timmins, ON P4N 2K1
(705) 264-9500
(705) 235-3105 Emergency
Contact: Mrs. Patricia Totten, secretary.

Toronto Musicians' Association
Local 149
101 Thorncliffe Park Dr.
Toronto, ON M4H 1M2
(416) 421-1020
Contact: Ms. Hazel Walker, secretary.

Vancouver Musicians' Association
Local 145
925 W. 8 Ave., Suite 100
Vancouver, BC V5Z 1E4
(604) 737-1110
FAX (604) 736-9023
Contact: Mr. Wayne Morris, secretary.

Victoria Musicians' Association
Local 247
485 C. Garbally Rd.
Victoria, BC V8T 2J9
(604) 385-3954
Contact: Mr. Paul Sparrow, secretary.

Windsor Federation of Musicians
Local 566
76 University Ave.
Windsor, ON N9A 5N7
(519) 258-2288
Contact: Mr. Gerry Brannagan, President

Winnipeg Musicians' Association
Local 190
167 Lombard Ave., Suite 238
Winnipeg, MB R3B 0T6
(204) 943-4803
Contact: Mr. Cornelius Godrl, secretary.

ARRAYMUSIC
343A Albany Ave.
Toronto, ON M5R 3E2
(416) 532-3019
Date Established: 1971.
Aims and Objectives: To perform, promote and commission contemporary Canadian music.
Membership Benefits: ARRAYMUSIC subscribers are entitled to a season poster, discount tickets and advance notice of all events.
Comments: ARRAYMUSIC is a performing ensemble of professional musicians dedicated to the interpretation and performance of Canadian contemporary music.

Arts Dunnville Cultural Association

P.O. Box 264
Dunnville, ON N1A 2X5
(416) 774-6033 (a.m.)
(416) 774-6526 (p.m.)
FAX (416) 774-9322
Date Established: 1988.
Aims and Objectives: To encourage, co-ordinate and promote activities related to the performing and/or creative arts within the town of Dunnville, and to provide local children with educational opportunities.
Membership Criteria: Members must be over 18 years of age, reside in the town of Dunnville and pay the dues of the association.
Number of Members: 13.
Membership Fees: $5.
Membership Benefits: Advance notice and re-duced rates for concerts or series package. Other benefits include a newsletter and an annual meet-ing.
Comments: This is a new, inexperienced but enthusiastic group that has hosted the Toronto Mendelssohn Choir, the Royal Brass Quintet, the Elmer Iseler Singers and the Tudor Singers of Montreal. In June 1990 the association will help the Dunnville Community Theatre produce its first play after a six-year period of inactivity.

Association for Native Development in the Performing and Visual Arts

9 St. Joseph St., Suite 204
Toronto, ON M4Y 1J6
(416) 972-0871
Date Established: 1974.
Membership Criteria: All who support the objectives of the association.
Number of Members: 530.
Membership Fees: $10.
Membership Fees: Newsletter, discounts for events.

Association des Professeurs du Conservatoire du Quebec

270 rue St. Amable
Quebec, PQ G1R 5G1
(418) 643-2190

Association of Canadian Orchestras

56 The Esplanade, Suite 311
Toronto, ON M5E 1A7
(416) 366-8834
FAX (416) 364-3311
Date Established: 1972.
Aims and Objectives: To assist in the devel-opment of Canadian orchestral life through the protection and enhancement of the artistic, administrative and financial health of its member orchestras.
Membership Fee: $35 individual, $20 stu-dents, $65 organizations, $125 corporations. For orchestra rates call the secretariat.
Membership Benefits: Newsletter, publications discounts and discounts on conferences and workshops.

Association of Canadian Women Composers

20 St. Joseph St.
Toronto, ON M4Y 1J9
(416) 239-5195
Date Established: 1980.
Aims and Objectives: To promote the performance of works by women composers (particularly Canadian women composers). The association also provides a support network for Canadian women composers.
Membership Criteria: Open to composers and supporters of serious classical music.
Number of Members: 75.
Membership Fees: $30 active, $25 affiliate/associate, $15 student composer.
Membership Fees: Quarterly newsletter and opportunities for performance.

Association of Cultural Executives

720 Bathurst St., Suite 503
Toronto, ON M5S 2R4
(416) 535-2858
Date Established: 1976.
Aims and Objectives: ACE is dedicated to the development of professional cultural executives and to the management of Canada's cultural resources.
Membership Criteria: Full membership is open to those individuals who carry the administrative and/or programming responsibilities of a recognized cultural organiza-tion or who are acknowledged as part of the management team.
Number of Members: 500.
Membership Fees: $150 full, $125 associate, $35 student.
Membership Benefits: ACE News (monthly newsletter), Cultural Executive Employment Exchange (monthly position listing), plus guideline employment contract, portable health benefits package, legal benefits fund.

AMNAQ (Association Musique Nouvel Age Quebec) Inc.

P.O. Box 640, Stn. Desjardins
Montreal, PQ H5B 1B7
(514) 327-6172
Aims and Objectives: AMNAQ is a new age music association which is organizing a conference in Montreal slated for September 1991.

ADISQ (Association Quebecoise de l'industrie du disque, du spectacle et de la video)

3575 St. Laurent, Suite 706
Montreal, PQ H2X 2T7
(514) 842-5147
FAX (514) 842-7762
Date Established: 1977.
Aims and Objectives: To bring together in a formal organization artisans and participants in the record, video and show business industries. The association also fosters the national and international development of Quebecois talent and represents its members' interests before all levels of government.
Membership Criteria: Members must be involved in the Quebec arts industry.
Number of Members: 500.
Membership Fees: $500 full corporate, $350 associate corporate, $60 academy.
Membership Benefits: *Informadisq*, a quarterly newsletter, group purchase program, group insurance, information services, promotional portfolio.

l'Atelier lyrique de l'Opera de Montreal

1008 Ste. Catherine e.
Montreal, PQ H2L 2G2
(514) 842-8436
FAX (514) 521-8751
Date Established: 1984.
Aims and Objectives: Training of young professional singers and other opera-related professionals.
Membership Criteria: Apprentices are chosen through auditions and must be Canadian citizens or landed immigrants, under 30 years of age and must demonstrate solid musical and vocal knowledge.
Number of Members: Can vary between 10 and 16.
Membership Fees: Apprentices receive a stipend of approximately $350 per week for a 40-week contract.

The Atlantic Canadian Composers' Association

Faculte des Arts, Universite de Moncton
P.O. Box 48
Moncton, NB E1A 2E9
(506) 858-4041
Date Established: 1979.
Aims and Objectives: To promote and assist in securing performances and recordings for the music of composers based in Atlantic Canada.
Membership Criteria: Completion of formal training, plus recommendation by two members, or by submission of works to committee.
Membership Fees: $30.
Membership Fees: Newsletter, eligibility to submit works for performance consideration and inclusion in the *Handbook of Atlantic Canadian Composers*.
Comments: Interested in applicants that compose serious concert music.

Bach-Elgar Choral Society

Hamilton Place, P.O. Box 2080, Stn. A
Hamilton, ON L8N 3Y7
(416) 527-5995
FAX (416) 521-0924
Date Established: 1905.
Aims and Objectives: To serve the community by providing choral symphonic music.
Membership Criteria: Vocal audition prior to membership.
Number of Members: 120.
Membership Fees: $85.
Membership Benefits: Professional voice training and performing experience.
Comments: This is a concert performance organization.

British Columbia Music Educators' Association

1734 Evelyn St.
North Vancouver, BC V7K 1V1
(604) 985-5722
Date Established: 1960.
Aims and Objectives: To promote the arts (music) as an essential component of basic education and to champion excellence in music instruction in all provincial schools.
Membership Criteria: Music educators and those interested in music education.
Number of Members: 860.
Membership Fees: $20 BC Teachers' Federation member, $40 non-BCTF member.
Membership Fees: Members receive two journals and four newsletters per year plus access to various services.

The Calgary Association of Professional Disc-Jockeys

928-7 Ave. N.E.
Calgary, AB T2E 0N8
(403) 276-8534
FAX (403) 287-3926
Date Established: April 1987.
Aims and Objectives: To promote dance music in Alberta.
Membership Criteria: Members must be practicing DJs. For record pool service, members must represent an established dance club.
Number of Members: 36.
Membership Fees: No membership fee. Record pool service charges vary according to courier charges ($40-60 per month).
Membership Benefits: Newsletters, chart service, record discounts and technical assistance.

Calgary Youth Orchestra Society

4825 Richard Rd. S.W.
Calgary, AB T3E 6K6
(403) 240-6839
Date Established: 1957.
Aims and Objectives: To provide talented young musicians with the finest possible training in orchestral performance. To generally promote appreciation of the orchestral repertoire.
Membership Criteria: By competitive audition.
Number of Members: 75.
Membership Fees: $200.
Membership Benefits: Workshops, clinics, coaching, performance opportunities and international tours.

The Canada Council

99 Metcalfe St., P.O. Box 1047
Ottawa, ON K1P 5V8
(613) 237-3400
FAX (613) 598-4390
Date Established: 1957.
Aims and Objectives: The Canada Council is an independent agency created by the Parliament of Canada to foster and promote the arts. The council provides a range of grants and services to professional Canadian artists and arts organizations in music.
Comments: Programs include tour assistance, funding for commissioning works and sound recordings, and grants for formal studies.

Canadian Academy of Recording Arts & Sciences (CARAS)

124 Merton St., 3rd Floor
Toronto, ON M4S 2Z2
(416) 485-3135
FAX (416) 485-4978
Date Established: 1975.
Aims and Objectives: CARAS is a non-profit organization established primarily for the purposes of administering the Juno Awards, a Canadian awards system which recognizes and celebrates achievements in recorded music. The awards are broadcast annually on national TV.
Membership Criteria: Open to individuals employed in the music and recording industries. Applications are accepted from individuals only, not from companies or organizations.
Number of Members: 1,300 members across Canada.
Membership Fees: $45.
Membership Benefits: Voting privileges for annual Juno Awards and discounted awards show tickets with preferential seating. Also, a quarterly newsletter, discounts on the industry's major trade magazines and industry-related products and services worth over $200. Members may also purchase mail order recordings by Canadian artists at half price.

The Canadian Aldeburgh Foundation

34 Glenallan Rd.
Toronto, ON M4N 1G8
(416) 481-1964
Date Established: 1975.
Aims and Objectives: To assist young qualified Canadian singers and string players to attend master classes at the Britten-Pears School for Advanced Musical Studies in Aldeburgh, England.
Number of Members: Approximately 100.
Membership Fees: $25.
Membership Benefits: Advance information and priority booking for the Aldeburgh Festival and other events at the Snape Maltings.

CAMMAC (Canadian Amateur Musicians)

P.O. Box 353
Westmount, PQ H3Z 2T5
(514) 932-8755
Date Established: 1952.
Aims and Objectives: To promote, encourage, stimulate and support the study, knowledge and practice of music. Established expressly for amateur musicians.
Number of Members: 1,500.
Membership Fees: $25 standard, $13 students, $12 seniors.
Membership Benefits: Newsletter and workshops.
Comments: CAMMAC operates a summer music centre in the Laurentians and a similar centre north of Toronto.

Canadian Association of Festivals and Events

P.O. Box 398, Stn. A
Ottawa, ON K1N 8V4
(613) 230-1552
FAX (613) 230-2153
Date Established: 1981.
Aims and Objectives: To provide a national, pro-Canadian organization which supports the aims of various provincial and territorial festival and event associations.
Membership Criteria: Must be a festival or event producer, supplier or government agency.
Number of Members: 500.
Membership Fees: $25 festival and event, $100 associate.
Membership Benefits: Data resources, newsletter, annual conference and networking.

Canadian Association of Music Libraries

395 Wellington St.
Ottawa, ON K1A 0N4
(613) 996-3377
FAX (613) 996-4424
Date Established: 1971.
Aims and Objectives: To encourage the development of music libraries; to initiate and participate in projects dealing with music and musical resources; to co-operate with organizations concerned with music in all aspects.
Number of Members: 143.
Membership Fees: $25 individuals.

Canadian Association of Youth Orchestras

The Banff Centre, P.O. Box 1020
Banff, AB T0L 0C0
(403) 762-6278
FAX (403) 762-6444
Date Established: 1974.
Aims and Objectives: To provide ongoing support and aid in the development of Canadian youth orchestras. The association also organizes the Canadian Festival of Youth Orchestras and provides training opportunities for youth orchestras in all regions of Canada.
Number of Members: 40 orchestras.
Membership Fees: $50 orchestra, $25 affiliate, $15 individual.
Membership Benefits: NOTES (newsletter), plus regional youth orchestra workshops, a biennial national festival and repertoire manual.

Canadian Association for Music Therapy

P.O. Box 2132
Sarnia, ON N7T 7L1
(519) 337-5592
Date Established: 1977.
Aims and Objectives: To promote the use and development of music therapy in the treatment of persons suffering from emotional, physical or mental handicaps.
Membership Criteria: Any person trained in music therapy.
Number of Members: 216.
Membership Fees: $60 active voting, $25 associate, $15 students.
Membership Benefits: Quarterly newsletters, printed proceedings of annual conference and membership directory.

The Canadian Band Association (Ontario) Incorporated

21 Tecumseh St.
Brantford, ON N3S 2B3
(519) 753-1858
Date Established: 1934.
Aims and Objectives: To promote and develop the musical, educational and cultural values of bands in Canada.
Membership Criteria: Band enthusiasts, players, teachers and composers.
Number of Members: 130.
Membership Fees: $25 standard, $50 commercial.
Membership Benefits: General information concerning bands, band music, personalities and advertising.

Canadian Conference of the Arts

189 Laurier Ave. E.
Ottawa, ON K1N 6P1
(613) 238-3561
FAX (613) 238-4849
Date Established: 1945.
Aims and Objectives: To strengthen public support and enhance public awareness of the role and value of the arts through research promotion and consultative activities.
Membership Criteria: Any person or organization interested in furthering the aims of the CCA.
Number of Members: Over 1,000.
Membership Fees: Varies according to budget of organization.
Membership Benefits: Newsletter, *Arts Bulletin* and *Artsnews*. Also, discounts on CCA publications and an annual conference.
Comments: The CCA is a national, non-profit association administered by a 23- member board of governors representing artists from across Canada.

Canadian Country Music Association

833 The Queensway, Suite 102
Toronto, ON M8Z 5Z1
(416) 252-1025
FAX (416) 252-9998
Date Established: 1976.
Aims and Objectives: CCMA is a federally chartered, non-profit organization. Its objectives are to further the interests of all segments of the Canadian country music industry.
Membership Criteria: Applicants must be directly and substantially involved in the field of country music.
Number of Members: 1,200.
Membership Fees: $35.
Membership Benefits: Quarterly newsletter, vote in Canadian Country Music Awards, and advance information on Country Music Week.

Canadian Disc Jockey Association

P.O. Box 163, Malton Postal Stn.
Mississauga, ON L4T 3B5
(416) 755-3898
Date Established: 1977.
Aims and Objectives: To promote the image of DJs in Canada, and to promote public awareness and quality standards.
Membership Criteria: Must be a professional DJ.
Number of Members: 160.
Membership Fees: $150.
Membership Benefits: Monthly newsletter, seminars, workshops, back-up service.

Canadian Federation of Music Teachers' Associations

812 Haig Rd.
Ancaster, ON L9G 3G9
(416) 648-4711
Date Established: 1935.
Membership Criteria: Music Degree from recognized university or school of music.
Number of Members: 3,200.
Membership Benefits: Quarterly magazine.
Comments: President: Prof. Matt Hughes, School of Music, Acadia University, P.O. Box 182, Wolfville, NS B0P 1X0.

Canadian Folk Music Society

P.O. Box 4232, Stn. C
Calgary, AB T2T 5N1
(403) 230-0340 (editor and mail order service)
(306) 652-9801 (president)
Date Established: 1956.
Aims and Objectives: To encourage the study, appreciation and enjoyment of Canadian folk music; to promote the publication and performance of Canadian folk music, and; to stimulate international understanding through a common interest in folk music.
Membership Criteria: Interest in Canadian folk music.
Number of Members: 859.
Membership Fees: $10 student/senior, $20 institution.
Membership Benefits: Quarterly magazine, annual journal, discounts on records, cassettes and books by mail.
Comments: The society has over 300 titles of records, books and cassettes available through mail order. The society publishes the *Canadian Folk Festival Directory* as well as magazines.

Canadian Independent Record Production Association (CIRPA)

144 Front St. W., Suite 330
Toronto, ON M5J 2L7
(416) 593-1665
Date Established: 1975
Objectives: To represent its membership to the recording industry, the press and the public of Canada and the world in a forceful and impressive manner. The association actively supports the growth of Canadian talent and acts as a forum for the gathering, discussion and dissemination of information relating to the recording industry.
No. of Members: 150
Membership Fee: $350 affiliate, $150 associate, $350-1000 voting based on gross annual sales of the company applying.

Canadian League of Composers

20 St. Joseph St.
Toronto, ON M4Y 1J9
(416) 964-1364
Date Established: 1951.
Aims and Objectives: To maintain the highest standards of musical composition and to foster a general appreciation for contemporary music. The league also encourages the establishment of scholarships in musical composition.
Membership Criteria: Applicants should show evidence of talent, musical integrity and ongoing professional activity.
Number of Members: 201.
Membership Fees: $50.
Membership Benefits: Newsletter.

Canadian Music Centre

20 St. Joseph St.
Toronto, ON M4Y 1J9
(416) 961-6601
FAX (416) 961-7198
Date Established: 1959.
Aims and Objectives: The centre collects, re-produces, promotes, records and distributes the music and recordings of its associate composers. The centre also works with Canadian and international musicians, conductors, educators and other creative artists and groups, and produces the Canadian recording label Centrediscs.
Membership Criteria: Selection process by jury.
Number of Members: 296.
Membership Benefits: Services as rendered by the centre.
National Headquarters and Branch Offices:
Executive Director: Simone Auger
National Office: Chalmers House
Ettore Mazzoleni Library
20 St. Joseph St.
Toronto, ON M4Y 1J9
(416) 961-6601
FAX (416) 961-7198
National Librarian: Mark Hand

430 rue St. Pierre
P.O. Box 300
Montreal, PQ
H2Y 2M5
(514) 849-9176
Regional Director: Mireille Gagne

Violet Archer Library
911 Library Tower
2500 University Dr. N.W.
Calgary, AB T2N 1N4
(403) 220-7403
FAX (403) 282-6837
Regional Director: John Reid

200-2021 W. 4 Ave.
Vancouver, BC V6J 1N3
(604) 734-4622
Regional Director: Colin Miles

Canadian Music Competitions Inc.

1600 Berri, Suite 3016
Montreal, PQ H2L 4E2
(514) 844-8836
Aims and Objectives: To organize Canadian competitions and provide scholarships.

Canadian Music Educators' Association

16 Royaleigh Ave.
Etobicoke, ON M9P 2J5
(416) 235-1833 or 244-3745
Date Established: 1959.
Aims and Objectives: To support and provide leadership for music education throughout Canada.
Membership Criteria: An interest in music education.
Number of Members: 3,000
Membership Fees: $20 individual, $75 corporate, $35 subscription.
Membership Benefits: *The Canadian Music Educator*, the *CMEA Newsletter*, biennial conference (1991 Vancouver), corporate members receive discounts on advertising.
Comments: CMEA is the official Canadian representative to the International Society of Music Educators.

Canadian Music Publishers Association

56 Wellesley St. W., Suite 320
Toronto, ON M5S 2S4
(416) 926-1966
FAX (416) 926-7521
Contact: David Basskin, General Manager.

Canadian Recording Industry Association

1255 Yonge St., Suite 300
Toronto, ON M4T 1W6
(416) 967-7272
FAX (416) 967-9415
Date Established: 1964.
Aims and Objectives: To foster the effective production and marketing of quality sound recordings.
Membership Criteria: Record companies, record manufacturers and recording studios.
Number of Members: 27.
Membership Fees: Information available from CRIA.

Canadian University Music Society

c/o Faculty of Music, Memorial University
St. John's, NF A1C 5S7
(709) 737-7486
FAX (709) 737-4569
Aims and Objectives: To enable Canadian university teachers to discuss common problems and to exchange scholarly ideas.
Membership Criteria: University school of music or faculty member.
Number of Members: 200 individual, 32 institutional.
Membership Fees: $15 individual, $160 institutional.
Membership Benefits: Scholarly journal, directory of members.

Celebrity Concert Society

5740 Cambie St., Suite 207
Vancouver, BC V5Z 3A6
(604) 325-0202
FAX (604) 325-4666
Date Established: 1985.
Aims and Objectives: To promote concert performances throughout British Columbia.
Membership Criteria: Attendance at one or more concerts sponsored by the Society.
Membership Fees: Local concert fee.
Membership Benefits: Cultural exposure and enrichment.

Chamber Concerts Canada

326 Brunswick Ave.
Toronto, ON M5R 2Y9
(416) 924-1766
FAX (416) 924-1951
Aims and Objectives: Chamber Concerts Canada fosters and promotes the development of chamber music through the sponsorship of festivals, special events, recording projects, and through commissioning new works by Canadian composers. Chamber Concerts Canada also produces *Musical Mondays*, an eclectic series of concerts ranging from Bach to jazz, with an emphasis on contemporary Canadian repertoire.

A Coeur Joie N-B

25 ave. Chatellerault, P.O. Box 440
Saint-Antoine, NB E0A 2X0
(506) 525-2707
Date Established: 1971.
Aims and Objectives: To promote the formation of choirs, and to organize workshops, festivals and music camps.
Membership Criteria: For choirs and small vocal ensembles.
Number of Members: Over 100.
Membership Fees: $45 per choir plus $1 per choir member.

Council for Business and the Arts in Canada

401 Bay St., P.O. Box 7, Suite 1507
Toronto, ON M5H 2Y4
(416) 869-3016
FAX (416) 869-0435
Aims and Objectives: An organization which encourages corporate support for the arts.
Membership Criteria: Must be a business corporation.
Number of Members: 125.
Membership Fees: $1,000-5,000.
Membership Benefits: *CBAC News* (newsletter) and various other publications.

Country Music Foundation of Canada Inc.

P.O. Box 7397, Stn. M
Edmonton, AB T5E 0G3
(403) 476-8230
Date Established: Incorporated 1987.
Aims and Objectives: The Country Music Foundation is a tax-exempt organization with a distinct purpose: to preserve and illuminate the rich heritage of country music. The foundation acts as a repository for information and artifacts relating to country music and its history. The foundation plans to open a museum designed to meet the needs of fans, students, journalists, filmmakers, scholars and special audiences. Exhibits will feature artifacts, costumes, musical instruments, photographs and manuscripts. The educational goal of the museum is to provide a world-class resource center for studies in contemporary and non-contemporary country music.

Deer Park Concerts

129 St. Clair Ave. W.
Toronto, ON M5V 1N5
(416) 962-3381
Date Established: 1970.
Aims and Objectives: To promote organ recitals in the Toronto area and to feature the Rathgeh memorial organ.
Membership Criteria: None.
Comments: The organization is totally voluntary and works to bring organists of the highest possible calibre to Toronto. In conjunction with this, the organization presents concerts by the Deer Park Vocal Ensemble.

The Detroit-Windsor Jazz Club

c/o Eric Gilbert
1872 George Ave.
Windsor, ON N8W 4L8
Number of Members: Approximately 350.
Comments: The club sponsors weekly Dixieland jazz sessions at the Knights of Columbus Hall, 1140 Goyeau St., Windsor, ON.

Edmonton Chamber Music Society

8359-120 St.
Edmonton, AB T6G 1X1
(403) 433-8102
Date Established: 1954.
Aims and Objectives: To present chamber concerts covering the musical range from medieval to contemporary.
Membership Criteria: None.
Number of Members: 400.
Membership Fees: $85.

Edmonton Jazz Society

10203-86 Ave., Yardbird Suite
P.O. Box 255, Sub Stn. 11
Edmonton, AB T6G 2E0
(403) 432-0428
FAX (403) 433-3779
Date Established: Incorporated 1973.
Aims and Objectives: To present quality jazz programs throughout Alberta and to increase public understanding of jazz music through educational workshops.
Membership Criteria: Open.
Number of Members: 1,100.
Membership Fees: $35 adults, $20 students/seniors.
Membership Benefits: Membership card, EJS newsletter (every six weeks), admission to the Yardbird Suite and an opportunity to sign-in up to eight guests an evening, plus special record deals and record draws.
Comments: Since September 1984, The Edmonton Jazz Society has operated the Yardbird Suite, which presents jazz all year. The Yardbird is fully licensed as a private club—the best of local, national and international jazz musicians.

FACTOR

100 Lombard St., Suite 304
Toronto, ON M5C 1M3
(416) 368-8678
FAX (416) 363-5021
Date Established: 1982.
Aims and Objectives: To assist Canadian artists with the production costs of sound recordings and videos. FACTOR also assists with the production costs of Canadian syndicated radio programs.

Federation des Associations Musicales du Quebec

4545 ave. Pierre-de-Coubertin
P.O. Box 1000, Stn. M
Montreal, PQ H1V 3R2
(514) 252-3025
FAX (514) 251-8038
Date Established: 1972.
Aims and Objectives: To bring together marching bands, majorettes and dance groups.
Membership Criteria: Must be actively involved with a marching band or dance group.
Number of Members: 5,000.
Membership Fees: $7 individual.
Membership Benefits: Group discount rates.

Federation des Harmonies du Quebec

4545 ave. Pierre-de-Coubertin
P.O. Box 1000, Stn. M
Montreal, PQ H1V 3R2
(514) 252-3026
FAX (514) 251-8038
Date Established: 1927.
Aims and Objectives: To develop and improve concert bands as cultural, educational and leisure activities; to allow greater accessibility to musical activities for Quebecers.
Membership Criteria: Concert bands, stage bands, individuals and corporations.
Number of Members: 5,022.
Membership Fees: $100 concert band, $50 all others.
Membership Benefits: Bulletins, publishing house, assistance for new groups, clinics, cultural exchange programs and travel contacts.

Federation of Canadian Music Festivals

1034 Chestnut Ave.
Moose Jaw, SK S6H 1A6
(306) 693-7087
Date Established: 1952.
Aims and Objectives: To advance, promote and develop the music festival movement in Canada, and to organize and operate a national competitive festival of music. The federation also encourages the study and practice of music, either in isolation or in conjunction with related arts.
Membership Criteria: An interest in the music festival movement in Canada.
Number of Members: 66 associate members, 30 life members, five honorary life members.
Membership Fees: $10 associate, $200 life membership.
Membership Benefits: Quarterly newsletter, *The Digest Report*; life members receive two complimentary tickets to the awards competition concert of the CIBC National Music Festival.

Georgian Bay Folk Society

P.O. Box 521
Owen Sound, ON N4K 5R1
(519) 371-2995
Date Established: 1978.
Aims and Objectives: The advancement and preservation of folk music generally and specifically to provide a forum for Canadian folk performers.
Membership Criteria: Open to all who are interested.
Number of Members: 200.
Membership Fees: $10 individuals, $15 families.
Membership Benefits: Newsletter and discounts on recordings and T-shirts. Also discounts on admission to events other than Summerfolk.
Comments: The society's main event is Summerfolk.

The Guitar Society of Toronto

9 Gibson Ave.
Toronto, ON M5R 1T4
(416) 922-8002
Date Established: 1956.
Aims and Objectives: To foster the interest in and love of the guitar by offering concerts, scholarships, competitions, commissions and publications.
Membership Criteria: Anyone interested in supporting these aims.
Number of Members: 300.
Membership Fees: $35-250, from single members to patrons.
Membership Benefits: *Guitar Toronto* magazine.

Hamilton and Region Arts Council

P.O. Box 2080, Stn. A
Hamilton, ON L8N 3Y7
(416) 529-9485
Date Established: 1969.
Aims and Objectives: A charitable organization which promotes, co-ordinates and provides the assistance necessary to stimulate cultural growth.
Number of Members: 600.
Membership Fees: $15 individual.
Membership Benefits: Publications, free meeting space, discounts on various workshops throughout the year and counselling on grant applications.

Harmony Inc.

150 Renfield St.
Guelph, ON N1E 4B2
(519) 824-5882
Date Established: 1959.
Aims and Objectives: Women united to promote and preserve barbershop music. Provides entertainment for civic and charitable purposes, and sponsors area and international chorus and quartet competitions. The group supports the Autism Society.
Membership Criteria: Available on request.
Number of Members: Approximately 2,200.
Membership Fees: $33 U.S. funds for new members.
Membership Benefits: Members receive issues of *The Key-Note* magazine and are tutored in the art of barbershop singing. Members can also be trained as directors, leaders and judges.
Comments: Awards are presented at an annual international contest and convention.

Hot Jazz Society of Vancouver

2120 Main St.
Vancouver, BC V5T 3C5
(604) 873-4131
Date Established: 1973.
Aims and Objectives: To encourage the playing of jazz, with an emphasis on works dating from the first half of this century.
Membership Criteria: Age of majority.
Number of Members: 1,200.
Membership Fees: $20.
Membership Benefits: Voting privileges, volunteer activities, eligibility for board membership and reduced admission.
Comments: The society is open Wednesday through Saturday during the evenings. This is a non-profit group and all work is done by volunteers. The society features both union and non-union musicians, but has a union agreement.

Instrumental Society of Calgary

4825 Richard Rd. S.W.
Calgary, AB T3E 6K6
(403) 240-6821
Date Established: 1975.
Aims and Objectives: To promote the live performance of instrumental music (largely classical).
Membership Criteria: None.
Number of Members: Eight.

International Foundation for the Arts

3737 Oak St.. Suite 103
Vancouver, BC V6H 2M4
(604) 736-3737
FAX (604) 736-8018
Comments: Generates funds which benefit four separate artistic and educational entities: Festival Concert Society, Johannesen International School of the Arts, the Victoria International Festival and Canada Opera Piccola.

Jazz Calgary (1982) Society

P.O. Box 2735, Stn. M
Calgary, AB T2P 3C2
(403) 233-2628
Date Established: 1974.
Aims and Objectives: To present and promote jazz music, and to encourage, foster and develop an understanding and recognition of jazz within the community.
Membership Criteria: Open.
Number of Members: 350.
Membership Fees: $20 single, $30 family, $15 student/senior.
Membership Benefits: Monthly newsletter, concert discounts and record store discounts.

Jazz City Festival Society

P.O. Box 255, Sub Stn. 11
Edmonton, AB T6G 2E0
(403) 432-7166
Date Established: 1979.
Aims and Objectives: To present the annual Jazz City International Jazz Festival which includes performances from local, national and international musicians over 10 days and features a variety of free and admission shows.
Membership Criteria: Open.
Number of Members: 400.
Membership Fees: $20 regular, $50 (sustaining with tax receipt $35).
Membership Benefits: Membership card, newsletter and identification in festival program.

Edward Johnson Music Foundation

P.O. Box 1718
Guelph, ON N1H 6Z9
(519) 821-3210
Date Established: 1957.
Aims and Objectives: Sponsors of the Guelph Spring Festival, the National Vocal Competition (every five years) and the annual Edward Johnson Music Competition.
Number of Members: 550.
Membership Fees: $35 and up.
Membership Benefits: Priority box office privileges, newsletter (*Notes from the Horn*) and early-bird discounts.

Kitchener-Waterloo Chamber Music Society

57 Young St. W.
Waterloo, ON N2L 2Z4
(519) 886-1673
FAX (519) 884-8995
Date Established: 1974.
Aims and Objectives: The society sponsors quality chamber music concerts in the Kitchener-Waterloo area. Touring artists of national and international standing are featured with occasional appearances by local professionals and amateurs.
Membership Criteria: Subscriber or donor.
Number of Members: Approximately 150.
Membership Fees: Range from $37-195.
Membership Benefits: Mailers and subscription discounts.
Comments: This volunteer organization presents approximately 50 concerts in a typical year, most of them in a large 85-seat room.

Kiwanis Music Festival of Greater Toronto Association

100 Adelaide St. W., Suite 501
Toronto, ON M5H 1S3
(416) 363-3238
Date Established: 1942.
Aims and Objectives: To administer an annual competitive music festival.
Number of Members: 60.
Membership Fees: Varies.
Comments: Syllabus available on request.

Manitoba Composers' Association

100 Arthur St., Suite 407
Winnipeg, MB R3B 1H3
(204) 942-6152
Date Established: 1982.
Aims and Objectives: To promote the creation and performance of contemporary music (especially the music of Manitobans) through concert performances and publications.
Membership Criteria: Professional composer and a resident of Manitoba.
Number of Members: 40.
Membership Fees: $25.
Membership Benefits: News bulletin, discounts and voting at general meetings.
Comments: Scores, recordings and brochures from the Manitoba Music Centre are available to musicians, scholars and teachers.

Mariposa Folk Foundation

95 Lavinia Ave., Suites 10-11
Toronto, ON M6S 3H9
(416) 769-3655
FAX (416) 769-9008
Date Established: 1961.
Aims and Objectives: To preserve and promote contemporary and traditional folk music and folk arts in Canada and the world.
Number of Members: Approximately 1,000.
Membership Fees: $30 individual, $45 family, $50 supporting, $300-500 patron.
Membership Benefits: 20% discount on festival tickets and concert admissions; 10% discount on records, tapes and books. Advance notice of all Mariposa events and a tax receipt for donations above the family membership price. The Foundation also produces a bi-monthly newsletter and runs a resource centre.
Comments: Activities include a summer festival, a free fall market in the park, a concert series, country dances, song circles and workshops. The focus is on participation.

Music and Entertainment Industry Educators Association (MEIEA)

c/o Trebas Institute
451 St. Jean St.
Montreal, PQ H2Y 2R5
(514) 845-4142
Date Established: 1978.
Aims and Objectives: To establish and maintain standards of music industry education throughout the world; to encourage contact between the educational community and the music industry; to foster interaction among people involved with music industry education; to assist institutions involved in the development of programs in music industry education; and to promote music industry-related research.
Membership Criteria: Open to anyone interested in furthering the objectives of the association.
Membership Fees: Various categories (contact MEIEA).
Membership Benefits: MEIEA *Notes* newsletter, annual conference, and networking.
Comments: MEIEA's 1990 conference is in Denver, Colorado. The 1991 conference is in Nashville. David P. Leonard, Canadian director and past president.

Music Industries Association of Canada (MIAC)

1210 Shepaprd Ave. E., Suite 109
North York, ON M2K 1E3
(416) 490-1871
FAX (416) 490-9739
Date Established: 1972.
Aims and Objectives: MIAC is a national, non-profit, trade association representing Canadian manufacturers, wholesalers and distributors of musical instruments, accessories, sound reinforcement products and published music.
Membership Criteria: Canadian manufacturers, wholesalers and distributors only.
Number of Members: 87 active members, four associate members.
Membership Fees: $350 basic fee (corporate membership).
Membership Benefits: Access to the MUSICANADA Trade Show, membership lists, product statistics, credit group, retailer lists and government/trade information.
Comments: For further information, please contact Al Kowalenko, MIAC executive secretary/secretariat manager (see number above).

Muskoka Concert Association

P.O. Box 908
Gravenhurst, ON P0C 1G0
(705) 687-2369
Date Established: 1949.
Aims and Objectives: To present fine classical concerts in the Muskoka area.
Number of Members: 410.
Membership Fees: $28.
Membership Benefits: A subscription series ticket to four or five concerts each season.

National Campus/ Community Radio Association Association Nationale des Radios Etudiantes et Communautaires

University of Guelph, Level 2 UC
Guelph, ON N1G 2W1
(519) 824-4120, ext. 8341
Date Established: 1981.
Aims and Objectives: To provide support for campus and community radio stations and to represent the interests of the organization and its members to government and business groups. The association also organizes a yearly conference.
Membership Criteria: Community or campus radio station or project.
Number of Members: 60.
Membership Fees: Range from $50-500 depending on budget.
Membership Benefits: Newsletter.

The National Professional Music Teachers' Association

483 W. 39 Ave.
Vancouver, BC V5Y 2T8
(604) 324-4415
Date Established: 1971.
Aims and Objectives: To elevate the status and improve the qualifications of all members of the music teaching profession, and to grant funds for the promotion of music.
Membership Criteria: Diploma or degree in music.
Number of Members: 37.
Membership Fees: $20-35.
Membership Benefits: Teacher/student referrals.

New Brunswick Choral Federation

Kings Place, P.O. Box 6000
Fredericton, NB E3B 5H1
(506) 453-3731
FAX (506) 453-3325
Date Established: 1979.
Aims and Objectives: To promote and encourage the art of choral music throughout New Brunswick.
Membership Criteria: Open to individuals, choirs and institutions.
Number of Members: 150.
Membership Fees: $30 for individuals. .
Membership Benefits: Quarterly newsletter, library privileges and reduced rates at workshops.

Nova Scotia Choral Federation

5516 Spring Garden Rd., Suite 304
Halifax, NS B3J 1G6
(902) 423-4688
Date Established: 1976.
Aims and Objectives: To promote the art of choral music in Nova Scotia.
Number of Members: 100 individuals, 70 choirs.
Membership Fees: $20 individual, $50 adult choir, $30 student choir.
Membership Benefits: Quarterly newsletter, access to choral library, discounts, workshops and provincial network.
Comments: NSCF receives grants from the Nova Scotia Department of Culture, Recreation and Fitness.

The Offshore International Jazz Society

P.O. Box 7213, Sandwich
Windsor, ON N9C 3Z1
Number of Members: Approximately 800.
Comments: Annual sponsors of a non-profit jazz festival and other events.

Ontario Choral Federation

20 St. Joseph St.
Toronto, ON M4Y 1J9
(416) 925-5525
FAX (416) 961-7198
Date Established: 1970.
Aims and Objectives: To encourage, support and promote participation and excellence in the choral arts throughout Ontario, and to provide representation for the choral arts in Ontario.
Membership Criteria: Open to individuals, choirs, institutions and corporations.
Number of Members: 900.
Membership Fees: $30 individual, $40 choral, $55 corporate, $15 institution.
Membership Benefits: *Choirs Ontario* newsletter, workshop grants and library score rentals.

Ontario Federation of Symphony Orchestras

56 The Esplanade, Suite 311
Toronto, ON M5E 1A7
(416) 366-8834
FAX (416) 364-3311
Date Established: 1955.
Aims and Objectives: To assist in the development of Ontario symphony orchestras, chamber orchestras and youth orchestras by providing workshops, courses and a forum for sharing concerns.
Membership Fees: $35 individual, $20 student, $65 organization, $125 corporate. For orchestra rates contact the secretariat.
Membership Benefits: Members receive a newsletter plus discounts on conferences, workshops and publications.

Ontario Guild of Piano Technicians Inc.

P.O. Box 623, Stn. B
Willowdale, ON M2K 2P9
(416) 491-3934
Date Established: 1970.
Aims and Objectives: A non-profit organization of professional craftsmen dedicated to maintaining the highest possible standards in piano tuning and servicing.
Membership Criteria: Examinations to qualify for membership.
Number of Members: 60, plus a number of associates and applicants.
Membership Fees: $100.
Membership Benefits: Monthly meetings which include technical sessions, information exchanges and dialogue between members.

Ontario Music Festivals Association

100 Adelaide St. W.
Toronto, ON M5H 1S3
(416) 363-2657
Date Established: 1972.
Aims and Objectives: To provide and promote a provincial level of competition for outstanding performers from all member festivals in the province.
Number of Members: 54 associate festivals.

Ontario Percussive Arts Society

97 Barton St.
London, ON N6A 1N1
(519) 439-0101
FAX (519) 657-2884
Date Established: 1980.
Aims and Objectives: To elevate the standards of percussion teaching and performance and to improve the general awareness of percussion-related arts. The society sponsors performances, clinics, workshops and research.
Membership Criteria: An interest in and involvement with percussion.
Number of Members: 5,500 worldwide, 200 Ontario.
Membership Fees: $40 U.S. professional, $20 U.S. student.
Membership Benefits: Quarterly magazine, monthly international newsletter and a bi-annual provincial newsletter.
Comments: The Ontario Chapter of the Percussive Arts Society is registered as a charity.

Ontario Registered Music Teachers' Association l'Association des Professeurs de Musique Enregistres de l'Ontario

63 South Marine Dr.
Scarborough, ON M1E 1A1
(519) 336-0744
Date Established: 1885.
Aims and Objectives: To promote quality music teaching throughout the province.
Membership Criteria: Applicants must have an Associate Diploma from a recognized conservatory or hold a university degree.
Number of Members: Approximately 1,400 in Ontario.
Membership Fees: Varies.
Membership Benefits: A magazine called *Notes* published three times a year. Also, the CFMTA newsletter published three times a year. The association holds an annual convention and workshops throughout the year in different centres across the province.
Comments: ORMTA is the only organization which represents Ontario's private music teachers.

Organization of Saskatchewan Arts Councils

4010 Pasqua St., Suite 600
Regina, SK S4S 7B9
(306) 586-1250
FAX (306) 586-1550
Date Established: 1968.
Aims and Objectives: OSAC is a provincial organization which represents numerous arts councils in Saskatchewan and across the country. It is a communications link for the councils, and specializes in co-ordinating events, developing new councils and funding members. OSAC members present performances, visual arts exhibitions, adjudications and special events.
Number of Members: OSAC has arts council members throughout Saskatchewan (69) as well as two affiliate members and 15 associate members.
Membership Fees: $150 member, $75 affiliate, $25 associate.
Membership Benefits: Members receive assistance with funding, the contracting of performers, and with publicity. All members receive the OSAC newsletter (printed three times per year) as well as OSAC's annual report and listings of annual performing and visual arts tours.

Pacific Music Industry Association

68 Water St., Suite 204
Vancouver, BC V6B 1A4
(604) 684-8841
FAX (604) 683-4298
Date Established: 1985.
Aims and Objectives: To stimulate employment, education and discourse throughout the music industry. The association also promotes regional talent and lobbies for a stronger voice in government and business.
Membership Criteria: Should be involved in the music industry.
Membership Fees: $40 corporate, $15 individual, $25 band or association.
Membership Benefits: Free or reduced admission to PMIA functions, a bi-monthly newsletter and industry representation.

Performing Arts Development Fund of Toronto

66 Gerrard St. E., Suite 104
Toronto, ON M5B 1G3
(416) 971-5568
FAX (416) 977-3759
Date Established: 1982.
Aims and Objectives: The Performing Arts Development Fund of Toronto is a charitable, non-profit organization dedicated to promoting the professional performing arts within Metro Toronto. Through numerous audience development campaigns, such as the Five Star Ticket program and the Special Audience Service, PADFOT endeavours to increase performing arts attendance throughout all sectors of Toronto's society.

Quebec Music Educators' Association

147 Chartwell Cr.
Beaconsfield, PQ H9W 1C2
(514) 630-1973
Aims and Objectives: To hold conferences, meetings and workshops for the discussion of matters relating to music education in Quebec.
Membership Criteria: Anyone interested in music education.
Number of Members: 50.
Membership Fees: $35 regular, $15 student, $50 corporate, $40 library, $20 retired.
Membership Benefits: Members receive journals, discounts at workshops and automatic membership in the CMEA.

The Rhythm 'n Greens Society

7249 Ashburn St.
Vancouver, BC V5S 2R6
(604) 321-7311 or 685-2644
FAX (604) 684-2590
Comments: A non-profit society for environmentally-concerned musicians. The group's goals are to provide a focus through which musicians can help promote environmental awareness and raise funds in support of "green" organizations and causes. Presently Vancouver-based. Plans are in progress for national and international representation.

Royal Canadian College of Organists

500 University Ave., Suite 614
Toronto, ON M5G 1V7
(416) 593-4025
Date Established: 1909.
Aims and Objectives: To promote high standards of organ playing, choral directing, church music and composition; to hold examinations in organ- playing, and related musical subjects; to encourage organ recitals and other musical events; to promote the welfare of church musicians.
Membership Criteria: Anyone who supports the aims of the College.
Number of Members: 1,300.
Membership Fees: $63 (approximately).
Membership Benefits: RCCO newsletter, *The American Organist*, an annual convention, job listings and resource materials.

Saskatchewan Band Association Inc.

1860 Lorne St.
Regina, SK S4P 2L7
(306) 780-9286
FAX (306) 781-6021
Date Established: 1983.
Aims and Objectives: To enhance instrumental music and the development of band programs in Saskatchewan through the provision and co-ordination of resources, programs, services and promotion.
Membership Criteria: Membership is open to all interested parties.
Number of Members: 237.
Membership Fees: $25 individual, $10 student, $200 corporate.
Membership Benefits: Newsletter, directory, *Band Journal*, CBA membership and discount rates at SBA-sponsored events.

Saskatchewan Choral Federation

1870 Lorne St.
Regina, SK S4R 2L7
(306) 780-9230
FAX (306) 781-6021
Date Established: 1978.
Aims and Objectives: To promote and assist the enhancement of choral music in the province of Saskatchewan.
Membership Criteria: All interested in furthering the objectives of the federation.
Number of Members: 400.
Membership Fees: $15 individual, $30-60 choirs.
Membership Benefits: Bulletins, member funding, workshops, ticket discounts, library services and equipment rental.
Comments: The Saskatchewan Choral Federation is a provincial cultural organization managed by a board of directors with an office staff of two.

Saskatchewan Music Festival Association

1819 Cornwall St., Suite 201
Regina, SK S4P 2K4
(306) 757-1722
Comments: Major events include 48 local competitive festivals, the SMFA Concerto Competition, the Saskatchewan National Playoffs and the SMFA provincial finals.

Saskatchewan Registered Music Teachers' Association

Regina Branch
1340 McNiven Ave.
Regina, SK S4S 3X8
(306) 586-3593
Date Established: 1925.
Aims and Objectives: To promote progressive ideas and methods related to the teaching of music; to encourage systematic preparation in the art of teaching; to foster the interest of the public; and to join with other associations having like aims and objectives.
Membership Criteria: Applicants must be 18 or over, have two years of teaching experience and hold a certificate from a recognized conservatory or school of music.
Number of Members: 58 in Regina branch, 297 in provincial association.
Membership Fees: $20 local branch, $30 provincial association.
Membership Benefits: Newsletters, student recitals, eligibility of students to receive scholarships in performance and composition.
Comments: A Regina music teachers' association was formed in 1925. Joining with other local groups, the Saskatchewan Music Teachers' Association was formed in 1930. The name was changed to the Saskatchewan Registered Music Teachers' Association in 1938 when an Act of Registration was passed in the Provincial Legislature.

Saskatoon Symphony Society

703 Hotel Bessborough, P.O. Box 1361
Saskatoon, SK S7K 3N9
(306) 665-6414
FAX (306) 664-8677
Date Established: 1931.
Aims and Objectives: To provide symphonic music.
Membership Criteria: A donation of $25 and over.
Number of Members: 300.
Membership Fees: $25 and over.

Scarborough Arts Council (formerly Arts Scarborough)

739 Ellesmere Rd.
Scarborough, ON M1P 2W1
(416) 755-2209
Date Established: 1979.
Aims and Objectives: The Scarborough Arts Council is a non-profit organization whose purpose is to promote and encourage development of the visual, literary and performing arts in Scarborough for the mutual benefit of artists and the community.
Membership Criteria: Anyone agreeing with the above.
Number of Members: 739 individuals, 65 groups.
Membership Fees: $20 individual, $20 senior/student, $45 groups.
Membership Benefits: Members receive a newspaper (mailed 10 times per year), benefits with various suppliers and free advertising of events in the council's newspaper.
Comments: At present, the Council deals mainly with individual visual artists; however, there are competitions for poets and songwriters. The winner of the songwriting competition is awarded a recording session plus a public performance.

Society for Reproduction Rights of Authors, Composers and Publishers of Canada Inc. (SODRAC)

54 rue Cour Leroyer o.
Montreal, PQ H2Y 1W7
(514) 845-3268
FAX (514) 845-3401
Date Established: 1985.
Aims and Objectives: Licensing and collection society for reproduction rights.
Membership Fees: None.

Songwriters Association of Canada

387 Bloor St. E., 5th Floor
Toronto, ON M4W 1H7
(416) 934-7664
Date Established: 1983.
Membership Criteria: Open to all songwriters.
Number of Members: 650.
Membership Fee for 1990: $35 Voting, $125 Associate.
Membership Benefits: Newsletter (*The Bridge*), workshops, song depository, song assessment.

South Side Folk Club

15016-62 St.
Edmonton, AB T5A 2B5
(403) 478-6417
Date Established: 1976.
Aims and Objectives: To promote live roots music.
Number of Members: 520.
Membership Fees: $65.
Membership Benefits: Discounts, newsletter and early admittance.

Toronto Blues Society

P.O. Box 1263, Stn. F
Toronto, ON M4Y 2V8
(416) 974-9213
Date Established: 1985.
Aims and Objectives: Promotion of blues music in the Toronto area and support for local musicians who perform blues.
Membership Criteria: None.
Number of Members: 750.
Membership Fees: $30 charter member, $15 general.
Membership Benefits: Newsletter and discounts at record stores and nightclubs.

Toronto Programmer's Association

465 King St. E., Unit 11
Toronto, ON M5A 1L6
(416) 366-7093
FAX (416) 366-3405
Date Established: 1981.
Aims and Objectives: To promote dance music and help generate record sales; to provide feedback on new releases to the respective record labels; and to report potential crossover products to radio.
Membership Criteria: Must be a DJ programming in a Toronto club on a regular basis.
Number of Members: 20.
Membership Fees: $960.
Membership Benefits: Bi-monthly newsletter, weekly dance chart, bi-monthly meeting (where record label reps discuss new material). Members also receive promotional 12-inch dance releases from major and independent record labels at no charge.

Vancouver New Music Society

206-6 Ave. E., Suite 108
Vancouver, BC V5T 1J8
(604) 874-6200
Date Established: 1972.
Aims and Objectives: To promote and encourage the performance of new music; to foster a greater interest in, and appreciation of, contemporary music; to arrange concerts and recitals of contemporary music, as well as lectures, workshops, etc.
Membership Criteria: Any person may become a member. Subscribers automatically become members.
Number of Members: Approximately 250.
Membership Fees: By donation.
Membership Benefits: Mailings, subscription information, discounts to concerts, newsletters on an irregular basis and invitations to receptions.
Comments: Concert season September-April annually. Programming is done by committee. Submissions by composers and performers are welcome and will be considered. VNMS also accepts proposals from choreographers and visual artists for multimedia work involving music.

Victoria Jazz Society

P.O. Box 542, Stn. E
Victoria, BC V8W 2P3
(604) 388-4423
FAX (604) 388-4407
Date Established: 1981.
Aims and Objectives: To present a year-round concert program (with internationally-acclaimed jazz artists), an annual international jazz festival and an annual three-day summer music festival. The society also supports regional jazz musicians.
Membership Criteria: Interest in helping to present and preserve jazz music as a recognized art form.
Number of Members: 326.
Membership Fees: $15 single, $20 couple, $25 family.
Membership Benefits: Current newsletter and discounts on select concerts.

West Coast Amateur Musicians' Society

943 Clements Ave.
North Vancouver, BC V7R 2K8
(604) 980-5341
Date Established: 1982.
Aims and Objectives: To foster and promote amateur music-making.
Membership Criteria: An interest in music.
Number of Members: 150.
Membership Fees: $25 individual, $13 senior, $12 student, $35 family.
Membership Benefits: A newsletter, access to a music library and membership list, and discounts at workshops.
Comments: The group's major activity is Shawnigan Lake Music Holiday, a music camp for adults and families to be held July 22-29, 1990 at Shawnigan Lake, Vancouver Island. Scholarships and family discounts available.

The Women's Musical Club of Toronto

27 Anderson Ave.
Toronto, ON M5P 1H5
(416) 322-7366
Date Established: 1898.
Aims and Objectives: To present chamber music concerts of a high standard in an annual five-concert series and to administer music scholarships and a biennial award given to exceptional young Canadian musicians.
Membership Criteria: An interest in chamber music.
Number of Members: Approximately 400.
Membership Fees: $50.
Membership Benefits: Opportunity to meet artists after the concert. Complimentary tea, coffee and cookies served after concerts. Most importantly: being part of a 93-year tradition of presenting music in Toronto.
Comments: Staffed by volunteers with one part-time secretary/treasurer.

ONTARIO
ARTS
COUNCIL

ONTARIO ARTS COUNCIL

The Music Office of the Ontario Arts Council offers grants to:

Chamber Ensembles
- Professional, Ontario-based groups organized on a permanent basis may be eligible for project grants.
- Full-time permanent ensembles may be eligible for operating grants.

Opera/Music Theatre
- General category: provides operating or project grants to Ontario-based professional music theatre companies, for performance activities.
- Developmental category: supports the development of new Canadian works in music theatre/opera.

Choirs
- Project grants: assist Ontario-based community choirs with professional artistic costs
- Operating grants: assist professional choirs (budgets over $100,000)

Commissioning
- Ontario-based performers (soloists or groups) can apply for a grant to commission new music from any Canadian composer.

For further information about applying, eligibility criteria and deadlines, please contact:

Music Office
ONTARIO ARTS COUNCIL
151 Bloor Street West, Suite 500, Toronto, Ontario M5S 1T6 (416) 961-1660

Youth and Music Canada/Jeunesses musicales du Canada

720 Bathurst St., Suite 501
Toronto, ON M5S 2R4
(416) 535-0660
FAX (416) 535-1024
Date Established: 1949 (in Canada).
Aims and Objectives: To promote the enjoyment of music and culture and to promote Canada's best young artists.
Membership Criteria: Purchase and present concert package of artists.
Number of Members: 40 (national), six (provincial).
Membership Fees: $4,800.
Membership Benefits: Newsletters, conferences, special events, tickets honoured in other member centres and international networking.
Comments: There are 52 member countries, the most recent of which is the U.S.S.R. There are also international exchanges including the Jeunesses Musicales World Orchestra, which was initiated by Canada in 1979. The young artists are offered performing advice and experience throughout the country and perhaps even throughout the world.

Gala de l'ADISQ

3575 St. Laurent, Suite 706
Montreal, PQ H2X 2T7
(514) 842-5147
FAX (514) 842-7762
Objectives: Televised annually, this gala recognizes Quebec artists who have excelled either on record or on the stage.
Prizes: Each winner receives a Felix trophy.
Dates & Locations: October 21, 1990 - Place des Arts, Montreal.
Deadline: June 30, 1990.

Arts Journalism Award

Canadian Conference of the Arts
189 Laurier Ave. E.
Ottawa, ON K1N 6P1
(613) 238-3561
FAX (613) 238-4849
Objectives: To recognize outstanding Canadian arts journalists.
Events & Artists: Journalists covering all arts-related disciplines.
Prizes: $1,000 cash prize and a certificate awarded to two recipients.
Dates & Locations: May 1991 - Saskatoon.
Deadline: December 31, 1990.
Comments: Members of the Canadian Conference of the Arts cast ballots to determine the winners.

Leslie Bell Prize

Ontario Choral Federation
20 St. Joseph St.
Toronto, ON M5R 2C2
(416) 925-5525
FAX (416) 961-7198
Objectives: Scholarship awarded to emerging choral conductors (aged 18-35) for further study in the field.
Prizes: $2,000.
Dates & Locations: Fall 1990 - TBA.
Deadline: August 1, 1990.

CASBY Music Awards

CFNY-FM
83 Kennedy Rd. S.
Brampton, ON L6W 3P3
(416) 453-7452
FAX (416) 453-7711
Objectives: To grant nationwide recognition to outstanding new Canadian talent.
Events & Artists: An annual televised awards dinner.
Prizes: Trophies are awarded.
Dates & Locations: Unconfirmed.
Deadline: Contact CFNY-FM.
Comments: Previously the U-Know Awards.

CMC Annual Awards

Canadian Music Council
189 Laurier Ave. E.
Ottawa, ON K1N 6P1
(613) 238-5893
Objectives: To promote (nationally and internationally) Canadian music and musicians.
Awards: CMC Medal, Artist of the Year, Composer of the Year, Firm of the Year, Media of the Year, Special Mention. The CMC also organizes the Jules Leger Prize and the Robert Fleming Prize.
Prizes: CMC Medal (a certificate), The Jules Leger Prize ($5,000), The Robert Fleming Prize ($1,000).
Dates & Locations: TBA.
Deadline: Various dates.
Comments: For further information, please contact the Canadian Music Council.

Prix de musique Calixa-Lavallee

Societe Saint-Jean-Baptiste de Montreal
82 rue Sherbrooke o.
Montreal, PQ H2X 1X3
(514) 843-8851
Objectives: To reward Quebecois(es) who have distinguished themselves in the field of music.
Events & Artists: Composers or performers of all types of music.
Prizes: $1,500 and the "Bene Merenti de Patria" medal.
Dates & Locations: June.
Deadline: February 25.

Canadian Country Music Awards

Canadian Country Music Association
833 The Queensway, Suite 102
Toronto, ON M8Z 5Z1
(416) 252-1025
FAX (416) 252-9998
Objectives: These awards are presented to honour those who have excelled as country music performers.
Events & Artists: Canadian country music artists.
Prizes: Trophies.
Dates & Locations: September 8, 1990 - Edmonton. September 14, 1991 - Calgary.
Deadline: Voting is restricted to CCMA members in good standing.

The Glenn Gould Prize

The Canada Council
99 Metcalfe St., P.O. Box 1047
Ottawa, ON K1P 5V8
(613) 598-4365
FAX (613) 598-4390
Objectives: Awarded for exceptional contribution to music through the use of any of the communications technologies.
Prizes: $50,000.

Juno Awards

Canadian Academy of Recording Arts and Sciences (CARAS)
124 Merton St., 3rd Floor
Toronto, ON M4S 2Z2
(416) 485-3135
FAX (416) 485-4978
Objectives: The Juno Awards celebrate excellence in Canadian recorded music.
Events & Artists: Annual awards open to all Canadian recording artists.
Prizes: Statuettes.
Dates & Locations: March 18, 1990 - O'Keefe Centre, Toronto. March 1991 - O'Keefe Centre, Toronto.
Deadline: November 30 (craft categories), January 7 (sales categories).

MIAC Scholarship

Music Industries Association of Canada
1210 Sheppard Ave. E., Suite 109
North York, ON M3K 1E3
(416) 490-1871
Objectives: The MIAC Scholarship is presented at the annual MusicFest Competitions.
Events & Artists: A competition for instrumentalists.
Prizes: $1,500 scholarship.
Dates & Locations: May 1990 - Winnipeg.
Comments: Contact MusicFest for more information (403) 247-2901.

Concours OSM

Orchestre Symphonique de Montreal
85 rue Ste. Catherine o., Suite 900
Montreal, PQ H2X 3P4
(514) 842-3402
Objectives: Promotion of young Canadian artists.
Events & Artists: String, wind, piano and voice categories.
Prizes: $7,500 in prizes.
Dates & Locations: Annual.
Deadline: November.
Comments: For Canadian citizens and landed immigrants only.

The Rock Express Awards

Rock Express Communications
47 Jefferson Ave.
Toronto, ON M6K 1Y3
(416) 538-7500
Objectives: National consumer ballot on the most popular albums and performances of the calendar year.
Events/Artists: Canadian and international artists.
Prizes: Gold Microphone awards.

SOCAN Awards

41 Valleybrook Dr.
Don Mills, ON M3B 2S6
(416) 445-8700
Sponsor: Society of Composers, Authors and Music Publishers of Canada.
Objectives: To honour composers, writers and publishers for the most performed songs in the areas of pop music, country and French language. Special awards are given for film music, concert music and jazz.

Toronto Arts Awards

Toronto Arts Awards Foundation
151 John St., Suite 402
Toronto, ON M5V 2T2
(416) 597-8223
Objectives: To heighten public awareness of Metro Toronto's arts and artists.
Events & Artists: Six $5,000 awards presented annually (one is for music). Also, two annual Lifetime Achievement Awards ($10,000 each).
Dates & Locations: Toronto, Ontario (dates TBA).
Deadline: Selection is by jury from nominations submitted by the general public.
Comments: Awards are open to Canadian citizens, landed immigrants or long-term Canadian residents. Nominees must have demonstrated ongoing creative excellence, and made an outstanding contribution to the arts and culture of greater Metropolitan Toronto.

Toronto Music Awards

CILQ-FM 107
2 Bloor St. E., Suite 3000
Toronto, ON M4W 1A8
(416) 967-3445
FAX (416) 924-2479
Objectives: To recognize and celebrate achievements in Toronto's music community.
Events & Artists: Music, entertainment and awards presentation broadcast live on radio.
Prizes: Statuettes.
Dates & Locations: TBA.

BOOKING AGENTS

ALBERTA

Banks Associated Music Ltd.
10310-102 Ave., Suite 305
Edmonton, AB T5J 2X6
(403) 424-0441
Preferred Musical Styles: Singles, duos,
Country Rock and casual bands, comics.
Services: Bookings only.

Barry's Pro Music Agency Ltd.
P.O. Box 526
Brooks, AB T0J 0J0
(403) 362-4204
Preferred Musical Styles: C&W.
Acts Represented: The Prisoners, Vicki Alynn,
Wilf Ducharme & Argus, Gordie West.
Venues Represented: Brooks Legion, Brooks
Hotel, Patricia Hotel.

Caldwell Entertainment Agency Ltd.
52 Castleburry Ct. N.E.
Calgary, AB T3J 1L5
(403) 285-7895
Preferred Musical Styles: Pop, MOR, C&W,
show groups.
Contact: Richard P. Caldwell.
Network Affiliations: A.F. of M., ITAA.

D&I Entertainment Agencies
36 Glacier Dr. S.W.
Calgary, AB T3E 5A1
(403) 242-3588
Contact: Irene Marjoram.

Encore Productions

P.O. Box 516, Stn. M
Calgary, AB T2P 2J2
(403) 274-1962
Contact: Judy Dalgliesh.

Fisher and Associates Music Ltd.

10525 Jasper Ave., Lower Level
Edmonton, AB T5J 1Z4
(403) 425-7500
FAX (403) 426-1392
Preferred Musical Styles: Top 40 and original recording acts.
Acts Represented: Famous Blue Raincoat, Grace Under Pressure, Blackboard Jungle.

Global Arts Inc.

11254-73 Ave.
Edmonton, AB T6G 0C6
(403) 438-2713
Contact: Josh H. Keller.

Guild Hall Productions

13427-130 St.
Edmonton, AB T5l 1M1
(403) 454-2997
Contact: Maureen Saumer.

Heritage Productions

1756-62 St.
Edmonton, AB T6L 1M6
(403) 862-8070
Contact: Miguel Neri.

Highwood Productions

P.O. Box 44
High River, AB T0L 1B0
(403) 558-3640
Contact: Keith Hitchner.

Donna Hopkins & Associates Ltd.

R.R. 1
Calgary, AB T2P 2G4
(403) 249-5255
Preferred Musical Styles: Pop, MOR, Rock, C&W, Dine & Dance.
Acts Represented: 50-100 acts, accept new acts.
Contact: Donna Hopkins.

Image Control Productions Ltd.

10852 Whyte Ave., Suite 203
Edmonton, AB T6E 2B3
(403) 433-2016
FAX (403) 439-4209
Preferred Musical Styles: Alternative, Country Rock, Rock & Roll, Reggae, Heavy Metal, Hardcore.
Acts Represented: Frank Carroll, Robb Gott and Hyrd Help, One Eyed Wendy.
Venues Represented: Fantasy Nightclub (W.E.M.), Andante, Sunset Club.

Interact Music Productions Inc.

71 Woodglen Close S.W.
Calgary, AB T2W 4M9
(403) 281-3149
Contact: Frank Scott.

International Musical Services

11714-113 Ave.
Edmonton, AB T5G 0J8
(403) 454-6848 or 454-9291
Preferred Musical Styles: Various.
Acts Represented: Kidd Country, Jenson Interceptor, Garry Lee & Showdown.
Venues Represented: The Ranchmans (Calgary), Tumbleweeds (Edmonton), Cook County (Edmonton), Desperados (Calgary).
Services: International Musical Services is a booking agency, management company and record company.

K.B.D. Enterprises Ltd.

8 Ave. S.W., Suite 630
Calgary, AB T2P 1G6
(403) 263-5480
Contact: Robert di Paolo.

Lucky Lee Agency

47 Rossland Rd. S.E.
Medicine Hat, AB T1B 2M4
(403) 526-8574
Contact: Lee Paguio.

Magnum Music Corporation Ltd.
8607-128 Ave.
Edmonton, AB T5E 0G3
(403) 476-8230
Preferred Musical Styles: Country.
Acts Represented: Catheryne Greenly, Billy Jay Legere, Cormier Country.
Affiliated Companies: Magnum Records, Ramblin' Man Music Publishing.

Maria Martell Productions
P.O. Box 5359
Edmonton, AB T5P 4C5
(403) 963-3111
Contact: Maria Martell.

Music Company
5809 MacLeod Tr. S., Suite 210
Calgary, AB T2H 0J9
(403) 259-5282
Preferred Musical Styles: All styles.
Contact: Frederick Thootenhoofd.
Acts Represented: 125, accept new acts.

Frank Pollard Entertainment Agency
1620-8 Ave. N.W., Suite 453
Calgary, AB T2N 1C4
(403) 289-9961
FAX (403) 289-0263
Preferred Musical Styles: All styles.
Acts Represented: R.D. Fisher, Ozark Mountain Daredevils (for Western Canada only).
Venues Represented: North Country Inn (Calgary), Gateway Hotel (High River).
Network Affiliations: A.F.of M.

R.O. One Talent Productions Inc.
10026-105 St., Room 202
Edmonton, AB T5J 1C3
(403) 422-2449
Contact: Alcide Gramigni.

Ann Randall Productions Ltd.
P.O. Box 5690, Stn. A
Calgary, AB T2H 1Y1
(403) 243-5431
Contact: Ann Randall Gray.

Roadside Attractions Inc.
11411-37A Ave.
Edmonton, AB T6J 0J6
(403) 438-6185
Contact: Bradley D. Welk.

The Rock Shop Entertainment
6607 Bowness Rd. N.W.
Calgary, AB T3B 0G2
(403) 247-1166
Contact: Allan Gibson.

Royalty Shows Ltd.
P.O. Box 8768, Stn. L.
Edmonton, AB T6C 4J5
(403) 467-5580
Preferred Musical Styles: C&W.
Contact: R.H. Smith.
Acts Represented: Four, accept new high-profile acts.

Stony Plain Recording Company Ltd.
9963-83 St.
Edmonton, AB T6A 3N3
(403) 468-6423
Contact: Kate Carey.

Unisphere Entertainment Agency
10333 Southport Rd. S.W., Suite 5
Calgary, AB T2W 3X6
(403) 743-0300
Contact: Peter Farnum.

Wildrose Entertainment
59 Sillak Cr., S.E.
Medicine Hat, AB T1B 2P9
(403) 526-0050
Preferred Musical Styles: Pop, MOR, Rock, C&W, 50s and 60s.
Acts Represented: Magenta, Tristan, Southeast Movement.
Venues Represented: Hotels, lounges, clubs.
Network Affiliations: A.F. of M.

BRITISH COLUMBIA

Catholine B. Egan
1315 W. 15 Ave., Suite 1
Vancouver, BC V6H 3B3
(604) 733-7827
Contact: Catholine B. Egan.

S.L. Feldman & Associates
1505 W. 2 Ave.
Vancouver, BC V6H 3Y4
(604) 734-5945
FAX (604) 732-0922
Preferred Musical Styles: Pop, MOR, Rock.
Contact: Samuel L. Feldman.
Acts Represented: 150, accept new acts.
Venues Represented: 40 venues.

Grace Germain Productions
1934 Bee St., Suite 204
Victoria, BC V8R 5E5
(604) 595-4821
Contact: Grace Elizabeth Germain.

Valley Hennell Productions
2736 W. 13 Ave.
Vancouver, BC V6K 2T4
(604) 736-7676
Contact: Valerie Hennell.

International Talent Services Incorporated
177 W. 7 Ave., 4th Floor
Vancouver, BC V5Y 1K5
(604) 872-2906
FAX (604) 873-0166
Preferred Musical Styles: Country.
Acts Represented: Ron Tarrant Band, The Marlaine Sisters, Silver City.

MPS Music Productions
P.O. Box 5666, Stn. B
Victoria, BC V8R 6S4
(604) 382-3153
Contact: Dave Paulson.

McDougall Mielnick and Associates Ltd.
1247 W. 7 Ave.
Vancouver, BC V6B 1H7
(604) 732-0321
Contact: Ingrid McDougall.

Ian McGlynn Entertainment Services
964 Bowron Ct.
North Vancouver, BC V7H 2T2
(604) 929-7851
Contact: Ian McGlynn.

More Music Entertainment
2856 Waterloo
Vancouver, BC V6R 3J3
(604) 732-7683
Contact: Bruce Messecar.

Music Unlimited (1979) Ltd.
4935 Cordova Bay Rd.
Victoria, BC V8Y 2K1
(604) 658-1111
FAX (604) 658-5111
Preferred Musical Styles: C&W, MOR.
Acts Represented: Doc & The Doo-Wops, The Kevin Erwin Band, Cactus Cats.
Network Affiliations: ITAA
Services: Service the night clubs throughout Western Canada.
Special Projects: Overseas tours (Europe and the Orient).

Overture Concerts
5740 Cambie St., Suite 207
Vancouver, BC V5Z 3A6
(604) 325-0202
FAX (604) 325-4666
Preferred Musical Styles: Classical soloists and ensembles.
Acts Represented: Arthur Polson (violinist), Vancouver Wind Trio, Cassenti Players.

Paizley Productions

P.O. Box 65751, Stn. F
Vancouver, BC V5N 5K7
(604) 255-2961
FAX (604) 255-2961
Preferred Musical Styles: Alternative,
Independent, Rock, Punk, Metal.
Acts Represented: U.K. Subs, Gwar, Toxic
Reasons.
Venues Represented: Commodore Ballroom
(Vancouver), Club Soda (Vancouver).
Services: Bookings, promotions and complete
performance production.
Special Projects: Ray Manzarek/Michael
McLure spoken words performance (Graceland,
1987).

Prairie Promotions Ltd.

9940 Lougheed, Suite 330
Burnaby, BC V3J 1N3
(604) 421-6699
Contact: Paul Mascioli.

Siegel Entertainment Ltd.

1648 W. 7 Ave., Suite 101
Vancouver, BC V6J 1S5
(604) 736-3896
FAX (604) 736-3464
Preferred Musical Styles: Pop, MOR, Rock,
C&W, Lounge, etc.

T.O.C. Talent/ Native Talent Agency

800-1115 West Georgia St.
Vancouver, BC V6E 3H4
(604) 683-4230 or 275-1696
FAX (604) 687-5519
Preferred Musical Styles: All styles.
Acts Represented: Arrows To Freedom Sing-
ers, Rick Patterson (country singer), Shaman
Singers.
Services: Public relations, promotion and
marketing.

Total Entertainment Network

68 Water St., Suite 504
Vancouver, BC V6B 1A4
(604) 689-3457
FAX (604) 689-5245.
Preferred Musical Styles: All styles.
Acts Represented: Champagne, Peter York &
the Continentals, Runaway Jukebox.
Venues Represented: Pan Pacific Hotel.

JW Whitefoot Entertainments Ltd.

5763 Oak St., Suite 18
Vancouver, BC V6M 2V7
(604) 266-7145
FAX (604) 266-1519
Preferred Musical Styles: Various.

MANITOBA

Hungry I Agency

2025 Corydon Ave., Suite 207
Winnipeg, MB R3P 0N4
(204) 489-8222
FAX (204) 489-8274
Preferred Musical Styles: Pop, Rock.
Acts Represented: The Watchmen, Harlequin,
Kenny Shields Band.

J.O.Y. Publishing Co.

209 Colony St., Suite 23
Winnipeg, MB R3C 1W2
(204) 775-2633
Contact: Eileen Marie Kovac-Buckingham.
Affiliated Companies: Key of E.

Morris Theatrical Agencies Incorporated

265 Portage Ave. Suite 406
Winnipeg, MB R3B 2B2
(204) 943-7236
Preferred Musical Styles: All.
Contact: Terry Morris.
Acts Represented: 60, accept new acts.
Network Affiliations: CART, ITAA.

Shelby Talent Agency

P.O. Box 244
Dominion City, MB R0A 0H0
(204) 427-2934
Contact: Mitzi Lee or Shelby Knox.

United Artists Productions

224 Beaverbrook
Winnipeg, MB R3N 1M8
(204) 489-3933
Contact: Warren Browne.

Zee Talent Agency Ltd.
3095 Sinclair St.
Winnipeg, MB R2P 1Y6
(204) 338-7094
Preferred Musical Styles: Rock, Country Rock, plus touring groups.
Acts Represented: The Wolf, Musiqa, Rockslyde.
Venues Represented: Local pubs, night clubs and high schools.

NEW BRUNSWICK

Atlantic Sounds Agency
333 St. George St.
Moncton, NB E1C 1W8
(506) 857-9466
Preferred Musical Styles: Mostly C&W.
Contact: Barbara Dunnville.

NOVA SCOTIA

Agency 2000
327 Prince Albert Rd., Suite 3
Dartmouth, NS B2Y 1N7
(902) 466-2000
FAX (902) 466-2200
Preferred Musical Styles: Top 40, MOR, Rock & Roll.
Acts Represented: Inbetween Days, Miss Paris, Ricochet.
Services: Booking, management, production, recording.

John Alphonse Productions Ltd.
7095 Churchill Dr.
Halifax, NS B3L 3H7
(902) 423-0656
Contact: John J. Alphonse.

Brookes Diamond Productions
World Trade and Convention Centre
1800 Argyle St., Suite 507
Halifax, NS B3J 3N8
(902) 422-7000
FAX (902) 422-2929
Preferred Musical Styles: All styles.
Acts Represented: Rita MacNeil, Joan Kennedy, John Allan Cameron.
Services: Tour co-ordination and convention entertainment.
Special Projects: Festivals, fairs, exhibitions.

Downeast Entertainment and Meeting Specialists
5663 Stairs St.
Halifax, NS B3K 2E1
(902) 423-1974
Contact: William Norton.

EMD United Artists
5 Oakwood Ave.
Dartmouth, NS B2W 3C8
(902) 434-7713
Contact: Eric McDow.

Eastern Entertainment Agency
P.O. Box 41, Site 3, R.R.5
Armdale, NS B3L 4J5
(902) 868-2440
Contact: Brian P. Doherty.

Eastern Talent International
P.O. Box 847, Stn. M
Halifax, NS B3J 2V2
(902) 423-0266
FAX (902) 423-0735
Preferred Musical Styles: Pop.
Acts Represented: Susan Dibbon, Crossfire, Magazine.
Venues Represented: The New Place Cabaret (Halifax).
Network Affiliations: A.F. of M.

Entertainment Etcetera
P.O. Box 2627, Stn. M
Halifax, NS B3J 3P7
(902) 420-0440
Contact: T.L. Buckley.

Everett Entertainment

290 Main Ave., Suite 1108
Halifax, NS B3M 3V3
(902) 422-3305
Contact: Belinda Gurnham.

Bruce Hudson Productions

P.O. Box 3250
Halifax South, NS B3J 3H5
(902) 429-7007
Preferred Musical Styles: Rock.
Contact: G.B. Hudson.

L.A. Talent Agency

P.O. Box 547
Bridgewater, NS B4V 2X6
(902) 543-1886
Contact: Lynn Anne Heisler.

F. Maillet Entertainment Agency

Site 12, P.O. Box 55, R.R. 2
Windsor Junction, NS B0N 2V0
(902) 861-3370
Contact: Francine Maillet.

Moonlight Promotions

22 York St., P.O. Box 42
Glace Bay, NS B1A 5V1
(902) 849-2344
Contact: Tanya MacIntyre.

Pepper Agency

1800 Argyle St., Suite 507
Halifax, NS B3J 3N8
(902) 422-9663
Contact: Fiona Diamond.

Razorloy Productions

16 Faulkner St.
Dartmouth, NS B3A 3A3
(902) 463-6268
Contact: John B. Smith.

T.K. Productions Ltd.

P.O. Box 8391, Stn. A
Halifax, NS B3K 5M1
(902) 423-8434
FAX (902) 422-2929
Preferred Musical Styles: Contemporary.
Acts Represented: Terry Kelly.
Services: Bookings, management and recordings.
Affiliated Companies: Gun Records Inc.

Talent Source Entertainment Coordinators Ltd.

1541 Barrington St., Suite 404
Halifax, NS B3J 1Z5
(902) 420-9550
FAX (902) 420-9558
Preferred Musical Styles: All styles.
Acts Represented: John Gracie, Paul Lawson, The Backstreet Boys.

ONTARIO

A.A.A. Entertainment Enterprises

3179 Bathurst St.
Toronto, ON M6A 2B2
(416) 783-0037
FAX (416) 787-8622
Preferred Musical Styles: All styles, traditional to rock.
Acts Represented: Attitude, The Studio Band.
Affiliated Companies: The Entertainment Co.
Services: Bookings for weddings, Bar Mitzvahs, etc. see below.
Special Projects: Planning consultation.

Aarin Entertainment Agency

P.O. Box 6112, Stn. J
Ottawa, ON K2A 1T2
(613) 726-1618
Preferred Musical Styles: Top 40.
Acts Represented: The Counter Clocks, The Paperboys, Bombay.
Services: Bookings.
Special Projects: Sub-contracting for other agencies.

Accent Agency

P.O. Box 2102
Kingston, ON K5L 5V8
(613) 542-9451
Preferred Musical Styles: C&W, Jazz, Folk,
Comtemporary.
Acts Represented: Bob Hearns Quartet, Paul
Chabot, Michael George.
Venues Represented: Downtown Hotels,
Chatz, Lucy's, others.
Services: Booking and management.

Ace International Entertainment Agency Ltd.

7 Pleasant Blvd., Suite 201B
Toronto, ON M4T 1G4
(416) 929-9305
FAX (416) 964-7076
Preferred Musical Styles: Variety, MOR,
Jazz, Show and Caribbean.
Acts Represented: Front Page, Hook & Ladder
Jazz Band, Syncona.
Special Projects: Wrestling shows.
Network Affiliations: CART.

Active Talent Agency

148 York St., Suite 224
London, ON N6A 1A9
(519) 679-0971
Contact: Brian Smith.

The Agency

41 Britain St., Suite 200
Toronto, ON M5A 1R7
(416) 365-7833
FAX (416) 365-9692
Preferred Musical Styles: Pop, MOR, Rock,
C&W.
Acts Represented: Lee Aaron, Kim Mitchell,
Glass Tiger.
Venues Represented: Clancy's Live
(Burlington), Rock 'n' Roll Heaven, The Nag's
Head.
Services: Touring and financial services.

Ron Albert Entertainment Agencies Ltd.

4600 Kingston Rd.
Scarborough, ON M1E 2P4
(416) 281-4447
Acts Represented: Lounge acts, solos, duos,
trios.
Services: Bookings.

Aldel Music

270 Evans Ave.
Toronto, ON M8Z 1J8
(416) 259-3713
Preferred Musical Styles: Various acts for
conventions.
Services: Booking.

Archie Alleyne & Associates

209 McCaffrey Rd.
Newmarket, ON L3X 1K1
(416) 773-2889
Contact: Archibald A. Alleyne.

Anderson Entertainment Agency

600 Southdale Rd. E.
London, ON N6E 1A6
(519) 685-9217
Contact: John Anderson.

Apricot Talent & Recording Industries Inc.

1449 Ridgebrook Dr., Suite 120
Gloucester, ON K1B 4T1
(613) 749-1116
FAX (613) 238-1687
Preferred Musical Styles: Top 40 Rock,
MOR, Rock, Metal.
Acts Represented: Antix, In & Out, Lexy
Jones, Johnny The Fox.
Venues Represented: Beachcomber Lounge
(Talisman), airforce bases (Ottawa),
Barrymore's (Ottawa).
Network Affiliations: CART.
Services: Booking agency.

Armstrong Entertainment

165 Ontario St., Suite 912
St. Catharines, ON L2R 5K4
(416) 684-2654
Preferred Musical Styles: Children's entertainment, weddings, bars.

Artists by Alyson Music Productions

220 Dovercourt Rd., Suite 2
Toronto, ON M6J 3C8
(416) 588-1908
Contact: Alyson Grannum.

August Music
P.O. Box 1774
Guelph, ON N1H 6Z9
(519) 763-9725
Contact: Paul E. Embro.

BBR Agency
104 Hamilton Rd.
Dorchester, ON N0L 1G0
(519) 268-7333
Preferred Musical Styles: Pop, MOR, Rock.
Acts Represented: Carmela Long, Ten Seconds Over Tokyo, Player.
Venues Represented: Gables Tavern (Grand Bend), Campbell St. Station (Sarnia).
Network Affiliations: COCA, CART.
Special Projects: Convention consultation.

BGS Music Promotions
64 Glen Manor Dr.
Toronto, ON M4E 2X2
(416) 698-0715
Preferred Musical Styles: Classical guitar, classical ensembles.
Acts Represented: Stepan Rak, Jukka Savijoki, Alan Torok, The Castellani-Andriaccio Duo, Savijoki/Helasvuo.

Gary Bailey Entertainment Agency
207 Queen St.
Port Stanley, ON N0L 2A0
(519) 782-3570
Preferred Musical Styles: Pop, MOR, 50s and 60s.
Acts Represented: Rudy Davis Band, Bustin Loose, Destiny.

Big G Enterprises
5754 Yonge St., Suite 805
Toronto, ON M2M 3T6
(416) 223-4771
Contact: Eardley A. Guthrie.

Black Arch Booking
P.O. Box 2476, Stn. B
Richmond Hill, ON L4E 1A5
(416) 773-1422
Preferred Musical Styles: Country, Country Rock, Country Blues.
Acts Represented: Ragtop Down, Julie Gibb, Kalle Rodemacker.

Brady's Booking Agency
2991 Barger Rd.
Stevensville, ON L0S 1S0
(416) 382-2349
Preferred Musical Styles: All styles.

Busker Entertainment Agency
R.R. 7
St. Thomas, ON N5P 3T2
(519) 633-6989
Preferred Musical Styles: Rock, MOR, Variety, singles to bands.
Acts Represented: Wrif Wraf.
Contact: Randy Dawdy.

C&C Entertainment
864 Eastern Ave.
Toronto, ON M4C 1A3
(416) 469-5961
FAX (416) 469-4273
Preferred Musical Styles: Pop, MOR, Classical, Variety.
Acts Represented: Liona Boyd, Nylons, Mary Wilson & The Supremes.
Venues Represented: Conventions, special events in the major hotels.
Network Affiliations: MTCVA, ISES.

CBD Enterprises
180 Duncan Mill Rd., Suite 400
Don Mills, ON M3B 1Z6
(416) 441-2144
FAX (416) 441-2259
Preferred Musical Styles: Pop, MOR, C&W.
Network Affiliations: ISES.
Services: Special event planning and consulting.

C.J.'s Entertainment Marketing Agency
38 Hubbell St.
Brockville, ON K6V 4K3
(613) 342-2599
Preferred Musical Styles: C&W, 50s, 60s, Folk, Big Band, and others.
Contact: James M. Murray.

C.O. Productions
52 Larch St.
Sudbury, ON P3E 1B9
(705) 673-5900
Contact: Nicole R. Godin.

Canadian Talent International
120 Carlton St.
Toronto, ON M5A 4K2
(416) 967-4444
FAX (416) 967-5664
Preferred Musical Styles: Pop, Rock, C&W.
Acts Represented: George Fox, Michelle Wright, Blushing Brides, Matt Minglewood.
Network Affiliations: ITAA.

Dave Caplan Entertainment

35 Canyon Ave., Suite 2009
Downsview, ON M3H 4Y2
(416) 630-1535
Preferred Musical Styles: R&B, Top 40, Jazz,
Rock & Roll.

Carlomar Productions Inc.

404 Soudan Ave.
Toronto, ON M4S 1W9
(416) 484-0258
FAX (416) 923-1277
Preferred Musical Styles: MOR, singles,
duos and bands.
Contact: Charles Rodrigues.

Carlton Enterprises

542 Edenvalley Cr.
Waterloo, ON N2T 1Y3
(519) 747-0929
Contact: Buddy Carlton.

Chicho Valley Orchestras and Agency Ltd.

1100 Eglinton Ave. E., Suite 223
Don Mills, ON M3C 1H8
(416) 445-6710
Contact: Lenore Valle.

Helen Chilcott Theatrical Agency

100 Antibes Dr., Suite 307
Willowdale, ON M2R 3N1
(416) 223-2621
Preferred Musical Styles: Pop, MOR, C&W.
Network Affiliations: A.F. of M., CART.

Christie Marketing Associates

265 Balliol St., Suite 2304
Toronto, ON M4S 1C9
Contact: Jane Christie.

Clark Agency

75 Wolfe St.
Kingston, ON K7M 1H4
(613) 546-3066
FAX (613) 542-1282
Preferred Musical Styles: Jazz.
Acts Represented: Oliver Jones, Jon
Ballantyne, Fraser MacPherson.

Classic The Show Biz People

P.O. Box 442, Stn. K
Toronto, ON M4P 2G9
(416) 481-5327
Preferred Musical Styles: Pop, MOR.
Acts Represented: Dino Grandi Band, The
Front Page Band, Hook & Ladder Jazz Band.
Services: Booking agency, sound and lighting
consultants, entertainment consultants.

Colwell Arts Management

R.R. 1
New Hamburg, ON
N0B 2G0
(519) 662-3499
FAX (519) 662-2210
Preferred Musical Styles: Classical singers
and vocal ensembles.
Venues Represented: Worldwide
representation.
Services: Management and booking of classical
soloists.

Complex Five Productions

465 Milner Ave., Unit 10
Scarborough, ON M1B 2K4
(416) 755-5523
Contact: Nick Fotes.

Concertmasters Inc.

22 Linden St.
Toronto, ON M4Y 1V6
(416) 922-9922
FAX (416) 960-6166
Preferred Musical Styles: Major classical mu-
sic attractions.
Concert Affiliations: Straightwire Digital Edit-
ing, Aaron Concert Management (Boston).

Cornerstone Entertain- ment Concepts Inc.

184 Glenview Dr.
Mississauga, ON L5G 2N6
(416) 271-7700
FAX (416) 271-7209
Preferred Musical Styles: Pop, MOR, C&W,
New Age, Classical, Jazz, Caribbean.
Acts Represented: Various.
Network Affiliations: A.F. of M.
Services: Comprehensive production and
planning of corporate events and conventions.

Country Music Connections Canada
188 Forest Ave.
Hamilton, ON L8N 1X9
(416) 528-3506
Preferred Musical Styles: C&W.
Acts Represented: Kitty Wells.
Contact: Sonny Tompkins.

Creative Arts Agency
401 Main St. W.
Hamilton, ON L8P 1K5
(416) 525-6644 or 823-4373
FAX (416) 525-8292
Preferred Musical Styles: Various (especially folk).
Acts Represented: Doug Reansbury, Jim Witter, Brent Titcomb.

Creative Entertainment
P.O. Box 473
Belleville, ON K8N 5B2
(613) 969-0446
FAX (613) 966-7933
Preferred Musical Styles: 50s, 60s, C&W.
Acts Represented: Debbie Post.
Contact: Stephen L. Graham.

Crossroads Entertainment Consultants
180 Duncan Mill Rd., Suite 400
Don Mills, ON M3B 1Z6
(416) 441-2144
FAX (416) 441-2259
Preferred Musical Styles: All kinds.
Network Affiliations: ISES, Toronto Musicians' Association.

Crystal Promotions
P.O. Box 2471
Ottawa, ON K1P 5W6
(613) 230-1524
Contact: Julie Hodgson.

DBC Ltd.
180 Duncan Mill Rd., Suite 400
Don Mills, ON M3B 1Z6
(416) 441-2144
FAX (416) 441-2259
Preferred Musical Styles: Pop, MOR, C&W.
Network Affiliations: Founding member of ISES.
Services: Special event planning and consulting.

Mike Danton Productions
1813 West Creek Dr.
Pickering, ON L1V 6K2
(416) 286-9513
Preferred Musical Styles: All styles, mainly dance bands and MOR.

Dobbin Agency
477A Princess St.
Kingston, ON K7L 1C3
(613) 549-4401
Preferred Musical Styles: Pop, MOR, Rock, C&W.
Network Affiliations: CART.

Double "D" Promotions
19 Acadia Cr.
St. Catharines, ON L2P 1H7
(416) 684-9058
Contact: Donald Hammond.

Double Time Music
7752 Jubilee Dr.
Niagara Falls, ON L2G 7J6
(416) 354-8053
Preferred Musical Styles: Pop, MOR, Rock.
Contact: Richard Richardson.

Ray Douglas Promotions
P.O. Box 7213-Sandwich
Windsor, ON N9C 3Z1
(519) 969-1203 or 258-2288
Preferred Musical Styles: MOR, Pop, C&W, Jazz, Big Band, Classical.
Acts Represented: Ray Douglas International Big Band, Joan Eastman and the Music Makers, The Kenny Crone Jazz Group.
Venues Represented: Victoria Tavern, Kozak's By The Sea Tavern, International Freedom Festival.
Network Affiliations: A.F. of M.
Special Projects: The Off Shore International Jazz Society.

ESP-Elwood Saracuse Productions Ltd.
6 Lansing Sq., Suite 129
Willowdale, ON M2J 1T5
(416) 499-7070
FAX (416) 492-4108
Preferred Musical Styles: All styles.
Acts Represented: Pharazon Dance Company, Video Hits Alive, Clazz flute and harp duo.
Network Affiliations: CAFE.
Services: Specializing in public and corporate special events.

Elmir Agency

15 Dundonald St., Suite 1903
Toronto, ON M4Y 1K4
(416) 926-1636
Contact: Alberto Gonzalo Elmir.

Elton Entertainment Agency

6 Manorhampton Dr.
Etobicoke, ON M9P 1E2
(416) 244-1500
Contact: Evelyn Mishko.

Gino Empry Public Relations and Personal Management Services Inc.

25 Wood St., Suite 104
Toronto, ON M4Y 2P9
(416) 977-1153
Preferred Musical Styles: Pop, MOR, Rock, C&W.
Contact: Gino Empry.
Network Affiliations: CART.

The Entertainment Agency

693 Bank St.
Ottawa, ON K1S 3T8
(613) 230-0704
Contact: Michael Weber.

Evergreen Talent Agency

472 Dover Place, P.O. Box 789
Port Stanley, ON N0L 2A0
(519) 782-3334
FAX (519) 631-3409
Preferred Musical Styles: Charlie Clements And The Justice Band, Dieter Boehme And The Risky Business Band, C.W. Post and Hocus Pocus.
Acts Represented: C&W, Rock.

Exclusive Management

55 Wynford Heights, Apt. 1910
Don Mills, ON M3C 1L4
(416) 449-9612
FAX (416) 792-1059.
Contact: Jerry C. Cameron.

Falcon Productions

20 Dean Park Rd.
Scarborough, ON M1B 3G9
(416) 247-7815
Preferred Musical Styles: Henry Falcon Cuesta.

Fete Accompli

133 Queen St.
St. Catharines, ON L2R 5H4
(416) 682-0587
Contact: Gail Burns.

First Impressions Entertainment

50 Shelley Dr., Suite 265
Sudbury, ON P3A 4S6
(705) 673-2122
Preferred Musical Styles: Singles to 10-piece bands: Rock, Pop, Country, Blues, Variety and specialty acts.
Acts Represented: Sweet Steeler, The Good Brothers, Pushy Pushy.
Venues Represented: Lakeview Hotel (Wawa), Empress Tavern (Timmins), Chimo's (Espanola).

Floyd Promotions

114 Franklin Way
Hyde Park, ON N0M 1Z0
(519) 657-0343
Preferred Musical Styles: Pop, Rock, MOR.
Contact: Edward F. Floyd.

Jim Ford and Associates Inc.

315 Soudan Ave.
Toronto, ON M4S 1W6
(416) 483-0663
FAX (416) 483-2866
Preferred Musical Styles: Jazz, Big Band, Swing, Pop.

The Fox Agency

P.O. Box 197
Elgin, ON K0G 1E0
(613) 359-5381
FAX (613) 546-4161
Preferred Musical Styles: MOR, Rock.
Acts Represented: The Rubels, The Fanatix, Wild Rose, Burnin' Bad.

Foxland Agency

P.O. Box 618, R.R.1
Carleton Place, ON K7C 3P1
(613) 257-5471
Contact: Ronald F. McMunn.

Fremont Promotions

2755 Jane St., Suite 202
North York, ON M3N 2H6
(416) 638-5578
Contact: Clairmont Monty Providence.

Frontline Attractions

P.O. Box 303
Waterloo, ON N2J 4A4
(519) 886-2530
Contact: Tim O'Donnell.

Gardner's Jazz Agency

40 Sunrise Ave., Suite 418
Toronto, ON M4A 2R4
(416) 751-8937
Contact: Harry M. Gardner.

Bill Gilroy Entertainment Agency

15 Villeneuve Cr.
London, ON N5V 1M7
(519) 455-0831
Preferred Musical Styles: C&W, Top 40, 50s and 60s.
Contact: William Gilroy.

Attila Glatz International Music Management

21 Webster Ave.
Toronto, ON M5R 1N6
(416) 923-6245
Preferred Musical Styles: Pop, MOR, Rock, Classical, Showbands.
Contact: Attila Glatz.
Comments: New acts accepted.

Golden Fiddle Music Company

R.R. 1
St. Agathe, ON N0B 2L0
(519) 886-3699
Contact: Carl Kieswetter.

John Goodwin Entertainment Agency

69 Shavian Blvd.
London, ON N6G 2P4
(519) 642-2190
FAX (519) 641-2584
Preferred Musical Styles: Pop, MOR.
Acts Represented: Fantasy, Venus, Dr. Henry.

Great Northern Vision Entertainment

P.O. Box 896
Lambeth, ON N0L 1S0
Contact: Michael Graham.
Network Affiliations: Dee Records Inc.

Great World Artists Management Inc.

66 Gerrard St. E., Suite 201
Toronto, ON M5B 1G3
(416) 971-9723
FAX (416) 971-9732
Preferred Musical Styles: Chamber Music, Classical and Contemporary.
Acts Represented: Nexus, Angela Hewitt, Elmer Iseler Singers.
Special Projects: International touring of foreign artists.

Hami Entertainment

204A St. George St.
Toronto, ON M5R 2N6
(416) 975-9266
Contact: Judy Simmonds or Deborah Perry.

Rolly Hammond Productions (1985) Inc.

135 York St., Suite 201
Ottawa, ON K1N 5T4
(613) 234-2886
FAX (613) 234-3377
Preferred Musical Styles: Various.
Acts Represented: Straightface Band, J.P. & Company, Dynasty Orchestra.
Services: Special events and convention co-ordinators.

Harbourlights Productions

P.O. Box 3656
Thunder Bay, ON P7B 6E3
(807) 344-8560
Contact: Marsha Ivall.

Hart/Murdock Artists Management

204A St. George St.
Toronto, ON M5R 2N6
(416) 922-5020
FAX (416) 922-6686
Preferred Musical Styles: Classical (voice and instrumental).
Acts Represented: Catherine Robbin (mezzo soprano), Jon Kimura Parker (pianist), The King's Singers.
Network Affiliations: Hami Entertainment.

Terry Hartman Enterprises
P.O. Box 500, Stn. A
Mississauga, ON L5A 3A2
(416) 569-1063
Contact: Terry Hartman.

Hollywood Productions
280 College St.
Toronto, ON M5T 1R9
(416) 975-0284
FAX (416) 363-6986
Preferred Musical Styles: All styles.
Acts Represented: Jr. Gone Wild, Pat Temple & The High Lonesome Players, Shotgun Rationale.
Services: Touring merchandise service.

In Tune Productions & Associates
1880 O'Connor Dr., Suite 303
Toronto, ON M4A 1W9
(416) 752-3520
Preferred Musical Styles: Rock, Pop, Top 40.
Contact: Richard Jozefacki.
Venues Represented: In Quebec and Ontario.

Isis Agency
164 Tragina Ave. N.
Hamilton, ON L8H 3C8
(416) 449-9600
Contact: Ricci Gene O'Reilly.

Jamrock Agencies
80 Highview Ave. E., Suite 910
London, ON N6C 5W8
(519) 649-7665
Contact: Mike Thomas

Jay-Coh Talent
407 Southcote Rd.
Ancaster, ON L9G 2W4
(416) 648-4059
Contact: J. Brian Oakes

The Jazz Agency
41 Mabelle Ave. Suite 1115
Islington, ON M9A 5A9
(416) 233-1574
Contact: Dick Wattam

KGB Management
107 Kennedy Rd. S.
Brampton, ON L6W 3G2
(416) 452-0211
Contact: Dan Kallinteris

Damian Kerr Agency
2133 Royal Windsor Dr., Unit 3
Mississauga, ON L5J 1K5
(416) 823-7633
Contact: Damian McKerr.

Krystal Tear Sounds
317 E. Victoria Ave. Suite 11
Thunder Bay, ON P7C 1A4
(807) 622-8847
Contact: Karen Augustine.

Lammert Entertainment Enterprises Inc.
47 Fieldgate Dr.
Nepean, ON K2J 1V3
(613) 825-3111
Contact: Pat Lammert, owner.
Preferred Musical Styles: Top 40, Variety plus mime, dancers, soloists and groups.
Acts Represented: Jon-E-Shakka, August Skyy (formerly Tiffany).
Services: Booking, management and sound production.

The Charles Lant Agency
(A Division of Lant International)
P.O. Box 1085, 569 Lynwood Dr.
Cornwall, ON K6H 5V2
(613) 938-1532
Contact: Charles W.B. Lant.
Preferred Musical Styles: All Styles.

Lapointe-Dubay Inc.
5117 Lakeshore Rd.
Burlington, ON L7L 1C1
(416) 681-0101
FAX 681-6488
Preferred Musical Styles: Top 40 Rock.
Acts Represented: Lost Johnny, Stiletto, T.O.Joker.
Network Affiliations: A.F. of M.
Services: Booking bands into clubs throughout Canada & the U.S.

Larabie Entertainment Agency
R.R.2, P.O. Box 62
Cumberland, ON K0A 1S0
(613) 833-3256
Contact: Edward Larabie.

Latino Productions Co. Ltd.
P.O. Box 310, Stn. T
Toronto, ON M6B 4A3
(416) 588-0703
Contact: Rodrigo Aranda.

Laurie-Ann Entertainment Agency Ltd.
71 Birchview Rd.
Nepean, ON K2G 3G3
(613) 224-6530
Contact: Ronald P. Sparling.

Ada Lee Entertainment Agency
813 Fairbairn St.
Peterborough, ON K9H 6B9
(705) 742-5250
Contact: Ada Lee.

Vita Linder Agency
64 St. Clair Ave. W.
Toronto, ON M4V 1N1
(416) 921-9536
Contact: Vita Linder.

Lindsay-Cooper Agency
40 Panorama Ct., Suite 1602
Rexdale, ON M9V 4M1
(416) 745-0523
Contact: Estiban Lindsay, Gwen Cooper.

M&G Promotions
15 Delroy Ave., Suite 201
Kitchener, ON N2A 2S2
(519) 741-0680
Preferred Musical Styles: Various.
Acts Represented: Beatlemania, Elvis Wade and the Jordanaires, Canadian Country Fever.
Venues Represented: Arenas and Theatres.
Network Affiliations: A.F. of M.
Services: Concert tours and management.
Special Projects: Outdoor festivals.

M.C. Talent Agency
134 Odessa Ave.
London, ON N6J 2Z8
(519) 686-5400
Preferred Musical Styles: C&W.
Contact: Marilynne Caswell.
Acts Represented: New acts accepted.

Major Talent Inc.
86 Queen St. N.
Kitchener, ON
N2H 2H5
(519) 894-5540
Contact: Rob Cressman.

Management West International
14 Sumach St.
Toronto, ON M5A 3J4
Contact: Gary Pring.

Bud Matton Enterprises Ltd.
119 Degrassi St.
Toronto, ON M4M 2K5
(416) 778-6890
Contact: Bud Matton.

Nancy McCaig All Star Productions Ltd.
19 Eastview Cr.
Toronto, ON M5M 2W4
(416) 486-0081
Contact: Nancy McCaig Higgins.

Larry Mercey Productions
Talent Division, 590 Hunters Place
Waterloo, ON N2K 3L1
(519) 746-8488

Merdella Music Agency
3482 Lawrence Ave. E., Suite 203
Scarborough, ON M1H 3E5
(416) 289-0236

Mid-City Pick-Crew's Talent Agency
151 John St.
Sarnia, ON N7T 2Z1
(519) 332-1869
Contact: James Starr Leblanc.

Mike's Entertainment Agency
R.R. 2
Nanticoke, ON N0A 1L0
(416) 776-3562
Preferred Musical Styles: Pop, MOR, Commercial Rock.
Contact: Mike Swainston.

John Moorhouse Entertainment Agency

3665 Arista Way, Suite 1910
Mississauga, ON L5A 4A3
(416) 277-3908
Preferred Musical Styles: Pop, MOR, C&W.
Acts Represented: John Moorhouse, The Keynotes, Canada's Solid Ivory Brothers' Band.
Network Affiliations: Bovine International Record Co.
Clients: Service clubs, Royal Canadian Legions.
Services: Live entertainment bookings.

Vivienne Murphy & Associates

1587 Summergrove Cr.
Pickering, ON L1X 2J5
(416) 283-7634
Acts Represented: Pop, MOR, C&W, show groups, orchestras.
Contact: Vivienne Murphy.
Network Affiliations: A.F. of M.

B. Murray Agency

106 Delaney Dr., R.R.2, Site 3, A 7
Carp, ON K0A 1L0
(613) 839-2533
Preferred Musical Styles: Bluegrass, Country.
Contact: Bruce Murray.

Music & Artists Placement Ltd.

47 Thorncliffe Park Dr., Suite 2609
Toronto, ON M4H 1J5
(416) 421-4424
Preferred Musical Styles: C&W, Rock, Pop, MOR.
Contact: Maureen Enright.

Music & Entertainment

18 Freeman St.
Scarborough, ON M1N 2B9
(416) 691-4430
Contact: Zena Cheevers.

Music Anyone? Inc.

1253 Baldwin Dr.
Oakville, ON L6J 2W4
(416) 338-3267
Preferred Musical Styles: Pop, MOR, Rock and Contemporary.
Network Affiliations: A.F. of M.
Services: Complete co-ordination and production of live variety presentations.
Special Projects: Complete theme night decor.
Branch:
90 Smirle Ave.
Ottawa, ON K1Y 0S3
(613) 725-9888

Night-Star Entertainment

1311 Cuthberson Ave.
Brockville, ON K6V 6Y2
(613) 345-2548
Services: Bookings.
Contact: Peter Dunn.

OHM Music International (OMI)

253 College St., Suite 340
Toronto, ON M5T 1R5
(416) 922-6297
FAX (416) 285-7104
Preferred Musical Styles: New Music, Roots-Related Rock & Roll.
Acts Represented: Dr. Limbo & His Fabulous Off-Whites.
Network Affiliations: A.F. of M.
Affiliated Companies: Dirty Little Nipper Records.
Services: Bookings, promotions, publicity and management.

Peever Talent & Management

7151 Tamar Rd.
Mississauga, ON L5N 1Y7
(416) 826-1701
Preferred Musical Styles: Country.
Contact: David Peever.
Venues Represented: Dallas Club, Hunt Club.
Services: Complete concert and club promotions.

Performance Presents

372 The Thicket
Mississauga, ON L5G 4P6
(416) 274-3055
Contact: Ann Footitt.

Phillips Promotions

416 1/2 Brock St. S.
Sarnia, ON N7T 2X2
(519) 332-6905
Contact: Anthony Mark Phillips.

Phil's Entertainment Agency Ltd.

889 Smyth Rd.
Ottawa, ON K1G 1P4
(613) 731-8983
Preferred Musical Styles: Various.
Acts Represented: Bruce Golden, the Debenhams, Andy Langley.
Venues Represented: Clubs, fairs, festivals and private functions.
Services: Booking agency.

Portinari Productions

49 Varley Dr.
Kanata, ON K2K 1G8
(613) 592-3627
Preferred Musical Styles: Pop, Classical, Jazz, MOR Cabaret Shows, Latin.
Acts Represented: Shuttlebus, Havana, Dr. Jazz.
Venues Represented: Ottawa venues: Chateau Laurier Hotel, Westin Hotel, National Arts Centre.
Network Affiliations: A.F. of M.

Pro-Talent

R.R. 1
Kingston, ON K7L 4V1
(613) 542-7212
Contact: Brian Hinchey.

Progressive Talent Productions Inc.

2 Melanie Dr., Unit 3A
Brampton, ON L6T 4K9
(416) 793-8133
Preferred Musical Styles: All styles.
Contact: John Kondis.
Venues Represented: Theatres, auditoriums.
Network Affiliations: CTO, ITAA.

R.I.B. Systems

384 1/2 George St. N., Unit 2
Peterborough, ON K9H 3R3
(705) 749-9565
Contact: Ian Osborne.

Marie Rakos Concert Management

14 Palsen St.
Nepean, ON K2G 2V8
(613) 224-6750
Contact: Marie Rakos.

Rastar International Promotion Co.

193 Leyton Ave.
Scarborough, ON M1L 3V5
(416) 694-6353
Contact: Robert Morgan.

Results by Mr. Mac

78 Ottawa St. S., Suite B
Hamilton, ON L8K 2E3
(416) 544-3134
Preferred Musical Styles: MOR, Rock, C&W.
Contact: John MacDougall.
Comments: New acts accepted.

Reynolds Agency Reg'd.

15 Parkland Cr.
Nepean, ON K2H 5V3
(613) 726-1285
Preferred Musical Styles: C&W.
Acts Represented: Howard Hayes and the Country Drifters.
Services: Management and promotion.

Roadhouse Entertainment Agency

29 Elizabeth St.
Thunder Bay, ON P7A 4J4
(807) 345-9296
Contact: Robert Jardine.

The ROCK Shoppe Booking Agency

P.O. Box 1329
Pembroke, ON K8A 6Y6
(613) 735-4060
Preferred Musical Styles: Pop, MOR, Rock.
Acts Represented: Prisoner, Paper Boys, Love Chain.
Venues Represented: The Embassy Tavern (Pembroke).

Rocklands Talent & Management Inc.

P.O. Box 1282
Peterborough, ON K9J 7H5
(705) 743-7354
FAX (705) 743-8847
Acts Represented: Country.
Contact: Brian Edwards.

Ross Booking Agency

1250 Brimley Rd., Unit 23
Scarborough, ON M1P 3G7
(416) 431-3979
Contact: Ann Ross-Johnson.

S.D.R. Promotions Ltd.
1700 Eglinton Ave. W.
Toronto, ON M6E 2H5
(416) 781-2850
Contact: Clifford Bancroft.

Secret Agency (C10592)
17 Paradise Rd. S., Unit 2
Hamilton, ON L8S 1S1
(416) 572-7474
Preferred Musical Styles: Country, Rock.
Acts Represented: Jack Diamond, Mark & The Sharks, Captain Skullsauce and the Schlonkhonkers.
Network Affiliations: A.F. of M.

Shoe String Booking Agency
935 The Queensway, P.O. Box 340
Toronto, ON M8Z 5P7
(416) 255-5166
Preferred Musical Styles: Rock, Pop, Country Rock.
Acts Represented: SAB, Bitchin', The Rockin' Rollers.
Network Affiliations: AEE.

Showmakers Inc.
P.O. Box 6288, Stn. A
Toronto, ON M5W 1P7
(416) 362-3353
Preferred Musical Styles: Pop, C&W, MOR.

Sibley Productions Inc.
208 Huron Cr.
Thunder Bay, ON P7A 3K4
(807) 344-8233
Contact: David Petrunka.

Silver Fox Agency
79 Dover Dr.
Hamilton, ON L8G 2M3
(416) 578-2665
Contact: Harry C. Doubledee.

Paul Simmons Management Inc.
125 Dupont St.
Toronto, ON M5R 1V4
(416) 920-1500
Contact: Paul Simonsky.

Joanne Smale Productions Ltd.
686 Richmond St. W.
Toronto, ON M6J 1C3
(416) 363-4051
FAX (416) 363-6986
Preferred Musical Styles: Songwriters.
Acts Represented: Murray McLauchlan, Willie P. Bennett, Jane Bunnett.

Something Bluegrass Agency
P.O. Box 697, Stn. A
Burlington, ON L7R 3Y5
Contact: Tony de Boer.

Sparkle Productions
119 Hanson St.
Toronto, ON M4C 5P3
(416) 691-6677
Preferred Musical Styles: Independent artists of all types.
Contact: Ruth Hotchkiss.
Venues Represented: Libraries, schools, theatres, auditoriums.
Network Affiliations: A.F. of M., PAPA, CPRS.

Sphere Entertainment
22 Rainsford Rd.
Toronto, ON M4L 3N4
(416) 694-6900
Preferred Musical Styles: Pop, Variety, Children's.
Acts Represented: Sphere Clown Band, Sphere Band.
Network Affiliations: CIRPA, CARAS, A.F. of M.

Suds Sutherland Management Projects Inc.
R.R. 2
Orillia, ON L3V 6H2
(705) 327-2521
Services: Booking agent.
Special Projects: Concert productions.
Clients: Entertainment Centre, The Agency, Orillia Community Centre.

TSS Technical Support Services
P.O. Box 1981
Huntsville, ON P0A 1K0
(705) 789-4682
Contact: Kenneth Kruse.

Talent City Booking
414B University Dr.
Thunder Bay, ON P7C 2C8
(807) 475-7417
Contact: Joseph Furoy.

Steve Thomson Agency
3015 Kennedy Rd., Suite 1
Scarborough, ON M1V 1E7
(416) 291-4913
Preferred Musical Styles: Pop, Rock, C&W.
Contact: Steve Thomson
Acts Represented: Numerous, accept new acts.

Valerie Thompson Entertainment Agency
79 Jameson Ave., Suite 610
Toronto, ON M6K 2W7
(416) 534-0099
Contact: Valerie Thompson.

Trick or Treat Agency
1971 Spruce Hill Rd.
Pickering, ON L1V 1S6
(416) 831-9191
FAX (416) 420-9140
Acts Represented: Long John Baldry, Alannah Myles, Blue Rodeo.

Ultimate Sound Inc.
247 Crosslane Gate
Newmarket, ON L3X 1B1
(416) 853-4241

Valley Star Productions
P.O. Box 3131, Stn. P
Thunder Bay, ON P7B 5G6
(807) 344-4832
Contact: Giuseppi Veltri.

Vehicle Entertainment Agency
1 Andria Lane
Hamilton, ON L8E 3K7
(416) 578-0533
FAX (416) 573-1919
Preferred Musical Styles: Rock.
Acts Represented: Powerhouse, Speck Jennings, 7th Veil.
Venues Represented: O'Toole's Restaurant (Burlington and Oakville, ON).

Willcock Enterprises
133 Council Cr.
Ancaster, ON L9G 1T9
(416) 648-2490
Contact: Herbert W.R. Lock.

Worries Promotions
814 Broadview Ave., Suite 28
Toronto, ON M4K 2P7
Contact: Warren Anderson.

Y.S. Enterprises
86 Olive Ave.
Toronto, ON M6G 1V1
(416) 534-2550
Preferred Musical Styles: Jazz, African, Latin.
Network Affiliations: A.F. of M.

Young Uprising Sound Production
3 Knightsbridge Rd., Unit 3
Bramalea, ON L6T 3X3
(416) 458-6210
Contact: John McMorris.

QUEBEC

Productions A&P
103 boul. de la Concorde, Suite 2
Laval, PQ H7N 1H8
(514) 383-1777
Contact: Jeannine Martin Demers.

All Styles Music Productions
1550 ave des Pins o.
Montreal, PQ H3G 1B4
(514) 933-0320
Contact: Nicole Beaudoin.

Agence George Angers (Anprom)
2695 boul. Gouin o.
Montreal, PQ H3M 1B5
(514) 355-3416
Contact: George Angers.

Black Tiger Productions
264 Ste. Catherine o.
Montreal, PQ H2X 2A1
(514) 954-1221
Preferred Musical Styles: Jazz, Blues,
Reggae, R&B, Afro-Caribbean.
Acts Represented: Mango Stars, Blue
Monday, Rising Sun Afro-Jazz Orchestra.
Venues Represented: Area universities,
CEGEPs, Place des Arts.

C.D.C.B. Production Inc.
813 rue Saint-Christophe, P.O. Box 1112
Trois-Rivieres, PQ G9A 5K4
(819) 376-0818
Venues Represented: Office parties and large
concerts.
Special Projects: Annual Grand Ball with the
Three-Rivers Symphony Orchestra.

Les Productions C.R. Inc.
1091 rue Notre Dame
Lachine, PQ H8S 2C3
(514) 637-4468
FAX (514) 636-6026
Preferred Musical Styles: Pop, MOR, Rock.
Acts Represented: Paradox, Kinky Foxx, Toyo.

Bob Carlisle Productions Inc.
P.O. Box 599
St-Basile-Le-Grand, PQ J0L 1S0
(514) 653-0442
FAX (514) 653-0272
Preferred Musical Styles: Bavarian, Big
Band, C&W, Dixieland, Ethnic, MOR, Pop.
Acts Represented: The Entertainers, Claude
Foisy, Remember.
Type of Events: Corporate shows, trade shows,
commercial centres and festivals.

Cory Entertainment Agency
960 Kipawa Rd.
Temiscaming, PQ J0Z 3R0
(819) 627-9479
Preferred Musical Styles: Duos, trios and
bands.
Contact: Simone E. Piquette.

Do-Re-Mi Agency
1055 Rochon St.
St. Laurent, PQ H4L 1V6
(514) 748-8270
Contact: Don Aress.

Daniele Dorice Productions Inc.
18 Balzac Ave.
Candiac, PQ J5R 2A6
(514) 659-0200
Contact: William A. Skerczak.

Centre des Orchestres du Quebec Alex Drolet Ltee.
905 de Nemours, Suite 215
Charlesbourg, PQ G1H 6Z5
(418) 628-9923
Contact: Alexandre Drolet, Germain Bilodeau.

Le Maison de Production Encart Ltee.
220C Duquette o.
Gatineau, PQ J8P 2Z4
(819) 643-9282
Contact: Lisette Brisbois.

Fiesta Smolash Productions Inc.
5027A Plamondon
Montreal, PQ H3W 1E9
(514) 737-9898
FAX (514) 342-6696
Preferred Musical Styles: Orchestra, Big
Band, Rock, Pop, Dance, Folk.
Acts Represented: Lorraine Klaasen, Line Up,
Trio Ambiance.

Fleming Artists' Management
5975 Park Ave.
Montreal, PQ H2V 4H4
(514) 276-5605
FAX (514) 495-4889
Preferred Musical Styles: Jazz, Folk, Roots.
Acts Represented: Karen Young/Michel
Donato, Jean Beaudet, Penny Lang.
Affiliated Companies: Justin Time, Fusion 111
(distribution).

Agence Gauthier & Rollins
5880 rue Giffard
St. Leonard, PQ H1P 1G6
(514) 322-5876
Contact: Roland Gauthier.

Les Productions Golden Enr.
2016-1 Ave.
Lac St. Charles, PQ G0A 2H0
(418) 849-1666
Contact: Sylvie Cloutier.

Pierre Gravel -Impresario
89 Alexandra St.
Granby, PQ J2G 2P4
(514) 372-7764
FAX (514) 372-4391
Preferred Musical Styles: Pop, MOR, Rock, C&W.
Acts Represented: Andre-Philippe Gagnon, Denis Lacombe.
Venues Represented: Worldwide.
Services: Management and booking.

In Motion Productions
P.O. Box 322, Stn. Longueuil
Longueuil, PQ J4K 5E6
(514) 679-8021
Preferred Musical Styles: Rock, Pop.
Acts Represented: Just For Mom, Pacific, The Motion. (Original acts and cover-bands).
Services: Management, mailing list and booking.

Productions Jazz Tempo Primo
5191 Brebeuf
Montreal, PQ H2J 3L8
(514) 523-4107
Contact: Bernard Primeau.

Sheldon Kagan Productions Ltd.
1020-5 Ave.
Dorval, PQ H9S 1J2
(514) 631-2160
FAX (514) 631-4430
Preferred Musical Styles: Pop, MOR, Big Band.

Kenmar Productions Ltd.
2555 Modugno, Suite 305
St. Laurent, PQ H4R 2L5
(514) 748-5144
Contact: Perry Carmen.

Les Productions Ghyslaine Lacoste & Associes.
6647-24 Ave.
Rosemont, PQ H1T 3M6
(514) 722-6861
Contact: Ghyslaine Lacoste.

Productions Musicales Richard Landry Inc.
706 ave. Moreau
Ste. Foy, PQ G1V 3A4
(418) 651-0453
Contact: Richard Landry.

Michael Laucke and Company
5261 Jeanne-Mance, Suite 3
Montreal, PQ H2V 4K3
(514) 277-8550
FAX (514) 278-2319
Preferred Musical Styles: Classical (mainly Spanish) and Flamenco.
Acts Represented: Michael Laucke (guitarist), The Michael Laucke Group, Fiesta Flamenco.
Venues Represented: Place des Arts (Montreal). Wigmore Hall (England) plus other halls worldwide.
Services: Local, national and international tours.
Special Projects: International negotiations for concerts, recordings, etc.

Pierre Leduc Musique Inc.
31 Archambault
Le Gardeur, PQ J5Z 2A9
(514) 581-4229
Contact: Pierre Leduc.

Marquee Productions
12 Cartier St.
Aylmer, PQ J9H 1B8
(819) 684-3043
Contact: William Grella.

Agence Musicale Roland Martel Inc.
6495 Place Monette
Charlesbourg, PQ G1H 6K1
(418) 626-0034
Contact: Roland J. Martel.

Steve Michaels Inc.
1390 Pine Ave. W., Suite 5A
Montreal, PQ H3G 1A8
(514) 849-5979
Contact: Saul Michael Shade.

Les Productions Johnny Monti Inc.
9033A rue Perinault
St. Leonard, PQ H1P 2L6
(514) 322-5785
Contact: Johnny Montenaro.

Brian Pombiere Productions Inc.
5405 Park Ave., 2nd Floor
Montreal, PQ H2V 4G9
(514) 276-9000
FAX (514) 270-7310
Preferred Musical Styles: Top 40, Rock.
Acts Represented: Cinema V, Indecent Xposure, Alma Faye Brooks, Worrall Brothers, and various duos.
Venues Represented: Bloomingdale's (Newmarket, ON), Palladium (Quebec City), American Rock Cafe (Montreal).
Network Affiliations: A.F. of M.

Centre Musical Quebec Plus Inc.
Halles Fleur de Lys
245 Soumande, Suite 282
Ville Vanier, PQ G1M 3H6
(418) 687-5540
Contact: Guylaine C. Lemieux.

Nat Raider Productions Inc.
5799 Eldridge Ave.
Montreal, PQ H4W 2E3
(514) 486-1676
FAX (514) 485-7237
Network Affiliations: A.F. of M.

Les Productions Rubicon
10960 ave. Laurentides, Unit 2
Montreal, PQ H1H 4V9
(514) 327-6172
Contact: Gilles Bedard.

Stella Productions
P.O. Box 23
Ste-Anne-de-Bellevue, PQ H9X 3L4
(514) 937-5590 or (514) 457-2266
Preferred Musical Styles: Hotel music.
Acts Represented: Steve Farrel, Denis Dean, Jerome Semay.

Les Productions Summertime Enr.
7259 ave. de Chateaubriand
Montreal, PQ H2R 2L4
(514) 276-1756
Contact: William St. Hilaire.

Superstrat Inc.
86 Cote Ste. Catherine
Montreal, PQ H2V 2A3
(514) 270-9556
FAX (514) 270-9556
Preferred Musical Styles: Pop, Folk.
Acts Represented: Edith Butler.
Services: Shows, touring, TV.

Les Productions Paul Tanguay Inc.
390 Peloquin, Suite 10
Montreal, PQ H2C 2K1
(514) 666-3695
FAX (514) 666-6331
Preferred Musical Styles: Folk, Classical, MOR.
Acts Represented: La Bottine Souriante (folk), Claude Garden (classical harmonica), Donald Poliquin (children's songs).
Services: Booking, management and productions.

SASKATCHEWAN

Drummond Music Services Ltd.
4332 Pasqua St.
Regina, SK S4S 6M5
(306) 584-8114
Preferred Musical Styles: MOR, C&W.
Contact: Doreen E. Brown.
Acts Represented: New acts accepted.

Music City Promotions

3410 Dieppe St.
Saskatoon, SK S7M 3S9
(306) 382-0330
Contact: David Calyniuk.

Platinum Productions

P.O. Box 2048
Yorkton, SK S3N 3X3
(306) 783-1150
Preferred Musical Styles: Country, Country Rock.
Acts Represented: Rob McLane (singer/songwriter), Against the Grain (country rock band).

State of the Art Productions

3230 Argyle Rd.
Regina, SK S4S 2B4
(306) 586-2992
FAX (306) 584-1187
Contact: Ria Kaal.
Preferred Musical Styles: All.
Acts Represented: Williams & Ree.

Universal Talent Associates

P.O. Box 645
Regina, SK S4P 3A3
(306) 586-9444
FAX (306) 584-5857
Contact: Tim Bleiler, Geoff Bjorgan.
Preferred Musical Styles: Rock, Country Rock.
Acts Represented: Fist, Buddy Knox, Rob Holden and Horizon.

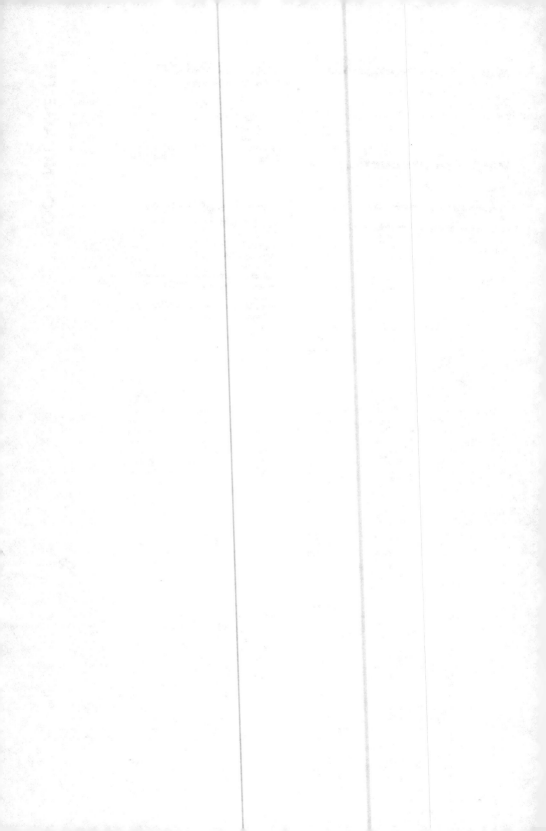

CHORAL GROUPS

A Cappella Singers

P.O. Box 699
Rossland, BC V0G 1Y0
(604) 362-5786
Venue: Rossland-Trail.
Music Director: Helen Dahlstrom.
Auditions: Throughout the year.
Comments: A 16-member group of women, which sings baroque, romantic, classical and contemporary repertoire.

Bach-Elgar Choir

Hamilton Place
P.O. Box 2080, Stn. A
Hamilton, ON L8N 3Y7
(416) 527-5995
FAX (416) 521-0924
Venue: Hamilton Place.
Music Director: Wayne Strongman.
Auditions: Throughout the year on Tuesdays.
Comments: The Bach-Elgar Choir, Hamilton's symphonic choir, is a 110-voice choir which features accomplished amateur singers from Hamilton and surrounding regions. In addition to its Hamilton Place subscription series, the Bach-Elgar Choir makes guest appearances with the Hamilton Philharmonic Orchestra and the Canadian Brass, and performs at many civic functions.

73

Barrhead Senior Singers

P.O. Box 1106
Barrhead, AB T0G 0E0
(403) 674-4346
Music Director: Margaret Hunt.
Comments: A group of 45 singers and musicians which gets together to share the joy of music. They sing regularly at the hospital, nursing home, seniors' lodge and at various local functions.

The Bel Canto Chorus

P.O. Box 426, Stn. B
Sudbury, ON P3E 4P6
(705) 522-0204
Venue: St. Andrew's United Church, Sudbury.
Music Director: Susan Marrier.
Auditions: January and September.
Comments: A 60-member community chorus.

Blyth Festival Singers

P.O. Box 10
Blyth, ON N0M 1H0
(519) 523-4345
FAX (519) 523-9140
Venue: Blyth Memorial Hall.
Music Director: Angus Sinclair.
Comments: Community-based choir (part of the Blyth Centre for the Arts).

Canadian Children's Opera Chorus

227 Front St. E., Suite 215
Toronto, ON M5A 1E8
(416) 366-0467
FAX (416) 363-5584
Venue: Harbourfront, Young People's Theatre and St. Simon's Church.
Music Director: John Tuttle.
Auditions: During April, May and June of each year.

Cantata Singers of Ottawa

P.O. Box 4396, Stn. E.
Ottawa, ON K1S 5B4
(613) 745-7651
Venue: National Arts Centre and other halls in and around Ottawa.
Music Director: Laurence Ewashko.
Auditions: Late August or early September.
Comments: Founded in 1964, the Cantata Singers of Ottawa is a highly skilled choir of about 40 voices. The Cantata Singers appear regularly at the National Arts Centre under the direction of well-known conductors. They also appear with other Ottawa groups in joint concerts, and do their own a cappella concerts in Ottawa and surrounding area.

Exultate Chamber Singers

383 Huron St.
Toronto, ON M5S 2G5
(416) 690-5775
Venue: St. James Cathedral.
Music Director: John Tuttle.
Auditions: Upon request.
Comments: Presents an annual four-concert subscription series.

The Halifax Chamber Choir

15 Alderwood Dr.
Halifax, NS B3N 1S6
(902) 477-7456
Venue: Halls in the Halifax/Dartmouth region.
Music Director: Paul Murray.
Auditions: As required.
Comments: A community choir which tours and performs at benefits, special anniversaries and festivals.

Johannes Brahms Choir

1594 Claymor Ave.
Ottawa, ON K2C 1T3
(613) 224-7467
Music Director: Dietrich P. Kiesewalter.
Auditions: January and September.

Kingston Symphony Association Chorus

P.O. Box 1616
Kingston, ON K7L 5C8
(613) 546-9729
Venue: Grand Theatre and Grant Hall.
Music Director: Brian Jackson.

Kitchener-Waterloo Philharmonic Choir

P.O. Box 2661, Stn. B
Kitchener, ON N2H 6N2
(519) 745-4711
Venue: Centre in the Square, Kitchener.
Music Director: Howard Dyck.
Auditions: May, September and December.
Comments: Subscription series of four-six concerts per season, with professional soloists and orchestra.

Mohawk College Singers

Department of Music, Mohawk College,
P.O. Box 2034
Hamilton, ON L8N 3T2
(416) 575-2043
Venue: Mohawk College Theatre and the Cathedral of Christ the King.
Music Director: Christopher Hunt.
Auditions: Wednesday after Labour Day and Wednesday after New Year's Day.
Comments: Performs twice a year with Symphony Hamilton, plus frequent appearances in Hamilton area churches. A college/community choral society.

North Bay Choral Society

P.O. Box 772
North Bay, ON P1B 8J8
(705) 472-4798
Venue: North Bay Arts Centre, North Bay.
Music Director: Dawn Wallis Sutton.
Auditions: January and September.
Comments: A community SATB choir of 60 voices which performs two concerts a year, plus other engagements for civic functions and church services.

North York Philharmonic Choir

c/o North York Arts Council
7 Edithvale Dr.
North York, ON M2N 2R4
(416) 443-9939
Music Director: Edward Moroney.
Auditions: June and September.

The Orpheus Choir of Toronto

P.O. Box 145, Stn. K
Toronto, ON M4P 2G1
(416) 462-0160
Music Director: Brainerd Blyden-Taylor.
Auditions: January, June and September.

Ottawa Choral Society

P.O. Box 952
Ottawa, ON K1P 5R1
(613) 725-2560
Venue: National Arts Centre.
Music Director: Brian Law.
Auditions: Annually in June.

Red Deer Boys Choir

P.O. Box 1041
Red Deer, AB T4N 6S5
(403) 347-7464
Music Director: Judy Buck.
Auditions: January and June of each year.
Comments: This choir is for boys aged seven to approximately 14. Two major concerts are given each year, at Christmas and in the spring. The boys are exposed to other local musicians and perform at many local functions in the community throughout the year.

Renaissance Singers

251 Neilson Ave.
Waterloo, ON N2J 2M2
(519) 886-8233
Music Director: R.S.J. Daniels.
Auditions: In September when rehearsals resume.
Comments: Rehearsals are every Tuesday evening between 7:30 and 10:00 p.m. The choir performs a four-concert season, with additional appearances in the community.

Shevchenko Musical Ensemble

626 Bathurst St.
Toronto, ON M5S 2R1
(416) 533-2725
Venue: Ryerson Theatre and area schools.
Music Director: Andrew Markow.
Comments: An ensemble including a male chorus, a mandolin orchestra (woodwinds, accordion and percussion), and a folk dance troupe. The group performs music from the folk traditions of the Ukraine, Canada and other countries, as well as contemporary compositions commissioned by the ensemble.

The Toronto Mendelssohn Choir

60 Simcoe St.
Toronto, ON M5J 2H5
(416) 598-0422
Venue: Roy Thomson Hall.
Music Director: Dr. Elmer Iseler.
Auditions: Spring/early summer.

The Toronto Mendelssohn Youth Choir
60 Simcoe St.
Toronto, ON M5J 2H5
(416) 598-0422
Music Director: Robert Cooper.
Auditions: May and September.

Tudor Singers of Montreal
1538 Sherbrooke St. W., Suite 412
Montreal, PQ H3G 1L5
(514) 932-3376
FAX (514) 932-3383
Venue: Various halls and churches.
Music Director: Patrick Wedd.
Auditions: Spring of every year.

Vancouver Cantata Singers
5115 Keith Rd.
West Vancouver, BC V7W 2M9
(604) 921-8588
FAX (604) 922-9167
Venue: Various Vancouver performance spaces.
Music Director: James Fankhauser.
Auditions: April and August.
Comments: A 40-member, mixed-voice choral ensemble. All members are auditioned.

Vancouver Chamber Choir
1254 W. 7 Ave.
Vancouver, BC V6H 1B6
FAX (604) 738-7832
Venue: Orpheum Theatre and Ryerson Church.
Music Director: Jon Washburn.
Auditions: Spring and fall.
Comments: This 20-voice chamber choir presents a regular concert series in Vancouver and is an accomplished touring, broadcasting and recording ensemble.

Whiteoaks Choral Society
53 Central St.
Toronto, ON M8V 2R6
(416) 259-9152
Venue: Sheridan College, Oakville.
Music Director: J.B. Stainton.
Auditions: No auditions. Registration held the first Tuesday after Labour Day, and in January.
Comments: A community-based choral group whose only entrance requirement is a love of singing and a willingness to learn. The group produces two major concerts each season as well as other occasional performances. The choir is listed as a course in the Extension Department of Sheridan College and members must pay a course fee. Rehearsals on Tuesday at 8:00 p.m., in Hall B125 at Sheridan College.

Winnipeg Philharmonic Choir
P.O. Box 1616
Winnipeg, MB R3C 2Z6
(204) 831-0056
Music Director: Henry Engbrecht.
Auditions: May and August.
Comments: A 90-voice choral group established in 1922 and incorporated in 1983. Holds its own subscription series and sings on commission with the Winnipeg Symphony Orchestra.

American Dream Festival/Canadian Dream Festival

4091 Pheasant Run
Mississauga, ON L5L 2C2
(416) 820-6400
FAX (416) 820-9512
Sponsor: JCO Communications/Barslow & Associates.
Aims and Objectives: Competitions for bands and comedians. Winners advance to finals in Las Vegas to perform, record and compete for gold, silver and bronze medals.
Events/Artists: Canadian preliminaries held in Toronto in association with Joyce Barslow & Associates.
Prizes: Varies depending on region and category.
Dates and Locations: January 1991—Las Vegas.
Deadline for Application: November 1990.
Comments: Preliminaries to be held across Canada. Winners advance to finals in 1991.

Banff International String Quartet Competition

P.O. Box 1020
Banff, AB T0L 0C0
(403) 762-6231
Sponsor: The Banff Centre for the Arts.
Aims and Objectives: To help launch the careers of young world-class quartets. Held every three years.
Prizes: $45,000 (total). First prize winner guaranteed a tour.
Dates and Locations: April 19-25, 1992.
Deadline for Application: December 1991.

Calgary Kiwanis Music Festival

417-14 St. N.W., 3rd Floor
Calgary, AB T2N 2A1
(403) 283-6009
Sponsor: Calgary Kiwanis Clubs.
Aims and Objectives: To provide a competitive music and speech festival for amateur performers.
Events/Artists: 800 classes, 45,000 participants.
Prizes: $36,000 in prizes and scholarships.
Dates and Locations: April 23—May 10, 1990.
Deadline for Application: February 1, 1990.

CBC National Competition for Young Performers

P.O. Box 500, Stn. A
Toronto, ON M5W 1E6
(416) 975-6037
FAX (416) 975-6040
Sponsor: CBC Radio Music.
Aims and Objectives: To encourage the development of young Canadian musicians, and to serve as a springboard for those musicians with a potential solo career.
Events/Artists: Voice and piano.
Prizes: $5,000, $3,000, $2,000, additional special prizes and scholarships.
Dates and Locations: June 4, 1991—Ottawa.
Deadline for Application: June 15, 1990.

CBC National Radio Competition for Amateur Choirs

P.O. Box 500, Stn. A
Toronto, ON M5W 1E6
(416) 975-6037
FAX (416) 975-6040
Sponsor: CBC Radio Music.
Aims and Objectives: To encourage the development of choral music in Canada.
Events/Artists: Various categories and forms of choral groups performing traditional, ethnocultural and contemporary music.
Prizes: $1,500, $1,000, $500.
Dates and Locations: Final adjudication: May 20-25, 1990—Montreal.
Deadline for Application: February 9, 1990.

CBC Radio Competition for Young Composers

P.O. Box 500, Stn. A
Toronto, ON M5W 1E6
(416) 975-6037
FAX (416) 975-6040
Sponsor: CBC Radio Music.
Aims and Objectives: To encourage the development of serious composition in Canada.
Events/Artists: Categories: String ensemble, electronic music, chamber music.
Prizes: $3,000-5,000, depending on placement.
Dates and Locations: Final presentation: November 1990—Quebec.
Deadline for Application: February 9, 1990.

Canadian Music Competitions Inc.

1600 rue Berri, Suite 3016
Montreal, PQ H2L 4E4
(514) 844-8836
Aims and Objectives: To discover and aid new talent, and to raise the level of music education.
Events/Artists: Various competitions.
Prizes: Bursaries.
Dates and Locations: Throughout the year, across Canada.

Canadian Open Championship Old Time Fiddlers' Contest

P.O. Box 27
Shelburne, ON L0N 1S0
(519) 925-2830
Sponsor: Shelburne Rotary Club.
Aims and Objectives: To raise money for charity.
Events/Artists: Fiddle competition.
Prizes: $8,500 in prize money plus 20 trophies.
Dates and Locations: August 10-11, 1990—Shelburne; August 9-10, 1991—Shelburne.
Deadline for Application: August 8, 1990.

Canadian Open Country Singing Contest

P.O. Box 426
Simcoe, ON N3Y 4K7
(519) 426-2005 or 426-3714
Sponsor: Board of directors of contest.
Aims and Objectives: To promote Canadian country singers.
Events/Artists: Eight categories including junior, senior and duet.
Prizes: Over $30,000 plus recording sessions for certain categories.
Dates and Locations: July 6-8, 1990—Simcoe, Ontario; July 5-7, 1991—Simcoe, Ontario.
Deadline for Application: June 1, 1990.
Comments: Founded in 1975, the Canadian Open Country Singing Contest attracts about 200 contestants and crowds approaching 5,000 for the three-day event.

Downtowners Optimist Band and Vocal Jazz Festival

1544 Albert St.
Regina, SK S4P 2S4
(306) 757-7272
Sponsor: Downtowners Optimist Club.
Aims and Objectives: To promote the development of bands to help youth and to raise the level of musical performance among participants.
Events/Artists: Concert bands, jazz bands, jazz combos, Dixieland, vocal jazz.
Prizes: Trophies to "A" grade performers, Canadian Stage Band Festival invitations and plaques.
Dates and Locations: February to March, 1991.
Deadline for Application: TBA.

Dundalk Square Dance Competition

c/o Dundalk Herald Newspaper, P.O. Box 280
Dundalk, ON N0C 1B0
Events/Artists: Square and stepdance competition.
Prizes: Cash prizes to $500 and trophies.
Dates and Locations: Last weekend of June.
Deadline for Application: Wednesday of prior week.
Comments: Camping available.

Edward Johnson Music Competition

P.O. Box 1718
Guelph, ON N1H 6Z9
(519) 821-3210
Sponsor: Edward Johnson Music Foundation.
Aims and Objectives: Part of the Guelph Spring Festival.
Events/Artists: Piano, voice, strings and instrumental categories open to residents of Wellington County and Waterloo region.
Prizes: $550, $350, $250.
Dates and Locations: May 14-15, 1990—University of Guelph.
Deadline for Application: March 30, 1990.

S.C. Eckhardt-Gramatte National Competition for the Performance of Canadian Music

Brandon University, School of Music
Brandon, MB R7A 6A9
(204) 727-9631
Aims and Objectives: To encourage young pianists, singers and string players to learn and perform the music of Canadian composers, and to commission new Canadian works for the competition.
Events/Artists: Opening concert by a major artist (also generally a juror) broadcast by CBC. Three sessions of semi-finals and finals.
Prizes: $2,500 (first, plus a major cross-Canada tour), $1,500 (second), $1,000 (third). Also a prize for best performance of a commissioned work.
Dates and Locations: May 4-6, 1990—Brandon.

Festival National de la Chanson de Granby

261 rue Laurier, P.O. Box 41
Granby, PQ J2G 8E2
(514) 375-7555
Aims and Objectives: To promote new talents and coach young professional and non-professional singers.
Events/Artists: National competition open to all non-professional authors, composers and performers of French song.
Prizes: For each category, cash prize plus a grant from Music Action for production of a record. Also, a cash prize for the best original song presented at the festival and a cash prize from the press.
Dates and Locations: TBA.
Deadline for Application: TBA.
Comments: All semi-finals and gala evenings are broadcast across Canada on the CBC radio network.

Fiddling and Stepdancing Competitions

P.O. Box 189
Mattawa, ON P0H 1V0
(705) 744-2311
Sponsor: Mattawa and District Chamber of Commerce.
Events/Artists: Fiddlers and stepdancers from around Ontario.
Prizes: Cash prizes and trophies.
Dates and Locations: Summer.
Deadline for Application: TBA.

Fleming Award for Young Composers

36 Elgin St.
Ottawa, ON K1P 5K5
(613) 238-5893
Sponsor: Canadian Music Council.
Aims and Objectives: To encourage young composers.
Events/Artists: Composer/competition.
Prizes: $1,000.
Deadline for Application: May 1, 1990.

Florence and Stanley Osborne Organ Competition

P.O. Box 688
Alliston, ON L0M 1A0
(705) 435-5786
Sponsor: Whitby Summer Institute of Church Music.
Aims and Objectives: To encourage gifted young Canadian organists to pursue a church music career by making possible further advanced study.
Events/Artists: Organists.
Prizes: $1,000, $500.
Dates and Locations: TBA.
Deadline for Application: TBA.

Godfrey Ridout Awards

1240 Bay St.
Toronto, ON M5R 2C2
(416) 974-4427
FAX (416) 924-4837
Aims and Objectives: To encourage and support Canadian composers pursuing a career in composition.
Events/Artists: Choral compositions written for mixed choir (SATB), a cappella or accompanied.
Prizes: $1,000, $500.
Deadline for Application: May 15, 1990.

Great Ontario Talent Search

83 Kennedy Rd. S.
Brampton, ON L6W 3P3
(416) 453-7452
Sponsor: CFNY-FM.
Aims and Objectives: To promote and encourage the large body of untapped Canadian talent.
Events/Artists: Artists involved cannot have current or past recording contracts.
Prizes: Various prizes include cash, studio time, musical instruments.
Dates and Locations: TBA.
Deadline for Application: TBA.

Hugh LeCaine Awards

1240 Bay St.
Toronto, ON M5R 2C2
(416) 924-4427
FAX (416) 924-4837
Sponsor: Composers, Authors and Publishers Association of Canada.
Aims and Objectives: To encourage and support Canadian composers pursuing a career in composition.
Events/Artists: Compositions realized on tape with electronic means (synthesizers, computers, etc.).
Prizes: $1,000, $500.
Deadline for Application: May 15, 1990.

International Guitar Competition

9 Gibson Ave.
Toronto, ON M5R 1T4
(416) 922-8002
Sponsor: The Guitar Society of Toronto.
Aims and Objectives: To encourage and foster talent, and to improve the standard of guitar performance.
Events/Artists: Guitarists from all over the world.
Prizes: Cash prizes.
Dates and Locations: TBA.
Deadline for Application: TBA.
Comments: Contact Anne Kassner.

Jules Leger Prize for New Chamber Music

36 Elgin St.
Ottawa, ON K1P 5K5
(613) 238-5893
Sponsor: Canadian Music Council.
Aims and Objectives: To encourage Canadian composers to write for chamber music groups and to foster the performance of Canadian music.
Events/Artists: All Canadian composers are eligible.
Prizes: $5,000, trophy, concert.
Dates and Locations: TBA.
Deadline for Application: TBA.

Kitchener-Waterloo Oktoberfest Thanksgiving Day Parade

77 Ontario St., P.O. Box 1053
Kitchener, ON N2G 4G1
(519) 576-0571 or 578-8300
Sponsor: K-W Oktoberfest Inc.
Aims and Objectives: The parade is the highlight of the 10-day Oktoberfest celebration.
Events/Artists: A parade including marching bands and floats.
Prizes: Band prizes awarded for best overall band. Also youth and senior band categories.
Dates and Locations: October 8, 1990; October 7, 1991.
Deadline for Application: May 1, 1990; May 1, 1991.
Comments: The Oktoberfest Parade attracts over 250,000 on the street and is viewed by many more through CTV's national coverage.

Kiwanis Music Festival of Stratford

P.O. Box 103
Stratford, ON N5A 6S8
(519) 273-3011
Sponsor: Kiwanis Club of Stratford.
Aims and Objectives: To promote musical experiences and encourage excellence in performance.
Events/Artists: Adjudicated competitions in voice, choral, piano, strings, orchestral instruments and speech arts.
Prizes: Trophies, scholarships and cash awards.
Dates and Locations: April 30—May 12, 1990.
Deadline for Application: February 8, 1990.

Leslie Bell Scholarships Competition

FAX (416) 961-7198
Sponsor: Ontario Choral Society.
Aims and Objectives: Competition in choral rehearsal technique.
Events/Artists: Choirs and conductors.
Prizes: $2,000 scholarship.
Dates and Locations: October 1990—Kingston.
Deadline for Application: 60 days in advance of competition.

Lethbridge and District Kiwanis Music Festival

26 Algonquin Bay
Lethbridge, AB T1K 5B6
(403) 381-6991
Sponsor: Kiwanis Club of Lethbridge.
Aims and Objectives: To encourage and promote excellence in music and speech arts.
Events/Artists: Competitors aged three years to adult.
Prizes: $15,000 in scholarships, some trophies.
Dates and Locations: March 29—April 7, 1990.
Deadline for Application: January 24, 1990.

Maritime Old Time Fiddling Contest

P.O. Box 3037
Dartmouth, NS B2W 4Y3
(902) 423-7389 or 434-5466
Sponsor: Saint Thomas More Council of Catholic Men.
Aims and Objectives: To promote the culture of old time fiddle music and to raise funds for numerous charitable organizations.
Events/Artists: Old time fiddling competition in five categories. Special headline entertainers.
Prizes: Trophies and cash prizes for all fiddle classes plus special awards for individual participants.
Dates and Locations: July 6-7, 1990; July 12-13, 1991.
Deadline for Application: July 6, 1990.

Midwestern Ontario Rotary Music Festival

P.O. Box 1960
Walkerton, ON N0G 2V0
(519) 881-1455

Sponsor: Hanover-Walkerton Ontario Registered Music Teachers & Walkerton Rotary Club.
Aims and Objectives: To give competitors unbiased criticism and an evaluation of their performances; to upgrade standards of teaching, and to improve music appreciation of music.
Events/Artists: Vocal, instrumental and dance; solo and ensemble, choirs, bands, children and adults. Professional and amateur. Competitive or non-competitive at entrant's desire.
Prizes: Many scholarships and certificates awarded.
Dates and Locations: April 24—May 5, 1990—various halls in Walkerton.
Deadline for Application: February 1, 1990.
Comments: Highlight concert on May 5 featuring the best of the festival and the award presentations.

Montreal International Music Competition

Place des Arts, 1501 rue Jeanne-Mance
Montreal, PQ H2X 1Z9
(514) 285-4380
FAX (514) 285-4266

Aims and Objectives: Competitions devoted to violin, piano and voice scheduled on a four-year cycle. Violin (1991), piano (1992), voice (1993).
Prizes: First prize of $15,000 plus eight additional prizes totalling $15,000.
Dates and Locations: 1991 (violin)—Montreal, Place des Arts.
Deadline for Application: February 1 each year (entrance fee: $35 Canadian).
Comments: Eligibility: 16-30 years old for violin and piano; 20-35 years old for voice. All nationalities are eligible.

Moose Jaw Kinsmen International Band and Choral Festival

P.O. Box 883
Moose Jaw, SK S6K 4P5
(306) 693-5933

Sponsor: Moose Jaw Kinsmen Club.
Aims and Objectives: To promote music among young students, using some of the best adjudicators in North America.
Events/Artists: Concert bands, stage bands, field marching, solos, ensembles, bagpipes, choral.
Prizes: Approximately $13,000 total.
Dates and Locations: TBA.
Deadline for Application: TBA.

1992 National Vocal Competition

P.O. Box 1718
Guelph, ON N1H 6Z9
(519) 821-3210

Sponsor: Edward Johnson Music Foundation.
Prizes: $15,000-plus.
Dates and Locations: 1992—Guelph.
Deadline for Application: November 1, 1991.

New Brunswick Competitive Festival of Music

P.O. Box 2022
Saint John, NB E2L 3T5
(506) 847-5800

Aims and Objectives: To hold a music festival in which children of all ages and musical disciplines compete on a friendly basis and learn by receiving expert adjudication.
Events/Artists: Competitive music classes for students of all ages in piano, violin and voice. Classes also for bands and choral groups.
Prizes: Trophies and many generous cash awards.
Dates and Locations: April 18-28, 1990. April 17-27, 1991.
Deadline for Application: February 17, 1990. February 16, 1991.
Comments: Out of province participants, university students and families welcome.

New Celebrity Competition

P.O. Box 57
Kamloops, BC V2C 5K3
(604) 372-5000

Sponsor: Kamloops Symphony Society.
Aims and Objectives: This piano competition is open to any Canadian citizen or landed immigrant meeting the following requirements: Applicants must have played with the Kamloops Symphony during the 12 months prior to the competition; applicants must also be engaged in studying their instrument.
Prizes: First prize $1,000, second prize $500.
Dates and Locations: March 17, 1990.
Comments: This is a national competition.

New Glasgow Folk Song Competition

294 Abercrombie Rd.
New Glasgow, ON B2H 1K9
(902) 752-6910
Sponsor: New Glasgow Music Festival Association.
Aims and Objectives: To acknowledge young talent and to provide an opportunity for amateur musicians to advance the art of folk music.
Events/Artists: Competition in music.
Dates and Locations: April 6-7, 1990—New Glasgow.
Deadline for Application: February 10, 1990.

The North American Radio Music Challenge

1209 King St. W., Suite 210
Toronto, ON M6K 1G2
(416) 820-6400
Sponsor: JCO Communications Inc.
Aims and Objectives: To discover new recording talent and send regional winners to the finals in November.
Prizes: Cash awards.
Dates and Locations: TBA.
Deadline for Application: TBA.

OSM Concours

85 St. Catherine St. W., Suite 900
Montreal, PQ H2X 3P4
(514) 842-3402
FAX (514) 842-0728
Sponsor: Orchestre symphonique de Montreal.
Aims and Objectives: To help and encourage Canadian musicians. Prize winners perform in concert with the OSM in a regular subscription series.
Events/Artists: 1989/90 (piano and voice), 1990/91 (strings and winds), 1991/92 (piano and voice).
Prizes: Total of $8,500.
Dates and Locations: January 5-10, 1990—Montreal. Dates in winter 1991 to be confirmed.
Deadline for Application: 1990/91 TBA.
Comments: Open to Canadian citizens or landed immigrants. Age restrictions: Strings and piano, Category A: 18-25, Category B: 17 and under; Winds: 16-25; Voice: 18-30.

Okanagan Valley Music Festival

P.O. Box 174
Penticton, BC V2A 6K3
(604) 492-3664
Sponsor: Okanagan Valley Music Festival Society of Penticton.
Aims and Objectives: To hold a competitive music and dance festival for students. Adjudicated by professionals.
Events/Artists: Competitive daily sessions concluding with dance and music highlight concerts.
Prizes: Scholarships and trophies awarded to winners in the various music and dance classes.
Dates and Locations: April 2-14, 1990—Penticton. 1991 dates TBA.
Deadline for Application: February 15, 1990.

Ontario Open Fiddle and Stepdance Competition

P.O. Box 119
Bobcaygeon, ON K0M 1A0
(705) 738-3569
Aims and Objectives: To promote and encourage old time fiddling and step dancing.
Events/Artists: Fiddle and stepdance contests for all ages in various classes.
Prizes: Cash awards and trophies for each class.
Dates and Locations: July 27-28, 1990—Bobcaygeon Arena.
Deadline for Application: July 15, 1990.

Oshawa-Whitby Kiwanis Music Festival

P.O. Box 921
Oshawa, ON L1H 7N1
(416) 263-2080
Aims and Objectives: To encourage the performance and appreciation of music.
Events/Artists: Adjudicated sessions for students entering instrumental, vocal, choral and speech arts classes.
Prizes: Scholarships and trophies.
Dates and Locations: April 1990—Oshawa.

COMPETITIONS

Pacific Northwest Music Festival

P.O. Box 456
Terrace, BC V8G 4B5
(604) 635-3215

Aims and Objectives: Opportunity for students to perform and grow artistically.
Events/Artists: For students and non-professionals.
Prizes: Various trophies and cash awards sponsored by businesses and individuals in the community.
Dates and Locations: March 8-16, 1990—Terrace, BC
Deadline for Application: January 10, 1990.

Pembroke Old Time Fiddling and Stepdancing Contest

P.O. Box 63, R.R. 1
Chalk River, ON K0J 1A0
(613) 584-3962

Aims and Objectives: To promote and encourage old time fiddling and stepdancing.
Events/Artists: 250 contestants.
Prizes: Cash and trophies.
Dates and Locations: September 1990.
Deadline for Application: Open to last minute.

Porcupine Music Festival de Musique

P.O. Box 662
Timmins, ON P4N 6K5
(705) 267-5310

Aims and Objectives: To promote music and music competitions in the Timmins area.
Events/Artists: Vocal, instrumental, piano.
Prizes: Scholarships, plaques, rose bowl (highest award).
Dates and Locations: February 26—March 7, 1990.
Deadline for Application: November 4, 1989.

Provincial Music Festival

45 Raymond Heights
Corner Brook, NF A2H 2S2
(709) 634-4735

Sponsor: Newfoundland Federation of Music Festivals.
Aims and Objectives: Competitors are selected by adjudicators to represent the province at the national Music Festival.
Events/Artists: Voice, piano, woodwinds, brass, strings. Amateur musicians.
Prizes: Cash awards from the Canadian Imperial Bank of Commerce.
Dates and Locations: TBA.
Comments: This festival is governed by the rules and regulations issued by the Federation of Canadian Music Festivals.

Q-107 Homegrown

2 Bloor St. E., Suite 3000
Toronto, ON M4W 1A8
(416) 967-3445
FAX (416) 924-2479

Sponsor: CILQ-FM 107.
Aims and Objectives: To foster and develop Canadian talent.
Events/Artists: Amateur-status Canadian artists, unsigned to a record label. Panel of judges rate bands on originality, performance and professionalism.
Prizes: Four finalists are selected to be released on one record. Other various prizes awarded.
Dates and Locations: TBA.
Deadline for Application: TBA.

The Rudolph Mathieu Awards

1240 Bay St.
Toronto, ON M5R 2C2
(416) 924-4427
FAX (416) 924-4837

Aims and Objectives: To encourage and support Canadian composers pursuing a career in composition.
Events/Artists: Solo or duet composition for one or two performers.
Prizes: $1,500, $1,000, $500.
Deadline for Application: May 15, 1990.

Sackville Music Festival

10 Lakeshore Dr.
Middle Sackville, NB E0A 2E0
(506) 536-2411
Sponsor: Sackville Music Festival Association.
Aims and Objectives: To have young players' performances assessed in a competitive music festival context.
Events/Artists: Piano, woodwind, strings, brass, vocal, chamber, choral; ages seven and up.
Prizes: Cash awards, plus a non-cash award for outstanding performance of a Canadian composition.
Dates and Locations: Early April—Sackville, NB and Amherst, NS.

Saskatchewan Music Festival Association Concerto Competition

1819 Cornwall St.
Regina, SK S4P 2K4
(306) 757-1722
Sponsor: Saskatchewan Music Festival Association.
Aims and Objectives: To provide an opportunity for the winner to play as a soloist with the RSO in the following year's concert season; to provide senior music students with a professional playing situation.
Prizes: $1,000, $300, $200.
Dates and Locations: March 1990.
Deadline for Application: TBA.

Sir Ernest MacMillan Awards

1240 Bay St., 9th Floor
Toronto, ON M5R 2C2
(416) 924-4427
FAX (416) 924-4837
Sponsor: Composers, Authors and Publishers Association of Canada.
Aims and Objectives: To encourage and support Canadian composers pursuing a career in composition.
Events/Artists: Composition for an orchestra of at least 12 performers (may include voice and/or tape).
Prizes: $1,500, $1,000, $500.
Deadline for Application: May 15, 1990.

The William St. Clair Low Awards

1240 Bay St.
Toronto, ON M5R 2C2
(416) 924-4427
FAX (416) 924-4837
Sponsor: Composers, Authors and Publishers Association of Canada.
Aims and Objectives: To encourage and support Canadian composers pursuing a career in composition.
Events/Artists: Chamber composition for an ensemble of three to 12 performers (may include voice and/or tape).
Prizes: $1,500, $1,000, $500.
Deadline for Application: May 15, 1990.

CONCERT PROMOTERS

ALBERTA

Brimstone Productions
P.O. Box 6834, Stn. D
Calgary, AB T2P 2E9
(403) 269-6806
FAX (403) 262-7139
Preferred Musical Styles: All styles.
Acts Represented: Anne Murray, Chris de Burgh, Doobie Brothers.

Celtic Productions Ltd.
15016-62 St.
Edmonton, AB T5A 2B5
(403) 478-6417
Preferred Musical Styles: Roots.
Acts Represented: Various, nationally.

Class Act International Inc.
1003 Woodward Towers, P.O. Box 1323
Lethbridge, AB T1K 4E1
(403) 320-5537
Preferred Musical Styles: Pop, MOR, Rock, C&W.
Acts Represented: 60-70 acts, accept new acts for Western Canada only.
Venues Represented: 20-30.

Heavelution Concert Productions
P.O. Box 762, Stn. G
Calgary, AB T3A 2G6
(403) 289-4073
Preferred Musical Styles: Pop, Rock, Metal.
Venues Represented: Calgary area venues.
Services: Promotion, production, security.
Special Projects: Promotion of local and regional talent.

Image Control Productions Ltd.
10852 Whyte Ave., Suite 203
Edmonton, AB T6E 2B3
(403) 433-2016
FAX (403) 439-4209
Preferred Musical Styles: Rock & Roll, Alternative, Country Rock, Reggae, Heavy Metal, Hardcore.
Acts Represented: Frank Carroll, Robb Gott and Hyrd Help, One Eyed Wendy.
Venues Represented: Fantasy Nightclub (W.E.M.), Andante, Sunset Club.

New Age Entertainment
107343-155 St.
Edmonton, AB T5P 2M7
(403) 476-6585
Preferred Musical Styles: Pop, Rock.

Jeff Parry Promotions
P.O. Box 1234, Stn. M
Calgary, AB T2P 2C2
(403) 230-5334
Preferred Musical Styles: All, accept new acts.

Pro Motion
P.O. Box 5663, Stn. L
Edmonton, AB T6C 4G1
(403) 437-4803
Contact: Al MacKechnie.

Revolutionary Happenings
9909-110 St., Suite 1402
Edmonton, AB T5K 2E5
(403) 428-8159
Preferred Musical Styles: Folk music that promotes social change.
Acts Represented: Jennifer Berezan, Lynn Lavner.
Services Offered: Specialize in producing fundraising concerts for progressive groups.

Shantero Productions
519-20 Ave. N.W.
Calgary, AB T2M 1C7
(403) 282-3680
Preferred Musical Styles: C&W, Folk, Blues, Comedy, Mime, Theatre.

Yardbird Productions Ltd.
9716-89 Ave.
Edmonton, AB T6E 2S2
(403) 433-4763
Preferred Musical Styles: Blues, Folk, Country, Rock, Pop.

BRITISH COLUMBIA

Crystal Concert Productions Ltd.
13876-102 Ave., Suite 408
Surrey, BC V3T 1P1
(604) 589-4510
Preferred Musical Styles: Pop, MOR, Rock, C&W.
Services Offered: Full-service concert promoter.

Famous Events Ltd.
68 Water St., Suite 504
Vancouver, BC V6B 1A4
(604) 689-3448
Services Offered: Special events production company.

Festival Concert Society
3737 Oak St., Suite 103
Vancouver, BC V6H 2M4
(604) 736-3737
Preferred Musical Styles: Classical and Folk music, plus opera and ballet.
Acts Represented: 70 artists and groups.
Services Offered: Established in 1961 to provide top quality artists to communities and school districts.

Front Row Productions
747 Cardero St.
Vancouver, BC V6B 3V7
(604) 681-8311
FAX (604) 684-0726
Preferred Musical Styles: MOR.
Network Affiliations: CARAS, CIRPA, BC Touring Council.

Just Jazz
1460 Nelson St., Unit 2
Vancouver, BC V6G 1L7
(604) 669-2698
Preferred Musical Styles: New Orleans and Dixieland Jazz.
Services Offered: Festival and Jazz promotion.

Paul Mercs/Craig McDowall Concerts

68 Water St., Suite 405
Vancouver, BC V6B 1A4
(604) 683-4233
FAX (604) 683-4298
Preferred Musical Styles: Pop, Rock, Broadway Musicals, MOR.
Acts Represented: Harry Belafonte, Crowded House, Honeymoon Suite, Amy Grant, INXS.
Venues Represented: All major markets from Vancouver to Toronto.
Services Offered: Pre-production, accommodation, local publicity plus all aspects of show production.

Pacific Show Productions

925 West Georgia St., Suite 316
Vancouver, BC V6C 1R5
(604) 684-3242
Preferred Musical Styles: Pop, MOR, Show Bands plus convention acts, music variety, lounge performers.
Network Affiliations: A.F. of M., BC Touring Council, Tourism Victoria.
Services Offered: Convention entertainment productions, stage shows, tours, lounge and casual bookings.

Perryscope Concert Productions Ltd.

2241 Oak St.
Vancouver, BC V6H 3W6
(604) 731-4621
FAX (604) 731-1318
Preferred Musical Styles: Concert, theatre and special events.
Venues Represented: All venues: British Columbia and Alberta.

Prestige Entertainment Agencies Ltd.

177 W. 7 Ave., 4th Floor
Vancouver, BC V5Y 1K5
(604) 846-5535
Preferred Musical Styles: Pop, Jazz.
Network Affiliations: CART, ITAA.

Ramcoff Productions Management Ltd.

339 E. 27 St.
N. Vancouver, BC V7N 1B9
(604) 986-6838
Preferred Musical Styles: Classical chamber ensembles.
Acts Represented: Vancouver Wind Quintet, North Vancouver Wind Trio, Vancouver Chamber Winds, I Musici; Vancouver, regionally.

Rogue Folk Club

2982 W. 3 Ave.
Vancouver, BC V6K 1N1
(604) 736-3022
Preferred Musical Styles: Folk.
Venues Represented: W.I.S.E. Hall (Vancouver).

T.O.C. Talent/ Native Talent Agency

800-1155 West Georgia St.
Vancouver, BC V6E 3H4
(604) 683-4230 or 275-1696
FAX (604) 687-5519
Preferred Musical Styles: All styles.
Acts Represented: Arrows to Freedom (singers/dancers), Rick Patterson (country singer), Shaman Singers.
Services Offered: Management, public relations, promotion and marketing.

MANITOBA

Nite Out Entertainment

70 Albert St., Suite 200
Winnipeg, MB R3B 1E9
(204) 943-8800
Preferred Musical Styles: All.
Venues Represented: Regional: Manitoba, Saskatchewan, Alberta.

University of Winnipeg Students' Association, Program Department

515 Portage Ave., Suite 2L30
Winnipeg, MB R3B 2E9
(204) 786-9126
FAX (204) 786-1824
Preferred Musical Styles: All styles.
Network Affiliations: COCA, CARAS.
Services Offered: Evening concerts, lunchtime entertainment, films and lectures.
Special Projects: Student orientation (September).

NEW BRUNSWICK

Bob Lee Productions Ltd.
698 Main St., P.O. Box 1354
Moncton, NB E1C 8T6
(506) 389-3730
Preferred Musical Styles: All styles.
Acts Represented: Various, regionally.

NEWFOUNDLAND

Donna DeCarlo Enterprises
P.O. Box 901
Bishops Falls, NF A0H 1C0
(709) 489-7144
Preferred Musical Styles: All styles.
Acts Represented: Ten, new acts accepted.
Network Affiliations: CART.

NOVA SCOTIA

Bruce Hudson Productions
P.O. Box 3250
Halifax, NS B3J 3H5
(902) 429-7007
Contact: Bruce Hudson.

Brookes Diamond Productions
World Trade and Convention Centre
1800 Argyle St., Suite 507
Halifax, NS B3J 3N8
(902) 422-7000
FAX (902) 422-2929
Preferred Musical Styles: A/C, Country, Classical, Traditional.
Acts Represented: Rita MacNeil, Joan Kennedy, John Allan Cameron, Abraxas Trio.
Services Offered: Artists management, booking and tour co-ordination.

ONTARIO

Apricot Talent & Recording Industries Inc.
1449 Ridgebrook Dr., Suite 120
Gloucester, ON K1B 4T1
(613) 749-1116
FAX (613) 238-1687
Preferred Musical Styles: Top 40 Rock, MOR, Rock, Metal.
Acts Represented: Antix, In & Out, Lexy Jones, Johnny The Fox.
Venues Represented: Beachcomber Lounge (Talisman), airforce bases (Ottawa), Coulonge Hotel (Quebec), Barrymores (Ottawa).
Network Affiliations: CART.
Services Offered: Booking agency.

BGS Music Promotions
64 Glen Manor Dr.
Toronto, ON M4E 2X2
(416) 698-0715
Preferred Musical Styles: Classical Guitar, Classical Ensembles.
Acts Represented: Stepan Rak, Jukka Savijoki, Alan Torok, The Castellani- Andriaccio Duo, Savijoki/Helasvuo.

Big Time Productions Ltd.
54 Duncombe Dr., Lower Level
Hamilton, ON L9A 2G2
(416) 389-4265
FAX (416) 389-4265
Preferred Musical Styles: Contemporary, Rock, Pop, Theatricals, Dixieland, Big Band, Jazz, Blues, C&W.
Acts Represented: Gowan, Kim Mitchell, Candi, Honeymoon Suite.
Venues Represented: Brantford Civic Centre, Hamilton Convention Centre, Niagara Falls Arena.
Clients: Department of Culture and Recreation, City of Hamilton, Hamilton Downtown Business Improvement Association, Burlington Sound of Music.

CBD Enterprises
180 Duncan Mill Rd., Suite 400
Don Mills, ON M3B 1Z6
(416) 441-2144
FAX (416) 441-2259
Preferred Musical Styles: Pop, MOR, C&W.
Network Affiliations: Founding member of ISES.
Services Offered: Special event planning and consulting.

Canadent Concerts Management

1534 Dearbourne Dr.
Sudbury, ON P3A 5A4
(705) 566-8465
FAX (705) 566-0380
Preferred Musical Styles: Classical, Light Classical.

Concert Productions International (CPI)

72 Fraser Ave., Suite 222
Toronto, ON M6K 3E1
(416) 538-0077
FAX (416) 538-0100
Preferred Musical Styles: All styles.
Contact: Arthur Fogel.

Crossroads Entertainment Consultants

180 Duncan Mill Rd., Suite 400
Don Mills, ON M3B 1Z6
(416) 441-2144
FAX (416) 441-2259
Preferred Musical Styles: All kinds.
Network Affiliations: ISES, Toronto Musicians' Association (A.F. of M.).

Dobbin Agency

477A Princess St.
Kingston, ON K7L 1C3
(613) 549-4401
Preferred Musical Styles: Pop MOR, Rock, C&W.
Network Affiliations: CART.

Ray Douglas Promotions

P.O. Box 7213, Sandwich
Windsor, ON N9C 3Z1
(519) 969-1203 or 258-2288
Preferred Musical Styles: MOR, Pop, C&W, Jazz, Big Bands, Classical Artists.
Acts Represented: Ray Douglas International Big Band, Joan Eastman and the Music Makers, The Kenny Crone Jazz Group.
Venues Represented: Victoria Tavern, Kozaks By The Sea Tavern, Tourist and Convention Bureau.
Network Affiliations: A.F. of M.
Special Projects: The Offshore International Jazz Society.

ESP — Elwood Saracuse Productions Ltd.

6 Lansing Sq, Suite 129
Willowdale, ON M2J 1T5
(416) 499-7070
FAX (416) 492-4108
Preferred Musical Styles: All styles.
Acts Represented: Pharazon Dance Company, Video Hits Alive, Clazz Flute & Harp Duo.
Network Affiliations: CAFE.
Services Offered: Specializing in public and corporate special events.

Elliott Lefko Productions

191 St. George St., Suite 507
Toronto, ON M5R 2M6
(416) 323-3936
FAX (416) 323-3936
Preferred Musical Styles: Alternative, Underground, Rock, Acoustic.
Venues Represented: Apocalypse Club (Toronto).

Richard Flohil & Associates

1240 Bay St., Suite 303
Toronto, ON M5R 2A7
(416) 925-3154
FAX (416) 925-0136
Preferred Musical Styles: Acoustic, Roots, Blues, Folk.
Acts Represented: Loreena McKennitt, Downchild Blues Band, Cromdale (Bobby Watt).
Clients: Stony Plain Records, RBI Productions, Mariposa Festival.
Services Offered: Full public relations, publicity and promotion services.
Special Projects: Also promote concerts in Toronto area venues.

Jim Ford & Associates Inc.

315 Soudan Ave.
Toronto, ON M4S 1W6
(416) 483-0663
FAX (416) 483-2866
Preferred Musical Styles: MOR, Pop, Musical Comedy.
Acts Represented: Peter Appleyard, John Arpin, Buddy Wasisname and the Other Fellers.

Attila Glatz International Music Management

21 Webster Ave.
Toronto, ON M5R 1N6
(416) 923-6245
Preferred Musical Styles: Classical, Pop, Rock, MOR.
Acts Represented: Accept new acts.
Services Offered: International tours for various show bands.

Golden Media Presentation Ltd.

P.O. Box 120
Carlisle, ON L0R 1H0
(416) 689-4421
Preferred Musical Styles: Bluegrass, Country.
Acts Represented: Accept new acts.
Special Projects: Organize Bluegrass Canada, annually.

The Gords of Barrymore's

323 Bank St.
Ottawa, ON K2P 1X9
(613) 238-5842
FAX (613) 238-1687
Preferred Musical Styles: All styles.
Acts Represented: Monkees, Kris Kristoferson, Violent Femmes.
Venues Represented: Barrymore's (Ottawa), Porter Hall (Carleton University), Ottawa Civic Centre.
Affiliated Companies: Barrymore's Imperial Theatre Ltd.

Gross National Product

425 University Ave., Suite 601
Toronto, ON M5G 1T6
(416) 977-8777
Preferred Musical Styles: American and English Funk.
Venues Represented: Montreal, Ottawa, Toronto and Vancouver.

Hollywood North Promotions

4544 Dufferin St., Suite 24
Downsview, ON M3H 5X2
(416) 736-6319
Preferred Musical Styles: All styles, original bands or single performers.
Venues Represented: Spectrum, Entex, plus others.
Services Offered: Concert production, promotions, videos and special events.

Hollywood Productions

280 College St.
Toronto, ON M5T 1R9
(416) 975-0284
FAX (416) 363-6986
Preferred Musical Styles: All.
Acts Represented: Jr. Gone Wild, Pat Temple & The High Lonesome Players, Shotgun Rationale.
Services Offered: Touring merchandise service.

Darina Hradkova Artists Management Services

238 Davenport Rd., Suite 37
Toronto, ON M5R 1Y6
(416) 968-0960
Preferred Musical Styles: Classical, MOR.
Services Offered: Publicity and promotion.

Jam Jam Talent Booking

2108 Queen St. E.
Toronto, ON M4E 1E2
(416) 698-2498
Preferred Musical Styles: Rock, New Wave, Reggae, Funk, Hardcore, Country, R&B, Soul.
Acts Represented: Nationally.

Jilljill Productions

1235 Lambeth Rd.
Oakville, ON L6H 2E2
(416) 849-0244
Preferred Musical Styles: Alternative, Punk, Hardcore.
Acts Represented: Various, regionally.
Services Offered: Individual concert promotion.

Lant-International

569 Lynwood Dr., P.O. Box 1085
Cornwall, ON K6H 5V2
(613) 938-1532
Contact: Charles W.B. Lant, CEO.
Acts Represented: All, mainly C&W.
Venues Represented: Across Canada and the United States.

Elliott Lefko Productions

101 St. George St., Suite 507
Toronto, ON M5R 2M6
(416) 323-3936
Acts Represented: Various, nationally and internationally.

M&G Promotions

5 Delroy Ave., Suite 201
Kitchener, ON N2A 2S2
(519) 741-0680
Preferred Musical Styles: Various.
Acts Represented: Beatlemania, Elvis Wade and The Jordanaires, Canadian Country Fever.
Venues Represented: Arenas and theatres.
Network Affiliations: A.F. of M.
Services Offered: Concert tours and management.
Special Projects: Outdoor festivals.

Mariposa Folk Foundation

95 Lavinia Ave.
Toronto, ON M6S 3H9
(416) 769-3655
FAX (416) 769-9008
Preferred Musical Styles: Folk, Traditional, Blues, Roots, Celtic.
Venues Represented: Mariposa, the festival of roots music, Molson Park, Barrie, ON (June '90). Also various venues in Toronto for concerts, including The Diamond, Transac, Harbourfront.
Network Affiliations: Ontario Council of Folk Festivals, Festivals Ontario.

Music Here and Now

1967 Main St. W., Suite 45
Hamilton, ON L8S 4P4
(416) 526-6579
Preferred Musical Styles: Chamber Ensembles, Contemporary Classical.

Ontario Place Corporation

955 Lakeshore Blvd. W.
Toronto, ON M6K 3B9
(416) 965-5225
Preferred Musical Styles: Pop, Classical, Rock, MOR, Folk, R&B, C&W.
Acts Represented: Accept new acts.

POP Music

P.O. Box 499, Stn. A
Ottawa, ON K1N 8V5
(613) 238-3906
Preferred Musical Styles: Pop, Rock, MOR.
Acts Represented: Avery Singer, Heaven's Radio, The Magic Circle.
Affiliated Companies: Lowertown Music.
Clients: Heaven's Radio.
Services Offered: Concert management, marketing and publicity.
Special Projects: Televised concerts.

Priceless Productions

P.O. Box 474
Welland, ON L3B 5R2
(416) 788-0055
Preferred Musical Styles: All styles.
Acts Represented: 12, accept new acts.

Progressive Talent Productions Inc.

2 Melanie Dr., Unit 3A
Brampton, ON L6T 4K9
(416) 793-8133
FAX (416) 793-8110
Preferred Musical Styles: All styles.
Acts Represented: Deerhurst Vegas-Style Review, Beatlemania, Rita MacNeil.
Venues Represented: Skyline Hotel (Toronto), Constellation Hotel (Toronto), Roy Thomson Hall (Toronto), Hamilton Place (Hamilton), O'Keefe Centre (Toronto).
Network Affiliations: ITAA.
Clients: Bell Canada, Northern Telecom, Apple.
Services Offered: Complete convention services, corporate functions and national tours.

Prologue to the Performing Arts

252 Bloor St. W., 12th Floor, Suite 200
Toronto, ON
Preferred Musical Styles: Folk, Jazz, Pop, Classical, for young audiences 13-18 years.
Venues Represented: Schools and libraries.

Skarratt Promotions Inc.

19 Hess St. S.
Hamilton, ON L8P 3M7
(416) 527-0552
Preferred Musical Styles: All styles.
Acts Represented: Nationally.

Star Attractions

P.O. Box 2154
Oshawa, ON L1H 7V4
(416) 723-6644
FAX (416) 436-9774
Preferred Musical Styles: Pop, MOR, Rock, C&W.
Acts Represented: Various.
Venues Represented: Various.
Special Projects: Corporate bookings.

Star Treatment

P.O. Box 1329
Pembroke, ON K8A 6Y6
(613) 735-4060
Preferred Musical Styles: Pop, MOR, Rock.

Lou Turco Presents (LTP)
P.O. Box 400
Sault Ste. Marie, ON P6A 5N2
(705) 942-7177
Preferred Musical Styles: All styles.
Acts Represented: Accept new acts.
Venues Represented: Serving Sault Ste. Marie, Northwestern Ontario and the upper peninsula of Michigan.

University of Western Ontario Students' Council
Room 268, U.C.C. Building
U.W.O.
London, ON N6A 3K7
(519) 661-3574
FAX (519) 661-3816
Preferred Musical Styles: All styles.
Venues Represented: Spoke Tavern (capacity 400), Alumni Hall (capacity 2,330).
Network Affiliations: COCA.

Warner Casselman Music
7305 Woodbine Ave., Suite 455
Markham, ON L3R 3V7
(416) 477-3780
Preferred Musical Styles: Rock, MOR.
Acts Represented: Three, accept new acts.

Womanly Way Productions
427 Bloor St. W.
Toronto, ON M5S 1X7
(416) 925-6568
Acts Represented: Primarily female artists.

QUEBEC

ARS Musicalis
P.O. Box 181
Montreal, PQ H3X 3T4
(514) 861-3485
Preferred Musical Styles: Classical.
Acts Represented: Six, accept new acts.

Les Productions BSST
16 rue Saint-Stanislas
Quebec City, PQ G1R 4G9
(418) 694-9327
Preferred Musical Styles: Classical.
Acts Represented: Duo Todd-Simard, L'Ensemble Instrumental du Quebec.
Services Offered: Concerts and recordings.

Stella Black Productions
P.O. Box 23
Ste. Anne de Bellevue, PQ H9X 3L4
(514) 457-6311
Preferred Musical Styles: Classical, Dance Music.
Venues Represented: Hotels, conventions, bars, salons.
Services Offered: Permanent music placements.

Black Tiger Productions
264 Ste. Catherine o.
Montreal, PQ H2X 2A1
(514) 954-1221
Preferred Musical Styles: Jazz, Blues, Reggae, R&B, Afro-Caribbean.
Acts Represented: Mango Stars, Blue Monday, Rising Sun Afro-Jazz Orchestra.
Venues Represented: Area universities, CEGEPs, Place des Arts.

Productions Bob Carlisle Enrg.
P.O. Box 1357, Stn. B
Montreal, PQ H3B 3K9
(514) 653-0442
Preferred Musical Styles: Pop, MOR, C&W, Bavarian, Dixieland, Ethnic, Big Band.
Acts Represented: Accept new acts.
Network Affiliations: A.F. of M., CARAS and others.

Donald K. Donald
6265 Cote-de-Liesse, Suite 200
Montreal, PQ H4T 1C3
(514) 735-2724
Preferred Musical Styles: All styles.
Acts Represented: Many international headliners.

Fogel-Sabourin Productions

3431 rue St. Denis
Montreal, PQ H2X 3L1
(514) 288-7500
Preferred Musical Styles: Pop, MOR, Rock and others.
Services Offered: 100 shows annually in Montreal and other eastern markets.

Pierre Gravel — Impresario

89 Alexandra St.
Granby, PQ J2G 2P4
(514) 372-7764
FAX (514) 372-4391
Preferred Musical Styles: Pop, MOR, Rock, C&W.
Acts Represented: Andre-Philippe Gagnon, Denis Lacombe.
Venues Represented: International.
Services Offered: Management and booking.

Great Artists Management

3575 boul. St. Laurent, Suite 810
Montreal, PQ H2X 2T7
(514) 842-2968
Preferred Musical Styles: Classical, Variety.
Acts Represented: Andre Gagnon, McGill Chamber Orchestra, nationally.

Sheldon Kagan Productions Ltd.

1020-5 Ave.
Dorval, PQ H9S 1J2
(514) 631-2160
FAX (514) 631-4430
Preferred Musical Styles: Pop, MOR, Big Band.

Les Productions Ghyslaine Lacoste & Associates

6647-24 Ave.
Montreal, PQ H1T 3M6
(514) 722-6861

Nouveau Spec Inc.

6370 Place des Outardes
Laval, PQ H7L 3T1
(514) 963-2726
FAX (514) 963-0608
Preferred Musical Styles: Pop, Rock, Theatre.
Acts Represented: Starmania, Lord of the Rings, Dixie Band.
Network Affiliations: ADISQ.
Services Offered: Entertainment consultant for corporations.

Productions RAM-16

3616 Ste-Famille
Montreal, PQ H2X 2L4
(514) 845-6475
Preferred Musical Styles: New Age.
Acts Represented: Ka, Flash Cube.
Affiliated Companies: SAGA disques.
Distributor: Distributions RAM-16.

SASKATCHEWAN

Roadside Attractions Inc.

718 Eastlake Ave.
Saskatoon, SK S7N 1A3
(306) 863-2890
Preferred Musical Styles: Folk, Blues, Rock, Jazz, Pop.
Acts Represented: Bruce Cockburn, Murray McLauchlan, Colin James and others.

Show-Time Productions

1418 College Dr.
Saskatoon, SK S7N 0W7
(306) 653-0901
Preferred Musical Styles: C&W, Pop.
Venues Represented: Regional.

State of the Art Productions

3230 Argyle Rd.
Regina, SK S4S 2B4
(306) 586-2992
FAX (306) 584-1187
Contact: Ria Kaal.
Preferred Musical Styles: All.
Acts Represented: Williams & Ree.
Services Offered: Festival consultation.

CONCERT VENUES

ALBERTA

Arden Theatre
5 St. Anne St.
St. Albert, AB T8N 3Z9
(403) 459-1540
FAX (403) 460-2394
Contact: Theatre Manager.
Style of Music: Pop, Country and Contemporary.
Seating Capacity: 529.
Liquor License: Theatre bar.
Booking Agent: Theatre Manager.
Comments: Available for rent by promoters. St. Albert is a dormitory suburb of Edmonton, located a 20 minute drive from downtown.

The Arena
155 Ash Ave. S.E.
Medicine Hat, AB
(403) 529-8344
Seating Capacity: 5,000.
Mailing Address:
c/o City Hall
580-1 St. S.E.
Medicine Hat, AB T1A 8E6

The Arts Centre
Red Deer College
56 Ave. and 32 St., P.O. Box 5005
Red Deer, AB T4N 5H5
(403) 342-3520
Style of Music: All styles (mainly classical).
Seating Capacity: 589.
Liquor License: Yes.

Calgary Centre for Performing Arts

205-8 Ave. S.E.
Calgary, AB T2G 0K9
(403) 294-7455
FAX (403) 294-7457
Contact: Marcia Elane, director of programming & marketing.
Style of Music: All styles.
Seating Capacity: 1,800.
Liquor License: Yes.

Canada Games Sportsplex

2510 Scenic Dr. S.
Lethbridge, AB T1J 0P6
(403) 329-4737
FAX (403) 320-9369
Style of Music: All.
Seating Capacity: 6,543 (reserve seating), 7,884 (festival), 2,996 (portable theatre).
Liquor License: No.
Booking Agent: Sportsplex promotes and co-promotes.
Comments: Full-service, multi-purpose facility. All rentals are negotiable.

Citadel Theatre

9828-101A Ave.
Edmonton, AB T5J 3C6
(403) 426-4811
FAX (403) 428-7194
Contact: Denis Themens.
Style of Music: All forms of music and theatre.
Seating Capacity: 240.
Liquor License: Yes.

Commonwealth Stadium/Clarke Stadium

P.O. Box 2359
Edmonton, AB T5J 2R7
(403) 428-5086
Style of Music: All types.
Seating Capacity: 60,000/20,000.
Liquor License: Yes.

Dinwoodie Lounge

University of Alberta Students' Union
256 Sub. University of Alberta
Edmonton, AB T6G 2J7
(403) 492-2048
FAX (403) 492-4643
Contact: Gerald Stoll.
Style of Music: Blues, Rock.
Seating Capacity: 620 (Dinwoodie Lounge), 720 (Horowitz Theatre).
Liquor License: Yes.
Booking Agent: All styles.

Edmonton Convention Centre

9797 Jasper Ave.
Edmonton, AB T5J 1N9
(403) 421-9797
FAX (403) 425-5121
Contact: Lloyd Fitzsimonds.
Style of Music: All.
Seating Capacity: 3,250.
Liquor License: Yes.

Genevieve E. Yates Memorial Centre

1010-4 Ave. S.
Lethbridge, AB T1J 0P6
(403) 320-3845
Style of Music: Classical, Folk.
Seating Capacity: 500.

Grande Prairie Regional College Theatre

10726-106 Ave.
Grande Prairie, AB T8V 4C4
(403) 539-9016
Style of Music: Classical, Jazz, Folk.
Seating Capacity: 487.

Jasper Activity Centre

Pyramid Ave., P.O. Box 1539
Jasper, AB T0E 1E0
(403) 852-3381
Style of Music: Pop, Folk, Jazz, Classical.
Seating Capacity: 350.
Liquor License: No.

Lethbridge and District Exhibition

3401-6 Ave. S.
Lethbridge, AB T1J 1G5
(403) 328-4491
Style of Music: All.
Seating Capacity: 2,800 (inside Exhibition Pavillion), 1,700 (bleachers), 1,100 (floor).
Liquor License: Yes.

Northern Alberta Jubilee Auditorium

87 Ave. and 114 St.
Edmonton, AB
(403) 427-2760
Style of Music: All types of music plus dance and opera.
Seating Capacity: 2,694.
Mailing Address:
14th Floor, CN Tower
10004-104 Ave.
Edmonton, AB T5J 0K5

Northlands Coliseum

P.O. Box 1480
Edmonton, AB T5J 2N5
(403) 471-7210
Style of Music: All.
Seating Capacity: 17,309 (18,500 with floor seats).
Liquor License: No.

Olympic Saddledome

P.O. Box 1060
Calgary, AB T2P 2K8
(403) 261-0400
FAX (403) 265-7172
Contact: Libby Raines.
Style of Music: Various.
Seating Capacity: 20,018.
Liquor License: For selected events only.

Performing Arts Centre, University of Lethbridge

4401 University Dr.
Lethbridge, AB T1K 3M4
(403) 329-2656
Style of Music: Pop, Jazz, Folk, Country, Classical.
Seating Capacity: 450 (University Theatre), 203 (Recital Hall).

Southern Alberta Jubilee Auditorium

1415-14 Ave. N.W.
Calgary, AB T2N 1M4
(403) 289-5531
Style of Music: Variety.
Seating Capacity: 2,719.
Liquor License: Yes.

University Theatre

2500 University Dr.
Calgary, AB T2N 1N4
(403) 220-4900
FAX (403) 220-4905
Contact: K. Hewitt.
Style of Music: All styles (mainly classical).
Seating Capacity: 500.
Liquor License: Yes.

Westerner Exposition Association

P.O. Box 176
Red Deer, AB T4N 5E8
(403) 343-7800
FAX (403) 341-4699
Contact: Larry Johnstone or Judy Herder.
Style of Music: Country, Folk.
Seating Capacity: 2,000.
Liquor License: No.

BRITISH COLUMBIA

Arts Club Theatres

1585 Johnson St.
Vancouver, BC V6H 3R9
(604) 687-5315
FAX (604) 687-3306
Contact: Micheal Cunningham.
Style of Music: All.
Seating Capacity: 480.
Liquor License: Yes.
Comments: Available Sundays.

Beban Park Recreation Centre

2300 Bowen Rd.
Nanaimo, BC V9R 3K7
(604) 758-1177
FAX (604) 390-4163
Contact: Joanne Sadler (Social Centre), Bill Bostwick (Arena).
Style of Music: All.
Seating Capacity: 630 (Social Centre), 2,755 (Arena).
Liquor License: Arena facility only.

Centennial Theatre Centre

2300 Lonsdale Ave.
North Vancouver, BC V7M 3L1
(604) 984-4484
FAX (604) 984-4294
Contact: Oksana Dexter.
Style of Music: All.
Seating Capacity: 718.
Liquor License: No (application in progress).
Booking Agent: No.
Comments: The Centennial Theatre is a fully-equipped, professionally staffed rental facility. The theatre produces some presentations throughout the season. Rental charges and a full technical package are available on request.

Commodore Ballroom

870 Granville St.
Vancouver, BC
(604) 681-7838
Style of Music: All.
Seating Capacity: 1,200.
Liquor License: Yes.

Kelowna Community Centre

1375 Water St.
Kelowna, BC V1Y 1J4
(604) 763-6011
Style of Music: All.
Seating Capacity: 865.
Liquor License: No.
Comments: Contact rental co-ordinator at ext. 249.

Massey Theatre

821-8 St.
New Westminster, BC V3L 4Z8
(604) 521-7430
FAX (604) 522-6653
Style of Music: All.
Seating Capacity: 880 (orchestra seats), 390 (balcony).
Liquor License: No.
Comments: Proscenium width 40 feet, stage depth 30 feet.

McPherson Playhouse

3 Centennial Sq.
Victoria, BC V8W 1P5
(604) 386-6400
Style of Music: All.
Seating Capacity: 837.
Liquor License: Yes.

Mount Elizabeth Theatre

1491 Kingfisher Ave.
Kitimat, BC V8C 1E9
(604) 632-7887
FAX (604) 632-4363
Contact: Yvonne Stowell.
Style of Music: All.
Seating Capacity: 512.
Liquor License: No.
Comments: This theatre is a combination rental/presenting facility which covers all disciplines.

The Orpheum

649 Cambie St.
Vancouver, BC V6B 2P1
(604) 665-3050
FAX (604) 665-3001
Contact: John Dyck.
Style of Music: All (emphasis on Classical music).
Seating Capacity: 2,788.
Liquor License: Yes.
Booking Agent: Ellen Greaves.
Comments: Owned and operated by the City of Vancouver, the Orpheum is a 2,788- seat facility located in Vancouver's downtown core. The Vancouver Symphony Orchestra is a principal tenant.

Pacific Coliseum

Pacific National Exhibition
P.O. Box 69020
Vancouver, BC V5K 4W3
(604) 253-2311
Style of Music: All.
Seating Capacity: 4,500-17,000.
Liquor License: Yes.
Booking Agent: Corinne Johnson.
Comments: Four different stage formats are available: theatre stage, in-the-round, full house and concert bowl.

Pacific National Exhibition

P.O. Box 69020
Vancouver, BC V5K 4W3
(604) 253-2311
Style of Music: Pop, Jazz, Country, MOR.
Seating Capacity: 15,000 (Coliseum), 3,000 (mainstage during annual exhibition).
Liquor License: Yes.
Booking Agent: Direct.

Penticton Community Centre Theatre

325 Power St.
Penticton, BC V2A 7K9
(604) 493-4171
Style of Music: All.
Seating Capacity: 443.
Liquor License: Yes.
Booking Agent: Ron Philpott.
Comments: The Community Centre Theatre staff facilitates sponsorship for performances at the Theatre. For sponsorship inquiries contact: The Penticton and District Community Arts Council Leir House, 220 Manor Park Ave. Penticton, BC (604) 492-7997

Prince Rupert Performing Arts Centre

1100 McBride St.
Prince Rupert, BC V8J 3H2
(604) 627-8888
Style of Music: All.
Seating Capacity: 700.
Liquor License: Yes.

Queen Elizabeth Theatre

649 Cambie St.
Vancouver, BC V6B 2P1
(604) 665-3050
FAX (604) 665-3001
Contact: John Dyck.
Style of Music: Broadway shows, dance, opera, pop, rock.
Seating Capacity: 2,815.
Liquor License: Yes.
Booking Agent: Ellen Greaves.
Comments: The Queen Elizabeth Theatre is owned and operated by the City of Vancouver and features a large proscenium stage, wings and fly spaces, and has well-equipped sound and lighting capabilities. This centrally located, 2,815-seat facility is available for rental throughout the year.

R.E.M. Lee Theatre

4920 Straume Ave.
Terrace, BC V8G 4V8
(604) 635-2101
Contact: T. Walker.
Style of Music: All.
Seating Capacity: 700.
Liquor License: No.
Booking Agent: T. Walker.

Royal Theatre

805 Broughton
Victoria, BC
(604) 386-6400
Style of Music: All.
Seating Capacity: 1,455.
Liquor License: Yes.

Sagebrush Theatre

821 Munro St.
Kamloops, BC V2C 5K3
(604) 374-3544
Style of Music: All.
Seating Capacity: 730.
Liquor License: Yes.

University of British Columbia, Music Recital Hall

6361 Memorial Rd.
Vancouver, BC V6T 1W5
(604) 228-4175
Style of Music: Classical.
Seating Capacity: 300.
Liquor License: No.

The Vancouver Playhouse

649 Cambie St.
Vancouver, BC V6B 2P1
(604) 665-3050
FAX (604) 665-3001
Contact: John Dyck.
Style of Music: Theatre, dance, recital, mini-opera and mini-musicals.
Seating Capacity: 670.
Liquor License: Yes.
Booking Agent: Ellen Greaves.
Comments: The 670-seat Vancouver Playhouse is owned and operated by the City of Vancouver. The Playhouse is centrally located and offers an intimate atmosphere.

Vernon Recreation Complex

3310-37 Ave.
Vernon, BC V1T 2Y5
(604) 545-6035
Seating Capacity: 1,070.
Liquor License: No.
Comments: The auditorium is available for rentals.

Victoria Memorial Arena
1925 Blanshard St.
Victoria, BC V8T 4J2
(604) 384-0444
Contact: J.H. Bate.
Style of Music: All.
Seating Capacity: Varies.
Liquor License: Yes.
Booking Agent: J.H. Bate.
Comments: Various size concert set-ups
from 2,000 to 6,500 seats.

Vincent Massey Theatre
835-8 St.
New Westminster, BC V3M 3S9
(604) 521-7430
Seating Capacity: 1,278.

Frederick Wood Theatre, University of British Columbia
6354 Crescent Rd.
Vancouver, BC V6T 1W5
Style of Music: All.
Seating Capacity: 400.
Liquor License: No.

MANITOBA

Keystone Centre
P.O. Box 122
Brandon, MB
(204) 728-2246
Style of Music: All.
Seating Capacity: 6,922 (including floor).
Liquor License: Yes.

Manitoba Centennial Concert Hall
555 Main St.
Winnipeg, MB R3B 1C3
(204) 956-1360
FAX (204) 944-1390
Contact: John C. Walton.
Style of Music: All.
Seating Capacity: 2,263.
Liquor License: Yes.
Booking Agent: John C. Walton.
Comments: The Centennial Concert Hall is
home to the Winnipeg Symphony Orchestra,
the Manitoba Opera Association and the Royal
Winnipeg Ballet and features over 250
performances of various kinds annually.

Pantages Playhouse Theatre
180 Market Ave. E.
Winnipeg, MB R3B 0P7
(204) 986-3004
FAX (204) 956-4502
Style of Music: All.
Seating Capacity: 1,475.
Liquor License: Yes.
Booking Agent: Contact theatre management.
Comments: This restored vaudeville theatre
is suited to intimate events.

Western Manitoba Centennial Auditorium
205-20 St.
Brandon, MB R7B 1L6
(204) 728-9510
Style of Music: Various.
Seating Capacity: 877.
Liquor License: Yes.
Comments: Contact theatre management for
rental costs, etc.

Winnipeg Convention Centre
375 York Ave.
Winnipeg, MB R3C 3J3
(204) 956-1720
FAX (204) 943-0310
Contact: Terry O'Reilly
Style of Music: Various.
Seating Capacity: 5,000.
Liquor License: Yes.
Comments: Venue available on a straight rental
basis or will consider a co- promotion arrange-
ment depending on nature of act, suitability and
target market.

NEW BRUNSWICK

Aitken University Centre, University of New Brunswick
University of New Brunswick
Fredericton, NB E3B 5A3
(506) 453-3555
FAX (506) 453-4599
Style of Music: Rock, Country, Jazz, Rap and
Contemporary.
Seating Capacity: 6,200.
Liquor License: Yes.
Booking Agents: Donald K. Donald, Jack
Roberts Agency, Maritime Concerts Productions
and Genesis Productions, Fredericton.

Lord Beaverbrook Rink
536 Main St.
Saint John, NB E2K 1J4
(506) 652-6710
Style of Music: All.
Seating Capacity: 4,000.
Liquor License: No.
Booking Agent: Same.

The Playhouse
686 Queen St.
Fredericton, NB E3B 5A6
(506) 458-8345
Contact: Theatre New Brunswick for rental
information.
Style of Music: All.
Seating Capacity: 723.
Liquor License: No.

NEWFOUNDLAND

Arts and Culture Centres

Corner Brook
University Ave., P.O. Box 100
Corner Brook, NF A2H 6C3
(709) 637-2581
Contact: Diane Butt, manager.
Style of Music: General programming.
Seating Capacity: 384.
Liquor License: Yes.
Booking Agent: Cultural Affairs
P.O. Box 1854
St. John's, NF A1C 5P9

Gander
50 boul. Airport
Gander, NF A1V 1K6
(709) 256-7575
Contact: Una Joseph, manager.
Style of Music: General programming.
Seating Capacity: 408.
Liquor License: No.
Booking Agent: Cultural Affairs
P.O. Box 1854
St. John's, NF A1C 5P9

Grand Falls
Cromer Ave.
Grand Falls, NF A2A 1W9
(709) 489-5741
Contact: Reg Pye, manager.
Style of Music: General programming.
Seating Capacity: 392.
Liquor License: No.
Booking Agent: Cultural Affairs
P.O. Box 1854
St. John's, NF A1C 5P9

Labrador
Hudson Dr., P.O. Box 69
Labrador City, NF A2V 2K3
(709) 944-7345
Contact: Karin Galliott, acting manager
Style of Music: General programming.
Seating Capacity: 348.
Liquor License: Yes.
Booking Agent: Cultural Affairs
P.O. Box 1854
St. John's, NF A1C 5P9

St. John's
Prince Philip Dr., P.O. Box 1854
St. John's, NF A1C 5P9
(709) 576-3867
FAX (709) 576-5952
Contact: Heather Morgan, manager.
Style of Music: General programming.
Seating Capacity: 1,013.
Liquor License: Yes.
Booking Agent: Cultural Affairs
P.O. Box 1854
St. John's, NF A1C 5P9

Stephenville
380 Massachusetts Dr.
Stephenville, NF A2N 3A5
(709) 643-4571
Contact: Janet White, manager.
Style of Music: General programming.
Seating Capacity: 447.
Liquor License: Yes.
Booking Agent: Cultural Affairs
P.O. Box 1854
St. John's, NF A1C 5P9

Humber Gardens
137 O'Connell Dr., P.O. Box 1080
Cornerbrook, NF A2H 6E1
(709) 634-2674
Style of Music: All.
Seating Capacity: 2,664 (3,000 in summer).
Liquor License: No.

St. John's Memorial Stadium - St. John's
Lake Ave., P.O. Box 908
St. John's, NF A1C 5H2
(709) 576-7820
FAX (709) 576-8467
Contact: Glenn Stanford.
Seating Capacity: 5,400 (festival), 4,200
(reserved).
Liquor License: Yes.
Comments: Will promote or co-promote on all
types of musical entertainment.

NORTHWEST TERRITORIES

Northern Arts and Cultural Centre

52 Ave. and 49 St., P.O. Box 1025
Yellowknife, NT X1A 2N7
(403) 873-4950
Contact: General manager.
Style of Music: All.
Seating Capacity: 313.
Liquor License: No.

NOVA SCOTIA

Convocation Hall, Acadia University

Main St.
Wolfville, NS B0P 1X0
(902) 542-2201
Style of Music: All.
Seating Capacity: 1,440.
Liquor License: No.
Comments: Convocation Hall is a university theatre situated in a population area of over 40,000. The student audience is in place from September through April, annually.

Dartmouth Sportsplex

110 Wyse Rd.
Dartmouth, NS B3A 1M2
(902) 464-2600
Seating Capacity: 5,200.
Liquor License: Yes.

Halifax Forum

2901 Windsor St.
Halifax, NS B3K 5E5
(902) 421-6574
Seating Capacity: 7,000.
Liquor License: Yes.
Booking Agent: Al Driscoll.

Halifax Metro Centre

5284 Duke St.
Halifax, NS B3J 3L2
(902) 421-8000
FAX (902) 422-2922
Contact: Colin Craig
Seating Capacity: 3,200 (concert bowl), 10,000 (full).
Liquor License: Yes.
Comments: 24 concerts in 1989, including Bruce Cockburn, The Irish Rovers and The Nylons.

The New Palace Cabaret

1721 Brunswick St.
Halifax, NS B3J 2G4
(902) 420-0015
Contact: Jerry Khoury.
Style of Music: Pop.
Seating Capacity: 1,000.
Liquor License: Yes.
Booking Agent: Eastern Talent International (Rick O'Grady).
Comments: The New Palace Cabaret is located in the heart of downtown Halifax.

Pictou County, North Colchester Exhibition

P.O. Box 773
Pictou, NS B0K 1H0
(902) 485-5858
Seating Capacity: 3,000.
Liquor License: No.
Comments: Agriculture exhibition held first week of September, Tues. to Sat. (inclusive), following Labour Day weekend.

Rebecca Cohn Auditorium

6101 University Ave.
Halifax, NS B3H 3J5
(902) 424-2267
Style of Music: All.
Seating Capacity: 1,041.
Liquor License: Yes.
Booking Agent: Brenda MacDonald.

ONTARIO

Alumni Auditorium, University of Ottawa
85 Hastey St.
Ottawa, ON K1N 6N5
(613) 564-3463
Seating Capacity: 300.
Liquor License: No.

Alumni Theatre, Carleton University
Colonel By Dr., Room 624, Southam Hall
Ottawa, ON K1S 5B6
(613) 788-3818 or 788-3821
FAX (613) 788-3928
Contact: Cedric B. Broten, theatre manager.
Style of Music: All.
Seating Capacity: 450.
Liquor License: No.
Booking Agent: Elizabeth Kingsbury.

Aultsville Hall
St. Lawrence College, Windmill Point
Cornwall, ON K6H 4Z1
(613) 993-6080, ext. 2176
Style of Music: Classical, Pop, Folk.
Seating Capacity: 680.

Bathurst Street Theatre
736 Bathurst St.
Toronto, ON
(416) 533-1161
Style of Music: All.
Seating Capacity: 600.

Bingeman Park Farms Ltd.
1380 Victoria St. N.
Kitchener, ON N2B 2E2
(519) 744-1555
Style of Music: All.
Seating Capacity: 1,850 (Marshall Hall), 1,250 (Ballroom), 600 (Lodge).
Liquor License: Yes.
Booking Agent: CPI plus an in-house agency.

Burwash Park
61 Demorest Ave.
Sudbury, ON P3C 3J5
(705) 522-1954
Style of Music: Country.
Seating Capacity: 30,000.
Liquor License: Yes.

Capitol Theatre
90 Dalhousie St., Suite 88, P.O. Box 1762
Brantford, ON N3T 5V7
(519) 752-9910
Style of Music: Opera, Classical, Jazz, Pop.
Seating Capacity: 1,200.
Liquor License: Yes.

The Centre in the Square
101 Queen St. N.
Kitchener, ON
(519) 578-5660
Style of Music: All.
Seating Capacity: 2,016.
Liquor License: Yes.

Chatham Cultural Centre
75 William St. N.
Chatham, ON N7M 4L4
(519) 354-8338
FAX (519) 436-3237
Contact: Margaret Eaton.
Style of Music: Jazz, Country, MOR.
Seating Capacity: 700.
Booking Agent: Margaret Eaton.

Cleary Auditorium and Convention Centre
201 Riverside Dr. W.
Windsor, ON N9A 5K4
(519) 252-8311
FAX (519) 973-4976
Contact: Theatre Manager.
Style of Music: Various.
Seating Capacity: 1,194.
Liquor License: Yes.

Convocation Hall, University of Toronto
King's College Circle
Toronto, ON M5S 1A5
(416) 978-2187
Seating Capacity: 1,730.
Liquor License: No.

Copps Coliseum
101 York Blvd.
Hamilton, ON L9G 3S4
(416) 527-7900
FAX (416) 527-6856
Contact: John T. Crane.
Style of Music: All.
Seating Capacity: 18,000.
Liquor License: No.

CONCERT VENUES

Cornwall Civic Centre
100 Water St.
Cornwall, ON
(613) 938-9400

Exhibition Stadium
Exhibition Place
Toronto, ON M6K 3C3
(416) 393-6209
Seating Capacity: 54,000.
Liquor License: No.

Fort William Gardens
901 Miles St.
Thunder Bay, ON P7C 1J9
(807) 625-2929
FAX (807) 623-4538
Contact: Bill Vass.
Seating Capacity: 4,100 (plus 700 standing room).
Liquor License: No.

The Grand Theatre
218 Princess St.
Kingston, ON K7L 1B2
(613) 546-1756
FAX (613) 546-5232
Contact: Nancy Helwig.
Style of Music: All.
Seating Capacity: 826.
Liquor License: Yes.

Grimsby Public Art Gallery
25 Adelaide St.
Grimsby, ON L3M 1X2
(416) 945-3246
Style of Music: Classical.

Guelph Memorial Gardens
50 Carden St.
Guelph, ON N1H 3A1
(519) 837-5620
Seating Capacity: 3,999 (plus 1,500 on floor).

Hamilton Place Theatre
P.O. Box 2080, Stn. A
Hamilton, ON L8N 3Y7
(416) 525-3100
FAX (416) 521-0924
Style of Music: All.
Seating Capacity: 2,181 (plus 10 wheelchair locations).
Liquor License: Yes.

Harbourfront Corporation
410 Queen's Quay W., Suite 500
Toronto, ON M5V 2Z3
(416) 364-7127
Seating Capacity: 410 (Water's Edge Cafe), 358 (Brigantine Room), 435 (Premiere Dance Theatre), 385 (du Maurier Theatre Centre).

Ivor Wynne Stadium
75 Balsam Ave. N.
Hamilton, ON L8L 6Y3
(416) 544-7978
Seating Capacity: 29,000.

Kingston Memorial Centre
303 York St., P.O. Box 671
Kingston, ON K7L 4X1
(613) 546-3183
Style of Music: Rock, Country, Pop.
Seating Capacity: 3,107.
Comments: Arena venue.

Kingswood Music Theatre
9560 Jane St.
Maple, ON L0J 1E0
(416) 832-8131
Style of Music: All.
Seating Capacity: 14,000.
Liquor License: No.
Booking Agent: Nederlander Concerts
(212) 730-0820.

Kitchener Memorial Auditorium
400 E. Ave.
Kitchener, ON N2H 1Z6
(519) 885-7396
Style of Music: All.
Seating Capacity: 6,300.
Liquor License: Yes.

Salle L.J. Fortin

7 Aurora Ave.
Kapuskasing, ON P5N 1J6
(705) 335-8461
Style of Music: Pop, Symphonic.
Seating Capacity: 677.
Liquor License: Yes.

Leah Posluns Theatre

4588 Bathurst St.
Toronto, ON M2R 1W6
(416) 636-2720
Box Office 630-6752
Style of Music: Classical chamber music.
Seating Capacity: 444.
Liquor License: No.

Lindsay Central Exhibition Grounds

37 Adelaide St. N.
Lindsay, ON K9V 4K8
(705) 324-5551
Contact: John Lester.
Seating Capacity: 3,500.
Liquor License: No.
Comments: 3,500 seat open air grandstand available to rent for concerts. Stage available.

MacMillan Theatre/ Walter Hall

Edward Johnson Building
80 Queen's Park
Toronto, ON M5S 1A1
(416) 978-3744
Contact: Wendy Deacon.
Style of Music: Opera, Classical, Jazz.
Seating Capacity: 815 (MacMillan Theatre), 450 (Walter Hall).
Liquor License: No.

Maple Leaf Gardens

60 Carleton St.
Toronto, ON M5B 1L1
(416) 977-1641
Style of Music: All.
Seating Capacity: 16,316.
Liquor License: No.

Markham Theatre for Performing Arts

171 Town Centre Blvd.
Markham, ON L3R 8G5
(416) 479-0201
FAX (416) 479-4870
Contact: Brenda Houston.
Style of Music: Pop, Symphony, Chamber, Jazz.
Seating Capacity: 528.
Liquor License: Yes.
Comments: A civic arts centre with an annual professional entertainment series. Computerized box office, lobby bar, free parking, state-of-the-art sound and lighting.

Massey Hall

178 Victoria St.
Toronto, ON M5B 1T7
(416) 363-7301
FAX (416) 363-5290
Style of Music: Pop, Jazz, Country, Classical, Ethnic.
Seating Capacity: 2,765.
Liquor License: No.
Booking Agent: Karen Killeen, manager.

Molson Park

100 Molson Park Dr.
Barrie, ON L4M 3V3
(705) 726-6272
FAX (705) 722-8357
Contact: Maggie McDaniel.
Style of Music: Varied.
Seating Capacity: 27,500.
Liquor License: Yes.
Booking Agent: Chart Toppers (Neill Dixon).

Music Gallery

1087 Queen St. W.
Toronto, ON M6J 1H3
(416) 534-6311
Style of Music: Alternative, Experimental, New Music.
Seating Capacity: Two theatres, 100 and 400.
Liquor License: Yes.
Comments: Leading centre for contemporary music in Canada. Concerts, workshops, programs and services. Recording studios and concert halls.

The Music Hall

147 Danforth Ave.
Toronto, ON M4K 1N2
(416) 465-0400
Style of Music: All.

National Arts Centre
Confederation Square
Ottawa, ON K1P 5W1
(613) 996-5051
Style of Music: All.
Seating Capacity: 350, 969, 2,326.
Liquor License: Yes.

North Bay Arts Centre
150 Main St. E., P.O. Box 911
North Bay, ON P1B 8K1
(705) 474-1944
Style of Music: Opera, Classical.
Seating Capacity: 1,014.
Liquor License: Yes.

O'Keefe Centre
1 Front St. E.
Toronto, ON M5E 1B2
(416) 393-7469
Style of Music: Various, mainly Opera.
Seating Capacity: 3,223.
Liquor License: Yes.
Booking Agent: Martin Onrot.

Ontario Place Forum
955 Lakeshore Blvd. W.
Toronto, ON M6K 3B9
(416) 965-5224
Style of Music: All.
Seating Capacity: 12,000.
Liquor License: No.
Booking Agent: Contact Ontario Place Corp., (416) 965-7810.

Orillia Opera House
20 Mississaga St. W.
Orillia, ON L3V 6K8
(705) 325-1311, ext. 25
FAX (705) 325-5178
Contact: David Fanstone.
Style of Music: All.
Seating Capacity: 691.
Liquor License: No.
Booking Agent: Eva O'Brien-Hurst.
Comments: This facility self-promotes and is also available for rentals.

Oshawa Civic Auditorium
99 Thornton Rd. S.
Oshawa, ON L1J 5Y1
(416) 728-5162
FAX (416) 436-5618
Contact: Robert Simon.
Seating Capacity: 3,418.
Liquor License: No.

Ottawa Civic Centre
1015 Bank St.
Ottawa, ON K1S 3W7
(613) 564-1485
FAX (613) 564-1619
Contact: Julie Chiasson.
Style of Music: Mostly rock concerts.
Seating Capacity: 9,355.
Liquor License: No.
Booking Agent: Bass Clef Entertainments.

Queen's University
Performing Arts Office
Kingston, ON K7L 3N6
(613) 545-2557
Style of Music: Classical, Dance, Theatre.
Seating Capacity: 953.
Liquor License: No.

Roy Thomson Hall
60 Simcoe St.
Toronto, ON M5J 2H5
(416) 593-4822
FAX (416) 593-4224
Style of Music: Pop, Jazz, Country, Classical, Ethnic.
Seating Capacity: 2,812.
Liquor License: Yes.
Booking Agents: Geoffrey Butler, executive director; Pat Taylor, production manager.
Comments: Reception and auditorium space available for private functions.

Ryerson Theatre
43 Gerrard St. E.
Toronto, ON M5B 2K3
(416) 979-5000
Style of Music: Classical, Jazz, Folk, Opera, Pop.
Seating Capacity: 1,250.
Comments: Theatre manager, ext. 6129.

Sault Memorial Gardens
269 Queen E.
Sault Ste. Marie, ON P6A 1Y9
(705) 759-5251
Style of Music: All.
Seating Capacity: 4,000.

Stratford Fairground Complex

20 Glastonbury Dr.
Stratford, ON N5A 6T1
(519) 271-5130
FAX (519) 271-5832
Contact: Brian Gropp.
Style of Music: All.
Seating Capacity: 1,400.
Liquor License: Yes.

Sudbury Community Arena

240 Elgin St. S.
Sudbury, ON P3E 3N6
(705) 675-7595
Seating Capacity: 6,000.
Liquor License: No.

Theatre Centre, University of Waterloo

200 University Ave. W.
Kitchener, ON N2L 3G1
(519) 885-1211, ext. 2126
FAX (519) 884-8995
Contact: Al Anderson, manager, ext. 6560.
Seating Capacity: 500/721 (two separate theatres).
Liquor License: No.
Booking Agent: Peter M.G. Houston, assistant manager in charge of rental clients.
Comments: Peter B. Carette, ext. 2128, technical director.

Thunder Bay Community Auditorium

P.O. Box 2209
Thunder Bay, ON P7B 5E8
(807) 343-2310
Style of Music: All.
Seating Capacity: 1,485.
Liquor License: Yes.

Victoria Hall, Concert Hall

55 King St. W.
Cobourg, ON K9A 2M2
(416) 372-4301 or 372-2210
FAX (416) 372-1533
Contact: Christine Sharp.
Style of Music: Various.
Seating Capacity: 320.
Liquor License: Yes.
Booking Agent: Christine Sharp.

QUEBEC

Salle Albert-Rousseau

2410 ch. Ste. Foy
Ste. Foy, PQ G1V 1T3
(418) 659-6710
Style of Music: Dance, Theatre and all styles of music.
Seating Capacity: 1,232.

Salle Andre-Mathieu

CEGEP Montmorency, 475 boul. de L'Avenir
Laval, PQ H7N 5H9
(514) 667-5100
Style of Music: Mostly Classical and Jazz.
Seating Capacity: 806.

Salle Andre-Prevost

535 rue Filion
St. Jerome, PQ J7Z 1J6
(514) 436-4330
Style of Music: Jazz, Pop.
Seating Capacity: 904.
Liquor License: No.

Salle des Argoulets

1111 rue Lapierre
La Salle, PQ H8N 2J4
(514) 364-3320
Style of Music: Folk, Jazz and dance presentations.
Seating Capacity: 784.

Auditorium Dufour

534 rue Jacques-Cartier e., P.O. Box 518
Chicoutimi, PQ G7H 5C8
(418) 549-3910
Style of Music: Classical, Jazz, Pop.
Seating Capacity: 1;013.
Liquor License: Yes.

Auditorium le Carrefour

600-7 rue.
Val d'Or, PQ J9P 3P3
(819) 825-3060
Style of Music: Jazz, Pop.
Seating Capacity: 798.
Liquor License: No.

Auditorium d'Almo

850 ave. Begin
Alma, PQ G8B 6J9
(418) 668-3033
Style of Music: Jazz, Folk, Dance.
Seating Capacity: 797.
Liquor License: Yes.

Centre Culturel de Jonquiere

4160 rue du Vieux-Pont, P.O. Box 2000
Jonquiere, PQ G7X 7W7
(418) 547-6631
Style of Music: All.
Seating Capacity: 350.
Liquor License: No.

Centre Culturel du CEGEP de Riviere-du-Loup

85 rue Ste. Anne
Riviere-du-Loup, PQ G5R 1R1
(418) 862-6009
Style of Music: Opera, Classical.
Seating Capacity: 1,000.
Liquor License: No.

Centre Culturel de Shawinigan

2100 des Saulles, P.O. Box 400
Shawinigan, PQ G9N 6V3
(819) 539-6676
FAX (819) 536-7255
Comments: One concert hall, two recital halls.

Salle Claude-Champagne de l'Universite de Montreal

Universite de Montreal, P.O. Box 6128, Stn. A
Montreal, PQ H3C 3J7
(514) 343-6000
Style of Music: Classical, Classical-Jazz, Folk.
Seating Capacity: 1,030.
Liquor License: On request.

Concordia University Concert Hall

7141 Sherbrooke St. W.
Montreal, PQ H4B 1R6
(514) 848-4718
FAX (514) 848-2808
Contact: Jane Needles, concert and concert hall manager.
Style of Music: All types (not heavy rock).
Seating Capacity: 620.
Liquor License: Yes.
Booking Agent: None.
Comments: This hall is new (opened in December 1989) and feature adjustable acoustics and flexible architecture.

Salle Georges-Beaulieu

CEGEP de Rimouski, 60 rue de l'Eveche o.
Rimouski, PQ G5L 4H6
(418) 723-1880
Style of Music: All.
Seating Capacity: 900.

Golem Concert Room

3460 Stanley St.
Montreal, PQ H3A 1R8
(514) 935-5066
Style of Music: Folk, Country, Bluegrass, singer/songwriters and new acoustic music, etc.
Seating Capacity: 80.
Liquor License: Yes.
Comments: The Golem is a non-profit venue presenting acoustic music.

Salle Maurice O'Bready

Universite de Sherbrooke, 2500 boul. Universite
Sherbrooke, PQ J1K 2R1
(819) 821-7742
Style of Music: All.
Seating Capacity: 1,564.
Liquor License: Yes.

Montreal Forum Inc.

2323 St. Catherine St. W.
Montreal, PQ H3H 1N2
(514) 932-2582
FAX (514) 932-8285
Contact: Aldo Giampaolo.
Style of Music: Rock, Symphonic, Opera.
Seating Capacity: Approximately 16,000.
Liquor License: Yes.
Booking Agent: Donald K. Donald Productions, (514) 735-2724.

Oboro Gallery

3981 St. Laurent, Suite 499
Montreal, PQ H2W 1Y5
(514) 844-3250

Palais Montcalm

995 place d'Youville
Quebec City, PQ G1R 3P9
(418) 691-2399
FAX (418) 691-6212
Contact: Denys Laforce.
Style of Music: All.
Seating Capacity: 1,367.
Liquor License: Yes.

Place des Arts

1501 Jeanne-Mance St.
Montreal, PQ H2X 1Z9
(514) 285-4200
Style of Music: Variety, no rock shows.
Seating Capacity: 3,000 (Salle Wilfred
Pelletier), 1,300 (Maisonneuve), 755 (Port Royale),
140 (Theatre du Cafe de la Place).
Liquor License: Yes.

Place Nikitoutagan

2330 rue de la Riviere-aux-Sables,
P.O. Box 2000
Jonquiere, PQ G7X 7W7
(418) 547-6631
Style of Music: All.
Seating Capacity: 800.
Liquor License: Yes.

Pollack Concert Hall

McGill University, Faculty of Music
555 Sherbrooke St. W.
Montreal, PQ H3A 1E3
(514) 398-4539
FAX (514) 398-8061
Contact: Richard Lawton, director of concerts
and publicity.
Style of Music: Classical, Jazz, Avant-Garde.
Seating Capacity: 600.
Liquor License: Receptions only.

Redpath Hall

McGill University, Faculty of Music
555 Sherbrooke St. W.
Montreal, PQ H3A 1E3
(514) 398-4539
FAX (514) 398-8061
Contact: Richard Lawton, director of concerts
and publicity.
Style of Music: Classical, Early Music,
Contemporary.
Seating Capacity: 350.
Liquor License: Receptions only.

Robert Guertin Sports Centre

125 Carillon, P.O. Box 351, Stn. A
Hull, PQ J8Y 6M9
(819) 777-2791
Style of Music: Pop, Country.
Seating Capacity: 3,580.
Liquor License: Yes.
Booking Agent: Yvon Sabourin.

Theatre de la Cite Universitaire

Universite Laval, 1358 Pavillon Pollack
Ste. Foy, PQ G1K 7P4
(418) 656-2765
Style of Music: All styles of music, dance and
theatre.
Seating Capacity: 686.
Liquor License: No.

Theatre Palace

135 rue Principale
Granby, PQ J2G 2V1
(514) 375-2262
Seating Capacity: 1,240.
Liquor License: Yes.

Universite de Montreal (CEPSUM)

2100 Edouard-Montpetit, P.O. Box 6128, Stn. A
Montreal, PQ
(514) 343-7826
FAX (514) 343-5721
Contact: Lyne McKay or Patrick Haccoun.
Style of Music: Pop, Jazz, Country.
Seating Capacity: 2,500-4,000.
Liquor License: Alcoholic beverages may be
sold according to a pre-established percentage.

Auditorium de Verdun

4110 boul. Lasalle
Verdun, PQ H4G 2A5
(514) 765-7130
Seating Capacity: 4,022.
Liquor License: No.

SASKATCHEWAN

The Agridome (Regina Exhibition Park)

P.O. Box 167
Regina, SK S4P 2Z6
(306) 781-9200
FAX (306) 565-3443
Contact: Glen Duck
Style of Music: All.
Seating Capacity: 8,500.
Liquor License: Yes.
Booking Agent: Glen Duck.

Broadway Theatre
715 Broadway Ave.
Saskatoon, SK S7N 1B3
(306) 652-6556
Style of Music: Classical, Jazz, Folk, Pop, Choral.
Seating Capacity: 540.
Liquor License: Yes.

Centennial Civic Centre
2001 Chaplin Ave. E.
Swift Current, SK S9H 3W1
(306) 778-2730
FAX (306) 778-2194
Contact: Bill Leggat.
Style of Music: Pop and Country.
Seating Capacity: 3,000.
Liquor License: Yes.
Mailing Address: P.O. Box 340
Swift Current, SK S9H 3W1

Darke Hall, University of Regina
College Avenue Campus, College Ave.
and Scarth St.
Regina, SK S4S 0A2
(306) 584-4810

The Globe Theatre
1801 Scarth St.
Regina, SK S4P 2G9
(306) 525-9553
Style of Music: Jazz.
Seating Capacity: 400.
Liquor License: Yes.

Prince Albert Exhibition Association
P.O. Box 1538
Prince Albert, SK S6V 5T1
(306) 764-1711
Seating Capacity: 2,500 (Grandstand), 1,000 (Hall).

Saskatchewan Centre of the Arts
200 Lakeshore Dr.
Regina, SK S4P 3V7
(306) 565-0404
FAX (306) 565-3274
Contact: Jim McCrum.
Style of Music: Various.
Seating Capacity: 2,029.
Liquor License: Yes.

Saskatoon Centennial Auditorium and Convention Centre
35-22 St. E.
Saskatoon, SK S7K 0C8
(306) 975-7777
FAX (306) 975-7804
Contact: Marilyn Dembisky, director of marketing and sales.
Style of Music: All types of music.
Seating Capacity: 2,000 (soft seat), 1,300 (cabaret).
Liquor License: Yes.

YUKON

Bonanza Centre
P.O. Box 308
Dawson City, YK Y0B 1G0
Seating Capacity: 475.

CONSUMER AUDIO/VIDEO SUPPLIERS

Alpine Electronics of Canada Inc.

605 Alden Rd.
Markham, ON L3R 3L5
(416) 475-7280
FAX (416) 474-9146
Type of Company: Distributor.
Product Specialty: Car and home audio.
Top Brands: Alpine, Luxman.

Ampex of Canada

1770 Argentia Rd.
Mississauga, ON L5N 3S7
(416) 821-8840
FAX (416) 858-1056
Type of Company: Distributor.
Product Specialty: Ampex tape and equipment.

Aralex Acoustics Ltd.

33 W. 8 Ave.
Vancouver, BC V5Y 1M8
(604) 873-4475
FAX (604) 872-1210
Type of Company: Distributor.
Top Brands: Sonance, Niles, Phoenix Gold.
Product Specialty: Architectural audio products.

Atlas Electronics Ltd.

50 Wingold Ave.
Toronto, ON M6B 1P7
(416) 789-7761
FAX (416) 789-3053
Type of Company: Distributor.
Top Brands: Amprobe, VNK, Atlas Soundalier.
Product Specialty: Components, instrumentation, sound.

113

Audio Video Specialists

2134 Trans-Canada Highway
Montreal, PQ H9P 2N4
(514) 683-1771
FAX (514) 683-5307
Type of Company: Distributor.
Top Brands: Audio Technica, General Electric, Klipsch.
Product Specialty: Cartridges, microphones, VCRs, loudspeaker systems and stereo equipment.

Audiosphere Audio Research Corp. Ltd.

25 Esna Park Dr.
Markham, ON L3R 1C9
(416) 474-1843
FAX (416) 474-9812
Type of Company: Manufacturer.
Product Specialty: Loudspeakers (over 150 models).
Special Services Offered: Custom programs for OEM and private label.
Top Brands: Audiosphere Research, KLA, Accusound.

Axiom Audio

Highway 60
Dwight, ON P0A 1H0
(705) 635-2222
FAX (705) 635-1972
Type of Company: Manufacturer.
Top Brands: Axiom.
Product Specialty: Loudspeaker systems.

B & W Loudspeakers of America

104 Carnforth Rd.
Toronto, ON M4A 2K7
(416) 751-4520
FAX (416) 751-4526
Type of Company: Distributor of B&W loudspeakers.

BASF Canada Inc.

5850 Cote-de-Liesse
Montreal, PQ H4T 1C1
(514) 341-5411
FAX (514) 340-1248
Type of Company: Manufacturer.
Top Brands: BASF LH-D, BASF Chrome dioxide.
Product Specialty: Bulk cassette tapes and mastering tapes. Suppliers to duplicators and studios.

Bose Ltd.

35 East Beaver Creek Rd., Unit 8
Richmond Hill, ON L4B 1B3
(416) 886-9123
FAX (416) 886-9134
Type of Company: Manufacturer of loudspeaker systems.
Special Services Offered: Sound system design (CAD).
Top Brands: Bose.

Bryston Ltd.

57 Westmore Dr.
Rexdale, ON M9V 3Y6
(416) 746-0300
FAX (416) 746-0308
Type of Company: Manufacturer.
Product Specialty: Pro audio amplifiers and crossovers.

Califone Industries Ltd.

1305 Odlum Dr.
Vancouver, BC V5L 3M1
(604) 254-5148
FAX (604) 254-9944
Type of Company: Manufacturer.
Product Specialty: A/V products.
Top Brands: Califone, Sumo.

Camber Acoustics Inc.

7101 Park Ave.
Montreal, PQ H3N 1X9
(514) 277-8852
Top Brands: Camber.
Product Specialty: Loudspeakers.

Cerwin-Vega Canada Ltd.

2360 Midland Ave., Unit 21
Scarborough, ON M1S 4A9
(416) 292-6645
FAX (416) 292-4330
Type of Company: Distributor.
Product Specialty: Speakers.

Commodore Business Machines Ltd.

3470 Pharmacy Ave.
Agincourt, ON M1W 3G3
(416) 499-4292
FAX (416) 494-9755
Type of Company: Manufacturer.
Special Services Offered: Seminars on multimedia (music and video).
Top Brands: Amiga: A500, A2000, A2500.
Product Specialty: Integrated music and video production, personal computers.

Elnova Professional Electronics Ltd.

325 rue Clement o.
La Salle, PQ H8R 4B4
(514) 364-2118
FAX (514) 364-0791
Type of Company: Distributor of professional audio products.
Top Brands: Beyer Dynamic, Schoeps, Klein & Hummel.
Product Specialty: Microphones, headphones, headsets, amplifiers and intercom equipment.

Evolution Audio Inc.

1131 South Service Rd. W.
Oakville, ON L6L 6K4
(416) 847-8888
FAX (416) 847-7408
Type of Company: Distributor, importer.
Top Brands: Carver, Polk Audio, Monster Cable, Audio Control.
Product Specialty: Amplifiers, speakers, cable, sound adjustment products.

Gentronic Marketing International Inc.

1495 Bonhill Rd., Unit 14
Mississauga, ON L5T 1M2
(416) 670-0894
FAX (416) 670-0896
Type of Company: Distributor.
Product Specialty: Quality audio equipment and software.
Top Brands: Beard, Musical Fidelity, Perpetua and Realtime Records.

Gould Marketing Inc.

6445 Cote de Liesse
Montreal, PQ H4T 1E5
(514) 342-4441
FAX (514) 342-5597
Type of Company: Distributor.
Product Specialty: Professional and consumer audio electronics, service.
Special Services Offered: Custom home automation systems.
Top Brands: JBL, AKG Acoustics, Otari.

H. Roy Gray Ltd.

14 Laidlaw Blvd.
Markham, ON L3P 1W7
(416) 294-4833
FAX (416) 294-7670
Type of Company: Distributor, importer, wholesaler.
Top Brands: Infinity, Onkyo, Discwasher.
Product Specialty: Consumer audio and video products.

Hitachi Sales Corporation of Canada

6740 Campobello Rd.
Mississauga, ON L5N 2L8
(416) 821-4545
FAX (416) 821-1101
Type of Company: Distributor.

Holborne Distributing

P.O. Box 309
Mount Albert, ON L0G 1M0
(416) 841-1254
FAX (416) 853-2955
Type of Company: Distributor, sales agency.
Product Specialty: A/V products.
Top Brands: Solitudes, Sounds of Nature, Total Records.

JVC Canada Inc.

21 Finchdene Sq.
Scarborough, ON M1X 1A7
(416) 293-1311
FAX (416) 293-8208
Type of Company: Distributor.
Branches:
29 Martin Dr.
Fall River Village
Fall River, NS B0N 2V0
(902) 861-1580

6839 boul. des Gradines
Charlesbourg o., PQ G2J 1B1
(418) 624-4085

900 Chemin St. Francois
Ville St. Laurent, PQ H4S 1N1

868 Marivale Rd., Suite 10
Ottawa, ON
(613) 729-0861

911-10 Ave. N.
Saskatoon, SK
(306) 242-6794

7503-35 St. S.E., Unit 1
Calgary, AB T2C 1V3
(403) 236-9090

11536-43 Ave.
Edmonton, AB
(403) 436-5864

13040 Worster Ct.
Richmond, BC
(604) 270-1311

115

Kenwood Electronics Canada Inc.
959 Gana Ct., P.O. Box 1075
Mississauga, ON L4T 4C2
(416) 670-7211
FAX (416) 670-7248
Type of Company: Manufacturer, distributor.
Top Brands: Kenwood.
Product Specialty: Home and car audio products.

Koss Ltd.
4112 S. Service Rd.
Burlington, ON
(416) 637-3849
FAX (416) 637-7622
Type of Company: Distributor, wholesaler.
Top Brands: Koss.
Product Specialty: Loudspeakers, stereophones and accessories.

Lenbrook Industries Limited
633 Granite Ct.
Pickering, ON L1W 3K1
(416) 831-6333
FAX (416) 831-6936
Type of Company: Distributor.
Top Brands: NAD, PSB, Proton, B&O.

ML Corporation
1925 Leslie St.
North York, ON
(416) 449-6446
FAX (416) 443-8810
Type of Company: Distributor.
Product Specialty: Audio equipment.

Marishita & Associates Ltd.
2857 Derry Rd. E., Unit 713
Mississauga, ON L4T 1A6
(416) 244-6200
FAX (416) 246-0829
Type of Company: Distributor.
Product Specialty: Audio equipment.

Mitsubishi Electric Sales
8885 Woodbine Ave.
Markham, ON L3R 5G1
(416) 475-7728
FAX (416) 475-7861
Type of Company: Distributor.
Product Specialty: A/V equipment.

Noresco Canada Inc.
50 Wingold Ave.
Toronto, ON M6B 1P7
(416) 787-2461
FAX (416) 789-9824
Type of Company: Distributor.
Top Brands: Marantz, Sherwood, Dual.
Product Specialty: Audio.

Paco Electronics
20 Steelcase Rd. W., Unit 10
Markham, ON L3R 1B7
(416) 475-0740
FAX (416) 475-0464
Type of Company: Distributor.
Top Brands: Paco, Paso, Fuji.
Product Specialty: Microphones, accessories, sound columns, amplifiers, audio and video cassettes.

Paradigm Electronics Inc.
569 Fenmar Dr.
Weston, ON M9L 2R6
(416) 749-2889
FAX (416) 749-2960
Type of Company: Distributor.
Product Specialty: Speaker systems.
Special Services Offered: Speaker stands and audio cables.

Perspective Audio Inc.
294 Marcel Giguere
Blainville, PQ J7E 4H4
(514) 435-2925
FAX (514) 437-8535
Type of Company: Distributor of audio and video products.
Prime Type of Business: Distribution of audio and video products.
Top Brands: LAST, FM Acoustics.
Product Specialty: Electronics and amplification.

Philips Electronics Industries Ltd.
601 Milner Ave.
Scarborough, ON M1B 1M8
(416) 292-5161
FAX (416) 297-1019
Type of Company: Manufacturer, distributor.
Product Specialty: Audio and video equipment.

Pioneer Electronics of Canada Inc.

505 Cochrane Dr.
Markham, ON L3R 8E3
(416) 479-4411
FAX (416) 474-9170
Type of Company: Distributor.
Top Brands: Pioneer.
Product Specialty: Home and car stereo equipment, TVs, laser disc players and software.

Plurison

P.O. Box 357, Station Youville
Montreal, PQ H2P 2W1
(514) 384-3697
Type of Company: Distributor.

Precor

140 Doncaster Ave., Unit 11
Thornhill, ON L3T 1L3
(416) 731-2022
FAX (416) 731-8139
Type of Company: Distributor.
Product Specialty: Audio and video electronics and accessories.
Special Services Offered: Professional maintenance accessories.
Top Brands: Acoustic Research, Snell Acoustic, AM Kemi Accessories.

Radio Shack

P.O. Box 34000
Barrie, ON L4M 4W5
(705) 728-6242
FAX (705) 728-2012
Type of Company: Distributor.
Product Specialty: Computers, assorted audio and visual equipment.

Rocelco Inc.

24 Viceroy Rd., Unit 1
Concord, ON L4K 2L9
(416) 738-0737
FAX (416) 738-0396
Type of Company: Distributor, importer.
Top Brands: Celestion.
Product Specialty: Musical instrument, PA, pro speakers.

Samsung Electronics Canada Inc.

445 Hood Rd.
Markham, ON L3R 8H1
(416) 470-2750
FAX (416) 470-2797
Type of Company: Distributor of consumer electronics.
Top Brands: Samsung.
Product Specialty: Audio, TV and VCR.

Shinon Inc.

400 Eastern Ave., Suite 290
Toronto, ON M4M 1B9
(416) 462-3500
FAX (416) 462-3526
Type of Company: Distributor.
Top Brands: Acoustic Energy, B&K electronics, Vandersteen loudspeakers.

Shriro (Canada) Ltd.

8145 Devonshire Rd.
Montreal, PQ H4P 2K6
(514) 735-4647
FAX (514) 342-1698
Type of Company: Distributor of audio equipment.
Top Brand: Aiwa.
Product Specialty: Single and double cassette recorders and microphones.
Branch:
99 Advance Rd.
Toronto, ON M8Z 2S6
(416) 236-1623

A.C. Simmonds & Sons Limited

975 Dillingham Rd.
Pickering, ON L1W 3B2
(416) 839-8041
FAX (416) 839-2667
Type of Company: Distributor.
Top Brands: Shure.
Product Specialty: Broadcast mixers, mic mixers, and wired and wireless microphones.
Branches:
4259 Canada Way, Suite 203
Burnaby, BC V5G 1H1
(604) 438-5267
FAX (604) 438-5269

5963-103A St.
Edmonton, AB T6H 2J7
(403) 438-4044
FAX (403) 437-4308

1700 boul. Taschereau, Suite 200
Ville Lemoyne, PQ J4P 3M9
(514) 466-5250
FAX (514) 466-5252

P.O. Box 815
Lower Sackville, NS B4C 3V3
(902) 865-1889
FAX (902) 865-5120

Smyth Sound Equipment Ltd.

595 rue du Parc Industriel
Longueuil, PQ J4H 3V7
(514) 679-5490
FAX (514) 679-1780
Type of Company: Distributor, importer.
Top Brands: KEF, Grado, Perreaux, Meridian, Creek.
Product Specialty: Speakers, amplifiers and phono cartridges.

Sony of Canada Ltd.

155 Gordon Baker Rd., Suite 216
Willowdale, ON M2H 3N5
(416) 499-5111
FAX (416) 499-0984
Type of Company: Distributor.
Product Specialty: Audio equipment.

Studer Revox Canada

14 Banigan Dr.
Toronto, ON M4H 1E9
(416) 423-2831
FAX (416) 425-6906
Type of Company: Manufacturer, distributor.
Top Brands: Studer and Revox.
Product Specialty: Consumer and professional audio products, sales and service.

Studio-Lab Audio Inc.

29 Bermondsey Rd.
Toronto, ON M4B 1Z7
(416) 757-3265
Type of Company: Manufacturer.
Product Specialty: Home and professional speakers.
Special Services Offered: Custom manufacturing and installations.
Top Brands: Studio-Lab.

Summit Magnetics (Canada) Ltd.

140 Advance Blvd., Unit 3
Brampton, ON L6T 4J4
(416) 791-6271
FAX (416) 791-8757
Type of Company: Distributor.
Top Brands: SML.
Product Specialty: Magnetic tapes, chrome dioxide cassettes, audio boxes and CD jewel boxes.
Branch:
8828 Osler St.
Vancouver, BC V6P 4G2
(604) 266-3520
FAX (604) 921-8873

TC Electronics

221 Labrosse Ave.
Pointe Claire, PQ
(514) 426-3010
FAX (514) 426-2979
Type of Company: Distributor.
Top Brands: Sennheiser, Marantz, Final Technology.
Product Specialty: Microphones, headphones and wireless microphones.

TEAC Canada Ltd.

340 Brunel Rd.
Mississauga, ON L4Z 2C2
(416) 890-8008
FAX (416) 890-9888
Type of Company: Distributor.
Top Brands: TEAC and TASCAM.

Tannoy North America Inc.

300 Gage Ave., Suite 1
Kitchener, ON N2M 2C8
(519) 745-1158
FAX (519) 745-2364
Type of Company: Manufacturer.
Product Specialty: Loudspeakers.

3M Canada Inc.

P.O. Box 5757
London, ON N6A 4T1
(519) 451-2500
FAX (519) 452-6262
Type of Company: Manufacturer.
Top Brands: Scotch, 3M.
Product Specialty: Video cassettes and open reel audio and video tapes.
Branches:
1001-53 Ave. N.E.
P.O. Box 3954, Stn. B
Calgary, AB T2M 4M5
(403) 275-7330
SK 1-800-661-8126

4808-87 St., Unit 120
Edmonton, AB T6E 5W3
(403) 275-7330

680 Lepine Blvd.
Dorval, PQ H9P 2S5
(514) 631-7600

1155 Lola St.
Ottawa, ON K1K 4C1
(613) 741-2007

155 Lesmill Rd., P.O. Box 1500
North York, ON M3C 2V3
(416) 449-8010
Outside Toronto 1-800-268-7770

7100 River Rd.
Richmond, BC V6X 1X5
(604) 273-2211

85 Muir Rd.
Winnipeg, MB R2X 2X7
(204) 633-6143

Toshiba of Canada Ltd.

3680 Victoria Park Ave.
Willowdale, ON M2H 3K1
(416) 499-5555
FAX (416) 499-4882
Type of Company: Distributor.
Product Specialty: A/V equipment.

Tri-Tel Associates Ltd.

105 Sparks Ave.
Willowdale, ON M2H 2S5
(416) 499-5044
FAX (416) 499-5044
Type of Company: Distributor.
Top Brands: Maxell, Thorens, Stanton.
Product Specialty: Blank audio and video tapes.

Yamaha Canada Music Ltd.

135 Milner Ave.
Scarborough, ON M1S 3R1
(416) 298-1311
FAX (416) 292-0732
Type of Company: Manufacturer, wholesaler.
Product Specialty: Consumer audio.

CONSUMER & TRADE SHOWS

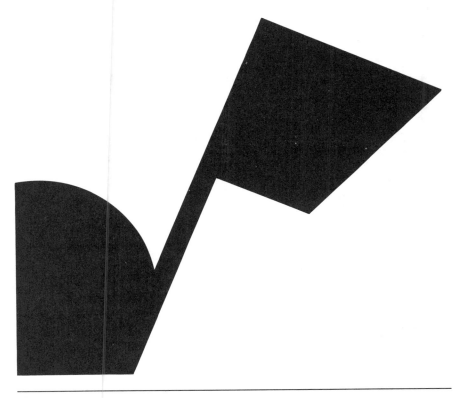

The CE-EX Show
1408 Kingston Rd.
Scarborough, ON M1N 1R3
(416) 691-2852
FAX (416) 691-2891
Aims & Objectives: A trade and audiophile show with the latest in high-end to mid-fi audio equipment and accessories for the professional, home and business.
Dates & Locations: September 8-10, 1990 - Toronto Airport Hilton. Dates for 1991 TBA - Toronto.
Comments: Also produces consumer and trade shows in a number of product categories. Member of CAEM (Canadian Association of Exhibitor Managers).

Combec
A.V. Shows Canada Ltd.
620 Wilson Ave., Suite 550
Toronto, ON M3K 1Z3
(416) 398-7606
FAX (416) 398-7611
Aims & Objectives: Visual communications conference and exhibition for Eastern Canada.
Dates & Locations: Dates TBA - Montreal Convention Centre.
Comments: Peter Dixon, exposition and conference manager.

Computer Expo

Task Corp.
119 Spadina Ave., Suite 804
Toronto, ON M5V 2L1
(416) 599-7579
FAX (416) 599-8876
Aims & Objectives: Public exhibition of
computers and micro-computers.
Events: Shows and seminars.
Dates & Locations: April 20-22, 1990 -
Toronto International Centre.
Comments: Cam MacDonald, president.

Comwest

A.V. Shows Canada Ltd.
620 Wilson Ave., Suite 550
Toronto, ON M3K 1Z3
(416) 398-7606
FAX (416) 398-7611
Aims & Objectives: Visual communications
exhibition and conference for Western Canada.
Dates & Locations: Dates TBA - Vancouver
Trade Convention Centre.
Comments: Peter Dixon, exposition and
conference manager.

Dimensions '90

A.V. Shows Canada Ltd.
620 Wilson Ave., Suite 550
Toronto, ON M3K 1Z3
(416) 398-7606
FAX (416) 398-7611
Aims & Objectives: Exhibition and conference
for visual communications technology.
Events: Full program of over 40 seminars and
workshops; over 200 exhibitors.
Dates & Locations: Oct. 2-4, 1990 - Metro
Toronto Convention Centre.
Comments: Peter Dixon, exposition and
conference manager.

Focus On Video '90

Premiere Magazine/Promex Productions
2231 Bloor St. W.
Toronto, ON M6S 1N7
(416) 763-2121
Dates & Locations: September 13-19, 1990 -
Canadian Exposition Conference Centre, Toronto.

International Lighting Exposition

Kerwill Publishing, Trade Show Division
393 Matheson Blvd. E.
Mississauga, ON L4Z 2H2
(416) 890-1846
FAX (416) 890-5769
Aims & Objectives: Consumer show, open to
public.
Events: Various workshops and seminars on
commercial lighting.
Dates & Locations: June 19-21, 1990 - Metro
Toronto Convention Centre.
Comments: Deborah Dugan, show manager.

Make Music Expo

Music Industries Association of Canada (MIAC)
1210 Sheppard Ave. E.
North York, ON M2K 1E3
(416) 490-1871
Events: Consumer music show, seminars,
workshops.
Dates & Location: May 5, 1990 - Automotive
Building, Exhibition Place, Toronto.
Comments: Brad Heintzman (show manager),
Al Kowalenko (MIAC executive secretary/
manager).

MUSICANADA '90

Music Industries Association of Canada (MIAC)
1210 Sheppard Ave. E.
North York, ON M2K 1E3
(416) 490-1871
Events: Music industry trade show.
Dates & Locations: May 6-7, 1990 -
Automotive Building, Exhibition Place, Toronto.
Comments: Brad Heintzman (show manager),
Al Kowalenko (MIAC executive secretary/
manager).

World Of Commodore

Hunter Nichols Inc.
204 Richmond St. W., Suite 410
Toronto, ON M5V 1V6
(416) 595-5906
FAX (416) 595-9093
Events: Ongoing demonstrations, seminars and
stage presentations including Casio and Roland
exhibits.
Dates & Locations: November 29 - December
2, 1990 - Toronto International Centre.
Comments: Contact Karen Jewell. Sponsored
by Commodore Business Machines.

CUSTOM DUPLICATORS

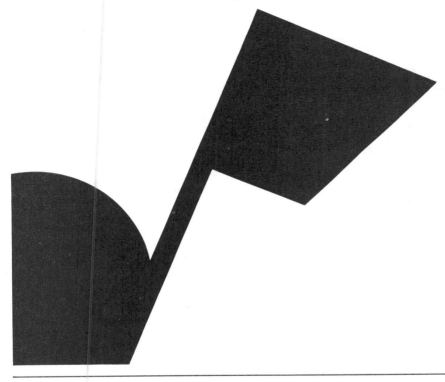

Accurate Audio
612 Yonge St., Suite 201
Toronto, ON M4Y 1Z3
(416) 928-2978
Type of Company: Real-time cassette duplication.
Special Services: Editing, rush service, blank cassettes.
Top Brands: BASF tape.

Accusonic
70 Bathurst St.
Toronto, ON M5V 2P5
(416) 368-1262
Type of Company: Custom real-time and audio duplicator.

Analogue Industries
6902 Park Ave.
Montreal, PQ H3N 1W9
(514) 278-8273
FAX (514) 273-8883
Type of Company: Manufacturer and audio cassette duplication.
Special Services: Real-time duplication, blank cassettes, recording supplies.
Top Brands: BASF, Ampex, Scotch.

Audio To Go
114 Yorkville Ave.
Toronto, ON M5R 1B9
(416) 927-0444
Type of Company: Custom duplication and production.

123

CUSTOM DUPLICATORS

Audiobec Recording Canada Inc.
60 Port Royal o.
Montreal, PQ H3L 2C5
(514) 384-6667
FAX (514) 388-1488
Type of Company: Custom duplicator.

Bastion City Mobile Recording Ltd.
3760 Departure Bay Rd.
Nanaimo, BC V9T 1C4
(604) 758-3424
Type of Company: Audio recording studio.
Special Services: Studio and cassette multitrack recording duplication.

Beam-103 Audio Arts
155 Liberty Ave.
Toronto, ON M6K 3G3
(416) 531-5443
Type of Company: Distributor.
Product Specialty: Strictly involved with experimental bands and labels. All recording, dubbing and distribution is done in-house.

Bullfrog Recording Co. Ltd.
2475 Dunbar St.
Vancouver, BC V6R 3N2
(604) 734-4617
Type of Company: Real-time digital mastering and cassette duplication.
Special Services: Full-length cassette releases and demo tapes. Will arrange preparation, printing and packaging services for cassette insert cards and labels.

C&L Audio Distributors
360 Supertest Rd.
Downsview, ON M3J 2M2
(416) 663-8273
FAX (416) 663-8277
Type of Company: Manufacturer and tape duplicator.
Special Services: Custom printing (rush and special projects).

Canatron
35 Stafford Rd. E., Suite 4
Nepean, ON K2H 8V8
(613) 726-1660
Type of Company: High-speed and real-time audio duplication.

The Cassette Plant
120 Harry Walker Parkway, Unit 2
Newmarket, ON L3Y 7B2
(416) 841-1478
FAX (416) 853-2955
Type of Company: Cassette duplication.

Cinelectric
2 Lake St., Upper Suite
St. Catharines, ON L2R 5W6
(416) 685-1234
Type of Company: Manufacturer and custom audio and video cassette duplicator.
Special Services: Real-time duplication, cassette labelling and packaging, and film and video production.
Product Specialty: Scotch and XHE audio and video tape.

Cinram Ltd.
2255 Markham Rd.
Scarborough, ON M1B 2W3
(416) 298-8190
FAX (416) 298-9307
Type of Company: Manufacturer of records, pre-recorded cassettes and CDs.
Special Services: Also manufacture cassette housings (c-zeros) cassette boxes and jewel boxes for CDs.

Comfort Sound Recording Studios.
26 Soho St., Suite 390
Toronto, ON M5T 1Z7
(416) 593-7992
FAX (416) 593-7301
Type of Company: Recording services.
Special Services: High-speed duplication.

Dynapak Music Services Ltd.
3121 Universal Dr.
Mississauga, ON L4X 2E2
(416) 625-8311
FAX (416) 625-5209
Type of Company: Manufacturer.
Special Services: Custom duplication, and cassette and CD packaging. Sonic welded PVC blister packs.
Product Specialty: Cassettes, 7- and 12-inch records and CDs.

Emmanuel Productions
31B Industrial St.
Toronto, ON M4G 1Z2
(416) 423-7131
Type of Company: Audio duplication.

Evergreen Audio-Visual Ltd.

7170 Warden Ave., Unit 3
Unionville, ON L3R 8B2
(416) 477-6322
FAX (416) 477-9299
Type of Company: Manufacturer.
Product Specialty: Blank and duplicated audio cassettes.

Golden Musicassette Ltd.

510 Coronation Dr., Unit 20
West Hill, ON M1E 4X6
(416) 284-9927
FAX (416) 281-8579
Type of Company: Manufacturer.
Special Services: Cassette duplication.

Metro Media Industries

532 Gordon Baker Rd.
Willowdale, ON M2H 3B4
(416) 493-8810
Type of Company: Manufacturer.
Special Services: Real-time audio and video tape duplication.

Music Manufacturing Services

101 Glen Rd., Suite 2
Toronto, ON M4W 2V8
(416) 928-6919
FAX (416) 928-6919
Type of Company: Custom manufacturing of records, cassettes and CDs.
Special Services: Complete product management and marketing consultation.
Comments: Major label experience. Suppliers of art and filmwork.

New Creation Productions

12013-76 St., Suite 202
Edmonton, AB T5B 2C9
(403) 471-2744
Type of Company: Manufacturer.
Special Services: Custom duplication.

Panfor Dubbing Ltd.

63 Lombard St.
Toronto, ON M5C 1M2
(416) 868-6002
FAX (416) 868-0366
Type of Company: Custom duplicator specializing in commercials and broadcast material.

Praise Sound Productions

7802 Express St.
Burnaby, BC V5A 1T4
(604) 420-4227
Type of Company: Manufacturer, distributor.
Special Services: Real-time and high-speed custom audio duplication.

Precision Sound Corporation

5614 Goring St.
Burnaby, BC V5B 3A3
(604) 299-4141
Type of Company: Manufacture, distribute, duplicate and package audio cassette tapes.
Special Services: Real-time duplication.
Product Specialty: Music duplication on TDK custom wound tape.

R.E.P. Sound Image Recording Ltd.

180 Sheldon Dr.
Cambridge, ON N1R 6V1
(519) 623-2269
FAX (519) 623-4448
Type of Company: Manufacturer of pre-recorded cassettes.

Disques RSB Inc.

8400 Cote-de-Liesse
St. Laurent, PQ H4T 1G7
(514) 342-8511
FAX (514) 342-0401
Type of Company: Record manufacturer.
Special Services: Mastering and record pressing, as well as CD and cassette duplication.

The Reel Supply Company

34 Vaughan Rd.
Toronto, ON M6G 2N3
(416) 925-3991
Type of Company: High-speed duplication and custom length cassette manufacturing.
Special Services: Complete cassette and album packaging.

Now that we have your attention we have to tell you that what you read doesn't count. *What you hear does !*

I'm Ron Drake. My company is
Canatron Electronics
35 Stafford Road
Nepean, K2H 8V8
ph. (613) 726-1660
fax (613) 726-1609

Call for brochure and sample. The things we do for you are : Master Editing; Signal Processing; Real-time, Loop-bin, in-cassette replication; Colour printing on cassette or computer labels; Award winner David Brynaert - graphics conception, design and layout; Assembly; Shrink wrap; and Quality.

Cathy, Martha, Debby, Chris, Ian, Derek, Peter, David, John, Ken, Gary.

Right Tracks Productions Inc.

226B Portage Ave., Sub P.O. Box 18
Saskatoon, SK S7H 0Y0
(306) 933-4949
Type of Company: Manufacturer and custom duplicator.

Roan Sound Productions Ltd.

1005 View St.
Vancouver, BC V8V 3L7
(604) 381-6151
Type of Company: Custom duplicator.

Smyth Sound Equipment Ltd.

595 rue du Parc Industriel
Longueuil, PQ J4H 3V7
(514) 679-5490
Type of Company: Manufacturer, distributor and custom duplicator.

Sonrise Cassette Duplication Ltd.

12840 Bathgate Way, Unit 7
Richmond, BC V6V 1Z4
(604) 278-1544
FAX (604) 270-2745
Type of Company: Custom high-speed and bin-loop duplication.

Sound Stage Niagara

7040 Thorold Stone Rd.
Niagara Falls, ON L2J 1B6
(416) 358-6592
Type of Company: High-speed and real-time audio and video duplication.

Soundhouse Inc.

409 King St. W., 3rd Floor
Toronto, ON M5V 1K1
(416) 598-2260
Type of Company: Manufacturer.
Special Services: Audio for video and film. Sound mixing, ADR, Foley.

Summit Sound Inc.

40 Main St., Unit 1, P.O. Box 333
Westport, ON K0G 1X0
(613) 673-2818
FAX (613) 273-3998
Type of Company: Manufacturer and high-speed and real-time audio cassette duplication.

T.D.C. Tape Duplicating Centre

2182 W. 12 Ave., Suite 109
Vancouver, BC V6K 2N4
(604) 734-4546
Type of Company: Real-time and high-speed tape duplication.

Western Imperial Magnetics Ltd.

7-12840 Bathgate Way
Richmond, BC V6V 1Z4
(604) 270-8682
FAX (604) 270-2745
Type of Company: Manufacturer and distributor of audio, video and motion picture products.
Special Services: Packaging and labelling, recording equipment supplies, custom duplication.
Top Brands: Adtec, DMC, Ampex, Scotch.
Product Specialty: Cassettes.

Alberta Provincial Government

Culture/Performing Arts Branch
10004-4 Ave., 11th Floor, CN Tower
Edmonton, AB T5J 0K5
(403) 427-6713

Requirements: All artists must be Alberta residents.

Assistance: Study grants, project grants and travel grants are available to the following: Performers and composers of classical music, conductors, performers in jazz, rock, folk, etc., and instrument-makers.

Deadline: See *Guide to Programs and Services* brochure, available for free.

Comments: The music section of Alberta Culture's Performing Arts Branch provides financial assistance to Alberta orchestras, opera companies, choirs, instrumental ensembles and service organizations.

British Columbia Ministry of Municipal Affairs, Recreation and Culture

Cultural Services Branch
Legislative Buildings
Victoria, BC V8V 1X4
(604) 356-1718
FAX (604) 387-1407

Requirements: Applicants must be registered, non-profit organizations.

Assistance: Project and operating grants are available for current or future operations. Eligibility in this category is reviewed on an annual basis. Organizations that have not previously received funding are requested to establish their eligibility with the Cultural Services Branch prior to filing an application. Note: Project grants must be approved before any application for operating grants are considered.

Deadline: January 15, May 15, September 15.

129

The Canada Council/ Le Conseil des Arts du Canada

99 Metcalfe St., P.O. Box 1047
Ottawa, ON K1P 5V8
(613) 598-4365 or 598-4366
FAX (613) 598-4390

Assistance: The Canada Council is an independent agency created by the Parliament of Canada in 1957 to foster and promote the arts. The Council provides a wide range of grants to professional Canadian artists and arts organizations.

Deadline: Varies.

Comments: For deadlines and other information contact the Communication Section of the Canada Council. The Council accepts station-to-station collect calls.

Canada Council Touring Office

99 Metcalfe St., P.O. Box 1047
Ottawa, ON K1P 5V8
(613) 598-4342
FAX (613) 598-4390

Assistance: To foster and promote the arts in Canada by providing grants and services to professional Canadian artists and arts organizations.

Centennial Scholarships

Red Deer and District Allied Arts Council
4836 Ross St.
Red Deer, AB T4N 5E8
(403) 346-1565

Requirements: Open to Red Deer and area residents who are over the age of 16 and attending school.

Assistance: Three $500 scholarships.

Deadline: TBA.

Conseil des arts de la Communaute urbaine de Montreal/ Montreal Urban Community Arts Council

3450 Saint-Urbain St.
Montreal, PQ H2X 2N5
(514) 280-3580
FAX (514) 280-3789

Assistance: Funding for professional companies in dance, music, theatre and the visual arts.

Deadline: Council meets four times a year.

Cultural Initiatives Program

Federal Department of Communications
300 Slater St., Suite 387
Ottawa, ON K1A 0C8
(613) 990-4170
FAX (613) 952-3632

Comments: Contact the Federal Department of Communications for details.

Department of Tourism, Recreation and Heritage

Arts Branch
P.O. Box 12345
Fredericton, NB E3B 5C3
(506) 453-2555
FAX (506) 453-2416

Assistance: To provide financial assistance to provincial music organizations and individuals for the development, implementation and monitoring of programs related to music.

Deadline: Varies.

Comments: Grants available in a range of areas. Contact Arts Branch for details.

Fort Macleod and District Allied Arts Council Association

P.O. Box 244
Fort Macleod, AB T0L 0Z0
(403) 553-3700

Fondation Leo Roy

540 ave. Royale
Beauport, PQ G1E 1Y1
(418) 667-2127

Comments: To promote the works of young Quebec artists.

Foundation to Assist Canadian Talent on Record (FACTOR)

146 Front St., Suite 355
Toronto, ON M5J 2L7
(416) 593-4545

Assistance: New Talent Demo award, Sound Recording loan, Video loan, Radio Syndication loan, International Tour Support loan.

Deadline: Last working day of each month.

Laidlaw Foundation

60 St. Clair Ave. E., Suite 203
Toronto, ON M4T 1N5
(416) 964-3614

Requirements: A reputation for influencing and enhancing the development of the performing arts in Canada.

Assistance: Support for creative and developmental phases of new and experimental Canadian works in the disciplines of dance, music, theatre and opera.

Comments: Consult with foundation staff prior to submitting a proposal. Grants are *not* made toward the following: general operating/capital building costs, equipment purchases, festivals, film projects, choral groups, local amateur arts associations, competitions, travel subsidies, conventional theatre music or dance for mainstage production.

Manitoba Arts Council

93 Lombard Ave., Suite 525
Winnipeg, MB R3B 3B1
(204) 945-2237

Requirements: Requirements, deadlines and available funding vary depending on the particular grant applied for.

Comments: Available funding includes grants for composers and performers, operations and special projects, touring and community access.

Manitoba Culture, Heritage and Recreation

Cultural Resources Branch
177 Lombard Ave., 8th Floor
Winnipeg, MB R3B 0W5
(204) 945-3847
FAX (204) 945-1369

Assistance: Special initiative funding only.

Ministere des Affaires culturelles

Direction generale des conservatoires
580 Grande Allee e., P.O. Box 420
Quebec, PQ G1R 2K2
(418) 644-4766
FAX (418) 646-0175

Newfoundland Department of Culture, Recreation and Youth

Project Grants
P.O. Box 5011
St. John's, NF A1C 5V3
(709) 726-2212

Requirements: Must be a resident of Newfoundland and at least 18 years of age.

Assistance: Grants awarded for staging concerts and tours, professional skills development and demo tapes.

Deadline: January 15, April 15, September 15.

Comments: Grant monies are directed toward artists' fees. No capital equipment costs covered or record production costs covered.

NWT Arts Council

Government of the Northwest Territories
Culture and Communications
P.O. Box 1320
Yellowknife, NT X1A 2L9
(403) 920-3103
FAX (403) 873-0107

Requirements: A resident of the NWT for two years or longer.

Assistance: Support for arts projects including demo recordings.

Deadline: January 31, April 30, and one flexible date.

Nova Scotia Performing Arts Policies

Department of Tourism and Culture
P.O. Box 456
Halifax, NS B3J 2R5
(902) 424-5929
FAX (902) 424-2668

Requirements: Grants available only to registered, non-profit groups.

Assistance: Funds are available for commissioning new works and grants are available to assist new and established community arts organizations.

Deadline: Applications are considered on a bi-weekly basis.

Ontario Arts Council

Music Office
151 Bloor St. W., Suite 500
Toronto, ON M5S 1T6
(416) 961-1660 or 1-800-387-0058
FAX (416) 961-7796
Requirements: All artists must be professional and Ontario-based.
Assistance: Grants are available to performing arts organizations, individual artists and composers of classical music.
Deadline: Consult the Music Office of the OAC.
Comments: Funding is also available for touring and multi-discipline projects.

Ontario Ministry of Culture and Communications

Cultural Industries and Agencies Branch
77 Bloor St. W., 6th Floor
Toronto, ON M7A 2R9
(416) 965-6487
FAX (416) 324-3448
Assistance: Project grant assistance is available to non-profit cultural industry and trade organizations in a variety of areas. Categories include internship training, skills training, resource material development, equipment purchases, special events, organizational development and membership services.

Organization of Saskatchewan Arts Councils

4010 Pasqua St., Suite 700, P.O. Box 1146
Regina, SK S4S 7B9
(306) 586-1250
Requirements: Members of the Organization of Saskatchewan Arts Councils.
Assistance: Performing arts grant (Stars for Saskatchewan, Koncerts for Kids), deficit protection grants, visual arts exhibition grants, and equipment grants.
Deadline: June 30
Comments: Visual arts program is designed to promote emerging Saskatchewan artists. One showcase conference per year (in June) in member community.

Prince Edward Island Council of the Arts

Department of Community and Cultural Affairs
P.O. Box 2234
Charlottetown, PE C1A 8B9
(902) 368-4410
Requirements: Must be member of the Council and a Canadian citizen or landed immigrant.
Assistance: Grants of up to $800, $2,000 and $5,000.
Deadline: April 30, September 15, December 15.

Princess Margaret Scholarship

Red Deer and District Allied Arts Council
4836 Ross St.
Red Deer, AB T4N 5E8
(403) 346-1565
Requirements: Open to area residents who are attending a post secondary institution and are committed to a career in the arts.
Assistance: $500 cash award.
Deadline: January 31, 1990
Comments: The Princess Margaret Scholarship is made possible by an endowment fund established by the City of Red Deer to commemorate the visit of Her Royal Highness, Princess Margaret, Countess of Snowdon, to Red Deer on the 26th day of July 1980.

Saskatchewan Arts Board

2550 Broad St.
Regina, SK S4P 3V7
(306) 787-4056
FAX (306) 787-4199
Requirements: Must be a Saskatchewan resident.
Assistance: The Saskatchewan Arts Board (an agency of the provincial government) has several grant programs for professional performers and arts groups.
Comments: Write or telephone for information.

Saskatchewan Culture, Multiculturalism and Recreation

Arts and Multicultural Branch
3211 Albert St.
Regina, SK S4S 5W6
(306) 787-5728
FAX (306) 525-0133
Requirements: Designated Provincial Cultural Organizations (PCOs) are eligible to apply through a program proposal for one resident artist in one fiscal year. Artists should be Saskatchewan residents.
Assistance: This program assists PCOs in placing resident artists in selected Saskatchewan communities for up to one year.
Deadline: June 15 annually for residencies commencing after October 1.
Comments: The program stimulates participation in the creation and interpretation of visual, performing and literary arts. The residencies are 12 months in duration and are non-renewable in the same community for the same artist.

Sound Recording Development Program

Department of Communications of Canada
295 St. Paul St. E.
Montreal, PQ H2Y 1H1
(514) 283-2873
FAX (514) 283-5157
Requirements: Varies.
Assistance: The following eight funding programs are available: sound recording production, music video production, syndicated radio programing, international touring, specialized music production, international marketing, business development, specialized music distribution.
Deadline: Six weeks before commencement of the activity.

Support to Northern Performers

Government of Northwest Territories
Culture and Communications
P.O. Box 1320
Yellowknife, NT X1A 2L9
(403) 920-3103
FAX (403) 873-0107
Requirements: Applicants must be residents of the NWT for at least two years.
Assistance: Support for the development of performing artists based in the NWT.
Deadline: Ongoing.

Vancouver Foundation

505 Burrard St., Suite 230
Vancouver, BC V7X 1M3
(604) 688-2204
FAX (604) 688-4170
Requirements: Limited to provincial organizations which are registered, non- profit societies and registered federal charities.
Assistance: Project assistance to established performing arts organizations in existence for at least two years, earning 25% of revenue through performance-related receipts.
Deadline: Beginning of January, April, July, October.
Comments: A letter of enquiry should be sent to the president giving description of group, particulars of project and budget. Applications sent if warranted. Four granting cycles annually.

VideoFACT

Sponsored by the MuchMusic/ MusiquePlus Network
51 John St., Suite 301
Toronto, ON M5V 2T2
(416) 596-8696
FAX (416) 596-6861
Requirements: Projects must be newly-conceived, Canadian-owned and satisfy CRTC Canadian content criteria.
Assistance: $12,500 non-recoupable award to a maximum of 50% of the total production cost.
Deadline: Five deadlines per year (call office for updated information).

Wintario

Ministry of Culture and Communications
Regional Services Branch
10 St. Mary St.
Toronto, ON M7A 2R9
(416) 965-6597
FAX (416) 324-4566

FINANCIAL SERVICES

Reginald Adelman, Chartered Accountant

The Madison Centre
4950 Yonge St., Suite 601
North York, ON M2N 6K1
(416) 733-1995

The Agency

41 Britain St., Suite 200
Toronto, ON M5A 1R7
(416) 365-7833
FAX (416) 365-9692
Services Provided: Bookkeeping, banking and cash management.
Specialization: Payroll and tax filing.

Canadian Finance Corporation

Madison Centre
4950 Yonge St., Suite 706
Toronto, ON M2N 6K1
(416) 226-6580
FAX (416) 226-6961
Services Provided: Credit guarantee and management of accounts receivable.

Jack R. Cayne, M.B.A., C.G.A.

500 Sheppard Ave. E., Suite 203
North York, ON M2N 6H7
(416) 733-8055
Services Provided: Accounting services and tax preparation.
Specialization: Small business accounting and taxation.
Clients: Main Frame Computer Graphics, Capstone Communications Group, Palace at 4 A.M.

Creative Arts Management Service

11 Pinewood Ave.
Toronto, ON M5C 2V2
(416) 652-CATS
FAX (416) 652-5969
Services Provided: Business management services.
Specialization: Specializing in issues affecting freelancers and small businesses in the arts, fashion, entertainment and communications industries.

R.V. Dodson

2249 Birchmount Rd., Suite 406
Scarborough, ON M1T 2M1
(416) 291-7338
Services Provided: Accounting services, tax planning and income tax preparation.
Specialization: Accounting for musicians and the music business in general.
Clients: Marigold Productions, Rosedale Records, Ariel Records.

Fields Tax Services Ltd.

P.O. Box 385, Stn. A
Toronto, ON M5W 1C2
(416) 481-5566
Services Provided: Tax preparation for self-employed musicians. All work done by former Revenue Canada employee.
Specialization: Tax returns prepared from any available records (receipts, cancelled cheques, whatever). Several years of experience.
Comments: Clients all over Canada. Write or phone collect.

Kazman & Associates

1110 Lodestar Rd.
Downsview, ON M3J 2Z4
(416) 630-9950
FAX (416) 630-9159
Specialization: Contract negotiation, management packages and financial consultation.

Kyle Management Group

41 Peter St., Suite 300
Toronto, ON M5V 2G2
(416) 971-6667
FAX (416) 971-6565
Services Provided: Business management, tax preparation and consulting for self-employed professionals in all facets of the entertainment industry.
Clients: Patricia Cullen, (composer), FM (recording artists) Richard Monette (actor/director).

Lant Financial Services

569 Lynwood Dr., P.O. Box 1085
Cornwall, ON K6H 5V2
(613) 938-1532
Services Provided: Income tax and bookkeeping services (Canada & U.S.), plus financial and management consulting.

Motion Picture Guarantors Ltd.

14 Birch Ave.
Toronto, ON M4V 1C8
(416) 968-0577
FAX (416) 960-0474
Services Provided: Completion guarantees.
Specialization: Completion guarantees to TV series and motion pictures.
Clients: Nelvana, Sunrise, Primedia.
Branch Office:
240 rue St. Jacques, Suite 700
Montreal, PQ H2Y 1L9
(514) 288-2544

POP Strategies

3284 Yonge St.
Toronto, ON M4N 3M7
(416) 485-8295
FAX (416) 485-8924
Services Provided: Business management, strategic planning, financial management.
Specialization: Entertainment Industry

Sprackman-Metcalfe, Chartered Accountants

789 Don Mills Rd., Suite 300
Don Mills, ON M3C 1T5
(416) 467-6984
Services Provided: Tour and royalty accounting, auditing, international taxation and general business management.
Specialization: Music recording industry.
Comments: Contact Lorne Sprackman.

Stanley M. Tepner, M.B.A.
Chartered Accountant

c/o Metfin
360 Bay St., Suite 200
Toronto, ON M5H 2V6
(416) 580-1740
FAX (416) 869-0249
Services Provided: Personal investment and tax counselling, partnerships, distribution.
Specialization: Canada's top mutual funds. Performers, producers, managers, senior executives and professionals shown how to participate in partnerships that acquire shopping centres, office buildings and medical centres.
Comments: Affiliated office in Calgary.
Clients: Clients are upper-income level performers, managers, business people and professionals.

Touche Ross & Co.

First Canadian Place, P.O. Box 12
Toronto, ON M5X 1B3
(416) 364-4242
FAX (416) 361-0601
Services Provided: Chartered accountants, management consultants.

Wheeler Accounting Services Inc.

671 Danforth Ave., Suite 304
Toronto, ON M4J 1L3
(416) 462-0811
FAX (416) 462-0608
Services Provided: Personal tax returns.
Specialization: Entertainment industry.
Clients: Rick Fox, Matthew Greenberg, Blair Packham.

Yada, Tompkins, Humphries, Palmer & Co.

1008 Homer St., Suite 301
Vancouver, BC V6B 2X1
(604) 669-4242
FAX (604) 669-2097
Services Provided: Accounting and tax services.
Clients: Bryan Adams, Jim Vallance, Paul Janz.

FINANCIAL SERVICES

137

INSURANCE COMPANIES

Clydesdale Insurance Brokerage Limited
2473 Ouellette Ave.
Windsor, ON N8X 1L5
(519) 966-2600
FAX (519) 966-6177
Services Provided: Musical instrument and equipment insurance.

Dale & Company Ltd.
595 Burrard St., Suite 873
Vancouver, BC V7X 1J1
(604) 681-0121
FAX (604) 681-4327
Specialization: Specializing in entertainment and equipment insurance.

Douglas Insurance Brokers
57 Main St.
Unionville, ON L3R 2E6
(416) 477-6566
FAX (416) 477-0965
Services Provided: Liability insurance, and coverage for equipment and studio contents.

Duggan West Insurance Service Ltd.
3515 Kingsway St., Unit 3
Vancouver, BC V5R 5L8
FAX (604) 433-0608
Services Provided: Equipment coverage.

139

Richards Melling

141 Adelaide St. W., Suite 806
Toronto, ON M5H 3L5
(416) 869-1320
Services Provided: Insurance for TV programs, recording studios and video advertising.

Sedgwick Tomenson Inc.

401 W. Georgia St., 6th Floor
Vancouver, BC V6B 5B8
FAX (604) 682-5867
Services Provided: Producer's liability, cast insurance, equipment insurance, plus props, sets and wardrobe coverage.

Warren G. Hogg Insurance

55 Wynford Heights. Cr., Suite 810
Don Mills, ON M3C 1L4
(416) 445-1692
FAX (416) 479-9653
Services Provided: Disability, extended health, dental, travel coverage and life insurance.
Specialization: Ten years of co-ordinating health benefits for musicians and film workers.
Comments: Endorsed by both the Toronto Musicians' Association and the Canadian Filmcrafts Association.

JINGLE PRODUCTION COMPANIES

Acoustic 1 Studios

1741 Leprohon
Montreal, PQ H4E 1P3
(514) 769-7032
FAX (514) 769-7032
Services Provided: Custom music composition.
Specialization: Jingles.
Clients: Thrifty Car Rentals, Publiart Inc., Aupercom Canada.

The Air Company

506 Adelaide St. E.
Toronto, ON M5A 1N6
(416) 364-8820
Services Provided: Original music and production for TV and radio commercials.

Airwaves Sound Design Ltd.

34 W. 8 Ave., 3rd Floor
Vancouver, BC V5Y 1M7
(604) 875-0114
FAX (604) 876-1087
Services Provided: Composition and production of music for jingles, A/V and film soundtracks. Also, sound design, music library, talent and sound effects.
Specialization: Effects, mixing and production for radio, TV and film.
Clients: Baker Lovick, FCB Ronalds Reynolds, Ogilvy Mather.

141

Audio Image Inc.
51 Quebec Ave.
Toronto, ON M6P 2T3
(416) 254-0808
FAX (416) 769-2190
Services Provided: Jingles.

B & C Productions
P.O. Box 1012
Trenton, ON K8V 6E6
(613) 392-5144 or 392-6296
Services Provided: Custom songwriting, plus record and jingle production. MIDI recording studio and services.
Comments: B & C Productions offers "Market Exclusive" jingles with over 300 clients.
Clients: Cadillac Fairview, Northumberland Mall, CFFX Radio.

Beta Sound Recorders Ltd.
10534-109 St., Suite 102
Edmonton, AB T5H 3B2
(403) 424-3063
Clients: Frame 30, Polaris Entertainment, CFRN-TV.

Bob Derkach Music
3023 Queen St. E.
Scarborough, ON M1N 1A5
(416) 698-5422
Services Provided: Filmscores and music composition and special effects for television and non-broadcast video. Pre-production service available.
Specialization: Human emotion.

Boomtalk Musical Production
406 River Ave.
Winnipeg, MB R3L 0L5
(204) 453-8972
Services Provided: Custom jingle packages for large or small accounts.
Specialization: MIDI production with digital mastering.
Clients: Re/Max Real Estate, CJOB Winnipeg, QX-104 Winnipeg.

Brad MacDonald Music Ltd.
151 John St., Suite 505A
Toronto, ON M5V 2T2
(416) 348-8901
FAX (416) 348-8902
Services Provided: Music and audio production for jingles and television.
Specialization: Sound design.
Clients: CBC, Kellogg's, Leon's Furniture and Appliance.

C.M.S. Studios
151 Mountain Rd.
Moncton, NB E1C 2K8
(506) 858-0073
FAX (506) 859-7406
Services Provided: Original music, film scoring, audio post production, computer animation.
Comments: 24-track recording facility with MIDI system.
Clients: National Film Board, CBC, Crystal Palace.

Les Productions D.A. Enr.
333B Kennedy S.
Sherbrooke, PQ J1G 2H8
(819) 822-0702
Services Provided: Production and recording of jingles and records.
Clients: Houbigant Perfumes, Canron, Arctic Cat.

DMX-2 Music Productions Inc.
2111 Montreal Rd., Suite 21
Gloucester, ON K1J 8M8
(613) 744-3339
Services Provided: Music for films, television series and documentaries. Arrangements and transcriptions.
Specialization: Background music and theme songs for film and television.
Comments: MIDI facility at reasonable rates.
Clients: TV Ontario, Turnelle Productions Inc., Sok Cinema Inc.

Echosphere Productions

37 Scarborough Rd.
Toronto, ON M4E 3M4
(416) 690-3888
Services Provided: Production and post-production for film, video, audio and multimedia.
Specialization: Complete in-house graphics, audio production and original music.
Comments: Priority given to peace, environmental and educational projects.
Clients: Cine Video Productions, Cornice Entertainment, Mako Films, First Choice.

Wayne Finucan Productions

697 Sargent Ave.
Winnipeg, MB R3E 0A8
(204) 786-5578
Services Provided: Recording studio and film post-production.
Specialization: Film post-production.
Clients: Palmer-Jarvis Advertising, McKim Advertising, Pradinuk Advertising Agency.

Bob Fuhr

Trillium Recording Centre Inc.
1253 Clarence Ave., Suite 3
Winnipeg, MB R3T 1T4
(204) 453-8484
FAX (204) 453-6437
Services Provided: Music composition for jingles, film and original recording projects.

FX Productions Musicales

11018 ave. Pigeons
Montreal, PQ H1G 5V3
(514) 322-3207
Services Provided: Musical production, composition, performance and arrangements in a MIDI studio.
Specialization: Film music, jingles, original music, arrangements, studio production.

Good Music Productions Ltd.

25 Southport St.
Toronto, ON M6S 4W7
(416) 761-9273
Services Provided: Producer of original recorded music for radio, TV and film industries, using acoustic and synthesized sound.
Clients: J. Walter Thompson, FCB Ronalds Reynolds, Baker Lovick.

Halsmith Music

986 Vanier Dr.
Mississauga, ON L5H 3T7
(416) 274-0471
Services Provided: Music for film, video, A/V and trade shows.
Specialization: Acoustic, vocal and MIDI scoring in all styles with a marked flair for "Theme Park" styled revues.
Clients: Hopwood Advertising, World Vision Canada, Pavillion of Promise/Expo '86.

Hark Productions

366 Adelaide St. E., Suite 540
Toronto, ON M5A 3X9
(416) 865-9611
FAX (416) 360-7811
Services Provided: Original music for commercials plus film orchestration and arrangements.
Comments: Personal service.
Clients: Texaco, Coors Light, Ontario Hydro.

Icedrum Inc.

P.O. Box 2310, Stn. A
Sudbury, ON P3A 4S8
(705) 560-3769
FAX (705) 560-1702
Services Provided: Complete custom production available for radio jingles and station IDs. Also, music scores for film and TV from conception to completion.

Intermede Musique Media Inc.

P.O. Box 609, Stn. Place du Parc
Montreal, PQ H2W 2P2
(514) 842-8661
FAX (514) 843-8278

The Jingle Works

220 Rideau St.
Ottawa, ON K1N 5Y1
(613) 236-5446
FAX (613) 235-5473
Services Provided: Original creative and music production for video, film and broadcast commercials.
Clients: Carlsberg Beer, Mr. Gas, Mr. Lube.

Kayzee Lou Productions Inc.

7 Roanoke Rd.
Don Mills, ON M3A 1E3
(416) 449-5155
FAX (416) 928-9412
Services Provided: Jingle production, independent record promotion and music marketing.
Specialization: Record promotion.
Clients: Duke Street Records, Unidisc Records, Einstein Brothers Music

Keen Communication Systems Inc.

11 Soho St., Suite 203
Toronto, ON M5T 1Z6
(416) 977-9845
FAX (416) 599-9714
Services Provided: Music production and composition, sound design, voice recording and direction.
Comments: Contact: Thomas Neuspiel or John Tucker.
Clients: Saatchi Saatchi (Toyota), Chiat/Day/Mojo (Labatt's), Laser Communications (Thomas Cook Travelers Cheques).

Leon Aronson Productions

901 Kenilworth Rd.
Montreal, PQ H3R 2R5
(514) 341-6721
Services Provided: Original music for film, TV, radio and A/V.
Comments: Demo tape available upon request.
Clients: The Gazette, Alliance Productions, NFB.

Marigold Productions Ltd.

P.O. Box 141, Stn. S
Toronto, ON M5M 2L6
(416) 484-8789
Services Provided: Writing, producing and recording any type of jingle, theme song or movie score.
Comments: 24-track recording facility. Top writers and musicians are available.

Mid-Ocean Recording

1578 Erin St.
Winnipeg, MB R3E 2T1
(204) 774-3715
Services Provided: Original jingle production for national and international advertisers.

Les Productions Minos Ltee.

P.O. Box 431, Stn. Victoria
Montreal, PQ H3Z 2V8
(514) 489-7009
FAX (514) 489-1972
Services Provided: Music composition for soundtracks.
Specialization: New Age music, electronic music.
Comments: IBM computer, 16-bit sampling, SMPTE Sync.

Musique Sur Mesure enr.

5717 Northmount
Montreal, PQ H3S 2H4
(514) 342-5013
Services Provided: Scoring films, composing jingles for TV and radio commercials.
Specialization: All styles of music.
Comments: Reasonable fees.
Clients: Blacksnow Snowboards, Rx Soleil, Metropolis

P.A.M. - Paul Anand Music

56 Saugeen Cr.
Scarborough, ON M1K 3N1
(416) 267-9413
Services Provided: Full-service music production.
Specialization: Jingles, stock music, music for film and TV.
Comments: A creative team with full digital production.
Clients: Caf-lib Coffee, Mr. Grocer

Pearcely Road Music

31B Industrial St.
Toronto, ON M4G 1Z2
(416) 423-7131
FAX (416) 467-6805
Services Provided: Promotional music for TV, radio and industrial video.
Clients: World Vision (Canada), Creative TV, Windborne Creations

Pi Music Productions
134 Peter St., Suite 314
Toronto, ON M5V 2H2
(416) 581-0198
Services Provided: Production of original music including composition, arranging, sound effects and recording.
Specialization: Music for most media applications.
Clients: CKVR (Barrie), BMW (Lens & Eye Films), PEI Tourism

Players Music Inc.
216 Carlton St.
Toronto, ON M5A 2L1
(416) 961-5290
FAX (416) 961-7254
Services Provided: Radio and TV jingles, voice-overs, film and A/V scores, broadcast IDs.
Clients: Cooper & Williamson, McCann Erikson, JWT Direct

Pyramid Productions
205A Lakeshore Rd. E.
Mississauga, ON L5G 1G2
(416) 891-0336
FAX (416) 278-1799
Services Provided: Custom music for radio, TV and film.
Specialization: Composing with ambience and special effects (Digital Foley); giving each project an image of its own.
Comments: A comprehensive recording studio offering post-audio and video.
Clients: Mountain Electronics, Golden Screen Films, Carrier Find

Pyrate Audio
(The Pyrate Group)
451 St-Sulpice, Studio L
Montreal, PQ H2Y 2V9
(514) 284-0761
FAX (514) 284-1838
Services Provided: Audio soundtrack production for TV, radio and internal communications.
Specialization: Popular song format music productions.
Comments: Integrated production services with Pyrate Films (cinematography) and Pyrate Animation (computer generated animation).
Clients: Kodak Canada, Honda Canada, Seagram's.

R.S. Music Productions
155 Deloraine Ave.
Toronto, ON M5M 2B1
(416) 480-1654
Services Provided: Jingle service, demo tapes, A/V and film music.
Comments: Excellent writers and professional sound production.
Clients: Sunquest Vacations, Crazy Lee's, Petro Partners.

Right Tracks Productions Ltd.
226B Portage Ave., Sub. P.O. 18
Saskatoon, SK S7H 0Y0
(306) 933-4949
Services Provided: Full jingle and soundtrack production, SMPTE sync for audio/visual projects.

Seacoast Sound
825 Broughton St.
Victoria, BC V8W 1E5
(604) 386-1131
FAX (604) 386-5775
Services Provided: Commercials, TV soundtracks, post score and radio programs.
Specialization: Custom music for advertising.
Comments: Full-service audio production company.
Clients: Kentucky Fried Chicken, Wendy's, Intra Travel.

Spencer Critchley Productions
62-12 St.
Toronto, ON M8V 3G7
(416) 252-0775
FAX (416) 251-7834
Services Provided: Film music, jingle and album production.
Specialization: Film music.
Clients: Bermuda Dept. of Tourism, General Motors of Canada, Bambi (album artist)

Sound Path Productions
11 Invicta Dr., Units 20-21
Oakville, ON L6H 2K9
(416) 842-1743
FAX (416) 849-3886
Services Provided: Complete custom jingle packages designed from concept through to final recording. Detailed special effects and music libraries.
Specialization: Custom jingle concepts and productions for award-winning results.
Comments: Facility houses a comprehensive multitrack recording studio for productions. Voice-over talent and custom script consultation can be provided.

Sound Source Productions

67 Mowat Ave., Suite 31
Toronto, ON M6K 3E3
FAX (416) 531-7439
Services Provided: Music for film, TV and radio. Complete jingle production.
Specialization: Theme songs and movie scores.
Comments: Musicians and writers available.

Studio A

190 Highway 7 W., Unit 6
Brampton, ON L7A 1A2
(416) 455-1043
Services Provided: Custom jingles written, produced and recorded.
Specialization: Studio musicians available.
Comments: 16-track recording on premises. Fully locked 24-track MIDI.
Clients: Power Boat Show (TSN), John Parry Music.

Studio West Productions

502-45 St. W., Suite 3
Saskatoon, SK S7L 6H2
(306) 244-2815
FAX (306) 242-3301
Services Provided: Jingles, music video, commercials and documentaries.
Clients: Saskatchewan Roughriders, Federated Co-Ops, Saskatchewan Tourism, Big Valley Jamboree.

Super Nova Sounds

141 Dunvegan Rd.
Toronto, ON M5P 2N8
(416) 488-0263
Services Provided: Composition, arranging and production.
Specialization: Commercials, film, video and album production.
Clients: Ronalds Reynolds (McCain Foods), BWS Advertising (Fuji Film)

Tanis Productions

4160 Dundas St. W.
Islington, ON M8X 1X3
(416) 233-7029
FAX (416) 445-5145
Services Provided: Concept development, demos, jingles, franchise packages, original music for TV and film.
Specialization: Franchise companies, food marketing and corporate slogans.
Comments: For demo tape and presentation call Tanis.
Clients: CHUM FM, Global-TV, City of Scarborough

Thinkmusic

473-1/2 Church St.
Toronto, ON M4Y 2C5
(416) 922-4438
FAX (416) 924-2499
Specialization: Jingles.
Clients: Coca-Cola, Apple Computers, American Express

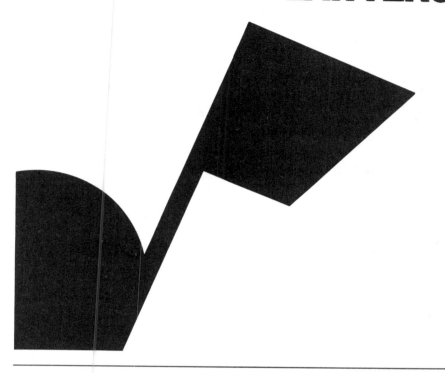

Alexander, Holburn, Beaudin & Lang

700 W. Georgia St., Suite 1800
Vancouver, BC V7Y 1B8
(604) 688-1351
FAX (604) 669-7642
Specialization: Booking contracts.
Entertainment Laywer: Glen Harder.

Cassels, Brock & Blackwell

Scotia Plaza, 40 King St. W.
Toronto, ON M5H 3C2
(416) 869-5300
FAX (416) 360-8877
Services Provided: Entertainment law.
Entertainment Lawyers: Peter Steinmetz, Frank Monteleone.

Epstein, Wood, Wong & Logie

1500 West Georgia St., Suite 650
Vancouver, BC V6G 3A9
(604) 685-4321
FAX (604) 685-7901
Services Provided: Negotiation and litigation of matters pertaining to the entertainment industry.
Entertainment Lawyer: Norman Wexler.

Goodman & Goodman

20 Queen St. W., Suite 3000
Toronto, ON M5H 1V5
(416) 979-2211
FAX (416) 979-1234
Services Provided: General representation for all artists in the entertainment field.
Specialization: TV and film.
Entertainment Lawyers: Michael Levine, Eric Kert, Daniel Gormley, David Zitzerman.

Griesdorf, Chertkoff, Levitt

100 University Ave., Suite 910
Toronto, ON M5J 1V6
(416) 593-5881
FAX (416) 593-6033
Services Provided: Full legal services for the entertainment industry.
Entertainment Lawyer: Norman Griesdorf.

Gowling & Henderson

1 First Canadian Place, Suite 5260
Toronto, ON M5X 1A0
(416) 862-8484
Entertainment Lawyer: Mark Tamminga.

Heenan Blaikie

1001 boul. de Maisonneuve o., Suite 1400
Montreal, PQ H3A 3C8
(514) 281-1212
FAX (514) 281-0639
Services Provided: Legal services for film production and distribution, financing and transferring of music rights for films.
Entertainment Lawyers: Michael Prupas, Yves Dupras, Pam Berliner.

Kazman & Associates

1110 Lodestar Rd.
Downsview, ON M3J 2Z4
(416) 630-9950
FAX (416) 630-9159
Specialization: Contract negotiation, management packages and financial consultation.
Entertainment Lawyer: Marshall Kazman.

Kerbel, Himelfarb,
Barristers and Solicitors

55 York St., Suite 305
Toronto, ON M5J 1R7
(416) 365-0505
Services Provided: Litigation for the entertainment industry.
Branch Office:
1185 W. Georgia St., Suite 1050
Vancouver, BC V6E 4E6

Anita Lerek,
Lawyer and Trademark Agent

559 Markham St.
Toronto, ON M6G 2L6
(416) 927-9222
FAX (416) 967-3510
Services Provided: Advice for contracts, business law and trademarks; copyright and incorporations.
Specialization: Drafting of arts and entertainment contracts.
Clients: Beverley Glenn-Copeland, Romaniac Brothers, Bradley/Francis.

Mark Lewis

2 Braemore Gardens
Toronto, ON M6G 2C8
(416) 658-9455
FAX (416) 654-9148
Services Provided: Representation for broadcast industry, plus production agreements and policy regulations for film, TV and radio.
Specialization: Entertainment, media communications and telecommunications.
Entertainment Lawyer: Mark Lewis.

Martineau, Walker

Stock Exchange Tower
Victoria Sq., Suite 3400
P.O. Box 242
Montreal, PQ M4Z 1E9
(514) 397-7400
FAX (514) 397-7600 or 397-7601
Services Provided: Communications and entertainment law.
Specialization: Motion picture, broadcasting and recording industries; copyright and trademarks.
Entertainment Lawyers: Francis Fox, Claude Brunet, Jean-Francois Buffoni, Lise Bertrand, Jean-Pierre Blais, Stephane Gilker.

McCarthy Tetrault

Toronto Dominion Bank Tower
Toronto Dominion Centre
Toronto, ON M5K 1E6
(416) 362-1812
FAX (416) 868-0673
Services Provided: Negotiating and drafting music contracts.
Entertainment Lawyers: Stephen Stohn, Graham Henderson, Peter Grant, Hank Intven.
Branch Office:
580-8 Ave., S.W., Suite 1600
Calgary, AB T2P 3S8
(403) 234-7200
FAX (403) 234-7208

McLennan Ross

12220 Stony Plain Rd., Suite 600 West
Chambers
Edmonton, AB T5N 3Y4
(403) 482-5802
FAX (403) 428-0015
Services Provided: Negotiating and drafting agreements, intellectual property registration and production contracts.
Specialization: Intellectual property protection and copyright.
Comments: Vice-president of Alberta Recording Industry Association.
Entertainment Lawyer: Gary W. Cable.

McMillan Binch

S. Tower, Royal Bank Plaza, P.O. Box 38
Toronto, ON
M5J 2J7
(416) 865-7111
FAX (416) 865-7048
Services Provided: Legal services in music, film, TV, broadcasting, stage and publishing.
Entertainment Lawyers: Douglas Barrett, Diana Cafazzo, Sheila Budd, David Matheson, David MacDonald, Peter Cathcart.

Merchant Burnett

810 Spadina Cr. E.
Saskatoon, SK
S7K 3H4
(306) 653-7777
FAX (306) 975-1983
Services Provided: Intellectual property and entertainment law.
Comments: Representing individual artists, producers and organizations.
Clients: SRTV Productions, Saskatoon Jazz Festival, *Billy Bob*.
Entertainment Lawyers: Robert Crowe, Juan Martinez.

Clark Miller,
Barrister and Solicitor
52 St. Patrick St., 2nd Floor
Toronto, ON M5T 1V1
(416) 971-6616
FAX (416) 971-4144
Services Provided: Legal services for the entertainment industry.
Specialization: Entertainment and media law.
Entertainment Lawyers: Clark Miller and Paul Sanderson.

Miller, Mills & Associates

571 Jarvis St.
Toronto, ON M5R 3L2
(416) 968-2023
FAX (416) 968-7958
Entertainment Lawyers: David Ruskin, George Miller.

Minden, Gross, Grafstein & Greenstein

111 Richmond St. W., Suite 600
Toronto, ON M5H 2H5
(416) 362-3711
FAX (416) 864-1099
Entertainment Lawyers: Ed Glinert, Len Glickman.

Moher & Associates,
Barristers and Solicitors
685 Queen St. W., 2nd Floor
Toronto, ON M6K 1E6
(416) 862-7892
FAX (416) 862-2626
Entertainment Lawyer: Brendan J. Moher.

Murrant Brown

52 St. Patrick St.
Toronto, ON M5T 1V1
(416) 971-6619
FAX (416) 340-0406
Services Provided: Entertainment law.
Specialization: Visual and musical arts.
Comments: Firm has over 14 years of experience in entertainment.
Clients: Sharon, Lois and Bram, Corey Hart, Ann Medina.
Entertainment Lawyers: Anthony Baker, Clark Miller.

Rogers, Bereskin & Parr

40 King St. W., P.O. Box 401
Toronto, ON M5H 3Y2
(416) 364-7311
FAX (416) 361-1398
Services Provided: Copyright law and litigation for licensing.
Entertainment Lawyers: Jill Jarvis-Tonus, Sharon Groom, Roger Hart, Daniel Bereskin.

Paul Sanderson,
Barrister and Solicitor
52 St. Patrick St., 2nd Floor
Toronto, ON M5T 1V1
(416) 971-6616
FAX (416) 971-4144
Services Provided: Legal services for the entertainment industry.
Specialization: Entertainment and media law.
Entertainment Lawyers: Clark Miller, Paul Sanderson.

Shibley, Righton & McCutcheon

401 Bay St., Suite 1800
Toronto, ON M5H 2Z1
(416) 363-9381
FAX (416) 365-1717
Services Provided: Full-service law firm.
Specialization: Acting for record labels and artists.
Entertainment Lawyers: Rupert F. Righton, Q.C.; William (Bill) L. Northcote, Helder M. Travassos.

Silverstein & Fodor

55 Avenue Rd., Suite 2500
Toronto, ON M5R 3L2
(416) 968-2939
FAX (416) 961-5350
Services Provided: Corporate and commercial law.
Specialization: All fields of the entertainment industry.
Entertainment Lawyers: Louis Silverstein, Joseph Fodor, Laurie Gelfand.

Sim, Hughes, Dimock

330 University Ave., Suite 701
Toronto, ON M5G 1R7
(416) 595-1155
FAX (416) 595-1163
Services Provided: Copyright law and litigation.
Entertainment Lawyer: Roger T. Hughes.

Smith, Lyons, Torrance, Stevenson & Mayer

2 First Canadian Place, Suite 3400
Toronto, ON M5X 1J3
(416) 369-7315
Services Provided: Communications and copyright law.

Strathy, Archibald & Seagram

Commerce Court W., 38th Floor
Toronto, ON M5L 1J3
(416) 862-7525
FAX (416) 862-2504
Services Provided: Full-service law firm.
Specialization: Music law, including recording, publishing, licensing, merchandising and copyright.
Entertainment Lawyers: Mark Tamminga, Michael Fleisher.

R. Bruce Torrie,

Barrister and Solicitor
1211 and 1221 Bidwell St.
Vancouver, BC V6G 2K7
(604) 683-8111
FAX (604) 685-0194
Services Provided: Contracts, litigation and business advice.
Specialization: Court work.
Entertainment Lawyer: R.B. Torrie.

Varty & Company

475 Howe St., Suite 302
Vancouver, BC V6E 2B3
(604) 684-5356
Services Provided: Copyright, contracts, licensing and royalties for film and video.

Roger Watts

3201-30 Ave., 4th Floor
Vernon, BC V1T 2C6
(604) 542-5353
FAX (604) 542-7273
Entertainment Lawyer: Roger Watts.

Wolinsky, Liffmann, Wolinsky

444 St. Mary Ave., Suite 900
Winnipeg, MB R3C 3T1
(204) 944-9777
FAX (204) 957-5482
Services Provided: Entertainment law.
Specialization: Recording, TV and film.
Clients: Fred Turner (BTO), Byron O'Donnell, Errol Ranville.
Entertainment Lawyer: David Wolinsky.

LIGHTING & SPECIAL EFFECTS SUPPLIERS

ALBERTA

Axe Music
11931-72 St.
Edmonton, AB T5B 1Y4
(403) 471-2001
FAX (403) 479-1443
Type of Company: Manufacturer, sales agency, rentals and installations.
Product Specialty: Sound and lighting for nightclubs and theatres.
Top Brands: TOA, JBL, QSC.
Special Services: Servicing.

Lighting By Monty Ltd.
9170 Yellowhead Tr.
Edmonton, AB T5B 1G2
(403) 477-5077
FAX (403) 477-8247
Type of Company: Distributor, sales and rentals.
Top Brands: Strand, Altman, Leprecon.

United Light and Sound (ULS) Ltd.
12915-146 St.
Edmonton, AB T5L 2H6
(403) 455-6482
FAX (403) 425-0329
Type of Company: Manufacturer, distributor.

BRITISH COLUMBIA

TMI
2530 Davies Ave., P.O. Box 279
Port Coquitlam, BC V3C 3V7
(604) 464-1341
Type of Company: Distributor, product specialists and clinicians.
Product Specialty: Stage lighting, PAs, amplification, musical instruments and recording equipment.
Top Brands: Fender, Akai, Alesis, Sunn.
Special Services: Inventory finance plans.

MANITOBA

Westsun Media Ltd.
120 James Ave.
Winnipeg, MB R3B 0N8
(204) 943-1690
FAX (204) 943-1081
Type of Company: Manufacturer, distributor, sales and rental agency.
Product Specialty: Theatrical, television and entertainment lighting systems.

NOVA SCOTIA

Atlantic Illumination
23 Sheridan St.
Dartmouth, NS B3A 2C9
(902) 463-7418
FAX (902) 469-3255
Type of Company: Distributor, sales agency, rentals, repairs and installations.
Product Specialty: Lights and dimmers for tours and theatre.
Top Brands: Altman, Celco, Leprecon
Special Services: Major warranty repair facility.

Tour Tech East Ltd.
200B Wyse Rd.
Dartmouth, NS B3A 1M9
(902) 466-6851
FAX (902) 466-3173
Type of Company: Distributor, sales agency, installations and rentals.
Top Brands: Dilor Industries, Thomas, Avolites, Altman Select, LMI.

ONTARIO

Ainsworth Productions
120 Bermondsey Rd.
Scarborough, ON M4A 1X6
(416) 585-8500
Type of Company: Distributor, sales agency, rentals and installations.
Product Specialty: Complete staging and design services for music, video, trade shows and industrials.

B.C.B. Sound & Lighting Productions
1535 Meyerside Dr., Unit 8
Mississauga, ON L5T 1M9
(416) 672-3444
Type of Company: Distributor, sales agency.
Product Specialty: Complete disco lighting and aluminum lighting fixtures.
Top Brands: JBL, Sennheiser, SF Marketing.
Special Services: Repairs.

Canadian Staging Projects
571 Adelaide St. E.
Toronto, ON M5A 1N8
(416) 947-9400
FAX (416) 367-8708
Type of Company: Distributor, sales and rental agency, service centre.
Product Specialty: Fibre optics, stage lighting.
Top Brands: Strand, Altman, Rosco

Carere Special Effects
P.O. Box 5818, Stn. A
Toronto, ON M5W 1P2
(416) 463-6656
(416) 460-0034 (mobile)
Type of Company: Manufacturer, distributor, sales agency.
Product Specialty: Special effects, designs and implementation.

Cinetrix Special Effects Inc.
32 Logan Ave.
Toronto, ON M4M 2M8
(416) 461-0977
FAX (416) 461-1067
Type of Company: Visual special effects and prop building.
Special Services: Equipment rentals.

D.J.U. Canada Ltd.
220 Pony Dr.
Newmarket, ON L3Y 7B6
(416) 836-6078
FAX (416) 836-6089
Type of Company: Distributor, sales agency, importer.
Top Brands: Megalite, WB, Pulsar.

E.T.I.

150 McLevin Ave., Unit 8
Scarborough, ON M1B 4Z7
(416) 754-7747
FAX (416) 291-0666
Type of Company: Manufacturer, sales agency, rentals
Product Specialty: Lighting equipment and special effects for concerts, theatres and discotheques.

Jack A. Frost Ltd.

3245 Wharton Way
Mississauga, ON L4X 2R9
(416) 624-5344
FAX (416) 624-2386
Type of Company: Motion picture and theatrical lighting sales and distribution.
Product Specialty: Specialty lamps.
Top Brands: Strand, Altman, Ushio.
Special Services: Custom manufacturing of power distribution equipment.

HNS Sound & Lights Ltd.

253 Regent St.
Sudbury, ON P3C 4C6
(705) 674-1450
FAX (705) 674-8392
Type of Company: Lighting and effects supplier, manufacturer and distributor.
Product Specialty: Gels, foggers, parcans, consoles and dimmers.
Top Brands: Rosco, Strand, CGE.
Special Services: Repairs and rentals.

Headwater Audio

635 Caron Ave.
Windsor, ON N9A 5B8
(519) 256-2454
FAX (519) 256-2522
Type of Company: Leasing and production company, professional sound system rentals.
Special Services: Lighting, staging and trucking.

KLS Electronics Group

1707 Sismet Rd., Unit 12
Mississauga, ON L4W 2K8
(416) 238-8244
FAX (416) 238-1073
Type of Company: Distributor of entertainment lighting products and smoke machines.
Product Specialty: Foggers, strobelights, dimmers, controllers, beam projectors.
Top Brands: JEM smoke machines, Anytronics, FAL lighting effects.

Laser F/X International

P.O. Box 1340, Stn. A
Toronto, ON M5W 1A0
(416) 247-3112
Product Specialty: Laser lighting for dance parties, film and video.

Laser Magic Productions Inc.

550 Alden Rd., Unit 112
Markham, ON L3R 6A8
(416) 470-7770
FAX (416) 470-9701
Type of Company: Manufacturer and supplier of laser effects.
Product Specialty: Laser projection systems.
Special Services: Laser beams and graphics, fibre optics, holographic imagery.

Laserlite F/X Inc.

70 Esna Park Dr., Units 3-A
Markham, ON L3R 1E3
(416) 479-0255
FAX (416) 470-0828
Type of Company: Manufacturer and distributor of laser effects.

Lumitrol Ltd. Theatre Lighting

253 Merton St.
Toronto, ON M4S 1A7
(416) 485-4817
FAX (416) 485-4826
Type of Company: Manufacturer, distributor, sales agency.
Product Specialty: Dimmers and drapes
Top Brands: Altman, Ash, Lee-Colortran
Special Services: Engineering services

Magic Lite Ltd.

1075 Meyerside Dr., Unit 3
Mississauga, ON L5T 1M3
(416) 564-0026
FAX (416) 564-1690
Type of Company: Distributor.
Product Specialty: Decorative lighting.
Top Brands: Fiberstars, Non Neon, Tubelite.

National Show Systems

36 Malley Rd.
Toronto, ON M1L 2E2
(416) 755-8666
FAX (416) 752-1382
Type of Company: Show services.
Special Services: Sound, lighting, staging and outdoor roofs.

Pierce Sound & Lighting
411 Industrial Rd., Unit 6
London, ON N5V 3L3
(519) 455-7041
FAX (519) 455-6506
Type of Company: Supplier.
Product Specialty: Sound and lighting contractors for TV production, tours, fashion shows and live industrials.
Top Brands: Meyer, MSL-3, UPA-1A, Thomas/Avolite.

Pyrotek Special Effects
617 Pharmacy Ave.
Scarborough, ON M1L 3H1
(416) 288-9938
FAX (416) 288-9483
Type of Company: Distributor, show designers, special effects for theatre and concerts.
Product Specialty: Pyrotechnics
Top Brands: Pyro Pak, Rosco, Le Maitre
Special Services: Indoor and outdoor fireworks

RMSCO Ltd.
9 Pullman Ct.
Scarborough, ON M1X 1E4
(416) 298-7766
FAX (416) 298-0225
Type of Company: Distributors of professional lighting and special effects for the entertainment industry.
Product Specialty: Lighting fixtures and controls, smoke machines and pyrotechnics.
Top Brands: F.E. Lighting, Light Design Systems, Le Maitre.
Special Services: System design assistance.

Rosco Laboratories
1271 Denison St., Suite 66
Markham, ON L3R 4B5
(416) 475-1400
FAX (416) 475-3351
Type of Company: Distributor
Product Specialty: Colour filmers, smoke/fog effects and other materials used in film, TV and theatre.
Special Services: Lighting consulting, and repair and service for Rosco fog machine.

Scoreworks Unlimited
656 Woodbine Ave.
Toronto, ON M4E 2J3
(416) 690-8632
Type of Company: Manufacturer of special effects.
Product Specialty: Flash powder and fog oils.
Top Brands: Steiner Binoculars, Davis & Sanford Tripods, Universal Cine Heads.
Special Services: Pyrotechnics, electronic displays and props.

Stagetech Inc.
275 Berkeley St.
Toronto, ON M5A 2X3
(416) 368-0839
FAX (416) 368-6856
Type of Company: Manufacturer, distributor, sales agency.
Product Specialty: Lighting systems and special effects for trade shows, fashion shows, touring and theatre.
Top Brands: Rosco, Times Square, Philips.
Special Services: Rentals and installations.

Ultrastage Inc.
4917 Bridge St.
Niagara Falls, ON L2E 2S2
(416) 356-0499
FAX (416) 356-9187
Type of Company: Distributor, rentals.
Product Specialty: Theatrical lighting and special effects, sales and rentals.
Top Brands: Rosco, Altman, Foto Engineering.

Westbury/National Show Systems
36 Malley Rd.
Scarborough, ON M1L 2E2
(416) 752-1371
FAX (416) 752-1382
Type of Company: Distributor, sales, service, and rentals of sound and lighting equipment.
Product Specialty: Concert sound and lighting equipment.
Top Brands: Electro-Voice, Yamaha, Adamson.
Special Services: Full audio, lighting, staging and production services.

William F. White Ltd.
36 Park Lawn Rd.
Toronto, ON M8Y 3H8
(416) 252-7171
FAX (416) 252-6095
Type of Company: Distributor.
Product Specialty: Lighting, grip and camera
supplies for theatre, film and TV.
Special Services: Sales and rentals.
Branches:
North Shore Studios
555 Brooksbank Ave.
N. Vancouver, BC V7J 3S5
(604) 983-5300
FAX (604) 983-5309

2185 rue Lariviere
Montreal, PQ H2K 1P5
(514) 866-3323
FAX (514) 866-8856

2616 16th St. N.E., Suite 2
Calgary, AB T2E 7J8
(403) 250-1719
FAX (403) 250-1537

QUEBEC

Ateliers Albert Inc.
2222 Ontario St. E.
Montreal, PQ H2K 1V8
(514) 521-2225
FAX (514) 521-2806
Type of Company: Distributor, sales agency.
Top Brands: Altman, Lee.
Special Services: Rentals, installation and
service.

Audesco Electronics Ltd.
1396 St. Patrick
Montreal, PQ H3K 1A6
(514) 931-5888
FAX (514) 931-2359
Type of Company: Distributor, sales agency.
Product Specialty: Custom designed sound
systems.
Top Brands: Discomotion, Miralum, Crystaline.

Conception Audio/ Visuels Projecson Inc.
176-13 St.
Rouyn-Noranda, PQ J9X 2H8
(819) 762-1404
FAX (819) 762-5532
Type of Company: Manufacturer, sales agency.
Product Specialty: Sound and lighting rentals
for shows, full design for clubs and discotheques,
manufacturer of road cases, sound and lighting
equipment.
Special Services: Rentals and service.

Kinpar
40 Windmere
Dollard-des-Ormeaux, PQ H9A 2C4
(514) 683-2477
Type of Company: Sound and lighting
suppliers for nightclubs and discotheques.

Kitsch Audio Ltd.
1565 Iberville
Montreal, PQ H2K 3B8
(514) 527-2323
FAX (514) 527-2326
Type of Company: Distributor.
Product Specialty: Tour-related products.
Top Brands: Hill, Soundcraft, Yamaha.
Special Services: Tours, trade shows and conferences.

Mephistronique Ltee.
990 Amherst St., Suite 400
Montreal, PQ H2L 3K5
(514) 281-1025
FAX (514) 281-1037
Type of Company: Manufacturer.
Product Specialty: Lighting control and
dimmer power packs.

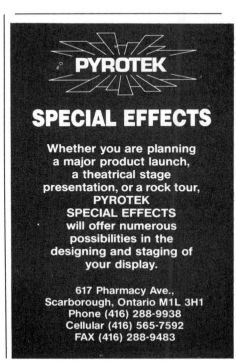

Protech Cases

1751 Richardson, Suite 4557
Montreal, PQ H3K 1G6
(514) 931-5023
FAX (514) 931-5023
Type of Company: Manufacturer.
Product Specialty: Transport cases.

Les Eclairages Projec Inc.

150-5 St.
Quebec, PQ G1L 2R4
(418) 529-8982
FAX (418) 529-8519
Type of Company: Manufacturer and lighting systems sales.
Product Specialty: Color Ray 2 System.
Top Brands: Le Maitre, NSI, Coemar.
Special Services: Sales and rental of Color Ray 2 System.

MANAGEMENT COMPANIES

ALBERTA

Tommy Banks Music Ltd.
12227-107 Ave., Suite 2
Edmonton, AB T5M 1Y9
(403) 482-3001
Preferred Musical Styles: Pop (mostly writers).

Barry's Pro Music Agency
P.O. Box 526
Brooks, AB T0J 0J0
(403) 362-4204
Preferred Musical Styles: C&W, Country Rock.
Acts Represented: Nine, accept new acts.
Network Affiliations: Nashville Connection.
Services Offered: Organizing tours for U.S. bands.

Caldwell Entertainment Agency
6720-43 Ave. N.E.
Calgary, AB T1Y 5P1
(403) 285-7895
Preferred Musical Styles: Show and lounge acts.
Network Affiliations: Actra, ITAA.

Image Control Management
(A Division of Image Control Productions Ltd.)
10852 Whyte Ave. Suite 203
Edmonton, AB T6E 2B3
(403) 433-2016
FAX (403) 439-4209
Preferred Musical Styles: Alternative, Rock & Roll, Country Rock, Reggae, Heavy Metal, Hardcore.
Acts Represented: Andy Rox, Red Rum, One Eyed Wendy.
Network Affiliations: Platinum Studio, Churchyard Publishing.
Services Offered: Management.

157

MKM Music Productions Ltd.
159 Harrison Dr.
Edmonton, AB T5A 2X5
(403) 476-0746
Preferred Musical Styles: Folk.
Acts Represented: The Michael Mitchell Band.
Network Affiliations: MKM.
Services Offered: Tour and booking management.

Magnum Music Corporation Ltd.
8607-128 Ave.
Edmonton, AB T5E 0G3
(403) 476-8230
Preferred Musical Styles: Country.
Acts Represented: Catheryne Greenly, Billy Jay Legere, Cormier Country (Gordon and Loretta.
Network Affiliations: Magnum Records, Ramblin' Man Music Publishing.

Danny Makarus Musical Services
11714-113 Ave.
Edmonton, AB T5G 0J8
(403) 454-6848 or 454-9291
Preferred Musical Styles: All styles.
Acts Represented: Mary Lou Sonmor, Miriam, Jenson Interceptor.
Venues Represented: Venues throughout Western Canada.

Robert Montgomery and Associates
9170 Yellowhead Tr.
Edmonton, AB T5B 1G2
(403) 477-1286
FAX (403) 477-8247
Preferred Musical Styles: Pop, Rock.
Network Affiliations: San Paku Music, Kartunes.

New Age Entertainment
107343-155 St.
Edmonton, AB T5P 2M7
(403) 476-6585
Preferred Musical Styles: Pop, Rock.

Jeff Parry Promotions
P.O. Box 1234, Stn. M
Calgary, AB T2P 2C2
(403) 230-5334
Preferred Musical Styles: All styles, accept new acts.

Pro Motion
P.O. Box 5663, Stn. L
Edmonton, AB T6C 4G1
(403) 437-4803
Contact: Al MacKechnie.

Roadside Attractions Inc.
11411-37A Ave.
Edmonton, AB T6J 0J6
(403) 438-6185
Preferred Musical Styles: Pop, Folk, Jazz, theatre and dance.
Acts Represented: Accept new acts.
Services Offered: Contacts with Alberta's tour networks.

SCM Recording & Management Services
12 Park Dr., Ridgewood Estates
P.O. Box 64, Site 16, R.R.2
Winterburn, AB T0E 2N0
(403) 962-3709
Preferred Musical Styles: Top 40, Rock, Pop, Commercial.
Acts Represented: Nationally.
Venues Represented: All Western Canada hotel venues and clubs.
Services Offered: Booking agency, consultants.

Shantero Productions
519-20 Ave. N.W.
Calgary, AB T2M 1C7
(403) 282-3680
Preferred Musical Styles: C&W, Folk, Blues plus comedy, mime and theatre.

Doug Wong Music
P.O. Box 1714, Stn. M
Calgary, AB T2P 2L7
(403) 265-1714
Preferred Musical Styles: All.
Acts Represented: Adventures in Paradise, nationally.
Services Offered: Management and music industry consulting.
Special Projects: Contract negotiation, licensing.

BRITISH COLUMBIA

Active Artists Promotion
P.O. Box 580, Stn. A
White Rock, BC V4B 5G4
(604) 535-0707
Preferred Musical Styles: Pop, Rock, Reggae.
Acts Represented: Recording acts on tour, nationally.

Bruce Allen Talent
68 Water St., Suite 406
Vancouver, BC V6B 1A4
(604) 688-7274
FAX (604) 688-7118
Preferred Musical Styles: Rock.
Acts Represented: Bryan Adams, Loverboy, BTO.

B&E Records
2233 W. 1 Ave., Suite 101
Vancouver, BC V6K 1E9
(604) 734-7090
Preferred Musical Styles: Rock.
Acts Represented: Saint Eves.
Affiliated Company: B&E Management.

Lou Blair Management Inc.
68 Water St., Suite 407
Vancouver, BC V6B 1A4
(604) 689-7070
FAX (604) 688-7118
Preferred Musical Styles: Pop, Rock.
Acts Represented: Loverboy, Alfie Zappacosta.

Brass Ring Productions Ltd.
P.O. Box 1266, Stn. A
Kelowna, BC V1Y 7V8
(604) 763-5502
Preferred Musical Styles: Pop and MOR.
Acts Represented: Kim Boz, Dalyn Norgard.
Network Affiliations: CARAS, SOCAN.
Affiliated Companies: Brass Ring Records.
Services Offered: Personal Management, publishing, music photography and recording.

Bumstead Productions
1616 W. 3 Ave.
Vancouver, BC V6J 1K2
(604) 736-3512
FAX (604) 736-0567
Preferred Musical Styles: General.
Acts Represented: k.d. lang and the reclines, nationally.
Affiliated Companies: Lars Music Publishing, WEA, Sive Records, Warner Bros., Bumstead.

Cloana Music Group
177 W. 7 Ave. 4th Floor
Vancouver, BC V5Y 1K5
(604) 876-3005
FAX (604) 873-0166
Preferred Musical Styles: Country, Contemporary.
Acts Represented: Alibi, Dianne Kauffman, Colette Wise.
Network Affiliations: CCMA, BCCMA.
Affiliated Companies: Cloana Publishing, Diclo Publishing, Cloana Records, ITS, Cloana Promotions.

Diversified Music Group
1969 Pandora St.
Vancouver, BC V5L 5B2
(604) 255-3536
FAX (604) 255-8711
Preferred Musical Styles: Rock, Country, Country Rock.
Acts Represented: Darby Mills, One Horse Blue, Lori Jordan, Bear Mountain Boys, Kenny Shaw and Danny Mack.
Network Affiliations: BCCMA, CCMA.
Services Offered: Marketing, publicity, management, publishing, rehearsal and production studios.

Donnelly Enterprises
68 Water St., Suite 203
Vancouver, BC V6B 1A4
(604) 681-1193
Acts Represented: Two, accept new acts.

S.L. Feldman & Associates
1534 W. 2 Ave., 3rd Floor
Vancouver, BC V6J 1H2
(604) 734-5945
Preferred Musical Styles: Pop, MOR, Rock, Blues plus comedy and lounge music.
Acts Represented: Approximately 150, accept new acts.
Venues Represented: Approximately 40 venues.

159

Front Row Productions
747 Cardero St.
Vancouver, BC V6B 3V7
(604) 681-8311
FAX (604) 684-0726
Preferred Musical Styles: MOR.
Network Affiliations: CARAS, CIRPA,
BC Touring Council.

Gangland Artists
810 W. Broadway Ave., Suite 707
Vancouver, BC V5Z 1J8
(604) 872-0052
FAX (604) 872-1715
Preferred Musical Styles: Pop Rock, Rock.
Acts Represented: Bolero Lava, Sons of Free-
dom, 54.40.
Network Affiliations: Love Mao Music Ltd.,
54.40 Songs Inc.
Services Offered: Personal management.

Jessica A. Gihon Management
68 Water St., Suite 303
Vancouver, BC V6B 1A4
(604) 684-5115
Preferred Musical Styles: Rock, Pop.
Clients: MCM Concert Promotions.
Services Offered: Bios, press releases, press
kits and newsletters.

Gillstrom Management
207 W. Hastings St., Suite 206
Vancouver, BC V6B 1H7
(604) 685-0818
FAX (604) 683-5357
Preferred Musical Styles: Rock.
Acts Represented: Paradise.

Michael Godin Management Inc.
218 W. 19 Ave.
Vancouver, BC V5Y 2B7
(604) 876-1208
Preferred Musical Styles: Rock, Pop.
Acts Represented: Paul Janz, worldwide.

Goldrush Productions
1234 W. 6 Ave.
Vancouver, BC V6H 1A5
(604) 733-4012
Contact: Simon Garber.

Homestead Productions
1616 W. 3 Ave.
Vancouver, BC V6J 1K2
(604) 736-2667
Preferred Musical Styles: General.
Acts Represented: Colin James, nationally.
Affiliated Companies: Instead Publishing,
Bumstead Productions.
Clients: Virgin Records, Warner Bros.

International Talent Services Incorporated
177 W. 7 Ave., 4th Floor
Vancouver, BC V5Y 1K5
(604) 872-2906
FAX (604) 873-0166
Preferred Musical Styles: Country.
Acts Represented: Ron Tarrant Band,
The Marlaine Sisters, Silver City.

Jaguar Entertainment
68 Water St., Suite 401
Vancouver, BC V6B 1A4
(604) 684-4455
FAX (604) 873-0166
Preferred Musical Styles: 50s Rock and
Country.
Acts Represented: Larry Branson (tribute to
Roy Orbison), Jess Lee.

Lizard Mountain Music
P.O. Box 251
Cranbrook, BC V1C 4H8
(604) 489-2036
Preferred Musical Styles: MOR, Rock, C&W.
Acts Represented: The Black Diamond Band.
Affiliated Companies: Lizard Mountain Rec-
ords.
Services Offered: Demo and record produc-
tion, singles and sound production, management
and promotion.
Services Offered: Annual East Kootenay Con-
cert - Cranbrook, BC.

Ted Mansfield Talent Management
68 Water St., Suite 302
Vancouver, BC V6B 1A4
(604) 687-8712
Preferred Musical Styles: Pop Rock.
Acts Represented: Amie Moore, Zombo X,
Paul Gregory.
Affiliated Companies: Trade Mark Music.
Services Offered: Artist development and
management.

Massop Communications

P.O. Box 970
Parksville, BC V0R 2S0
(604) 248-5960
Preferred Musical Styles: Country music recording artists.
Acts Represented: Two, accept new acts.
Services Offered: Career guidance and consulting management.
Special Projects: Promo kits, bios, media service.

Opus Promotions

35236 McKae Rd.
Abbotsford, BC V2S 6K6
(604) 850-3901
Preferred Musical Styles: Pop, Classical.
Acts Represented: Accept new acts.

Pacific Show Productions

925 W. Georgia St., Suite 316
Vancouver, BC VC6 1R5
(604) 684-3242
Preferred Musical Styles: Pop, MOR, convention acts, music variety, lounge performers and show bands.
Network Affiliations: A.F. of M., BC Touring Council, Tourism Victoria.
Services Offered: Convention entertainment production, stage shows, tours, lounge and casual bookings.

Parallel One Artists Inc.

1622 W. 7 Ave., Suite 301
Vancouver, BC V6J 1S5
(604) 736-0434
Preferred Musical Styles: Pop.
Acts Represented: Body Electric, JATO, nationally.
Affiliated Companies: Parallel One Productions, Parallel One Music, Parallel One Records.

Prestige Entertainment Agencies Ltd.

177 W. 7 Ave., 4th Floor
Vancouver, BC V5Y 1K5
(604) 876-5535
Preferred Musical Styles: Pop, Jazz.
Network Affiliations: CART, ITAA.

Ramcoff Productions Management Ltd.

339 E. 27 St.
N. Vancouver, BC V7N 1B9
(604) 986-6838
Preferred Musical Styles: Classical chamber ensembles.
Acts Represented: Vancouver Wind Quintet, North Vancouver Wind Trio, Vancouver Chamber Winds, I Musici, Vancouver regionally.

Saddlestone Publishing, Recording and Distribution

2954 O'Hara Lane
Surrey, BC V4A 3E5
(604) 531-1771 or (206) 332-8688
Preferred Musical Styles: C&W, Rock, MOR, Gospel, Pop, Easy Listening.
Acts Represented: Matt Audette, Dorrie Alexander, Patty Mayo.
Affiliated Companies: Saddlestone International.
Services Offered: Distribution, publishing, recording, promotion and production.
Special Projects: Worldwide record promotion.

Siegel Entertainment Ltd.

1648 W. 7 Ave., Suite 101
Vancouver, BC V6J 1S5
(604) 736-3896
FAX (604) 736-3464
Preferred Musical Styles: Pop, MOR, Rock, C&W, Lounge, etc.

Skywalk

1967 Panorama Dr.
North Vancouver, BC V7O 1V2
(604) 929-8397
Preferred Musical Styles: Instrumental Jazz Fusion.
Acts Represented: Skywalk.
Network Affiliations: SOCAN.
Services Offered: General business for Skywalk only.

Straight Ahead Productions

2416 Vine St.
Vancouver, BC V6K 3K8
(604) 731-4460
Preferred Musical Styles: Pop, Rock.
Network Affiliations: CARAS, PMIA.
Clients: *Georgia Straight* newspaper.
Services Offered: Advertising, multimedia and special events.

MANAGEMENT COMPANIES

T.K.O. Entertainment Inc.
6556 Kitchener St.
Burnaby, BC V5B 2J7
(604) 467-0709
FAX (604) 467-6924
Acts Represented: Annihilator, Rocky Swanson, Tommy Floyd, Jess Lee, Eddie Carrigan.

Teamworks Production & Management
867 Hamilton St., 2nd Floor
Vancouver, BC V6B 2R7
(604) 683-6535
FAX (604) 688-7155
Services Offered: Management and bookings for national and regional artists.
Specialization: Personal artist management.
Comments: Not actively seeking new clients. Only musicians with demo and promotional materials need apply.
Clients: Bob's Your Uncle, Brent Lee, Hard Rock Miners, Persuaders.

Timeless Productions
207 W. Hastings St., Suite 206
Vancouver, BC V6B 1H7
(604) 681-3029
FAX (604) 683-5357
Preferred Musical Styles: Kick Axe, Paradise, The Law, plus 30 other acts.
Venues Represented: Club Soda, Commodore, 86 St. (Vancouver), South Centre (Calgary).
Network Affiliations: I Told You So Publishing.

MANITOBA

Dallas Productions
P.O. Box 1843
Winnipeg, MB R3C 3R1
(204) 775-7250
Preferred Musical Styles: Rock, Pop, original.

Direction Four Artist Management Ltd.
140 Bannatyne Ave., Suite 301
Winnipeg, MB R3B 3C5
(204) 947-9200
FAX (204) 943-3588
Preferred Musical Styles: All.

Morris Theatrical Agency
265 Portage Ave.
Winnipeg, MB R3B 2B2
(204) 943-7236
Preferred Musical Styles: All styles.
Acts Represented: 60, accept new acts.
Network Affiliations: CART, ITAA.

Showcase Productions
2003 Portage Ave., Suite 201
Winnipeg, MB R3J 0K3
(204) 889-5567
Preferred Musical Styles: Rock, Pop, MOR, C&W.
Acts Represented: Singles, duos and bands, regionally.

NEW BRUNSWICK

A. Couturier & Company Inc.
304 George St.
Fredericton, NB E3B 1J7
(506) 450-9422
Preferred Musical Styles: Classical, Folk.
Acts Represented: The Duo Pach, Barbara Ann Quigley.
Network Affiliations: A.F. of M.

NEWFOUNDLAND

Donna DeCarlo Enterprises
P.O. Box 901
Bishops Falls, NF A0H 1C0
(709) 489-7144
Preferred Musical Styles: All.
Acts Represented: 10, accept new acts.
Network Affiliations: CART.

Fabian James
363 Blackmarsh Rd.
St. John's, NF A1E 1T3
(709) 722-5868

162

NOVA SCOTIA

Backstage Productions
1541 Barrington St., Suite 400
Halifax, NS B3J 1Z5
(902) 423-9284
Preferred Musical Styles: Pop, R&B.
Network Affiliations: Sara Hope Music.

Brookes Diamond Productions
World Trade and Convention Centre
1800 Argyle St., Suite 507
Halifax, NS B3J 3N8
(902) 422-7000
FAX (902) 422-2929
Preferred Musical Styles: A/C, Country,
Classical, Traditional.
Acts Represented: Rita MacNeil, Joan
Kennedy, John Allan Cameron, Abraxas Trio.
Services Offered: Artist management, booking,
tour co-ordination and production.

T.K. Productions Ltd.
P.O. Box 8391, Stn. A
Halifax, NS B3K 5M1
(902) 423-8434
FAX (902) 422-2929
Preferred Musical Styles: Mass appeal con-
temporary.
Acts Represented: Terry Kelly.
Services Offered: Booking, management and
recordings.

Targe Productions
1586 Queen St.
Halifax, NS B3J 2J1
(902) 422-1342
Preferred Musical Styles: Military, Classical,
Pop.

ONTARIO

A.C.E. Management
4544 Dufferin St., Suite 24
Toronto, ON M3H 5X2
(416) 736-6319

A.T.I. (Access to the Industry)
75 Parkway Ave.
Markham, ON L3P 2H1
FAX (416) 294-5538
Preferred Musical Styles: Country, variety.
Acts Represented: James H. Robinson, J.D.
Sheridan, Elvis Aaran Presley Jr., GEM.
Services Offered: Management and promotion.

Active Talent Agency
148 York St., Suite 224
London, ON N6A 1A9
(519) 679-0971
Preferred Musical Styles: Commercial Top
40 acts.
Services Offered: Booking agency and
management.

Adelman/O'Connell Enterprises
505 Parliament St., Suite Z
Toronto, ON M4X 1P3.
(416) 923-2256 or 924-4251.
Preferred Musical Styles: Pop, Rock, Funk.
Acts Represented: The Jitters, Phase IV.

The Agency
41 Britain St., Suite 200
Toronto, ON M5A 1R7
(416) 365-7833
FAX (416) 365-9692
Preferred Musical Styles: Pop, MOR, Rock,
C&W.
Acts Represented: Downchild Blues Band,
Over The Garden Wall.
Services Offered: Banking Cash Management,
A/P, A/R, bookkeeping.
Special Projects: Payroll, tax preparation.

Alert Management
41 Britain St., Suite 305
Toronto, ON M5A 1R7
(416) 364-4200
Acts Represented: Kim Mitchell, The Box.
Branch Office:
3510 St. Laurent, Suite 209
Montreal, PQ H2Y 2P6

Apricot Talent & Recording Industries Inc.
1449 Ridgebrook Dr., Suite 120
Gloucester, ON K1B 4T1
(613) 749-1116
Preferred Musical Styles: Top 40, MOR, Rock, Heavy Metal.
Acts Represented: Various, regionally.
Venues Represented: Talisman Motor Inn, Le Spectra, Barrymore's.
Services Offered: Booking and promotion of all acts.

The Artist Consulting Team Inc.
25 Draper St.
Toronto, ON M5V 2M3
(416) 596-0353
FAX (416) 596-8120
Preferred Musical Styles: Pop, MOR, Rock, Reggae.
Acts Represented: Crash Vegas, Blue Rodeo, The Sattalites.
Network Affiliations: Risque Disque Music (publishing), Risque Disque Inc. (recording), WEA Music of Canada Ltd. (distribution).

Artistic Canadian Entertainers Management Associates
4544 Dufferin St., Unit 24
Downsview, ON M3H 5X2
(416) 736-6319
Preferred Musical Styles: All styles (original acts only).
Acts Represented: Flipside, Joyride, Tyra.
Services Offered: Management consultation, music videos, special events and concerts.

Audio Plus Productions
409 King St. W., Suite 508
Toronto, ON M5V 1K1
(416) 340-9871
Acts Represented: The Bourbon Tabernacle Choir.
Network Affiliations: CIRPA, AES.

Azumuve Management
600 Queen St. E.
Toronto, ON M4M 1G3
(416) 463-2797
FAX (416) 463-0989
Preferred Musical Styles: Rock.
Acts Represented: Bambi.

BGS Music Promotions
64 Glen Manor Dr.
Toronto, ON M4E 2X2
(416) 698-0715
Preferred Musical Styles: Classical Guitar, Classical Ensembles.
Acts Represented: Stepan Rak, Jukka Savijoki, Alan Torok, The Castellani-Andriaccio Duo, Savijoki/Helasvuo.

Backstage Productions International
3015 Kennedy Rd., Suite 1
Scarborough, ON M1V 1E7
(416) 291-4913
FAX (416) 297-7784
Preferred Musical Styles: Pop, MOR, C&W.
Acts Represented: Ronnie Hawkins, Jannetta, J.K. Gulley.
Network Affiliations: Melmar Publishing, Star Sattelite Publishing, Trilogy Records.

Balmur Ltd.
4881 Yonge St., Suite 412
Willowdale, ON M2N 5X3
(416) 223-7700
FAX (416) 223-7808
Preferred Musical Styles: A/C, Pop, Country.
Acts Represented: Anne Murray, George Fox, Frank Mills.
Services Offered: Personal and business management.

Bandstand (International) Entertainment Agency
P.O. Box 1010
Simcoe, ON N3Y 5B3
(519) 426-3799
Preferred Musical Styles: MOR, Rock, Top 40.
Acts Represented: Many.
Venues Represented: Hotels in Southern Ontario.
Network Affiliations: A.F. of M.
Affiliated Companies: Thrust Management.

Blue Train Music
56 Braemar Ave.
Toronto, ON M5P 2L2
(416) 925-7557
Preferred Musical Styles: Roots-oriented Rock & Roll.
Acts Represented: The Phantoms, The Jack De Keyzer Band.
Affiliated Companies: Fried Publishing, Paradise Audio Visual.
Services Offered: Music management.

Bounty Enterprises

1474 Wallace Rd.
Oakville, ON L6L 2Y2
(416) 847-ROCK
FAX (416) 847-6608
Preferred Musical Styles: Top 40.
Acts Represented: Various.
Venues Represented: Various.
Clients: CBS.
Services Offered: Recording direction.
Special Projects: Full promotion plus in-house photography and video.

CBD Enterprises

180 Duncan Mill Rd., Suite 400
Don Mills, ON M3B 1Z6
(416) 441-2144
FAX (416) 441-2259
Acts Represented: Pop, MOR, C&W.
Network Affiliations: ISES (founding member).
Services Offered: Special event planning and consulting.

Call Yes Management and Consulting

533 Lakeshore Rd.
Cobourg, ON K9A 1S4
(416) 372-8469
FAX (416) 372-1754
Preferred Musical Styles: Rock, Pop, Alternative Jazz.
Acts Represented: Big Bang Theory.
Services Offered: Artist management, publicity and promotion.

Jerry C. Cameron Exclusive Management

1474 Wallace Rd.
Oakville, ON L6L 2Y2
(416) 847-0144
Preferred Musical Styles: Pop, Rock, MOR, Top 40.
Acts Represented: Various, nationally.
Network Affiliations: A.F. of M.

Canadent Concerts Management

1534 Dearbourne Dr.
Sudbury, ON P3A 5A4
(705) 566-8465
FAX (705) 566-0380
Preferred Musical Styles: Classical, Light Classical.

Chart Toppers

1908 Beechknoll Ave.
Toronto, ON
(416) 625-6007
Contact: Neill Dixon.

Children's Hour Productions

750 Oakdale Rd., Suite 60
North York, ON M3N 2Z4
(416) 740-5105
FAX (416) 740-6449
Preferred Musical Styles: Children's entertainment.
Venues Represented: Ontario Place Forum.

Citation Records

191A Wolseley St., Suite 200
Thunder Bay, ON P7A 3G5
(807) 345-2448
Preferred Musical Styles: Country, Country Rock.
Network Affiliations: CCMA.
Services Offered: Production, artist direction.

Cityspeak

20 Fairford Ave.
Toronto, ON M4L 2J7
(416) 461-9538
Contact: Ian Gregory Wright.

Clark Agency

75 Wolfe St.
Kingston, ON
(613) 546-3066
FAX (613) 548-1282
Preferred Musical Styles: Jazz.
Acts Represented: Oliver Jones, Fraser MacPherson, Jon Ballantyne.
Network Affiliations: A.F. of M.
Affiliated Companies: Justin Time Records Inc. (Recording), Distribution Fusion III (Distributing).

Collegium Arts Management

427 Bloor St. W.
Toronto, ON M5S 1X7
(416) 920-9797
Preferred Musical Styles: Baroque music.
Acts Represented: Tafelmusik Baroque Orchestra and Tafelmusik Chamber Choir, nationally.

Colwell Arts Management

R.R. 1
New Hamburg, ON N0B 2G0
(519) 662-3499
FAX (519) 662-2210
Preferred Musical Styles: Classical vocalists and ensembles.
Venues Represented: Worldwide representation.
Services Offered: Management and booking of classical soloists.

Concertmasters Inc. Artists' Management

22 Linden St.
Toronto, ON M4Y 1V6
(416) 922-9922
FAX (416) 960-6166
Preferred Musical Styles: Major classical music attractions.
Affiliated Companies: Straightwire Digital Editing, Aaron Concert Management (Boston).

Randall Cousins Management

17 Paradise Rd. S., Unit 2
Hamilton, ON L8S 1S1
(416) 572-7474
Preferred Musical Styles: Rock, Country, Country Rock.
Acts Represented: Jack Diamond, Mark and the Sharks, Frequency.
Affiliated Companies: Roto-Noto Music.

Covert Communications

36 Wright Ave.
Toronto, ON M6R 1K8
(416) 531-2185
FAX (416) 869-0017
Preferred Musical Styles: Rock.
Acts Represented: Flatland, Michael Phillip Wojewoda, Neil Sternberg, Neil Exall, Matthew Myers, Jellyfishbabies.
Services Offered: Artist representation, contract consulting, biography writing, small tour management.

Crossroads Entertainment Consultants

180 Duncan Mill Rd., Ste. 400
Don Mills, ON M3B 1Z6
(416) 441-2144
FAX (416) 441-2259
Preferred Musical Styles: All kinds.
Network Affiliations: ISES, Toronto Musicians' Association.

Current Management

366 Adelaide St. E., Suite 437
Toronto, ON M5A 3X9
(416) 361-1101
FAX (416) 867-9501
Preferred Musical Styles: Pop, Rock, Dance.
Acts Represented: Strange Advance, Alta Moda, Mystery Romance, nationally.
Network Affiliations: Current Records, Current Sounds.

DBC Ltd.

180 Duncan Mill Rd.
Don Mills, ON M3B 1Z6
(416) 441-2144
FAX (416) 441-2259
Preferred Musical Styles: Pop, MOR, C&W.
Network Affiliations: ISES (founding member).
Services Offered: Special event planning and consulting.

Dobbin Agency

477A Princess Street
Kingston, ON K7L 1C3
(613) 549-4401
Preferred Musical Styles: Pop, MOR, Rock, C&W.
Network Affiliations: CART.

Double A Entertainment Inc.

3611 Mavis Rd., Unit 5
Mississauga, ON L5C 1T7
(416) 279-4008
FAX (416) 279-4006
Preferred Musical Styles: Pop.
Acts Represented: Regatta, nationally.

Ray Douglas Promotions

P.O. Box 7213-Sandwich
Windsor, ON N9C 3Z1
(519) 969-1203 or 258-2288
Preferred Musical Styles: MOR, Pop, C&W, Jazz, Big Bands, Classical.
Acts Represented: Ray Douglas International Big Band, Joan Eastman And The Music Makers, The Kenny Crone Jazz Group.
Venues Represented: Victoria Tavern, Kozak's By The Sea Tavern, International Freedom Festival.
Network Affiliations: A.F. of M.
Special Projects: The Off Shore International Jazz Society.

EKG Management Inc.

P.O. Box 577
Waterloo, ON N2J 4B8
(519) 744-4350
FAX (519) 742-3398
Acts Represented: Syre, Nasty Klass, The Warning.
Network Affiliations: EKG Music.

E.M.E. International
(Effective Management of Entertainers)
696 The Queensway
Toronto, ON M8Y 1K9
(416) 259-4164
FAX On request
Preferred Musical Styles: Pop, Rock.
Network Affiliations: Canadian Music Publishers.

ESP - Elwood Saracuse Productions Ltd.
6 Lansing Sq., Suite 129
Willowdale, ON M2V T5
(416) 499-7070
FAX (416) 492-4108
Preferred Musical Styles: All styles.
Acts Represented: Pharazon Dance Company, Video Hits Alive, Clazz Flute and Harp Duo.
Network Affiliations: C.A.F.E.
Services Offered: Specializing in public and corporate special events.

Early Morning Productions
1365 Yonge St., Suite 207
Toronto, ON M4T 2P7
(416) 924-1146
Acts Represented: Gordon Lightfoot, no new acts.

Elliot & Associates
P.O. Box 1010
Simcoe, ON N3Y 5B3
(519) 426-0000
FAX (519) 426-3799
Preferred Musical Styles: MOR, Rock.
Services Offered: Management.
Branch Office:
1475 Flamingo Dr., Unit 392
Englewood, Fl 34224 USA

Entertainment Management Corporation
P.O. Box 490, Stn. K
Toronto, ON M4P 2G9
(416) 481-3369
Preferred Musical Styles: All styles.
Acts Represented: Various.
Network Affiliations: ALUCAA, CAPACOA.
Affiliated Companies: William James Publishing, Revenge Records.

Exclusive Management
55 Wynford Heights, Apt. 1910
Don Mills, ON M3C 1L4
(416) 449-9612
FAX (416) 792-1059
Services Offered: Management and booking.
Special Projects: Production.

Falcon Productions
3080 Lenworth Dr.
Mississauga, ON L4X 2G1
(416) 625-3865
FAX (416) 277-1356
Acts Represented: New acts accepted.

B.C. Fiedler Management
40 Alexandra, Penthouse 2
Toronto, ON M4Y 1B5
(416) 967-1421
Preferred Musical Styles: Pop, Rock, MOR, Classical guitar.
Acts Represented: Canadian Brass, Dan Hill, accept new acts.

The Finkelstein Management Co. Ltd.
151 John St., Suite 301
Toronto, ON M5V 2T2
(416) 596-8696
FAX (416) 596-6861
Services Offered: Record Company and recording artists' management.

Jim Ford & Associates Inc.
315 Soudan Ave.
Toronto, ON M4S 1W6
(416) 483-0663
FAX (416) 483-2866
Preferred Musical Styles: Jazz, Big Band Swing (for listening and dancing), Popular, Classical plus galas and musical comedy concerts.
Acts Represented: Peter Appleyard, John Arpin, Buddy Wasisname and the Other Fellers.
Contact: Jim Ford.

Gandhi Management
70 Plunkett Rd., Suite 3
Weston, ON M9L 2J5
(416) 749-4104
FAX (416) 271-4115
Preferred Musical Styles: Commercial Pop.
Acts Represented: Kumari, nationally and internationally.
Network Affiliations: CIRPA, CARAS, BMAC.
Affiliated Companies: Justice Records.
Services Offered: Personal management and career development.

General Arts Management Inc. (GAMI)
651 Queen St. E.
Toronto, ON M4M 1G4
(416) 461-0301
Preferred Musical Styles: Classical, Chamber and Jazz recitalists.
Acts Represented: 11, accept new acts.

Ginjoy & Associates Inc.
25 Wood St., Suite 104
Toronto, ON M5J 2P9
(416) 977-1153
Acts Represented: All, nationally.
Network Affiliations: CART.
Services Offered: Publicity, advertising, management and bookings.

Attila Glatz International Music Management
21 Webster Ave.
Toronto, ON M5R 1N6
(416) 923-6245
Preferred Musical Styles: Classical, Pop, Rock, MOR.
Acts Represented: Accept new acts.
Services Offered: North American and European tours for pianists, show bands and recording artists.

Jacob J. Gold & Associates
372 Richmond St. W.
Toronto, ON M5V 1X6
(416) 977-8022
FAX (416) 971-7759
Preferred Musical Styles: Pop, Rock.
Acts Represented: Tragically Hip, and others nationally.

Great World Artists Management Inc.
66 Gerrard St. E., Suite 201
Toronto, ON M5B 1G3
(416) 971-9723
FAX (416) 971-9732
Preferred Musical Styles: Classical and contemporary chamber music.
Acts Represented: Nexus, Angela Hewitt, Elmer Iseler Singers.
Special Projects: International touring of foreign artists.

Hart/Murdock Artists Management
204A St. George St.
Toronto, ON M5R 2N6
(416) 922-5020
FAX (416) 922-6686
Preferred Musical Styles: Classical singers and instrumentalists.
Acts Represented: Catherine Robbin (mezzo-soprano), Jon Kimura Parker (pianist), The King's Singers.
Services Offered: Canadian tours for foreign artists and ensembles.

Head Office Management
296 Richmond St. W., Suite 305
Toronto, ON M5V 1X2
(416) 979-8455
FAX (416) 979-8766
Preferred Musical Styles: Rock, Pop.
Acts Represented: Brighton Rock, Michael Hanson, Big House.
Affiliated Companies: Fraze Songs, Steeler Music, Autotunes Publishing, Dee Songs, Boomtown Music, Boom Songs, Town Songs, Suite Music Inc., Eleven Music Inc.
Services Offered: Management and publishing services.

Headquarters Entertainment Corporation
157 Princess St., Suite 300
Toronto, ON M5A 4M4
(416) 363-7363
FAX (416) 363-1203
Preferred Musical Styles: Pop, Rock.
Acts Represented: The Nylons, Canadian Brass, nationally.

Davina Hradkova Artists Management Services
238 Davenport Rd., Suite 37
Toronto, ON M5R 1Y6
(416) 968-0960
Preferred Musical Styles: Classical, MOR.
Acts Represented: Three, nationally.
Services Offered: Publicity and promotion.

Hulen Enterprises
2447 Falcon Ave., Suite 2
Ottawa, ON K1V 8C8
(613) 738-2373
FAX (613) 521-2673
Preferred Musical Styles: Pop, Rock Country.
Services Offered: Artist management, tour support and marketing.
Special Projects: National and international services as well as Bootcamp.

In Tune Productions
1450 O'Connor Dr., Suite 118
Toronto, ON M4B 2T8
(416) 752-4616
Preferred Musical Styles: Pop, Rock, Top 40.
Acts Represented: Regionally in Ontario and Quebec.

International Theatrical Services/ITS Agency
562 Brock St.
Windsor, ON N9L 2T2
(519) 252-8663
Preferred Musical Styles: All kinds.
Acts Represented: New acts accepted.

Jimjam Talent Booking
2108 Queen St. E.
Toronto, ON M4E 1E2
(416) 698-2498
Preferred Musical Styles: Rock, New Wave, Reggae, Punk/Hardcore, Country, R&B, Funk/Soul.
Acts Represented: Nationally.

D.R. Jellis & Associates
32 Roblocke Ave.
Toronto, ON M6G 3R7
(416) 537-6947
Services Offered: Public relations plus personal and financial management.

John W. Jones Management & Communications Direction
123 Scadding Ave., Suite 817
Toronto, ON M5A 4J3
(416) 361-5009
Preferred Musical Styles: Jazz.
Acts Represented: Exclusive management for Manteca, nationally.

Jonwhite Productions
44 Wardell St.
Toronto, ON M4M 2L5
(416) 461-6742
Acts Represented: Calypso, Soca, Reggae, Latin, Funk, Pop.

Key Artist Management & Entertainment Consultants
500 Newbold St.
London, ON N6E 1K6
(519) 686-5060
Services Offered: Career management, artist direction, image consultation and record promotion.

Kitchen Music
R.R. 4
Shelburne, ON L0N 1S0
(519) 925-5009
FAX (519) 925-6313
Preferred Musical Styles: Family and children's entertainment.
Acts Represented: Eric Nagler.
Network Affiliations: ACTRA, A.F. of M.
Affiliated Companies: Snagglepuss Music.
Clients: Eric Nagler.
Special Projects: Touring, TV.

Lant Management Services
(Management Division of Lant International)
P.O. Box 1085
569 Lynwood Dr.
Cornwall, ON K6H 5V2
(613) 938-1532
Preferred Musical Styles: All.
Acts Represented: Serendipity Singers.
Services Offered: Artist management, tax preparation and consulting, and revenue services.
Contact: Charles W.B. Lant.

Robert Luhtala Management
342 Jarvis St.
Toronto, ON M4Y 2G6
(416) 920-6969
Services Offered: Management services provided for both producers and bands.
Clients: Bob Potter (producer), Rain, Kelso, Slik Toxik.

The Management Company
41 Britain St. Suite 200
Toronto, ON M5A 1R7
(416) 365-7833
FAX (416) 365-9692
Preferred Musical Styles: Rock.
Acts Represented: The White, Over the Garden Wall, Riff Raff, Partland Brothers.
Affiliated Companies: The Agency.
Services Offered: Complete tour support.

Management West International

14 Sumach St.
Toronto, ON M5A 3J4
(416) 360-5775
FAX (416) 360-5772
Preferred Musical Styles: Pop, Rock, MOR.
Acts Represented: Glass Tiger, The Kings, Green River.
Services Offered: Management and consultation.

Mark III Management

191A Wolseley St., Suite 200
Thunder Bay, ON P7A 3G5
(807) 345-2448
Preferred Musical Styles: Country, Country Rock.
Network Affiliations: CCMA.

John Mars

P.O. Box 1583
Brantford, ON N3T 5V6
(519) 753-2081
Preferred Musical Styles: Pop, Rock, New Jazz.
Acts Represented: The Children, Stu Broomer & John Mars, The Popp Tarts.
Network Affiliations: A.F. of M., SOCAN.
Affiliated Companies: Ugly Dog Records, Utter Nonsense Publishing.
Services Offered: Management, direction and production.

Media & Entertainment Development

P.O. Box 1015
Waterloo, ON N2J 4S1
(519) 747-0274
Preferred Musical Styles: Rock, Pop.
Acts Represented: Fax, Rude Boyz, Driver.
Network Affiliations: A.F. of M.
Affiliated Companies: Encore Productions, Elora Sound.
Services Offered: Artist representation, management and direction.

Modern Artists Management

221 Balliol St., Suite 811
Toronto, ON M4S 1C8
(416) 483-1403
Preferred Musical Styles: Pop, Rock.

Moffatt Corporation

1 Stewart St., Suite 200
Ottawa, ON K1N 6H7
(613) 563-2416
FAX (613) 235-5843
Preferred Musical Styles: Rock.
Acts Represented: Blazing Apostles, Jeff Moffatt (two acts only).

Music Matters Management

P.O. Box 417, Stn. C
Toronto, ON
(416) 534-4297
Preferred Musical Styles: Pop, Rock.
Acts Represented: Skydiggers.
Affiliated Companies: Enigma, Capitol.
Services Offered: Management, consulting, promotion.

Musicon Management

3611 Mavis Rd., Unit 3
Mississauga, ON L5C 1T7
(416) 279-4000
FAX (416) 279-4006
Preferred Musical Styles: Rock.
Acts Represented: Triumph, no new acts.

New Management

383 Parkdale Ave.
Ottawa, ON K1Y 4R4
(613) 722-2553
FAX (613) 722-3918
Contact: Allan White.

Carmen Nunez Artists Management

P.O. Box 293, Stn. F
Toronto, ON M4Y 2L7
(416) 549-7614
Preferred Musical Styles: Classical.
Services Offered: Management, booking, consulting and publicity.

OHM Music International (OMI)

253 College St., Suite 340
Toronto, ON M5T 1R5
(416) 922-6297
FAX (416) 285-7104
Preferred Musical Styles: Roots-related Rock & Roll, New Music.
Acts Represented: Dr. Limbo & His Fabulous Off-Whites.
Network Affiliations: A.F. of M.
Affiliated Companies: Dirty Little Nipper Records.
Services Offered: Management, bookings, promotions, publicity.

Open Heart Productions

246 James St. N., Suite 2
Hamilton, ON L8R 2L3
(416) 521-0560
Acts Represented: Pop, Rock.

P.R.E.S. Management Services Inc.

32 Voyageur Ct. S.
Rexdale, ON M9W 5M7
(416) 674-7211
Preferred Musical Styles: Pop, Rock.
Acts Represented: Eye Eye, nationally.

The Pangaea Music House

P.O. Box 609, Stn. F
Toronto, ON M4Y 2L8
(416) 922-1600
FAX (416) 922-0799
Preferred Musical Styles: Pop.
Acts Represented: Ken Tobias.
Clients: Pangaea Music Publishing, Mispec Music.

Tony Paniccia Management Inc.

391 Hopewell Ave.
Toronto, ON M6E 2S1
(416) 785-5621
FAX (416) 782-8574
Preferred Musical Styles: Pop, Rock.
Acts Represented: Debbie Johnson, Dezire.
Affiliated Companies: Marigold Records, Electric Distributing.
Clients: Debbie Johnson, Dezire.
Services Offered: Personal Management.

Pizazz Productions

35 Hambly Ave.
Toronto, ON M4E 2R5
(416) 699-3359
Preferred Musical Styles: Pop, Rock, C&W.
Acts Represented: Various, nationally.
Network Affiliations: CART.

Pop Music

P.O. Box 499, Stn. A
Ottawa, ON K1N 8V5
(613) 238-3906
Preferred Musical Styles: Pop, Rock, MOR.
Acts Represented: Avery Singer, Heaven's Radio, The Magic Circle.
Affiliated Companies: Lowertown Music.
Clients: Heaven's Radio.
Services Offered: Concert management, marketing and publicity.
Special Projects: Televised concerts.

Priceless Productions

P.O. Box 474
Welland, ON L3B 5R2
(416) 788-0055
Preferred Musical Styles: All.
Acts Represented: 12, accept new acts.

Propas Management Corporation

6A Wellesley St. W.
Toronto, ON M4Y 1E7
(416) 964-2621
FAX (416) 925-0661
Preferred Musical Styles: Pop, Rock.
Acts Represented: Lee Aaron, Dan Hill, Frank Marino.
Affiliated Companies: Attic, A&M, Spy.

Marie Rakos Concert Management

14 Palsen St.
Nepean, ON K2G 2V8
(613) 224-6750
FAX (613) 727-1626
Preferred Musical Styles: Classical, Folk, Jazz, Pop.
Acts Represented: Stephane Lemelin, Manfred Trio, Cathy Miller.
Network Affiliations: A.F. of M.
Services Offered: Management and booking for musicians.

MANAGEMENT COMPANIES

Random Entertainment Inc.
3100 Ridgeway Dr., Unit 26
Mississauga, ON L5L 5M5
(416) 569-3100
FAX (416) 569-1221
Preferred Musical Styles: Rock, Pop.
Acts Represented: Rik Emmett, Danny Brooks, Simon Chase.
Affiliated Companies: Toon Town Music (publishing).

Regal Recording Ltd.
2421 Hammond Rd.
Mississauga, ON L5K 1T3
(416) 855-2370
Preferred Musical Styles: Jazz.
Acts Represented: Oscar Peterson, exclusively.

Resource One
1235 Bay St., Suite 501
Toronto, ON M5R 3K4
(416) 922-3633
Preferred Musical Styles: Jazz, Pop.
Acts Represented: Hugh Marsh.

Rock Power Management (RPM)
85 Wellesley St. E.
Toronto, ON M4Y 1H8
(416) 967-5356
Preferred Musical Styles: Rock, Heavy Metal.
Acts Represented: Jade.

SKU Productions
P.O. Box 805, Stn. P
Toronto, ON M5S 2Z1
Preferred Musical Styles: Pop, Jazz, Funk.
Acts Represented: Rare Air.

SPI
(Spontaneous Promotions Inc.)
P.O. Box 116, Stn. C
Toronto, ON M6J 3M7
(416) 769-1281
Preferred Musical Styles: Pop, Rock, MOR.
Affiliated Companies: Spontaneous Records, IPS music.

S.R.O. Productions
189 Carlton St.
Toronto, ON M5A 2K7
(416) 923-5855
FAX (416) 923-1041
Preferred Musical Styles: Rock.
Acts Represented: Rush, Gowan, Spoons, Images in Vogue, internationally.
Affiliated Companies: Anthem Records, Anthem Entertainment Group, Brandy Publishing, Core Music Publishing, Mark-Cain Music.

Steve Sechi Management
18 The Donway E., Suite 607
Toronto, ON M3C 1X9
(416) 445-0678
Preferred Musical Styles: Commercial Rock, Pop.
Acts Represented: Joe Vincent, internationally.
Affiliated Companies: Rippin' Music, Riptide Records.

William Seip Management Incorporated
P.O. Box 515
Waterloo, ON N2J 4A9
(519) 741-1252
FAX (519) 742-3398
Preferred Musical Styles: Commercial Rock, Hard Rock.
Acts Represented: Helix, Ray Lyell and The Storm, Big Bang.
Affiliated Companies: Lyell Communications (A Division of William Seip Music Incorporated), William Seip Music Incorporated, H&S Records (A Division of William Seip Management Incorporated).
Services Offered: Artist management, publishing and recording label.

Seventh Sword Productions
312 Adelaide St. W., Suite 415
Toronto, ON M5V 1R2
(416) 960-3123
Preferred Musical Styles: Rock.
Acts Represented: City Speak, Those Guys.
Network Affiliations: SOCAN.
Services Offered: Music management.

Shemac Entertainment Group Inc.
89 Clarence St.
Woodbridge, ON L4L 1L4
(416) 850-3630
FAX (416) 850-2830
Preferred Musical Styles: Pop, Rock.
Acts Represented: Dorian Gray, Benjamin's Kite.

Renee Simmons Artists Management

117 Ava Road
Toronto, ON M6C 1W2
(416) 782-7712
FAX (416) 785-5099
Preferred Musical Styles: Classical musicians.
Acts Represented: Norbert Kraft, Kraft/Silver Duo, Marina Piccinini/Robert Kortgaard Duo, Marina Piccinini, Robert Kortgaard, Stephanie Sebastian, Steven Isserlis.
Network Affiliations: ASOL, CAAM, CAPACOA, ASO/OFSO, APAP, WAAA.
Services Offered: Personal management.

Sky Is Falling Inc.

2027 Dickson Rd.
Mississauga, ON L5B 1Y7
(416) 566-5907
FAX (416) 848-7718
Preferred Musical Styles: Rock.
Acts Represented: Tom Cochrane and Red Rider, Saga.
Affiliated Companies: Chesterfield Entertainment, Falling Sky Music.
Services Offered: Music Entertainment.

Joanne Smale Productions Ltd.

686 Richmond St. W.
Toronto, ON M6J 1C3
(416) 363-4051
FAX (416) 363-6986
Preferred Musical Styles: Songwriters.
Acts Represented: Murray McLauchlan, Willie P. Bennett, Jane Bunnett.
Star Treatment
P.O. Box 1329
Pembroke, ON K8A 6Y6
(613) 735-4060
Acts Represented: Pop, MOR, Rock.

Starrider Productions

16 Cayuga Ave.
Mississauga, ON L5G 3S7
(519) 855-4951
Preferred Musical Styles: Rock, Pop.
Network Affiliations: CARAS, CIRPA, ITAA.

Stars Management Group

3336 Mainway
Burlington, ON L7M 1A7
(416) 332-4424
FAX (416) 847-0308
Preferred Musical Styles: Pop, Dance, Rock, R&B.
Acts Represented: Never...But Always, accepting new acts.
Affiliated Companies: Prime Time Records, W.E.T. Productions.
Services Offered: Career development, management and music publishing.

Suds Sutherland Management Projects Inc.

R.R. 2
Orillia, ON L3V 6H2
(705) 327-2521
Services Offered: Booking agent and manager.
Special Projects: Concert productions.
Clients: Entertainment Centre, The Agency, Orillia Community Centre.

Supervision

807 Sweetwater Cr.
Mississauga, ON L5H 4A7
(416) 274-3215
Preferred Musical Styles: C&W.
Acts Represented: Terry Carisse, Anita Perras & Tim Taylor, Matt Minglewood, Michelle Wright, nationally.

Swell Inc.

7 Fraser Ave., Suite 7
Toronto, ON M6K 1Y7
(416) 532-2340
FAX (416) 533-5177
Preferred Musical Styles: Pop, Rock.
Acts Represented: The Pursuit of Happiness, One Free Fall.

TBA

120 Carlton St.
Toronto, ON M5A 4K2
(416) 961-7000
Preferred Musical Styles: Rock, Pop.

William Tenn Management

25 Bay Mills Blvd., Suite 502
Agincourt, ON M1T 3P4
(416) 292-3510
FAX (416) 596-1239
Preferred Musical Styles: Rock.
Acts Represented: Andrew Cash.
Network Affiliations: CARAS.
Affiliated Companies: Positively music.

3L Productions

3578 Silverplains Dr.
Mississauga, ON L4X 2P4
(416) 238-2901
FAX (416) 625-2165
Preferred Musical Styles: Pop, Rock.
Acts Represented: Various, nationally.
Network Affiliations: CTO, CART.

20/20 Management Limited

175 Jardin Dr., Unit 1
Concord, ON L4K 1B1
(416) 738-9777
FAX (416) 738-9779
Preferred Musical Styles: Rock, Folk, Blues.
Acts Represented: Frozen Ghost, The Tony
Springer Band, Cindy & The Slammers.
Services Offered: Personal management and
direction.

Two-Tone Productions

9 Gillespie Cr., Unit 21
Ottawa, ON K1V 9T5
(613) 526-3390
Preferred Musical Styles: Pop, Rock.
Network Affiliations: CARAS, SOCAN.
Affiliated Companies: The House of Attitude
Readjustment.
Services Offered: Management, promotion,
merchandising and consulting.

The Ultimate Umbrella Corporation

68 Summerhill Gardens
Toronto, ON M4T 1B4
(416) 944-0435
FAX (416) 944-1149
Preferred Musical Styles: Original non-Rock.
Acts Represented: Norm Hacking, Katharine
Wheatley.

VKD International Artists

220 Sheppard Ave. E.
Willowdale, ON M2N 3A9
(416) 225-5882
Preferred Musical Styles: Classical singers,
conductors and instrumentalists.
Acts Represented: Various.

Victory Artist Management

P.O. Box 1059, Stn. F
Toronto, ON M4Y 2T7
(416) 367-4677
Preferred Musical Styles: Pop, Rock.
Acts Represented: Chalk Circle, Sheep Look
Up, Touchstones.

Wagers and Co.

31 Parkside Dr.
Toronto, ON M6R 2Y7
(416) 531-4823
Acts Represented: Neo A4, nationally.
Affiliated Companies: A4 Publishing.

Peter Ware, Artist Representative

P.O. Box 61, Stn. K
Toronto, ON M4P 2G1
(416) 787-3481
Preferred Musical Styles: Classical.
Acts Represented: Lynn Harting-Ware
(guitarist), Ware/Wells Duo (violin and guitar).
Network Affiliations: Acoma Company,
Acoma Recordings.
Services Offered: Management and
promotions.

Warner Casselman Music

7305 Woodbine Ave., Suite 455
Markham, ON L3R 3V7
(416) 477-3780
Preferred Musical Styles: Rock, MOR.
Acts Represented: Three, accept new acts.

Wren Management

511 St. Johns Rd.
Toronto, ON M6S 2L7
(416) 762-6789
FAX (416) 925-7344
Preferred Musical Styles: Country.
Acts Represented: Mary Lynn Renn,
exclusively.

Barry Yaffa Management

164 York Hill Blvd.
Thornhill, ON L4J 2P6
(416) 881-7927
Preferred Musical Styles: All styles.
Network Affiliations: SOCAN, CIRPA, A.F.of M., FACTOR.
Services Offered: Contract negotiation (record, publishing and booking).
Special Projects: Merchandising for all events.

QUEBEC

ARS Musicalis

P.O. Box 181
Montreal, PQ H3X 3T4
(514) 861-3485
Preferred Musical Styles: Classical.
Acts Represented: Six, accept new acts.

Rene Angelil

4410 rue Louis-Payette
Laval, PQ H7T 1V2
(514) 687-4501
Preferred Musical Styles: Pop, New Music.
Acts Represented: Celine Dion.

Black Tiger Productions

264 Ste. Catherine o., Suite 203
Montreal, PQ H2X 2A1
(514) 875-6795
Preferred Musical Styles: R&B, Jazz.
Acts Represented: B.B. King, Koko, Taylor, approximately 40 others.

Gina Brown Management

P.O. Box 534
Montreal, PQ H2W 2P1
(514) 842-6791
FAX (514) 276-2696
Preferred Musical Styles: Jazz and New Music.
Acts Represented: The Beards.
Network Affiliations: Bloc-Notes Notation (publishing).

Bob Carlisle Productions Inc.

P.O. Box 599
St. Basile-le-Grand, PQ J0L 1S0
(514) 653-0442
FAX (514) 653-0272
Preferred Musical Styles: Bavarian, Big Band, C&W, Dixieland, Ethnic, MOR, Pop.
Acts Represented: The Entertainers, Claude Foisy, Remember.
Special Projects: Corporate events, trade shows and festivals.

Bernardo Carrara Management

3733 Hutchison
Montreal, PQ H2X 2H4
(514) 844-7832
Preferred Musical Styles: Pop, Rock.
Acts Represented: MollyBelle & Dax.
Network Affiliations: Venus Landing Records.

Productions Musicales CIBE

1183 ave. Colbert, Suite 12
Sainte-Foy, PQ G1V 3Z2
(418) 658-3778
Preferred Musical Styles: Classical.
Acts Represented: Soloists and chamber musicians.
Network Affiliations: CIBE Recordings.
Services Offered: Booking, promotion, publicity and management.
Special Projects: Record promotion and distribution.

Les Productions Guy Cloutier

2322 Sherbrooke St. E.
Montreal, PQ H2K 1E5
Preferred Musical Styles: Pop.
Acts Represented: Rene Simard, Natalie Simard.

DB Management Reg'd

5405 Park Ave., 2nd Floor
Montreal, PQ H2V 4G9
(514) 276-9000
FAX (514) 270-7310
Preferred Musical Styles: Pop Rock.
Acts Represented: Cinema V.

Darkhouse Musical Productions Reg'd

P.O. Box 687, Stn. NDG
Montreal, PQ H4A 3P5
(514) 735-3061
Preferred Musical Styles: Pop, MOR, New Age and contemporary instrumental.
Acts Represented: John Horrocks, Melodies On Canvas.
Affiliated Companies: Les Editions Wingspirit Enr., Empress Records Reg'd.
Special Projects: Production, promotion and management of artists. Rental of sound reinforcement equipment.

Equus Management

3405 Thimens Blvd.
Montreal, PQ H4R 1V5
(514) 335-9501
Preferred Musical Styles: Rock.
Affiliated Companies: Aquarius, EMI.

Fleming Artists' Management

5975 Park Ave.
Montreal, PQ H2V 4H4
(514) 276-5605
FAX (514) 495-4889
Preferred Musical Styles: Jazz, Folk, Roots.
Acts Represented: Karen Young/Michel Donato, Jean Beaudet, Penny Lang.
Clients: Justin Time, Fusion III.

Terry Flood Management

6265 Cote-de-Liesse, 2nd Floor
Montreal, PQ H4T 1C3
(514) 735-4777
Preferred Musical Styles: Pop, Rock.
Acts Represented: Accept new acts.

Pierre Gravel, Impresario

89 Alexandra St.
Granby, PQ J2G 2P4
(514) 372-7764
FAX (514) 372-4391
Preferred Musical Styles: Pop, MOR, Rock, C&W.
Acts Represented: Andre-Philippe Gagnon, Denis Lacombe.
Venues Represented: International.
Services Offered: Management and booking.

Great Artists Management

3575 boul. St. Laurent, Suite 810
Montreal, PQ H2X 2T7
(514) 842-2968
Preferred Musical Styles: Classical, Variety.
Acts Represented: Andre Gagnon, McGill Chamber Orchestra, nationally.

Josie Productions

1859 Everett St., Suite 4
Montreal, PQ H2E 1N8
(514) 729-0416
Preferred Musical Styles: Pop, Rock, MOR.
Acts Represented: Niky Nero.
Clients: Niky Nero.
Services Offered: Artist representation.

Sheldon Kagan Promotions

1020-5 Ave.
Dorval, PQ H9S 1J2
(514) 631-2160
FAX (514) 631-4430
Preferred Musical Styles: Pop, MOR, Rock.
Acts Represented: Three acts, accept new acts.

Latitude 45/Arts Promotion

109 boul. St. Joseph o.
Montreal, PQ H2T 2P7
(514) 276-2694
FAX (514) 276-2696
Preferred Musical Styles: Contemporary, Classical.
Acts Represented: Alain Trudel, Les Granules and Louise Bessette.
Network Affiliations: CAAM.

Paul Levesque Management Inc.

154 Grande Cote
Rosemere, PQ J7A 1H3
(514) 437-7625
FAX (514) 430-9751
Preferred Musical Styles: Pop, Rock.
Acts Represented: Paradox, All The Tribes, Sonia Papp, Xcuse, Silver Saddle, The Weapon, Broken Hearts.
Affiliated Companies: Artiste Records.
Clients: Management of record producers Pierre Bazinet and John Farley.
Services Offered: Management, record label and publishing.

Francine Loyer-Hershorn
3525 Marlowe
Montreal, PQ H4A 3L8
(514) 487-9474
Preferred Musical Styles: R&B, Pop, Rock, Funk.

MCM Entertainment Management Inc.
1327 boul. St. Joseph e.
Montreal, PQ H2J 1M1
(514) 522-4722
FAX (514) 525-7550
Preferred Musical Styles: Pop, Rock, Dance.
Acts Represented: Paris Black & Diodati.
Network Affiliations: ISBA Records Inc., ISBA Music Publishing Inc.
Services Offered: Management.

Moffet Management
36 Dandelin
Kirkland, PQ H9J 1L8
(514) 694-3515
Preferred Musical Styles: Pop, Rock.
Acts Represented: Gilt, See Spot Run, nationally.
Network Affiliations: Fyada Music.
Services: Career guidance, accounting and business management.

Out Of The Blue Management
2315 Belgrave Ave.
Montreal, PQ H4A 2L9
(514) 486-5699
Preferred Musical Styles: Rock, R&B, Pop.
Acts Represented: Dorion & The Freeriders, Riopel.
Network Affiliations: Freeride Music, Spin Music.
Services Offered: Personal management.

Les Productions Rubicon Inc.
P.O. Box 1370, Stn. Desjardins
Montreal, PQ H5B 1H3
(514) 327-6172
Preferred Musical Styles: New Age.
Acts Represented: Raoul Duguay & Michel Robdoux, Daniel Blanchet.
Services Offered: Promotion, music consultants and booking agency.
Special Projects: Production of New Age music radio program.

Showbiz International Inc.
137 St. Pierre, Suite P121
Montreal, PQ H2Y 2L6
(514) 843-3443
Preferred Musical Styles: Pop, Rock.
Acts Represented: Veronique Beliveau, Lucien Francoeur, and others nationally.

Spectra Scene
355 Ste. Catherine o., Suite 700
Montreal, PQ H3B 1A5
(514) 288-5363
FAX (514) 499-0956
Preferred Musical Styles: Quebec Pop Rock.
Acts Represented: Michel Rivard, Paul Piche, Jim Corcoran, Louise Forestier.
Venues Represented: Spectrum (Montreal).
Special Projects: Festival International de Jazz de Montreal.

Hendrica Verheyden Artist Management
4175 Jean Brillant
Montreal, PQ H3T 1P2
(514) 737-1851
FAX (514) 731-5678
Preferred Musical Styles: All kinds.
Acts Represented: Favorite Nation, Daniel Weaver, First Kick.
Affiliated Companies: FN Productions, One Nation Music.

YUL Arts Promotion
Latitude 45/Arts Promotion
109 St. Joseph boul., o.
Montreal, PQ H2T 2P7
(514) 276-2694
FAX (514) 276-2696
Preferred Musical Styles: New and Contemporary Music, Musique Actuelle and Improvisational Performance.

SASKATCHEWAN

Platinum Productions
P.O. Box 2048
Yorkton, SK S3N 3X3
(306) 783-1150
Preferred Musical Styles: Country, Country Rock.
Acts Represented: Rob McLane (singer/songwriter), Against The Grain.

MUSIC CAMPS

Academy of Music and Dance

Domaine Forget
398 ch. les Bains
St. Irenee, Charlevoix, PQ G0T 1V0
(418) 452-8111
FAX (418) 452-3503
1990 Session Dates: Brass and percussion, June 3-17; woodwinds, June 17-July 1; guitar and dance, July 1-22; strings and conducting, July 22-August 12; choral singing, August 12-19.
Age Range: No age consideration (admission based on qualifcations).
Rates: $300 (one week), $550 (two weeks), $790 (three weeks).
Entrance Requirements: Applications end when classes are full. Letter of recommendation and, if possible, a demo tape.

Acadia Piano Camps and Summer Workshop

Acadia University, School of Music
Wolfville, NS B0P 1X0
(902) 542-2201, ext. 512
FAX (902) 542-4727
1990 Session Dates: July 28—August 4, 1990.
Programs: Piano camps, advanced piano performance seminar, teachers' workshop.
Age Range: Eight years to university level.
1989 Rates: $75-150 (tuition only), $120-300 (tuition plus room and board).
Deadline for 1990: Approximately July 1, 1990.
Entrance Requirements: Piano performance seminar campers must be advanced highschool players (grade nine and up).
Comments: Beautiful Anapolis Valley setting. All theory subjects plus chorus are part of the program and supervised recreation program and evening concerts are included.

179

Adventures in Summer Music

Red Deer College
P.O. Box 5005
Red Deer, AB T4N 5H5
(403) 342-3527 or 342-3526
FAX (403) 340-8940
1990 Session Dates: August 13-17, 1990.
Programs: Introductory, junior and intermediate band plus ensemble classes, music theory, sectional rehearsals and master classes.
Rates: $75 (plus $5 materials fee). $15 instrument rental if required.
Deadline for 1990: June 29, 1990.
Entrance Requirements: None for introductory band, one year minimum experience for junior band, two or more years of experience for intermediate band.

Algoma Music Camp

505 Albert St. E.
Sault Ste. Marie, ON P6A 2K3
(705) 949-3933
1990 Session Dates: Early August, 1990.
Programs: Classical: strings, brass, woodwinds, orchestra, choir.
Age Range: From eight years to late teens.
Rates: Approximately $400.
Deadline for 1990: June 1, 1990.
Entrance Requirements: Must have some musical background.

Camp Musical D'Asbestos Inc.

P.O. Box 6
Asbestos, PQ J1T 3M9
(819) 879-4342
1990 Session Dates: Session 1, July 1-13; Session 2, July 15-27; Session 3, July 29-August 10; Session 4, August 11-17.
Programs: Stage band and harmony.
Age Range: 10 to 18 years.
Rates: $200 per session, plus $50 registration fee.
Deadline for 1990: May 25, 1990.

CAMMAC Music Centre at Cedar Glen

220 St. Germaine Ave.
Toronto, ON M5M 1W1
(416) 489-4770
1990 Session Dates: July 29—August 12, 1990.
Programs: Large and small choirs, recorder playing, orchestra, chamber music and jazz.
Age Range: All ages.
Rates: TBA.
Deadline for 1990: TBA.
Entrance Requirements: None.

Canadian Conservatory of Music

6065 Cunard St.
Halifax, NS B3K 1E6
(902) 422-6561
FAX (902) 423-0633
1990 Session Dates: July 30—August 11, 1990.
Programs: Rock music workshops and seminars.
Age Range: 14-21 years.
Rates: $290 for two weeks, includes everything except accommodation.
Deadline for 1990: July 20, 1990.

Courtenay Youth Music Centre

Courtenay Youth Music Centre Society
P.O. Box 3056
Courtenay, BC V9N 5N3
(604) 338-7463
FAX (604) 338-1969
1990 Session Dates: Two- and three-week programs between July 8 and August 5.
Programs: Suzuki violin, musical theatre, jazz, strings, piano, band, classical guitar, harp and orchestra.
Age Range: Open.
Rates: $650 (two-week residential), $400 (two-week days), $80 (Suzuki program).
Deadline for 1990: May 31, 1990.
Entrance Requirements: Should be able to read music.

Inter-Provincial Music Camp

251 Davenport Rd.
Toronto, ON M5R 1J9
(416) 922-1591
1990 Session Dates: August 25-September 2, 1990.
Programs: Orchestral, symphonic and stage bands.
Age Range: High school students.
Rates: $425, all inclusive.
Deadline for 1990: Flexible.
Entrance Requirements: Must be studying music in school.

International Symphony Summer Strings

774 London Rd.
Sarnia, ON N7T 5T9
(519) 337-7775
1990 Session Dates: July 9—July 13, 1990; concert on July 14, 1990.
Programs: Master class lessons, chamber music, string orchestra, daily recitals and other outdoor activities.
Age Range: From pre-school to 16 years.
Rates: TBA.
Deadline for 1990: July 1, 1990.
Entrance Requirements: Entrants must own instrument and have minimal playing ability. Pre-schoolers must be accompanied by an adult.

The Jazz Camp

251 Davenport Rd.
Toronto, ON M5R 1J9
(416) 922-1591
1990 Session Dates: August 18—August 24, 1990.
Programs: Big band, combos, ensembles, vocal and improvisation.
Age Range: No age restrictions.
Rates: $425, all inclusive.
Deadline for 1990: Flexible.
Entrance Requirements: Interest in jazz.

Lake MacDonald Music Centre

CAMMAC
P.O. Box 353
Westmount, PQ H3Z 2T5
(514) 932-8755
1990 Session Dates: June 24—August 19, 1990.
Programs: Early music, choral, jazz, opera, guitar and children's programs.
Age Range: From four years of age and up.
Rates: Approximately $115-400 (children-adults, all inclusive).
Deadline for 1990: May 15, 1990.
Entrance Requirements: Annual membership: $25 adults, $13 seniors, $12 students, $35 families.
Comments: Reduced rates for families.

Music Camp '90

Memorial University of Newfoundland, Sir Wilfred Grenfell College
Sir Wilfred Grenfell College, University Dr.
Corner Brook, NF A2H 6P9
(709) 637-6324
FAX (709) 639-8125
1990 Session Dates: August 16-19 and August 19-25, 1990.
Programs: Jazz band camp, concert band camp.
Age Range: Applicants must have celebrated their 11th birthday by August 1, 1990.
Rates: Concert band camp: $310 (live-in early registration), $330 (live-in late registration), $230 (day campers registration), $195 (jazz band camp).
Deadline for 1990: Those who apply before Friday May 18, 1990 will be eligible for discount rates.
Entrance Requirements: Applicants must have played their instrument for a minimum of one year. As in previous years, campers will be selected according to their playing ability (audition) and attitude.
Comments: Campers will be assigned to a band based on their performance at placement auditions which will take place on August 16 (jazz band camp) and August 19 (concert band camp).

National Music Camp of Canada

1749 Bathurst St.
Toronto, ON M5P 3K5
(416) 489-5104
FAX (416) 489-5108
1990 Session Dates: Junior: August 17-August 25, 1990; Highschool and jazz: August 25-September 2, 1990.
Programs: Band, stage band, orchestra, voice, jazz, improvisation, oboe, music theatre. Also, master classes, staff and faculty concerts.
Age Range: Junior, nine-14; highschool, 14-18; jazz, 11-18.
Rates: $399, includes program costs and accommodation (transportation not included).
Deadline for 1990: Open, subject to accommodation space availability.
Entrance Requirements: One year of experience in a school music program.
Comments: Some scholarship assistance available.

New Brunswick Youth Orchestra
(Summer Session)

P.O. Box 6249
Saint John, NB B2N 1L9
(506) 634-8379
FAX (506) 634-0843

1990 Session Dates: TBA, approximately late August.

Programs: Orchestral and chamber music. Full/sectional rehearsals and workshops.

Age Range: 11-24 years of age.

Deadline for 1990: TBA, auditions in April.

Entrance Requirements: Entrants must play an orchestral instrument and pass an audition.

Comments: For information, contact Ellen Buckley (506) 847-8508.

Shawnigan Lake Music Holiday

West Coast Amateur Musicians' Society
943 Clements Ave.
North Vancouver, BC V7R 2K8
(604) 980-5341

1990 Session Dates: July 22-29, 1990.

Programs: Chamber, choral, orchestral, computer and early music. Plus children's, relaxation and fitness programs.

Age Range: Children six-12, adults 13 and up.

Rates: $370 adults, $305 students aged 13-21, $185 children.

Deadline for 1990: June 30, 1990.

Entrance Requirements: Children must have adult sponsors.

Comments: Extra activities include swimming and hiking. Scholarships are available.

MUSIC CONSULTANTS

Tommy Banks Music Ltd.
12227-107 Ave., Suite 2
Edmonton, AB T5M 1Y9
(403) 482-3001
Acts: Pop.

Black Tiger Productions
264 rue Ste. Catherine o.
Montreal, PQ H2X 2A1
(514) 954-1221
Acts: Jazz, Blues, Reggae, R&B and Afro-Caribbean.
Roster: Mango Stars, Blue Monday, Rising Sun Afro-Jazz Orchestra.
Venues: CEGEPs, universities, Place des Arts.

Bootcamp
2447 Falcon Ave., Suite 2
Ottawa, ON K1V 8C8
(613) 738-2373
FAX (613) 521-2673
Acts: All types.
Venues: Worldwide.
Services: Bootcamp is a professional consulting firm specializing in teaching performers stagecraft and deportment. The training emphasizes the need for mental and physical preparation.

Boss Productions Inc.
1220 Shaw St.
Toronto, ON M6G 3N6
(416) 538-6761
Clients: CBC, TV Ontario, CHCH-TV.
Services: Music and post-production studio. Promotions and publicity.
Special Projects: *Sketches of Our Town, Science en Images, And There Were Seven.*

183

CBD Enterprises

180 Duncan Mill Rd., Suite 400
Don Mills, ON M3B 1Z6
(416) 441-2144
FAX (416) 441-2259
Acts: Pop, MOR, C&W.
Network Affiliations: Founding member of ISES.
Services: Special event planning and consulting.

Bob Carlisle Productions Inc.

P.O. Box 599
St. Basile-Le-Grand, PQ J0L 1S0
(514) 653-0442
FAX (514) 653-0272
Acts: Bavarian, Big Band, C&W, Dixieland, Ethnic, MOR and Pop.
Roster: The Entertainers, Claude Foisy, Remember.
Type of Engagements: Corporate events, trade shows, commercial centres and festivals.

Jim Chapman Music Services

197 Ridout St. S.
London, ON N6C 3X8
(519) 679-1396
Clients: Blackburn Communications, P.R.I.D.E., Sunshine Foundation, London Tigers Baseball Club, London Participaction, Easter Seals.
Services: Original music and marketing concepts created, recorded and/or implemented.

Chart Toppers

1908 Beechknoll Ave.
Mississauga, ON L4W 2G3
(416) 238-8682
FAX (416) 625-2189
Clients: Molson, Juno Awards, Music Industry Conference.

Mona Coxson

25 Mabelle Ave., Suite 2615
Toronto, ON M9A 4Y1
(416) 233-4700
Acts: All.
Services: Expert guidance on all music-related careers.

Crossroads Entertainment Consultants

180 Duncan Mill Rd., Suite 400
Don Mills, ON M3B 1Z6
(416) 441-2144
FAX (416) 441-2259
Acts: All.
Network Affiliations: ISES, Toronto Musicians' Association.
Services: Event planning and consulting.

De Wolfe Music of Canada Ltd.

211 Yonge St., 3rd Floor
Toronto, ON M5B 1M4
(416) 364-5778
Services: Music consultant, recorded library of background music.

Ray Douglas Promotions

P.O. Box 7213—Sandwich
Windsor, ON N9C 3Z1
(519) 969-1203 or 258-2288
Acts: Mainstream pop, C&W, Jazz and Classical.
Roster: Ray Douglas International Big Band, Joan Eastman and the Music Makers, The Kenny Crone Jazz Group.
Venues: Victoria Tavern, Kozaks By The Sea Tavern, Tourist and Convention Bureau, International Freedom Festival.
Network Affiliations: A.F. of M.
Special Projects: The Offshore International Jazz Society.

Diversified Music Group

1969 Pandora St.
Vancouver, BC V5L 5B2
(604) 255-3536
FAX (604) 255-8711
Acts: Rock, Country, Country Rock.
Roster: Darby Mills, One Horse Blue, Lori Jordan, Bear Mountain Boys, Kenny Shaw, Danny Mack.
Network Affiliations: ITAA, BCCMA (British Columbia Country Music Association), CCMA (Canadian Country Music Association).
Services: Marketing and publicity, management, publishing, rehearsal and production studios.

Dobbin Agency

477A Princess St.
Kingston, ON K7L 1C3
(613) 549-4401
Acts: Pop, MOR, Rock, C&W.
Network Affiliations: CART.

Entertainment Media Corporation

513 Broadview Ave.
Toronto, ON M4K 2N5
(416) 469-8300
Acts: DJs specializing in Top 40, Rock and Dance music.
Venues: O'Toole's, Pat & Mario's, PM Toronto.
Affiliated Companies: Effective Marketing Concepts.
Services: DJs and music programming.

The Garys
19 Sandford Ave.
Toronto, ON M4L 2E6
(416) 466-3081
Roster: All areas of music and entertainment.
Internationally.

Group One Communications
3416 W. 2 Ave.
Vancouver, BC V6R 1J2
(604) 737-0399
Acts: Pop, Rock, MOR.
Clients: Sez-U, bang, Mya Max, Mushroom Studios, Roy Salmond.
Services: Image development and positioning, marketing, market research, merchandising.

Morley R. Halsmith Creative Services
986 Vanier Dr.
Mississauga, ON L5H 3T7
(416) 274-0471
Network Affiliations: A.F. of M., SOCAN.
Clients: Crossroads Inc., World Vision Canada, Roland Canada.
Services: TV music director, conductor, producer/arranger and MIDI applications clinician.
Special Projects: Television credits include *Salute to Canada* (1981), *Tears of Famine* (1986) and *Crossroads TV Orchestra* (New Year's Eve 1988). Other projects include music at the Pavillion of Promise, Expo '86.

The Independent Network
66 Joseph St.
Brampton, ON L6X 1H8
(416) 454-3865
Acts: The Network's indie database accepts all music categories.
Clients: Star Search U.S.A., *Music Express* magazine, Norris Publications, CBC-Radio and TV.
Services: Information on independent recording artists plus referrals and consulting. To register a release in the Network database, call for more information.

Intermede Plus
P.O. Box 609, Stn. Place du Parc
Montreal, PQ H2W 2P2
(514) 842-8661
FAX (514) 843-8278
Acts: All.

International Talent Services Incorporated
177 W. 7 Ave., 4th Floor
Vancouver, BC V5Y 1K5
(604) 872-2906
FAX (604) 873-0166
Acts: Country.
Roster: Ron Tarrant Band, The Marlaine Sisters, Silver City.

Joint Communications Corp.
41 Peter St., Suite 200
Toronto, ON M5V 2G2
(416) 593-1136
FAX (416) 593-7589
Services: Radio, record, TV consulting and research.
Contact: David Oakes.

Jon-E-Shakka
176B Woodridge Cr.
Nepean, ON K2B 7S9
(613) 596-5918
Services: Choreography for music, dance, video and film performances.
Special Projects: 15 years of experience in all areas of street dances and Afro-rhythm dances.
Comments: As choreographer and director, Shakka has performed with Jermaine Jackson, Celion Dion, Nancy Martinez and Tckuhon.

Key Artist Management and Entertainment Consultants
500 Newbold St.
London, ON N6E 1K6
(519) 686-5060
Services: Career management, image consultation and record promotions.

Larry LeBlanc and Associates
15 Independence Dr.
Scarborough, ON M1K 3R7
(416) 265-3277
FAX (416) 265-3280
Clients: CRTC, Ralph Mellanby Associates.
Services: Research on music for radio licensing and programming.

Paul Levesque Management Inc.

154 Grande Cote
Rosemere, PQ J7A 1H3
(514) 437-7625
FAX (514) 430-9751
Acts: Pop, Rock.
Roster: Paradox, All The Tribes, Sonia Papp, Xcuse, Silver Saddle, The Weapon, Broken Hearts.
Affiliated Companies: Artiste Records.
Clients: Management of record producers, Pierre Bazinet and John Farley.
Services: Management and publishing.

Danny Makarus Musical Services

11714-113 Ave.
Edmonton, AB T5G 0J8
(403) 454-6848 or 454-9291
Acts: All.
Roster: Garry Lee & Showdown, Jenson Interceptor, Pam Henry.

Match-Music

92 Avenue Rd., Suite 200
Toronto, ON M5R 2H2
(416) 960-3130
FAX (416) 960-8264
Acts: All.
Roster: Various Toronto-based acts.
Services: Matching musicians, singers, songwriters and technical music professionals with bands.

The Music Brokers

92 Avenue Rd., Suite 200
Toronto, ON M5R 2H2
(416) 960-3130
FAX (416) 960-8264
Network Affiliations: CARAS, CIRPA.
Services: Full consulting service to the music industry.
Special Projects: Marketing and promotion at all levels.

Musician's Listing Service

4544 Dufferin St.
North York, ON M3H 5X2
(416) 665-5844
Acts: All styles.
Services: Free listing for individual musicians plus a musicians' networking service.
Branch:
3050 Constitution Blvd., Suite 74
Mississauga, ON L4Y 3X1
(416) 848-0874

Musician's Referral of Montreal

P.O. Box 298, Stn. H
Montreal, PQ H3G 2K8
(514) 933-3301
Acts: Any style.
Roster: Simply Dashing, Chris Bonnet, Fabrice Rouah.
Venues: Montreal universities and colleges, Le Spectrum, Club Soda and Cafe Campus.
Special Projects: The firm also acts as a broker for several recording studios in the Montreal area.

On The Line Music Collective

Bathurst St. Centre for Peace and Justice
736 Bathurst St., Suite 212
Toronto, ON M5S 2R4
(416) 537-7702
FAX (416) 531-6214
Acts: Folk, political content.
Roster: Arlene Mantle, Rick Fielding, The Mantlepeaces.
Network Affiliations: People's Music Network.
Clients: Canadian Autoworkers, the Steelworkers' Union and various community organizations.
Services: Production of educational materials, including cassettes, albums, songbooks and audio/visuals.

Pearcely Road Music

31B Industrial St.
Toronto, ON M4G 1Z2
(416) 423-7131
FAX (416) 467-6805
Network Affiliations: SOCAN.
Clients: Russ Reid Company, GM, Subaru.
Services: Creation of broadcast production music.
Special Projects: World Vision Canada TV themes 1987-1990.

Pop Music

P.O. Box 499, Stn. A
Ottawa, ON K1N 8V5
(613) 238-3906
Acts: Pop, Rock, MOR.
Roster: Avery Singer, Heaven's Radio, The Magic Circle.
Affiliated Companies: Lowertown Music.
Clients: Heaven's Radio.
Services: Concert management, marketing and publicity.
Special Projects: Televised concerts.

POP Strategies
3284 Yonge St.
Toronto, ON M4N 3M7
(416) 485-8295
FAX (416) 485-8924
Services Provided: Promotion, publicity, marketing, sponsorship, special events, business management, financial management.
Special Projects: POP Strategies specializes in the Canadian music and entertainment industries, with extensive media and industry contacts, and associations with top freelance writers and photographers.

Promofrica
264 rue Ste. Catherine o.
Montreal, PQ H2X 2A1
(514) 954-1221
Venues: Video, movies, television.
Services: Casting for minorities: black, latino etc.

Regal Recordings Limited
2421 Hammond Rd.
Mississauga, ON L5K 1T3
(416) 855-2370
FAX (416) 855-1773
Acts: Jazz.
Roster: Oscar Peterson.

Frank Regan Productions
15 Martha Eaton Way, Suite 1506
Toronto, ON M6M 5B5
(416) 245-6795
Services: Consultation plus choreography for music video, film and performance.
Special Projects: All areas of dance, theatre, film and TV.

Roadside Attractions
718 Eastlake Ave.
Saskatoon, SK S7N 1A3
(306) 653-2890
Acts: All aspects of performing arts.
Services: Programming and consulting in the performing arts.

Siegel Entertainment Ltd.
1648 W. 7 Ave., Suite 101
Vancouver, BC V6J 1S5
(604) 736-3896
FAX (604) 736-3464
Acts: Pop, MOR, Rock, C&W, Lounge, etc.

State of the Art Productions
3230 Argyle Rd.
Regina, SK S4S 2B4
(306) 586-2992
FAX (306) 584-1187
Acts: All.
Roster: Big Valley Jamboree.
Services: Booking agency, consultants on outdoor shows, plus staging, lighting, sound services.

Steel City Meltdown Record Pool
82 Mohawk Rd. E.
Hamilton, ON L9A 2G9
(416) 385-6116
Acts: All forms of recorded music.
Venues: O'Toole's (chain-wide), Mellows.
Clients: O'Toole's, Mellows, Benis, Murf Music DJ Service.
Services: DJ services and equipment installation.
Special Projects: Promoting dance music in Hamilton, Burlington and surround areas.

Stella Black Productions
P.O. Box 23
St. Anne de Bellevue, PQ H9X 3L4
(514) 937-5590
Acts: Classical, Dance Music.
Venues: Hotels, conventions, bar salons.
Services: Permanent music placements and conventions.

W/A Music Corporation
P.O. Box 9, Stn. O
Toronto, ON M4A 2M9
(416) 299-2222
FAX (416) 299-2232
Services: Production music library, original music and music clearance services, music business consulting.
Special Services: Services in many aspects of the music industry. Specializing in television, corporate videos and film.

Doug Wong Music
3560-1 St. N.E.
Calgary, AB T2E 3C9
(403) 277-9292
FAX (403) 276-8187
Acts: All.
Services: Management and music industry consulting.
Special Projects: Contract negotiating and licensing.

MUSIC EDUCATION

Alberta College

Conservatory of Music
10041-101 St.
Edmonton, AB T5J 0S3
(403) 428-1851
FAX (403) 424-6371
Instruction Language: English.
Programs: Private and group instruction.
Annual Admission: 2,500 students.
Tuition: Varies with instruction.
Grants/Scholarships: Several scholarships available for talented students. Financial aid available for students demonstrating need.

Athabasca University

Humanities Department
P.O. Box 10000
Athabasca, AB T0G 2R0
(403) 675-6111
Instruction Language: English.
Programs: Arts, general studies.
Degrees/Certificates: B.A., B.G.S.
Tuition Fees: See calendar.
Grants/Scholarships: See calendar.
Comments: Humanities department offers two courses in the history of popular music (1900-1940, 1940-1970). Other music courses are being developed.

The Banff Centre for the Arts

Department of Music
P.O. Box 1020
Banff, AB T0L 0C0
(403) 762-6213
FAX (403) 762-6699
Instruction Language: English.
Programs: Summer and winter music programs.
Duration: 12-week summer program, 27-week winter program.
Annual Admission: 150-200 in summer, 50 in winter.
Tuition Fees: $225 per week.
Additional Costs: $209 per week (room and board).
Application Deadline: January 15, February 20, March 1, 1990.
Grants/Scholarships: Full scholarships (tuition and partial room and board); tuition scholarships.
Department Heads: Thomas Rolston, artistic director (summer music program), Isobel Moore (Rolston), artistic director (winter music program).
Comments: Many different programs offered as part of the summer music program, ranging from two weeks to six weeks. The winter music program is broken into two- and three-month terms. Both or only one term may be attended.

CamTek Audio Productions Inc.

Student Engineering
15112-116A Ave.
Edmonton, AB T5M 3W8
(403) 452-6910
Instruction Language: English.
Programs: Recording and engineering, the business of music.
Duration: Six months.
Annual Admission: Approximately 100 students.
Comments: Courses are taught in one of Canada's largest recording studios.

Grant MacEwan Community College

Department of Music
10045-156 St.
Edmonton, AB T5P 2P7
(403) 483-2312
FAX (403) 483-4300
Instruction Language: English.
Programs: General, performance, composition, recording arts.
Degrees/Certificates: Diploma.
Duration: Two years.
Annual Admission: 110 students.
Tuition Fees: $608 per year.
Additional Costs: $550 per year.
Application Deadline: June 30 (for upcoming fall session).
Grants/Scholarships: 11 awards in the music program, many college awards.
Head of Department: Richard Garn, chairman.
Comments: Two trimesters per year, plus a seven-week preparatory course (in May and June) if needed to upgrade certain skills.

The King's College

Department of Music
10766-97 St.
Edmonton, AB T5H 2M1
(403) 428-0727
Instruction Language: English.
Programs: Music.
Degrees/Certificates: B.A., Church Music Diploma.
Duration: Two-three years.
Annual Admission: Two-ten students.
Tuition Fees: $2,650 per year (five or more courses).
Application Deadline: August 31 for fall term, December 29 for winter term.
Grants/Scholarships: Various small bursaries in music.
Head of Department: Dr. Jacobus Kloppers.

Medicine Hat College

Department of Music and Dance
299 College Dr. S.E.
Medicine Hat, AB T1A 3Y6
(403) 529-3880
Instruction Language: English.
Programs: University transfer, private lessons.
Duration: 35 weeks.

Mount Royal College

Conservatory of Music and Speech Arts
4825 Richard Rd. S.W.
Calgary, AB T3E 6K6
(403) 240-6821
Instruction Language: English.
Programs: Band, choral, orchestral and chamber ensembles; piano, theory, speech arts and voice; early childhood program and an academy program for gifted children.
Degrees/Certificates: Post-secondary diploma in music performance.
Duration: Up to two years.
Grants/Scholarships: Exam-based and special scholarships available.
Comments: The conservatory offers instruction in all areas of music and speech arts to all ages at all levels. Faculty of 75 plus 30 associate branch teachers.

Northern Alberta Institute of Technology

11762-106 St.
Edmonton, AB T5G 2R1
(403) 471-8641

Pianosonics/ Guitar Magic

LOve KNOw PLAy Music Institute of Alberta Ltd.
246 Kaska Rd.
Sherwood Park, AB T8A 4G7
(403) 464-3851
Comments: For information, contact Paulette Breault or D'Arcy Greaves (403) 433-6209.

Prairie Bible College

Fine Arts Department
Three Hills, AB T0M 2A0
(403) 443-5511, ext. 5392
FAX (403) 443-5540
Instruction Language: English.
Programs: Church music.
Degrees/Certificates: Bachelor.
Duration: Four years.
Annual Admission: 20 students.
Tuition Fees: $1,150.
Additional Costs: $221-422.
Additional Costs: August 1 (for fall semester),
December 1 (for winter semester), April 1 (for
spring semester).
Head of Department: Thomas Holm.
Comments: The Bachelor of Church Music
program offers a double major in both music and
Bible courses.

Red Deer College

Music Department
P.O. Box 5005
Red Deer, AB T4N 5H5
(403) 342-3305

Southern Alberta Institute of Technology

1301-16 Ave. N.W.
Calgary, AB T2M 0L4
(403) 284-8110

University of Alberta

Department of Music
3-82 Fine Arts Building
Edmonton, AB T6G 2C9
(403) 432-3263
Instruction Language: English.
Programs: Music.
Degrees/Certificates: B.Mus., B.Mus. (Hon.),
M. Mus., Doc. Mus.
Duration: Two-four years.
Tuition Fees: See calendar.
Application Deadline: See calendar.
Grants/Scholarships: Write for information.
Head of Department: Dr. Wesley Berg,
chairman.

University of Lethbridge

Music Department
4401 University Dr.
Lethbridge, AB T1K 3M4

Western Board of Music Examining Institute

University of Alberta
Edmonton, AB T6G 2E1
(403) 492-3264
Instruction Language: English.
Programs: Various.
Degrees/Certificates: A.Mus.
Duration: 11 years.
Annual Admission: Approximately 40 students.
Tuition Fees: $30-125.
Application Deadline: November 25 and
March 10 (for theory courses), November 25 and
March 10 (for practical courses).
Grants/Scholarships: Various scholarships
are available to all candidates and are awarded
on the basis of overall standing.
Head of Department: Marguerite Abbot, exec-
utive director.
Comments: The Western Board of Music is af-
filiated with the Universities of Alberta, Calgary,
Lethbridge, Manitoba, Regina, Saskatchewan and
Brandon.

BRITISH COLUMBIA

B.C. Conservatory of Music

250 Willington Ave.
Burnaby, BC V5C 5E9
Instruction Language: English.
Programs: Various.
Degrees/Certificates: Associateships.
Annual Admission: Four students.
Tuition Fees: $35.
Head of Department: Christian Meyers.

B.C. Institute of Technology

3700 Willingdon Ave.
Burnaby, BC V5G 3H2
(604) 432-8748

Bullfrog Recording School

2475 Dunbar St.
Vancouver, BC V6R 3N2
(604) 734-4617
Instruction Language: English.
Programs: Training at three levels, plus a MIDI workshop.
Degrees/Certificates: Certificate.
Duration: Three-six weeks.
Annual Admission: Four-eight students per class.
Tuition Fees: Varies with level.
Comments: The Summer School of Sound program offers levels One through Three in a week-long intensive schedule. All courses emphasize hands-on training in the fields of recording and engineering. All courses are trade school-certified and are tax deductible.

Capilano College

Music Department
2055 Purcell Way
North Vancouver, BC V7J 3H5
(604) 986-1911
FAX (604) 984-4985
Instruction Language: English.
Programs: Bachelor of Music transfer program, plus courses in commercial music and music therapy.
Degrees/Certificates: College Diploma.
Tuition Fees: Approximately $700 per semester.
Grants/Scholarships: Yes, write or call for information.
Comments: A recording studio, computer music labs and many practice rooms are available 14 hours a day, seven days a week.

Cedar Grove School of Music

10330-144 St.
Surrey, BC V3T 4V3
(604) 581-8933
Instruction Language: English.
Programs: Private lessons in piano, violin, flute and voice, in preparation for ARCT.
Duration: One-four years.
Annual Admission: 50-60 students.
Tuition Fees: $260 per year.
Additional Costs: $50.
Grants/Scholarships: Half-year scholarships for tuition.
Head of Department: John Taylor.
Comments: This school operates out of the Cedar Grove Baptist Church.

Central Valley Academy of Music

P.O. Box 8000-334
Abbotsford, BC V2S 6H1
(604) 852-3242
Programs: Various, including Suzuki violin and piano programs, and a Royal Conservatory music program.
Duration: Minimum of two 16-week semesters.
Annual Admission: Approximately $350.
Grants/Scholarships: Various bursaries and scholarships.
Comments: For more information, write for brochure.

Columbia Academy of Radio, TV and Recording Arts.

1295 W. Broadway
Vancouver, BC V6H 3X8
(604) 736-3316
FAX (604) 731-5458
Instruction Language: English.
Programs: Multitrack recording, and audio for video post-production.
Degrees/Certificates: Certificate.
Duration: 40 weeks (full time), 44 weeks (part time).
Tuition Fees: Varies with number of courses.
Grants/Scholarships: Federal and provincial student loans, in-house payment plans.
Comments: Established in 1967. All recording courses are taught in a 48-channel Neve/Necam/Ampex recording studio by award-winning engineers.

Douglas College

Music Department
700 Royal Ave.
New Westminster, BC V3L 5B2
(604) 520-5400
FAX (604) 527-5097
Instruction Language: English.
Programs: General studies, elementary music, secondary music education. All university transfer programs.
Degrees/Certificates: B.Mus., B.A., B.Ed.
Duration: One-two years.
Annual Admission: 40 students.

Drums Only! Percussion Academy

1272 Granville St.
Vancouver, BC
(604) 689-2978
FAX (604) 662-3856
Instruction Language: English.
Comments: Complete percussion instruction.

Elementary Music Theory School

2409 Dunbar St.
Vancouver, BC V6R 3N2
(604) 734-7788

Institute of Communication Arts (I.C.A.)

Music/Recording Arts/Video Department
5787 Marine Dr.
Burnaby, BC V5J 3H1
(604) 876-0451
FAX (604) 876-1087
Instruction Language: English.
Programs: Recording arts, commercial music performance, music technology.
Degrees/Certificates: Certificate.
Duration: One-two years
Tuition Fees: $6,000-12,500.
Application Deadline: April, August, December.
Grants/Scholarships: $1,000-7,000 (commercial music performance program only).
Head of Department: John Sereda.

Johannesen International School of the Arts

Summer Music School
3737 Oak St., Suite 103
Vancouver, BC V6H 2M4
(604) 736-1611
Programs: Master classes for advanced young musicians.
Duration: Six weeks.
Head of Department: J.J. Johannesen.
Comments: Classical music.

Kelowna Community Music School

599 Harvey Ave., P.O. Box 456, Stn. A
Kelowna, BC V1Y 7P1
(604) 860-1737
Instruction Language: English.
Programs: Instruction in all areas of instrumental music, voice, history and theory. Group instruction for pre-schoolers.
Duration: September to June each year.
Annual Admission: To a total enrollment of 300 students.
Tuition Fees: $12-17 per half hour.
Additional Costs: $20 registration fee.
Application Deadline: Registrations accepted throughout the year.
Grants/Scholarships: Students are invited to apply for bursaries.
Head of Department: School is operated by a volunteer board of directors.
Comments: A non-profit society.

Langley Community Music School

Department of Music
4899-207 St.
Langley, BC V3A 2E4
(604) 530-2848
FAX (604) 530-9780
Instruction Language: English.
Programs: Private instruction in piano, guitar, voice, winds, strings and brass. Orff and Suzuki pre-school programs are offered.
Duration: 36 weeks per year.
Annual Admission: 650 students.
Tuition Fees: $540 per year.
Additional Costs: $33 registration fee.
Grants/Scholarships: Scholarships awarded and bursaries available.

Orff Music for Children

1793 Glenella Pl.
Kelowna, BC V1Y 4M7
(604) 376-4430

Pacific Radio Arts Ltd.

Radio Broadcast Department
400 Smithe St., Suite 103
Vancouver, BC V6B 5E4
(604) 685-3899
Instruction Language: English.
Programs: Radio broadcasting.
Duration: 52 weeks.
Annual Admission: 70 students.
Tuition Fees: $5,650.
Grants/Scholarships: Canadian and provincial student loans.

193

Powell River Academy of Music

P.O. Box 334
Powell River, BC V8A 5C2
(604) 485-7662

Selkirk College

Professional Music
2001 Silver King Rd.
Nelson, BC V1L 1C8
(604) 352-6601
FAX (604) 352-3180
Instruction Language: English.
Programs: Music performance (jazz, pop and rock) and music production.
Degrees/Certificates: Diploma.
Duration: Two years.
Annual Admission: 50 students.
Tuition Fees: $575.
Additional Costs: $200.
Application Deadline: May 31.
Grants/Scholarships: Canada Student Loans, B.C. Student Assistance, college-adminstered scholarships.
Head of Department: Davey Hepner.
Comments: Individual instruction in guitar, bass, woodwinds, voice and keyboards. MIDI lab facility on campus.

Simon Fraser University

Centre for the Arts
Burnaby, BC V5A 1S6
(604) 291-3363
FAX (604) 291-3039
Programs: Major in fine and performing arts, and a concentration in music.
Degrees/Certificates: B.A., M.F.A.
Comments: Focus on contemporary and new music. Collaborative work with dance, film, theatre and visual arts is encouraged. Faculty has an on-site electronic music studio.

Surrey Academy of Music

6962-124 St.
Surrey, BC V3W 3W7
(604) 589-7698

Trebas Institute of Recording Arts

112 E. 3 Ave., Suite 305
Vancouver, BC V5T 1C8
(604) 872-2666
FAX (604) 872-3001
Instruction Language: English.
Programs: Recorded music production, audio engineering, music industry management.
Degrees/Certificates: Diploma in Recording Arts and Sciences.
Duration: 15 months.
Tuition Fees: Contact admissions office.
Grants/Scholarships: One $6,000 entrance scholarship, Pierre Juneau Scholarship for second year studies ($2,500), Dr. David Baskerville Memorial Scholarship for second year studies, Sam Sniderman Scholarship for music business studies in second year, Dr. Peter C. Goldmark Memorial Scholarship for second year studies, Canada and provincial student loans. Guaranteed Student Loans (GSL) and Pell Grants for American students are also available.
Comments: Full time and part time day or evening studies. 80 courses offered in three programs. A limited number of internships are available. Transfer credits between all five campuses of the Trebas Institute. Facilities include: multitrack recording studio, an electronic music lab, a disc mastering lab, and a resource centre. Fully accredited by ACCET (USA). Jaob placement assistance available.

Trinity Western University

Music Department
7600 Glover Rd.
Langley, BC V3A 4R9
(604) 888-7511
Instruction Language: English.
Programs: Church music performance, general music and music education.
Degrees/Certificates: B.A., B.Ed.
Tuition Fees: Approximately $2,000.
Additional Costs: $150.
Grants/Scholarships: President's entrance scholarship ($2,500). For other sources of financial assistance, write to the Department of Financial Aid.
Comments: Trinity Western University is a private Christian university located in the Fraser Valley, about 40 minutes from downtown Vancouver. Trinity is a member of the Association of Universities and Colleges of Canada.

United Conservatory of Music

623 Tranquille Rd.
Kamloops, BC V2B 3H6
(604) 554-1222

Universal Recording Inc.

2190 W. 12 Ave.
Vancouver, BC V6K 2N2
(604) 734-2922
Comments: Audio production school.

University of British Columbia

Music Faculty
6361 Memorial Rd.
Vancouver, BC V6T 1W5
(604) 228-3113
Instruction Language: English.
Programs: Piano, organ, voice, orchestral
instruments, opera, general studies, secondary
music education, music history and literature,
composition, theory, musicology.
Degrees/Certificates: D.M.A., B.Mus., M.A.,
Ph.D.
Tuition Fees: See calendar.
Grants/Scholarships: University graduate
fellowships and teaching assistantships are
available. For a list of available scholarships and
bursaries, contact the University Awards Office.

University of Victoria

School of Music
P.O. Box 1700
Victoria, BC V8W 2Y2
(604) 721-7902 or 721-7903
FAX (604) 721-7748
Instruction Language: English.
Programs: Composition, history, music
education, performance, musicology.
Degrees/Certificates: B.Mus., M.Mus., M.A.,
Ph.D.
Duration: Four years.
Annual Admission: Approximately 60 students.
Tuition Fees: $1,650.
Additional Costs: $400.
Application Deadline: March 31 for
undergraduates.
Grants/Scholarships: $30,000 annually for
undergraduates, as well as university
scholarships and bursaries. Work-study funds are
also available.
Head of Department: Gordana Lazarevich.

Victoria Conservatory of Music

839 Academy Close
Victoria, BC V8V 2X8
(604) 386-5311
Instruction Language: English.
Programs: Teacher training.
Degrees/Certificates: A.V.C.M., A.A.Mus
Duration: Two years.
Tuition Fees: Approximately $1,100.
Additional Costs: $300 annual studio fee.
Application Deadline: April 30.
Grants/Scholarships: Provincial student as-
sistance loans and grants available to approved
full time senior students. Those in Camosun/VCM
program apply directly to Camosun College.
Head of Department: Dr. Robin Wood.

MANITOBA

Brandon University School of Music

School of Music
Brandon, MB R7A 6A9
(204) 727-9631
FAX (204) 726-4573
Instruction Language: English.
Programs: General, school music, school music
specialist, applied music.
Degrees/Certificates: B.Mus.
Duration: Four-five years.
Tuition Fees: $1,500.
Dean: Dr. Lawrence Jones.

Professional Musicians College

1369 Erin St.
Winnipeg, MB R3C 2J8
(204) 774-8210
Instruction Language: English.
Programs: Audio engineering, voice, guitar,
keyboards, percussion, bass guitar.
Degrees/Certificates: Diploma.
Duration: One-two years.
Annual Admission: 25 students.
Tuition Fees: $5,895.
Additional Costs: $250 book purchase.
Application Deadline: August 30, 1990.
Grants/Scholarships: Registered with Canada
Student Loans.
Head of Department: Mr. Greg Dunstan.
Comments: Instruction in all contemporary
musical styles. Identical programs are offered at
the Regina campus.
Branch Campus:
2614-6 Ave.
Regina, SK.
S4T 0N0

University of Manitoba

School of Music
65 Dafoe Rd.
Winnipeg, MB R3T 2N2
(204) 474-9310
FAX (204) 269-6629
Instruction Language: English.
Programs: Music, music education.
Degrees/Certificates: B.Mus., B.Ed.
Duration: Four-five years.
Annual Admission: 90 students.
Tuition Fees: $1,158.
Additional Costs: $300.
Application Deadline: July 1.
Grants/Scholarships: Various, from $100-4,000. Write for information.
Head of Department: Dr. Richard Wedgewood.
Comments: A recording studio, keyboard lab and electronic music lab are available.

NEW BRUNSWICK

Mount Allison University

Music Department
Sackville, NB E0A 3C0
(506) 364-2374
Instruction Language: English.
Programs: Various.
Degrees/Certificates: B.Mus., B.A., B.Ed.
Duration: Four-five years.
Annual Admission: 30-35 students.
Tuition Fees: See calendar.
Grants/Scholarships: Yes, write for information.

Universite de Moncton

Music Department, Faculte des Arts
Moncton, NB E1A 3E9
(506) 858-4000
Instruction Language: French.
Programs: General, history and literature, music education.
Degrees/Certificates: B.Mus.
Tuition Fees: See calendar.

University of New Brunswick

P.O. Box 4400
Fredericton, NB E3D 3C5
(506) 453-4666
Instruction Language: English.
Programs: Resident artists program, lectures, recitals, private lessons.
Comments: Stimulating music activity at the provincial level: This program works in conjunction with degree programs at Mount Allison University and Universite de Moncton.

NEWFOUNDLAND

Memorial University of Newfoundland

School of Music
St. John's, NF A1C 5S7
(709) 737-7480
FAX (709) 737-4569
Instruction Language: English.
Programs: General, history, theory, performance.
Degrees/Certificates: B.Mus., B.Mus.Ed.
Duration: Four-five years.
Tuition Fees: $755 per semester.
Application Deadline: January 31.
Head of Department: Dr. D.F. Cook.

NOVA SCOTIA

Acadia University

School of Music
Wolfville, NS B0P 1X0
(902) 542-2201, ext. 512
FAX (902) 542-4727
Instruction Language: English.
Programs: General, performance, composition, history, theory, music education.
Degrees/Certificates: B.A., B.Mus., B.Mus.Ed.
Duration: Four-five years.
Tuition Fees: $1,720.
Additional Costs: $240.
Application Deadline: Open.
Grants/Scholarships: Many.
Head of Department: Peter H. Riddle.

Canadian Conservatory of Music

6065 Cunard St.
Halifax, NS B3K 1E6
(902) 422-6561
FAX (902) 423-0633
Programs: Music lessons for all instruments, plus summer rock camps.

Dalhousie University

Arts Centre, Room 514
Halifax, NS B3H 3J5
(902) 424-2418
Instruction Language: English.
Programs: Various.
Degrees/Certificates: B.A., B.Mus., B.Mus.Ed.

Maritime Conservatory of Music

Music Department
5820 Spring Garden Rd.
Halifax, NS B3H 1X8
(902) 423-6995
Instruction Language: English.
Programs: Instruction in keyboard, organ, piano, orchestral instruments, guitar, voice, theory, ballet, ballroom dancing.
Degrees/Certificates: Diploma.
Comments: Write for calendar.

St. Francis Xavier University

Music Department
P.O. Box 108
Antigonish, NS B2G 1C0
(902) 867-2106
FAX (902) 867-5153
Instruction Language: English.
Programs: Classical, jazz and jazz pedagogy.
Degrees/Certificates: B.A., Jazz Diploma.
Duration: Two-four years.
Annual Admission: Approximately 60 students.
Tuition Fees: $1,800.
Application Deadline: June 30.
Head of Department: Gene Smith, chairman.

ONTARIO

Bayview Music Clinic

1650 Bayview Ave.
Toronto ON M4G 3C2
(416) 488-0664
Instruction Language: English, some French.
Programs: Private lessons on most instruments including piano, guitar and flute.
Tuition Fees: Lessons are sold in sets of six. Teachers set their own rates.
Application Deadline: Lessons are ongoing all year.
Grants/Scholarships: None.
Head of Department: Doreen Hunter.

Brock University

Music Department
Merrittville Highway
St. Catharines, ON L2S 3A1
(416) 688-5550 or 688-5544, ext. 3817
FAX (416) 688-2789
Instruction Language: English.
Programs: History, theory, pedagogy, piano, organ, voice, orchestral instruments.
Degrees/Certificates: B.A.
Duration: Three-four years.
Annual Admission: 20 students.
Tuition Fees: $327 per course.
Head of Department: Harris Loewen, coordinator.
Comments: History, theory, performance (piano, organ, voice, orchestral instruments), pedagogy (choral, piano, vocal, classroom).

Cambrian College of Applied Arts and Technology

School of Communication and Creative Arts
1400 Barrydowne Rd.
Sudbury, ON P3A 3V8
(705) 566-8101
FAX (705) 671-7329
Instruction Language: English.
Programs: Music
Degrees/Certificates: Diploma.
Duration: Three years.
Annual Admission: 35 students.
Tuition Fees: $802.
Grants/Scholarships: Contact the Financial Aid Office.
Head of Department: Dr. Metro Kozak.

Carleton University

Music Department
A911 Loeb
Ottawa, ON K1S 5B6
(613) 564-3633
FAX (613) 788-4467
Instruction Language: English.
Programs: History, theory, composition, performance, early music, popular music, ethnomusicology, sociology and aesthetics of music, Canadian music, electronic music and computer music.
Degrees/Certificates: B.A., B.Mus.
Duration: One-four years.
Tuition Fees: Varies with credits.
Grants/Scholarships: Jack Barwick and Douglas Duncan Memorial Scholarships for Music, Music Department Award, Bettina Oppenheimer Scholarship.

Centennial College

651 Warden Ave.
Scarborough, ON M1L 3Z6
(416) 694-3241

Confederation College

Performing Arts Department
P.O. Box 398
Thunder Bay, ON P7C 4W1
(807) 475-6320
FAX (807) 623-6230
Instruction Language: English.
Programs: Performing arts management.
Duration: Two years.
Annual Admission: 30 students.
Grants/Scholarships: Some aid through various provincial culture departments; check your home province.
Comments: A program designed to provide entry-level management skills to performing arts administration students.

Cosmo School of Music

9201 Yonge St.
Richmond Hill, ON L4C 6Z2
(416) 889-6382
FAX (416) 889-4061

Domenic's Music Academy Ltd.

1767 Carling Ave.
Ottawa, ON K2A 1C9
(613) 722-1021
FAX (613) 722-2022
Comments: Organizers of an annual music festival featuring over 900 students from various parts of Canada.

Durham College

2000 Simcoe St. N., P.O. Box 385
Oshawa, ON L1H 7L7
(416) 576-0210
FAX (416) 436-9774

Fanshawe College of Applied Arts and Technology

Music Industry Arts Program
P.O. Box 4005
London, ON N5W 5H1
(519) 452-4470
FAX (519) 452-3570
Instruction Language: English.
Programs: Recording engineering, recorded music production.
Duration: Two years.
Annual Admission: 30 students.
Tuition: $600 per year.
Comments: Applicants must show proof of Ontario residency, must be musicians, and are required to submit an audition tape. Courses offered include practical instruction, lectures, and lab time with synthesis and MIDI technology.

The Halton Academy of Music and the Arts

P.O. Box 564, Stn. U
Toronto ON M8Z 5Y9
(416) 849-0388
Instruction Language: English.
Programs: Instruction to prepare students for accredited examinations from Grade one to associate degrees offered by the following institutions: The Associated Board of The Royal Schools of Music (LRSM), Trinity College of Music (ATCL), Western Ontario Conservatory of Music (A.Mus.), Western Board of Music (A.Mus.), and the Royal Conservatory of Music (ARCT).
Grants/Scholarships: Write to the financial director.
Comments: Students accepted at any time during the year. All instruction is private and courses are specifically designed for each individual.

Hands On School of Modern Recording

Recording Technology Department
3886 Chesswood Dr.
Downsview, ON M3J 2W6
(416) 638-3869
Instruction Language: English.
Programs: Recording technology.
Duration: Six months.
Annual Admission: 24 students.
Tuition Fees: $3,900.
Application Deadline: February 28, 1990.
Head of Department: Steven Dell'Angelo.
Comments: An intensive course which emphasizes the practical aspects of the recording business. Courses taught in a 24-track studio.

Harris Institute For The Arts

The Office of the Registrar
296 King St. E.
Toronto ON M5A 1K4
(416) 367-0178
FAX (416) 367-0271
Instruction Language: English.
Programs: Producing, engineering and recording arts management.
Degrees/Certificates: Diploma.
Duration: 12 months.
Annual Admission: 96 students.
Tuition Fees: Information available on request.
Application Deadline: Full and part time programs start every February, June and October.
Grants/Scholarships: R. Richard Hahn Scholarship for excellence in the recording arts management program, and the CJEZ-FM Scholarship for excellence in the producing and engineering program.
Registrar: Stan Janes.
Comments: Harris Institute is registered and approved by the Ministry of Colleges and Universities. One-year diploma programs are taught by leading industry professionals and culminate in the formation of production and managment companies and internship placements in studios and companies within the industry.

Humber College of Applied Arts and Technology

Music Department
205 Humber College Blvd.
Rexdale, ON M9W 5L7
(416) 675-3111, ext. 4427
Instruction Language: English.
Degrees/Certificates: Diploma in Music.
Tuition Fees: Approximately $400 per semester.
Grants/Scholarships: Contact the Financial Aid Office.

Huntington College, Laurentian University

Department of Music
935 Ramsey Lake Rd.
Sudbury, ON P3E 2C6
(705) 673-4126
FAX (1-800) 461-6366
Instruction Language: English, French.
Programs: General music, church music.
Degrees/Certificates: B.A., B.A. (Hon.), Certificate of Church Music.
Duration: Two-four years.
Tuition Fees: $1,808.
Additional Costs: $150.
Application Deadline: Date differs each year: September (week-four), January (week-two).
Grants/Scholarships: Various, see Laurentian University calendar under Financial Aid.
Head of Department: Charlotte Leonard.
Comments: Huntington College, Laurentian University hopes to have a Bachelor of Music degree program in performance, music education and pedagogy by September 1991. Jazz studies are available.

Lakehead University

Music Department
Oliver Rd.
Thunder Bay, ON P7B 5E1
(807) 343-8787
FAX (807) 343-8023
Instruction Language: English.
Degrees/Certificates: Honours B.A.
Duration: Four years.
Annual Admission: 15 students.
Tuition Fees: $1,517.
Grants/Scholarships: A wide variety of entrance and in-course scholarships are available. Consult Student Services for details.
Head of Department: Dr. Glen B. Carruthers.
Comments: An Honours Bachelor of Music program and concurrent Honours B.A. (Music)/B.Ed. program are currently under consideration. Consult the department for details.

Loomis Academy of Music

3044 Lindenlea Dr.
Mississauga, ON L5C 2C2
(416) 848-5428
Programs: Private instruction in organ, voice, recorder, and all levels of theory.
Tuition Fees: Available on request.

Maestro Music Academy

323 Talbot St. W.
St. Thomas, ON N5P 1B5
(519) 631-1530

McMaster University

Music Department
1280 Main St. W.
Hamilton, ON L8S 4M2
(416) 525-9140
Instruction Language: English.
Programs: Music education, music criticism, theory, history.
Degrees/Certificates: B.Mus., M.A.
Annual Admission: Approximately 30 students.
Grants/Scholarships: Merril Francis Gage Scholarship (value $1,000), Frank Thorolfson Memorial Scholarship ($750).

Metropolitan Academy of Music

860 College St.
Toronto ON M6H 1A2
(416) 532-6601
Programs: Pre-kindergarten instrumental (piano, organ, guitar and drums) and theory programs available. The programs are designed for beginner and intermediate students.
Degrees/Certificates: Certificate of Achievement (piano and theory).
Comments: Practice facilities available for enrolled students.

Mohawk College

P.O. Box 2034
Hamilton, ON L8N 3T2
(416) 575-2044
Instruction Language: English.
Programs: Applied music program.
Duration: Three years.

Music for Young Children

72 Kingsford Ct.
Kanata, ON K2K 1T9
(613) 592-7565
Instruction Language: English.
Programs: Various levels of musical training, up to Grade one, Royal Conservatory of Music.
Annual Admission: To a total of 5,000 students, nationwide.
Comments: There are 18 coordinators across Canada who conduct teacher training. The program is also offered in the U.S., England and Germany.

Music School of St. Christopher House

248 Ossington Ave.
Toronto ON M6J 3A2
(416) 532-4828, ext. 127.
Instruction Language: English.
Programs: Piano, violin, guitar, accordion, theory and harmony.
Duration: Ongoing.
Annual Admission: 125 students.
Tuition Fees: Varies.
Grants/Scholarships: Available through limited financial resources.
Head of Department: Stephan van Heerden.

Musica School

882-1 St. E.
Cornwall, ON K6H 1N1
(613) 932-8625
Programs: Royal Conservatory training at all levels.
Duration: September-June of each year.
Annual Admission: 75 students.
Tuition Fees: Varies with each teacher.

National Institute of Broadcasting

1497 Yonge St.
Toronto, ON M4T 1Z2
(416) 922-2793

Ontario Bible College

25 Ballyconnor Ct.
Willowdale, ON M2M 4B3
(416) 226-6380
Instruction Language: English.
Programs: Religious education (major in music), church music, sacred music.
Degrees/Certificates: Bachelor Degree and Certificate.
Tuition Fees: Charged per hour.
Grants/Scholarships: A number of scholarships and bursaries are available. Loans are also available through OSAP.
Comments: The college specializes in training students to be church musicians.

Ontario College of Percussion and Music

1656 Bayview Ave.
Toronto ON M4G 3C2
(416) 483-9117
Programs: Various full and part time instruction in drums and percussion, guitar, bass and keyboards.
Duration: Varies, up to six years.
Tuition Fees: Varied.
Application Deadline: Monthly applications.
Grants/Scholarships: Available for workshops and master classes.
Head of Department: Robin Boers.
Comments: Rates vary according to private teachers and workshops.

Ontario Institute of Audio Recording Technology

500 Newbold St.
London, ON N6E 1K6
(519) 686-5010
Instruction Language: English.
Programs: Audio recording/engineering.
Duration: Eight months.
Annual Admission: 50 students.
Tuition Fees: $4,750.
Additional Costs: $275.
Application Deadline: September of each year.
Grants/Scholarships: Grants and loans are available for those who qualify.
Head of Department: Peter Kryshtalovich.

Queen's University

Music Department
Harrison-LeCaine Hall
Kingston, ON K7L 3N6
(613) 547-5783
Instruction Language: English.
Programs: Theory, composition, performance, history and literature.
Degrees/Certificates: B.Mus.
Tuition Fees: See calendar.
Grants/Scholarships: Yes, write for information.

Recording Arts Program of Canada

28 Valrose Dr.
Stoney Creek, ON L8E 3T4
(416) 662-2666
Instruction Language: English.
Programs: Recording arts.
Degrees/Certificates: Graduating Diploma
Duration: 13-19 weeks.
Annual Admission: 40 students.
Grants/Scholarships: Available to eligible students.
Comments: Call or write for interviews and information.

Royal Conservatory of Music

273 Bloor St. W.
Toronto, ON M5S 1W2
(416) 978-3797
FAX (416) 978-3793
Instruction Language: English, French.
Programs: Numerous.
Grants/Scholarships: Various.
Head of Department: Gordon Kushner, acting principal.

The Royans School for the Musical Performing Arts

1694 St. Clair Ave. W.
Toronto, ON M6N 1J1
(416) 656-0028
Instruction Language: English, Italian, Russian.
Programs: Voice, piano, and guitar instruction.
Duration: Four weeks.
Annual Admission: 120 students.
Tuition Fees: Varies with program.

Ryerson Polytechnical Institute

50 Gould St.
Toronto, ON M5B 1E8
(416) 595-5107

St. Michael's Choir School

66 Bond St.
Toronto, ON M5B 1X2
(416) 393-5518
Instruction Language: English, French.
Programs: Secondary school education with an emphasis on choral training.
Duration: Up to Grade 13.
Application Deadline: Contact the Choir School Office.
Grants/Scholarships: Scholarships and bursaries are available through the St. Michael's Choir School Foundation.

Saved by Technology Arts Academy

10 Breadalbane St.
Toronto, ON M4Y 1C3
(416) 928-5957

Seneca School of Communication Arts

Audio-Visual Techniques
1124 Finch Ave. W.
Downsview, ON M3J 3J3
(416) 491-5050, ext. 4864
FAX (416) 739-1856
Instruction Language: English.
Programs: Audio-visual techniques, radio-TV broadcasting.
Duration: Two years.
Annual Admission: 140 students.
Tuition Fees: $700.
Additional Costs: $200.
Application Deadline: February.
Head of Department: Alex Hall, coordinator.
Comments: Courses are given in music mixing in both AVT and RTV.

Sheridan College

Music Theatre Department
1430 Trafalgar Rd.
Oakville, ON L6H 2L1
(416) 845-9430
Instruction Language: English.
Programs: Training in carpentry, theatre management, properties and scenic art, wardrobe, and lighting and sound.
Head of Department: Marilyn Lawrie.

Sir Sanford Fleming College

Brealy Dr.
Peterborough, ON K9J 7B1
(705) 743-5610
Programs: Arts Administration (visual performing).

Trebas Institute of Recording Arts

290 Nepean St.
Ottawa, ON K1R 5G3
(613) 232-7104
FAX (613) 233-6945
Instruction Language: English.
Programs: Recorded music production, audio engineering, music industry management.
Degrees/Certificates: Diploma in Recording Arts and Sciences.
Duration: 15 months.
Tuition Fees: Contact Admissions Office.
Grants/Scholarships: One Entrance Scholarship ($6,000 value), Pierre Juneau Scholarship for second year studies ($2,500), Dr. David Baskerville Memorial Scholarship for second year studies, Sam Sniderman Scholarship for music business studies in second year, Dr. Peter C. Goldmark Memorial Scholarship for second year studies. Federal and provincial loans available. GSL and PELL grants for American students are also available.
Comments: Full time and part time, day or evening studies. 80 courses offered in three programs and a limited number of internships are available. Transfer credits accepted between all five campuses of the Trebas Institute. Facilities include a multitrack recording studio, an electronic music lab, a disc mastering lab and a resource centre. Fully accredited by ACCET (USA). Job placement assistance available.
Branch Campus:
410 Dundas E.
Toronto, ON M5A 2A8
(416) 966-3066
FAX (416) 966-0030

Trent National Centre for Music

Peter Robinson School of Music
Trent University
Peterborough, ON K9J 7B8
(705) 748-1778
Instruction Language: English.
Programs: All instruments, voice, theory, Suzuki.
Degrees/Certificates: All grades and diplomas of the Associated Board of Royal Schools of Music.
Comments: Canadian representative for Associated Board of Royal Schools of Music, London, England.

Unison Academy of Music

3852 Finch Ave. E.
Scarborough, ON M1T 3E8
(416) 297-8997

University of Ottawa

Department of Music
1 Stewart St.
Ottawa, ON K1N 6N5
(613) 564-2481
Instruction Language: French, English.
Programs: Various.
Degrees/Certificates: B.Mus., B.A.
Duration: Three-four years.
Tuition Fees: See calendar.
Grants/Scholarships: Firestone Scholarship ($1,000), Friends of the Department Scholarship ($1,000), Beaudet Scholarship ($1,000), MacDonal Club Scholarship ($1,000), Frederick Karam Scholarship ($1,000), Keith and Ross MacMillan Scholarship ($1,000).
Comments: Instruction given on all orchestral instruments as well as on piano; musicians from the National Arts Centre Orchestra teach orchestral students.

University of Toronto

Faculty of Music
Edward Johnson Building
80 Queen's Park Cr.
Toronto, ON M5S 1A1
(416) 978-3750
FAX (416) 978-5771
Instruction Language: English.
Programs: Performance, composition, theory, history and literature, music education, musicology.
Degrees/Certificates: B.A., Mus.Bac., M.A., M.Mus., Doc.Mus., Ph.D., Artist Diploma.
Duration: Three-four years (undergraduate).
Annual Admission: Approximately 100 students.
Grants/Scholarships: Yes, contact above address.

University of Waterloo

Conrad Trebel College
Music Department
Waterloo, ON N2L 3G6
(519) 885-0220
Instruction Language: English.
Programs: Various music programs.
Degrees/Certificates: B.A.
Grants/Scholarships: Clemens Scholarship in Music (up to $250 for students continuing in the music program). Financial aid based on need.
Comments: The music program examines music in the context of the liberal arts, thus this faculty offers a B.A. rather than a B.Mus. program.

University of Western Ontario

Faculty of Music
Talbot College, Room 210
London, ON N6A 3K7
(519) 661-3767
FAX (519) 661-3292
Instruction Language: English.
Programs: Music.
Degrees/Certificates: B.Mus., B.M.A., B.A., B.A. (Hon).
Duration: Three-four years.
Tuition Fees: $1,600.
Additional Costs: $300.
Application Deadline: February 1.
Grants/Scholarships: Please inquire.
Head of Department: Dean Jeffrey L. Stokes.
Comments: Call (519) 661-2044 for enrollment information, (519) 661-3767 for other information.

University of Windsor

School of Music
Windsor, ON N9B 3P4
(519) 253-4232, ext. 2780
Instruction Language: English.
Programs: Music, music theatre.
Degrees/Certificates: B.A., B.M.A., Honours Certificate.
Duration: Three-four years.
Annual Admission: 50-60 students.
Tuition Fees: $785.50 per semester.
Application Deadline: September.
Grants/Scholarships: As listed in the calendar.
Head of Department: Dr. E. Gregory Butler.

University Settlement Music School

23 Grange Rd.
Toronto, ON M5T 1C3
(416) 598-3444
Instruction Language: English.
Programs: Individual and class instruction for children and adults. Courses include piano, violin, viola, guitar, flute, clarinet, saxophone, tuba, cello, recorder, voice, theory and harmony.
Duration: 11 months.
Annual Admission: 300 students.
Tuition Fees: Varies.
Grants/Scholarships: Financial aid is available when a need is identified.

Upstage Music

199 Lakeshore Rd. E.
Mississauga, ON L5G 2G1
(416) 278-3524
Instruction Language: English.
Programs: Guitar, brass, woodwinds, vocal, strings, piano.
Degrees/Certificates: Royal Conservatory Certificate.
Tuition Fees: Charged on a monthly basis.
Additional Costs: Registration fee.
Comments: All lessons are private and are based on minimum half-hour lesson rates. Lessons are taught by qualified professionals.

Western Ontario Conservatory of Music

Conservatory Building
University of Western Ontario
London, ON N6A 5B7
(519) 661-3485
Instruction Language: English.
Programs: Instruction and examinations accredited by the Ministry of Education in all instruments and in theory.
Degrees/Certificates: Certificates for Grades I-X, practical I-V and theory. Associate of Music Diploma.
Grants/Scholarships: A limited number of scholarships are administered annually on the basis of performance record, including examination results, musical potential, effort, achievement and financial need.

Wilfrid Laurier University

Faculty of Music
75 University Ave. W.
Waterloo, ON N2L 3C5
(519) 884-1970, ext. 2432
Instruction Language: English.
Programs: Comprehensive music education, including studies in baroque and early music, church music, composition, music history, performance and theory.
Tuition Fees: See university calendar for full details.
Degrees/Certificates: B.Mus., B.A., Opera Diploma, Performance Diploma.
Financial Aid: Contact the Student Awards Office.
Deadline for Application: Auditions are held in April and May. For more information contact the audition coordinator, Carol Raymond at ext. 2150.

York University

Music Department
4700 Keele St.
North York, ON M3J 1P3
(416) 736-5186
Instruction Language: English.
Programs: Music performance, opera.
Degrees/Certificates: B.A., B.F.A., Opera Diploma, Diploma in Performance.
Duration: Four years.
Tuition Fees: On request, call 736-5000.
Grants/Scholarships: Yes, call for information.

Youth and Music Canada

720 Bathurst St., 5th Floor
Toronto, ON M5S 2R4
(416) 364-2959
Instruction Language: English, French.
Programs: Workshops, educational concerts for children in schools and libraries.
Comments: Artists selected by Youth and Music Canada gear their performances and workshops to the average age of each audience, making each concert educational and entertaining for children.

QUEBEC

Bishop's University

Music Department
Lennoxville, PQ J1M 1Z7
(819) 822-9642
Instruction Language: English, French.
Programs: Comprehensive musical studies.
Degrees/Certificates: B.A., B.A. Hon.
Duration: One-four years.
Annual Admission: 20-30 students.
Tuition Fees: $460 per semester.
Application Deadline: March 1.
Grants/Scholarships: Numerous scholarships, up to $4,000 per year.
Head of Department: Tom Gordon.

Concordia University

Music Department
7141 Sherbrooke St. W.
Montreal, PQ H4V 2A8
(514) 848-4707
FAX (514) 848-2808
Instruction Language: English, French.
Programs: Music.
Degrees/Certificates: B.F.A.
Duration: Three years.
Annual Admission: 60 students.
Tuition Fees: $540.
Additional Costs: $500.
Application Deadline: March 1.
Grants/Scholarships: Rector's Entrance
Scholarships, loans and bursaries.
Head of Department: Sherman Friedland.

Conservatoire de musique a Montreal

100 rue Notre-Dame e.
Montreal, PQ H2Y 1C1
(514) 873-4031
FAX (514) 873-7943

Conservatoire de musique du Quebec

580 Grande Allee e., 4th Floor, Unit 420
Quebec City, PQ G1R 2K2
(418) 643-7427
Instruction Language: French.

Jeunesses Musicales du Canada

Oxford Arts Centre
P.O. Box 280
Magog, PQ J1X 3W8
(819) 843-3981
Instruction Language: English, French.
Programs: Summer music school with courses
in all major instruments, including voice.
Tuition Fees: Charged per week.
Grants/Scholarships: Scholarships may be
applied for upon completion of registration.
Comments: Registration in the spring. Audition
pieces must be recorded and sent in for
consideration.

College de Jonquiere

2505 St. Hubert St.
Jonquiere, PQ G7X 7W2
(418) 547-2191

Institut Marguerite-Bourgeoys

Musicotheque
4873 ave. Westmount
Montreal, PQ H3Y 1X9

Marianopolis College CEGEP

Department of Music
3880 Cote-des-Neiges Rd.
Montreal, PQ H3H 1W1
(514) 931-8792
Instruction Language: English.
Programs: Music.
Degrees/Certificates: D.E.C. (Diplome
d'etudes collegiales).
Duration: Two years.

McGill University

Faculty of Music
555 rue Sherbrooke o.
Montreal, PQ H3A 1E3
(514) 398-4535
FAX (514) 398-8061
Instruction Language: English, French.
Programs: General, including studies in performance, composition, history, theory, school music, early music and jazz.
Degrees/Certificates: B.Mus., Concert Diploma, Music Licentiate Diploma.
Duration: Two-four years.
Annual Admission: Approximately 120 students.
Tuition Fees: $570.
Additional Costs: $450, not including living expenses or supplies.
Application Deadline: March 1.
Grants/Scholarships: Faculty-established scholarships and university- established scholarships for entrance or upon completion of 27 credits.
Dean: Professor John Rea.

Musitechnic Education- al Services Inc.

1259 Berri St., Suite 909
Montreal, PQ H2L 4C7
(514) 844-2141
Instruction Language: French, English.
Programs: Computer-assisted sound design.
Degrees/Certificates: Attestation of Collegial Studies.
Duration: 12 months.
Annual Admission: 40 students.
Tuition Fees: $11,000.
Additional Costs: $600 book fee.
Application Deadline: June 30.
Grants/Scholarships: Grants and loans are available.
Head of Department: Gilles Valiquette.
Comments: The only school of this nature which is recognized by The Ministry of Higher Education and Sciences.

Trebas Institute of Recording Arts

451 St. Jean St.
Montreal, PQ H2Y 2R5
(514) 845-4141
FAX (514) 845-2581
Instruction Language: English and French.
Programs: Recorded music production, audio engineering, music industry management.
Degrees/Certificates: Diploma in Recording Arts and Sciences.
Duration: 15 months.
Tuition Fees: Contact the Admissions Office.
Grants/Scholarships: See Trebas Institute in the Ontario educational listings.

CEGEP de Trois-Rivieres

Department of Music
3500 de Courval
Trois Rivieres, PQ G9A 5E6
(819) 376-1721
FAX (819) 376-1026
Instruction Language: French.
Programs: Music concentration, music for adults, professional music copying.
Degrees/Certificates: D.E.C. (Diplome d'etudes collegiales).
Duration: One-two years.
Annual Admission: 45 students.
Tuition Fees: Free for full-time students.
Application Deadline: March 1.
Grants/Scholarships: Contact the CEGEP Foundation of Trois-Rivieres.
Head of Department: Claude Parenteau.

Universite Laval

Ecole de musique
Pavillon Casault, Cite Universitaire
Ste. Foy, PQ G1K 7P4
(418) 656-7061
Instruction Language: French.
Programs: Performance, composition, history and literature, music education, accompaniment, musicology.
Degrees/Certificates: B.Mus., M.Mus., Mus.Doc.
Head of Department: Joel Pasquier.
Comments: Write for other information.

Universite de Montreal

P.O. Box 6128, Stn. A
Montreal, PQ H3C 3J7
(514) 343-6432

Universite du Quebec à Montreal

Ecole Preparatoire de Musique
4873 ave. Westmount
Montreal, PQ H3Y 1X9
(514) 987-3939 or 488-6274
Instruction Language: French.
Programs: Theory, ear-training, harmony, instrumental and vocal performance.
Annual Admission: 250 students.
Tuition Fees: Theory courses: $110 for 45 hours. Instrumental: $250 for 15 hours.
Additional Costs: $15 registration fee.
Grants/Scholarships: None.
Head of Department: Marcelle Corneille, C.N.D.
Comments: Special Orff and Dalcroze courses for children 4-1/2 and up. Also, courses to prepare for entrance to CEGEP and university.

Vanier College CEGEP

Music Department
821 St. Croix Blvd.
St. Laurent, PQ H4L 3X9
(514) 744-7689
Instruction Language: English.
Programs: Music.
Degrees/Certificates: D.E.C. (Diplome d'etudes collegiales).
Duration: Two-three years.
Annual Admission: 85 students.
Head of Department: Lessy Kimmel.
Comments: A general music program to prepare students for more specialized study or professional work. The first two years, common to all students, is classically oriented. The third year is geared to preparing students for studio work, arranging and performance.

Ecole de Musique Vincent d'Indy

628 de la Cote Ste. Catherine
Outremont, PQ H2V 2C5
(514) 735-5261
FAX (514) 735-5266

MUSIC EDUCATION

CARLETON UNIVERSITY

MUSIC

PROGRAMS

Bachelor of Music

Bachelor of Arts

Bachelor of Arts (Hons.)

Diploma in Music

CONCENTRATIONS

History

Theory

Composition

Performance

Early Music

Popular Music

Ethnomusicology

Sociology and
Aesthetics of Music

Canadian Music

Electronic Music

Computer Music

For further information, contact:

The Department of Music
Room 911, Loeb Building
Carleton University
Ottawa, Ontario
K1S 5B6
Telephone: (613) 788-3733

The Office of Admissions
Room 315, Administration Building
Carleton University
Ottawa, Ontario
K1S 5B6
Telephone: (613) 788-3663

SASKATCHEWAN

Briercrest Bible College
Caronport, SK S0H 0S0
(306) 756-2321
Instruction Language: English.
Programs: Sacred music and theological training.
Degrees/Certificates: B.R.E., B.S.M.
Duration: Four years.
Annual Admission: 10 students.
Tuition Fees: On a per-credit basis.
Grants/Scholarships: Write to the director of admissions.

University of Regina
Department of Music
College Avenue Campus
Regina, SK S4S 0A2
(306) 779-4832
FAX (306) 779-4825
Instruction Language: English (music appreciation offered in French).
Programs: Performance, composition, music education, conducting.
Degrees/Certificates: B.A., B.A. (Hon.), B.Mus., B.Mus.Ed, M.Mus.
Duration: Three-four years.
Annual Admission: 40 students.

Tuition Fees: $1400 per year.
Additional Costs: $3850 (fees, books, accommodations).
Application Deadline: March 15 (for Master's), August 15 (for undergrads).
Grants/Scholarships: Entrance, and several others in voice, piano and strings, for upper-class students.
Head of Department: H. Bruce Lobaugh, B.Sc., M.Mus.Lit, Ph.D.

University of Saskatchewan
Music Department
1045 Education Building
Saskatoon, SK S7N 0W0
(306) 966-6171
FAX (306) 966-8719
Instruction Language: English.
Programs: Various.
Degrees/Certificates: B.Mus., B.Mus.Ed., M.Mus., Ph.D.
Annual Admission: 120 students.
Tuition Fees: $1344.
Additional Costs: $120.
Application Deadline: July 31.
Grants/Scholarships: Write for Scholarships Booklet from Awards office.

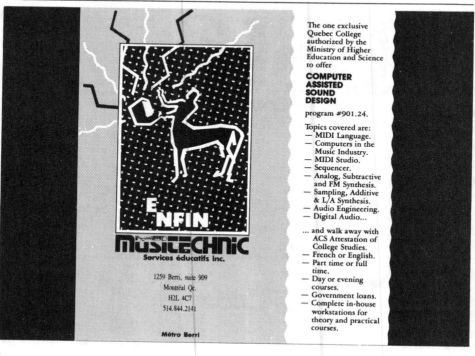

MUSIC FESTIVALS

Banff Festival of the Arts

P.O. Box 1020
Banff, AB T0L 0C0
(403) 762-6100
Sponsor: Banff Centre School of Fine Arts.
Aims and Objectives: To provide specialized training for dedicated and advanced artists in all disciplines.
Events/Artists: Music concerts and recitals. Chamber music, orchestral, jazz, opera, musical theatre, ballet and drama.
Dates and Locations: Dates TBA—Banff Centre.
Comments: Auditions held across Canada in February.

Big Valley Jamboree

P.O. Box 200
Regina, SK S4P 2Z6
(306) 721-6060
FAX (306) 584-1187
Sponsor: Bosco Society.
Aims and Objectives: Country music festival.
Events/Artists: Past participants include Willie Nelson, Kenny Rogers, Johnny Cash, Charlie Pride, George Strait, Randy Travis, Reba McEntire, Rick Van Shelton.
Dates and Locations: July 19-22, 1990—Saskatchewan. July 18-21, 1991—Saskatchewan.
Comments: Largest country music festival in Canada.

CIBC National Music Festival

Sponsor: Federation of Canadian Music Festivals.
Dates and Locations: August 27-29, 1990—Regina.

Calgary International Jazz Festival

P.O. Box 2735, Stn. M
Calgary, AB T2P 3C2
(403) 233-2628
Aims and Objectives: To present a quality jazz festival.
Events/Artists: Concerts, club shows, street performances and a two-day island park event.
Dates and Locations: June 17-24, 1990—Calgary. June 16-23, 1991—Calgary.
Deadline for Application: March.

Canadian Festival of Youth Orchestras

P.O. Box 1020
Banff, AB T0L 0C0
(403) 762-6278
Sponsor: Canadian Association of Youth Orchestras.
Dates and Locations: April 5-15, 1990—The Banff Centre.

Cariboo Festival

P.O. Box 4506
Williams Lake, BC V2G 2V5
(604) 398-5333
Sponsor: Cariboo Festival Society.
Aims and Objectives: To create and cultivate various art forms throughout the communities of central British Columbia.
Events/Artists: Vocal, choral, band, piano, instrumental, speech arts, creative writing.
Dates and Locations: TBA.
Deadline for Application: January 25, 1991.

Club Boreal Jubilee — Adult Concert Series

P.O. Box 1236, Stn. B
Sudbury, ON P3E 4S7
(705) 674-5512
Sponsor: Northern Lights Festival Boreal.
Dates and Locations: Annually during winter and spring—Jubilee Centre.

Country Music Week

833 The Queensway
Toronto, ON M8Z 5Z1
(416) 252-1025
Sponsor: Canadian Country Music Association.
Dates and Locations: September 3-9, 1990 —Edmonton. September 9-15, 1991—Hamilton. September 14-20, 1992—Calgary.

Dance Hilights Concert

P.O. Box 174
Penticton, BC V2A 6K3
(604) 493-3287
Sponsor: Okanagan Valley Music Festival Society.
Aims and Objectives: To develop the skills of student dancers, and to have their performances evaluated by competent adjudicators.
Events/Artists: Performances by students of dance at all age levels. Various competitive classes offered.
Dates and Locations: April 7, 1990—Community Centre Theatre.

Downtowners Optimist Band and Vocal Jazz Festival

1544 Albert St.
Regina, SK S4P 2S4
(306) 757-7272
FAX (306) 757-0577
Sponsor: Downtowners Optimist Club of Regina.
Aims and Objectives: To help promote and develop bands in Saskatchewan. To give participants an opportunity to be evaluated by outstanding North American adjudicators.
Events/Artists: Festival includes classes for concert band, jazz band, jazz combo, Dixieland combo and vocal jazz. Open to all ages.
Prizes: Optimist plaques to groups receiving an 'A' grade. Also, invitations are given to outstanding groups to attend MusicFest Canada.
Dates and Locations: March 13-16, 1991.
Deadline for Application: January 1991.

Dreaming of Beauty

1087 Queen St. W.
Toronto, ON M6J 1H3
(416) 534-6311
Sponsor: CCMC.
Dates and Locations: March 8, 1990— Music Gallery.

The Elora Festival

78 Metcalfe St., P.O. Box 990
Elora, ON N0B 1S0
(519) 846-0331
Aims and Objectives: To present a summer classical music festival in the scenic setting of Elora, Ontario.
Events/Artists: Top Canadian and international vocal and instrumental artists perform works dating from the Baroque to the modern age.
Dates and Locations: July 27—August 12, 1990—Elora. Date for 1991 TBA.
Deadline for Application: December.

Festival annuel des Harmonies du Quebec

4545 ave. Pierre-de-Coubertin
Montreal, PQ H1V 3R2
Sponsor: Federation des Harmonies du Quebec.
Dates and Locations: May 17-20, 1990— Universite de Sherbrooke.

Festival de Musique Classique de Montreal

3880 Cote-des-neiges
Montreal, PQ H3H 1W1
(514) 931-8792
Sponsor: Marianopolis College.
Events/Artists: Classical music festival.
Dates and Locations: April 21-22, 1990—
Montreal.

Festival International de Jazz de Montreal

355 Ste. Catherine o., Suite 301
Montreal, PQ H3B 1A5
(514) 289-9473
Aims and Objectives: To present a variety of
international jazz musicians.
Events/Artists: Street and club performances.
Dates and Locations: June 29—July 8,
1990—Montreal.

Festival International de Lanaudiere

1500 Base-de-Roc
Joliette, PQ J6E 3Z1
(514) 759-7636
FAX (514) 759-3082
Aims and Objectives: To promote the
creation, development and promotion of the arts
in general. Particular stress is given to music,
theatre and dance.
Events/Artists: Concerts, opera productions
and dance programs.
Dates and Locations: From June through to
the end of August, 1990. Exact dates TBA.
Comments: The festival now has its own
amphitheatre which can accommodate up to
10,000 people (2,000 covered and 8,000 on
the grass).

Festival Musical 1990

308 Frigon
Repentigny, PQ J6A 4B1
(514) 585-2593
Sponsor: Federation des Associations
Musicales du Quebec.
Dates and Locations: August 25, 1990—
Universite de Montreal, 2100 Edouard-Monpetit.

Festival National de la Chanson de Granby

P.O. Box 41
Granby, PQ J2G 8E2
(514) 375-7555

Festival of Friends

401 Main St. W.
Hamilton, ON L8P 1K5
(416) 525-6644
FAX (416) 525-8292
Sponsor: City of Hamilton.
Dates and Locations: August 10-12, 1990—
Hamilton.
Deadline for Application: March 1990.

Festival of the Sound

50 James St., P.O. Box 750
Parry Sound, ON P2A 2Z1
(705) 746-2410
Aims and Objectives: To administer a summer
music festival.
Events/Artists: Festival features chamber
music, jazz, Dixieland, operetta, musical comedy,
a children's series, brunches and musical cruises
aboard a 500-passenger cruise vessel.
Dates and Locations: Dates TBA—Festival
Hall, 111 Isabella St., Parry Sound, ON.

Francofolies de Montreal

355 Ste. Catherine o., Suite 301
Montreal, PQ H3B 1A5
(514) 289-9473
Dates and Locations: November 30—
December 9, 1990—Place des Arts, Montreal.

The Guelph Spring Festival

P.O. Box 1718
Guelph, ON N1H 6Z9
Sponsor: Edward Johnson Music Foundation.
Aims and Objectives: To promote young
singers and composers.
Events/Artists: Operas, concerts, dance
programs, theatre events.
Dates and Locations: TBA.

l'International Montreal 1990

308 Frigon
Repentigny, PQ J6A 4B1
(514) 585-2593
Sponsor: Federation des Associations
Musicales du Quebec.
Dates and Locations: Complexe Sportif
Claude Robillard, 1,000 rue Emile- Journeault.
Deadline for Application: March 3, 1990.

Jazz City Festival

P.O. Box 255, Sub Stn. 11
Edmonton, AB T6G 2E0
(403) 458-0404
Aims and Objectives: To present a week-long festival of jazz music featuring local, national and international musicians.
Events/Artists: Free outdoor concerts and paid-admission indoor concerts.
Dates and Locations: Late June, early July—various locations.

Jazzfest International Victoria B.C.

P.O. Box 542, Stn. E
Victoria, BC V8W 2P3
(604) 384-1189
Sponsor: Victoria Jazz Society.
Dates and Locations: June 20—July 3, 1990—Newcombe Theatre, Market Square Courtyard.

Lakes District Performing Arts Festival

c/o M. Long, P.O. Box 878
Burns Lake, BC V0V 1E0
(604) 692-7425
Sponsor: Lakes District Festival Association.
Events/Artists: Amateur music, speech arts and highland dance competitions.
Prizes: Challenge trophies.
Dates and Locations: April 19-28, 1990—Burns Lake, BC.
Deadline for Application: February 16, 1990.
Comments: This will be the association's 33rd annual festival.

Mariposa: The Festival of Roots Music

525 Adelaide St. E.
Toronto, ON M4A 3W4
(416) 363-4009
Sponsor: Mariposa Folk Foundation.
Aims and Objectives: To preserve and promote contemporary and traditional folk music and art.
Events/Artists: Participatory folk play, children's area, crafts, concerts, workshops and activities. Approximately 50 artists and musicians.
Dates and Locations: June 22-24, 1990—Molson Park, Barrie.

Mariposa in the Park

525 Adelaide St. E.
Toronto, ON M4A 3W4
(416) 363-4009
Sponsor: Mariposa Folk Foundation.
Aims and Objectives: To preserve and promote contemporary and traditional folk music and art.
Dates and Locations: September 8, 1990—Christie Pits, Toronto.

Maritime Old Time Fiddling Contest

P.O. Box 3037, Dartmouth E.
Dartmouth, NS B2W 4Y3
(902) 423-7389
Sponsor: St. Thomas More Council of Catholic Men
Aims and Objectives: To provide exposure for maritime talent.
Events/Artists: Individual and group fiddling.
Dates and Locations: July 6-7, 1990—Prince Andrew High School Auditorium.

Maritime Old Time Jamboree

P.O. Box 3037, Dartmouth E.
Dartmouth, NS B2W 4Y3
(902) 423-7389
Sponsor: St. Thomas More Council of Catholic Men.
Aims and Objectives: To foster maritime musical talent.
Events/Artists: Outdoor variety show featuring individual and group fiddling.
Dates and Locations: July 8, 1990—Beazley Sport Field.

The Montreal New Music Festival

P.O. Box 1176, Stn. B
Montreal, PQ H3B 3K9
(514) 457-3691
FAX (514) 457-4724
Aims and Objectives: The festival is formatted to promote independent and upcoming artists. Past participants include the Jazz Butcher, The Hodads, Condition, Change of Heart, Timbuk3.
Events/Artists: Everything from rock, pop, punk to country and reggae.
Dates and Locations: The fifth New Music Festival will take place in October, 1990—Montreal.
Deadline for Application: Apply with press kit and demo by July 30, 1990.
Comments: Venues and clubs with capacities of 450 to 1,200 seats.

Music Hilights Concert

P.O. Box 174
Penticton, BC V2A 6K3
(604) 493-3287
Sponsor: Okanagan Valley Music Festival
Society.
Aims and Objectives: To develop the musical
skills of participants and have their performances
evaluated by competent adjudicators.
Events/Artists: Performances by students of
piano, string, brass, woodwind, vocal and choral
music at various class and age levels.
Dates and Locations: April 14, 1990—
Penticton Secondary School Auditorium.

MusicFest Canada

4500-16 Ave. N.W.
Calgary, AB T3B 0M6
(403) 247-2901
FAX (403) 247-4548
Sponsor: General Motors, Yamaha Music,
Moffat Communications.
Aims and Objectives: To promote a lifelong
interest in music in particular and the arts in
general. To provide an opportunity for students
and educators to share musical achievements.
Events/Artists: Canadian Stage Band Festival,
Canadian Concert Band Festival, Canadian
Choral Festival. Guests include clinicians,
adjudicators and artists.
Prizes: Over $100,000 available in scholarships.
Standards of Performance prizes awarded to
participating ensembles (gold, silver, bronze).
Dates and Locations: May 16-20, 1990—
Winnipeg. Dates for 1991 TBA.
Deadline for Application: Applications done
on regional basis. Refer to MusicFest newsletter
for specifics.

New Brunswick Competitive Festival of Music

P.O. Box 2022
Saint John, NB E2L 3T5
(506) 847-5800
Aims and Objectives: To hold a music festival
where children of all ages may meet, compete on
a friendly basis and learn by receiving expert
adjudication.
Events/Artists: Competitive classes in piano,
violin, voice and other instruments. Also classes
for band and choral groups.
Prizes: Trophies and many generous cash
awards.
Dates and Locations: April 18-28, 1990. April
17-27, 1991—Saint John, New Brunswick.
Deadline for Application: February 16, 1991.
Comments: The festival welcomes out of
province participants and university students.

New Westminster Hyack Jazz Festival

835-8 St.
New Westminster, BC V3M 3S9
(604) 522-0644
FAX (604) 522-6653
Sponsor: New Westminster Hyack Jazz Festival.
Events/Artists: Jazz festival.
Comments: The festival involves over 80
groups and features professional guest artists.
The event takes place at the Massey Theatre,
New Westminster.

Northern Lights Festival Boreal

176 Larch St., Suite 301
P.O. Box 1236, Stn. B
Sudbury, ON P3E 4S7
(705) 674-5512
Aims and Objectives: To promote the
development of various art forms which have
roots in the folk tradition.
Events/Artists: An annual festival featuring
child and adult programming. Also a fall and
winter performance series.
Dates and Locations: Festival: July 6-8,
1990—Sudbury. Series: Fall and winter 1990/91.
Deadline for Application: Festival (February
15, 1990), Series (July 31, 1990).

Northern Music Festival

P.O. Box 14
North Bay, ON P1B 8J6
(705) 476-5889
Sponsor: North Bay Symphony Orchestra and
Candore College.
Events/Artists: 16 concerts are performed
during the six-week festival.
Dates and Locations: Last week of June to
first week of August.

Ottawa International Jazz Festival

P.O. Box 3104, Stn. D
Ottawa, ON K1P 6H7
(613) 594-3580
FAX (613) 235-5473
Sponsor: Labatt's Breweries (Eastern Ontario).
Aims and Objectives: To stage a ten-day jazz
festival in early July.
Events/Artists: Jazz programming featured at
Confederation Park and at many satellite
locations throughout Ottawa and Hull.
Dates and Locations: July 13-22, 1990—
Ottawa and Hull. Dates for 1991 TBA.
Comments: Groups wishing to participate must
forward a biography of the ensemble, and a letter
stating preferred performance dates and technical
requirements. A diagram of equipment layout for
stage management is also required.

Popsicles and Piccolos—Children's Concert Series

P.O. Box 1236, Stn. B
Sudbury, ON P3E 4S7
(705) 674-5512
Sponsor: Northern Lights Festival Boreal.
Dates and Locations: Winter, spring, 1990/91—Sheridan Auditorium.

Quinte Summer Music Festival

P.O. Box 500
Picton, ON K0K 2T0
(613) 476-5806
FAX (613) 476-7588
Aims and Objectives: To present a summer music festival featuring the best in Canadian talent in a variety of styles with a focus on vocal music.
Events/Artists: Classical, jazz, folk, country, children's and choral concerts in both formal and informal settings.
Dates and Locations: July 6-22, 1990.

The Red Deer International Folk Festival

P.O. Box 224
Red Deer, AB T4N 5E8
(403) 346-0055
Sponsor: The Red Deer International Folk Festival Society.
Aims and Objectives: To celebrate Canada's multicultural make-up through showcasing local and international performing artists.
Events/Artists: Ethnic music, food and dance. Also craft and costume exhibits.
Dates and Locations: Annually on July 1—Bower Ponds, Red Deer.
Deadline for Application: April 1st each year.

Regina Folk Festival

P.O. Box 1203
Regina, SK S4P 3B4
(306) 757-7684
Sponsor: Regina Guild of Folk Arts.
Aims and Objectives: To preserve and promote folk music through live performances.
Events/Artists: Three evening concerts plus workshops and a children's area.
Dates and Locations: June 8-10, 1990—Victoria Park. June 7-9, 1991—Victoria Park.
Deadline for Application: March of each year.
Comments: Oldest continuously running folk festival in Canada (22nd year in 1990). No admission charge.

Saskatchewan Talent Showcase

Studio West Canada Inc.
Saskatoon, SK S7L 6H2
(306) 244-2818
Sponsor: Saskatchewan Recording Industry Association.
Dates and Locations: November 9-11, 1990—Saskatoon.

Summer Music From The Comox Valley

P.O. Box 3056
Courtenay, BC V9N 5N3
(604) 338-7463
FAX (604) 338-1969
Sponsor: Courtenay Youth Music Centre Society.
Aims and Objectives: To provide a musical environment that nurtures the teachers, audiences and stars of tomorrow.
Events/Artists: Jazz, musical theatre, classical guitar, plus music for harp, piano, band and orchestra.
Prizes: Some scholarships.
Dates and Locations: July 8—August 5, 1990.

Sunderland Lions Music Festival

R.R. 4
Sunderland, ON L0C 1H0
(705) 357-3092
Sponsor: Sunderland Lions Club.
Dates and Locations: February 12-23, 1990—Sunderland Town Hall, Sunderland United Church.

Sunfest Victoria B.C.

P.O. Box 542, Stn. E
Victoria, BC V8W 2P3
(604) 384-1189
Sponsor: Victoria Jazz Society.
Dates and Locations: April 17-19, 1990—Newcombe Theatre, Market Square Courtyard.

Toronto Arts Week

151 John St., Suite 402
Toronto, ON M5V 2T2
(416) 597-8223
FAX (416) 597-6956
Sponsor: Toronto Arts Awards Foundation.
Aims and Objectives: To heighten public awareness of the arts and artists of greater Metropolitan Toronto.
Events/Artists: Tours, panel discussions, screenings and exhibitions. Also large-scale public performances in non-traditional venues.
Dates and Locations: Sept. 22-30, 1990—Metro Toronto.

Vancouver Folk Music Festival

3271 Main St.
Vancouver, BC V5V 3M6
(604) 879-2931
FAX (604) 879-4315
Sponsor: Vancouver Folk Music Festival Society.
Aims and Objectives: To preserve and promote traditional and contemporary folk music.
Events/Artists: Eclectic mix of international performers.
Dates and Locations: July 13-15, 1990—Jericho Beach Park.
Comments: Festival Society also produces concerts throughout the year and distributes over 3,000 recorded music titles.

World Music—Cymbali

1087 Queen St. W.
Toronto, ON M6J 1H3
(416) 534-6311
Sponsor: CCMC.
Dates and Locations: May 12, 1990—Music Gallery.

World Music—Staro Selo

1087 Queen St. W.
Toronto, ON M6J 1H3
(416) 534-6311
Sponsor: CCMC.
Dates and Locations: January 2, 1990—Music Gallery.

Valerie Alia

Graduate School of Journalism - Middlesex
College
University of Western Ontario
London, ON N6A 5B7
(519) 661-3383, ext. 6663
FAX (519) 661-3848
Freelance: Yes.
Publications: *London Free Press, Up Here
Magazine, London Magazine, Globe and Mail*
(book reviews). Also U.S. dailies and weeklies.
Area of Expertise: Classical and Folk music,
plus some Jazz.
Language: English.
Comments: Alia is a member of the broadcast
faculty at the U.W.O., and also teaches a course
in arts criticism. She used to cover the
Tanglewood and Saratoga seasons for public TV
and for various Boston and Albany papers.

Richard Allen

76 Constance St.
Toronto, ON M6R 1S6
(416) 766-5349
Freelance: Yes.
Publications: *Canadian Music Trade, CBC
Radio Guide, Opera Canada, Music Directory
Canada.*
Area of Expertise: Classical and Folk music.
Language: English.

Bill Anderson

Canadian Press
36 King St. E.
Toronto, ON M5C 2L9
(416) 364-0321
FAX (416) 364-0207
Freelance: Yes.
Publication: Canadian Press.
Area of Expertise: Music, TV.
Language: English.

Rick Andrews

1315 Camosun St., Suite 2
Victoria, BC V8V 4L3
(604) 385-1350 (home), (604) 382-6188 (office)
FAX (604) 381-2662 (*Monday Magazine*)
Staff Writer: Yes.
Publication: *Monday Magazine*, a weekly news and entertainment paper.
Area of Expertise: Alternative music.
Language: English.
Comments: Andrews also co-owns Funhouse Records, a local retail store specializing in underground music. Any bands with independent releases are welcome to get in touch.

Greg Barr

1101 Baxter Rd., P.O. Box 5020
Ottawa, ON K2G 3M4
(613) 596-3664
FAX (613) 726-1198
Staff Writer: Yes.
Publication: *Ottawa Citizen*.
Area of Expertise: Pop music.
Language: English.

Jason Beck

6727 Betsworth Ave.
Winnipeg, MB R3R 1V6
(204) 895-7727
Freelance: Yes.
Staff Writer: Yes.
Publications: *Winnipeg Entertainment Network* (staff writer), *Winnipeg Sun* (freelance), *Music Express* (freelance).
Area of Expertise: Pop, Rock and Alternative music.
Language: English.

Karen Bliss

49 Anvil Millway
Willowdale, ON M2L 1P9
(416) 447-0930
Freelance: Yes.
Publications: *Music Express, Melody Maker, Metal Hammer, Illinois Entertainer, SMASH, JAM, M.E.A.T., Canadian Composer, Campus Canada*.
Area of Expertise: Blues, Folk, Rock, Pop, Reggae.
Language: English.

Alison Broddle

21 Macdonell Ave.
Toronto, ON M6R 2A3
(416) 928-2909
FAX (416) 928-2909
Freelance: Yes.
Staff Writer: Yes.
Publications: *JAM* (freelance), *Network* (staff writer), *Campus Canada* (editor).
Area of Expertise: Pop music and personalities.
Language: English.

Terry Burman

1580 Sandhurst Circle, Suite 1802
Agincourt, ON M1V 2L3
(416) 291-3384
Freelance: Yes.
Publications: *Inside Tracks*, Caribbean Chinese Association Newsletter.
Area of Expertise: Pop/Rock, Dance, Funk, Caribbean, Country, Classical.
Language: English.
Comments: Can also do publicity writing (bios, press releases, etc.).

Rod Campbell

P.O. Box 2421
Edmonton, AB T5J 2S6
(403) 429-5348
FAX (403) 429-5500
Freelance: Yes.
Publication: *Edmonton Journal*.
Area of Expertise: Country.
Language: English.

Allan Casey

369 York St.
London, ON N6A 4G1
(519) 679-0230
FAX (519) 667-4528
Staff Writer: Yes.
Publication: *London Free Press*.
Area of Expertise: Pop, Country, Jazz, Children's.
Language: English.

Andrew J. Charron

3284 Yonge St.
Toronto, ON M4N 3M7
(416) 485-1049
FAX (416) 485-8924
Freelance: Yes.
Publications: *Guitar Toronto, Music Directory Canada*.
Area of Expertise: Classical music, especially related to the guitar; features, analyses.
Language: English.

Ashley Collie

154 Spadina Rd.
Toronto, ON M5R 2T8
(416) 961-0876
Freelance: Yes.
Publications: *Performance, Spin, Toronto Life, Maclean's, Canadian Music Trade.*
Area of Expertise: Features, articles on the business of music and personality profiles.
Languages: English, Welsh.
Comments: Ashley "Rugby Legs" Collie has written music videos for David Gibson and episodic TV scripts about the music business e.g., *Diamonds.*

Gisele Cote

305 Mont-Royal e.
Montreal, PQ H2T 1P8
(514) 845-4108
FAX (514) 845-8241
Staff Writer: Yes.
Publication: *Behind the Scenes/En Sourdine.*
Area of Expertise: Music.
Languages: English, French.

Tony Davis

300 Carlton St.
Winnipeg, MB R3C 3C1
(204) 943-9331
FAX (204) 942-7805
Staff Writer: Yes.
Publication: *Winnipeg Free Press.*
Area of Expertise: Arts reporter covering classical music, ballet, contemporary dance and performance art.
Language: English.

David Daw

P.O. Box 3
Westport, ON K0G 1X0
(613) 273-2818
FAX (613) 273-7325
Freelance: Yes.
Staff Writer: Yes.
Publication: *Gospel Music News* (editor for 10 years).
Area of Expertise: Specialist on Canadian Christian music. Also artist promotions.
Language: English.
Comments: Owner of Summit Sound Inc. (recording studio and custom cassette duplication facility) and Peak Productions (graphic design and typesetting studio). Member of gospel group The Proverbs (since l967).

Eric Dawson

P.O. Box 2400, Stn. M
Calgary, AB T2P 0W8
(403) 235-7580
FAX (403) 235-7379
Staff Writer: Yes.
Publication: *Calgary Herald.*
Area of Expertise: Classical.
Language: English.

Larry Delaney

P.O. Box 7323 (Vanier Terminal)
Ottawa, ON K1L 8E4
(613) 745-6006
FAX (613) 745-0576
Publications: *Country Music News* (editor, publisher), Country Music Awards Program, and bio material for Country Music Hall of Fame.
Area of Expertise: Canadian Country music.
Language: English.
Comments: Publisher of *Country Music News.*

Denise Donlon

299 Queen St. W.
Toronto, ON M5V 2Z5
(416) 591-5757
FAX (416) 591-7791
Freelance: Yes.
Staff Writer: Yes.
Programs: City-TV's *The New Music* and *MuchMusic.*
Area of Expertise: *MuchMusic* (Country and Roots), *The New Music* (all styles plus business-oriented stories, profiles and behind-the-scenes stories).
Language: English.
Comments: Laurie Brown, host and associate producer of *The New Music.*

Kerry Doole

47 Jefferson Ave.
Toronto, ON M6K 1Y3
(416) 538-7500
FAX (416) 538-7503
Staff Writer: Yes.
Publications: *Music Express* (features editor), *Sound & Vision* (record reviews).
Area of Expertise: Contemporary music from country to jazz. Will also write on film topics.

Howard Druckman

16 St. Joseph St., Suite 33
Toronto, ON M4Y 1J9
(416) 922-3620
Freelance: Yes.
Publications: *Musician, Spin, Canadian Musician, Metropolis, Network, Park Press, Canadian Business, Music Scene, Canadian Composer, Graffiti* (now defunct), *T.O.* (now defunct).
Area of Expertise: Rock & Roll, Folk, Jazz, Blues, Country, New Music, Rap, Reggae, Hardcore, World Beat, Noise, Industrial, Soul, R&B, Punk.
Languages: English, French.
Comments: Random sampling and resume available on request.

Doug Gallant

P.O. Box 2394
Charlottetown, PE C1A 8C1
(902) 892-2908
FAX (902) 566-3808
Staff Writer: Yes.
Publications: *The Guardian, The Evening Patriot.*
Area of Expertise: Pop Rock, R&B, Country, Soul, plus film scores and musicals.
Language: English.
Comments: Produces a regular record column that covers everything except classical music and serious jazz.

Marty Gorvais

167 Ferry St.
Windsor, ON N9A 4M5
(519) 256-5533
FAX (519) 255-5515
Staff Writer: Yes.
Publications: *Windsor Star.*
Area of Expertise: Classical music, book editor.
Language: English.

Allan Gould

31 Glen Rush Blvd.
Toronto, ON M5N 2T4
(416) 486-7425
Freelance: Yes.
Publications: *Chatelaine, Toronto Life, Canadian Living, Canadian Forum,* and others.
Area of Expertise: Rock, Classical.
Language: English.

Stuart Green

5 Cheyenne Drive
Scarborough, ON M1J 2Y5
(416) 439-0237
FAX (416) 292-8661
Staff Writer: Yes.
Publications: *Scarborough Mirror, M.E.A.T.*
Area of Expertise: Alternative and underground music.
Languages: English and some French.

Shaleem Hosein

72 Donald St., Suite 1709
Winnipeg, MB R3C 1L7
(204) 942-6886
Staff Writer: Yes.
Publication: *Winnipeg Entertainment Network.*
Area of Expertise: Hard Rock, Heavy Metal, Art Rock.
Language: English.
Comments: Also hosts a radio show.

Marc Andre Joanisse

47 Clarence
Ottawa, ON K1N 9K1
(613) 560-2711
FAX (800) 267-6960
Staff Writer: Yes.
Publication: *Le Droit.*
Area of Expertise: Music.
Languages: French, English.

Andrew Jones

1820 Baile, Suite 2
Montreal, PQ H3H 1T4
(514) 932-2363
Freelance: Yes.
Staff Writer: Yes.
Publications: *Montreal Mirror* (music editor), *Option Magazine* (contributing editor), *Coda, Montreal Gazette* (freelance).
Area of Expertise: Musique Actuelle, World Beat, Jazz, Improvised, and New Music, Pop.
Languages: English (written), English and French (spoken).
Comments: *Montreal Mirror,* 400 McGill Montreal, PQ H2Y 2G1 (514) 393-1010.

Mark Kearney ~ 817

18 Braemar Cr.
London, ON N6H 2X1
(519) 472-4509
Freelance: Yes
Publications: *Toronto Sun, Music Express, Goldmine, Oshawa Times, Halifax Chronicle, Moncton Times-Transcript, London Free Press.*
Area of Expertise: Canadian music of the 50s, 60s and 70s. Some current.
Language: English.
Comments: Contributor to 1989 book *Shakin' All Over: The Rock 'n' Roll Years in Canada.* Occasional scriptwriter for syndicated radio show *Street Corner.*

John Kendle

1700 Church Ave.
Winnipeg, MB R2X 3A2
(204) 632-2783
FAX (204) 632-8709
Staff Writer: Yes.
Publication: *Winnipeg Sun.*
Area of Expertise: Rock, Country, Folk, Alternative.
Language: English.

John Laycock

167 Ferry St.
Windsor, ON N9A 4M5
(519) 256-5533
FAX (519) 255-5515
Staff Writer: Yes.
Publication: *Windsor Star.*
Area of Expertise: Pop music, film, theatre.
Language: English.

Larry Leblanc

15 Independence Dr.
Scarborough, ON M1K 3R7
FAX (416) 265-3280
Freelance: Yes.
Publication: Co-founder of Canadian trade paper, *The Record.*
Area of Expertise: Pop, Country, Folk, all forms of Rock.
Language: English.
Comments: Freelancer since 1965. Has written for the *The Record, Record World, Rolling Stone, Circus, Network.* Extensive TV and radio work as well. Regular on CTV's *Canada A.M.*

Roger Levesque

P.O. Box 2421
Edmonton, AB T5J 2S6
(403) 429-5348
FAX (403) 429-5500
Freelance: Yes.
Publication: *Edmonton Journal.*
Area of Expertise: Jazz.

Rachel Lussier

1950 rue Roy
Sherbrooke, PQ J1K 2X8
(819) 564-5454
FAX (819) 564-5455
Publication: *Journal La Tribune.*
Area of Expertise: Music.
Language: French.

Mairi Maclean

P.O. Box 2421
Edmonton, AB T5J 2S6
(403) 429-5348
FAX (403) 429-5500
Staff Writer: Yes.
Publication: *Edmonton Journal.*
Area of Expertise: Classical music.
Language: English.

Ross McLennan

1700 Church Ave.
Winnipeg, MB R2X 3A2
(204) 632-2777
FAX (204) 632-8709
Freelance: Yes.
Publication: *Winnipeg Sun.*
Area of Expertise: Jazz.
Language: English.

A.J. McMullan

39 Brier Park Rd.
Brantford, ON N3R 3P9
(416) 482-1091
Freelance: Yes.
Publications: Canadian correspondent for *Blitz* magazine (Los Angeles)
Area of Expertise: Retro-Rock, Roots, Blues, Rock, New Country.
Language: English, French.

Helen Metella

P.O. Box 2421
Edmonton, AB T5J 2S6
(403) 429-5348
FAX (403)429-5500
Staff Writer: Yes.
Publication: *Edmonton Journal.*
Area of Expertise: Pop music.
Languages: English, some French.
Comments: Metella also reviews records for CBC Radio's *Prime Time.*

Mark Miller

c/o The Globe & Mail
444 Front St. W.
Toronto, ON M5V 2S9
(416) 585-5500
FAX (416) 585-5085
Freelance: Yes.
Publications: *Globe and Mail, Encyclopedia of Music in Canada, Jazz Forum* (Warsaw), *down beat* (Chicago).
Area of Expertise: Jazz.
Language: English.

Donalee Moulton-Barrett

19 Oakhill Dr.
Halifax, NS B3M 2V3
(902) 443-9600
FAX (902) 445-4364
Freelance: Yes.
Publications: *Graffiti, Performing Arts, Arts Atlantic, Atlantic Insight, Chatelaine, Chronicle-Herald, Globe & Mail.*
Area of Expertise: Music, medicine, women, environmental issues.
Language: English.

James O'Connor

1700 Church Ave.
Winnipeg, MB R2X 3A2
(204) 632-2782
FAX (204) 632-8709
Staff Writer: Yes.
Publication: *Winnipeg Sun.*
Area of Expertise: Country, Rock, local club scene.
Language: English.

Ellie O'Day

1715 Cook St., Suite 101
Vancouver, BC V5Y 3J6
(604) 873-9686
FAX (604) 872-1715
Freelance: Yes.
Publications: *Canadian Musician, Hook Line & Singer.*
Area of Expertise: Pop, Rock, Ethnic, the music business.
Language: English.

Stephen Ostick

300 Carlton St., 4th Floor
Winnipeg, MB R3C 3C1
(204) 943-9331
FAX (204) 942-7805
Staff Writer: Yes.
Publications: Pop music columnist as well as concert and recorded music reviewer for the *Winnipeg Free Press.*
Area of Expertise: Pop and Rock music.
Language: English and French.
Comments: Former professional rock musician (bassist) for eight years.

William C. Paisley

700 King's College Rd.
Fredericton, NB E3B 2G9
(506) 457-2130
FAX (506) 450-2619
Freelance: Yes.
Publications: *Fredericton Daily Gleaner,* University of New Brunswick's *The Brunswickian,* CHSR-FM Radio (Fredericton).
Area of Expertise: Classical, Jazz, Electronic.
Language: English.
Comments: Reviews, interviews and promotions in daily newspaper and on radio. Also programs and produces classical and jazz music for radio.

Stephen Pedersen

2561 Beech St.
Halifax, NS B3L 2X9
(902) 420-8636
Freelance: Yes.
Publications: *Halifax Chronicle Herald and Mail Star* (criticism and features), *Arts Atlantic, Music Magazine, Maclean's, Canadian Composer, Music Scene, Broadcaster.*
Area of Expertise: Classical, New Music, Jazz, Folk and Traditional, Country.
Language: English.
Comments: Currently under contract with Nimbus Publishing Ltd. to co-author a book with Virginia Beaton on 50 years of maritime country music and musicians.

Tim Perlich

c/o Now Magazine
150 Danforth Ave.
Toronto, ON M4K 1N1
(416) 461-0871
FAX (416) 461-2886
Staff Writer: Yes.
Publications: *Now, Soul Survivor.*
Area of Expertise: Contemporary Pop Rock (North American, Australian), Alternative, 60s Soul, R&B, Blues, 50s Gospel.
Language: English.

Mitch Potter

1 Yonge St.
Toronto, ON M5E 1E6
(416) 869-4487
FAX (416) 869-4417
Staff Writer: Yes.
Publications: *Toronto Star, Rolling Stone,* various freelance assignments.
Area of Expertise: Pop, Rock, Folk, Country, Newfoundland Traditional.
Language: English.

Randy C. Ray

48 Dunbarton Ct.
Ottawa, ON K1K 4L4
(613) 746-9017
FAX (613) 995-5795
Freelance: Yes.
Publications: *Toronto Sun, Music Express, Oshawa Times, Moncton Times- Transcript, London Free Press.*
Area of Expertise: Music Nostalgia (mainly Canadian 50s-80s) plus Canadian music book *Shakin' All Over.*
Language: English.

Glenn Reid

136 Coxwell Ave.
Toronto, ON M4L 3B2
(416) 463-9842
Freelance: Yes.
Publication: *Canadian Musician.*
Area of Expertise: Rock, Pop, Country, Folk, plus humour and profiles.
Language: English.

Ann Ruebottom

567 Arlington Ave.
Toronto, ON M6C 3A6
(416) 653-6218
Freelance: Yes.
Publications: *Music Magazine, Opera Canada, Musicanada, Toronto Star, Gramophone.*
Area of Expertise: Profiles, especially classical musicians.
Language: English.
Comments: Also experienced publicist.

Darlene St. Pierre

1772 Comox St., Suite 501
Vancouver, BC V6G 1P8
Publications: *Westender/Eastender* (music critic), *Plus* magazine (contributing editor).
Area of Expertise: Rock, Blues, Jazz.
Language: English.

Ben Salem

95 Chavolais Blvd.
Brampton, ON L6Y 2R9
(416) 450-7445
Freelance: Yes.
Publications: *Scope Magazine* (Toronto), *Front* magazine (Montreal).
Area of Expertise: Dance Music (in general); R&B, Hip Hop, House, NRG, and Latin (specifically).
Language: English.

Marc Samson

390 rue St. Vallier e.
Quebec, PQ G1K 7J6
(418) 647-3394
FAX (418) 647-3374
Staff Writer: Yes.
Publication: *Le Soleil.*
Area of Expertise: Classical music.
Language: French.

Ted Shaw

167 Ferry St.
Windsor, ON N9A 4M5
(519) 256-5533
FAX (519) 255-5515
Staff Writer: Yes.
Publication: *Windsor Star.*
Area of Expertise: Pop music, TV.
Language: English.

Jacob Siskind

c/o The Ottawa Citizen
1101 Baxter Rd.
Ottawa, ON K2C 3M4
(613) 596-3730
FAX: (613) 726-1198
Comments: Classical music critic for the *Ottawa Citizen.*

Bill C. Smith

P.O. Box 335
West Hill, ON M1E 4R8
(416) 266-2152 (p.m. only)
Freelance: Yes.
Area of Expertise: Rock music, with specific expertise in 80s Rock, Alternative Rock and independents.
Language: English, French.
Comments: Smith is the publisher and author of *Heard It On The Radio* (1986), and publisher and co-author of *The Rock Music Handbook* (1988). He is a former campus radio station programmer and administrator.

Perry Stern

47 Jefferson Ave.
Toronto, ON M6K 1Y3
(416) 538-7500
FAX (416) 538-7503
Freelance: Yes.
Staff Writer: Yes.
Publication: *Music Express*.
Area of Expertise: Music.
Language: English.

Peter Stevens

167 Ferry St.
Windsor, ON N9A 4M5
(519) 256-5533
FAX (519) 255-5515
Freelance: Yes.
Publication: *Windsor Star*.
Area of Expertise: Jazz.
Language: English.

Hugo Trottier

3981 rue St. Laurent, Suite 715
Montreal, PQ H2W 1Y5
(514) 849-1236
FAX (514) 849-2076
Freelance: Yes.
Staff Writer: Yes.
Publications: *Radioactivite* (only French and English weekly trade publication).
Area of Expertise: Les pages jaunes de l'industrie (annual music business and services guide).
Comments: Also organizes panels and business seminars with simultaneous English translations.

Harry van Vugt

167 Ferry St.
Windsor, ON N9A 4M5
(519) 256-5533
FAX (519) 255-5778
Staff Writer: Yes.
Publication: *Windsor Star*.
Area of Expertise: Classical music critic, radio columnist.
Language: English, Dutch.
Comments: Mr. van Vugt is also entertainment editor of the *Windsor Star*.

Barry Yaffa

164 York Hill Blvd.
Thornhill, ON L4J 2P6
(416) 881-7927
Freelance: Yes.
Area of Expertise: Press releases, biographies, interviews.
Language: English.
Comments: Will write straight news, action, fact, travel, light satire, editorial, features and human interest pieces.

Alfred Whitehead Memorial Music Library

Mount Allison University
Sackville, NB E0A 3C0
(506) 364-2561
FAX (506) 364-2617

Book Holdings: 8,000 monographs, 75 periodical subscriptions, 1,300 bound periodicals.

Score, Sheet Music Holdings: 11,000 scores or books of music.

Record, Tape, Video Holdings: 6,000 LPs and 250 CD sound recordings, 112 reels of microfilm, 500-plus tapes, 3,287 microfiche (99 titles).

Comments: Subjects include music (theory, history, criticism, biography, musicology, music education). Special collections include 20th century Canadian music scores and recordings, and the Musical Canadiana Mary Mellish Collection of Folk Music. Publications include *Canadian Music Scores and Recordings* (Mount Allison University holdings) and *Sources in Canadian Music*.

Association of Canadian Orchestras Educational Resources Centre

56 The Esplanade, Suite 311
Toronto, ON M5E 1A7
(416) 366-8834
FAX (416) 364-3311

Book Holdings: Library consists of over 150 publications, as well as extensive files and recordings. Materials relate to general arts education as well as specific materials for orchestral education programs.

Record, Tape, Video Holdings: Large collection of children's recordings (primarily Canadian artists), and a collection of cassettes and videos pertaining to arts/music education and youth programming.

Comments: Established in 1984, the centre aids programmers, music directors and managers in planning more innovative orchestral education programs. The resource centre is not a lending library and research must be done at the ACO office. The centre is equipped with an excellent sound system for recordings and cassettes, as well as a FX4-VHS recorder.

MUSIC LIBRARIES

The Banff Centre Library

P.O. Box 1020
Banff, AB T0L 0C0
(403) 762-6265
Book Holdings: 17,000 books and 240 periodicals on the arts and related subjects.
Score, Sheet Music Holdings: 9,000 performance music scores and parts.
Record, Tape, Video Holdings: 6,000 recordings (records, CDs and cassettes), 450 video tapes on performance art, dance, jazz, music and music theatre.
Special Services: Listening facilities and video cassette players (VHS and 3/4").

Bibliotheque Municipale de Montreal

1210 Sherbrooke St. E.
Montreal, PQ H2L 1L9
Administration: 5500 Fullum St., Suite 300
Montreal, PQ H2G 2H3
(514) 872-5923 (main library)
(514) 872-1608 (administration)
FAX (514) 872-1626
Score, Sheet Music Holdings: Approximately 7,000 book titles and 80 periodical titles. Also has the Edouard-Zotique Massicotte Collection (82 books).
Record, Tape, Video Holdings: Over 70,000 tapes and 13,000 records.
Comments: The main library has an important collection of Canadiana and Laurentiana documents (Gagnon Collection).

Bibliotheque nationale du Quebec—Secteur des collections speciales, Section Musique

1700 rue St. Denis
Montreal, PQ H2X 3K6
(514) 873-4512
Book Holdings: 75,000 pieces of sheet music, 400 boxes of clippings.
Score, Sheet Music Holdings: 20,000 records (from Quebec 1900-1965).
Special Services: Music from Quebec, Canada and other countries.

Brandon University Music Library

270-18 St.
Brandon, MB R7A 6A9
(204) 727-9630
Booking Holdings: Approximately 10,000 music books and scores.
Record, Tape, Video Holdings: 3,200 records, 2,000 tapes and 400 CDs.
Special Services: Extensive collection in music theatre.

Calgary Public Library

616 MacLeod Tr. S.E.
Calgary, AB T2G 2M2
(403) 260-2600
FAX (403) 237-5393
Book Holdings: 5,000 circulating and 750 reference.
Score, Sheet Music Holdings: 4,500 (including some performing editions).
Record, Tape, Video Holdings: 90,000 LPs, cassettes, and CDs located in 16 libraries.

Cambrian College of Applied Arts & Technology

1400 Berrydowne Rd.
Sudbury, ON P3A 3V8
(705) 566-8101
Book Holdings: 700 general and reference works and over 20 current periodical subscriptions.
Score, Sheet Music Holdings: 900 scores.
Record, Tape, Video Holdings: Approximately 1,800 classical recordings and 40 videos.
Special Services: Apple computer programs.

Canadian Broadcasting Corporation Music and Record Libraries

P.O. Box 500, Stn. A
Toronto, ON M5W 1E6
(416) 975-5858 (music)
(416) 975-5900 (records)
Book Holdings: 1,500 books, 100 periodicals.
Score, Sheet Music Holdings: 200,000 popular song sheets, 5,000 scores (choral, orchestral, solo and chamber).
Record, Tape, Video Holdings: 200,000 LPs, 15,000 CDs (popular, classical, jazz, stage, film, ethnic, etc.), 8,000 Canadian content singles.
Comments: Circulation for CBC use only. Researchers by appointment.

Canadian Music Centre Library

20 St. Joseph St.
Toronto, ON M4Y 1J9
(416) 961-6601
FAX (416) 961-7198
Book Holdings: 100 monographs and 300 vertical files with biographical information, program notes, reviews and photographs. For reference only.
Score, Sheet Music Holdings: Free lending library of approximately 10,000 scores by Canadian composers.
Record, Tape, Video Holdings: 3,000 recordings for reference use only.
Special Services: Scores, recordings and manuscript paper available for purchase.
Comments: No-cost loans are available. Contact CMC in person or by mail or telephone.
Branches:
430 rue Saint-Pierre, Suite 300
Montreal, PQ H2Y 2M5
(514) 849-9175

Violet Archer Library
911 Library Tower
2500 University Dr. N.W.
Calgary, AB T2N 1N4
(403) 220-7403

2021 W. 4 Ave., Suite 200
Vancouver, BC V6J 1N3
(604) 734-4622

The Canadian National Institute for the Blind Music Library

1929 Bayview Ave.
Toronto, ON M4G 3E8
(416) 480-7546
FAX (416) 480-7700
Book Holdings: 200 printed titles for reference.
Score, Sheet Music Holdings: 18,000 braille music scores and a selection of taped lessons.
Special Services: Music archives and transcription services available. CNIB produces *Mouthpiece* magazine on tape.
Comments: Restricted to print-handicapped persons.

Centre de musique Canadienne

430 rue St. Pierre, Suite 300
Montreal, PQ H2Y 2M5
(514) 849-9176
Book Holdings: 260 books and 35 journals and magazines.
Score, Sheet Music Holdings: 10,000 scores.
Record, Tape, Video Holdings: 2,000 records and 3,000 cassettes.
Special Services: Tape duplication for study purposes only.
Comments: Scores are available for sale and rental (two months). Books, records and tapes cannot leave the library.

Carleton University

A911, Loeb
Ottawa, ON K1S 5B6
(613) 788-7400
Book Holdings: 2,800 books, 73 journals.
Record, Tape, Video Holdings: 13,000 audio cassettes, 35 video cassettes and 250 CDs.

Conservatoire de Musique de Montreal

100 rue Notre-Dame e.
Montreal, PQ H2Y 1C1
(514) 873-4031
Book Holdings: Approximately 54,000 books and journals, 12 microfilms.
Record, Tape, Video Holdings: Approximately 9,300 discs and 500 other audio/visual documents.
Special Services: Inter-library service.
Comments: Special collections: Emil Cooper, Jean Deslauriers, Arthur Garami.

Dalhousie University

Killiam Library, Special Collections
Halifax, NS B3H 3J5
(902) 424-3615
Book Holdings: Music journals.
Score, Sheet Music Holdings: 1,500 scores by 17th and 18th century composers.
Record, Tape, Video Holdings: 6,500 recordings.

Douglas College Library

700 Royal Ave.
New Westminster, BC V3L 5B2
(604) 520-5400
Book Holdings: Approximately 2,500 music books.
Special Services: Listening centre, video viewing room and use of rhythm tap machines.
Comments: The library has tape recorders and video equipment available for use.

835

Edmonton Public Library

7 Sir Winston Churchill Sq.
Edmonton, AB T6J 2V4
(403) 423-2331
Book Holdings: Housed in A/V department.
Record, Tape, Video Holdings: 60,000 records, 25,000 cassettes and 1,000 videos.

Grant MacEwan Community College

840

Jasper Place Campus
10045 156 St.
Edmonton, AB T5P 2P7
(403) 483-4415
Book Holdings: Approximately 1,800 book titles and 1,200 scores. Emphasis is on jazz, musical theatre, and popular music. Special collection (SUNWAPTA) of about 17,000 78s and LPs from the 1920-1950 era.
Record, Tape, Video Holdings: 2,300 cassettes, 300 CDs (music and sound effects), 100 video cassettes, computer software.
Special Services: Learner Centre with CML, A/V and computer hardware, including a Macintosh/synthesizer interface.

Hamilton Public Library

55 York Blvd.
Hamilton, ON L8R 3K1
(416) 529-8111
Book Holdings: 6,000 books on music.
Score, Sheet Music Holdings: 2,800 scores and performance parts.
Record, Tape, Video Holdings: 9,800 records, 4,500 cassettes.
Special Services: Audio listening centre and a practice studio with room for seven players.

Laurentian University

Tate Library
Sudbury, ON P3E 2C6
(705) 673-4126, ext. 30
Book Holdings: 3,250.
Score, Sheet Music Holdings: 750.
Record, Tape, Video Holdings: 3,000.
Special Services: An Otari high-speed audio cassette copier provides copies for in-library use only.
Comments: Books and scores available to Laurentian University students and through inter-library loan. Records, tapes and videos available for in-library use only.

The Leon & Thea Koener Music Library

Victoria Conservatory of Music
839 Academy Close
Victoria, BC V8V 2X8
(604) 386-5311
Book Holdings: 5,000.
Score, Sheet Music Holdings: 10,000.
Record, Tape, Video Holdings: 4,000.

McGill University

Marvin Duchow Music Library
555 Sherbrooke St. W.
Montreal, PQ H3A 1E3
(514) 398-4695
FAX (514) 398-8061
Book Holdings: 18,351.
Score, Sheet Music Holdings: 20,028.
Record, Tape, Video Holdings: 18,325.

McMaster University

Mills Memorial Library
1280 Main St. W.
Hamilton, ON L8S 4L6
(416) 525-9140, ext. 2069
Book Holdings: 10,000 monographs, 20,000 scores, 130 microfilm reels and 200 microfiche sheets. Special collections holdings include letters of Havergal Brian, Franz Liszt, Sir Charles H.H. Parry and Ethel Smyth; archives of Sir Robert Mayer, Herbert Menges and Klaus Pringsheim; opera collection of Eric Walter White; Dorothy Farquarson Collection of Musical Canadiana.
Record, Tape, Video Holdings: 21,000 record albums, 700 music cassettes, 500 spoken cassettes.
Comments: The library collection supports undergraduate courses in music education as well as graduate courses in musical criticism.

Metropolitan Toronto Reference Library, Arts Department

789 Yonge St.
Toronto, ON M4W 2G8
(416) 393-7077
FAX (416) 393-7229
Book Holdings: 16,000 volumes, approximately 180 magazine titles.
Score, Sheet Music Holdings: 43,000 items/volumes.
Record, Tape, Video Holdings: 24,000 recordings (vinyl and CDs).
Special Services: 30 listening carrels and two piano studios for trying out printed music. The library's clippings files include over 6,000 files on musicians and music subjects with Canadian emphasis.
Comments: A large part of the printed music collection circulates; other materials for in-library use only. Taping of recordings is not permitted. A retrospective collection of Canadian sheet music is indexed by six points of access.

Mississauga Public Library, Central Branch

110 Dundas St. W.
Mississauga, ON L5B 1H3
(416) 279-7002
Book Holdings: 1,600.
Score, Sheet Music Holdings: 150 miniature scores.
Record, Tape, Video Holdings: 15,000 audio tapes.
Special Services: Listening facilities.
Comments: Tapes circulate for three weeks and can be renewed once if not reserved. Reservations taken on classical titles.

National Library of Canada

395 Wellington St.
Ottawa, ON K1A 0N4
(613) 996-3377
FAX (613) 996-4424
Book Holdings: 18,500
Score, Sheet Music Holdings: 31,000 scores and 65,000 items of sheet music.
Record, Tape, Video Holdings: 113,000 sound recordings.
Special Services: Dubbings of sound recordings and photo reproductions of printed and manuscript material within terms of the copyright law and upon proof of clearance when required; maintenance of a Union Catalogue of Canadian Sheet Music Publications pre-1950; indexing of Canadian music periodicals.
Comments: The library specializes in Canadian music and music in Canada but also houses and maintains an extensive international collection of books, scores and periodicals. Goals are to support Canadian studies and to provide back-up services to other libraries and communities without music library services. Printed materials available through inter-library loan. Reference and consultation services by mail, telephone, electronic mail and in person.

Niagara Falls Public Library

4848 Victoria Ave.
Niagara Falls, ON L2E 4C5
(416) 356-8080
Record, Tape, Video Holdings: Approximately 3,100 records, 470 cassettes and 90 videos.

Queen's University

Music Library
Harrison-LeCaine Hall
Kingston, ON K7L 5C4
(613) 545-2839
Book Holdings: 110 current periodical subscriptions, 13,000 books, 13,000 scores and 150 titles on microfiche/microfilm. Also 2,000 performance scores and 1,500 chamber music titles.
Record, Tape, Video Holdings: 8,000 record albums and 400 tapes (cassettes and reel-to-reel).
Special Services: 25 listening stations and audio carrels.
Comments: Included in the university libraries' on-line catalog (GEAC). Separate computer listing of sound recordings. Recordings for in-library use only.

Saint John Regional Library

Audio Visual Department
1 Market Sq.
Saint John, NB E2L 4Z6
(506) 648-1191
Book Holdings: Yes.
Score, Sheet Music Holdings: No.
Record, Tape, Video Holdings: Vinyl and CDs.
Special Services: Loan of A/V equipment to non-profit community organizations.
Comments: This department also handles loans and bookings for the National Film Board of Canada.

Saskatoon Public Library

Fine & Performing Arts Department
311-23 St. E.
Saskatoon, SK S7K 0J6
(306) 975-7597
FAX (306) 975-7542
Book Holdings: 3,200 titles.
Score, Sheet Music Holdings: 750 titles.
Record, Tape, Video Holdings: 31,000 LPs, cassettes and CDs including music, spoken word and sound effects.
Special Services: Two listening stations.

Stratford Public Library

19 St. Andrew St.
Stratford, ON N5A 1A2
(519) 271-0220
FAX (519) 273-5041
Book Holdings: General.
Score, Sheet Music Holdings: Bound volumes of easy listening, big band, war music, musicals and rock.
Record, Tape, Video Holdings: Broad collection of LPs, CDs and spoken word tapes. Wide selection of film classics and "infotainment" videos.
Comments: Books circulate for three weeks. LPs circulate for three weeks, CDs and videos for one week.

University of Alberta

Music Resources Centre
Department of Music, 3-82 Fine Arts Building
Edmonton, AB T6G 2C9
(403) 432-5708
Book Holdings: 19,000 monographs and bound journals, 150 current journal subscriptions.
Score, Sheet Music Holdings: 26,000 volumes of music scores and 5,000 performance titles.
Record, Tape, Video Holdings: 10,000 items.

University of British Columbia

Wilson Recordings Collection
1958 Main Mall, UBC
Vancouver, BC V6T 1W5
(604) 228-2534
Book Holdings: None.
Score, Sheet Music Holdings: None.
Record, Tape, Video Holdings: 30,000 LPs, 5,000 CDs.
Comments: The collection, which has a yearly circulation of 85,000, contains mostly classical music with some spoken word recordings as well. Wheelchair access. Annual fee for borrowing.

University of Calgary

Music Library
2500 University Dr. N.W.
Calgary, AB T2N 1N4
(403) 220-6162
FAX (403) 282-6837
Book Holdings: 30,000 literature titles.
Score, Sheet Music Holdings: 30,000 scores.
Record, Tape, Video Holdings: 25,000 records, CDs and cassette tapes.
Special Services: Listening facilities for records, CDs and cassette tapes. Special collections include the Morris Surdin Collection of scores and scripts relating to the CBC drama series; *Lute Society of America* microfilm collection; *Canadian Folk Music Society Collection*; manuscript collections of contemporary Canadian composers.

Universite Laval Bibliotheque de musique

Pavillon Bonenfant
Quebec City, PQ G1K 7P4
(418) 656-7990
FAX (418) 651-3419
Book Holdings: 23,000 titles plus 7,000 microfilms on musicology, music education, music history, instrumental teaching and learning.
Score, Sheet Music Holdings: 29,000 scores and 2,000 sheets including standard repertory, 20th century music, early Canadian music and a collection of 144 pieces of printed music dating from before 1800 (mainly from France and England).
Record, Tape, Video Holdings: 14,300 LPs, 1,000 78s, 6,200 tapes, 600 CDs, 50 films and 75 videos.
Special Services: On-line CD-ROM reference service.
Comments: Inter-library loan. Special borrowing privileges available from choral/orchestral library located in the music department.
Contact: Music librarian, Claude Beaudry.

The University of Manitoba Libraries

223 School of Music, The University of Manitoba
Winnipeg, MB R3T 2N2
(204) 474-9567
FAX (204) 275-2597
Book Holdings: 17,500.
Score, Sheet Music Holdings: 31,800.
Record, Tape, Video Holdings: 950
audiotapes, 6,100 records and 160 videos.
Comments: Circulation (fiscal 1988/89) 46,792.

Universite de Montreal

Bibliotheque de musique
200 ave. Vincent D'Indy, P.O. Box 6128
Montreal, PQ H3C 3J7
(514) 343-6432
Book Holdings: 10,602 books, 444 periodicals,
10,679 microforms.
Score, Sheet Music Holdings: 23,255.
Record, Tape, Video Holdings: Approximate-
ly 13,000 tapes, CDs, records, slides and videos.
Comments: In-house listening facilities.

Universite du Quebec a Montreal, Bibliotheque de musique

P.O. Box 8889, Stn. A
Montreal, PQ H2L 4E7
(514) 987-3934
FAX (514) 987-4070
Book Holdings: Approximately 6,000 books
and 200 serial titles.
Score, Sheet Music Holdings: Approximately
14,000.
Record, Tape, Video Holdings: 10,000.
Special Services: Inter-library loan of
circulating materials. Holdings include CBC
Montreal's archival collection.
Comments: This library, although modest in
size, has some unusual strengths such as CBC
broadcast recordings, popular music, Brazilian
music, and books on music therapy.

University of Regina

Fine Arts Branch Library
Regina, SK S4S 0A2
(306) 779-4826
Book Holdings: 7,000.
Score, Sheet Music Holdings: 7,000.
Record, Tape, Video Holdings: 8,000.

University of Toronto

Edward Johnson Library
Toronto, ON M5S 1A1
(416) 978-3734
Book Holdings: 130,000 books, scores and
bound journals, 5,600 microforms.
Record, Tape, Video Holdings: 80,000 LPs,
85,000 78s and 3,500 tapes.

University of Victoria

Music and Audio Collection
McPherson Library
P.O. Box 1800
Victoria, BC V8W 3H5
(604) 721-8232
Book Holdings: 47,000 volumes of books and
music scores.
Record, Tape, Video Holdings: 33,000 LPs,
4,500 78s, 250 CDs and 3,000 tapes.
Special Services: In-house listening stations
and advisory services.

The University of Western Ontario

Music Library
London, ON N6A 3K7
(519) 679-2111, ext. 4850
Book Holdings: 34,000 books and periodical
volumes.
Score, Sheet Music Holdings: 62,000 scores
and parts, 5,500 choral, band, orchestral and
method book titles, 2,100 rare books and 8,900
microforms.
Record, Tape, Video Holdings: 29,000
sound recordings and CDs.
Special Services: Inter-library loan and special
borrowing privileges available from the choral/
band/orchestral library.
Comments: Special collections include: The
Opera Collection, comprised chiefly of rare manuscripts and first editions of operas composed
and/or printed between 1597 and 1900; The
Mahler-Rose Collection, containing letters, documents and related musical materials pertaining to
the life of Gustav Mahler and his nephew Alfred
Rose; The Matastasio Cumulation, consisting of
opera scores and librettos, chiefly on microfilm,
based on texts by Pietro Metastasio.
Contact: Librarian-in-charge, William Guthrie.

Vancouver Public Library

Fine Arts and Music Division
750 Burrard St.
Vancouver, BC V6Z 1X5
(604) 665-3591
Book Holdings: 16,000 books about music.
Score, Sheet Music Holdings: 2,000 scores,
2,500 sets of orchestra and chamber music parts
and 2,500 popular songbooks.
Record, Tape, Video Holdings: 200 video
cassettes, 500 audio cassettes.
Special Services: Extensive title index to
songs in collections.

Greater Victoria Public Library

735 Broughton St.
Victoria, BC V8W 3H2
(604) 382-7241
Book Holdings: 3,500 books.
Score, Sheet Music Holdings: 3,000 scores.
Record, Tape, Video Holdings: 9,000 records, 2,000 cassettes.

Westmount Public Library

4574 Sherbrooke St. W.
Montreal, PQ H3Z 1G1
(514) 935-8531 ext. 290
Book Holdings: 775 music books.
Score, Sheet Music Holdings: 950 scores.
Record, Tape, Video Holdings: 2,000 tapes.

Winnipeg Public Library

251 Donald St.
Winnipeg, MB R3C 3P5
(204) 986-6462 (business office)
FAX (204) 942-5671
Book Holdings: Circulating and reference books.
Score, Sheet Music Holdings: 1,200 volumes in system.
Record, Tape, Video Holdings:
Approximately 40,000 records, 12,000 tapes, 3,300 CDs and 4,500 video cassettes in the system.
Special Services: Talking books loaned to print-handicapped persons. Approximately 1,000 16mm films (rental of projectors available).
Comments: Three-day video loan period. Three-week loan period for all other materials.

York University

Scott Library Listening Room
409 Scott Library, 4700 Keele St.
Downsview, ON M3J 1P3
(416) 736-2100, ext. 8880
Book Holdings: 3,500 collected works and publishers' series study scores, 15 periodical titles and 700 discographies, dictionaries and encyclopediae.
Score, Sheet Music Holdings: 8,000 study and performance scores housed in main stacks.
Record, Tape, Video Holdings: 11,000 phonodisc volumes, 6,000 tapes and 50 CDs.
Special Services: Dubbing and group listening rooms for class use only.
Comments: Extended reference and course materials reservation available.

MUSIC MERCHANDISING

Anthem Merchandising
189 Carlton St.
Toronto, ON M5A 2K7
(416) 923-5855
FAX (416) 923-1041
Services Provided: Licensing.
Specialization: Rock artists.
Artists Represented: Rush, Gowan, Spoons.
Comments: International service.

Backstage Pass
37 Kodiak Cr.
Downsview, ON M3J 3E5
(416) 631-7743
FAX (416) 631-7745
Services Provided: Custom clothing, buttons, stickers and posters.
Specialization: Rock and Rap merchandising.
Artists Represented: New Kids on the Block, Paula Abdul, Depeche Mode.

Blue Live Merchandising
19 Hess St. S.
Hamilton, ON L8P 3M7
(416) 527-0552
FAX (416) 529-4006
Specialization: All styles of music.
Artists Represented: Gowan, Kim Mitchell, Lee Aaron
Comments: National

Canadian Graphics West Inc.
8285 Main St.
Vancouver, BC V5X 3L7
(604) 324-1246
FAX (604) 327-6379
Services Provided: Customized T-shirts and sweatshirts.

Capital Crest & Garments

1361 Powell St.
Vancouver, BC V5L 1G8
(604) 255-6588
FAX (604) 255-7625
Services Provided: Embroidery for garments and crests.
Artists Represented: *Molson Canadian Rocks* as well as various local bands.

Chesterfield Entertainment Corp.

2027 Dickson Rd.
Mississauga, ON L5B 1Y7
(416) 566-5865
FAX (416) 848-7718
Services Provided: Concert merchandising.
Specialization: Rock.
Artists Represented: Tom Cochrane and Red Rider, Bruce Cockburn.
Comments: National.

Contract Promotions

89 Reiner Rd.
Downsview, ON M3H 2L4
(416) 633-5780
Services Provided: Design and production of buttons, sets and point of purchase displays.

Custom Apparel & Promotions Ltd.

601 Magnetic Dr., Suite 34
Downsview, ON M3J 3J2
(416) 736-4166
FAX (416) 736-9991
Services Provided: Clothing with logos.
Artists Represented: Sabian, Warner/Chappell.
Comments: Tim Devries, account executive

Sandy Flett Unlimited

68 Water St., Suite 205
Vancouver, BC V6B 1A4
(604) 684-0165
FAX (604) 684-0165
Services Provided: Design of T-shirts, buttons, logos.
Specialization: Commercial artwork related to the entertainment industry.
Artists Represented: Bryan Adams, Trooper, Doug and the Slugs.

H.A.S. Novelties

545 King St. W.
Toronto, ON M5V 1M1
(416) 598-9757
Services Provided: Production of buttons, T-shirts, sweatshirts and calendars.
Specialization: International distribution.
Artists Represented: Ray Lyell and the Storm, Blue Rodeo, The Jeff Healey Band, Alannah Myles.

The Master's Collection

960 Gateway
Burlington, ON L7L 5K7
(416) 681-2760
FAX (416) 333-6684
Specialization: All types but specialize in Christian music.

Lorne Merkur & Sister Inc.

801 Eglinton Ave. W., Suite 404
Toronto, ON M5N 1E3
(416) 785-0777
FAX (416) 785-6016
Services Provided: Custom printing and embroidering for T-shirts, jackets, etc.
Specialization: Promotional textiles
Artists Represented: Messenjah, Hamilton Philharmonic, various ad agencies.

Non-Fiction Design Studios Inc.

136 Powell St.
Vancouver, BC V6A 1G1
(604) 684-9834
FAX (604) 684-1333
Services Provided: Design and silk screening of T-shirts.
Artists Represented: Doug and the Slugs, Young Guns.

PSST

75 Sherbourne St.
Toronto, ON M5A 2P9
(416) 365-7957
FAX (416) 365-7169
Services Provided: Screenprinting and promotional items.
Artists Represented: Skydiggers, Andrew Cash, Sacrifice.

Rock Merchandise Inc.

68 Water St., Suite 405
Vancouver, BC V6B 1A4
(604) 684-3926
FAX (604) 683-4298
Services Provided: Tour merchandising.
Artists Represented: Bryan Adams, Rock and
Hyde.

Arizona Jules Photography

70 Confederation Way
Thornhill, ON L3T 5R5
(416) 889-2707
Services Provided: Photography - anything but weddings, babies or prize winning dogs.
Clients: Canadian Children's Opera Chorus, Amadeus Choir, Perfect Strangers.

Ateliers Photographiques Artec

1798 ch. Galvin
Fleurimont, PQ J1G 3E9
(819) 569-4060
Services Provided: Design and photography for album jackets.
Specialization: Commercial photography, advertising.
Clients: Levis Bouliane, manager and producer for various artists.

Biserka

25 Liberty St., Studio 102
Toronto, ON M6K 1A6
(416) 537-7790
Services Provided: Photo sessions on location or in studio; band promo shots, parties, events, awards shows and concerts.
Specialization: Design and graphic work for album covers and posters. Specialize in air-brushing for backgrounds and colouring B&W photos.
Clients: *Metropolis, Music Scene, TV Guide.*

Joness Bowie

Main P.O. Box 4757
Vancouver, BC V6B 4A4
(604) 875-8300
Services Provided: Photos for record companies, album covers and band promotion. Location shoots, backstage and live in-concert photography.
Specialization: Music industry events and stills on movie and video sets.
Comments: Colour and B&W.

Ralph Brodie Photographics

1499 Queen St. W., Studio 304
Toronto, ON M6R 1A3
(416) 536-9463
Services Provided: Photography for bands, promo, album covers, etc.
Clients: Images in Vogue, Eros, Picture Comes to Life.

Douglas Buchan Photography

314 W. Pender St.
Vancouver, BC V6B 1T1
(604) 687-1933
Services Provided: Band promotions and some album covers.

Chris Buck

3 Belvedere Blvd.
Toronto, ON M8X 1J9
(416) 231-4337

Wolf Butz Photography

18 Croft St.
Toronto, ON M6K 2N7
(416) 254-3408
Services Provided: Music videos, concert stills and album covers. Also promotional events.
Specialization: Album cover photography.
Clients: Aquarius, WEA.

Canapress Photo Service

36 King St. E.
Toronto, ON M5C 2L9
(416) 364-0321
FAX (416) 364-9283
Services Provided: Concerts, promotional events and awards shows.
Clients: Juno Awards.

Mark Caporal

41 Valleybrook Dr.
Toronto, ON M3B 2S6
(416) 445-8700
Services Provided: B&W photography for trade papers.
Clients: Contributor to *Music Scene* magazine.

David Cooper Photography

1150 Homer St.
Vancouver, BC V6B 2X8
(604) 685-8715
Services Provided: Production stills and promotional portraits.
Specialization: The performing arts.
Clients: Shaw Festival, Ballet B.C., Vancouver New Music Society.

Country Image

5468 Dundas St. W., Suite 570
Toronto, ON M9B 6E3
(416) 626-0124
Services Provided: Promotional photography and in-concert stills.
Clients: *Country Music News*, International Fan Club Organization (IFCO), LinRon Productions.

FOTOWORK

11 Carlaw Ave., Unit 9
Toronto, ON M4M 2R6
(416) 465-6716
Services Provided: Publicity and album cover photography.
Comments: Jim Dawson, photographer.
Clients: Promotionally Yours, The Talent Group, *Western Report* magazine.

Galbraith Reproductions Ltd.

201 Dufferin St.
Toronto, ON M6K 1Y9
(416) 531-6913
FAX (416) 588-2289
Services Provided: Quality photo reproduction service. B&W and colour photographs duplicated in any quantity, fast and at a low cost per print.

Patrick Harbron Photography

366 Adelaide St. E., Suite 331
Toronto, ON M5A 3X9
(416) 462-0128
Services Provided: Album covers, promotions and motion pictures stills.

Inner Spirit Photography
711-84 Ave. S.W.
Calgary, AB T2V 0V8
(403) 252-2662
Services Provided: Photography service for musicians.
Clients: Tad Music, Raw Material, Jonathan Livingston.

K.W.O.I.
(Kamera Works On Ice)
474 Bathurst St., Suite 401
Toronto, ON M5T 2S6
(416) 924-4883
Services Provided: Experimental portraiture and conceptual illustrations.
Specialization: Manipulated photography.

Kevin Kelly Photography
89 McCaul St., Suite 922
Toronto, ON M5T 2X3
(416) 340-6377
Services Provided: Location, studio and concert photography in B&W or colour.
Clients: *Canadian Musician, Metropolis, Canadian Art.*

David Lee
16 Nesbitt Dr.
Toronto, ON M4W 2G3
(416) 921-3085
Services Provided: Music photography and concert photos, album jacket concept and photos, plus portraits, group photos and editorial photos.

John Loper
8 Ovendon Sq.
Toronto, ON M1S 2M5
(416) 292-3010
Services Provided: Event, performance, studio and location photography.
Specialization: Hand-colouring B&W images.
Clients: Jeff Healey Band, Forte Records, Smash.

Lu Taskey
Photographics
170 Martin Grove Rd.
Toronto, ON M9B 4L1
(416) 233-2323
Services Provided: Photojournalism, theatrical photography and special effects.
Specialization: Concert and promotional photography.
Clients: Magnetic North, Kayla Popp.

M&M Production Photography
272 Avenue Rd.
Toronto, ON M4V 2G7
(416) 927-8383
Specialization: Album covers and promotional photography.

O'Mara & Ryan Ltd.
2897 Bellevue Ave.
West Vancouver, BC V7V 1E7
(604) 926-9155
FAX (604) 926-9152
Services Provided: Complete marketing services including photography, graphic design and art direction, plus music video production and direction.
Specialization: Concepts for creative marketing in the music industry.
Comments: A full spectrum of creative and marketing services for music clients.
Clients: A&M Records, MCA Records, Bruce Allen Talent, S.L. Feldman & Associates.

John Ortner
Photography and Design
53 Regal Rd.
Toronto, ON M6H 2J6
(416) 656-6919
Services Provided: Creative photography, full design work to finished product.
Specialization: Portraiture.
Comments: Will work with band to build concept and create an image.
Clients: Ras Lee, S.P.I. Productions, *Metropolis* magazine.

Keith Penner
Photography
276 Carlaw Ave., Studio 302
Toronto, ON M4M 3L1
(416) 778-7763
Services Provided: Album photography and promo photos. Live, studio and on location.
Specialization: Solo artists.
Clients: Andy Warhol, George Olliver, Yuk Yuk Comedians.

Photo Works
222 The Esplanade, Suite 730
Toronto, ON M5A 4J6
(416) 361-0520
Services Provided: Studio or location promotional photos, concerts, album covers.
Clients: *Music Express, Campus Canada,* CITY-TV.

MUSIC FOR THE EYES...

KEVIN KELLY
PHOTOGRAPHY

(416) 340-6377, 89 McCAUL ST., SUITE 922, TORONTO, ONTARIO CANADA M5T 2X3

Plum Studios

1209 King St. W., Suite 210
Toronto, ON M6K 1G2
(416) 535-4484
Services Provided: Creative photography,
publicity stills and album design.

Pete Ryan Photographic Design

1 Atlantic Ave., Suite 204
Toronto, ON M6K 3E7
(416) 230-2552 (24 hour cellular)
FAX (416) 660-2492
Services Provided: Creative album design (on
location or in studio) and motion picture stills.
Specialization: All formats up to, and including,
8x10.
Clients: CBC, *Flare*, *Time-Life*.

Deborah Samuel Photography

104 Sumach St.
Toronto, ON M5A 3J9
(416) 359-0122
FAX (416) 359-0450
Services Provided: Album cover and
promotional photography.

Shutter Priority

(416) 287-0033
Services Provided: Album cover, promotional
and live photography.
Clients: BMG, Norris Publications, Risque
Disque, Current Records.

Cliff Spicer Photography

104 Portsdown Rd.
Scarborough, ON M1P 1V5
(416) 752-0640

Helen Stokell Photography

2250 Lawrence Ave. E., Apt. G1
Scarborough, ON M1P 2R1
(416) 757-9074
Services Provided: Live and promotional
photography done on location.
Specialization: Hand-coloured B&W prints
Clients: Dorian Gray, Mark Kelso, Norris
Publications.

Paul Till, Photographer

680 Queen's Quay W., Suite 521
Toronto, ON M5V 2Y9
(416) 595-5085
Services Provided: Manipulated photography,
hand-colouring and solarization.
Specialization: Live concert photography
Clients: *NOW* magazine, Maja Bannerman,
Nash the Slash

Umbrella Communications

90 Northline Rd.
Toronto, ON M4B 3E8
(416) 288-8739
FAX (416) 759-5007
Services Provided: Concert stills, album
covers and musical equipment.
Clients: AMI, Sony.

MUSIC PUBLICATIONS

AMI

18 Basaltic Rd., 2nd Floor
Concord, ON L4K 1G6
(416) 660-3753
FAX (416) 660-3741
Type of Publication: Music Industry Directory.
Content: Entertainment industry listings and information.
Music Coverage: 90%.
Frequency: Twice annually.
Distribution: National.
Publisher: Shelagh Rogers.
Editor: Jim Samson.

A l'Ecoute

4545 Pierre-de-Coubertin
Montreal, PQ H1V 3R2
(514) 252-3020
FAX (514) 251-8038
Type of Publication: Newsletter.
Content: Articles on concerts, workshops, activities, score reviews etc.
Music Coverage: 100%.
Frequency: Quarterly.
Circulation: 7,000.
Annual Subscription: $20.
Distribution: National.
Publisher: Alliance des Chorales du Quebec.
Comments: Distributed free of charge to the members of the alliance.

243

Arts Bulletin

189 Laurier Ave. E.
Ottawa, ON K1N 6P1
(613) 238-3561
FAX (613) 238-4849
Type of Publication: Newsletter.
Content: Information on current issues of interest to artists.
Frequency: Quarterly.
Circulation: 1,500 (to CCA members).
Annual Subscription: $25.
Distribution: National.
Publisher: The Canadian Conference of the Arts.
Editor: Director of Communications.

B.C. Music Educator

c/o B.C. Music Teachers' Federation
2235 Burrard St.
Vancouver, BC V6J 3H9
Type of Publication: Journal for music educators.
Content: Scholarly articles and commentary on music education in British Columbia.
Frequency: One-three issues per school year.
Circulation: 650.
Annual Subscription: $20 (members).
Distribution: Regional (British Columbia).
Publisher: B.C. Teachers' Federation.

Bravo!

30 St. Clair Ave. W.
Toronto, ON M4V 1L6
(416) 926-7595
FAX (416) 926-0407
Type of Publication: Program.
Content: Specifically relates to shows at Roy Thomson Hall and Massey Hall and features profiles of performing artists.
Frequency: Bi-monthly.
Circulation: One million per year.
Annual Subscription: $15.
Distribution: Regional.
Publisher: National Theatre Publications Ltd.
Editor: Laurie Payne.

CAML Newsletter/ ACBM Nouvelles

c/o Music Division, National Library of Canada
Ottawa, ON K1A 0N4
(613) 996-7510
Type of Publication: Newsletter.
Content: Articles, association news, conference reports, plus book, music and record reviews.
Frequency: Three times per year.
Circulation: 200 (approximately).
Annual Subscription: Varies, includes membership fee.
Distribution: National.
Publisher: Canadian Association of Music Libraries.
Editor: Kathleen McMorrow, Edward Johnson Music Library, University of Toronto.

CARAS News

124 Merton St., 3rd Floor
Toronto, ON
(416) 485-3135
FAX (416) 485-4978
Type of Publication: Newsletter.
Content: Juno news, plus aspects of the Canadian music industry.
Frequency: Quarterly.
Circulation: 1,300.
Annual Subscription: Free to members.
Distribution: National.
Publisher: Canadian Academy of Recording Arts and Sciences.
Editor: Maureen Littlejohn.

C.B.A. Newsletter
(Ontario)
21 Tecumseh St.
Brantford, ON N3S 2B3
(519) 753-1858
Type of Publication: Newsletter.
Content: General information concerning bands, band music, personalities and advertising.
Music Coverage: 75%.
Frequency: Quarterly.
Circulation: 135.
Annual Subscription: $25 (includes membership fee), $50 (for commercial members).
Distribution: Regional (Ontario).
Publisher: The Canadian Band Association (Ontario) Incorporated.
Editor: Frank McKinnon.

Campus Canada

287 MacPherson Ave.
Toronto, ON M4V 1A4
(416) 928-2909
FAX (416) 928-1357
Type of Publication: Campus publication.
Content: Information for and about university and college people.
Frequency: Four times, September to May.
Circulation: 50,000.
Annual Subscription: $5.
Distribution: National.
Publisher: Kim Locke.
Editor: Alison Broddle.

Canadian Band Journal

P.O. Box 5005
Red Deer, AB T4N 5H5
(403) 342-3216
Type of Publication: Professional journal.
Content: Articles and news items.
Music Coverage: 100%.
Frequency: Quarterly.
Circulation: 3,500.
Annual Subscription: $15.
Distribution: National.
Publisher: Unison.
Editor: K. Mann.

Canadian Composer/ Compositeur Canadien

41 Valleybrook Dr.
Don Mills, ON M3H 2S6
(416) 925-5138
Type of Publication: Trade magazine.
Content: Music industry news, composer profiles and notes promoting the activities of SOCAN members.
Music Coverage: 100%.
Frequency: Quarterly.
Annual Subscription: $10.
Distribution: National, international.
Publisher: SOCAN.
Editor: Richard Flohil.

Candian Folk Music Journal/Revue de Musique Folklore Canadienne

Canadian Folk Music Society
P.O. Box 4232, Stn. C
Calgary, AB T2N 5N1
Type of Publication: Educational.
Content: Articles on Canadian folk music.
Frequency: Annual.
Circulation: 500.
Annual Subscription: $15 individual, $20 institutions. Includes membership fees.
Distribution: National.
Publisher: Canadian Folk Music Society.
Editor: Edith Fowke.

Canadian Music Trade

3284 Yonge St.
Toronto, ON M4N 3M7
(416) 485-8284
FAX (416) 485-8924
Type of Publication: Trade magazine.
Content: News and features of interest to Canadian retailers of musical instruments, sound equipment, related products and accessories.
Music Coverage: 100%.
Frequency: Bi-monthly.
Distribution: National.
Publisher: Jim Norris, Norris Publications.
Editor: David Henman.

Canadian Musician

3284 Yonge St.
Toronto, ON M4N 3M7
(416) 485-8284
FAX (416) 485-8924
Type of Publication: Consumer magazine.
Content: Features, departments and columns on musicians, equipment, technique and other articles of interest to Canadian musicians.
Music Coverage: 100%.
Frequency: Bi-monthly.
Distribution: National.
Publisher: Jim Norris, Norris Publications.
Editor: David Henman.

Canadian Opera Company News

227 Front St. E.
Toronto, ON M5A 1E8
(416) 363-6671
FAX (416) 363-5584
Type of Publication: Newsletter.
Content: Upcoming COC productions and other COC events.
Music Coverage: 40%.
Frequency: Three times a year.
Circulation: 14,000.
Annual Subscription: $35 (membership in COC "Friends").
Distribution: National.
Publisher: Canadian Opera Company.
Editor: Colin Eatock.

Cheer Sheet

59 Chester Hill Rd.
Toronto, ON M4K 1X4
(416) 463-8880
Type of Publication: Newsletter.
Content: Dance music tip sheet containing charts, reviews and events.
Music Coverage: 100%.
Frequency: Weekly.
Circulation: 2,500.
Annual Subscription: $12.
Distribution: National.
Publisher: Val Caudeiron.
Editor: Daniel Caudeiron.

Coda Magazine

P.O. Box 87, Stn. J
Toronto, ON M4J 4X8
(416) 593-7230
Type of Publication: Consumer magazine.
Content: Jazz and improvised music.
Music Coverage: 100%.
Frequency: Bi-monthly.
Circulation: 4,000.
Annual Subscription: $18.
Distribution: International.
Publisher: William E. Smith and John Norris.
Editor: William E. Smith.

Country

160 Eastbourne Ave.
Toronto, ON M5P 2G6
(416) 485-6205
Type of Publication: Consumer magazine.
Content: Feature stories, columns and reviews.
Music Coverage: 100%.
Frequency: Bi-monthly.
Circulation: 5,000.
Annual Subscription: $12.
Distribution: National.
Publisher: Jim Baine.
Editor: Jim Baine.

Country Music News

P.O. Box 7323, Vanier Terminal
Ottawa, ON K1L 8E4
(613) 745-6006
Type of Publication: Consumer and trade magazine.
Content: Coast-to-coast coverage of Canada's country music scene, including record reviews, hit charts and hundreds of photos.
Music Coverage: 100%.
Frequency: Monthly.
Circulation: 4,000.
Annual Subscription: $18.
Distribution: National.
Publisher: Larry Delaney.
Editor: Larry Delaney.

Crescendo

101 Thorncliffe Park Dr.
Toronto, ON M4H 1M2
(416) 421-1020
FAX (416) 421-7011
Type of Publication: Association magazine.
Content: Reports on negotiated agreements, meetings, claims and disputes actioned by the association, plus articles of interest to musicians. Directory of live music - listing of musicians, groups and their specialties.
Frequency: Bi-monthly.

Directory of Canadian Orchestras and Youth Orchestras

56 The Esplanade, Suite 311
Toronto, ON M5E 1A7
(416) 366-8834
Type of Publication: Directory.
Content: Comprehensive information about Canadian orchestras.
Music Coverage: 100%.
Frequency: Annual.
Annual Subscription: $10.
Distribution: National.
Publisher: Association of Canadian Orchestras/ Ontario Federation of Symphony Orchestras.
Editor: Madeleine Fiala.

Directory of the Arts

189 Laurier Ave. E.
Ottawa, ON K1N 6P1
(613) 238-3561
FAX (613) 238-4849
Type of Publication: Music industry directory.
Content: Listings of national arts associations.
Frequency: Annually.
Annual Subscription: $15 (for non-members).
Distribution: National.
Publisher: Canadian Conference of the Arts Publications.
Editor: Carol Villeneuve.

Discorder Magazine

c/o CITR-FM,
University of British Columbia Radio
6138 SUB Blvd.
Vancouver, BC V6T 2A5
(604) 228-3017
Type of Publication: Campus publication.
Content: Alternative local music and arts scene.
Music Coverage: 80%.
Frequency: Monthly.
Circulation: 17,500.
Annual Subscription: $12.
Distribution: Local (Vancouver and area).

Edition Sonances

857 ave. du Chanoine-Martin
Ste. Foy, PQ G1V 3P6
(418) 651-1967
Type of Publication: Consumer magazine.
Content: French-language music magazine devoted to serious music.
Music Coverage: 100%.
Frequency: Quarterly.
Distribution: Regional (Quebec).

Ensemble

Faculty of Music, University of Western Ontario
London, ON N6A 3K7
(519) 661-3767
FAX (519) 661-3292
Type of Publication: Newsletter.
Content: Alumni News.
Music Coverage: 100%.
Frequency: Semi-annual.
Circulation: 3,000.
Annual Subscription: Free to alumni.
Distribution: International.
Publisher: J.L. Stokes.
Editor: Peter Somerville.

Fan Club

P.O. Box 400, Nun's Island Station
Verdun, PQ H3E 1K1
(514) 762-9272
Type of Publication: Consumer magazine.
Content: Music.
Music Coverage: 80%.
Frequency: Monthly.
Circulation: 85,000.
Annual Subscription: $20.
Distribution: National.
Publisher: Magazine Fan Club Inc.
Editor: Pierre Tremblay.

Forte

305 ave. Mont-Royal e.
Montreal, PQ H2T 1P8
(514) 845-4108
FAX (514) 845-8241
Type of Publication: Consumer magazine.
Content: Updates on musical events associated with youth and music organizations around the world.
Frequency: Quarterly.
Circulation: 5,000.
Distribution: International.
Editor: By committee.

Frame by Frame

92 Sumach St.
Toronto, ON M5A 3J9
(416) 862-7766
FAX (416) 862-2375
Type of Publication: Directory.
Content: Audio-video guide for Ontario.
Music Coverage: 20%.
Frequency: Annual.
Distribution: Regional (Ontario).
Publisher: Frame by Frame Publications.

Georgia Straight

1235 W. Pender St.
Vancouver, BC V6E 2V6
(604) 681-2000
FAX (604) 681-0272
Type of Publication: Consumer magazine.
Content: Entertainment guide.
Music Coverage: 15%.
Frequency: Weekly.
Annual Subscription: $25.
Distribution: Regional (Vancouver and area).
Publisher: Dan McLeod.
Editors: Dan McLeod, Charles Campbell.

Gerrmail

363 Adelaide St. E.
Toronto, ON M5A 1N3
(416) 868-0528
Type of Publication: Newsletter.
Content: Product news.
Music Coverage: 100%.
Annual Subscription: Free.
Publisher: Gerr Electro-Acoustics.

I.C.E. Magazine

103 Church St., Suite 202
Toronto, ON M5C 2G3
(416) 363-7118
FAX (416) 363-0816
Type of Publication: Consumer magazine.
Content: Champions of Canada's unexplored cosmopolitan character.
Music Coverage: 30%.
Frequency: 10 times a year.
Circulation: 30,000.
Annual Subscription: Free in Toronto, $1.75 in other major cities.
Distribution: National.
Publisher: John Katsouras.
Editor: Laura MacDonald.

Impulse

16 Skaey Lane
Toronto, ON M6J 3F4
(416) 537-9551
Type of Publication: Consumer magazine.
Content: Arts and culture, architecture, music, politics and art technology.
Frequency: Quarterly.
Circulation: 5,000.
Annual Subscription: $24-36.
Distribution: International.
Editor: Eldon Garnet, Peter Day.

Inside Tracks

93 Goulding Ave.
North York, ON M2M 1L3
(416) 229-9213
Type of Publication: Aimed at musicians with some consumer features.
Content: News and views for the Toronto musician.
Music Coverage: 100%.
Frequency: Monthly.
Circulation: 3,500.
Annual Subscription: $25.
Distribution: Regional (Metro Toronto).
Publisher: Stephen L. Hubbard.
Editor: Stephen L. Hubbard.
Comments: Inside Tracks' mandate is to cover the issues that affect the Toronto music industry—particularly those which impact on musicians—as well as events and developments in the Toronto Music scene. Also profiles of alternative and up-and-coming artists.

THE Magazine

593 Yonge St.
Toronto, ON M4Y 1Z4
(416) 964-8700
FAX (416) 964-8403
Type of Publication: Consumer magazine.
Contents: Popular music features.
Music Coverage: 100%.
Frequency: Bi-monthly.
Circulation: 25,000.
Annual Subscription: $15.
Distribution: National.
Publisher: Buy & Sell Newspaper Ltd.
Editor: Rob Stewart.
Comments: Looking for North American circulation in excess of 100,000 copies.

The Jazz Report

22 Helena Ave.
Toronto, ON M6G 2H2
(416) 656-7366
FAX (416) 651-0142
Content: Jazz magazine covering national and international improvisational music. Includes interviews, profiles, record reviews, top 30, new releases, club listings, radio listings and more.
Editor: Greg Sutherland
Comments: Written by musicians for musicians.

Juno Awards Program

333 King St. E.
Toronto, ON M5A 3X5
(416) 947-3212
Type of Publications: Awards program.
Content: Profiles, industry news features, listings of past winners and current nominees.
Music Coverage: 100%.
Frequency: Annual.
Distribution: National.
Publisher: Sun Controlled Ventures Inc.
Editor: David Henman.
Comments: Production by Norris Publications.

Live! le Journal Rock

P.O. Box 281, Laval des Rapides
Laval, PQ H7N 4Z9
(514) 687-1428
Type of Publication: Consumer magazine.
Content: Interviews, articles, profiles on national and international rock bands.
Music Coverage: 98%.
Frequency: Every three weeks.
Circulation: 25,000.
Annual Subscription: $14.
Distribution: Regional (Eastern Canada).
Publisher: Publications Arc en Ciel.
Editor: Marie-France Remillard.

M.E.A.T

P.O. Box 35, Stn. O
Toronto, ON M4A 2M8
(416) 699-8486
Type of Publication: Consumer magazine.
Content: Stories and interviews with local and international metal artists.
Music Coverage: 100%.
Frequency: Monthly.
Circulation: 20,000.
Annual Subscription: $12.
Distribution: National.
Publisher: M.E.A.T Communications Inc.
Editor: Drew Masters.
Comments: M.E.A.T stands for Metal Events Around Toronto.

Metropolis

355 Adelaide St. W., 2nd Floor
Toronto, ON M5V 1S2
(416) 971-6614
FAX (416) 971-6660
Type of Publication: Consumer magazine.
Content: Arts and entertainment listings.
Frequency: Weekly.
Circulation: 150,000.
Annual Subscription: $30.
Distribution: Local (Toronto and area).
Publisher: Richard E. Rotman.
Editor: Richard E. Rotman.

Monday Magazine

1609 Blanchard
Victoria, BC V8W 2J5
(604) 382-6188
FAX (604) 381-2662
Type of Publication: Consumer magazine.
Content: Arts and entertainment, urban social
comment and local alternative news.
Music Coverage: 10%.
Frequency: Weekly.
Circulation: 65,000.
Annual Subscription: $30.
Distribution: National.
Publisher: Andrew Lynch.
Editor: Sid Tafler.

Montreal Mirror

400 McGill St., 2nd Floor
Montreal, PQ H2Y 2G1
(514) 393-1010
Type of Publication: Consumer magazine.
Content: Emphasis on local alternative music
and cultural news.
Frequency: Weekly.
Circulation: 50,000.
Annual Subscription: $30-60.
Publishers: Eyal Kattan, Catherine Salisbury.
Editors: Brendan Weston, Marian MacNair.

Music Directory Canada

3284 Yonge St.
Toronto, ON M4N 3M7
(416) 485-1049
FAX (416) 485-8924
Type of Publication: Music directory.
Content: Comprehensive listings of individuals,
companies and organizations involved in the
Canadian music scene.
Music Coverage: 100%.
Frequency: Bi-annual.
Distribution: National.
Publisher: Jim Norris, CM Books.
Editors: Richard Allen, Andy Charron.

Music Express

47 Jefferson Ave.
Toronto, ON M6K 1Y3
(416) 538-7500
FAX (416) 538-7503
Type of Publication: Consumer magazine.
Content: Pop, contemporary rock, movies and
videos.
Music Coverage: 80%.
Frequency: Monthly.
Annual Subscription: $15.50.
Distribution: North America.
Publisher: Keith Sharp, Rock Express
Communications Inc.
Editor: Perry Stern.

Music McGill

555 rue Sherbrooke o.
Montreal, PQ H3A 1E3
(514) 398-4535
FAX (514) 398-8061
Type of Publication: Newsletter.
Music Coverage: 100%.
Frequency: Summer, fall, winter.
Annual Subscription: Free.
Distribution: Local.
Publisher: Independent.
Editors: Nathalie Boivert, Richard Nantel, Sheila
Miller.
Comments: Music McGill is circulated to
university staff, students and alumni.

Musicworks: The Canadian Journal of Sound Explorations

1087 Queen St. W.
Toronto, ON M6J 1H3
(416) 533-0192
Type of Publication: Consumer magazine.
Content: Electronic, improvised and
contemporary classical musics, native and
ancient musics, audio art, sound sculpture, music
for original instruments, jazz, liturgical music.
Music Coverage: 100%.
Frequency: Three times a year.
Circulation: 1,300.
Annual Subscription: $12 magazine only, $26
magazine and cassette.
Distribution: National and international.
Publisher: CCMC Music Gallery.
Editors: Gayle Young, Lauren Pratt.
Comments: Journal welcomes queries and proposals from composers and other artists working
with sound. Proposals can include both written
and audio material, as each issue is published
with an accompanying cassette.

NETWORK Magazine

287 MacPherson Ave.
Toronto, ON M4V 1A4
(416) 928-2909
FAX (416) 928-1357
Type of Publication: Consumer magazine.
Content: Music and entertainment.
Music Coverage: 80%.
Frequency: Six times a year.
Circulation: 150,000.
Annual Subscription: $9.
Distribution: National.
Publisher: Harvey Wolfe, Canadian Controlled
Media Communications.
Editor: Maureen Littlejohn.

The Newfoundland Herald

P.O. Box 2015
St. John's, NF A1C 5R7
(709) 726-7060
FAX (709) 726-8227
Type of Publication: Consumer magazine.
Content: Entertainment information and reviews.
Frequency: Weekly.
Circulation: 45,000.
Annual Subscription: $39 (in Newfoundland).
Distribution: Regional (Newfoundland).
Publisher: G.W. Stirling.
Editor: Carina Thomas-Pilgrim.

Nite Moves

109 Carrall St., Suite 201
Vancouver, BC V6B 2H9
(604) 688-4610
Type of Publication: Consumer magazine.
Content: Entertainment music publication.
Music Coverage: 90%.
Frequency: Monthly.
Circulation: 35,000.
Annual Subscription: $14.
Distribution: Regional (Vancouver, Victoria).
Publishers: Dave Bryant, Stephen Bennett.
Editor: Bob Colebrook.

NOW

150 Danforth Ave.
Toronto, ON M4K 1N1
(416) 461-0871
FAX (416) 461-2886
Type of Publication: Consumer magazine.
Content: Alternative newsweekly.
Frequency: Weekly.
Circulation: 75,000.
Annual Subscription: $39.
Distribution: Local (Toronto).
Publisher: NOW Communications Inc.
Editors: Alice Klein, Michael Hollett.

Opera Canada

366 Adelaide St. E., Suite 433
Toronto, ON M5A 3X9
(416) 363-0395
FAX (416) 361-6337
Type of Publication: Consumer magazine.
Content: Articles on opera, reviews and calendar listing of opera performances.
Frequency: Quarterly.
Circulation: 8,000.
Annual Subscription: $14.
Distribution: International.
Publisher: Foundation for Coast to Coast Opera Publication.
Editor: Harvey Chusid.

Orchestra Canada

56 The Esplanade, Suite 311
Toronto, ON M5E 1A7
(416) 366-8834
Type of Publication: Newsletter.
Content: Government information, Canadian music, concerts and orchestra-related news.
Frequency: 10 times a year.
Circulation: 3,000.
Annual Subscription: $10.
Distribution: National.
Publisher: Association of Canadian Orchestras.
Editor: Jack Edds.

Playback

111 Queen St. E., Suite 330
Toronto, ON M5C 1S2
(416) 366-2300
FAX (416) 366-3581
Type of Publication: Trade magazine.
Content: Production news relating to film and broadcast industries.
Music Coverage: 5%.
Frequency: Bi-weekly.
Circulation: 15,000.
Annual Subscription: $42.
Distribution: National.
Publisher: James Shenkman.
Editor: Mark Smyka.
Associate Editor: Siobhan Grennan.

Pop Rock

3646 St. Germain
Montreal, PQ H1W 2V5
(514) 521-3262
Content: Information covering music shows, interviews and calendar of pop and rock events.
Frequency: Monthly.
Circulation: 18,000.
Annual Subscription: $16.
Distribution: Regional (Quebec).
Publisher: Ultra Monde.
Editor: Geo Giguere.

Probe/Le Milieu

41 Valleybrook Dr.
Don Mills, ON M3B 2S6
(416) 925-5138
Type of Publication: Monthly trade newsletter reporting on SOCAN news and music industry topics of interest to composers and music publishers.
Distribution: National, international.
Publisher: Society of Composers, Authors and Music Publishers of Canada (SOCAN).
Editor: Richard Flohil.

Professional Sound

3284 Yonge St.
Toronto, ON M4N 3M7
(416) 485-8284
FAX (416) 485-8924
Type of Publication: Trade magazine for the professional sound industry.
Distribution: National industry.
Publisher: Norris Publications.

Qui Fait Quoi

1276 Amherst
Montreal, PQ H2L 3K8
(514) 842-5333
FAX (514) 842-6717
Type of Publication: Consumer magazine.
Content: Quebec music industry "who's who."
Frequency: Monthly.
Circulation: 10,000.
Annual Subscription: $48.
Distribution: Regional (Quebec).
Publisher: Claude Desjardins.
Editor: Emilie Devienne.

RPM Weekly

6 Brentcliffe Rd.
Toronto, ON M4G 3Y2
(416) 425-0257
FAX (416) 425-8629
Type of Publication: Trade Magazine.
Content: Record charts and industry news.
Frequency: Weekly.
Annual Subscription: $176.
Distribution: National.
Publisher: Walter Grealis.
Editor: Walter Grealis.

Radio Activite Plus

3981 boul. St. Laurent, Suite 715
Montreal, PQ H2W 1Y5
(514) 849-1236
FAX (514) 849-2678
Type of Publication: Trade magazine.
Content: Charts and music news.
Music Coverage: 100%.
Frequency: Weekly.
Circulation: 500.
Annual Subscription: $300.
Distribution: International.
Publisher: Luc Martel.
Editor: Hugo Trottier.
Comments: The only French publication of its kind in North America.

Radio Guide

1040 W. Georgia, Suite 450
Vancouver, BC V6E 4H1
(604) 688-0382
FAX (604) 688-3105
Type of Publication: Consumer magazine.
Content: CBC Radio and CBC Stereo program listings plus feature articles.
Music Coverage: 50%.
Frequency: Monthly.
Circulation: 37,000.
Annual Subscription: $23.95.
Distribution: National.
Publisher: Core Group Publishing.
Editor: Catherine Robertson.

The Record

P.O. Box 201, Stn. M
Toronto, ON M6S 4T3
(416) 533-9417
FAX (416) 533-0367
Type of Publication: Trade magazine.
Content: Charts and sales information pertaining to record sales and airplay.
Music Coverage: 100%.
Frequency: Weekly.
Annual Subscription: $200.
Distribution: National.
Publisher: David Farrell & Associates.
Editor: David Farrell.

Reel West Digest

811 Beach Ave., Suite 310
Vancouver, BC V6Z 2B5
(604) 669-4797
Type of Publication: Directory.
Content: Companies and services in the audio-video industry in Western Canada.
Music Coverage: 20%.
Distribution: Regional (Western Canada).
Publisher: Reel West Productions Inc.

Sound & Vision

250 The Esplanade, Suite 500
Toronto, ON M5A 1J2
(416) 365-9366
FAX (416) 365-7235
Type of Publication: Consumer magazine.
Content: Hi-Fi and video technology, CD, LP and video reviews, "techie" features and product test reports.
Music Coverage: 20%.
Frequency: six times annually.
Circulation: 45,000.
Annual Subscription: $15.95.
Distribution: National.
Publisher: Michael Briant.
Editor: Alan Lofft.
Comments: Canada's Electronic Entertainment Magazine.

MUSIC PUBLICATIONS

Streetsound Magazine

427 Yonge St.
Toronto, ON M4S 1T4
(416) 597-0873
FAX (416) 597-3896
Type of Publication: Consumer magazine.
Content: Charts, articles and record reviews plus classifieds. Focus on international dance music.
Music Coverage: 100%.
Frequency: Monthly.
Circulation: Unavailable.
Annual Subscription: $20.
Distribution: National.
Publisher: Sepehr Azari.
Editor: Mike Mannix.

Toronto Arts Awards Program

3284 Yonge St.
Toronto, ON M4N 3M7
(416) 485-8284
FAX (416) 485-8924
Type of Publication: Program.
Content: List of past award recipients, current nominees and Toronto Arts Awards personnel.
Music Coverage: 20%.
Frequency: Annual.
Distribution: Local (Toronto).
Publisher: Jim Norris, Norris Publications.
Editor: David Henman.

Toronto Hot Spots Magazine

4091 Pheasant Run
Mississauga, ON L5L 2C2
(416) 820-6400
FAX (416) 820-9512
Type of Publication: Consumer magazine.
Content: Features on nightlife and nightclub activities. Guide to clubs in greater Toronto.
Music Coverage: 10%.
Frequency: Quarterly.
Circulation: 30,000.
Annual Subscription: $10.
Distribution: Regional (Southern Ontario); Local (greater Toronto).
Publisher: JCO Communications Inc.
Editor: Joey Cee.
Comments: Also distributed to the nightclub trade.

Toronto Music Awards Program

3284 Yonge St.
Toronto, ON M4N 3M7
(416) 485-8284
FAX (416) 485-8924
Type of Publication: Program.
Content: List of past award recipients, current nominees plus articles and features.
Music Coverage: 100%.
Frequency: Annual.
Distribution: Local (Toronto).
Publisher: Jim Norris, Norris Publications.
Editor: David Henman.

Toronto Programmers' Association

(T.O.P.A.) Newsletter
465 King St. E., Unit 11
Toronto, ON M5A 1L6
(416) 366-7093
Type of Publication: Newsletter.
Content: Dance charts, events and dance club news.
Frequency: Bi-monthly.
Circulation: 2,000.
Annual Subscription: $25.
Distribution: Regional (Ontario).
Publisher: Randy Brill.
Editor: Randy Brill.

Trans FM

c/o CKCV-FM
Carleton University
5th Floor Unicentre
Ottawa, ON K1S 5B6
(613) 788-2898
Type of Publication: Radio station program guide.
Content: Program listings, features, profiles, interviews and columns.
Music Coverage: 70%.
Frequency: 10 times a year.
Circulation: 8,000.
Annual Subscription: $25.
Distribution: Local (Ottawa).
Publisher: Radio Carleton Inc.

MUSIC PUBLICATIONS

Vox Magazine

127C MacEwan Hall, University of Calgary
Calgary, AB T2N 1N4
(403) 220-3904
Content: Alternative arts and music news.
Music Coverage: 80%.
Frequency: Monthly.
Circulation: 18,000.
Annual Subscription: $20.
Distribution: National, Regional (Alberta), Local (Calgary).
Publisher: University of Calgary Studio Radio Society, CJSW.
Editor: Lee G. Hill.
Comments: Distributed free of charge in Calgary.

What's On/ Voici Ottawa-Hull

400 Cumberland St.
Ottawa, ON K1N 8X3
(613) 238-4736
FAX (613) 238-3281
Type of Publication: Consumer magazine.
Content: Listings of major events and tour information.
Frequency: Monthly.
Circulation: 30,000.
Annual Subscription: $15.
Publisher: Capitol Guide Publishers.
Editor: Marc Shoma.
Comments: Controlled circulation to major hotels in the city.

MUSIC PUBLISHERS

Acoma Company/ Nambe Edition

P.O. Box 61, Stn. K
Toronto, ON M4P 2G1
(416) 787-3481
Services Provided: Music publishing.
Comments: Specializes in classical music.

Les editions Albani Inc.

P.O. Box 28
Chambly, PQ J3L 4B1
(514) 658-6983
Preferred Musical Styles: Pedagogy.

Alfred Publishing Ltd.

487 Westney Dr., Unit 1
Ajax, ON L1S 6W7
(416) 428-7790
FAX (416) 428-7792
Comments: Music book publisher and manufacturer.

Alleged Iguana Music

148 Erin Ave.
Hamilton, ON L8K 4W3
(416) 572-7474
Preferred Musical Styles: Pop, Rock, Country Rock, Country, R&B.
Acts Represented: Michael Terry, Lynne and the Rebels, Rapid Transit, Randall Cousins & Frequency.
Network Affiliations: BMI, SOCAN.
Services Provided: Production and publishing.

Alliance des Chorales du Quebec Inc.

4545 Pierre-de-Coubertin Ave.
Montreal, PQ H1V 3R2
(514) 252-3020
FAX (514) 251-8038
Preferred Musical Styles: Choral music (Pop, Sacred, Folk, etc.) for mixed voices or treble voices.
Special Projects: Choral workshops, public concerts, conducting training programs.

255

Almo/Irving/Rondor Music of Canada
939 Warden Ave.
Scarborough, ON M1L 4C5
(416) 752-7191
FAX (416) 752-0059
Preferred Musical Styles: Rock, Pop.
Acts Represented: Paul Janz, The Works, Craig Jacks.

Anti-Conscious Music
4352 Kingston Rd., P.O. Box 11
Scarborough, ON M1E 2M8
(416) 428-2461
Preferred Musical Styles: Pop, Rock, New Wave, Alternative, Post Modern, Roots Rock.
Acts Represented: Swedish Fish, Simon Truth, Moving Targetz.
Services Provided: Publish music by self-financed acts.
Special Projects: Currently supporting recordings by Moving Targetz.

ART-TEC Publishing
323 Talbot St., 2nd Floor
St. Thomas, ON N5P 1B5
(519) 633-6518
FAX (519) 633-6518
Preferred Musical Styles: Pop, MOR, Rock, Metal, C&W, Christian.
Acts Represented: Over 30 Canadian song writers represented.
Network Affiliations: CMRRA.
Services Provided: Recorded music publisher, international promotion.

Ashita Music
1201 W. Georgia St., Suite 19
Vancouver, BC V6E 3J5
(604) 684-2282
Preferred Musical Styles: Rock, Pop, Country, Metal, Dance.
Network Affiliations: CMPA, SOCAN.

Attic Music Limited
624 King St. W.
Toronto, ON M5V 1M7
(416) 862-0352
FAX (416) 862-0915
Preferred Musical Styles: All styles.

Autotunes Publishing
296 Richmond St. W., Suite 305
Toronto, ON M5V 1X2
(416) 979-8455
FAX (416) 979-8766
Preferred Musical Styles: Rock, Pop.
Acts Represented: Honeymoon Suite.

Axe Music Group
180 Bloor St. W., Suite 300
Toronto, ON M5S 2V6
(416) 924-5781
FAX (416) 924-9966
Preferred Musical Styles: Pop, MOR, Rock, C&W.
Acts Represented: Sattalites, Three Stand Out.

BMG Music Publishing Canada Inc.
151 John St., Suite 309
Toronto, ON M5V 2T2
(416) 586-0022
FAX (416) 586-0454
Preferred Musical Styles: Various.
Network Affiliations: CMRRA, CMPA, CARAS, CIRPA, SOCAN.

Barking At The Ants Music
29 Brennan Rd.
Ajax, ON L1T 2G2
(416) 686-4868
Preferred Musical Styles: Rock, Alternative.
Acts Represented: Swindled, Moving Targetz, Why?!
Services Provided: Publish music by self-financed acts.
Special Projects: Currently supporting recordings by Moving Targetz.

Berandol Music Ltd.
110A Sackville St.
Toronto, ON M5A 3E7
(416) 869-1872
FAX (416) 869-1873
Preferred Musical Styles: Instrumental.
Acts Represented: Rob Liddell, Toronto Pops Orchestra.

Boom Songs
296 Richmond St. W., Suite 305
Toronto, ON M5V 1X2
(416) 979-8455
FAX (416) 979-8766
Preferred Musical Styles: Rock, Pop.
Acts Represented: Big House.
Services Provided: Publishing.

Boosey & Hawkes (Canada) Limited
279 Yorkland Blvd.
Willowdale, ON M2J 1S7
(416) 491-1900
FAX (416) 491-8377
Preferred Musical Styles: Classical concert music and compositions used in music education.

Broadland Music Ltd.
298 Gerrard St. E.
Toronto, ON M5A 2G7
(416) 968-6587
FAX (416) 966-3614
Preferred Musical Styles: C&W.

C.M.S. Records Publishing
151 Mountain Rd.
Moncton, NB E1C 2K8
(506) 858-0073
FAX (506) 859-7406
Preferred Musical Styles: All styles.
Acts Represented: Will accept new acts.

Canadian Musical Heritage Society
P.O. Box 262, Stn. A
Ottawa, ON K1N 8V2
(613) 232-3406
FAX (613) 233-0698
Preferred Musical Styles: The CMHS publishes an anthology of early Canadian music.

Churchyard Publishing
(A Division of Image Control Productions Ltd.)
10852 Whyte Ave., Suite 203
Edmonton, AB T6E 2B3
(403) 433-2046
FAX (403) 439-4209
Preferred Musical Styles: All styles.

Cod Oil Productions Limited
P.O. Box 8568
St. John's, NF A1B 3P2
(709) 745-3304
Comments: Promotion and marketing of recorded music published by Cod Oil Productions only.

Dawn of Creation
P.O. Box 8, Stn. 13
Toronto, ON M9C 4X9
(416) 869-1872
Preferred Musical Styles: Pop, C&W, Gospel.

Dee Songs
296 Richmond St. W., Suite 305
Toronto, ON M5V 1X2
(416) 979-8455
FAX (416) 979-8766
Preferred Musical Styles: Rock, Pop.
Acts Represented: Honeymoon Suite.
Services Provided: Publishing.

Diversified Music Group
1969 Pandora St.
Vancouver, BC V5L 5B2
(604) 255-3536
FAX (604) 255-8711
Preferred Musical Styles: Rock, Country, Country Rock.
Acts Represented: Darby Mills, One Horse Blue, Lori Jordan, Bear Mountain Boys, Kenny Shaw, Danny Mack.
Network Affiliations: BCCMA (British Columbia Country Music Association), CCMA (Canadian Country Music Association).
Services Provided: Publishing, management, marketing and publicity, plus rehearsal and production studios.

Dobbin Agency
477A Princess St.
Kingston, ON K7L 1C3
(613) 549-4401
Preferred Musical Styles: Pop, MOR, Rock, C&W.
Network Affiliations: CART.

Doberman-Yppan (les editions)
P.O. Box 2021
Saint-Nicolas, PQ G0S 3L0
(418) 831-1304
Preferred Musical Styles: Publishers of contemporary Canadian concert music and music for classical guitar.

The Ear Music Company
526 Brentwood Ave.
Oshawa, ON L1G 2T1
(416) 723-8916
Preferred Musical Styles: Pop, MOR, Rock, C&W.
Acts Represented: Scott Forrester, Screaming Blue Blood Turtles.
Services Provided: Record label (EMC Records of Canada).

First International Records

11602-75 Ave.
Edmonton, AB T6G 0J2
(403) 436-3096
Comments: First International is primarily a means of distributing the songs published by Manhole Music and Phillet/MacIver Music (same address as above).

Fraze Songs

296 Richmond St. W., Suite 305
Toronto, ON M5V 1X2
(416) 979-8455
FAX (416) 979-8766
Preferred Musical Styles: Rock, Pop.
Acts Represented: Brighton Rock.

The Frederick Harris Music Co. Limited

529 Speers Rd.
Oakville, ON L6K 2G4
(416) 845-3487
FAX (416) 845-1208
Preferred Musical Styles: Educational, Classical.
Affiliated Companies: Irwin Publishing (A division of General Publishing).
Comments: Exclusive publisher of official Royal Conservatory of Music materials.

Gamma Publishing Co.

300 Leo Pariseau, Suite 701
P.O. Box 1010, Place du Parc
Montreal, PQ H2W 2S2
(514) 842-4666
Preferred Musical Styles: Pop, Rock.
Acts Represented: Robert Charlebois, Stef Carse.

Gibney Music Publications

3455 W. 4 Ave., Suite 308
Vancouver, BC V6R 1N7
(604) 732-5355
Product Specialty: Manuscript.

Gilpin Publishing

P.O. Box 597
Alliston, ON L0M 1A0
(705) 424-6507
Comments: Piano publications (PIANO Plus! Series). Also distribute other publishers' materials.

Ginn Publishing Canada Inc.

3771 Victoria Park Ave.
Scarborough, ON M1W 2P9
(416) 497-4600
FAX (416) 497-5927
Preferred Musical Styles: Music programs in English and French for elementary grades.

Gordon V. Thompson Music

29 Birch Ave.
Toronto, ON M4V 1E2
(416) 923-7329
FAX (416) 923-4821
Preferred Musical Styles: Print publication of classical music.
Comments: Quality teaching materials.

Green Dolphin Music

201 Queen Victoria Dr., Suite 141
Hamilton, ON L8W 1W7
(416) 574-2272
Preferred Musical Styles: Pop, A/C.
Acts Represented: Rikki Rumball.
Services Provided: Song placement, demo tapes.
Comments: Several writers represented. Call before submitting tape(s).

Hel-Luk Publishing Co.

1151 Drouillard Rd.
Windsor, ON N8Y 2R2
(519) 973-4944

Horton Music Publishing Inc.

1201 W. Georgia St., Suite 19
Vancouver, BC V6E 3J5
(604) 684-2282
FAX (604) 688-1142
Preferred Musical Styles: Pop, Rock, Metal, Country, Dance, A/C.
Services Provided: Copyright exploitation and publishing administration.

Icedrum Records Inc.

P.O. Box 2310, Stn. A
Sudbury, ON P3A 4S8
(705) 560-3769
FAX (705) 560-1702
Contact: J.J. Hartman.

Les Editions Intermede Inc.

P.O. Box 609, Place du Parc
Montreal, PQ H2W 2P2
(514) 842-8661
FAX (514) 843-8278
Preferred Musical Styles: Pop, MOR.

ISBA Music Publishing Inc.

1327 boul. St. Joseph e.
Montreal, PQ H2J 1M1
(514) 522-ISBA
FAX (514) 525-7550
Preferred Musical Styles: Pop, MOR, A/C, Rock, Dance.
Acts Represented: Mitsou, Diodati, Nuance, Paris Black.
Services Provided: Publishing, administration.

Janijam Music

5455 rue Pare, Suite 101
Montreal, PQ H4P 1P7
(514) 738-9533
FAX (514) 737-9780
Preferred Musical Styles: Pop, Jazz, Comedy.
Acts Represented: Oliver Jones, Bowser & Blue, Sonny Greenwich.

Jennie Music Publishing Co.

21 Cutler Ct., P.O. Box 421
Schomberg, ON L0G 1T0
(416) 939-7900
Preferred Musical Styles: Country, MOR, Easy Listening, A/C.
Acts Represented: Ross Allen, Ray St. Germain, Sherisse Laurence, Razzy Bailey (U.S.).

Jobina Communications Ltd.

298 Gerrard St. E.
Toronto, ON M5A 2G7
(416) 968-6587
FAX (416) 966-3614
Preferred Musical Styles: All types.

Les Editions Roy Jourdan/ Vibration Records

P.O. Box 245, Place du Parc
Montreal, PQ H2W 2N8
(514) 987-1198
FAX (514) 987-1204
Preferred Musical Styles: Pop, MOR, Soft Rock.
Affiliated Companies: William Production (Paris).

Justin Publications

986 Vanier Dr.
Mississauga, ON L5H 3T7
(416) 274-0471
Comments: Desk-top music publishing (Macintosh Professional Composer).

Justin Time Publishing

5455 rue Pare, Suite 101
Montreal, PQ H4P 1P7
(514) 738-9533
FAX (514) 737-9780
Preferred Musical Styles: Pop, Jazz, Comedy.
Acts Represented: Denny Christianson, Bowser & Blue, Pat LaBarbera.

Kara Music Publishing

177 W. 7 Ave., Suite 400
Vancouver, BC V5Y 1L8
(604) 872-2906
Preferred Musical Styles: C&W.
Acts Represented: Various country songwriters.

LTM Music

7305 Woodbine Ave., Suite 467
Markham, ON L3R 3V7
(416) 449-4035
Preferred Musical Styles: All styles.

La Nash Music

11714-113 Ave.
Edmonton, AB T5G 0J8
Preferred Musical Styles: All styles.
Acts Represented: Pam Henry, Bill Hanson, DMT All Stars.
Services Provided: One-stop publishing.

Leslie Music Supply Inc.

211 Southview Rd.
Oakville, ON L6K 2P2

Lincoln Park Music

191A Wolseley St., Suite 200
Thunder Bay, ON P7A 3G5
(807) 345-2448
Preferred Musical Styles: Country, Country Rock.
Network Affiliations: CCMA.

Lucky Trio Publishing

7305 Woodbine Ave., Suite 467
Markham, ON L3R 3V7
(416) 449-4035
Preferred Musical Styles: All styles.

Danny Makarus Music

11714-113 Ave.
Edmonton, AB T5G 0J8
(403) 454-6848 or 454-9291
Preferred Musical Styles: All styles.
Acts Represented: Good Friends, Priscilla Morin, China White.
Services Provided: One-stop publishing.

Manhole Music

11602-75 Ave.
Edmonton, AB T6G 0J2
(403) 436-3096
Acts Represented: Magic Music.
Affiliated Companies: Phillet/MacIver Music.

The Master's Collection

960 The Gateway
Burlington, ON L7L 5K7
(416) 681-2760
FAX (416) 333-6684
Preferred Musical Styles: Religious.
Acts Represented: Ruth Fazal, Jerry Manus, Mark Moore.

Larry Mercy Music

590 Hunters Place
Waterloo, ON N2K 3L1
(519) 746-8488

Micah Music

43 Applemore Rd.
Scarborough, ON M1B 1R7
Preferred Musical Styles: Gospel, Children's.
Acts Represented: Karen Burke, Carlton Wright, Paul McPherson.
Services Provided: Music publishing, copyright consulting.
Special Projects: Various music workshops.

Morning Music Limited

5200 Dixie Rd., Suite 203
Mississauga, ON L4W 1E4
(416) 625-2676
FAX (416) 625-2092
Preferred Musical Styles: Pop, MOR, C&W, A/C, instrumental, serious, background.
Acts Represented: Stompin' Tom, Eddie Eastman, Werner Drexler.
Services Provided: Song exploitation worldwide, stock music for corporate A/V, film and TV productions.

Mundi Music

3491 Ouellette Ave.
Windsor, ON N9E 3M1
(519) 969-6585
Contact: Richard Janik.
Preferred Musical Styles: Pop, Novelty, Comedy.
Acts Represented: Sufferin' Catfish.
Comments: Send S.A.S.E. with submissions.

One-Eyed Duck Recording and Publishing

22 Rainsford Rd.
Toronto, ON M4L 3N4
(416) 694-6900
Preferred Musical Styles: Children's.
Acts Represented: Sphere Clown Band.
Network Affiliations: A.F. of M.

Les Editions Jacques Ostiguy

12790 rue Yamaska
St. Hyacinthe, PQ J2T 1B3
(514) 773-4911

The Pangaea Music House

P.O. Box 609, Stn. F
Toronto, ON M4Y 2L8
(416) 922-1600
FAX (416) 922-0799

Pape Publishing

7 Tansley Ave.
Scarborough, ON M1J 1P2
(416) 267-7482
Preferred Musical Styles: All styles.
Acts Represented: Bobby Blake, Sean Lynch, Pape Gang.

Peer Southern Organization

180 Bloor St. W., Suite 300
Toronto, ON M5S 2V6
(416) 924-5781
FAX (416) 924-9966
Preferred Musical Styles: Pop, MOR, Rock, C&W.

Pentachord/Pentarch Music

68 Water St., Suite 407
Vancouver, BC V6B 1A4
(604) 688-0077
FAX (604) 688-7118
Preferred Musical Styles: All styles.
Acts Represented: Paul Laine, Scramblers, Boulevard, Neil James Harnett.

PolyGram Music Publishing Companies

3575 St. Laurent, Suite 114
Montreal, PQ H2X 2T7
(514) 842-8663
FAX (514) 843-8278
Preferred Musical Styles: All styles.
Acts Represented: Men Without Hats, Sue Medley, Boot Sauce.

Ramblin' Man Music Publishing

8607-128 Ave.
Edmonton, AB T5E 0G3
(403) 476-8230
Preferred Musical Styles: Country.

Random Image Music

209 Madison Ave.
Toronto, ON M5R 2S6
(416) 929-2349
Preferred Musical Styles: Pop, MOR, Rock, Dance, C&W.
Acts Represented: Timeline, The Fact, Shaun Firth.
Services Provided: Standard publishing services.
Special Projects: Horizon's '89 (yearly compilation).

Renegade Productions Inc.

814 East Hastings St.
Vancouver, BC V6A 1R6
(604) 255-0435
FAX (604) 254-8311
Preferred Musical Styles: Rock, Pop.
Network Affiliations: A.F. of M., SOCAN.
Branches:
Arpieye Music
970 Homer St., Suite 206
Vancouver, BC V6B 1W6
(604) 669-7696

Renegade Productions Inc.
4146-148 Ave. N.E.
Redmond, WA 98052 USA
(206) 885-1731

Rock Headquarters

68 Water St., Suite 406
Vancouver, BC V6B 1A4
(604) 688-0077
FAX (604) 688-7118
Preferred Musical Styles: All styles.
Acts Represented: Boulevard, Scramblers, Neil James Harnett.

Schmoozic Music

1201 West Georgia St., Suite 19
Vancouver, BC V6E 3J5
(604) 684-2282
Preferred Musical Styles: Pop, Rock, Metal, Country, Dance.
Network Affiliations: SOCAN, CMPA.

Secret Agency Music

148 Erin Ave.
Hamilton, ON L8K 4W3
(416) 572-7474
Preferred Musical Styles: All styles.
Acts Represented: Mark LaForme Band, Jenny Lee West, Manon, Randall Cousins and Frequency.
Services Provided: Full-service publishing.

Seldom Tunes

11714-113 Ave.
Edmonton, AB T5G 0J8
(403) 454-9291 or 454-6848
Preferred Musical Styles: All styles.
Acts Represented: Sassy Donna Lee, P.J. McDonald, Five Wheel Drive.
Services Provided: One-stop publishing.

Shandan Music

590 Hunters Place
Waterloo, ON N2K 3L1
(519) 746-8488

Shemac Entertainment Group Inc.

89 Clarence St.
Woodbridge, ON L4L 1L4
(416) 850-3630
FAX (416) 850-2830
Preferred Musical Styles: Pop, Rock.
Acts Represented: Dorian Gray, Benjamin's Kite.

Sky Is Falling Inc.

2027 Dickson Rd.
Mississauga, ON L5B 1Y7
(416) 566-5907
FAX (416) 848-7718
Acts Represented: Tom Cochrane and Red Rider, Saga.
Affiliated Companies: Chesterfield Entertainment, Falling Sky Music.
Services Provided: Music entertainment.

Snagglepuss Music

R.R. 4
Shelburne, ON L0N 1S0
(519) 925-5009
FAX (519) 925-6313
Preferred Musical Styles: Family, Children's.
Acts Represented: Eric Nagler.

Southern Music Publishing Co. (Canada) Ltd.
180 Bloor St. W., Suite 300
Toronto, ON M5S 2V6
(416) 924-5781
FAX (416) 924-9966
Preferred Musical Styles: All styles.
Acts Represented: Sattalites.

Sparkus Maximus Publishing
40 Cherokee Bay
Winnipeg, MB R2J 2C5
(204) 257-4403
FAX (204) 452-2399
Preferred Musical Styles: Country.

Steeler Music
296 Richmond St. W., Suite 305
Toronto, ON M5V 1X2
(416) 979-8455
FAX (416) 979-8766
Preferred Musical Styles: Rock, Pop.
Acts Represented: Brighton Rock.

Stiff Riff Music
349 West Georgia St., P.O. Box 2987
Vancouver, BC V6B 3X4
(604) 875-6860
Preferred Musical Styles: Pop, Rock, AOR, CHR.

Stonehand Publishing
P.O. Box 895, Stn. E
Victoria, BC V8W 2R9
(604) 386-0507
Preferred Musical Styles: All styles.
Acts Represented: Kin Cain & Band, Mark Franklin, Bert Goulet.

Stony Plain Recording Co. Ltd.
P.O. Box 861
Edmonton, AB T5J 2L8
(403) 468-6423
FAX (403) 465-8941
Preferred Musical Styles: Roots, Traditional.
Acts Represented: Amos Garrett, Ian Tyson, Downchild.

Sunset Beach Music/ Rippin' Music
18 The Donway E., Suite 607
Don Mills, ON M3C 1X9
(416) 461-0895
Preferred Musical Styles: Pop, Dance, Hip Hop, A/C, MOR.
Acts Represented: Chris Cage.
Services Provided: Publishing demos, song placement.
Special Projects: Release singles for airplay (in-house label).

TMC Publishing
P.O. Box 362, Stn. A
Rexdale, ON M9W 5L3
(416) 747-1901
Preferred Musical Styles: Religious, Gospel.
Acts Represented: Ruth Fazal, Andrew Donaldson, Bill Davidson.

TMP— The Music Publisher
29 Birch Ave.
Toronto, ON M4V 1E2
(416) 922-2909
FAX (416) 923-4821
Preferred Musical Styles: Pop, Rock, MOR, C&W, New Age, Jazz.
Acts Represented: Exchange, Murray McLauchlan, Steve Kujala.

To Want It Music Publishing
177 W. 7 Ave., Suite 400
Vancouver, BC V5Y 1K5
(604) 872-2906
Preferred Musical Styles: Gospel, C&W.
Acts Represented: Step By Step, Karyn Esark, plus any new songwriters.

Town Songs
296 Richmond St. W., Suite 305
Toronto, ON M5V 1X2
(416) 979-8455
FAX (416) 979-8766
Preferred Musical Styles: Rock, Pop.
Acts Represented: Big House.

Tree Stump Publishing
P.O. Box 1217, R.R. 2
Odessa, ON K0H 2H0
(613) 386-3582
FAX (613) 386-3582
Preferred Musical Styles: Country.
Acts Represented: Dieter Boehme, Anne Banks, Dan Kennedy.
Affiliated Companies: Flyin' High Records.

W/A Music Corporation
P.O. Box 9, Stn. O
Toronto, ON M4A 2M9
(416) 299-2222
FAX (416) 299-2232

Warner/Chappell Music Canada Ltd.
85 Scarsdale Rd., Suite 101
Don Mills, ON M3B 2R2
(416) 445-3131
FAX (416) 445-2473
Preferred Musical Styles: All styles.
Acts Represented: Exclusive writers: David Roberts, Stan Meissner, Michael Hanson, Colin Linden, Myles Hunter.
Network Affiliations: CMRRA, CMPA, SOCAN.

Wilson and LeBlanc Music Inc.
15 Independence Dr.
Scarborough, ON M1K 3R7
(416) 265-3277
FAX (416) 265-3280
Preferred Musical Styles: Rock, Country.
Affiliated Companies: Hildyard Music, Brycemoor Music.

Les Editions Wingspirit Enr.
P.O. Box 137, Stn. NDG
Montreal, PQ H4A 3P5
(514) 735-3061

Word Communications Ltd.
7720 Alderbridge Way
Richmond, BC V6X 2A2
(604) 270-7231
Preferred Musical Styles: Christian, Gospel.
Acts Represented: Amy Grant, Michael W. Smith, Connie Scott.
Network Affiliations: CRIA, CARAS.

Xanthus
P.O. Box 7405
Ancaster, ON L9G 4G4
(416) 526-6579
Services Provided: Computer copying of scores and parts.

YMX MeDIA
(A Subsidiary of DIFFUSION i MeDIA)
4487 rue Adam
Montreal, PQ H1V 1T9
(514) 254-7794
FAX (514) 844-6263
Preferred Musical Styles: New Music, Electro-acoustic and Media Art.

Zauberer Music Publishing
Main P.O. Box 5087
Vancouver, BC V6B 4A9
(604) 525-9194
Preferred Musical Styles: All styles, except MOR and Country.
Comments: Sub-publishing with EMI Publishing (West Germany) since 1982.

MUSIC SERVICES

This category is new to the Directory, and the types of companies listed here represent a variety of services which are available to the music industry. To define the parameters of the category we have focussed mainly on tour specialists and referral services, neither of which could constitute a section of its own, but both of which have recently been gaining a fair amount of importance in the industry.

Dr. Darke
982 Semlin Dr.
Vancouver, BC V5L 4J8
(604) 253-7974
Services Provided: Specialists in tour support and technical direction.

The Independent Network
66 Joseph St.
Brampton, ON L6X 1H8
(416) 454-3865
Services Provided: Information on independent recording artists plus referrals and consulting.
Comments: The network's indie database accepts all music categories. To register a release in the network database, call for more information.

Match-Music
92 Avenue Rd., Suite 200
Toronto, ON M5R 2H2
(416) 960-3130
FAX (416) 960-8264
Services Provided: Matching musicians, singers, songwriters and technical professionals with bands.
Comments: Toronto-based acts.

The Music Bookstore
3284 Yonge St.
Toronto, ON M4N 3M7
(416) 485-1049
FAX (416) 485-8924
Services Provided: Sales of music-related books by mail-order.
Comments: List of books available free upon request.

Musician's Listing Service
4544 Dufferin St.
North York, ON M3H 5X2
(416) 665-5844
Services Provided: Free listing for individual musicians plus a musicians networking service.
Branch Office:
3050 Constitution Blvd., Suite 74
Mississauga, ON L4Y 3X1
(416) 848-0874

Musician's Referral of Montreal
P.O. Box 298, Stn. H
Montreal, PQ H3G 2K8
(514) 933-3301
Services Provided: The firm also acts as a booker for several recording studios in the Montreal area.

On Tour
15717-92 Ave.
Edmonton, AB T5R 5C5
(403) 483-1084
FAX (403) 452-2464
Services Provided: Booking of hotel accommodation, customized itineraries and ground transportation for musicians touring in Canada.
Contact: Dorothy McAuley, president and general manager.

POP Strategies
3284 Yonge St.
Toronto, ON M4N 3M7
(416) 485-1049
FAX (416) 485-8924
Services Provided: Marketing support and customized research.

MUSIC TELEVISION

NATIONAL PROGRAMMING

Big Valley Jamboree
1112 Winnipeg St., Suite 103
Regina, SK
(306) 569-8711
FAX (306) 352-8099
Network: Full CTV network.
Content: Variety specials from world's largest country music festival.
Contact: Murray MacDonald.

Good Rockin' Tonite CBC-TV
P.O. Box 4600
Vancouver, BC V6B 4A2
(604) 662-6180
Network: CBC.
Channel: Various.
Frequency: Once a week, Friday nights.
Format: 60 minutes.
Content: TV rock video magazine.
Language and Market: English, national.
Contact: Ken Gibson.

The Tommy Hunter Show / CBC-TV
P.O. Box 500, Stn. A
Toronto, ON M5W 1E6
(416) 975-3311
Network: CBC.
Channel: 5.
Cable Channel: 6.
Frequency: Once a week, Saturday nights.
Format: 60 minutes.
Content: C&W, special guests along with regular cast.
Language and Market: English, national.
Contact: Joan Tosoni, producer/director.

MuchMusic / City-TV

299 Queen St. W.
Toronto, ON M5V 2Z5
(416) 591-5757
FAX (416) 591-MUCH
Network: Independent.
Channel: 57 (Toronto area).
Cable Channel: 7 (Toronto area).
Frequency: 24 hours, seven days a week, eight hours live each day. Repeated.
Content: Music videos, interviews, news magazine, special events programming.
Language and Market: English, national.
Contact: John Martin (director of music programming), Nancy Oliver (director of music operations).

The New Music / City-TV

299 Queen St. W.
Toronto, ON M5V 2Z5
(416) 591-5757
FAX (416) 591-7791
Network: Independent.
Channel: 57 (Toronto area).
Cable Channel: 7 (Toronto area).
Frequency: Weekly.
Format: 60 minutes.
Content: Entertainment journalism.
Language and Market: English, national.
Contact: Denise Donlon.

The Performers / BCTV

P.O. Box 4700
Vancouver, BC V6B 4A3
(604) 420-2288
FAX (604) 421-9427
Network: CTV.
Channel: 8.
Cable Channel: 11.
Frequency: Weekly.
Format: 30 minutes.
Content: Artist profiles.
Language and Market: English, national.
Contact: Michael Meade.

Video Hits / CBC-TV

P.O. Box 500, Stn. A
Toronto, ON M5W 1E6
(416) 975-3311
Network: CBC.
Channel: 5.
Cable Channel: 6.
Frequency: Five days a week, Mon.-Fri.
Content: Music videos with host and guests.
Language and Market: English, national.
Contact: Sandra Faire, executive producer.

LOCAL AND REGIONAL PROGRAMMING

ALBERTA

Connections

CFAC-TV
1401-28 St. N., P.O. Box 1120
Lethbridge, AB T1J 4A4
(403) 327-1521
Network: Independent.
Channel: 7.
Cable Channel: 2.
Frequency: Weekly, Thursday nights.
Content: Talk, guests, performances and videos.
Language and Market: English, local.
Contact: Dan Germain.

BRITISH COLUMBIA

BC Music Project

CHEK-TV
780 King's Rd.
Victoria, BC V8T 5A2
(604) 383-2435

Soundproof Shaw Cable North/West Vancouver

1471 Pemberton Ave.
North Vancouver, BC V7P 2R9
(604) 985-2151
FAX (604) 985-7495
Network: Shaw Cablesystems.
Cable Channel: 4.
Frequency: Twice weekly.
Format: Two hours.
Content: Alternative music videos.
Language and Market: English, local.
Contact: David Toddington, producer.

NOVA SCOTIA

Shanty Town
ATV Cape Breton Ltd.
P.O. Box 469
Sydney, NS B1P 6H5
(902) 562-5511
Network: CTV.
Channel: 4.
Cable Channel: 8.
Frequency: Weekly.
Format: 60 minutes.
Content: Children's.
Language and Market: English, regional.
Contact: Jerome Campbell.

ONTARIO

CHUM-FM 30 / City-TV
299 Queen St. W.
Toronto, ON M5V 2Z5
(416) 591-5757
FAX (416) 591-MUCH
Network: Independent.
Channel: 57 (Toronto area).
Cable Channel: 7 (Toronto area).
Frequency: Weekly.
Content: Top 30 videos according to CHUM-FM album charts.
Language and Market: English, regional (Southwestern Ontario).
Contact: David Kines.

Toronto Rocks / City-TV
299 Queen St. W.
Toronto, ON M5V 2Z5
(416) 591-5757
FAX (416) 591-MUCH
Network: Independent, commercial.
Channel: 57.
Cable Channel: 7.
Frequency: Live daily, Mon.-Fri. Repeats every morning and Saturday.
Format: 60 minutes.
Content: Rock videos with guests.
Language and Market: English, regional (Southwestern Ontario).
Contact: Joel Goldberg, producer.

You Gotta Be Kiddin! Cable 10 Parkdale/ Trinity (Maclean Hunter)
47 Lisgar St.
Toronto, ON M6J 3T4
(416) 534-3341
Network: Maclean Hunter Cable TV.
Cable Channel: 10.
Frequency: Once a month.
Content: Indie music.
Language and Market: English, regional.
Contact: Manny Floriano.

QUEBEC

MusiquePlus
3518 St. Laurent
Montreal, PQ H2X 2V2
(514) 284-7587
Network: Independent, commercial.
Channel: Various.
Language and Market: French, regional.
Contact: Pierre Parent (promotion), Pierre Marchand (programming).

Video Star
3330 King St. W.
Sherbrooke, PQ J1L 1C9
(819) 565-7777
Network: Six stations (Pathonic).
Language and Market: French, regional.
Contact: Michel Bernier.

SASKATCHEWAN

Entertainment Saskatchewan
95 East Broadway
Yorkton, SK S3N 0L1
(306) 783-3685
FAX (306) 782-3433
Network: CTV.
Content: Music magazine with 50% Saskatchewan content.
Contact: Mike James.

Waiting on the Midnight Hour / Telecable 10

345-4 Ave. S.
Saskatoon, SK S7K 5S5
(306) 665-6610
Cable Channel: 10.
Frequency: Three times a week.
Content: Music videos, alternative music and concert updates.
Language and Market: English, local.
Contact: Luke Smith.

MUSICAL INSTRUMENT & SOUND EQUIPMENT SUPPLIERS

AFC Ltd.
3839 Burnsland Rd. S.E.
Calgary, AB T2G 3Z4
(403) 287-1311
FAX (403) 243-5603
Type of Company: Manufacturer.
Top Brands: Zarges, AFC.
Product Specialty: Custom aluminum cases.

A&M Wood Specialty
358 Eagle St. N., P.O. Box 3204
Cambridge, ON N3H 4S6
(519) 653-9322
FAX (519) 653-3441
Type of Company: Sales agency.
Product Specialty: Parts for stringed instruments and other wood instruments.

ASC Acoustic Sciences Corporation
P.O. Box 1179
Kaslo, BC V0G 1M0
(604) 353-2626
FAX (604) 353-7370
Type of Company: Manufacturer and distributor of Tube Traps.
Special Services: Applied acoustics research, design and development.
Top Brands: Tube Traps
Product Specialty: Portable, retrofit and broadband acoustic systems for studio, broadcast, performing and playback environments.

271

AVS Technologies Inc.
2100 Trans-Canada Highway S.
Montreal, PQ H9P 2N4
(514) 683-1771
FAX (514) 683-5307
Type of Company: Distributor, importer.
Product Specialty: Consumer electronics.
Top Brands: TDK, Nikko, Audio-Technica.

Acoustic Design Group Inc.
2465 Cawthra Rd., Suite 128
Mississauga, ON L5A 3P2
(416) 272-4495
FAX (416) 273-9756
Type of Company: Manufacturer of loudspeakers.
Special Services: Custom-built products.

Adamson Acoustic Design Corporation
850 Brock Rd., Unit 1
Pickering, ON L1W 1Z8
(416) 420-6279
FAX (416) 420-0813
Type of Company: Manufacturer, distributor.
Product Specialty: Commercial sound reinforcement systems and associated electronics.
Top Brands: Adamson Acoustic (manufacture), McCauley loudspeakers (distribute).

Airjack Wireless Systems
70 Neptune Cr.
Dartmouth, NS B2Y 4M9
(902) 465-8877
FAX (902) 466-6889
Type of Company: Manufacturer of the Airjack wireless guitar transmitter.
Top Brands: Airjack.

Amber Electro Design Ltd.
6969 Trans-Canada Highway
St. Laurent, PQ H4T 1V8
(514) 333-8748
FAX (514) 333-1388
Type of Company: Manufacturer, distributor.
Top Brands: Amber.
Product Specialty: Audio test equipment for noise and distortion.

Anatek Microcircuits Inc.
400 Brooksbank Ave.
North Vancouver, BC V7J 1G9
(604) 980-6850
FAX (604) 980-2722
Type of Company: Manufacturer of electronic products for the music industry.
Special Services: Customer support.
Top Brands: Pocket Products.
Product Specialty: MIDI accessories.

Apple Canada
7495 Birchmount Rd.
Markham, ON L3R 5G2
(416) 477-5800
FAX (416) 477-6305
Type of Company: Manufacturer, distributor.
Top Brands: Apple, Macintosh.
Product Specialty: Computer hardware.

Armor Case
R.R. 6
Woodstock, ON N4S 7W1
(519) 462-2882
Type of Company: Manufacturer.
Special Services: Fast delivery for standard and custom sizes.
Product Specialty: Standard and heavy-duty flight cases.

Artistic Developments Corp.
24 Fallingbrook Rd.
Scarborough, ON M1N 2T4
(416) 691-9650
Top Brands: Musicians' Almanac Time Organizer.

Aspri Creative Acoustics
6963 St. Hubert, Suite 200
Montreal, PQ H2S 2N1
(514) 274-3658
FAX (514) 271-9342
Type of Company: Manufacturer.
Top Brands: Aspri.
Product Specialty: Mechanical reverb for acoustic guitars.

Atari Canada Corp.
90 Gough Rd.
Markham, ON L1X 1A9
(416) 479-1266
FAX (416) 479-1439
Type of Company: Manufacturer of computers.
Special Services: MIDI systems.
Top Brands: Atari Mega, Atari Stacy, Atari ST.
Product Specialty: Computers with built-in MIDI capability.

Atlas Electronics Ltd.
50 Wingold Ave.
Toronto, ON M6B 1P7
(416) 789-7761
FAX (416) 789-3053
Type of Company: Distributor.
Top Brands: Amprobe, VNK, Atlas Soundalier.
Product Specialty: Electronic instrumentation and components.

Audionova Inc.
2083 Chartier Ave.
Dorval, PQ H9P 1H3
(514) 631-5787
FAX (514) 631-5789
Type of Company: Distributor.
Product Specialty: Pro audio and lighting equipment.
Top Brands: NSI, EAW, SCS.

Avalanche Effects
P.O. Box 582, Stn. C
Toronto, ON M6J 3R9
(416) 864-0306
Type of Company: Manufacturer.
Product Specialty: Brianizer Leslie speaker emulator.

Ayotte Drum Company
1272 Granville St.
Vancouver, BC V6Z 1M4
(604) 689-2978
FAX (604) 662-3856
Type of Company: Manufacturer.
Top Brands: Ayotte custom drums.

B&J Music
469 King St. W.
Toronto, ON M5V 1K4
(416) 596-8361
FAX (416) 596-8822
Type of Company: Distributor of musical instruments and accessories.
Special Services: Complete repair service.
Top Brands: Takamine guitars, Charvel guitars, Ross electronics.
Product Specialty: Guitars and music electronics.

B.P. Industries
6650-62B St.
Delta, BC V4K 4E2
(604) 940-0585
Type of Company: Distributor, wholesaler.
Top Brands: Switchcraft, Neutrik.
Product Specialty: Specialty case hardware, audio connectors and adaptors.

Bingley Distributors
280 Dufferin Ave.
Trenton, ON K8V 5G2
(613) 394-4729
Type of Company: Distributor of acoustic pianos and organs.

Boosey & Hawkes (Canada) Ltd.
279 Yorkland Blvd.
Willowdale, ON M2J 1S7
(416) 491-1900
FAX (416) 491-8377
Type of Company: Distributor, wholesaler.
Special Services: Band instrument repairs.
Top Brands: Buffet, Besson, Washburn.
Product Specialty: Brass and woodwind instruments; guitars, stringed instruments and accessories.

Bose Ltd.
35 East Beaver Creek Rd., Unit 8
Richmond Hill, ON L4B 1B3
(416) 886-9123
FAX (416) 886-9134
Type of Company: Manufacturer of loudspeaker systems.
Special Services: The CAD sound design system.
Top Brands: Bose.

Bridges Musical Instruments
80 Laird Dr.
Toronto, ON M4G 3V1
(416) 689-2978
FAX (416) 429-2704
Type of Company: Manufacturer.
Product Specialty: Custom-built contemporary bowed string instruments.

Bryston Ltd.
57 Westmore Dr.
Rexdale, ON M9V 3Y6
(416) 746-0300
FAX (416) 746-0308
Type of Company: Manufacturer.
Product Specialty: Pro audio amplifiers and crossovers.

C.M.S. Music Inc.
8660 Jeanne-Mance
Montreal, PQ H2P 2S6
(514) 387-7331
FAX (514) 383-3576
Type of Company: Distributor.

Calato Manufacturing (Canada) Ltd.
8407 Stanley Ave., Unit 1
Niagara Falls, ON L2E 6X8
(416) 357-2680
1-800-263-7145
FAX (416) 374-3981
Type of Company: Distributor.
Top Brands: Regal Tip sticks, Sabian cymbals, Remo.
Product Specialty: Percussion and accessories.

Califone Industries Ltd.
1305 Odlum Dr.
Vancouver, BC V5L 3M1
(604) 254-5148
FAX (604) 254-9944
Type of Company: Manufacturer of electronics.
Prime Type of Business: Manufacturing of electronics.
Product Specialty: Amps, PAs, microphones.

Canadian Musical Distributors
249 Betty Ann Dr.
Willowdale, ON M2R 1A6
(416) 225-5089
FAX (416) 225-5965
Type of Company: Distributor, importer.
Top Brands: Dave Wyre Musical Accessories.
Product Specialty: Strings and accessories.

Canwood Percussion
P.O. Box 615
Lloydminster, SK S9V 0Y7
(306) 825-2813
Type of Company: Manufacturer.
Product Specialty: Custom wood drums.

Casio Canada Ltd.
2100 Ellesmere Rd.
Scarborough, ON M1H 3B7
(416) 431-3747
FAX (416) 431-3664
Type of Company: Manufacturer of consumer electronics.
Top Brands: Music keyboards, SK1, SA20, CT650.
Product Specialty: Music keyboards, calculators, digital diaries, watches and cash registers.

Cerwin-Vega Canada Ltd.
2360 Midland Ave., Unit 21
Scarborough, ON M1S 4A9
(416) 292-6645
FAX (416) 292-4330
Type of Company: Distributor.
Product Specialty: Speakers.

Classe Audio
9414 Cote-de-Liesse Rd.
Lachine, PQ H8T 1A1
(514) 636-6384
FAX (514) 636-1428
Type of Company: Manufacturer, distributor.
Product Specialty: Amplifiers and pre-amplifiers.
Top Brands: Classe.

Classic Organ Company Ltd.
300 Don Park Rd., Unit 12
Markham, ON L3R 3A1
(416) 475-1263
FAX (416) 475-2735
Type of Company: Manufacturer.
Product Specialty: Builders of sampled-wave digital electronic organs for professional musicians. Builders of pipe organ control systems.
Special Services: Complete digital samples including all attack parameters. Tonal Bloom and full waveforms are used and different samples are utilized throughout the compass of each voice. Completely MIDI-compatible.

Clydesdale Case Co. Ltd.
80 Sinnott Rd.
Scarborough, ON M1L 4M7
(416) 755-6543
FAX (416) 755-0533
Type of Company: Manufacturer.
Product Specialty: Road cases.

Coast Music Ltd.
378 Isabey
St. Laurent, PQ H4T 1W1
(514) 738-3000
FAX (514) 737-5069
Type of Company: Distributor and wholesaler of musical instruments.
Special Services: Repair and service centres in Montreal, Toronto and Vancouver.
Top Brands: Samick, Vic Firth, GHS.
Product Specialty: Percussion.
Branches:
111 Graton Dr., Units 404 & 406
Richmond Hill, ON L4B 1L5
(416) 764-6350

3496 Vanness Ave.
Vancouver, BC V5R 5A9
(604) 438-9212

Cobra Road Cases
52 Guildhall Dr.
Scarborough, ON M1R 3Z9
(416) 398-0743
FAX (416) 251-3354
Type of Company: Manufacturer.
Product Specialty: Custom-made road cases.

Commodore Business Machines Limited
3470 Pharmacy Ave.
Agincourt, ON M1W 3G3
(416) 499-4292
FAX (416) 494-9755
Type of Company: Manufacturer of personal computers with built-in synthesizer.
Special Services: Seminars on multimedia, music and video.
Top Brands: Amiga - A500, A2000, A2500.
Product Specialty: Integrated music and video production.

Conception Case Co.
550 Coronation Dr., Unit 14
West Hill, ON M1E 2K1
(416) 282-4858
FAX (416) 251-2370
Type of Company: Manufacturer.
Product Specialty: Cases.

Contact Distribution
60 Venture Dr., Suite 6
Scarborough, ON M1B 1S4
(416) 287-1144
FAX (416) 287-1204
Type of Company: Distributor.
Top Brands: Rane, Crest, Technical Projects.
Product Specialty: Pro audio products including amplifiers, crossovers and mixers.

Custom Acoustics
2526 Leitrim Rd.
Gloucester, ON K1G 3N3
(613) 822-0620
FAX (613) 822-0620
Type of Company: Manufacturer.
Product Specialty: Shipping cases and speaker enclosures.

D&W Intercontinental Music
R.R. 2
Norwal, ON L0P 1K0
(416) 452-0082
Type of Company: Organ manufacturer.

D.M. Best
4640 Decarie Blvd., Suite 220
Montreal, PQ H3X 2H5
(514) 489-0443
FAX: (514) 489-0443
Type of Company: Manufacturer, Wholesaler.
Top Brands: D.M. Best.
Product Specialty: Piano parts, tools, accessories.

DJU Entertainment Group
220 Pony Dr.
Newmarket, ON L3Y 7D6
(416) 836-6078
FAX (416) 836-6089
Type of Company: Distributor.
Top Brands: Dobro, WB, Hohner.
Product Specialty: Guitars, drums, accordions, harmonicas and DJ sound systems.

J. D'Addario & Co. (Canada) Ltd.
50 West Wilmot St., Unit 13
Richmond Hill, ON L4B 1M5
(416) 889-0116
FAX (416) 889-8998
Type of Company: Distributor.
Product Specialty: Music accessories.
Top Brands: D'Addario, Vandoren, Sharkfin.

Doyle Custom Enclosures
3 Budworth Dr.
West Hill, ON M1E 3H8
(416) 755-9101
Type of Company: Manufacturer.
Product Specialty: PA, stage and guitar monitors, amp racks, crossovers and processors.

E.E.L.

(previously Garnet Amplifiers Ltd.)
1360 Sargent Ave.
Winnipeg, MB R3E 0G5
(204) 775-8201
Type of Company: Manufacturer of tube amplifiers and pre-amplifiers.

E.M.P. Canada Ltd.

18 Basaltic Rd.
Concord, ON L4K 1G6
(416) 660-4699
FAX (416) 660-4699
Type of Company: Sales agency.
Special Services: Service and warehousing.
Top Brands: Casio, Randall.
Product Specialty: Computers, cases, keyboards.

Efkay Musical Instruments Ltd.

2165-46 Ave.
Lachine, PQ H8T 2P1
Type of Company: Distributor.
Top Brands: Marshall, Ibanez, Tama.

Elnova Professional Electronics Ltd.

325 rue Clement o.
Lasalle, PQ H8R 4B4
(514) 364-2118
FAX (514) 364-0791
Type of Company: Distributor of professional audio products.
Top Brands: Beyer Dynamic, Schoeps, Klein & Hummel.
Product Specialty: Microphones, headphones, amplifiers, intercom equipment.

Equity Sound Investments

629 Eastern Ave., Unit 2
Toronto, ON M4M 1E4
(416) 465-4888
FAX (416) 465-3919
Type of Company: Manufacturer of loudspeakers.
Special Services: Custom-design and analysis.
Top Brands: Intersonics ServoDrive, BOND, Gane.

Erikson

(A Division of JAM Industries)
378 rue Isabey
St. Laurent, PQ H4T 1W1
(514) 738-3000
FAX (514) 737-5069
Type of Company: Distributor.
Top Brands: Pearl, Fostex, Kramer, Seymour Duncan, Valley, DIC, KMD, Vantage, Rapco, Biamp, Gorilla, Remo, Nomad.
Branches:
111 Granton Dr., Units 404 & 406
Richmond Hill, ON L4B 1L5
(416) 764-6350/1
FAX (416) 764-6799

3496 Vanness Ave.
Vancouver, BC V5K 5A9
(604) 438-9212
FAX (604) 438-7911

Evolution Audio Inc.

1131 South Service Rd. W.
Oakville, ON L6L 6K4
(416) 847-8888
FAX (416) 847-7408
Type of Company: Distributor, importer.
Top Brands: Carver, Polk Audio, Monster Cable.
Product Specialty: Amplifiers, speakers, cable and sound adjustment products.

Excelsior Supply Co.

1285 Hodge St., Suite 203
St. Laurent, PQ H4N 2B6
(514) 747-2922
Type of Company: Distributor, importer, wholesaler.
Product Specialty: Accordions (standard and Midivox).
Special Services: Sales and service.

FRM Enterprises

7000 Park Ave., Suite 202
Montreal, PQ H3N 1X1
(514) 274-9793
FAX (514) 495-9035 "Attn: FRM"
Type of Company: Distributor.
Product Specialty: Electronic accordions and piano bar accompaniment machines.
Special Services: Keyboard and piano parts available.
Top Brands: Elka, Sultan, FRM.

Fretter Guitars

21750-96 Ave., R.R. 10
Langley, BC V3A 4P9
(604) 888-8073
FAX (604) 888-0881
Type of Company: Manufacturer of solid-body electric guitars.

Fury Guitar Manufacturing Co.

902 Ave. JN
Saskatoon, SK S7L 2L2
(306) 744-4063
Type of Company: Manufacturer of electric guitars and basses.

Gerraudio Distribution

363 Adelaide St. E.
Toronto, ON M5A 1N3
(416) 361-1667
FAX (416) 868-0528
Type of Company: Distributor of exclusive products to the live sound, MI and contractor markets.
Top Brands: Meyer, Ashly, HM Electronics, Allen & Heath.

Gould Marketing Inc.

6445 Cote-de-Liesse
Montreal, PQ H4T 1E5
(514) 342-4441
FAX (514) 342-5597
Type of Company: Distributor of professional and consumer audio electronics.
Special Services: Custom home automation systems.
Top Brands: JBL, AKG Acoustics, Otari.

Grooves Percussion Inc.

220 Industrial Parkway S., Unit 24
Aurora, ON L4G 3V6
(416) 841-5055
Type of Company: Manufacturer of drumsticks.
Special Services: Custom drumsticks and an endorsement program.
Top Brands: Grooves drumsticks, Gambal mallets, Stingray drums.

H&A Selmer Ltd.

95 Norfinch Dr.
Downsview, ON M3N 1W8
(416) 667-9622
FAX (416) 667-0075
Type of Company: Distributor of band instruments as well as drums and percussion accessories.
Top Brands: Selmer, Ludwig, Sabian.

H.D.S. Industries

P.O. Box 4374, Stn. E
Ottawa, ON K1V 8P1
(613) 733-6892
Type of Company: Manufacturer of Combat loudspeakers.

Hammond Keyboards Canada Ltd.

50 Mural St., Unit 6
Richmond Hill, ON L4B 1E4
(416) 764-0044
FAX (416) 764-0126
Type of Company: Distributor of Kurzweil pianos and Hammond organs and pianos.
Special Services: Complete service department.

Hanseatic Overseas Trading Inc.

181 University Ave., Suite 1202
Toronto, ON M5H 3M7
(416) 367-9072
FAX (813) 251-1621
Type of Company: Sales agency.
Prime Type of Business: Representative for musical instruments from Demusa and Klingenthal, Germany.
Top Brands: Bandmaster, Sonora, Musima.
Product Specialty: Pianos, accordions, concertinas, band and stringed instruments.
Branch:
212 S. Magnolia Ave.
Tampa, FL 33606
(813) 251-2342
Telex: WU 52864
FAX (813) 251-1621

Frederick Harris Music Co.

529 Speers Rd.
Oakville, ON L6K 2G4
(416) 845-3487
FAX (416) 845-1208
Type of Company: Distributor, publisher.
Product Specialty: Official publisher for the Royal Conservatory of Music.

Headwater Imports

635 Caron Ave.
Windsor, ON N9A 5B8
(519) 256-5665
FAX (519 256-2522
Type of Company: Manufacturer and distributor of audio equipment.
Special Services: Custom electronics and manufacturing.
Top Brands: Drawmer, Hill Audio, OHM Ind. Speaker Systems.
Product Specialty: Noise gates, dynamic processors, amps and consoles.

Geo. Heinl & Co. Ltd.

201 Church St.
Toronto, ON M5B 1Y7
(416) 363-0093
FAX (416) 363-0053
Type of Company: Manufacturer and distributor of stringed musical instruments and accessories.
Special Services: Repairs and evaluations.
Top Brands: Hofner, Pirastro, Thomastik.
Product Specialty: Violins.

The Russ Heinl Group

41 Industrial Park Place S.
Aurora, ON L4G 3Y5
(416) 727-1951
FAX (416) 841-1312
Type of Company: Agency.
Prime Type of Business: Distribution agency.
Top Brands: DOD Electronics, Gallien Kruger, AB Systems amps.
Product Specialty: Amplifiers, signal processing, sound reinforcement and guitars.

Charles Heintzman Pianos

3447 Kennedy Rd., Suite 9
Scarborough, ON M1V 3S5
(416) 299-8084
Type of Company: Distributor.
Product Specialty: Grand and upright pianos.

Jean Hepburn Enterprises

125 West 5 Ave.
Vancouver, BC V5Y 1H9
FAX (604) 879-9799
Type of Company: Distributor, importer.
Top Brands: Harrion, Clay Paky, Coemar.
Product Specialty: Amplifiers, crossovers, plus sound, laser and lighting supplies.

D. Hinschberger Distributors

3447 Kennedy Rd., Unit 9
Scarborough, ON M1V 3S5
(416) 297-0304
FAX (416) 479-9081
Type of Company: Distributor.
Special Services: Repairs to most makes of keyboards.
Top Brands: Hohner, Ronisch, C. Heintzman, Singing Machine.
Product Specialty: Pianos and organs.

ILP Manufacturing Inc.

250 Wildcat Rd.
Downsview, ON M3J 2M5
(416) 667-9914
FAX (416) 667-8928
Type of Company: Manufacturer, distributor.
Product Specialty: Toroid transformers and high-power amplifiers and loudspeakers. Manufacturing of custom-designed products.

I.V.L. Technologies

3318 Oak St.
Victoria, BC V8X 1R2
(604) 383-4320
FAX (604) 386-2632
Type of Company: Manufacturer, distributor, designer.
Top Brands: Digitec, IVL.
Product Specialty: Electronic sound measuring equipment and MIDI interfaces for musical instruments.

The Imaginative Marketing Group (IMG)

1444 Hymus Blvd.
Dorval, PQ H9P 1J6
(514) 685-2046
FAX (514) 685-2094
Type of Company: Distributor.
Top Brands: ADA guitar amplification, Phonic, Hosa
Product Specialty: Quality guitar amplification systems.

Impact Cases Inc.

150 Ferrier St., Suite 3
Markham, ON L3R 3K3
(416) 470-7888
FAX (416) 470-7843
Type of Company: Manufacturer.
Product Specialty: Carrying and shipping cases.

Internote Canada Limited

1645 Bonhill Rd., Unit 11
Mississauga, ON L5T 1C8
(416) 564-7171
FAX (416) 564-3448
Type of Company: Distributor.
Top Brands: Bontempi, Farfisa, Furstein.
Product Specialty: Pianos, electronic organs and keyboards.

Irmbach Canada Ltd.

Clearview Rd., R.R. 3
Red Deer, AB T4N 5E3
(403) 347-5432
FAX (403) 347-1811
Type of Company: Manufacturer, distributor.
Top Brands: Irmbach, Fazer.
Product Specialty: Pianos and piano supplies.

James Designs

311 Robinson St.
Woodstock, ON N4S 3B8
(519) 539-1826
Type of Company: Manufacturer, sales agency.
Product Specialty: Custom-design of chin-rests and tail-pieces for violins and violas.

Janson Piano Co.

P.O. Box 5428, Stn. A
Toronto, ON M5W 1N6
(416) 536-4114
Type of Company: Piano repair.
Product Specialty: Rebuilding and tuning of pianos.

Kada Music

166 Toryork Dr., Suite 9
Weston, ON M9L 1W6
(416) 749-8069
FAX (416) 740-8097
Type of Company: Manufacturer.
Product Specialty: Guitar straps.

Kawai Canada Music Ltd.

6400 Shawson Dr., Unit 1
Mississauga, ON L5T 1L8
(416) 670-2345
FAX (416) 670-3646
Type of Company: Distributor, wholesaler.
Product Specialty: Pianos, organs, electronic keyboards, sequencers and MIDI accessories.

Korg Canada

378 rue Isabey
St. Laurent, PQ H4T 1W1
(514) 738-3000
FAX (514) 737-5069
Type of Company: Distributor of electronic musical instruments.
Top Brands: Korg, Oktal Software.
Branches:
111 Granton Dr., Units 404-406
Richmond Hill, ON L4B 1L5
(416) 764-6350
FAX (416) 764-6799

3496 Vanness Ave.
Vancouver, BC V5R 5A9
(604) 438-9212
FAX (604) 438-7911

Lado Guitars

689 Warden Ave., Suite 6
Scarborough, ON M1L 3Z5
(416) 690-5010
FAX (416) 690-5022
Type of Company: Manufacturer.
Product Specialty: Custom-built electric guitars.

Jean Larrivee Guitars Ltd.

267 E. 1 St.
North Vancouver, BC V7L 1B4
(604) 985-6520
FAX (604) 985-2169
Type of Company: Manufacturer of acoustic and electric guitars.

Lasido Inc.

R.R. 1
La Patrie, PQ H2J 2Z8
(819) 888-2255
FAX (819) 888-2780
Type of Company: Manufacturer.
Top Brands: Norman, Seagull, Simon and Patrick.
Product Specialty: Guitars.

Levy's Leathers

1780 Eglinton Ave. E.
Toronto, ON M4A 2T2
(416) 752-1795
FAX (416) 863-6744
Type of Company: Manufacturer.
Product Specialty: Leather goods and accessories for the music trade.

MUSICAL INSTRUMENT & SOUND EQUIPMENT SUPPLIERS

Linkon Guitar Co.

1549 Charleswood Rd.
Winnipeg, MB R3N 1X4
(204) 895-0115
Type of Company: Manufacturer of pedal steel guitars and accessories.
Comments: Distributor of strings.

R.R. Loewen Distributors Ltd.

1555 Dublin Ave., Unit 1
Winnipeg, MB R3E 3M8
(204) 783-7123
FAX (204) 774-4351
Type of Company: Distributor.
Product Specialty: Pianos
Top Brands: Samick, Hyundai.

Louis Musical Ltee.

529 Deslauriers St.
St. Laurent, PQ H4N 1W2
(514) 332-6907
1-800-363-1884
FAX (514) 332-0255
Type of Company: Distributor, importer and wholesaler of musical instruments.
Top Brands: Hohner electric guitars, Sonor drums, EMG pickups.
Product Specialty: Rexer wireless systems.

Don MacMillan Ent. Ltd.

14832-103A Ave.
Surrey, BC V3R 1L7
(604) 581-3063
FAX (604) 581-7512
Type of Company: Distributor, jobber for music books.
Top Brands: Hal Leonard, Warner-Chappell, Mel Bay, Gordon V. Thompson.

Mark IV Audio Canada Inc.

345 Herbert St., P.O. Box 520
Gananoque, ON K7G 2V1
(613) 382-2141
FAX (613) 382-7466
Type of Company: Manufacturer of professional audio products.
Special Services: Design and technical assistance.
Top Brands: Electro-Voice, Altec-Lansing, University Sound.
Product Specialty: Microphones, loudspeaker systems, loudspeaker components, amplifiers, EQs, audio instrumentation equipment, etc. Complete audio systems for musicians and concert sound. Fixed installations (churches, theatres, cinemas, schools and office buildings).

Marquis Music Inc.

144 Front St. W., Suite 460
Toronto, ON M5J 2L7
(416) 595-5498
FAX (416) 595-5487
Type of Company: Manufacturer.
Product: Midia computer music workstation.

The Martin Organisation Canada Ltd.

1080 Brock Rd., Unit 14
Pickering, ON L1W 3H3
(416) 831-8544
FAX (416) 831-3445
Type of Company: Distributor, wholesaler.
Top Brands: Martin, Goya, Crate, Ampeg.

Frank May Music Enterprises

26 Harris Ave.
Toronto, ON M4C 1P4
(416) 352-2442
FAX (416) 887-1525
Type of Company: Manufacturer.
Product Specialty: Drums, pads and practice books.

Mayfair Music Publications Inc.

2600 John St., Suite 209
Markham, ON L3R 2W4
(416) 475-1848
FAX (416) 474-9870
Type of Company: Publisher.
Product Specialty: Assorted music books and accessories.

McBride Loudspeaker Source Inc.

638 Colby Dr.
Waterloo, ON N2V 1A2
(519) 884-3500
FAX (519) 884-0193
Type of Company: Distributor of all types of loudspeaker driver units.
Top Brands: Eminence, Motorola, Marsland.
Product Specialty: 1-inch to 18-inch loudspeakers up to 400 watts.

McGill University Samples

555 Sherbrooke St. W.
Montreal, PQ H3A 1E3
(514) 398-4548
FAX (514) 398-3594
Type of Company: Manufacturer.
Product Specialty: CDs covering a range of instrumental sounds for sampling.

Merrari Guitars

20 Marlboro Rd.
Edmonton, AB T6J 2C6
(403) 435-1955
Type of Company: Manufacturer of solid body electric guitars.
Special Services: Custom made guitars.

R.D. Minz Co., Ltd.

1285 Hodge Ave.
St. Laurent, PQ H4N 2B6
(514) 748-5242
FAX (514) 748-1865 or 284-2282, ext. 302
Type of Company: Importer and distributor of violins and violin-related accessories and parts.
Top Brands: Sandner, Eberle, Pfretzschner.
Product Specialty: Canadian bow hair.

Morelli's Music

95-10 St. E.
Owen Sound, ON N4K 1S1
(519) 376-5533
Type of Company: Manufacturer, distributor.
Top Brands: Note-for-Note guitar solos, Starlicks, Lightning Licks.
Product Specialty: Instructional cassette tapes and videos.

Multi-Caisses Inc.

1135 Taillon St.
Quebec City, PQ G1N 4G7
(418) 527-2549
FAX (418) 527-5856
Type of Company: Manufacturer of custom shipping and carrying cases for music dealers.
Special Services: Roto-molded keyboard cases and a full line of standard cases.
Top Brands: Catalog available.
Branches:
85 Albert St.
Ottawa, ON K1P 6A4
(613) 235-3628
FAX (613) 563-1992

P.O. Box 622
Jackman, ME USA
04945
FAX (418) 527-5856

The Music Stand

1045 North Service Rd. E.
Oakville, ON L6H 1A6
(416) 849-4346
FAX (416) 849-0206
Type of Company: Distributor, franchisor.
Prime Type of Business: Distributing pianos, organs, keyboards and accessories through a franchise system. Franchise outlets available.
Top Brands: Heintzman/Gerhard Heintzman, Hohner, G.E.M.
Product Specialty: Acoustic pianos, keyboards, and digital pianos.

Musicware Distributors Inc.

1573 Eglinton Ave. W., Suite 3
Toronto, ON M6E 2G9
(416) 785-3311
FAX (416) 785-6416
Type of Company: Distributor of computer music software.
Prime Type of Business: Distribution of computer music software.
Special Services: In-store clinics and demonstrations.
Top Brands: Passport, Grey Matter, Pixel.

Nomad Cases

13250 Crowland Ave., R.R. 1
Welland, ON L3B 1X5
(416) 384-2368
FAX (416) 384-2322
Type of Company: Manufacturer.
Product Specialty: Drum cases.

Omnimedia Corporation Ltd.

9653 Cote-de-Liesse Rd.
Dorval, PQ H9P 1A3
(514) 636-9971
FAX (514) 636-5347
Type of Company: Distributor.
Top Brands: Crown, Clark-Technik, Samson, Soundtracs, Turbosound.
Product Specialty: Pro audio for the recording and broadcast industries.

M.J. Pacey's Distributing Ltd.

1411 West Broadway
Vancouver, BC V6H 1H6
(604) 732-8835
FAX (604) 732-0694
Type of Company: Distributor.
Top Brands: Sojin pianos.

Pacific Sound and Signal Inc.

2851 Simpson Rd., Suite 100
Richmond, BC V6X 2R2
(604) 270-6010
FAX (604) 270-0841
Type of Company: Manufacturer.
Special Services: Custom acoustic design.
Top Brands: Pacific, JBL, Sansui.
Product Specialty: Speakers.

Paco Electronics

20 Steelcase Rd. W., Unit 10
Markham, ON L3R 1B2
(416) 475-0740
FAX (416) 475-0464
Type of Company: Distributor.
Top Brands: Paco, Paso, Fuji.
Product Specialty: Amplifiers, microphones, audio and video cassettes.

Panasonic Canada Ltd.

5770 Ambler Dr.
Mississauga, ON L4W 2T3
(416) 624-5010
Type of Company: Distributor.
Product Specialty: A/V and RAMSA pro audio equipment.

Ken Parisien Pianos Ltd.

203 Colonnade
Nepean, ON K2E 7K3
(613) 226-4770
FAX (613) 226-3546
Type of Company: Sales agency.
Top Brands: Sojin.
Product Specialty: Piano restoration and sales.

Peate Musical Supplies Ltd.

6410 Abrams St.
Montreal, PQ H4S 9Z7
(514) 956-0077
FAX (514) 956-0711
Type of Company: Distributor, wholesaler.
Top Brands: Aspri, Fiesta, Mapes.
Product Specialty: Acoustic instruments.

Penn Fabrication

635 Caron Ave.
Windsor, ON N9A 5B8
(519) 256-5889
FAX (519) 256-2522
Type of Company: Manufacturer and distributor of case and cabinet hardware.
Special Services: Custom manufacturing and finishes.
Top Brands: Penn.

Perspective Audio Inc.

294 Marcel Giguere
Blainville, PQ J7E 4H4
(514) 435-2925
FAX (514) 437-8535
Type of Company: Distributor of home and professional A/V products.
Top Brands: LAST, FM Acoustics, Coldmund.

Phase Four Distributors

1235-64 Ave. S.E., Bay 4
Calgary, AB T2H 2J7
(403) 252-0911
FAX (403) 259-8394
Type of Company: Distributor.
Top Brands: Amiga Commodore, IBM.
Product Specialty: Computer music software.

Pianotek Ltd.

21 Canadian Rd.
Scarborough, ON M1R 5G2
(416) 759-8050
Type of Company: Manufacturer, distributor.
Top Brands: Imadegawa piano parts, Nippon Denro tuning pins.
Product Specialty: Piano parts (stock or custom-made) plus custom bass strings and bridges.

Pibroch Productions Two

12 Flanders Rd.
Toronto, ON M6C 3K6
(416) 789-3777
Type of Company: Distributor.
Prime Type of Business: Canadian distributor of Underwood bass pickups.

PIKA Technologies Inc.

155 Terrence Matthews Cr.
Kanata, ON K2M 1W8
(613) 591-1555
FAX (613) 591-1488
Type of Company: Manufacturer.
Product Specialty: The d-MIDI-16 drum processor.

Pixel Publishing

1573 Eglinton Ave. W., Suite 3
Toronto, ON M6E 2G9
(416) 785-3036
FAX (416) 785-6416
Type of Company: Manufacturer of computer software.
Top Brands: Super Librarian (compatible with Mac and Atari).

Prezmith Engineering

50 Carroll St., Suite 304
Toronto, ON M6M 3G3
(416) 461-4891
Type of Company: Manufacturer.
Product Specialty: MIDI thru and junction boxes.

Protech Cases

1751 Richardson, Suite 4557
Montreal, PQ H3K 1G6
(514) 931-5023
FAX (514) 931-5023
Type of Company: Manufacturer of road and flight cases.
Special Services: Custom silk screening of company or band logo.

Rexx Acoustics Inc.

3 Industrial Place, P.O. Box 2040
Canmore, AB T0L 0M0
(403) 678-4452
FAX (403) 678-4520
Type of Company: Manufacturer of quality instrument amplification products.
Top Brands: Rexx Acoustics.
Product Specialty: Rack-mounted, modular products.

Rhodes Canada

13880 Mayfield Place
Richmond, BC V6V 2E4
(604) 270-6332
FAX (604) 270-7150
Type of Company: Manufacturer of electronic musical instruments.

Rodam Manufacturing (Canada) Ltd.

91 Pelham Ave.
Toronto, ON M6N 1A5
(416) 656-8462
FAX (416) 656-8695
Type of Company: Manufacturer.
Top Brands: Rodam, Rimshot.
Product Specialty: Cables, drumsticks.

Roland Canada Music Ltd.

13880 Mayfield Place
Richmond, BC V6V 2E4
(604) 270-6626
FAX (604) 270-6552
Type of Company: Manufacturer of electronic musical instruments.
Branches:
346 Watline Ave.
Mississauga, ON L4Z 1X2

9425 Trans-Canada Service Rd. N.
St. Laurent, PQ H4S 1V3

Rosco

1271 Denison St., Suite 66
Markham, ON L3R 4B5
(416) 475-1400
FAX (416) 475-3351
Type of Company: Distributor, importer.
Top Brands: Rosco.
Product Specialty: Accessories for TV, theatre and film lighting.

Rumark Video Inc.

534 Lawrence Ave. W., Suite 215
Toronto, ON M6A 1A2
(416) 789-7881
FAX (416) 789-4725
Type of Company: Distributor of music instruction videos and audio tapes.

S.F. Marketing Inc.

3254 Griffith St.
Ville St. Laurent, PQ H4T 1A7
(514) 733-5344
FAX (514) 733-7140
Type of Company: Manufacturer of cables.

MUSICAL INSTRUMENT & SOUND EQUIPMENT SUPPLIERS

From a whisper to a scream.

Suddenly, all other speakers are outdated.
Adamson is the first to incorporate the Acoustic Waveguide Theory*
into speaker design. Combined with advanced driver technology,
with three patents pending, Adamson delivers
unsurpassed sound clarity.

*Presented by Dr. E.R. Geddes at the 83rd AES Convention. Oct. 1987.

ADAMSON

ADVANCED CONCERT SYSTEMS

Adamson Acoustic Design Corporation, 850 Brock Road South, Unit 1, Pickering, Ontario L1W 1Z8
Telephone: (416) 420-6279 Fax (416) 420-0813

Sabian Ltd.
Main Street
Meductic, NB E0H 1L0
(506) 272-2019
FAX (506) 328-9697
Type of Company: Manufacturer.
Special Services: Custom selection, warranty and accessories program.
Top Brands: AA, HH, B8 series.
Product Specialty: Cymbals.

St. John's Music Ltd.
633 Portage Ave.
Winnipeg, MB R3B 2Z9
(204) 775-0428
FAX (204) 786-6814
Type of Company: Sales agency, wholesaler.
Top Brands: Torque, Encore.
Product Specialty: Band instruments, guitars, electronic keyboards, sound reinforcement and percussion.

Saved By Technology Marketing
10 Breadalbane St.
Toronto, ON M4Y 1C3
(416) 928-5984
FAX (416) 928-0262
Type of Company: Distributor.
Top Brands: Atari, Macintosh.
Product Specialty: Computer music software and accessories.

Scott's Highland Services
1464 Beckworth Ave.
London, ON N5V 2K7
(519) 543-0892
FAX (519) 453-6303
Type of Company: Importers.
Top Brands: Legato, Gillanders McLeod, Canmore.
Product Specialty: Bagpipes, drums, music books and cassette tapes.

Sennheiser Canada
221 Labrosse Ave.
Pointe Claire, PQ H9R 1A3
(514) 426-3010
FAX (514) 426-2979
Type of Company: Distributor of conventional and wireless microphones, and infrared equipment.
Special Services: Theatre installations and sound enhancement for the hard of hearing.
Top Brands: Sennheiser.

Sherlock Manning Music Inc.
P.O. Box 99
Clinton, ON N0M 1L0
(519) 482-5444
FAX (519) 482-5448
Type of Company: Manufacturer of acoustic pianos.

A.C. Simmonds & Sons Ltd.
975 Dillingham Rd.
Pickering, ON L1W 3B2
(416) 839-8041
FAX (416) 839-2667
Type of Company: Distributor.
Top Brands: Shure.
Product Specialty: Microphones (conventional and wireless), broadcast consoles and microphone mixers.
Branches:
4259 Canada Way, Suite 203
Burnaby, BC V5G 1H1
(604) 438-5267
FAX (604) 438-5269

5963-103A St.
Edmonton, AB T6H 2J7
T6H 2J7
(403) 438-4044
FAX (403) 437-4308

1700 boul. Taschereau, Suite 200
Ville Lemoyne, PQ
J4P 3M9
(514) 466-5250
FAX (514) 466-5252

P.O. Box 815
Lower Sackville, NS B4C 3V3
(902) 865-1889
FAX (902) 865-5120

Sony of Canada Ltd.
155 Gordon Baker Rd., Suite 216
Willowdale, ON M2H 3N5
(416) 499-5111
FAX (416) 499-0984
Type of Company: Distributor of pro audio equipment.

Sound Music Distributors Ltd.
20 Melham Ct., Unit 9
Scarborough, ON M1B 2T6
(416) 299-4799
FAX (416) 299-4707
Type of Company: Distributor, importer.
Product Specialty: Musical instrument accessories.
Top Brands: Dunlop, Huang, Maxima Gold Strings, Schaller.

SM58

SHURE®

THE SOUND OF THE PROFESSIONALS®...WORLDWIDE
A.C. Simmonds & Sons Ltd., 975 Dillingham Road, Pickering, Ontario, 416-839-8041

Soundcraft Canada Inc.
1444 Hymus Blvd.
Dorval, PQ H9P 1J6
(514) 685-1610
FAX (514) 685-2094
Type of Company: Distributor.
Special Services: Maintenance and service.
Top Brands: Soundcraft mixing consoles.

Studer Revox Canada
14 Banigan Dr.
Toronto, ON M4H 1E9
(416) 423-2831
FAX (416) 425-6906
Type of Company: Manufacturer and
distributor of Studer and Revox products.
Product Specialty: Consumer and professional
audio products, sales and service.

StudioLab Audio Inc.
29 Bermondsey Rd.
Toronto, ON M4B 1Z7
(416) 757-3265
Type of Company: Manufacturer of
loudspeakers.
Prime Type of Business: Consumer and
professional loudspeakers.
Special Services: Custom speaker systems.
Top Brands: StudioLab.

TC Electronics
221 Labrosse Ave.
Pointe Claire, PQ
(514) 426-3010
FAX (514) 426-2979
Type of Company: Distributor.
Top Brands: Sennheiser, Marantz, Final
Technology.
Product Specialty: Microphones, headphones
and wireless microphones.

TMI
2530 Davies Ave., P.O. Box 279
Port Coquitlam, BC V3C 3V7
(604) 464-1341
FAX (604) 464-9275
Type of Company: Distributor.
Special Services: Product clinics and invento-
ry finance plans for retailers.
Top Brands: Fender, Akai, Alesis, Sunn.
Product Specialty: Stage lighting, PA systems,
amplification and recording equipment.

TOA Electronics Inc.
1351 Matheson Blvd. E., Unit 3
Mississauga, ON L4W 2A1
(416) 624-2317
FAX (416) 624-7348
Type of Company: Manufacturer of
professional sound systems.
Special Services: Distribution and service.
Product Specialty: Mixers, amps, speakers
and home recording systems.
Branches:
10712-181 St.
Edmonton, AB T5S 1K8
(403) 489-5511
FAX (403) 489-7038

19691 Shellbridge Way, Suite 130
Richmond, BC V6X 2W8
(604) 273-5212
FAX (604) 270-3644

1396 St. Patrick St.
Montreal, PQ H3K 1A6
(514) 931-5888
FAX: (514) 931-2359

Tannoy North America Inc.
300 Gage Ave., Suite 1
Kitchener, ON N2M 2C8
(519) 745-1158
FAX (519) 745-2364
Type of Company: Manufacturer of
loudspeakers.

TEAC Canada Ltd.
340 Brunel Rd.
Mississauga, ON L4Z 2C2
(416) 890-8008
FAX (416) 890-9888
Type of Company: Distributor of TEAC and
TASCAM recording equipment.

Technical Magic
P.O. Box 3939, Stn. C
Ottawa, ON K1Y 4M5
(613) 596-9114
FAX (6130 596-3304
Type of Company: Sales of custom modifica-
tion kits.
Special Services: MT-32 modifications.

Technics
3331 Jacombs Rd.
Richmond, BC V6V 1Z6
(604) 273-4976
FAX (604) 273-5931
Type of Company: Distributor, wholesale.
Special Services: Technics Music Academy
(teaching system).
Top Brands: Technics, PCM.
Product Specialty: Home organs, portable
keyboards and digital pianos.

Gordon V. Thompson

29 Birch Ave.
Toronto, ON M4V 1E2
(416) 923-7329
FAX (416) 923-4821
Type of Company: Distributor, sales agency, publisher.
Product Specialty: Printed music.

Thorvin Electronics Inc.

720 Burnhamthorpe Rd. W., Units 15-16
Mississauga, ON L5C 2R9
(416) 276-7271
FAX (416) 276-4196
Type of Company: Distributor of commercial and industrial sound systems.
Special Services: Rental of spectrum analyzer to dealer base.
Top Brands: Soundsphere, Anchor Audio, Williams Sound.
Product Specialty: Sound systems.

Timeless Instruments

P.O. Box 51
Tugaske, SK S0H 4B0
(306) 759-2042
Type of Company: Manufacturer of luthier supplies and accessories.
Special Services: Guitar construction seminars.
Top Brands: Fishman transducers, Matchman pre-amps, Labella strings.
Product Specialty: Wood for instruments plus instrument kits and finishing supplies.

Unisson

5276 boul. Levesque
Laval, PQ H7C 1N1
(514) 661-7171
FAX (514) 662-1922
Type of Company: Manufacturer.
Product Specialty: Speaker cabinets.

Vibration Technology Ltd.

1950 Ellesmere Rd., Unit 12
Scarborough, ON M1H 2V8
(416) 438-9320
FAX (416) 439-1937
Type of Company: Manufacturer and distributor of audio equipment.
Product Specialty: Industrial PAs plus guitar and bass amplifiers.

Art White Music Service

(A Division of DJU Entertainment Group)
220 Pony Dr.
Newmarket, ON L3Y 7D6
(416) 836-6078
FAX (416) 836-6089
Type of Company: Distributor of musical instruments, DJ equipment and lighting effects.
Top Brands: Vester, GHS, Dunlop, WB.

Yamaha Canada Music Ltd.

135 Milner Ave.
Scarborough, ON M1S 3R1
(416) 298-1311
FAX (416) 292-0732
Type of Company: Manufacturer, wholesaler of musical instruments.
Special Services: Music education courses.

Yorkville Sound Ltd.

80 Midwest Rd.
Scarborough, ON M1P 4R2
(416) 751-8481
FAX (416) 751-8746
Type of Company: Manufacturer, distributor.
Top Brands: Elite, Audiopro, Gibson.
Product Specialty: PA systems.

Young Chang Canada Corp.

5240 Finch Ave. E.
Scarborough, ON M1S 5A2
Type of Company: Distributor.
Top Brands: Young Chang, Weber.
Product Specialty: Grand and upright pianos.

ALBERTA

CALGARY

Country Roads Saloon

2120-16 Ave. N.E.
Calgary, AB T2E 1L4
(403) 291-4666
FAX (403) 291-6498
Contact: Kevin MacNeil.
Style of Music: Country, Rock.
Seating Capacity: 250.
Liquor License: Yes.
Booking Agent: Same as contact.

Crossroads Motor Hotel

2120-16 Ave. N.E.
Calgary, AB T2E 1L4
(403) 291-4666
FAX (403) 291-6498
Contact: Kevin MacNeil.
Style of Music: Country.
Seating Capacity: 250.
Liquor License: Yes.

Franky & Johnny's

1621 Centre St. N.
Calgary, AB T2E 2S2
(403) 243-5511
Contact: John Bitonti.
Style of Music: Heavy Rock, Metal, Top 40.
Seating Capacity: 250.
Liquor License: Yes.
Booking Agent: Commodore Entertainment.

Kensington's Delicafe

1414 Kensington Rd. N.W.
Calgary, AB T2N 3P9
(403) 283-0771
Contact: Linda Kitchin.
Style of Music: All styles.
Seating Capacity: 46.
Liquor License: Yes.

NIGHT CLUBS

Live Wire
9030 MacLeod Tr. S.E.
Calgary, AB T2H 0N4
(403) 253-1101
Contact: Jamie Wong.
Style of Music: Hard Rock, Metal.
Seating Capacity: 350.
Liquor License: Yes.
Booking Agent: Commodore Booking Agency.

The Old Scotch
820-10 St. S.W.
Calgary, AB T2P 2X1
(403) 269-7440
Contact: Garth Redmond.
Style of Music: Rock, Country, Jazz, Blues,
Alternative.
Seating Capacity: 400.
Liquor License: Yes.
Booking Agent: Garth Redmond.

Port O'Call Inn
1935 McKnight Blvd. N.E.
Calgary, AB T2E 6V4
(403) 291-4600
FAX (403) 250-6827
Contact: Mr. Paul Burgess.
Style of Music: Single lounge-style musicians.
Seating Capacity: 60.
Liquor License: Yes.
Booking Agent: In-house.

Top of the Inn
4404 Calgary Tr.
Edmonton, AB
(403) 434-6415
Contact: Paul Doucette, ext. 250
Style of Music: Wide variety of music ranging
from 30s to 80s.
Seating Capacity: 278.
Liquor License: Yes.
Booking Agent: Booked through Arturo
Domingo and Paul Doucette.

The Westward Club
119-12 Ave. S.W.
Calgary, AB T2R 0G8
(403) 266-4611
Contact: Alex Hazine.
Style of Music: Blues, Rock & Roll, New Wave.
Seating Capacity: 240.
Liquor License: Yes.
Booking Agent: Alex Hazine.
Comments: International attractions.

EDMONTON

Saxony
15540 Stony Plain Rd.
Edmonton, AB T5P 3Z2
(403) 484-3311
Style of Music: Hard Rock, Variety.
Seating Capacity: 120 (cocktail lounge),
450 (tavern).
Liquor License: Yes.

Sidetrack Cafe
10333-112 St.
Edmonton, AB T5K 1M9
(403) 421-1326
Contact: Clare Anderson.
Style of Music: R&B, Roots.
Seating Capacity: 175.
Liquor License: Yes.

University of Alberta Students' Union
256-SUB, University of Alberta
Edmonton, AB T6G 2J7
(403) 492-2048
FAX (403) 492-4643
Contact: Gerald Stoll.
Style of Music: Blues, Rock, Pop, Jazz,
Country.
Seating Capacity: 620 (Dinwoodie),
720 (Horowitz Theatre).

Yesteryear's Bar & Grill
10620-82 Ave.
Edmonton, AB
(403) 433-9411
Contact: Shirley Kopiak.
Style of Music: 60s Rock, New Music.
Seating Capacity: 120.
Liquor License: Yes.
Booking Agent: Network Entertainment.

BRITISH COLUMBIA

FORT ST. JOHN

The Woods "After Dark"
Northwoods Inn
10627 Alaska Rd.
Fort St. John, BC V1J 5P4
(604) 787-1616
FAX (604) 787-7078
Contact: Dale Plourde.
Style of Music: Pop.
Seating Capacity: 225.
Liquor License: Yes.

NANAIMO

Wichita North
25 Victoria Rd.
Nanaimo, BC V9R 4N9
(604) 753-5244
Contact: Melva White.
Style of Music: Country Rock, Vintage Rock &
Roll, some R&B.
Seating Capacity: 329.
Liquor License: Yes.

NORTH VANCOUVER

Coach's Lounge
Coach House Inn
700 Lillooet Rd.
North Vancouver, BC V7J 2H5
(604) 985-3111
Contact: Steve Webster.
Style of Music: Suitable for Light Pop and
Country acts (singles or duos). Catering to 30-60
age group.
Seating Capacity: 85.
Liquor License: Yes.
Booking Agent: Whitefoot Entertainment, 5763
Oak St., Suite 18, Vancouver, BC (604) 266-
7145.
Comments: Live MOR music Wed.-Thurs. 9
p.m.—1 a.m.

VANCOUVER

Arlington Cabaret
1236 W. Broadway
Vancouver, BC V6H 1G6
(604) 733-2220
FAX (604) 946-8163
Contact: M. Cerveny.
Style of Music: C&W, Rock, Latin Ballroom.
Seating Capacity: 300.
Liquor License: Yes.
Comments: Latin Ballroom (Thurs.-Sat.),
Country Rock (Fri.-Sat.). Two dance floors,
two bands.

Debonnaires Club
212 Carrall St.
Vancouver, BC V6B 2J1
(604) 681-2814
Contact: Mr. James Galant.
Style of Music: Folk, Standards, video
sing-a-long.
Seating Capacity: 150.
Liquor License: Yes.
Booking Agent: In-house.
Comments: Located in historic Gastown.

Frams
1450 S.W. Marine Dr.
Vancouver, BC V6P 5Z9
(604) 261-7277
Contact: Bruce Hatch.
Style of Music: Rock & Roll.
Seating Capacity: 250.
Liquor License: Yes.
Booking Agent: Same as contact.

Hot Jazz Club of Vancouver
2120 Main St.
Vancouver, BC V5T 3C5
(604) 873-4131
Contact: Bruce McCrea.
Style of Music: Jazz, Pop (dance band
standards).
Seating Capacity: 225.
Liquor License: Yes.

Hotel Georgia

801 West Georgia
Vancouver, BC V6C 1P7
(604) 682-5566
FAX (604) 682-8192
Contact: Martin Pucher, assistant general manager.
Style of Music: Sing-a-long with a "drop-in" jam policy, Thurs.-Sat.
Seating Capacity: 180.
Liquor License: Yes.
Booking Agent: None.

The Metro

1136 West Georgia St.
Vancouver, BC V6G 3H7
(604) 687-5566
FAX (604) 684-1302
Contact: Phil Coelho or Candi Amado
Style of Music: Rock & Roll. Caters to acts such as Lee Aaron, Killer Dwarfs and Loverboy.
Seating Capacity: 500.
Liquor License: Yes.
Booking Agent: Lenny Goddard (S.L. Feldman & Associates).

Pacific Bluegrass & Heritage Society

P.O. Box 46515, Stn. G
Vancouver, BC V6R 4G7
(604) 255-4779
FAX (604) 255-9496
Contact: Les Mortimer, president.
Style of Music: Bluegrass, Acoustic.
Seating Capacity: 120.
Liquor License: Yes.
Booking Agent: Roger Pilkey.
Comments: Society books touring groups approximately once every five weeks. Special events throughout April.

Soft Rock Cafe

1925 W. 4 Ave.
Vancouver, BC V6J 1M7
(604) 736-8480
FAX (604) 736-2590
Contact: David Payne.
Style of Music: Jazz (Sundays), Musical Dinner Theatre (Mon.-Tues.), Top 40 (Wed.-Sat.).
Seating Capacity: 300.
Liquor License: Yes.
Booking Agent: Feldman & Associates.
Comments: Fine dining combined with various music formats. Dancing Wednesday to Saturday.

Town Pump

66 Water St.
Vancouver, BC V6B 1A4
(604) 683-6695
Contact: Joe McLean, owner.
Style of Music: Original Rock.
Seating Capacity: 300.
Liquor License: Yes.
Booking Agent: Phantom Enterprises.
Comments: Food available.

VICTORIA

The Forge

919 Douglas St.
Victoria, BC V8W 2C7
(604) 383-7137
Contact: Kirk Olson, Bill Tilden.
Style of Music: Pop, Rock, Top 40.
Seating Capacity: 575.
Liquor License: Yes.
Booking Agents: Feldman & Associates, various others.
Comments: Mon. to Sat. Up to three or four special concerts per month, including such artists as 54•40, Trooper, David Lindley, Meatloaf, and others.

The Sting

919 Douglas St.
Victoria, BC V8W 2C2
(604) 383-7137
Contact: Kirk Olson, Bill Tilden.
Style of Music: R&B, 60s, 70s, some Folk.
Seating Capacity: 200.
Liquor License: Yes.
Booking Agents: Feldman & Associates, various others.
Comments: Live music nightly.

MANITOBA

WINNIPEG

Bullwinkle's

826 Regent Ave. W.
Winnipeg, MB
(204) 222-0081
Style of Music: Rock.

Rorie Street Marble Club
65 Rorie St.
Winnipeg, MB R3B 1A1
(204) 943-4222
FAX (204) 942-1765
Contact: Harry Holbrook.
Style of Music: Light Rock, R&B.
Seating Capacity: 305.
Liquor License: Yes.
Booking Agent: Hungry I Agency.

NEW BRUNSWICK
MONCTON

Urban Corral
333 St. George St.
Moncton, NB E1C 1W8
(506) 857-4116
Style of Music: C&W.
Seating Capacity: 300.
Liquor License: Yes.
Booking Agent: Roger Dupois.

Ziggy's
730 Main St.
Moncton, NB E1C 1E4
(506) 858-8844
FAX (506) 859-1301
Contact: Don Gautreau.
Style of Music: Top 40, Clones, New Music, Novelty.
Seating Capacity: 400.
Liquor License: Yes.
Booking Agents: The Agency, George Elm, and others.

NOVA SCOTIA
HALIFAX

Misty Moon Cabaret
1595 Barrington St.
Halifax, NS B3J 3N1
(902) 422-5871
Contact: Geoff Palmeter.
Style of Music: Pop.
Seating Capacity: 1,500.
Liquor License: Yes.

Privateer's Warehouse
Historic Properties
Halifax, NS B3J 1S9
(902) 422-1289
Style of Music: MOR, R&B, Jazz, Rock, Pop, Irish Traditional, Celtic, Maritime.
Liquor License: Yes.
Comments: Accommodations for band members.

ONTARIO
BRAMPTON

Hot Rocks
107 Kennedy Rd. S.
Brampton, ON L6W 3G3
(416) 452-0211
Contact: Rick Kaczmarek.
Style of Music: Hard Rock.
Seating Capacity: 450.
Liquor License: Yes.
Booking Agent: The Agency.

KITCHENER

Bingeman Park
1380 Victoria St. N.
Kitchener, ON N2B 3E2
(519) 744-1555
Contact: Brian Banks.
Seating Capacity: 1,900.
Liquor License: Yes.
Comments: Four licensed halls.

MARKHAM

Nag's Head North
7720 Woodbine Ave.
Markham, ON L3R 4B9
(416) 475-6405
Style of Music: Rock.
Seating Capacity: 480.
Liquor License: Yes.
Booking Agent: The Agency.

MISSISSAUGA

ENTEX
1325 Eglinton Ave. E.
Mississauga, ON L4W 4L9
(416) 238-9868
FAX (416) 624-6465
Contact: Paul Blais.
Style of Music: Primarily Rock but will showcase other forms.
Seating Capacity: 984.
Liquor License: Yes.
Booking Agent: Don Blais, in-house booker.
Comments: Open Wed.-Sat. every week, but will open on Mondays and Tues. for national touring acts.

Madame's
1554 Dundas St. E.
Mississauga, ON L4X 1L4
(416) 276-6474
Style of Music: R&B.
Seating Capacity: 150.
Liquor License: Yes.

Richard's
3170 Erin Mills Parkway
Mississauga, ON L5L 1A1
(416) 828-1666
Contact: Rick Kaczmarek
Style of Music: Commercial Rock.
Seating Capacity: 400.
Liquor License: Yes.
Booking Agent: The Agency.

Superstars
6487 Dixie Rd.
Mississauga, ON L5T 1A4
(416) 670-2211
Contact: Dale Murray.
Style of Music: All styles.
Seating Capacity: 1,620.
Liquor License: Yes.

OTTAWA

Auberge de la Salle Inn
245 Dalhousie St.
Ottawa, ON K1N 7E1
(613) 233-0201
FAX (613) 238-7345
Contact: Marc LePage.
Style of Music: Recorded dance music only.
Seating Capacity: 100.
Liquor License: Yes.

Bank Cafe
294 Bank St.
Ottawa, ON K2P 1X8
(613) 238-1757
Style of Music: Folk (guitar, piano).
Liquor License: Yes.

Barrymore's Imperial Theatre Ltd.
323 Bank St.
Ottawa, ON K2P 1X9
(613) 238-5842
FAX (613) 238-1687
Contact: Gord Kent or Gord Rhodes.
Style of Music: All styles.
Seating Capacity: 450.
Liquor License: Yes.
Booking Agents: In-house and Apricot Talent & Recording Industries Inc. (613) 749-1116.
Comments: Seven levels for patrons. Full in-house sound and lighting systems.

Hitching Post
363 Bank St.
Ottawa, ON
(613) 232-0718
Style of Music: C&W.
Seating Capacity: 300.
Liquor License: Yes.

The New Penguin Dinner Theatre
292 Elgin St.
Ottawa, ON K2P 1M3
(613) 233-0057
FAX (613) 233-9152
Contact: Mark Monohan.
Style of Music: Jazz, Swing, Pop.
Seating Capacity: 250.
Liquor License: Yes.

RICHMOND HILL

Paparazzi
270 West Beaver Creek Rd.
Richmond Hill, ON L4B 1B4
(416) 886-6239
Contact: Peter Elios.
Style of Music: Latin, Salsa.
Seating Capacity: 350.
Liquor License: Yes.

TORONTO

Albert's Hall/Ye Olde Brunswick House
481 Bloor St. W.
Toronto, ON M5S 1X9
(416) 964-2242
Contact: Pierre Tremblay.
Style of Music: Blues, R&B, Rock.
Seating Capacity: 250.
Liquor License: Yes.

Apocalypse Club
750 College St.
Toronto, ON M6G 1C4
(416) 533-5787
Contact: Al Miller.
Style of Music: Alternative, others.
Seating Capacity: 367.
Liquor License: Yes.

BamBoo Club
312 Queen St. W.
Toronto, ON M5V 2A2
(416) 593-5771
Contact: Richard O'Brien.
Style of Music: African, Latin American, Caribbean.
Seating Capacity: 325.
Liquor License: Yes.
Booking Agent: Richard O'Brien.

Beaton's Lounge
475 Yonge St.
Toronto, ON M4Y 1X7
(416) 924-0611
Contact: Dave Caplan.
Style of Music: MOR, Top 40.
Seating Capacity: 175.
Liquor License: Yes.

Ben Wick's
424 Parliament St.
Toronto, ON M5A 3A2
(416) 961-9425
Contact: Robert McEnirney
Style of Music: Country, Blues, Jazz, Dixieland.
Seating Capacity: 175.
Liquor License: Yes.

Berlin
2335 Yonge St.
Toronto, ON M4P 2C8
(416) 489-7777
Contact: John Dandurand.
Style of Music: Jazz, Blues, R&B.
Seating Capacity: 500.
Liquor License: Yes.

Black Bull
298 Queen St. W.
Toronto, ON M5V 2A1
(416) 593-2766
Contact: J.R. Taylor.
Style of Music: Rock, Rockabilly, some R&B.
Seating Capacity: 25.
Liquor License: Yes.

Black Swan
154 Danforth Ave.
Toronto, ON M4K 1N1
(416) 469-0537
Contact: Gary Kendall.
Style of Music: Blues, R&B.
Seating Capacity: 110.
Liquor License: Yes.

Blue Moon Saloon
372 Bloor St. W.
Toronto, ON M5S 1X2
(416) 944-1160
Contact: Chris Orleck.
Style of Music: Local acts, all styles.
Seating Capacity: 51.
Liquor License: Yes.

Bluenote
128 Pears Ave.
Toronto, ON M5R 1T2
(416) 924-8244
Contact: Alyson Grennum.
Style of Music: R&B.
Seating Capacity: 300.
Liquor License: Yes.

Blues & Cues
3477 Kennedy Rd.
Scarborough, ON M1V 4Y3
(416) 292-8000
Contact: Derek Andrews.
Style of Music: Blues, Jazz, R&B.
Seating Capacity: 250.
Liquor License: Yes.

Brigantine Room
235 Queen's Quay W.
Toronto, ON M5J 2G8
(416) 973-3000
Contact: Derek Andrews.
Style of Music: Various.
Seating Capacity: 350.
Liquor License: Yes.

Bronco's
1214 Queen St. W.
Toronto, ON M6J 1J6
(416) 531-4635
Contact: Herb Appelby.
Style of Music: C&W.
Seating Capacity: 300.
Liquor License: Yes.

C'est What?

67 Front St. E.
Toronto, ON M5E 1B5
(416) 867-9791
Contact: Georgie Milbrandt.
Style of Music: Jazz, Folk, Pop, Rock, Country, Classical.
Seating Capacity: 140.
Liquor License: Yes.
Comments: Prefer to book original acts. No cover bands.

Cabana Room

460 King St. W.
Toronto, ON M5V 1L7
(416) 368-2864
Contact: Jim Scopes.
Style of Music: New Age, Pop, Rock, Blues, Jazz.
Seating Capacity: 200.
Liquor License: Yes.

Cadillac Jack's

401 King St. W.
Toronto, ON M5V 1K1
(416) 977-2982
Contact: Dave Caplan.
Style of Music: R&B, Top 40.
Seating Capacity: 250.
Liquor License: Yes.

Cafe des Copains

48 Wellington St.
Toronto, ON M5E 1C7
(416) 869-0148
Contact: Lothar Lang.
Style of Music: Jazz.
Seating Capacity: 110.
Liquor License: Yes.

Cameron Public House

408 Queen St. W.
Toronto, ON M5V 2A7
(416) 364-0811
Contact: Cindy Matthews.
Style of Music: All styles.
Seating Capacity: 100 (back room), 100 (front room).
Liquor License: Yes.
Booking Agent: Cindy Matthews.
Comments: The Cameron has a diversified booking policy. Bands are given access to the club's in-house 12-track recording studio.

Canada House Tavern

134 Sherbourne St.
Toronto, ON M5A 2R4
(416) 364-3779
Contact: Joe Bagorro.
Style of Music: C&W, Nostalgia Rock.
Seating Capacity: 243.
Liquor License: Yes.

Cap's

572 Jarvis St.
Toronto, ON M4Y 2H9
(416) 924-8555
Contact: Brenda Perry.
Style of Music: R&B, Rock, Pop, Top 40.
Seating Capacity: 135.
Liquor License: Yes.

Chandler's

11 St. Clair Ave. W.
Toronto, ON M4V 1K6
(416) 922-3737
Contact: Craig Norton.
Style of Music: Duos.
Seating Capacity: 160.
Liquor License: Yes.

Chicago's

335 Queen St. W.
Toronto, ON M5V 2A4
(416) 593-3301
Contact: Lisa.
Style of Music: R&B, Blues.
Seating Capacity: 120.
Liquor License: Yes.

Chick 'n' Deli

744 Mount Pleasant Rd.
Toronto, ON M4S 2N6
(416) 489-3363
Contact: Dave Caplan.
Style of Music: R&B, Top 40.
Seating Capacity: 210.
Liquor License: Yes.

Clinton's

693 Bloor St. W.
Toronto, ON M6G 1L5
(416) 535-9541
Contact: Serge Slaimovits.
Style of Music: Rock, R&B, Jazz, Funk.
Seating Capacity: 200.
Liquor License: Yes.

Club 2000

530 Guelph St.
Toronto, ON
(416) 840-3251
Contact: Brian Jennings.
Style of Music: All styles.
Seating Capacity: 1,000.
Liquor License: Yes.
Booking Agent: The Agency.
Comments: Live music Thursday nights only.

Club Bedrock

2240 Midland Ave.
Scarborough, ON M1S 1P8
(416) 291-0888
Contact: Brian Jennings.
Style of Music: Hard Rock.
Seating Capacity: 400.
Liquor License: Yes.
Booking Agent: The Agency.

Club OV's

1184 The Queensway
Toronto, ON M8Z 1R6
(416) 252-3131
Style of Music: Rock, R&B, Top 40.
Seating Capacity: 250.
Liquor License: Yes.

The Copa

21 Scollard
Toronto, ON M5R 1G1
(416) 922-6500
Contact: George Mendes.
Style of Music: All styles.
Seating Capacity: 1,100.
Liquor License: Yes.

Crooks

106 Front St. E.
Toronto, ON M5A 1E1
(416) 365-8906
Contact: Derek Andrews.
Style of Music: Blues and Roots.
Seating Capacity: 100.
Liquor License: Yes.

Danforth Cafe

60 Bowden
Toronto, ON M4K 2X4
(416) 778-4810
Style of Music: All styles.
Seating Capacity: 100.
Liquor License: Yes.

The Diamond

410 Sherbourne St.
Toronto, ON M4X 1K2
(416) 927-9010
FAX (416) 927-7961
Contacts: Randy Charlton (talent buyer),
Michele Bateman (publicity manager), Caroline
Toth (general manager).
Style of Music: A showcase venue for all styles
of music.
Seating Capacity: 750.
Liquor License: Yes.

Doubles

580 Rogers Rd.
Toronto, ON M6M 1B6
(416) 656-2446
Contact: Gerry Peters.
Style of Music: Rock, Blues, R&B.
Seating Capacity: 138.
Liquor License: Yes.

Down Towne Browne's

49 Front St. E.
Toronto, ON M5E 1B3
(416) 367-4949
Contact: Lee Clancy.
Style of Music: Rock, Blues, R&B, Top 40.
Seating Capacity: 250.
Liquor License: Yes.

The Duke

1225 Queen St. E.
Toronto, ON M4M 1L6
(416) 463-5302
Contact: Tom Kapsimalis.
Style of Music: Top 40, Tribute.
Seating Capacity: 270.
Liquor License: Yes.

El Mocambo

464 Spadina Ave.
Toronto, ON M5T 2G8
(416) 961-8991
Style of Music: All styles.
Seating Capacity: 600 total.
Liquor License: Yes.

Flick's

2409 Yonge St.
Toronto, ON M4P 2E7
(416) 481-7533
Contact: Tom O'Connor.
Style of Music: Rock, R&B, Top 40.
Seating Capacity: 125.
Liquor License: Yes.

Free Times Cafe

320 College St.
Toronto, ON M5T 1S3
(416) 967-1078
Style of Music: Solos, Folk, Jazz, Acoustic.
Seating Capacity: 40.
Liquor License: Yes.

Gasworks

585 Yonge St.
Toronto, ON M4Y 1Z2
(416) 922-9367
Contact: Robbie Justin.
Style of Music: Hard Rock, Metal.
Seating Capacity: 600.
Liquor License: Yes.
Booking Agent: The Entertainment Centre.

Graceland

1199 Kennedy Rd.
Scarborough, ON M1P 2L2
(416) 755-3311
Contact: Wayne King.
Style of Music: C&W.
Seating Capacity: 1,000.
Liquor License: Yes.

Hemingway's

142 Cumberland St.
Toronto, ON M5R 1A8
(416) 968-2828
Contact: Craig Norton.
Style of Music: Piano Bar.
Seating Capacity: 125.
Liquor License: Yes.

Horseshoe Tavern

368 Queen St. W.
Toronto, ON M5V 2A2
(416) 598-2162
Contact: X-ray MacRae.
Style of Music: Roots, Rock, Blues, Country.
Seating Capacity: 250.
Liquor License: Yes.

Hotel Isabella

556 Sherbourne St.
Toronto, ON M4X 1L3
(416) 921-5450
Style of Music: Roots, Rock, Blues, Reggae.
Seating Capacity: 150.
Liquor License: Yes.

Hurricane's Road House Restaurant

3351 Ellesmere Rd.
Scarborough, ON M1C 1H1
(416) 281-1885
Contact: Danny Tsai.
Style of Music: Blues.
Seating Capacity: 140.
Liquor License: Yes.
Booking Agent: Danny Tsai.

The Imperial Room

100 Front St. W.
Toronto, ON M5J 1E3
(416) 368-2511
Style of Music: Dinner Theatre.
Seating Capacity: 350.
Liquor License: Yes.

JJ's Inn

2847 Lakeshore Blvd. W.
Toronto, ON M8V 1H8
(416) 259-1287
Contact: Robbie Justin.
Style of Music: Hard Rock, Tribute Bands.
Seating Capacity: 250.
Liquor License: Yes.
Booking Agent: The Entertainment Centre.

Jailhouse Cafe

97 Main St. (Community Centre 55)
Toronto, ON M4E 2V6
(416) 691-1113
Contact: Topaz Dawn.
Style of Music: Folk, Blues, Jazz, Poetry, Soft Rock, Classical.
Seating Capacity: 60.
Liquor License: No.
Comments: The Jailhouse Cafe offers an open stage format with occasional feature performers. It has a workshop-type atmosphere with a 60's flavour.

Last Temptation

12 Kensington
Toronto, ON M5T 2J7
(416) 599-2551
Contact: David Kelly.
Style of Music: All styles.
Seating Capacity: 100.
Liquor License: Yes.

Lee's Palace

529 Bloor St. W.
Toronto, ON M5S 1Y5
(416) 532-7383
Contact: Craig Morrison.
Style of Music: All types of music but primarily original rock.
Seating Capacity: 300.
Liquor License: Yes.

Lido's

1971 Queen St. E.
Toronto, ON M4L 1H9
(416) 699-0233
Contact: Michele Prieur.
Style of Music: R&B, Top 40.
Seating Capacity: 150.
Liquor License: Yes.

Marquee Club

280 Coxwell Ave.
Toronto, ON M4L 3B6
(416) 466-3784
Contact: Dawna Vennells.
Style of Music: All styles.
Seating Capacity: 1,000.
Liquor License: Yes.

Matador Club

466 Dovercourt Rd.
Toronto, ON M6H 2W4
(416) 533-9311
Contact: Charmaine Dunn.
Style of Music: C&W.
Seating Capacity: 250.
Liquor License: No.
Comments: After-hours club.

Meyer's Deli

69 Yorkville Ave.
Toronto, ON M5K 1B8
(416) 960-4780
Contact: Paul Iskader.
Style of Music: Jazz.
Seating Capacity: 140.
Liquor License: Yes.
Booking Agent: Helen Chilcott Theatrical
Agency.
Comments: Jazz, evenings Thurs.-Sat.

Mother's

130 Eglinton Ave. E.
Toronto, ON M4P 1A6
(416) 485-6666
Contact: Joanne Hutchinson.
Style of Music: Rock, Tribute.
Liquor License: Yes.
Comments: Weekends only.

Music Gallery

1087 Queen St. W.
Toronto, ON M6J 1H3
(416) 534-6311
Contact: Jim Montgomery.
Style of Music: Avant-garde, Experimental.
Seating Capacity: 100.
Liquor License: No.

Network

138 Pears Ave.
Toronto, ON M5R 3K6
(416) 924-1768
Contact: Lucie Carr.
Style of Music: R&B, Top 40.
Seating Capacity: 275.
Liquor License: Yes.

Nuts and Bolts

277 Victoria St.
Toronto, ON M5B 1W2
(416) 977-1356
Style of Music: Dance, Alternative, Pop, Rock.
Liquor License: Yes.

PWD

88 Yorkville Ave.
Toronto, ON M5R 1B9
(416) 923-9689
Contact: Paul Dinkel.
Style of Music: Blues, Jazz, R&B.
Seating Capacity: 200.
Liquor License: Yes.

Queensbury Arms

1212 Weston Rd.
Toronto, ON M6M 4P4
(416) 243-0660
Contact: Brian Jennings.
Style of Music: Rock, Tribute.
Seating Capacity: 400.
Liquor License: Yes.
Booking Agent: The Agency.
Comments: Live music Thursday nights only.

Rivoli

334 Queen St. W.
Toronto, ON M4V 2A2
(416) 596-1908
Contact: Carson.
Style of Music: Various.
Seating Capacity: 150.
Liquor License: Yes.

Rock 'N' Roll Heaven

2 Bloor St. E.
Toronto, ON M4W 1A7
(416) 968-2711
Contact: Gareth Brown.
Style of Music: Hard Rock, Tribute.
Seating Capacity: 700.
Liquor License: Yes.
Booking Agent: The Agency.

RPM

132 Queen's Quay E.
Toronto, ON M4X 1B2
(416) 869-1462
Contact: Murray Ball.
Style of Music: New Music.
Seating Capacity: 900.
Liquor License: Yes.

Siboney
169A Augusta
Toronto, ON M5T 2L4
(416) 977-4277
Contact: Danny K.
Style of Music: Rock.
Seating Capacity: 291.
Liquor License: Yes.

Silver Dollar
484 Spadina Ave.
Toronto, ON M5S 2H1
(416) 921-2141
Contact: Joe Risk.
Style of Music: Alternative.
Seating Capacity: 150.
Liquor License: Yes.

Skyline Toronto Airport Hotel
655 Dixon Rd.
Rexdale, ON M9W 1J4
(416) 244-1711
Style of Music: Pop, Rock.
Seating Capacity: 2,000.
Liquor License: Yes.

Sneaky Dee's Uptown
1954 Yonge St.
Toronto, ON M4S 1Z4
(416) 482-2414
Contact: Andrew Kilgour.
Style of Music: Piano Bar, Jazz.
Seating Capacity: 60.
Liquor License: Yes.
Booking Agent: Andrew Kilgour.
Comments: Open to ideas.

Solitaires
3032B Danforth Ave.
Scarborough, ON M4C 1N2
(416) 690-8048
Contact: Donna Kimber.
Style of Music: Rock, R&B, Top 40.
Seating Capacity: 245.
Liquor License: Yes.

Soup Club
178 Bathurst St.
Toronto, ON M5V 2R4
(416) 364-0605
Contact: William New.
Style of Music: Alternative.
Seating Capacity: 150.
Liquor License: Yes.

Southern Accent
595 Markham Rd.
Scarborough, ON M1H 2A3
(416) 536-3211
Contact: Frances Wood.
Style of Music: Cajun, Blues, Jazz.
Seating Capacity: 75.
Liquor License: Yes.

Spectrum
2714 Danforth Ave.
Toronto, ON M4C 1L7
(416) 699-9913
Contact: Bill Delingat.
Style of Music: Rock, New Music.
Seating Capacity: 800.
Liquor License: Yes.

Stratenger's
1130 Queen St. E.
Toronto, ON M4M 1L1
(416) 466-8934
Contact: Serge Slaimovits.
Style of Music: Blues, Jazz, Rock.
Seating Capacity: 300.
Liquor License: Yes.

Water's Edge Cafe
235 Queen's Quay W.
Toronto, ON M5J 2G8
(416) 973-3000
Contact: Derek Andrews.
Style of Music: All styles.
Seating Capacity: 300.
Liquor License: Yes.

Zanis
4353 Kingston Rd.
Scarborough, ON M1E 2M9
(416) 286-4827
Contact: John.
Seating Capacity: 260.
Liquor License: Yes.

Zydeco
583 Markham Rd.
Scarborough, ON M1H 2A3
(416) 536-3211
Contact: Frances Wood.
Style of Music: Cajun, Blues, Jazz.
Seating Capacity: 85.
Liquor License: Yes.

WINDSOR

Kozak's by the Sea Tavern
1444 Ottawa St.
Windsor, ON N8X 2G2
(519) 253-8081

The Victoria Tavern
400 Chilver Rd.
Windsor, ON N8Y 2J7
(519) 254-1535
Style of Music: Blues, Jazz.

QUEBEC

HULL

Bar Louis Jose
106 Eddy St.
Hull, PQ
(819) 777-4467
Style of Music: Pop, Country.
Seating Capacity: 115.
Liquor License: Yes.

MONTREAL

l'Air du Temps
191 St. Paul o.
Montreal, PQ H2Y 1Z5
(514) 842-2003
Style of Music: Jazz.
Seating Capacity: 150.
Liquor License: Yes.

American Rock Cafe
2080 Aylmer St.
Montreal, PQ H3A 2E3
(514) 288-9272
Style of Music: 50s and 60s, Top 40 (current).
Seating Capacity: 250.
Liquor License: Yes.

Club Balattou
4372 boul. St. Laurent
Montreal, PQ H2W 1Z5
(514) 499-9239
FAX (514) 499-9215
Contact: Catherine Collorec.
Style of Music: African and Caribbean music.
Seating Capacity: 200.
Liquor License: Yes.
Booking Agent: Catherine Collorec—Productions Nuits d'Afrique Inc.

Biddles
2060 Aylmer St.
Montreal, PQ H2A 2N3
(514) 842-8656
Style of Music: Jazz.
Seating Capacity: 110.
Liquor License: Yes.

Cafe Campus
3315 Queen Mary Rd.
Montreal, PQ H3B 1A1
(514) 735-1259
Style of Music: C&W, Alternative, Rock, Reggae.
Seating Capacity: 400.
Liquor License: Yes.

Checkers
4514 ave. du Parc
Montreal, PQ H2V 4E3
(514) 276-8525
Style of Music: Funk.
Seating Capacity: 208.
Liquor License: Yes.

Club Soda
5420 ave. du Parc
Montreal, PQ
(514) 270-7848
Style of Music: Pop, Rock, Jazz, Comedy.
Seating Capacity: 450.
Liquor License: Yes.

El Coyote Bar & Restaurant
1202 Bishop St.
Montreal, PQ H3G 2E3
(514) 875-7082
Seating Capacity: 65.
Liquor License: Yes.

Les Foufounes Electriques
97 rue Ste. Catherine e.
Montreal, PQ H2X 1K5
(514) 845-5484
Style of Music: All styles.
Seating Capacity: 300.
Liquor License: Yes.
Booking Agent: Goliath Productions Inc.

Haraiki Bar
1492 Shevchenko
Montreal, PQ
(514) 363-3111
Style of Music: Rock.
Seating Capacity: 80.
Liquor License: Yes.

Hotel Maritime
1155 Guy St.
Montreal, PQ H3H 2K5
(514) 932-1411
Seating Capacity: 250.
Liquor License: Yes.

Kicks
2051 de la Montagne
Montreal, PQ
(514) 288-2660

Puzzles
333 Prince Arthur St.
Montreal, PQ H2W 2P4
(514) 288-6666
Style of Music: Light Jazz.
Seating Capacity: 130.
Liquor License: Yes.

Rising Sun
286 rue Ste. Catherine o.
Montreal, PQ H2X 2A1
(514) 861-0657
Contact: Roue-Doudou Boicel or Roosmarie
Maten.
Style of Music: Jazz, Blues, Reggae, R&B,
Afro-Caribbean music.
Seating Capacity: 200.
Liquor License: Yes.
Booking Agent: Black Tiger Productions.
Comments: The club features international
headliners such as Dizzy Gillespie and Muddy
Waters.

Spectrum
318 rue Ste. Catherine o.
Montreal, PQ H2X 2A1
(514) 276-6286
Style of Music: Dance, Pop, Jazz.
Seating Capacity: 1,100.
Liquor License: Yes.

Station 10 Bar
2071 rue Ste. Catherine o.
Montreal, PQ H3H 1M6
(514) 934-0484
Style of Music: Original, Alternative.
Seating Capacity: 100.
Liquor License: Yes.
Comments: Bands must perform at least 90%
original material.

Le Tycoon
96 Sherbrooke St. W.
Montreal, PQ H2X 1X3
(514) 849-8094
FAX (514) 849-7476
Contact: A. Cocos.
Style of Music: Pop, Jazz, Country, Rock,
Alternative (no Metal or Hardcore).
Seating Capacity: 100.
Liquor License: Yes.

Yellow Door
3625 Aylmer St.
Montreal, PQ H2X 2C5
(514) 398-6243
Liquor License: Yes.

MORIN HEIGHTS

The Commons
73 ch. Lac Echo, P.O. Box 584
Morin Heights, PQ J0R 1H0
(514) 226-2211
Style of Music: Various, including Pop.
Seating Capacity: 400.
Liquor License: Yes.

SASKATCHEWAN

REGINA

The Pump
641 Victoria Ave. E.
Regina, SK S4N 0P1
(306) 522-0977
Style of Music: C&W.
Seating Capacity: 196.
Liquor License: Yes.

W.H. Shooter
2075 Broad St.
Regina, SK S4P 1Y4
(306) 525-3525
Contact: Ryan or Tracy Citynski.
Style of Music: Top 40 Rock.
Seating Capacity: 300.
Liquor License: Yes.
Booking Agent: Universal Talent Associates.
Comments: Interested in road and recording bands. Always looking for new talent, preferably Top 40 with a slight edge.

SASKATOON

Sheraton Cavalier (Lorenzo's Lounge)
612 Spadina Cr. E.
Saskatoon, SK S7K 3G9
(306) 352-6770
Style of Music: Pop.
Seating Capacity: 100.
Liquor License: Yes.

OPERA COMPANIES

Atelier Lyrique

1008 Ste. Catherine St. E.
Montreal, PQ H2L 2G2
(514) 842-8436
FAX (514) 521-8751
Venue: Various.
Music Director: Bernard Uzan.

Calgary Opera Company

125 9th Ave. S.E., Suite 800
Calgary, AB T2G 0P8
(403) 262-7286
FAX (403) 263-5428
Venue: Southern Jubilee Auditorium.
Music Director: David Speers.
Auditions: Springtime in Calgary. Others in New York, Toronto, and Vancouver in the fall.

Canadian Children's Opera Chorus

227 Front St. E., Suite 215
Toronto, ON M5A 1E8
(416) 366-0467
FAX (416) 363-5584
Venue: Harbourfront, Young People's Theatre and St. Simon's Church.
Music Director: John Tuttle.
Auditions: During April, May and June of each year.

Canadian Opera Company

227 Front St. E.
Toronto, ON M5A 1E8
(416) 363-3371
FAX (416) 363-5584
Venue: The O'Keefe Centre, Toronto.
Music Director: Mr. Richard Bradshaw.
General Director: Mr. Brian Dickie.
Auditions: September.

Cosmopolitan Opera Association

1142 Eglinton Ave. W.
Toronto, ON M6C 2E7
(416) 787-0501
Venue: Various.
Music Director: Michele Estrano.
Auditions: Auditions in winter and summer.
Comments: Provides young Canadian singers with an opportunity to sing professionally.

Edmonton Opera

11456 Jasper Ave., Suite 202
Edmonton, AB T5K 0M1
(403) 482-7030
FAX (403) 482-0916
Venue: Northern Alberta Jubilee Auditorium.
General Director: Robert J. Hallam.
Artistic Director: Irving Guttman.
Auditions: Spring and fall in Toronto, Montreal, New York and Vancouver.

Manitoba Opera Association

555 Main St., Suite 121
Winnipeg, MB R3B 1C3
(204) 942-7479
Venue: Centennial Concert Hall, Winnipeg.
Artistic Director: Irving Guttman.

Opera Atelier

1471 Flaminia Ct.
Mississauga, ON L5J 3Z5
(416) 822-3754
FAX (416) 822-3611
Venue: MacMillan Theatre, University of Toronto.
Music Director: David Fallis.
Auditions: Main auditions in October, others throughout the year.

Opera Hamilton

P.O. Box 2080, Stn. A
Hamilton, ON L8N 3Y7
(416) 527-7627
FAX (416) 526-9935
Venue: The Great Hall of Hamilton Place, Hamilton, Ontario.
Music Director: Maestro Daniel Lipton.
Auditions: Usually during the spring in Hamilton and during the fall in New York.

Opera in Concert

27 Front St. E.
Toronto, ON M5E 1B4
(416) 366-1656
FAX (416) 947-1387
Venue: Jane Mallett Theatre, St. Lawrence Centre, Toronto.
Music Director: Stuart Hamilton.
Auditions: For information, contact Katherine Brown (416) 921-3905.

Opera Lyra

2 Daly Ave.
Ottawa, ON K1N 6E2
(613) 233-9200
FAX (613) 233-5431
Venue: National Arts Centre.
Music Director: Jeannette Aster.
Auditions: Autumn and spring.
Comments: Committed to the development and promotion of Canadian artists.

l'Opera de Montreal

1157 Ste. Catherine St. E.
Montreal, PQ H2L 2G8
(514) 521-5577
FAX (514) 521-8751
Venue: Place des Arts
Music Director: Bernard Uzan
Auditions: Prior to performance

Opera Ora

4 Woodthorpe Rd.
Toronto, ON M4A 1S4
(416) 759-5424

Pacific Opera Victoria

1316 Government St.
Victoria, BC V8W 1Y8
(604) 385-0222
FAX (604) 382-4944
Venue: McPherson Playhouse.
Music Director: Timothy Vernon.
Auditions: Each summer.

Opera de Quebec

580 Grande Allee e., Suite 575
Quebec, PQ G1R 2K2
(418) 529-3735
Venue: Grand Theatre de Quebec.
Music Director: Guy Belanger.
Auditions: None scheduled regularly.

Saskatoon Opera

509 Copelang Cr.
Saskatoon, SK S7N 2Z4
(306) 374-1630

Toronto Operetta Theatre

752 Yonge St., Suite 304
Toronto, ON M4Y 2B6
(416) 920-6705
Venue: Bluma Appel Theatre, St. Lawrence Centre, Toronto.
Artistic Director: Guillermo Silva-Marin.
Auditions: As required.
Comments: The Toronto Operetta Theatre has as its mandate the production of classic works from the golden and silver age of operetta utilizing the finest Canadian talent in all areas of production. The company is a registered non- profit performing arts organization and a registered charitable organization.

Vancouver Opera

1132 Hamilton St.
Vancouver, BC V6B 2S2
(604) 682-2871
FAX (604) 682-3981
Venue: The Queen Elizabeth Theatre, Vancouver.
Artistic Director: Guus Mostart.
Auditions: Various.
Comments: Currently, Vancouver Opera performs four productions a year, one in October, January, March and April. Vancouver Opera also has an extensive community outreach program and a school outreach program, Opera in the Schools, where the Vancouver Opera Touring Ensemble travels through the province bringing opera to school children. Vancouver Opera also has a Resident Artist Program.

OPERA COMPANIES

Orchestre Symphonique Regional d'Abitibi-Temiscamingue

P.O. Box 2305
Rouyn-Noranda, PQ J9X 5A5
(819) 762-0043
Regular Venue: Rouyn-Noranda.
Music Director: Jacques Marchand.
Auditions: November.

Brantford Symphony Orchestra Association

P.O. Box 101
Brantford, ON N3T 5M3
(519) 759-8781
Music Director: Dr. Stanley Saunders.
Auditions: September.

CBC Vancouver Orchestra

P.O. Box 4600
Vancouver, BC V6B 4A2
(604) 662-6979
Regular Venue: The Orpheum.
Music Director: Mario Bernardi.
Auditions: As required.
Comments: 20 programs are broadcast nationally each year. Also produce records.

Calgary Philharmonic Orchestra

205-8 Ave. S.E.
Calgary, AB T2G 0K9
(403) 294-7420
FAX (403) 294-7424
Regular Venue: Jack Singer Concert Hall.
Music Director: Mario Bernardi.
Auditions: Varies.

Canadian Association of Youth Orchestras

The Banff Centre, P.O. Box 1020
Banff, AB T0L 0C0
(403) 762-6278
FAX (403) 762-6444
Executive Director: Peter Gardner.
Auditions: Orchestra adjudication held in off-festival year.
Comments: CAYO is a national service organization for the youth orchestras of Canada. It is also the operating association for the biennial Festival of Canadian Youth Orchestras.

Cathedral Bluffs Symphony Orchestra

37 Earl Rd.
Scarborough, ON M1M 1E9
(416) 261-4597
FAX (416) 291-3669
Regular Venue: Midland Avenue Collegiate, Scarborough.
Music Director: Clifford Poole.
Auditions: Usually in the fall.

Chamber Players of Toronto

24 Ryerson Ave., Suite 209
Toronto, ON M5T 2P3
(416) 862-8311
FAX (416) 860-0826
Regular Venue: Jane Mallet Theatre, St. Lawrence Centre.
Music Director: Agnes Grossmann.
Auditions: As required.
Comments: A 15-member chamber orchestra which presents a 12-concert series in the greater Toronto area. Also a touring and guest ensemble.

Chebucto Symphony Orchestra

P.O. Box 332
Dartmouth, NS B2Y 3Y5
(902) 835-9272
President: Mrs. Wietske Gradstein.
Comments: Presents an annual six-concert tour.

Crowsnest Pass Symphony

P.O. Box 268
Blairmore, AB T0K 0E0
(403) 562-2159
Regular Venue: Horace Allen School.
Music Director: Dick Burgman.
Auditions: No specific dates.
Comments: A 45-piece orchestra of amateur musicians, which presents four concerts each season.

Deep River Symphony Orchestra

P.O. Box 1496
Deep River, ON K0J 1P0
(613) 584-4230
Regular Venue: MacKenzie High School.
Music Director: James Wegg.
Auditions: No specific dates.
Comments: Three concerts each year plus children's concerts.

East York Symphony Orchestra

110 Rumsey Rd.
Toronto, ON M4G 1P2
(416) 467-7142
Regular Venue: Ontario Science Centre Auditorium.
Music Director: David Ford.
Auditions: As required.

Eastern Ontario Concert Orchestra

P.O. Box 102
Belleville, ON K8N 4Z9
(613) 477-2003
Regular Venue: Robert Horwood Auditorium, Centennial Secondary School.
Music Director: Dezso Vaghy.
Auditions: By appointment.
Comments: A community-based orchestra which presents four concerts each year.

Edmonton Symphony Orchestra

10010-109 St.
Edmonton, AB T5J 1M4
(403) 428-1108
FAX 403) 425-0167
Regular Venue: Northern Alberta Jubilee Auditorium.
Music Director: Uri Mayer.
Auditions: When vacancies occur.
Comments: Season series of 95-100 concerts.

Edmonton Youth Orchestra Association

P.O. Box 4172
Edmonton, AB T6E 4T2
(403) 436-7932
Regular Venue: University of Alberta.
Music Director: Michael Massey.
Auditions: September.

Etobicoke Philharmonic Orchestra

19 Hilldowntree Rd.
Etobicoke, ON M9A 2Z4
(416) 239-5665
Regular Venue: Martingrove Collegiate Institute.
Music Director: Tak Ng Lai.
Auditions: Regular auditions held in early September. Individual auditions held as required.

Fanshawe Community Orchestra

1551 Ryerside Rd.
London, ON N6G 2S2
(519) 432-4461
Regular Venue: Aeolian Hall.
Music Director: Erna Van Daele.
Auditions: At conductor's discretion.
Comments: Four concerts with soloists per season, from September to May. Rehearsals held once a week.

Georgian Bay Symphony

P.O. Box 133
Owen Sound, ON N4K 5P1
(519) 371-4065
Regular Venue: Owen Sound Collegiate and Vocational Institute.
Music Director: Guest conductors at time of publication.
Comments: Seven concerts each season.

The Halton Youth Symphony

P.O. Box 494
Oakville, ON L6J 5B5
(416) 827-2232
Regular Venue: Loyola High School, Oakville.
Music Director: Dr. Wayne Jeffry.
Auditions: June and September.
Comments: In addition to a senior symphony, the HYS has junior and intermediate string programs as well as training ensembles in flute, woodwinds and brass. Over 130 musicians are involved.

Hamilton Philharmonic Orchestra

P.O. Box 2080, Stn A
Hamilton, ON L8N 3Y7
(416) 526-8800
Regular Venue: Great Hall, Hamilton Place.
Music Director: Boris Brott.
Auditions: As needed.
Comments: Approximately 150 concerts per season.

Hamilton Philharmonic Youth Orchestra

P.O. Box 2080, Stn. A
Hamilton, ON L8N 3Y7
(416) 526-8800
Regular Venue: Hamilton Place and The Scottish Rule.
Music Director: Glen Mallory.
Auditions: First two weeks of September.
Comments: A 65-piece student orchestra (average age 16-17) that plays standard repertoire, from Baroque to Contemporary, as well as commissioned works and premiere performances.

Hart House Orchestra

Hart House, University of Toronto
7 Hart House Circle
Toronto, ON M5S 1A1
(416) 978-5362
Regular Venue: Great Hall, Hart House.
Music Director: Dr. Errol Gay.

Huronia Symphony

P.O. Box 904
Barrie, ON L4M 4Y6
(705) 728-3638
Regular Venue: Georgian Theatre.
Music Director: Arthur Burgin.
Comments: Four concerts annually.

Huronia Symphony Youth Orchestra

168 Parkview Ave.
Orillia, ON L3V 4M3
(705) 326-7548
Music Director: Mayumai Kumagai.
Auditions: September.

International Symphony Orchestra

774 London Rd.
Sarnia, ON N7T 4Y1
(519) 337-7775
Regular Venues: Various locations.
Conductor & Music Director: Zdzislaw Kopac.
Auditions: September (for choir and orchestra).

Kamloops Symphony Orchestra

P.O. Box 57
Kamloops, BC V2C 3K5
(604) 372-5000
FAX (604) 372-2358
Regular Venue: Sagebrush Theatre.
Music Director: Ches Gladyszewski.
Auditions: Late summer.
Comments: Seven concerts annually.

Kamloops Symphony Society

P.O. Box 57
Kamloops, BC V2C 2H9
(604) 372-5000
Regular Venue: 235 Lansdowne St.,
Kamloops.
Music Director: Cheslaw Gladyszewski.
Auditions: May and June.

Kingston Symphony Association

P.O. Box 1616
Kingston, ON K7L 5C8
(613) 546-9729
Regular Venues: Grand Theatre, Grant Hall.
Music Director: Brian Jackson.

Kitchener-Waterloo Chamber Orchestra

P.O. Box 937
Waterloo, ON N2J 4C3
(519) 744-3828
Regular Venue: St. John's Lutheran Church.
Music Director: Graham Coles.

Kitchener-Waterloo Community Orchestra

P.O. Box 938
Waterloo, ON N2J 4C3
(519) 885-1211
President: John Wine.
Comments: Four concerts annually.

Kitchener-Waterloo Symphony Orchestra

101 Queen St. N.
Kitchener, ON N2H 6P7
(519) 745-4711
FAX (519) 578-9230
Regular Venue: Centre in the Square.
Music Director: Raffi Armenian.
Auditions: When vacancies occur.
Comments: 85-90 concerts per season.

Kootenay Chamber Orchestra

P.O. Box 512
Cranbrook, BC V1C 4J1
(604) 426-2924
Regular Venues: Wildhorse Theatre, McKim
Auditorium.
Music Director: Ronald Edinger.
Comments: Season consists of approximately
16 concerts.

Orchestre Symphonique de Laval

5495 boul. St. Martin o.
Laval, PQ H7W 3S6
(514) 681-5269
Regular Venue: Maison des Arts, Laval.
Music Director: Paul Andre Boivin.

Lethbridge Symphony

P.O. Box 1101
Lethbridge, AB T1J 4A2
(403) 328-6808
(403) 327-9790
Regular Venue: Yates Memorial Centre
Music Director: Stewart Grant
Auditions: When vacancies occur.
Comments: Maintains a professional core (a
resident music director and *Musaeus*, a professional string quartet). Presents chamber and full
orchestra series' and offers a Suzuki string program and a young artists' competition.

London Youth Symphony

P.O. Box 553, Stn. B.
London, ON N6A 4W8
Music Director: Edit Haboczki.
Auditions: May and September.

Manitoba Chamber Orchestra

1317A Portage Ave., Suite 202
Winnipeg, MB R3G 0V3
(204) 783-7377
FAX (204) 783-0898
Regular Venues: Westminster Church, Fort
Garry Hotel.
Music Director: Simon Streatfeild.
Auditions: Auditions help upon special request.

McGill Chamber Orchestra

1745 Cedar Ave.
Montreal, PQ H3G 1A7
(514) 487-5190
FAX (514) 487-7390
Music Director: Alexander Brott.

Medicine Hat Symphony

P.O. Box 1295
Medicine Hat, AB T1A 7N1
(403) 527-0559
Regular Venue: Medicine Hat College Theatre.
President: Lynda Mastel.
Comments: Three concerts annually.

Mississauga Symphony

161 Lakeshore Rd. W.
Mississauga, ON L5H 1G3
(416) 274-1571
Regular Venue: Cawthra Park Auditorium.
Music Director: John Barnum.
Auditions: September.

Montreal Chamber Orchestra

5825 Esplanade Ave.
Montreal, PQ H2T 3A2
(514) 271-3301
Regular Venue: Redpath Hall.
Music Director: Wanda Kaluzny.

Orchestre Symphonique de Montreal

85 rue Ste. Catherine o., Suite 900
Montreal, PQ H2X 3P4
(514) 842-3402
FAX (514) 842-0728
Regular Venue: Place des Arts.
Music Director: Charles Dutoit.
Auditions: As required.
Comments: Approximately 150 concerts each season.

Nanaimo Symphony Orchestra

P.O. Box 661
Nanaimo, BC V9R 5L9
(604) 758-6176
Music Director: LLoyd Blackman.
Auditions: September.

National Arts Centre Orchestra

P.O. Box 1534, Stn. B
Ottawa, ON K1P 5W1
(613) 996-5051
FAX (613) 996-2828
Music Director: Jack Mills.

National Youth Orchestra of Canada

1032 Bathurst St.
Toronto, ON M5R 3G7
(416) 532-4470
FAX (416) 532-6879
Regular Venue: Major Canadian cities.
Music Director: Music director appointed on an annual basis.
Auditions: Each December in approximately 30 major centres across Canada.
Comments: Comprised of 100 of Canada's most talented classical music students, the NYO assembles for an intensive seven-week training session. Entry into the NYO is based on the results of nationwide auditions held in over 30 centres throughout Canada. The faculty for the NYO hails from symphony orchestras and universities throughout the world. All musicians, aged 14-26, are eligible. For details/application forms call (416) 532-4470.

Nepean Symphony Orchestra

35 Stafford Rd., Suite 11
Nepean, ON K2H 8V8
(613) 820-7483
Regular Venue: Centrepointe Theatre.
Music Director: S. James Wegg.
Auditions: As required.
Comments: A professional orchestra which presents a six-concert main series, an extensive summer series, as well as in-school concerts.

New Brunswick Chamber Orchestra

P.O. Box 6249
Saint John NB E2L 4R7
(506) 634-8379
FAX (506) 634-0843
Regular Venues: Saint John High School, Centenary Queen Square United Church.
Music Director: Nurhan Arman.
Auditions: By appointment.
Comments: The NBCO is a group of professional musicians. They prepare three programs and present eight concerts each season. The group performs in Moncton, Saint John, and Fredericton.

New Westminster Symphony Orchestra

P.O. Box 832
New Westminster, BC V3L 4Z8
(604) 594-5271
Comments: This organization has been part of the community for 45 years and continues to thrive. All organizational duties and fund raising are done by a volunteer board of directors.

Newfoundland Symphony Orchestra

Arts and Culture Centre
Saint John's, NF A1C 5P9
(709) 753-6492
Regular Venue: Arts and Culture Centre.
Music Director: Mario Duschenes.
Auditions: As required.
Comments: 16 concerts annually.

Niagara Symphony

P.O. Box 401
St. Catharines, ON L2R 6V9
(416) 687-4993
Regular Venues: Brock Theatre, Shaw Festival Theatre.
Music Director: Ermanno Florio.

North Bay Symphony Orchestra

P.O. Box 14
North Bay, ON P1B 8J6
(705) 476-5889
FAX (705) 476-1302
Regular Venue: North Bay Arts Centre.
Music Director: Nurhan Arman.
Auditions: As required.
Comments: Eight concerts per season.

North York Symphony Association

1210 Sheppard Ave. E., Suite 109
North York, ON M2K 1E3
(416) 499-2204
FAX (416) 490-9739
Regular Venue: Minkler Auditorium, Seneca College.
Music Director: Kerry Stratton.
Auditions: September.
Comments: The North York Symphony offers a regular subscription series of classical music from October through May. For further ticket information contact the Minkler Auditorium box office (416) 491-8877.

Northumberland Orchestra Society

P.O. Box 1012
Cobourg, ON K9A 4W4
(416) 342-2009
Regular Venue: Trinity United Church
Music Director: Philip Schaus.
Auditions: Throughout the year.
Comments: Four-concert series annually.

Nova Scotia Youth Orchestra

1541 Barrington St., Suite 200
Halifax, NS B3J 1Z5
(902) 423-5984
Music Director: Gregory Burton.
Auditions: May.
Comments: Members 14-22 years of age.

Symphony Nova Scotia

1646 Barrington St.
Halifax, NS V3J 2A3
(902) 421-7311
FAX (902) 422-1209
Regular Venue: Rebecca Cohn Auditorium, Dalhousie Arts Centre.
Music Director: Georg Tintner.
Auditions: As required.
Comments: Approximately 60 concerts annually.

Oakville Symphony Orchestra

P.O. Box 125
Oakville, ON L6J 4Z5
(416) 849-7630
Regular Venue: The Oakville Centre.
Music Director: David Miller.
Comments: Five-concert series annually.

Orchestra London Canada

520 Wellington St.
London, ON N6A 3P9
(519) 679-8558
FAX (519) 432-2020
Regular Venue: Centennial Hall.
Music Director: Maestro Uri Mayer.
Auditions: Audition dates/times vary according to the availability of positions within the orchestra.

Orchestre des Jeunes du Quebec

1501 rue Jeanne-Mance
Montreal, PQ H2X 1Z9
(514) 282-9465
Auditions: January or February.

Oshawa Symphony Association

P.O. Box 444
Oshawa, ON L1H 7L5
(416) 579-6711
Regular Venue: Eastdale Collegiate Theatre.
Music Director: Winston Webber.
Auditions: Early September.

Ottawa Symphony Orchestra

P.O. Box 3644, Stn C
Ottawa, ON K14 4J7
(613) 224-4982
Regular Venue: National Arts Centre.
Music Director: Brian Law.
Auditions: Early fall.
Comments: 85-member community orchestra.

Peterborough Symphony Orchestra

P.O. Box 1135
Peterborough, ON K9J 7H4
(705) 742-3844
Regular Venue: P.C.V.S. Auditorium.
Contact: Mary Ruth O'Brien.
Comments: Six concerts each season.

Prince Edward Island Symphony Orchestra

P.O. Box 185
Charlottetown, PE C1A 7K4
(902) 894-3566 or 892-5637
Regular Venue: Confederation Centre of the Arts.
Music Director: Dr. Brian Ellard.
Auditions: Early September.
Comments: The Prince Edward Island Symphony Orchestra is a community orchestra which depends on local and regional musicians for its personnel. It presents four concerts a year: in October, December, February and April.

Prince George Symphony Orchestra

2880-15 Ave.
Prince George, BC V2M 1T1
(604) 562-0800
Regular Venue: Vanier Hall.
Music Director: John Unsworth.
Comments: Approximately 20 concerts each season.

Pro Arte Orchestra

1692 Danforth Ave.
Toronto, ON M4C 1H8
(416) 466-4515
Music Director: Victor DiBello.

Orchestre Symphonique de Quebec

580 Grand Allee e., Suite 150
Quebec, PQ G1R 2K2
(418) 643-5598
FAX (418) 644-2380
Regular Venue: Grand Theatre de Quebec.
Music Director: Simon Streatfeild.
Comments: Approximately 80 concerts annually.

Regina Symphony Orchestra

200 Lakeshore Dr.
Regina, SK S4P 3V7
(306) 586-9555
FAX (306) 586-2133
Regular Venue: Saskatchewan Centre of the Arts.
Music Director: Vladimir Conta.
Auditions: May and September.

Royal Conservatory Orchestra

Royal Conservatory of Music
273 Bloor St. W.
Toronto, ON M5S 1W2
(416) 978-6257
Regular Venues: Church of the Redeemer, Royal Conservatory Concert Hall.
Music Director: John Barnum.

Orchestre Symphonique du Saguenay Lac St. Jean

520 rue Jacques Cartier e.
Chicoutimi, PQ G7H 1Z5
(418) 545-3409
FAX (418) 545-9859
Music Director: Jacques Clement.
Auditions: September.

Saint John Symphony

P.O. Box 6249
Saint John, NB E2L 4R7
(506) 634-8379
FAX (506) 634-0843
Regular Venues: Saint John High School, Centenary Square United Church.
Music Director: Nurhan Arman.
Auditions: By appointment.
Comments: The SJS is a community orchestra, and while the majority of members are from the Saint John area, some come from Moncton, Sackville, St. Steven and St. George.

Saskatoon Symphony

703 Hotel Bessborough, P.O. Box 1361
Saskatoon, SK S7K 3N9
(306) 665-6414
Regular Venue: Saskatoon Centennial Auditorium.
Music Director: Daniel Swift.
Comments: 15-concert season series.

Sault Symphony Orchestra

P.O. Box 695
Sault Ste. Marie, ON P6A 5N2
(906) 632-4047
Regular Venue: White Pines Auditorium.
Music Director: John Wilkinson.

Scarborough Philharmonic Orchestra

3663 Danforth Ave.
Scarborough, ON M1N 2G2
(416) 690-1769
Regular Venue: Birchmount Park Auditorium.
Music Director: Christopher Kitts.
Auditions: General auditions in September.
Comments: Nine concerts a year.

Scotia Chamber Players

1541 Barrington St., Suite 317
Halifax, NS B3J 1Z5
(902) 429-9467
Regular Venue: Dalhousie Arts Centre.
Music Director: Christopher Wilcox, managing and artistic director.
Auditions: Mid-April to mid-May for admission into the Young Artist Program of the Scotia Festival of Music.
Comments: The Scotia Festival Chamber Orchestra presents festival highlight concerts during the two-week Spring Festival. Personnel is drawn from guest artists and musicians in the Young Artist Program.

Sinfonia Chamber Ensemble

161 Lakeshore Rd. W.
Mississauga, ON L5H 1G3
(416) 274-1571
Regular Venue: St. Dominic's Church
Music Director: John Barnum.
Auditions: September.

Sir Ernest MacMillan Ensemble

221 Fairleigh Ave. S.
Hamilton, ON L8M 2K6
(416) 549-1665
Regular Venue: First Pilgrim Church.
Music Director: Marta Hidy.
Auditions: No auditions required.
Comments: 12-member string orchestra. Four-concert subscription series plus repeat performances featuring guest soloists.

South Shore String Association

81 place Courcelles
Saint-Hilaire PQ J3H 2S6
(514) 467-0955
Regular Venues: Beloiel, Saint-Hilaire.
Music Director: Ben Stolow.
Auditions: September and June.

Sudbury Symphony Orchestra Inc.

St. Andrew's Place
111 Larch St., 9th Floor
Sudbury, ON P3E 4T5
(705) 673-1280
FAX (705) 674-6098
Regular Venue: Fraser Auditorium, Laurentian University.
Music Director: Dr. Metro Kozak.
Auditions: September.

Symphony Hamilton

P.O. Box 7439
Ancaster, ON L9G 4G4
(416) 648-2813
Regular Venues: Mohawk College Theatre, Cathedral of Christ the King.
Artistic Advisor: Roberto DeClara.
Auditions: First week of September or on request.
Comments: Community orchestra serving the Hamilton-Wentworth region. Formerly called the McMaster Symphony.

Tafelmusik Baroque Orchestra

427 Bloor St. W.
Toronto, ON M5S 1X7
(416) 964-9562
FAX (416) 964-2782
Regular Venue: Trinity-St. Paul's United Church, Toronto.
Music Director: Ms Jean Lamon.
Auditions: Throughout the year.
Comments: Tafelmusik is Canada's Baroque orchestra on original instruments. In addition to a 25-concert Toronto season, Tafelmusik tours internationally and holds an exclusive recording contract with BMG/RCA of New York.

Te Deum Orchestra

105 Victoria St.
Dundas, ON L9H 2C1
(416) 628-4533
Regular Venues: Christ's Church Cathedral, Hamilton; St. Andrews, Toronto.
Music Director: Richard Birney-Smith.
Comments: Approximately 12 concerts each season.

Thunder Bay Symphony Orchestra Association Inc.

681 Oliver Rd., P.O. Box 2004
Thunder Bay, ON P7B 5E7
(807) 345-4331
FAX (807) 345-8915
Regular Venue: Thunder Bay Community Auditorium.
Personnel: Glenn Mossop (music director and conductor), Howard Cable (principal pops conductor).
Auditions: As required.

Timmins Symphony Orchestra

P.O. Box 1365
Timmins, ON P4N 7N2
(705) 267-5314
Regular Venue: Ecole Secondaire Theriault.
Music Director: Roy Takayesu.
Comments: Four concerts annually.

Toronto Philharmonic Orchestra

297 Victoria St.
Toronto, ON M5B 1W1
(416) 595-0404
Regular Venue: Various.
Music Director: Paul Robinson.

Toronto Pops Orchestra

180 Victoria St.
Toronto, ON M5B 1T6
(416) 365-7677
FAX (416) 363-5290
Regular Venue: Massey Hall.
Music Director: Norman Reintamm.

The Toronto Symphony

60 Simcoe St.
Toronto, ON M5J 2H5
(416) 593-7769
FAX (416) 593-6788
Regular Venue: Roy Thomson Hall
Music Director: Gunther Herbig.

Orchestre Symphonique de Trois-Rivieres

P.O. Box 1281
Trois-Rivieres, PQ G9A 5K8
(819) 373-5340
FAX (819) 375-6623
Regular Venue: Salle J. Antonio-Thompson.
Music Director: Gilles Bellemare.

University of Toronto Symphony Orchestra

Faculty of Music, Edward Johnson Building
80 Queen's Park Cr.
Toronto, ON M5S 1A1
(416) 978-6160
Regular Venue: MacMillan Theatre.
Music Director: Michel Tabachnik.
Comments: Credit course for students registered at the faculty.

University of Western Ontario Symphony Orchestra

Faculty of Music, University of Western Ontario
London, ON N6A 3K7
(519) 679-2111
Regular Venue: Alumni Hall
Music Director: Prof. Jerome Summers.
Auditions: September.
Comments: The 85-member U.W.O. Symphony presents a series of five programs each season, along with numerous additional chamber orchestra and run-out concerts.

Vancouver Symphony Orchestra

601 Smithe St.
Vancouver, BC V6B 5G1
(604) 684-9100
FAX (604) 684-9264
Regular Venue: Orpheum Theatre.
Music Director: Peter McCoppin.
Auditions: As required.
Comments: The VSO performs over 130 concerts during its September-July season.

Victoria Symphony

846 Broughton St., Lower level
Victoria, BC V8W 1E4
(604) 385-9771
Regular Venue: Royal Theatre.
Music Director: Peter McCoppin.
Auditions: Varies.

Wilfrid Laurier University Symphony

Faculty of Music, 75 University Ave. W.
Waterloo, ON N2L 3C5
(519) 884-1970, ext 2432
FAX (519) 886-9351
Regular Venue: J.B. Aird Centre Recital Hall.
Music Director: Paul Pulford.

Windsor Symphony Orchestra

198 Pitt St. W., 3rd Floor, Suite 174
Windsor, ON N9A 5L4
(519) 973-1238
Regular Venue: Cleary Auditorium.
Music Director: Dwight Bennett.
Auditions: Early spring, early summer.
Comments: 13-concert series each session.

Winnipeg Symphony Orchestra

555 Main St., Suite 101
Winnipeg, MB
R3B 1C3
(204) 942-4576
FAX (204) 956-4271
Regular Venue: Centennial Concert Hall.
Artistic Director: Bramwell Tovey.
Comments: Over 70 concerts annually.

York Symphony Orchestra

P.O. Box 355
Richmond Hill, ON L4C 4Y6
(416) 881-2886
Regular Venues: Markham Theatre, Aurora High School and Marylake Shrine.
Music Director: Guest conductors in the l989/90 season.
Comments: The York Symphony Orchestra is a community orchestra serving the regional municipality of York.

PACKAGING & LABELLING COMPANIES

Audio Video Packaging
132B-6 St.
Etobicoke, ON M8V 3A5
(416) 251-1557
FAX (416) 251-1557
Type of Company: Custom duplicator.
Special Services: Packaging of cassettes, LPs and CDs.

Audiobec Recording Canada Inc.
600 Port Royal o.
Montreal, PQ H3L 2C5
(514) 384-6667
FAX (514) 388-1488
Type of Company: Custom duplicator.

Bernard Album Graphic
179 Carlton Rd.
Unionville, ON L3R 3L7
(416) 477-3991
Type of Company: Manufacturer.
Product Specialty: Colour separations.
Special Services: Packaging, design and final film.

C&L Audio Distributors
360 Supertest Rd.
Downsview, ON M3J 2M2
(416) 663-8273
FAX (416) 663-8277
Type of Company: Manufacturer, distributor.
Special Services: Custom audio duplication with full packaging services.

319

Cinelectric Motion Picture and Sound Production
2 Lake St.
St. Catharines, ON L2R 5W6
(416) 685-1234
Type of Company: Manufacturer.
Product Specialty: Scotch professional-grade tape for video, audio and open reel. Custom audio and video cassette duplication, real time duplication, and cassette labelling and packaging.

Dover Pad Ltd.
57 Colville Rd.
Toronto, ON M6M 2Y2
(416) 245-7100
FAX (416) 245-4617
Type of Business: Supplier of packaging materials, wood-finishing products and furniture blankets.
Top Brands: Star Chemical Finishing Products, Dover Cordage.
Branch:
335 boul. Laurentien
Montreal, PQ
H4M 2L7

Dynapak Music Services Ltd.
3121 Universal Dr.
Mississauga, ON L4X 2E2
(416) 625-8311
FAX (416) 625-5209
Type of Company: Manufacturer.
Product Specialty: Cassettes, 12-inch and 7-inch records, and CDs. Also, pre-recorded stereo cassettes, sonic welded PVC blister packs, and cassette and CD special packaging.

Evergreen Audio-Visual Ltd.
7170 Warden Ave., Unit 3
Unionville, ON L3R 8B2
(416) 477-6322
FAX (416) 477-9299
Type of Business: Blank and duplicated audio cassettes.
Special Services: Audio production.

Multi-Caisses Inc.
1135 Taillon St.
Quebec City, PQ G1N 4G7
(418) 527-2549
FAX (418) 527-5856
Type of Business: Manufacturing custom shipping and carrying cases for music dealers.
Special Services: Plastic roto-molded keyboard case for distributors, plus a full-line of standard cases. Catalog available.
Branches:
85 Albert St.
Ottawa, ON K1P 6A4
(613) 235-3628
FAX (613) 563-1992

P.O. Box 622
Jackman ME, USA 04945
FAX (418) 527-5856

Music Manufacturing Services
101 Glen Rd., Suite 2
Toronto, ON M4W 2V8
(416) 928-6919
FAX (416) 928-6919
Type of Business: Custom manufacturing of vinyl, cassettes, and CDs.
Special Services: Complete product management and marketing consultation. Major label manufacturing experience and suppliers including artwork and filmwork.

Parr's Print and Litho Ltd.
111 Ferier St.
Markham, ON L3R 3K6
(416) 475-3300
FAX (416) 475-9201
Special Services: Packaging and labelling

Praise Sound Productions Ltd.
7802 Express St.
Burnaby, BC V5A 1T4
(604) 420-4227
Type of Business: Pressing and packaging of records and cassettes.

Precison Sound Corp.
5614 Goring St.
Burnaby, BC V5B 3A3
(604) 299-4141
Type of Business: Audio cassette manufacturing, duplication and packaging.
Product Specialty: Music duplication on TDK tape.
Top Brands: Canadian industrial distributor of TDK products.
Special Services: Real-time duplication.

R.E.P. Sound Image Recording Ltd.
180 Sheldon Dr.
Cambridge, ON N1R 6V1
(519) 623-2269
FAX (519) 623-4448
Type of Business: Manufacturing of recorded cassettes.

Ross-Ellis Ltd.
300 Ann St.
Montreal, PQ H3C 2K2
(514) 861-2411
FAX (514) 861-7610
Type of Business: Lithography.
Special Services: Record packaging.
Branch:
45 Esna Park Dr.
Markham, ON L3R 1C9
(416) 475-9811
FAX (416) 475-9814

Disques SNB
8400 Cote-de-Liesse
St. Laurent, PQ H4T 1G7
(514) 342-8513
FAX (514) 342-5139
Type of Company: Manufacturer.
Special Services: Labelling.

Shorewood Packaging Corp. of Canada Ltd.
2220 Midland Ave., Unit 50
Scarborough, ON M1P 3E6
(416) 292-3990
FAX (416) 292-0480
Type of Company: Manufacturer.
Special Services: Tape and CD graphics and boxes, record jackets and video cartons; printing and packaging.

Summit Sound Inc.
40 Main St., Unit 1, P.O. Box 333
Westport, ON K0G 1X0
(613) 673-2818
FAX (613) 273-3998
Type of Company: Manufacturer.
Special Services: High-speed and real-time audio cassette duplication.

Unity Gain Records Ltd.
5456 Young St.
Halifax, NS B3K 1Z4
(902) 455-7588
Type of Company: Manufacturer.
Special Services: Design, packaging and labelling.

Western Imperial Magnetics Ltd.
12840 Bathgate Way, Unit 7
Richmond, BC V6V 1Z4
(604) 270-8682
FAX (604) 270-2745
Type of Company: Manufacturer, distributor, sales agency.
Product Specialty: Cassettes.
Top Brands: Adtec, DMC, Ampex.
Special Services: Service department.

World Records
1712 Baseline Rd. W., P.O. Box 2000
Bowmanville, ON L1C 3Z3
(416) 433-0250 (Bowmanville)
(416) 686-2828 (Toronto)
Type of Company: Manufacturer.
Special Services: Complete record manufacturing and packaging service. Mailers in stock.

PERFORMING & MECHANICAL RIGHTS SOCIETIES

CEO Copyright Clearance Corp.

1423 Howe St.
Vancouver, BC
V6Z 1R9
(604) 684-1536
FAX (604) 669-7173
Services Provided: Music clearance for film, TV, video and commercial producers.
Specialization: Copyright tracking and license negotiation.

Canadian Musical Reproduction Rights Agency Ltd.

56 Wellesley St. W., Suite 320
Toronto, ON M5S 2S4
(416) 926-1966
FAX (416) 926-7521
Services Provided: Mechanical and synchronization licensing of music in Canada for more than 20,000 music publishers.
Comments: CMRRA issues more than 50,000 mechanical licenses yearly and collects and distributes revenue to publishers throughout Canada.

Society of Composers, Authors and Music Publishers of Canada (SOCAN)

(formerly CAPAC and PROCAN)

41 Valleybrook Dr.
Don Mills, ON M3B 2S6
(416) 445-8700
FAX (416) 445-7108

Services Provided: Administering performance royalties on behalf of Canadian composers, authors and music publishers.

Branches:

600 boul. de Maisonneuve o., Suite 500
Montreal, PQ H3A 3J2
(514) 844-8377
FAX (514) 849-8446

842 Thurlow St., Suite 200
Vancouver, BC V6E 1W2
(604) 688-7851
FAX (604) 684-7932

1201 W. Pender St., 4th Floor
Vancouver, BC V6E 2V2
(604) 669-5569

1240 Bay St., 9th Floor
Toronto, ON M5R 2C2
(416) 924-4427
FAX (416) 924-4837

8704-51 Ave., Suite 104
Edmonton, AB T6E 5E8
(403) 468-0905

6080 Young St., Suite 300
Halifax, NS B3K 5L2
(902) 454-6475

Society for Reproduction Rights of Authors, Composers and Publishers of Canada Inc. (SODRAC)

54 rue Cour Leroyer o.
Montreal, PQ H2Y 1W7
(514) 845-3268
FAX (514) 845-3401

Services Provided: Licensing and collection society for mechanical reproduction rights.
Comments: Charge is 10% to Canadian members and 5% to international members.

At last — One Performing Rights Society for Canada

Society of Composers,
Authors
and Music Publishers
of Canada

Société canadienne
des auteurs,
compositeurs
et éditeurs de musique

SOCAN

The merger of Canada's two performing rights societies, CAPAC and PROCAN, is a blending of the best elements of two successful organizations. The objective is a stronger, more effective and unified society to enhance and protect the performing rights of copyright owners — composers, lyricists, songwriters and music publishers — and to better serve the users of music in an increasingly complex world.

For the immediate future, head offices will remain at:
9th floor, 1240 Bay Street, Toronto, Ontario, M5R 2C2 • (CAPAC) • Tel: (416) 924-4427 • Fax: (416) 924-4837
41 Valleybrook Drive, Don Mills, Ontario, M3B 2S6 • (PROCAN) • Tel: (416) 445-8700 • Fax: (416) 445-7108

PROMOTION & PUBLICITY COMPANIES

ATI (Access To The Industry)
75 Parkway Ave.
Markham, ON L3P 2H1
(416) 294-5538
Acts: Country.
Artists Represented: Ray Griff, Jason McCoy, Floyd Tolman.
Services Provided: The ATI record label.
Special Projects: Distribution.

Apricot Talent and Recording Industries Inc.
1449 Ridgebrook Dr., Suite 120
Gloucester, ON K1B 4T1
(613) 749-1116
Acts: Top 40 Rock, MOR, Rock and Heavy Metal.
Artists Represented: Johnny the Fox, Lexy Jones, Red Syren, Network, In and Out.
Venues Represented: Talisman Motor Inn (Ottawa), Le Spectra (Gatineau), Barrymore's (Ottawa).
Contacts: Gord Kent, Rick Paquette, Monique Paquette.
Services Provided: Booking and promotion.

Backstage Productions
3015 Kennedy Rd., Suite 1
Scarborough, ON M1V 1E7
(416) 291-4913
FAX (416) 297-7784
Acts:
Pop, Rock, C&W.
Artists Represented: Ronnie Hawkins, Patti Jannetta, Wiz Bryant, JK Gulley.
Venues Represented: International.

Barry's Pro Music Agency Ltd.
P.O. Box 526
Brooks, AB T0J 0J0
(403) 362-4204
Acts: C&W.
Artists Represented: Various, will accept new acts.
Services Provided: Organizing tours for travelling U.S. bands.

325

Barslow & Associates Inc.

65 Helena Ave.
Toronto, ON M6H 2H3
(416) 652-1302
Network Affiliations: CARAS, CPRS, PRSA, The Fashion Group.
Clients: Miss Canada Pageant, Miss Teen Canada Pageant (seven years), International Motorcycles (14 years), CHIN International Picnic (24 years).

Big Time Productions Ltd.

54 Duncome Dr., Lower Level
Hamilton, ON L9A 2G2
(416) 389-4265
FAX (416) 389-4265
Acts: Contemporary, Rock, Pop, Theatricals, Dixieland, Big Band, Jazz, Blues, C&W.
Artists Represented: Gowan, Kim Mitchell, Candi, Honeymoon Suite.
Venues Represented: Brantford Civic Centre, Hamilton Convention Centre, Niagara Falls Arena, Gage Park.
Clients: Department of Culture and Recreation, City of Hamilton, Hamilton Downtown Business Improvement Association, Burlington Sound of Music, It's Your Festival, Gage Park.

Brookes Diamond Productions

1800 Argyle St., Suite 507
Halifax, NS B3J 3M8
(902) 422-7000
FAX (902) 422-2929
Acts: A/C.
Artists Represented: Rita MacNeil, Mary O'Hara, John Allan Cameron, Murray McLauchlan, Valdy, Bruce Cockburn, Edith Butler and Liona Boyd.
Services Provided: Tour booking, promotion for trade shows and entertainment production for conventions and conferences.

Gina Brown Management

P.O. Box 534
Montreal, PQ H2W 2P1
(514) 842-6791
FAX (514) 276-2696
Acts: Jazz, New Music.
Artists Represented: The Beards.
Services Provided: Biographies, press releases, press kits and tour management.

CBD Enterprises

180 Duncan Mill Rd., Suite 400
Don Mills, ON M3B 1Z6
(416) 441-2144
FAX (416) 441-2259
Acts: Pop, MOR, C&W.
Network Affiliations: Founding member of ISES.
Services Provided: Special event planning and consulting.

Call Yes Management and Consulting

533 Lakeshore Rd.
Cobourg, ON K9A 1S4
(416) 372-8469
FAX (416) 372-1754
Acts: Rock, Pop, Alternative, Jazz.
Artists Represented: Big Bang Theory.
Services Provided: Artist management, publicity and promotion.

Jim Chapman Music Services

197 Ridout St. S.
London, ON N6C 3X8
(519) 679-1396
Clients: Blackburn Communications, P.R.I.D.E., Sunshine Foundation, London Tigers Baseball Club.
Services Provided: Original music and marketing concepts created, recorded and/or implemented.

Chart Toppers

1908 Beechknoll Ave.
Mississauga, ON L4W 2G3
(416) 238-8682
FAX (416) 625-2189
Clients: Molson, Juno Awards, Music Industry Conference.

Cod Oil Productions Limited

P.O. Box 8568
St. John's, NF A1B 3P2
(709) 745-3304
Comments: Promotion and marketing of recorded music published with Cod Oil Productions only.

Concertmasters Inc.

22 Linden St.
Toronto, ON M4Y 1V6
(416) 922-9922
FAX (416) 960-6166
Acts: Classical.
Artists Represented: Major attractions.
Affiliated Companies: Straightwire Digital Editing, Aaron Concert Management (Boston).

Contract Promotions

89 Reiner Rd.
Downsview, ON M3H 2L4
(416) 633-5780
Services Provided: Set design, graphic design and production of promotional materials including buttons and point of purchase displays.

DBC Ltd.

180 Duncan Mill Rd., Suite 400
Don Mills, ON M3B 1Z6
(416) 441-2144
FAX (416) 441-2259
Acts: Pop, MOR and C&W.
Network Affiliations: Founding member of ISES.
Services Provided: Special event planning and consulting.

d'Anjou et Poirier

P.O. Box 5418, Stn. B
Montreal, PQ H3B 4P1
(514) 277-5771
FAX (514) 499-0332
Acts: All.
Clients: Kebec Disc, Spec d'ici.
Services Provided: Co-ordination and art direction for record jackets and programs.

Darkhorse Musical Productions

P.O. Box 687, Stn. N.D.G.
Montreal, PQ H4A 3P5
(514) 735-3061
Acts: Pop, MOR, New Age and Contemporary Instrumental.
Artists Represented: John Horrocks, Melodies on Canvas.
Affiliated Companies: Les Editions Wingspirit Enr., Empress Records.
Services Provided: Production, promotion and management of artists. Rental of sound reinforcement equipment.

Decent Exposure

161 Coxwell Ave., Suite 6
Toronto, ON M4L 3B4
(416) 463-9766
FAX (416) 944-1149
Acts: All artists and musical styles considered.
Artists Represented: Danny Gatton, Andrew Tosh, The Phantoms, Jack De Keyzer.

Diversified Music Group

1969 Pandora St.
Vancouver, BC V5L 5B2
(604) 255-3536
FAX (604) 255-8711
Acts: Rock, Country, Country Rock.
Artists Represented: Darby Mills, One Horse Blue, Lori Jordan, Bear Mountain Boys, Kenny Shaw and Danny Mack.
Network Affiliations: British Columbia Country Music Association, CCMA.
Services Provided: Marketing and publicity, management, publishing, rehearsal and production studios.

Dobbin Agency

477A Princess St.
Kingston, ON K7L 1C3
(613) 549-4401
Acts: Pop, MOR, Rock, C&W.
Network Affiliations: CART.

Ray Douglas Promotions

P.O. Box 7213, Sandwich
Windsor, ON N9C 3Z1
(519) 969-1203 or 258-2288
Acts: MOR, Pop, C&W, Jazz, Big Bands, Classical.
Artists Represented: Ray Douglas International Big Band, Joan Eastman and the Music Makers, The Kenny Crone Jazz Group.
Venues Represented: Victoria Tavern, Kozaks By The Sea Tavern, International Freedom Festival.
Network Affiliations: A.F. of M.
Special Projects: The Off-Shore International Jazz Society.

E.M.C. Presents

387 Bloor St. E., 5th Floor
Toronto, ON M4W 1H7
(416) 925-5437 or 960-9917
FAX (416) 962-6805
Acts: All.
Artists Represented: Hagood Hardy, Domenic Troiano, David Gibson, Body Electric, JATO.
Network Affiliations: PAPA.
Services Provided: Artist and tour sponsorship, artist and corporate endorsements.
Special Projects: TV Production and special events.

Gino Empry

25 Wood St., Suite 104
Toronto, ON M4Y 2P9
(416) 977-1153
Acts: All types.
Artists Represented: Estonia (Ultima Thule), Michael Danso, Norm Amadio.
Network Affiliations: CART, ITAA.
Services Provided: Various.

Entertainment Media Corporation

513 Broadview Ave.
Toronto, ON M4K 2N5
(416) 469-8300
Acts: Top 40, Rock & Roll, Dance.
Artists Represented: DJs.
Venues Represented: General Toronto and Montreal areas, including various O'Toole's and Pat & Mario's Franchises.
Services Provided: Music programming and DJs.
Special Projects: Promotional events.

Extravaganza Promotions Inc.

P.O. Box 1, Stn. Q
Toronto, ON M4T 2L7
(416) 929-9305
FAX (416) 964-7076
Acts: Shows.
Artists Represented: Samantha Jones.
Clients: Miss Nude World and the Casino Beauty International Pageant.
Services Provided: Promotes talent and beauty contests.
Comments: Head office: New York, U.S.A. (607) 753-6897.

Richard Flohil & Associates

1240 Bay St., Suite 303
Toronto, ON M5R 2A7
(416) 925-3154
FAX (416) 925-0136
Acts: Acoustic, Roots, Blues, Folk.
Artists Represented: Loreena McKennitt, Downchild Blues Band, Cromdale (Bobby Watt).
Clients: Stony Plain Records, RBI Productions, Mariposa Festival.
Services Provided: Full public relations, publicity and promotional services.
Special Projects: Also promotes concerts in Toronto-area venues.

Jim Ford & Associates Inc.

315 Soudan Ave.
Toronto, ON M4S 1W6
(416) 483-0663
FAX (416) 483-2866
Acts: Pop, MOR, Musical Comedy.
Artists Represented: Peter Appleyard, John Arpin, Buddy Wasisname and the Other Fellers.

Galbraith Reproductions Ltd.

201 Dufferin St.
Toronto, ON M6K 1Y9
(416) 531-6913
FAX (416) 588-2289
Services provided: Quality photo reproduction service. B&W or colour photographs available in any quantity and at a low cost per print. Fast service.

The Garys

19 Sandford Ave.
Toronto, ON M4L 2E6
(416) 466-3081
Acts: All areas of musical entertainment. International in scope.
Artists Represented: World-class groups.

Ginjoy and Associates Inc.

25 Wood St., Suite 104
Toronto, ON M5J 2P9
(416) 977-1153
FAX (416) 977-2006
Acts: All styles.
Network Affiliations: CART.
Services Provided: Publicity, advertising, management and bookings.

Group One Communications

3416 W. 2 Ave.
Vancouver, BC V6R 1J2
(604) 737-0399
Acts: Pop, Rock, MOR.
Clients: Sez-U, bang, Mya Max, Mushroom Studios.
Services Provided: Image development, marketing and merchandising.

Hollywood North Promotions

4544 Dufferin St., Suite 24
Downsview, ON M3H 5X2
(416) 736-6319
Acts: All styles, original bands or single performers.
Venues Represented: Spectrum, Entex, and others.
Services Provided: Video and concert production, promotion and special events.

Hollywood Productions

280 College St.
Toronto, ON M5T 1R9
(416) 975-0284
FAX (416) 363-6986
Acts: All styles.
Artists Represented: Jr. Gone Wild, Pat Temple & The High Lonesome Players, Shotgun Rationale.
Services Provided: Touring merchandise service.

Darina Hradkova Artists Management Services

238 Davenport Rd., Suite 37
Toronto, ON M5R 1Y6
(416) 968-0960
Acts: Classical, MOR.
Clients: Arthur Ozolins, publicity.
Services Provided: Publicity and promotion, touring and performance co- ordination. Contacts in Great Britain and Europe.

Hulen Enterprises

2447 Falcon Ave., Suite 2
Ottawa, ON K1V 8C8
(613) 738-2373
FAX (613) 521-2673
Acts: Pop, Rock, Country.
Services Provided: Artist management and tour support.
Special Projects: National and international services, as well as Bootcamp (see Music Consultants).

D.R. Jellis & Associates

32 Roblocke Ave.
Toronto, ON M6G 3R7
(416) 537-6947
Services Provided: Personal and financial management, and public relations.
Special Projects: Charged on a fee basis only.

Kayzeelou Productions Inc.

7 Roanoke Rd.
Don Mills, ON M3A 1E3
(416) 449-5155
FAX (416) 928-9412
Clients: Duke Street Records, Unidisc Records, Einstein Brothers Music.
Services Provided: Independent record promotion and music marketing.
Special Projects: Record promotion.
Comments: Also produces jingles.

Les Productions Ghyslaine Lacoste & Associates

6647-24 Ave.
Montreal, PQ H1T 3M6
(514) 722-6861

Lant Advertising Agency

(A Division of Lant-International)
569 Lynwood Dr., P.O. Box 1085
Cornwall, ON K6H 5V2
(613) 938-1532
Contact: Charles W.B. Lant, CEO.
Acts: All.
Network Affiliations: Cornwall Advertising and Sales Association (CASA).

Lizard Mountain Music

P.O. Box 251
Cranbrook, BC V1C 4H8
(604) 489-2036
Acts: MOR, Rock, C&W.
Artists Represented: The Black Diamond Band.
Affiliated Companies: Lizard Mountain Records.
Services Provided: Demo and record production, jingles, management and promotion.
Special Projects: Annual East Kootenay Concert, Cranbrook, BC.

Cliff Lorimer

75 Eastdale Ave., Suite 614
Toronto, ON M4C 5N3
(416) 699-4454
Acts: All.
Services Provided: Biographies, press materials.

Marigold Productions

P.O. Box 141, Stn. S
Toronto, ON M5M 4L6
(416) 484-8789
Acts: All.
Artists Represented: Nationally.

Gerry L. Massop

P.O. Box 970
Parksville, BC V0R 2S0
(604) 248-5960
Acts: Pop, C&W.
Services Provided: Office services and trans-Atlantic radio mailing labels.

MediaRep Public Relations

4091 Pheasant Run
Mississauga, ON L5L 2C2
(416) 820-6400
FAX (416) 820-9512
Acts: All categories.
Artists Represented: Power Patrol, Joey Cee, Ron Victors.
Clients: Niteluse (Toronto), Vicom 90, Curzons (Etobicoke).
Services Provided: Public relations, media services and consulting.
Special Projects: Shooting Stars Gallery at Vicom, Sportathlon at Curzons, Showcan in Los Angeles.

Moffatt Entertainment Group

19 Hess St. S.
Hamilton, ON L8P 3M7
(416) 522-8359
Venues Represented: National.

The Music Brokers

92 Avenue Rd., Suite 200
Toronto, ON M5R 2H2
(416) 960-3130
FAX (416) 960-8264
Acts: All.
Artists Represented: Rita MacNeil, Gipsy Kings, Roch Voisine, etc.
Comments: An independent promotion company.

Music Matters Management

P.O. Box 417, Stn. C
Toronto, ON
(416) 534-4297
Acts: Pop, Rock.
Artists Represented: Skydiggers.
Affiliated Companies: Enigma, Capitol.
Services Provided: Management, consulting and promotion.

O'Day Productions

177 W. 7 Ave., Suite 400
Vancouver, BC V5Y 1K5
(604) 873-9686
FAX (604) 872-1715
Acts: Pop, Rock, Country, Family/Children's, Ethnic.
Artists Represented: The Dots, Robert Minden Ensemble, Marty Gillan.
Clients: DMG, Prestige Entertainment, Sam's (Vancouver).
Services Provided: Promotion, publicity and career consultation.
Special Projects: Arts Umbrella fundraisers, BC Epilepsy media advisor, West Coast Music Conference, Country Music Conference.

OHM Music International (OMI)

253 College St., Suite 340
Toronto, ON M5T 1R5
(416) 922-6297
FAX (416) 285-7104
Acts: New Age, roots-related Rock & Roll.
Artists Represented: Dr. Limbo and His Fabulous Off-Whites.
Network Affiliations: A.F. of M.
Affiliated Companies: Dirty Little Nipper Records.
Services Provided: Management, bookings, promotion and publicity.

PSST

75 Sherbourne St.
Toronto, ON M5A 2P9
(416) 365-7957
FAX (416) 365-7169
Artists Represented: PSST has produced shirts for the Skydiggers, Andrew Cash and Sacrifice.
Services Provided: Screen-printing and promotional items.

Pierce Communications

56 Scollard St.
Toronto, ON M5R 1E9
(416) 961-5328
FAX (416) 961-4251
Clients: Best Foods, CAIN, Jack Daniel's, CCH, FBM Distillery, Becton-Dickinson, Kraft General Foods, Board of Trade.
Services Provided: Media relations, publicity, special events and corporate sponsorships.
Special Projects: Radio contest, broadcast advertising, concert promotions and sponsorships.

Platinum Publicity

68 Water St., Suite 203
Vancouver, BC V6B 1A4
(604) 682-1588
FAX (604) 683-4298
Acts: All.
Artists Represented: Crowded House, Harry Belafonte, Cabaret (the musical).
Services Provided: Artists and event publicity/promotion.
Special Projects: Pacific National Exhibition, Ice Capades.

POP Music

P.O. Box 499, Stn. A
Ottawa, ON K1N 8V5
(613) 238-3906
Acts: Pop, Rock, MOR.
Artists Represented: Avery Singer, Heaven's Radio, The Magic Circle.
Affiliated Companies: Lowertown Music.
Clients: Heaven's Radio.
Services Provided: Concert management, marketing and publicity.
Special Projects: Televised concerts.

POP Strategies

3284 Yonge St.
Toronto, ON M4N 3M7
(416) 485-8295
FAX (416) 485-8924
Services Provided: Promotion, publicity, marketing, sponsorship, special events, business management, financial management.
Special Projects: POP Strategies specializes in the Canadian music and entertainment industries, and has extensive media and industry contacts, and associations with top freelance writers and photographers.

Pro Motion

P.O. Box 5663, Stn. L
Edmonton, AB T6C 4G1
(403) 437-4803

Productions Musicales CIBE

1183 ave. Colbert, Suite 12
Ste. Foy, PQ G1V 3Z2
(418) 658-3778
Acts: Classical.
Artists Represented: Various soloists and chamber music ensembles.
Affiliated Companies: CIBE (recordings).
Services Provided: Booking, promotion, publicity and management.
Special Projects: Disc promotion and distribution.

The Promotion Network (A Division of Image Control Productions Ltd.)

10852 Whyte Ave., Suite 203
Edmonton, AB T6E 2B3
(403) 433-2096
FAX (403) 439-4209
Acts: Country Rock, Rock & Roll, Heavy Metal, Alternative.
Artists Represented: Robb Gott and Hyrd Help, Frank Carroll, Red Rum.
Venues Represented: Fantasy Night Club.
Comments: Full marketing and promotion.

Public Access

3810 boul. St. Laurent
Montreal, PQ H2W 1X6
(514) 843-4858
Services Provided: Publicity, press kits, design, graphics and typesetting.
Special Projects: Data-base of over 3,000 music industry contacts.

The Publicity Company

364 Richmond St. W., 4th Floor
Toronto, ON M5V 1X6
(416) 323-1500
FAX (416) 323-9520
Clients: Co-writer for 1986 Juno Awards, *It's Only Rock 'n' Roll* (CBC).
Services Provided: Publicity and promotions (local and national). Promo tours, live tours, single events, awards shows and all types of special projects.

Reynolds Agency Reg'd.

15 Parkland Cr.
Nepean, ON K2H 5V3
(613) 726-1285
Acts: C&W.
Artists Represented: Howard Hayes and the Country Drifters.
Services Provided: Bookings, management, promotions.

Roadside Attractions (Alberta) Inc.

11411-37A Ave.
Edmonton, AB T6J 0J6
(403) 438-6185
FAX (403) 438-6183
Acts: Jazz, Blues, Folk, Country.
Artists Represented: The Romaniacs, Tribute to Harry James Orchestra.
Venues Represented: Numerous venues throughout Alberta: soft seat 200-2,000 capacity.
Services Provided: Publicity and promotional services. Tour co-ordination for artists wishing to tour Alberta.
Special Projects: Innovative dance presentations done on a regular basis.

Les Productions Rubicon Inc.

P.O. Box 1370, Stn. Desjardins
Montreal, PQ H5B 1H3
(514) 327-6172
Acts: New Age.
Artists Represented: Raoul Duguay and Michel Robidoux, Daniel Blanchet.
Services Provided: Promotions, consulting and booking.
Special Projects: Production of new age music radio program.

SECT Talent

9371 Iberville St.
Montreal, PQ H1Z 2R5
(514) 384-5708
Artists Represented: Weather Permitting, The Pink Zone, The Darned, Two Men Laughing.
Services Provided: Press kits, photography and international mailing lists.
Special Projects: Record launches, radio distribution with kits, media relations.

S.J.R. Promotional Services Ltd.

1091 Broughton St., Suite 22
Vancouver, BC V6G 2A9
(604) 731-4621
Acts: All styles.
Services Provided: Biographies, press releases and tour support.

Joanne Smale Productions Ltd.

686 Richmond St. W.
Toronto, ON M6J 1C3
(416) 363-4051
FAX (416) 363-6986
Acts: Songwriters.
Artists Represented: Murray McLauchlan, Willie P. Bennett, Jane Bunnett.

Sphere

22 Rainsford Rd.
Toronto, ON M4L 3N4
(416) 694-6900
Acts: Children's, MOR, variety shows.
Artists Represented: Many, accepting new acts.
Services Provided: Planning and producing shows for shopping mall promotions, conventions, resorts and children's concerts.

Spinners Promotions

134 Pleasant Ave.
Willowdale, ON M2M 1M1
(416) 221-9332
Acts: Pop, Rock, R&B, Funk, Rap, New Music, House.
Services Provided: Record promotion to club DJs.

Star Treatment

P.O. Box 1329
Pembroke, ON K8A 6Y6
(613) 735-4060
Services Provided: Artist promotion packages, press releases, poster design.

Steel City Meltdown Record Pool

82 Mohawk Rd. E.
Hamilton, ON L9A 2G9
(416) 385-6116
Acts: All forms of music.
Venues Represented: O'Toole's (chain wide), Mellows (Hamilton).
Services Provided: DJ services and music equipment installation.
Special Projects: Promoting dance music in Hamilton, Burlington and surrounding areas.

T.O.C./ Native Talent Agency

1155 West Georgia St., Suite 800
Vancouver, BC V6E 3H4
(604) 683-4230 or 275-1696
FAX (604) 687-5519
Acts: All styles.
Artists Represented: Arrows to Freedom (singers/dancers), Rick Patterson (country singer) and the Shaman Singers.
Services Provided: Management, promotions and marketing.

Ultimate Enterprises

177 W. 7 Ave., Suite 400
Vancouver, BC
Acts: Gospel, C&W.
Artists Represented: Step by Step, New Wine, Kimberley.
Affiliated Companies: Roadside Records.

Peter Ware - Artist Representative

P.O. Box 61, Stn. K
Toronto, ON M4P 2G1
(416) 787-3481
Acts: Classical.
Artists Represented: Lynn Harting-Ware (guitarist), Ware/Wells Duo (violin and guitar).
Affiliated Companies: Acoma Recordings.
Services Provided: Management and promotions.

Western Event Marketing Group

1112 Winnipeg St., Suite 103
Regina, SK S4R 1J6
(306) 525-8546
FAX (306) 352-8099
Contact: Tom Lukiwski.
Services Provided: Event management and planning, public relations, communications and marketing.

Karen Williams Personal Publicity Services

P.O. Box 793, Stn. Q
Toronto, ON M4T 2N7
(416) 960-8376
FAX (416) 960-8376
Acts: Jazz, Rock.
Artists Represented: Manteca, Uzeb and various Duke Street Records artists.
Network Affiliations: ACCT (Academy of Canadian Cinema and Television).
Clients: Megan Follows, Gordon Clapp, Manteca, Illustrated Men, Gabrielle Rose, Mump & Smoot.
Services Provided: Publicity, promotion and personal management for the music, film and theatre industries.

Anya Wilson Promotion and Publicity

15 Independence Dr.
Scarborough, ON M1K 3R7
(416) 265-6263 or 265-5900
FAX (416) 265-3280
Acts: All styles.
Artists Represented: Ian Tyson, Mad About Plaid, The Paul James Band.
Services Provided: Radio promotion and tracking services.
Special Projects: Publicity campaigns, radio promotional tours and interviews.

Deborah Wood Productions

35 Churchill Rd.
Ajax, ON L1S 2K9
(416) 428-8426
FAX (416) 428-7715
Acts: Country.
Artists Represented: Tim Taylor, Albert Hall, The Good Brothers, Matt Minglewood, Terry Carisse, Michelle Wright, Heather Brooks, Dick Damron.

Wurdsand Inc.

10503-109 St., P.O. Box 1500
Edmonton, AB T5J 2M7
(403) 486-1386
Acts: All.
Artists Represented: The Kim Kastle Show, nationally.
Clients: Kim Kastle, Stained Glass, Tokyo, Vogue, The Shades.
Services Provided: Media representation plus complete press kit assembly and logo design.

YUL Arts Promotion

c/o Latitude 45/Arts Promotion
109 boul. St. Joseph o.
Montreal, PQ H2T 2P7
(514) 276-2694
FAX (514) 276-2696
Acts: New and Contemporary Music, Musique Actuelle and improvisational performance.

PROMOTION • PUBLICITY • MARKETING

Pop Strategies is a national publicity promotion and marketing firm specializing in the music and entertainment fields.
The company is a division of Norris-Whitney Communications Inc., publishers of numerous entertainment-related magazines and books.

Pop Strategies is a broad-based marketing company with skills and expertise to tackle a wide variety of challenges: media relations, promotions, special events, sponsorships, contests, research, new product launches, management consulting, graphic design, media monitoring and much more.

Pop Strategies is a full service publicity company with up-to-the-minute general and specialized media mailing lists on our computer.

3284 YONGE ST.,
TORONTO ON M4N 3M7
(416) 485-8295

Pop Strategies is an experienced, aggressive and professional company. We are proud of our competitive position among the leaders in our industry.

RACKJOBBERS

Century Sound and Music

1330 Cornwall St.
Regina, SK S4R 2H5
(306) 352-1838
FAX (306) 757-3561
Lines Carried: All major record labels plus audio equipment and accessories.
Accounts: Record and stereo stores, drug stores and variety accounts.
New Lines: Yes.
Coverage: Saskatchewan.

Continental Records Co. Ltd.

P.O. Box 2103
Bramalea, ON L6T 3S3
(416) 450-6660
Lines Carried: 45s exclusively. All labels including imports.
Accounts: Specialty and collector stores.
New Lines: Yes.
Coverage: Worldwide.
Comments: 12,000 title record catalog ($5 postage paid).

Cove Distributors

381A McAloney Rd.
Prince George, BC V2K 4L2
(604) 562-6172
FAX (604) 562-1538
Lines Carried: Domestic LPs, cassettes and CDs, plus care products and accessories.
Accounts: All types of music retailers and electronics stores.
New Lines: Yes.
Coverage: British Columbia, Alberta and Northwest Territories.

Global Distribution Inc.

740 Columbia St.
New Westminster, BC V3M 1B4
(604) 520-5037
Lines Carried: All general music cassette tapes, CDs and records. Also T-shirts, flags and music accessories.
Accounts: 120 convenience stores. Global also owns and operates three retail music stores.
New Lines: Yes.
Coverage: Vancouver, Lower Mainland and Fraser Valley.
Comments: Also distributes magazines, pocket books and comics. New titles accepted.

Handleman Company of Canada Ltd.

140 Barr St.
St. Laurent, PQ H4T 1W6
(514) 341-1822
FAX (514) 735-4003
Lines Carried: Cassettes, CDs, cassette singles and video cassettes.
Accounts: Retail merchants.
New Lines: No.
Coverage: Quebec and the Ottawa Valley.
Branches:
10 Newgale Gate, Units 1-3
Scarborough, ON M1X 1C5
(416) 298-0411

7408-40 St. S.E., Suite 5
Calgary, AB T2C 2H5
(403) 236-3868

450 Edinburgh Dr.
P.O. Box 2158
Moncton, NB E1C 3B2
(506) 857-8590

Impact Music Promotions

(A Division of Stereodyne)
3121 Universal Dr.
Mississauga, ON L4X 2E2
(416) 625-8311
FAX (416) 625-5209
Lines Carried: Impact, Starpak, Original Music Masters, Christmas products.
Accounts: K-Mart, Woolworth, Towers, Zellers and Canadian Tire Corporation.
New Lines: Yes.
Coverage: Canada.

National Record Distributors Ltd.

30 Plymouth St.
Winnipeg, MB R2X 2V7
(204) 633-1412
FAX (204) 694-9430
Lines Carried: All major lines.
Accounts: Music retailers.
New Lines: Yes.
Coverage: Northern Ontario to British Columbia.

Pindoff Record Sales Ltd.

166 Norseman St.
Toronto, ON M8Z 2R4
(416) 234-9211
FAX (416) 234-9213
Lines Carried: Pre-recorded music and video-related accessories.
Accounts: Major chain retailers and independents.
New Lines: Yes.
Coverage: National.
Branches:
837 Granville St.
Vancouver, BC V6Z 1K9
(604) 683-4086

4432-10 St. N.E.
Calgary, AB T2E 6K3
(403) 291-9881

277A Brunswick
Pointe Claire, PQ
H7B 5S1
(514) 694-0429

RMP Record Sales Co. Ltd.
300 Bates Rd.
Montreal, PQ H3S 1A3
(514) 739-5662
FAX (514) 735-9252
Lines Carried: All major record labels, imports and independents.
Accounts: Grocery chains, pharmacies, music stores, variety stores and CD rental clubs.
New Lines: Yes.
Coverage: Quebec, Ottawa and the Ottawa Valley.

The Shanook Corporation
4222 Manor St.
Burnaby, BC V6G 1B2
(604) 433-3331
FAX (604) 433-4815
Lines Carried: Records, cassettes, CDs (all major labels) and video movies (all major studios).
Accounts: Grocery chains, plus video, record and department stores.
New Lines: Yes.
Coverage: National.

Starsound Ltd.
427 Yonge St.
Toronto, ON M4S 1T4
(416) 977-0525
FAX (416) 977-2422
Lines Carried: Specializing in dance, rap, R&B and reggae cassettes, records and CDs.
Accounts: Clubs, DJs and DJ services.
New Lines: Yes.
Coverage: Ontario.
Comments: Starsound is a large importer and exporter of dance music which services both Canada and the U.S. The company handles mail order and wholesale accounts.

Sunrise Record Distributors
4069 Gordon Baker Rd.
Scarborough, ON M1W 2P3
(416) 498-6601
FAX (416) 494-8467
Lines Carried: All major and minor record labels (including CDs).
Accounts: Independent bookstores and record stores.
New Lines: Yes.
Coverage: Southern Ontario.

Total Sound Ltd.
10333-174 St.
Edmonton, AB T5S 1H1
(403) 483-3217
FAX (403) 486-0589
Lines Carried: All major manufacturers.
Accounts: Racks and record stores.
New Lines: Yes.
Coverage: Western provinces, central Canada and Ontario.

Western Imperial Magnetics Ltd.
12840 Bathgate Way, Suite 7
Richmond, BC V6V 1Z4
(604) 270-8682
FAX (604) 270-2745
Lines Carried: Pre-recorded: ERA, K-Tel, Dominion, Arrival, Headfirst.
Accounts: Government and education, plus the retail, church, broadcast and medical markets.
New Lines: Yes.
Coverage: Canada.
Comments: Western has been a major supplier of audio and video products, accessories and equipment since 1927. Western has been servicing musicians with tape, equipment and duplication for 11 years and now carries their own retail line of product.

RACKJOBBERS

RADIO PROGRAM DISTRIBUTORS

Bison Recording Ltd.
311 Kenny St.
Winnipeg, MB R2H 3E7
(204) 233-4464
FAX (204) 233-4464
Personnel: Howard Kazuska, Lucette Boulet.
Format: All.
Method of Distribution: Stereo tape.
Special Services: Sports and information.

Canadian Radio Networks Inc.
61 James St.
St. Catharines, ON L2R 5B9
(416) 687-8595
FAX (416) 687-9638
Personnel: Chuck Camroux (president), Ron Dale (VP/marketing director), Al Chonka (VP/program director).
Format: Contemporary, soft rock and contemporary country.
Method of Distribution: Stereo satellite.
Special Services: Music Radio Network, Star Country Network.

CFMX-FM/Different Drummer Productions
468 Queen St. E., Suite 101
Toronto, ON M5A 1T7
(416) 367-5353
FAX (416) 367-1742
Personnel: Mike Forrester, executive producer.
Format: Classical.
Producers Represented: Different Drummer Productions.
Method of Distribution: Stereo tape, stereo satellite.
Special Services: Distributors of one- and two-hour, category 6 (CRTC) Canadian content shows and specials featuring various major ensembles.

Hark Productions
366 Adelaide St. E., Suite 540
Toronto, ON M5A 3X9
(416) 865-9611
FAX (416) 360-7811
Personnel: Edward Henderson, producer/writer.
Format: All.
Method of Distribution: Stereo tape.
Special Services: Original music for commercials and film.

Hot Cable FM

Videotron Communications
10450-178 St.
Edmonton, AB T5S 1S2
(403) 486-6868 or 486-6558 (Saturdays)
FAX (403) 426-3244
Personnel: Howard Belnavis (station manager/
sales rep), Stan Redford (news director).
Format: World Beat, Black and Dance R&B.
Method of Distribution: Stereo tape, stereo
disk, compact disc.
Special Services: Cable radio service
(pay radio).

Jazz Inspiration Ltd.

90 Durie Lane
Thornhill, ON L3T 5H5
(416) 449-3322
FAX (416) 449-4406
Personnel: Arne (Larsen) Schwisberg (general
manager), Katherine Brodie (marketing manager).
Format: Jazz.
Producers Represented: Sonic Workshop,
Overtime Sports Programs.
Method of Distribution: Stereo tape, stereo
satellite.
Special Services: Largest jazz network in
Canada. This firm also provides in-house legal
services for clients.

Joyful Sounds

P.O. Box 303
Aurora, ON L4G 3H4
Personnel: Rob Green, Jerry Verhovsek, Cyril
Harper, Terry Whitfield, Boris Kuruc, Catharine
Green, Anny Verhovsek, Les Roberts.
Format: Two weekly shows: Joyful Sounds
(A/C Christian), County Line (Country Christian).
Method of Distribution: Stereo tape.
Special Services: Christian music program-
ming and annual Christmas music specials.
Barter basis for weekly programs. Consulting
services also available.
Branch:
720 Lakepointe Rd.
Grosse Pointe Parm, MI 48230
(313) 822-0024

Lutheran Radio/ Lutheran Laymen's League

270 Lawrence Ave., P.O. Box 481
Kitchener, ON N2G 4A2
(519) 578-7420
FAX (519) 742-8091
Personnel: Gary Ritter (director), Stephen
Klinck (manager and media programming).
Format: Contemporary, Rock, Classical,
Religious.
Method of Distribution: Stereo satellite,
agency.
Special Services: Seasonal specials, PSAs,
Ethnic language programming.

Michael Morgan & Associates Ltd.

1200 W. Pender St., Suite 411
Vancouver, BC V6E 2S9
(604) 688-0203
FAX (604) 688-7778
Personnel: Michael Morgan (president), Paul
MacDonald (studio manager).
Format: Rock.
Method of Distribution: Stereo tape.

Quasarts Productions

P.O. Box 1360, Stn. B
Oshawa, ON L1J 6P8
(416) 427-9156
FAX (416) 489-5430
Personnel: Jill Walters, Ian Sutton.
Format: Country.
Method of Distribution: Stereo tape, stereo
satellite.
Special Services: Quasarts also produces 90-
second information mosaics for radio stations
across Canada (i.e., consumer and lifestyle
programs).

Les Productions Rubicon Inc.

P.O. Box 1370, Stn. Desjardins
Montreal, PQ H5B 1H3
(514) 327-6172
Personnel: Gilles Bedard, president.
Format: New Age.
Special Services: "Nouvel Air", a weekly
program on Telemedia FH Radio Network
(Quebec).

Seacoast Sound

825 Broughton St.
Victoria, BC V8W 1E5
(604) 386-1131
FAX (604) 386-5775
Personnel: Geoffrey Bate (general manager),
Jerry Lucky (network services), Dale Baglo
(production manager).
Format: All.
Method of Distribution: Stereo tape, stereo
satellite.

Sound Source

2 St. Clair Ave. W.
Toronto, ON M4V 1L6
(416) 922-1290
FAX (416) 323-6828
Personnel: Canadian radio syndication
company.
Format: All.
Method of Distribution: Stereo satellite.
Special Services: Creating and distributing
Canadian radio programs.

SupeRadio

151 John St., Suite 407
Toronto, ON M5V 2T2
(416) 599-3949
FAX (416) 599-3958
Personnel: Robert K. Whyte (president), Helen
Lenthall (network director), Stacey Troster (traffic
manager).
Format: Syndicated radio broadcasts.
Method of Distribution: Stereo satellite.
Special Services: Presenters of Open House
Party.

Telemedia Broadcasting Systems

40 Holly St.
Toronto, ON M4S 3C3
(416) 482-4164
FAX (416) 482-9469
Personnel: Paul Williams (vice president) Allan
Davis (sports network manager), Dani Eisler
(network manager), Leslie Nelson (station
relations manager), Paul Wortley (sales manager).
Format: Information and entertainment.
Producers Represented: Various freelancers.
Method of Distribution: Stereo tape, stereo
disk, stereo satellite.
Special Services: Overnight format service.

Westwood One Canada

260 Richmond St. W., Suite 400
Toronto, ON M5V 1W5
(416) 597-8529
FAX (416) 597-0802
Personnel: Don Bradley (director of marketing/
advertising), Roger Pierce (affiliate relations
supervisor), Bruce Hennie (traffic co-ordinator),
Doughan Huska (production co-ordinator).
Format: Contemporary, Rock, Classical, Jazz,
Country, Comedy and Information.
Producers Represented: Westwood One
International, plus independent Canadian
producers.
Method of Distribution: Stereo disk, stereo
satellite.
Special Services: Distributors/syndicators of
Canadian and foreign radio programs, features
and specials. Developing networks for Canadian
radio productions and generating national
advertising involvement and sponsorship.

ALBERTA

CJPR

P.O. Box 840
Blairmore, AB T0K 0E0
(403) 562-8119
FAX (403) 562-8633
Frequency: 1490 kHz (AM).
Format: C&W.
Station Manager: Daryl Ferguson.

CIBQ

P.O. Box 180
Brooks, AB T0J 0J0
(403) 362-3418
Frequency: 1340 kHz (AM).
Format: C&W.
Station Manager: Monte Solberg.

CBR

CBC
P.O. Box 2640
Calgary, AB T2P 2M7
(403) 283-8361
FAX (403) 270-8505
Frequency: 1010 kHz (AM).
Format: Varied.
Station Manager: Mike Shea.

CBR

CBC
P.O. Box 2640
Calgary, AB T2P 2M7
(403) 283-8361
FAX (403) 270-8505
Frequency: 102.1 MHz (FM).
Format: A/C.
Station Manager: Mike Shea.

CFAC

3320-17 Ave. S.W.
Calgary, AB T3E 6X6
(403) 246-9696
FAX (403) 246-6660
Frequency: 960 kHz (AM).
Format: C&W.
Program Director: Bob Spitzer.

CFCN

80 Patina Rise
Calgary, AB T3C 3L9
(403) 240-5800
FAX (403) 240-5801
Frequency: 1060 kHz (AM).
Listening Area: Calgary, Banff, Red Deer, Lethbridge.
Cable: Yes.
Format: Top 40, CHR.
Program Director: Dean Sinclair.
Language: English.
Affiliates: CJAY 92 FM.

CFFR

2723-37 Ave. NE
P.O. Box 660, Stn. M
Calgary, AB T2P 3Z2
(403) 291-0000
FAX (403) 291-0037
Frequency: 660 kHz (AM).
Format: A/C.
Program Director: Shannon Cooke.

CFHC

3320-17 Ave. S.W.
Calgary, AB T3E 6X6
(403) 246-9696
FAX (403) 246-6660
Frequency: 1450 kHz (AM).
Format: A/C.
Program Director: Bob Spitzer.

CHFM

804-16 Ave. S.W.
Calgary AB T2R 0S9
(403) 228-9600
FAX (403) 244-3343
Frequency: 95.9 MHz (FM).
Format: A/C.
Program Director: Cal Walker.

CISS

804-16 Ave. S.W.
Calgary, AB T2R 0S9
(403) 228-2477
FAX (403) 244-3343
Frequency: 1140 kHz (AM).
Format: Golden Oldies.
Station Manager: Roy Hennessy.

CJAY

80 Petina Rise, P.O. Box 7060, Stn. E
Calgary, AB T3C 3L9
(403) 240-5850
FAX (403) 240-5801
Frequency: 92.1 MHz (FM).
Listening Area: Calgary, Banff Lake Louise, Invermere, Bassano.
Cable: Yes.
Format: A/C, AOR.
Program Director: Stewart J. Meyers.
Language: English.
Rebroadcasts: 95 FM-Banff, 97.5 FM-Lake Louise, 99.7 FM-Inveremere, 106.1- Bassano.

CKIK

1324-17 Ave. S.W., Suite 500
Calgary, AB T2T 5S8
(403) 244-4422
FAX (403) 244-8160
Frequency: 107.3 MHz (FM).
Listening Area: Calgary (Central).
Cable: Yes.
Format: AOR.
Specialty Programming: *Calgary Inside Out*, Public Affairs Program (weekdays 11:00 a.m-noon).
Program Director: Wes Erickson.
Language: English.
Affiliates: CHEZ FM-Ottawa, C-JET and Q 101 FM-Smith Falls, ON.

CKRY

609-14 St. N.W., Suite 300
Calgary, AB T2N 2A1
(403) 283-6105
FAX (403) 270-8295
Frequency: 105.1 MHz (FM).
Format: C&W.
Program Director: Greg Heraldson.

CHQR

125-9 Ave. S.E., Suite 1900
Calgary, AB T2G 0P6
(403) 233-0770
FAX (403) 265-7807
Frequency: 770 kHz (AM).
Format: MOR.
Program Director: Dave Rutherford

CKDQ

515 Highway 10 E.
Drumheller, AB T0J 0Y0
(403) 823-3384
FAX (403) 823-7241
Frequency: 910 kHz (AM).
Format: C&W.
Program Director: Mark Woods.

CBX

8861-75 St.
Edmonton, AB T5J 2P4
(403) 468-7500
FAX (403) 468-2638
Frequency: 740 kHz (AM).
Format: Varied.
Program Director: Val Boser.

CBX

8861-75 St.
Edmonton, AB T5J 2P4
(403) 468-7500
FAX (403) 468-2638
Frequency: 90.9 MHz (FM).
Format: Varied.
Station Manager: Ted North.

CFCW

4752-99 St.
Edmonton, AB T6E 5H5
(403) 437-7879
FAX (403) 436-9803
Frequency: 790 kHz (AM).
Format: C&W.
Program Director: Pete Hicks.

CFRN

18520 Stony Plain Rd.
Edmonton, AB T5S 1A8
(403) 483-3311
FAX (403) 486-5121
Frequency: 1260 kHz (AM).
Format: A/C.
Program Director: Walt Gidyk.
Specialty Programming: Edmonton Oilers Hockey.

CHED

5204-84 St.
Edmonton, AB T6E 5N8
(403) 468-6300
FAX (403) 468-6739
Frequency: 630 kHz (AM).
Format: AOR.
Program Director: Kevin McKanna.

CHFA

8861-75 St.
Edmonton, AB T5J 2P4
(403) 468-7500
FAX (403) 468-7812
Frequency: 680 kHz (AM).
Format: Contemporary.
Station Manager: Denis Collette.
Program Director: Denis Collette.
Language: French.
Ownership: Radio Canada.

CHQT

10130-103 St., Suite 2200
Edmonton, AB T5J 3N9
(403) 424-8800
FAX (403) 425-1201
Frequency: 880 kHz (AM).
Format: MOR.
Program Director: Jay Charland.

CIRK

10250-108 St.
Edmonton, AB T5J 2X3
(403) 428-8597
FAX (403) 428-7168
Frequency: 97.3 MHz (FM).
Format: AOR.
Program Director: Neil Edwards.

CISN

10550-102 St.
Edmonton, AB T5H 2T3
(403) 428-1104
FAX (403) 428-6502
Frequency: 103.9 MHz (FM).
Listening Area: North Central Alberta (coast to coast on satellite anik c-1).
Cable: Yes.
Format: Contemporary Country.
Program Director: Ruth Blakely.
Language: English.
Affiliates: Shaw Radio: CKGY-Red Deer, CFEZ-Taber, CHEC-Lethbridge.
Rebroadcasts: Overnight only on CKGY 1170 AM Red Deer, AB.
Comments: Awaiting CRTC approval on CHAY FM-Barrie, ON.

CJCA

10250-108 St.
Edmonton, AB T5J 2X3
(403) 423-4930
FAX (403) 428-7168
Frequency: 930 kHz (AM).
Listening Area: North Central Alberta.
Cable: Yes.
Format: A/C, News and Information.
Specialty Programming: *Dateline*, a show for the single people of Edmonton and area.
Program Director: Rick Lewis.

CJKE

18520 Stony Plain Rd.
Edmonton, AB T5T 1V3
(403) 484-2553
FAX (403) 489-6927
Frequency: 100.3 MHz (FM).
Listening Area: Edmonton and area.
Cable: Yes.
Format: Soft A/C.
Specialty Programming: New Age.
Program Director: Stephen L. Moore.
Affiliates: CFRN, CFRN-TV.

CKER

4443-99 St.
Edmonton, AB T6E 5B6
(403) 438-1480
FAX (403) 437-5129
Frequency: 1480 kHz (AM).
Listening Area: Edmonton.
Cable: Yes.
Format: Ethnic.
Program Director: Diana Parker.

CKNG
10326-81 Ave.
Edmonton, AB T6E 1X2
(403) 469-5464
FAX (403) 439-8017
Frequency: 92.5 MHz (FM).
Format: A/C.
Program Director: Wayne Bryant.

CKRA
4752-99 St.
Edmonton, AB T6E 5H5
(403) 437-4996
FAX (403) 436-9803
Frequency: 96.3 MHz (FM).
Format: A/C.
Program Director: Len Thuesen.

CKUA
10526 Jasper Ave.
Edmonton, AB T5J 1Z7
(403) 428-7595
FAX (403) 428-7628
Frequency: 580 kHz (AM).
Format: Varied.
Ownership: Alberta Educational Communications Corp.
Program Director: J. Rollans.
Rebroadcasts: On stations throughout Alberta.

CKUA
10526 Jasper Ave.
Edmonton, AB T5J 1Z7
(403) 428-7595
FAX (403) 428-7628
Frequency: 94.9 MHz (FM).
Format: Varied.
Ownership: Alberta Educational Communications Corp.
Program Director: J. Rollans.
Rebroadcasts: On stations throughout Alberta.

CKXM
18520 Stony Plain Rd.
Edmonton, AB T5P 4C2
(403) 483-2596
FAX (403) 486-5121
Frequency: 100.3 MHz (FM).
Format: Adult Contemporary.
Ownership: Sunwapta Broadcasting Ltd.
Station Manager: D. Nevett.
Program Director: George Kelso.

CKYR
P.O. Box 1450
Edson, AB T0E 0P0
(403) 723-4461
FAX (403) 723-4462
Frequency: 1450 kHz (AM).
Format: Contemporary Hit Radio.
Ownership: Yellowhead Broadcasting Ltd.
Station Manager: Mel Lazarenko.
Program Director: Dave Schuck.

CKYX
9912 Franklin Ave.
Fort McMurray, AB T9H 2K5
(403) 743-2246
FAX (403) 791-7250
Frequency: 97.9 MHz (FM).
Format: AOR.
Program Director: John B. Shields.

CJOK
9912 Franklin Ave.
Fort Murray, AB T9H 2K5
(403) 743-2246
FAX (403) 791-7250
Frequency: 1230 kHz (AM).
Format: C&W.
Program Director: Bill Bergen.

CFGP
9835-101 Ave.
Grand Prairie, AB T8V 0X6
(403) 532-1050
FAX (403) 539-0367
Frequency: 1050 kHz (AM).
Format: A/C.
Program Director: Ken White.

CJXX
9817-101 Ave., Suite 202
Grande Prairie, AB T8V 0V1
(403) 539-5599
FAX (403) 538-1266
Frequency: 1430 kHz (AM).
Listening Area: Grande Prairie and area.
Cable: Yes.
Format: C&W.
Program Director: Tom Bedore.
Affiliates: Monarch Broadcasting.

CHRB
P.O. Box 1280
High River, AB T0L 1B0
(403) 652-2472
FAX (403) 652-7861
Frequency: 1280 kHz (AM).
Format: C&W.
Ownership: Palliser Broadcasting Ltd.
Program Director: Lorne Ball.

CHEC
401 Mayor Magrath Dr.
Lethbridge, AB T1J 4A3
(403) 329-1090
FAX (403) 329-0195
Frequency: 1090 kHz (AM).
Format: A/C.
Program Director: Mike Leblanc.

CILA

1015-3 Ave. S.
Lethbridge, AB T1J 3Z9
(403) 328-1077
FAX (403) 327-5879
Frequency: 107.7 MHz (FM).
Format: AOR.
Ownership: Lethbridge Broadcasting Co.
Program Director: David Larsen.

CJOC

1015-3 Ave. S.
Lethbridge, AB T1J 3Z9
(403) 320-1220
FAX (403) 327-5879
Frequency: 1220 kHz (AM).
Format: C&W.
Program Director: David Larsen.
Ownership: Lethbridge Broadcasting Co.
Rebroadcasts: CJPR - Crowsnest Pass, CJEV
- Elkford, BC.

CKSA

5026-50 St.
Lloydminster, AB T9V 1P3
(403) 875-3321
FAX (403) 875-4704
Frequency: 1080 kHz (AM).
Format: CHR.
Program Director: Pat Thomas.
Ownership: Saskatchewan/Alberta
Broadcasters Ltd.

CHAT

P.O. Box 1270
Medicine Hat, AB T1A 7H5
(403) 529-1270
FAX (403) 529-1292
Frequency: 1270 kHz (AM).
Format: C&W.
Program Director: Pat O'Connor.
Ownership: Monarch Broadcasting Ltd.

CJCY

457-3 St. S.E., 2nd Floor
Medicine Hat, AB T1A 0G8
(403) 529-1390
FAX (403) 527-5971
Frequency: 1390 kHz (AM).
Format: A/C.
Program Director: John Carter.
Ownership: Medicine Hat Broadcasting Ltd.

CHCL

Barrack Block 24, 3rd Floor, CFB Cold Lake.
P.O. Box 1220
Medley, AB T0A 2M0
(403) 594-1450
Frequency: 1450 kHz (AM).
Listening Area: 30-mile radius.
Cable: No.
Format: A/C.
Language: English, French.
Affiliates: CBC.

CKYL

9811-100 Ave.
Peace River, AB T8S 2X0
(403) 624-2535
FAX (403) 624-5424
Frequency: 610 kHz (AM).
Format: MOR.
Program Director: Kieth Wasmuth.
Ownership: Peace River Broadcasting Corp.
Rebroadcasts: CKHL-High Level.

CIZZ

4920-59 St.
P.O. Bag 5339
Red Deer, AB T4N 6W1
(403) 342-7625
FAX (403) 346-1230
Frequency: 98.9 MHz (FM).
Listening Area: Central Alberta.
Cable: Yes.
Format: AOR.
Specialty Programming: *Jazz Inspiration,*
Sundays 6 a.m.-8 a.m., *Christian Rock,*
Sundays 9:30 p.m.-12p.m.
Program Director: Bob Mills.
Language English.
Affiliates: CKGY-AM, CISN-FM, CFEZ, CHEC.

CKGY

4920-59 St.
P.O. Bag 5339
Red Deer, AB T4N 6W1
(403) 343-1170
FAX (403) 346-1230
Frequency: 1170 kHz (AM).
Listening Area: Central Alberta.
Cable: Yes.
Format: Contemporary country.
Specialty Programming: *Gospel Show,* Sunday 8:00 p.m.-11:00 p.m.
Program Director: Bob Mills.
Language: English.
Affiliates: CIZZ-FM, CISN-FM, CFEZ, CHEC.

CKRD

2840 Bremner Ave.
P.O. Bag 5700
Red Deer, AB T4N 6V5
(403) 343-0700
FAX (403) 343-2573
Frequency: 700 kHz (AM).
Listening Area: Central Alberta.
Cable: Yes.
Format: A/C Gold.
Program Director: Marv Casey.
Language: English.

CKWA

P.O. Box 2470
Slave Lake, AB T0G 2A0
(403) 849-2577
FAX (403) 849-4833
Frequency: 1210 kHz (AM).
Format: MOR.
Program Director: Darrell Sebzda.

CHMG

22 Sir Winston Churchill Ave., Suite 602
St. Albert, AB T8N 1B4
(403) 458-1200
FAX (403) 460-9671
Frequency: 1200 kHz (AM).
Format: Gold.
Program Director: Kirk Elliott.
Specialty Programming: Original Rock 'n'
Roll, Amateur Sports Report.

CHLW

5117-50 Ave.
St. Paul, AB T0A 3A0
(403) 645-4425
FAX (403) 645-2383
Frequency: 1310 kHz (AM).
Format: C&W.
Program Director: J.B. Cartwright.

CKSQ

4703-58 St.
Stettler, AB T0C 2L0
(403) 742-2930
Frequency: 1400 kHz (AM).
Format: C&W.
Program Director: Brad Bazin.
Ownership: CHUM Ltd.

CFEZ

5331-48 Ave.
P.O. Box 2199
Taber, AB T0K 2G0
(403) 223-4455
FAX (403) 223-1035
Frequency: 1570 kHz (AM).
Format: Contemporary Easy Listening.
Listening Area: Lethbridge, Southern Alberta.
Cable: No.
Program Director: Steve Armstrong.
Language: English.
Affiliates: Shaw Radio Ltd. (CHEC-Lethbridge).

CILW

10137-2 Ave.
Wainwright, AB T0B 4P0
(403) 842-4311
FAX (403) 842-4636
Frequency: 1230 kHz (AM).
Format: C&W.
Program Director: Brian Hepp.
Ownership: Nor Net Communications.

CFOK

P.O. Box 1800
Westlock, AB T0G 2L0
(403) 349-6125
FAX (403) 349-6259
Frequency: 1370 kHz (AM).
Format: Country.
Listening Area: Westlock-Barrhead.
Cable: No.
Specialty Programming: Portugese Program-
ming (Sunday afternoons).
Program Director: Phyllis Shepard.
Language: English.
Affiliates: Central Alberta Radio Network.
Program Director: CKBA, CKWA, CHLW,
CILW, CJO1.

CJOI

5220-51 Ave.
Wetaskiwin, AB T9A 3E2
(403) 352-0144
FAX (403) 352-0606
Frequency: 1440 kHz (AM).
Listening Area: Central Alberta.
Cable: No.
Format: C&W.
Specialty Programming: Christian
programming, weekday evenings and all day
Sunday.
Program Director: Sandi Zenari.
Languages: English, Greek, German, Italian and
Polish.

BRITISH COLUMBIA

CFVR
2722 Allwood St.
Abbotsford, BC V2T 3R8
(604) 859-5277
FAX (604) 859-9907
Frequency: 850 kHz (AM).
Format: A/C.
Ownership: Fraser Valley Broadcasters.
Program Director: Bob Singleton.

CFWB
909 Ironwood St.
Campbell River, BC V9W 3E5
(604) 287-7106
Frequency: 1490 kHz (AM).
Listening Area: Campbell River - Gold River.
Cable: Yes.
Format: A/C.
Specialty Programming: Solid Gold.
Program Director: Brian Langston.
Affiliates: Coast Radio CHQB, CFCP, CFNI.

CJGR
909 Ironwood St.
Campbell River, BC V9W 3E5
(604) 287-7106
Frequency: 100 MHz (FM).

CKQR
525-11 Ave.
Castlegar, BC V1N 1J6
(604) 365-7600
FAX (604) 365-8480
Frequency: 760 kHz (AM).
Format: A/C.
Station Manager: Gordon Brady.
Program Director: Ross Hawse.

CHWK
P.O. Box 386
Chilliwack, BC V2P 6J7
(604) 795-5711
FAX (604) 792-6946
Frequency: 1270 kHz (AM).
Format: A/C.
Ownership: Fraser Valley Broadcasters.
Program Director: Bryan Laver.

CKSR
P.O. Box 386
Chilliwack, BC V2P 6J7
(604) 795-7827
FAX (604) 792-6946
Frequency: 104.9 MHz (FM).
Format: MOR.
Ownership: Star Radio Inc.
Program Director: Barrie McMaster.

CFCP
1595 Cliff Ave.
Courtenay, BC V9N 2K6
(604) 334-2421
Frequency: 1440 kHz (AM).
Format: CHR.
Program Director: Ken Armstrong.

CKEK
19-9 Ave. S.
Cranbrook, BC V1C 2L9
(604) 426-2224
FAX (604) 426-5520
Frequency: 570 kHz (AM).
Format: A/C.
Ownership: Columbia Kootenay Broadcasting.
Program Director: Ray Wilson.

CJDC
901-102 Ave.
Dawson Creek, BC
V1G 2B6
(604) 782-3341
FAX (604) 782-1809
Frequency: 890 kHz (AM).
Format: CHR.
Ownership: Mega Communications Inc.
Program Director: Mike Michaud.

CKAY
435 Trunk Rd., Suite 102
Duncan, BC V9L 2P5
(604) 748-2529
Frequency: 1500 kHz (AM).
Format: A/C.
Ownership: CKAY Radio (1979) Inc.
Program Director: Jay Longpre.

CFEK
P.O. Box 1170
Fernie, BC V0B 1M0
(604) 423-4449
FAX (604) 423-4440
Frequency: 1240 kHz (AM).
Format: A/C.
Ownership: Columbia Kootenay Broadcasting.
Program Director: Howard Ashmore.

CJEK
P.O. Box 1170
Fernie, BC V0B 1M0
(604) 423-4449
FAX (604) 423-4440
Frequency: 1400 kHz (AM).
Format: A/C.
Ownership: Columbia Kootenay Broadcasting.
Program Director: Howard Ashmore.

CKNL

P.O. Box 6310
Fort St. John, BC V1J 4H8
(604) 785-6634
FAX (604) 785-4544
Frequency: 560 kHz (AM).
Format: MOR.
Program Director: Paul Larsen.

CKGF

P.O. Box 1570
Grand Forks, BC V0H 1H0
(604) 442-8221
Frequency: 1340 kHz (AM).
Listening Area: Boundary Country.
Cable: Yes.
Format: Contemporary Country.
Language: English, Russian.
Affiliates: WIN, Seltech.
Rebroadcasts: Station has three LPRT: CKGF
1-Christina Lake, CKGF 2-FM -Green Midway,
CKGF 3-FM-Rock Creek.

CKGO

P.O. Box 1600
415 Wallace St.
Hope, BC V0X 1L0
(604) 869-9313
Frequency: 1240 kHz (AM).
Format: A/C.
Ownership: Fraser Valley Broadcasters.
Program Director: Greg Phillips.

CFJC

460 Pemberton Terrace
Kamloops, BC V2C 1T5
(604) 372-3322
FAX (604) 374-0445
Frequency: 550 kHz (AM).
Listening Area: Kamloops and area.
Format: C&W.
Ownership: Twin Cities Radio Ltd.
Program Director: Doug Collins.
Rebroadcasts: CFJC-FM - Merritt, CFJC-FM -
Clearwater.

CHNL

611 Lansdowne St.
P.O. Box 610
Kamloops, BC
(604) 372-2292
FAX (604) 372-0682
Frequency: 610 kHz (AM).
Listening Area: Kamloops, Merritt, Ashcroft/
Cache Creek, Clearwater/Shuswap.
Cable: Yes.
Format: A/C.
Specialty Programming: Live play by play of
Vancouver Canucks hockey, Kamloops Blazers
hockey, and B.C. Lions football.
Program Director: Jim Reynolds.
Affiliates: CJNL 1230 - Merritt.

CIFM

460 Pemberton Terrace
Kamloops, BC V2C 1T5
(604) 372-3322
FAX (604) 374-0445
Frequency: 98.3 MHz (FM).
Listening Area: Kamloops and Southern
Cariboo.
Cable: Yes.
Format: A/C.
Specialty Programming: Jazz.
Program Director: Doug Collins.
Rebroadcasts: 95.3 - Ashcroft, 105.9 -
Barriere, 92.7 - Clearwater 92.7, 101.3 - Clinton,
103.9 - Merritt, 106.3 - Pritchard.

CJNL

611 Landsdowne St.
Kamloops, BC V2C 1Y6
(604) 372-2292
FAX (604) 372-0682
Frequency: 1230 kHz (AM).
Format: A/C.
Program Director: Joan Gulliford.

CHIM

P.O. Box 100
Kelowna, BC V1Y 7N3
(604) 762-3331
FAX (604) 762-2141
Frequency : 104.7 MHz (FM).
Format: AOR.
Ownership: Seacoast Communications Group
Program Director: Rob Bye.

CILK

1598 Pandosy St.
Kelowna, BC V1Y 1P4
(604) 860-1010
FAX (604) 860-0505
Frequency: 101.5 MHz (FM).
Format: MOR.
Ownership: CILK-FM Broadcasting Ltd.
Program Director: Douglas Johnston.

CKIQ

2417 Highway 97 N.
Kelowna, BC V1X 4S2
(604) 860-8600
FAX (604) 860-8856
Frequency: 1150 kHz (AM).
Listening Area: South-Central Okanagan.
Cable: Yes.
Format: A/C.
Program Director: Dave Pears.
Affiliates: CKNW Vancouver.

CKOV

P.O. Box 100
Kelowna, BC V1Y 7N3
(604) 762-3331
FAX (604) 762-2141
Frequency: 630 kHz (AM).
Format: A/C.
Program Director: Bill Barnes.

CKTK

350 City Center
Kitimat, BC V8C 1T6
(604) 632-2102
Frequency: 1230 kHz (AM).
Format: A/C.
Program Director: Ron Langridge (Director).
Specialty Programming: *Home Town*, Fridays
at 9:30 a.m.

CKST

20627 Fraser Highway, Suite 201
Langley, BC V3A 4G4
(604) 534-0800
FAX (604) 534-4140
Frequency: 800 kHz (AM).
Format: A/C.
Program Director: Chuck Chandler.
Ownership: Western World Communs. Ltd.

CKMK

P.O. Box Box 1210
Mackenzie, BC V0J 2C0
(604) 997-3400
Frequency: 1240 kHz (AM).
Format: MOR.
Program Director: Edward Barr.

CHUB

22 Esplanade
Nanaimo,BC V9R 4Y7
(604) 753-4341
FAX (604) 753-4819
Frequency: 1570 kHz (AM).
Format: MOR.
Program Director: Henry Brilz.

CKEG

2231 McGarrigle Rd. E.
Nanaimo, BC V9S 4M5
(604) 758-1131
FAX (604) 758-4644
Frequency: 1350 kHz (AM).
Format: C&W.
Program Director: Mike Obrien.

CFMI

815 McBride Plaza
New Westminster, BC V3L 2C1
(604) 521-4808
FAX (604) 522-3413
Frequency: 101.1 MHz (FM).
Format: AOR.
Program Director: Rick Shannon.

CKNW

815 McBride Plaza
New Westminster, BC V3L 2C1
(604) 522-2711
FAX (604) 522-3413
Frequency: 980 kHz.
Format: MOR.
Program Director: Doug Rutherford.

CKOO

P.O. Box 539
Osoyoos, BC V0H 1V0
(604) 495-7226
Frequency: 1240
Format: MOR.
Program Director: Ron Clark.

CHPQ

162 W. Harrison Ave., Suite 4
P.O. Box 1370
Parksville, BC V0R 2S0
(604) 248-4211
FAX (604) 753-4819
Frequency: 1370 kHz (AM).
Listening Area: Central Vancouver Island.
Cable: Yes.
Format: A/C.
Specialty Programming: Tuesday afternoon
talk show.
Program Director: Robert Barrie.
Affiliates: CHUB - Nanaimo.

CIGV

125 Nanaimo Ave. W.
Penticton, BC V2N 1N2
(604) 493-6767
FAX (604) 493-0098
Frequency: 100.7 MHz (FM).
Format: C&W.
Ownership: Great Valley Radio Ltd.
Station Manager: R.J. Robinson.

CJMG

33 Carmi Ave.
Penticton, BC V2A 3G4
(604) 492-5919
FAX (604) 493-0370
Frequency: 97.1 MHz (FM).
Listening Area: South Okanagan.
Cable: Yes.
Format: Light Rock.
Specialty Programming: Jazz, comedy,
contemporary gospel, dance club, kids' show.
Program Director: Doug Turnbull.
Affiliates: CKOK.

CKOK

33 Carmi Ave.
Penticton, BC V2A 3G4
(604) 492-2800
FAX (604) 493-0370
Frequency: 800 kHz (AM).
Format: A/C.
Ownership: Okanagan Skeena Grp. Ltd.
Station Manager: Harry Levant.
Program Director: Grant Sherwood.

CJAV

2970 - 3 Ave.
Port Alberni, BC V9Y 7N4
(604) 723-2455
FAX (604) 723-0797
Frequency: 1240 kHz (AM).
Format: A/C.
Station Manager: Bill Gibson.
Program Director: Ike Patterson.

CFNI

P.O. Box 1240
5050 Beaver Harbour Rd.
Port Hardy, BC V0N 2P0
(604) 949-6500
Frequency: 1240 kHz (AM).
Format: C&W.
Ownership: CFCP Radio Ltd.
Station Manager: Bob McInnes.

CHQB

6816 Courtenay St.
Powell River, BC V8A 1X1
(604) 485-4207
Frequency: 1280 kHz (AM).
Format: C&W.
Station Manager: Brian Langston.
Program Director: Brian Langston.

CIOI

1220 6 Ave.
Prince George, BC V2L 3M8
(604) 562-2101
FAX (604) 562-8768
Frequency: 101 MHz (FM).
Format: C&W.
Ownership: Radio Station CKPG Ltd.
Station Manager: G.M. Leighton.
Program Director: Randy Seabrook.

CIRX

1940-3 Ave.
Prince George, BC V2M 1G7
(604) 564-2524
FAX (604) 562-6611
Frequency: 94.3 MHz (FM).
Listening Area: Prince George, BC.
Cable: Yes.
Format: Light Rock.
Program Director: Gary Russell.
Affiliates: Cariboo Central Interior Radio
Network.
Rebroadcasts: CIRX-1 (FM 96) - Nechako
Valley.

CIBC

1940-3 Ave.
Prince George, BC V2M 1G7
(604) 562-2236
FAX (604) 563-6218
Frequency: 620 kHz (AM).
Format: A/C.
Ownership: Cariboo Cent. Interior Radio.
Station Manager: Terry Shepherd.
Program Director: Wayne Pederson.

CJCI

1940-3 Ave.
Prince George, BC V2M 1G7
(604) 564-2524
FAX (604) 562-6611
Frequency: 620 kHz (AM).
Format: A/C.
Program Director: Wayne Pederson.

CKPG

1220-6 Ave.
Prince George, BC V2L 3M8
(604) 564-8861
FAX (604) 562-8768
Frequency: 550 kHz (AM).
Format: A/C.
Ownership: Radio Station CKPG Ltd.
Station Manager: G.M. Leighton.
Program Director: Randy Seabrook.

CFPR

CBC
222-3 Ave. W.
Prince Rupert, BC V8J 1L1
(604) 624-2161
FAX (604) 627-8594
Frequency: 860 kHz (AM).
Format: Varied.
Ownership: Radio Canada.

CHTK

346 Stiles Place
Prince Rupert, BC V8J 3S5
(604) 624-9111
FAX (604) 624-3100
Frequency: 560 kHz (AM).
Listening Area: Prince Rupert and the Queen
Charlotte Islands.
Cable: Yes.
Format: A/C days, CHR nights.
Program Director: Kevin McConville.
Affiliates: CFTK-Terrace, BC.

CKXR

360 Ross St.
P.O. Box 69
Salmon Arm, BC V1E 4N2
(604) 832-2161
FAX (604) 832-2240
Frequency: 580 MHz (FM).
Listening Area: Columbia-Shuswap.
Cable: No.
Format: Country, A/C.
Program Director: J. Susoeff.
Affiliates: SRN.
Rebroadcasts: CKCR-Revelstoke, CKGR-Golden, FM-102-North Shuswap-Sorrento, CKIR-Radium.

CKCQ

160 Front St.
Quesnel, BC V2J 2K1
(604) 992-7046
FAX (604) 992-2354
Frequency: 920 kHz (AM).
Ownership: Cariboo Broadcasters Ltd.
Station Manager: Terry Shepherd.
Program Director: Brian Miles.

CISL

11151 Horseshoe Way, Suite 20
Richmond, BC V7A 4S5
(604) 272-6500
FAX (604) 272-5428
Frequency: 650 kHz (AM).
Format: CHR.
Ownership: South Fraser Broadcasting Ltd.
Station Manager: Bill Waddington.
Program Director: Arnie Celsie.

CKCR

P.O. Box 69
Salmon Arm, BC V1E 4N2
(604) 832-2161
FAX (604) 832-2240
Frequency: 1340 kHz (AM).
Format: MOR
Ownership: Copper Is. Broadcasting.
Station Manager: Harvey Davidson.
Program Director: Jae Susoeff.

CKGR

P.O. Box 69
Salmon Arm, BC V1E 4N2
(604) 832-2161
FAX (604) 832-2240
Frequency: 1400 kHz (AM).
Format: A/C.
Ownership: Copper Is. Broadcasting.

CKIR

P.O. Box 69
Salmon Arm, BC V1E 4N2
(604) 832-2161
FAX (604) 832-2240
Frequency: 870 kHz (AM).
Format: A/C.
Ownership: Copper Is. Broadcasting.
Station Manager: Harvey Davidson.
Program Director: Jae Susoeff.

CFBV

P.O. Box 335
Smithers, BC V0J 2N0
(604) 847-2521
FAX (604) 847-9411
Frequency: 870 kHz (AM).
Format: MOR.
Station Manager: Allan Collison.
Program Director: Tom Stokes.

CFLD

P.O. Box 335
Smithers, BC V0J 2N0
(604) 847-2521
FAX (604) 692-3020
Frequency: 760 kHz (AM).
Format: MOR.
Station Manager: Allan Collison.
Program Director: Tom Stokes.

CKSP

P.O. Box 1170
Summerland, BC V0H 1Z0
(604) 494-0333
FAX (604) 494-9610
Frequency: 1450 kHz (AM).
Format: MOR.
Ownership: Okanagan Skeena Crp. Ltd.
Station Manager: Geoff Miller.
Program Director: Geoff Miller.

CFTK
4625 Lazelle Ave.
Terrace, BC V8G 1S4
(604) 635-6316
FAX (604) 638-6320
Frequency: 590 kHz (AM).
Format: A/C.
Ownership: Okanagan Skeena Crp. Ltd.
Station Manager: Sharon Taylor.

CJFW
4625 Lazelle Ave.
Terrace, BC V8G 1S4
(604) 635-6316
FAX (604) 638-6320
Frequency: 103.1 MHz (FM).
Format: C&W.
Ownership: Okanagan Skeena Crp. Ltd.
Station Manager: Sharon Taylor.
Program Director: Sharon Taylor.

CFKC
1560 2 Ave.
Trail,BC V1R 1M4
(604) 368-5510
FAX (604) 428-5311
Frequency: 1340 kHz (AM).
Format: MOR.
Ownership: Four Seasons Radio Ltd.
Station Manager: Dennis Gerein
Program Director: Karl Johnston.

CJAT
1560 2 Ave.
Trail, BC V1P 1M4
(604) 368-5510
FAX (604) 428-5311
Frequency: 610 kHz (AM).
Format: MOR.
Ownership: Four Seasons Radio Ltd.
Station Manager: Dennis Gerein.

CBU
CBC
700 Hamilton St.
Vancouver, BC V6B 2R5
(604) 662-6000
Frequency: 690 kHz (AM).
Format: Varied.
Ownership: Radio Canada.
Station Manager: Robert Sunter.

CBU
700 Hamilton St.
Vancouver, BC V6B 2R5
(604) 662-6000
Format: Varied.
Frequency: 105.7 MHz (FM).

CBUF
CBC
700 Hamilton St.
Vancouver, BC V6B 2R5
(604) 662-6000
FAX (604) 662-6161
Frequency: 97.7 MHz (FM).
Format: Varied.
Ownership: Radio Canada.
Station Manager: Michel Lacombe.
Program Director: Jacques Bernard.
Language: French.

CFMI
815 McBride Plaza
Vancouver, BC V3L 2C1
(604) 521-4808
FAX (604) 522-3413
Frequency: 101 MHz (FM).
Listening Area: Lower Mainland.
Cable: Yes.
Format: AOR, PRO, CHR.
Specialty Programming: *What's New in Music*, a two-hour music show Sunday evenings at 6 p.m.
Program Director: Rick Shannon.
Affiliates: Q107-Toronto, KIS-Winnipeg, WIN Network.

CFOX
1006 Richards St.
Vancouver, BC V6B 1S8
(604) 684-7221
FAX (604) 681-9134
Frequency: 99.3 MHz (FM).
Format: AOR.
Ownership: Moffat Communications Ltd.
Station Manager: Alden Diehl.
Program Director: Jim Johnston.

CFRO
337 Carrall St.
Vancouver, BC V6B 2J4
(604) 684-8494
Frequency: 102.7 MHz (FM).
Listening Area: Greater Vancouver-Victoria.
Cable: Yes (Across British Columbia).
Format: Eclectic.
Specialty Programming: Community programming.
Program Director: Allan Jensen.
Language : 85% English, plus Farsi, Armenian and Cantonese.

CFUN

1900 W. 4 Ave.
Vancouver, BC V6J 1M6
(604) 731-9222
FAX (604) 731-6143
Frequency: 1410 kHz (AM).
Listening Area: Lower Mainland, Fraser Valley,
Vancouver Island.
Cable: Yes.
Format: A/C., Favourites of yesterday and today.
Program Director: Neil Gallagher.
Affiliates: CHUM Group.

CHQM

1134 Burrard St.
Vancouver, BC V6Z 1Y8
(604) 682-3241
FAX (604) 682-5564
Frequency: 1320 kHz (AM).
Format: MOR.
Ownership: Q Broadcasting Ltd.
Station Manager: Noel Hullah.
Program Director: Dave Geddes.

CHQM

1134 Burrard St.
Vancouver, BC V6Z 1Y8
(604) 682-3241
FAX (604) 682-5564
Frequency: 103.5 MHz (FM).
Format: CHR.
Ownership: Q Broadcasting Ltd.
Station Manager: Noel Hullah.
Program Director: David Geddes.

CHRX

1410 W. 8 Ave.
Vancouver, BC V6H 1C9
(604) 731-6111
FAX (604) 731-0493
Frequency: 90.0 kHz (AM).
Format: CHR.
Station Manager: George Madden.
Program Director: Bob Morris.

CJJR

1401 W. 8 Ave.
Vancouver, BC V6H 1C9
(604) 731-7772
FAX (604) 731-0493
Frequency: 93.7 MHz (FM).
Listening Area: Vancouver and Lower
Mainland.
Cable: Yes.
Format: Country.
Program Director: John Beaudoin.
Affiliates: CIFM-Kamloops, CFFM-Williams
Lake.

CJVB

814 Richards St.
Vancouver, BC V6B 3A7
(604) 688-9931
FAX (604) 688-6559
Frequency: 1470 kHz (AM).
Listening Area: Greater Vancouver and the
East Coast of Vancouver Island.
Cable: Yes.
Format: Multilingual.
Specialty Programming: Ethnic
Programming.
Program Director: Theo Donnelly, Pat Karl.
Languages: English, Cantonese, Italian, Dutch,
German and 20 other languages.

CKKS

2440 Ash St.
Vancouver, BC V6B 1S8
(604) 872-2557
FAX (604) 873-0877
Frequency: 96.9 MHz (FM).
Format: A/C.
Ownership: Selkirk Broadcasting Ltd.
Station Manager: Tom Peacock.
Program Director: Dale Buote.

CKLG

1006 Richards St.
Vancouver, BC V6B 1S8
(604) 681-7511
FAX (604) 681-9134
Frequency: 730 kHz (AM).
Format: CHR.
Ownership: Moffat Communications Ltd.
Station Manager: Alden Diehl.
Program Director: Brad Phillips.

CKWX

2440 Ash St.
Vancouver, BC V5Z 4J6
(604) 873-2599
FAX (604) 873-0877
Frequency: 1130 kHz (AM).
Format: C&W.
Ownership: Selkirk Broadcasting Ltd.
Station Manager: Tom Peacock.
Program Director: Ted Farr.

CKXY

1199 W. Pender St., Suite 101
Vancouver, BC V6E 2R1
(604) 669-1040
FAX (604) 684-7911
Frequency: 1040 kHz (AM).
Format: CHR.
Ownership: Ocean Pacific Broadcasters.
Station Manager: Tom E. McBride.
Program Director: P. McKnight.

CIVH

150 W. St.
Vanderhoof, BC V0J 3A0
(604) 567-4914
FAX (604) 567-4928
Frequency: 1340 kHz (AM).
Format: Varied.
Ownership: Prince George Broadcasting.
Station Manager: Mel Brundige.
Program Director: Stan Sterdan.

CKAL

8808 Clerke Rd.
Vernon, BC V1B 1W2
(604) 545-9222
FAX (604) 545-6510
Frequency: 1050 kHz (AM).
Format: C&W.
Ownership: High Sierra Broadcasting Ltd.
Station Manager: Gordon Colledge.
Program Director: Steve Robinson.

CJIB

3313-32 Ave.
Vernon, BC V1T 2E1
(604) 545-2141
FAX (604) 545-9008
Frequency: 940 kHz (AM).
Format: A/C.
Ownership: Interior Broadcasters Co.
Station Manager: Patrick Nicol.
Program Director: Don Weglo.

CFAX

825 Broughton St.
Victoria, BC V8W 1E5
(604) 386-1070
FAX (604) 386-5775
Frequency: 1070 kHz (AM).
Format: A/C.
Ownership: CFAX Radio 1070 Ltd.
Station Manager: Mel Cooper.
Program Director: Terry Spence.

CFMS

P.O. Box 1200
Victoria, BC V8W 2S5
(604) 388-5544
FAX (604) 384-1213
Frequency: 98.9 MHz (FM).
Format: MOR.
Station Manager: John B. Sitter.
Program Director: Terry Giffiths.

CJVI

CBC
P.O. Box 900
Victoria, BC V8W 2S2
(604) 382-0900
FAX (604) 382-4358
Frequency: 900 kHz (AM).
Format: CHR.
Station Manager: Kim Hesketh.
Program Director: Ken Geiger.

CKDA

P.O. Box 1200
Victoria, BC V8W 2S5
(604) 384-9311
FAX (604) 384-1213
Frequency: 1200 kHz (AM).
Format: A/C.
Station Manager: John B. Sitter.
Program Director: Terry Griffiths.

KARI

P.O. Box 9
White Rock, BC V4B 4Z7
(604) 536-7733
Frequency: 550 kHz (AM).
Format: Gospel.
Ownership: Radio Kari Ltd.
Station Manager: Don Bevilacqua.
Program Director: Gary Nawman.

CFFM

197 North 2 Ave., Suite 102
Williams Lake, BC V2G 1Z5
(604) 398-2336
FAX (604) 392-4046
Frequency: 100 kHz (AM).
Listening Area: Williams Lake, Quesnel and 100 Mile House.
Cable: Yes.
Format: Country.
Program Director: Ken Wilson.

MANITOBA

CFAM

9 Centre Ave. E.
P.O. Box 950
Altona, MB R0G 0B0
(204) 324-6464
FAX (204) 324-8918
Frequency: 950 kHz (AM).
Listening Area: South Central Manitoba.
Cable: No.
Format: Country, MOR.
Specialty Programming: Classical, Ethnic.
Program Director: Al Friesen.
Affiliates: Golden West Broadcasting.
Rebroadcasts: Boissevain, Manitoba.

CKMW

P.O. Box 950
Altona, MA R0G 0B0
(204) 325-7602
FAX (204) 324-6464
Ownership: Golden West Broadcasting Ltd.
Station Manager: David Wiebe.
Program Director: Al Friesen.

CKLQ

624-14 St. E.
Brandon, MB R7A 6N6
(204) 726-8888
FAX (204) 726-1270
Frequency: 880 kHz (AM).
Format: C&W.
Ownership: Riding Mountain Broadcasting.
Program Director: Steve Antaya.

CKX

2940 Victoria Ave.
Brandon, MB R7B 0N2
(204) 728-1150
FAX (204) 727-4697
Frequency: 1150 kHz (AM).
Format: MOR.
Ownership: Western Manitoba Broadcasters.
Station Manager: A.S. Craig.
Program Director: Glenn Hildebrand.

CKX

2940 Victoria Ave.
Brandon, MB R7A 6A5
(204) 728-1150
FAX (204) 727-4697
Frequency: 96.1 MHz (FM).
Format: AOR.
Ownership: Western Manitoba Broadcasters.
Station Manager: A.S. Craig.
Program Director: Murray Redman.

CKDM

27-3 Ave. N.E.
Dauphin, MB R7N 2V5
(204) 638-3230
FAX (204) 638-8257
Frequency: 730 kHz (AM).
Format: C&W.
Ownership: Dauphin Broadcasting Co. Ltd.
Station Manager: Linus J. Westberg/S.
Marcynuk.
Program Director: Kevin Anderson.

CFAR

316 Green St.
Flin Flon, MB R8A 1N3
(204) 687-3469
Frequency: 590 kHz (AM).
Format: A/C.
Ownership: Arctic Radio (1982) Ltd.
Station Manager: Doug O'Brien.
Program Director: Joe McCormick.

CFRY

1500 Saskatachewan Ave. W.
Portage La Prairie, MB R1N 0N6
(204) 239-5111
FAX (204) 857-3456
Frequency: 920 kHz (AM).
Format: C&W.
Station Manager: Red Hughes.
Program Director: Bob Turner.

CFQX

P.O. Box 400
Selkirk, MB R1A 2B#
(204) 785-2929
FAX (204) 772-0060
Frequency: 104.1 MHz (FM).
Format: C&W.
Ownership: Radio QX-FM Inc.
Station Manager: James A. Millican.
Program Director: James A. Millican.

CKSB

CBC
607 Rue Langevin
St. Boniface, MB R2H 2W2
(204) 786-0240
FAX (204) 786-0793
Frequency: 1050 kHz (AM).
Format: Varied.
Ownership: Radio Canada.
Language: French.

CJAR

General Delivery
The Pas, MB R9A 1R7
(204) 623-5307
Frequency: 1240 kHz (AM).
Format: Varied.
Ownership: Arctic Radio (1982) Ltd.
Station Manager: Jim Hamm.
Program Director: Jim Hamm.

CHSM

Main St., P.O. Box 1250
Steinbach, MB R0A 2A0
(204) 326-1010
FAX (204) 324-8918
Frequency: 1250 kHz (AM).
Listening Area: South Eastern Manitoba.
Cable: Yes.
Format: MOR, Country.
Specialty Programming: Classical, Ethnic.
Program Director: Al Friesen.
Affiliates: Golden West Broadcasting.

CBWK

CBC
7 Selkirk Ave.
Thompson, MB R8N 0M4
(204) 677-2307
Frequency: 100.9 MHz (FM).
Format: News and information.
Ownership: Radio Canada.
Station Manager: Keran Sanders.

CHTM

201 Hayes Rd.
Thompson, MB R8N 1M5
(204) 778-7361
Frequency: 610 kHz (AM).
Format: MOR.
Ownership: Arctic Radio (1982) Ltd.
Station Manager: Bunny Kane.
Program Director: Ron Krane.

CBW

CBC
541 Portage Ave.
Winnipeg, MB R3C 2H1
(204) 775-8351
FAX (204) 786-0586
Frequency: 98.3 MHz (FM).
Format: Varied.
Ownership: Canadian Broadcasting Corp.
Station Manager: Marv Terhoch.
Program Director: John Coutanche.
Language: English, French.

CKMW

561 Main St.
P.O. Box 1570
Winkler, MB R0G 2X0
(204) 325-7602
FAX (204) 324-8918
Frequency: 1570 kHz (AM).
Listening Area: South Central Manitoba.
Cable: No.
Format: Country.
Specialty Programming: Sports, Old Time Music.
Program Director: Al Friesen.
Languages: English, French.
Affiliates: Golden West Broadcasting.

CBW

541 Portage Ave.
Winnipeg, MB R3C 2H1
(204) 775-8351
FAX (204) 786-0586
Frequency: 990 kHz (AM).
Format: Varied.
Ownership: Canadian Broadcasting Corp.
Station Manager: Marv Terhoch.
Program Director: John Coutanche.

CIFX

1445 Pembina Hwy.
Winnipeg, MB R3T 5C2
(204) 477-5120
FAX (204) 453-0815
Frequency: 1290 KHz (AM).
Ownership: CHUM Ltd.
Program Director: Mark Mahen.

CFQX

276 Colony St.
Winnipeg, MB R3C 1W3
(204) 284-8591
FAX (204) 772-0060
Frequency: 104.1 MHz (FM).
Listening Area: Southern Manitoba.
Cable: Yes.
Format: Contemporary Country.
Specialty Programming: Country Gospel, and *Touch The Earth*, a weekly folk and roots music program.
Program Director: Jim Millican.

CHIQ

1445 Pembina Highway
Winnipeg, MB R3T 5C2
(204) 477-5120
FAX (204) 453-0815
Frequency: 94.3 MHz (FM).
Format: A/C.
Ownership: CHUM Ltd.
Station Manager: Bob Laine.
Program Director: Pat Holliday.

CITI

Polo Park
Winnipeg, MB R3G 0L7
(204) 786-6181
FAX (204) 775-5978
Frequency: 92.1 MHz (FM).
Format: AOR.
Ownership: Moffat Communications Ltd.
Station Manager: Don Kay.
Program Director: Ross Winters.

CJOB

930 Portage Ave.
Winnipeg, MB R3G 0P8
(204) 786-2471
FAX (204) 783-4512
Frequency: 680 kHz (AM).
Format: News and information.
Ownership: Western Manitoba Broadcasters.
Station Manager: John Cochrane.
Program Director: Del Sexsmith.

CKIS

930 Portage Ave.
Winnipeg, MB R3G 0P8
(204) 786-6884
FAX (204) 783-4512
Frequency: 97.5 MHz (FM).
Format: A/C.
Ownership: Western World Communications Ltd.
Station Manager: Peter Grant.
Program Director: Jake Edwards.

CKJS

520 Corydon Ave.
Winnipeg, MB R3L 0P1
(204) 477-1221
FAX (204) 453-8244
Frequency: 810 kHz (AM).
Format: Varied.
Station Manager: Tony Carta.
Program Director: Tony Carta.

CKRC

P.O. Box 9700
Winnipeg, MB R3C 3E5
(204) 942-2231
FAX (204) 943-7687
Frequency: 630 kHz (AM).
Format: C&W.
Ownership: Armadale Communications Ltd.
Station Manager: William C. Gorrie.
Program Director: John Norris.

CKWG

P.O. Box 9700
Winnipeg, MB R3C 3E5
(204) 942-2231
FAX (204) 943-7687
Frequency: 103.1 MHz (FM).
Format: A/C.
Ownership: Armadale Communications Ltd.
Station Manager: William C. Gorrie.
Program Director: John Norris.

CKY

Polo Park
Winnipeg, MB R3G 0L7
(204) 786-6181
FAX (204) 775-5978
Frequency: 580 kHz (AM).
Format: CHR.
Ownership: Moffat Communications Ltd.
Station Manager: Don Kay.
Program Director: Gary Russell.

NEW BRUNSWICK

CKBC

176 Main St.
Bathurst, NB E2A 3Z2
(506) 547-1360
FAX (506) 547-1367
Frequency: 1360 kHz (AM).
Format: Varied.
Ownership: Radio Atlantic Ltd.
Station Manager: Jim Duncan.
Program Director: Al Hebert.
Language: English, French.

CKNB

100 Water St.
Campbellton, NB E3N 1B1
(506) 753-4415
FAX (506) 753-2672
Frequency: 950 kHz (AM).
Format: Adult Contemporary.
Station Manager: Dick Alberts
Program Director: Dick Alberts.

CJVA

P.O. Box 970
Caraquet, NB E0B 1K0
(506) 727-4426
FAX (506) 727-6707
Frequency: 810 kHz (AM).
Format: Varied.
Ownership: Radio-Acadie Ltd.
Station Manager: Rufino Landry.
Program Director: Armand Roussy.
Language: French.

CKNB

100 Water St.
P.O. Box 340
Campbellton, NB E3N 3G7
(506) 753-4415
FAX (506) 753-2672
Frequency: 950 kHz (AM).
Listening Area: Northern New Brunswick, Gaspe Peninsula, PQ.
Cable: Yes.
Format: Varied.
Program Director: Dick Alberts.
Language: English, French.
Affiliates: MacLean Hunter.

CJEM

174 Rue De L'Eglise
Edmundston, NB E3V 1K2
(506) 735-3351
FAX (506) 739-5803
Frequency: 570 kHz (AM).
Format: Contemporary.
Ownership: Radio Edmunston Ltee.
Station Manager: Jean M. Michaud.
Program Director: Claude Boucher
Language: French.

CBZ

CBC
P.O. Box 2200
Fredericton, NB E3B 5G4
(506) 452-8974
FAX (506) 452-1019
Frequency: 970 kHz (AM).
Format: News and Information.
Ownership: Radio Canada.
Station Manager: Mike Daigneault.
Program Director: Tom Grand.

CBZ

CBC
P.O. Box 2200
Fredericton, NB E3B 5G4
(506) 452-8974
FAX (506) 452-1019
Frequency: 101.5 MHz (FM).
Format: News and Information.
Ownership: Radio Canada.
Station Manager: Mike Daigneault.
Program Director: Tom Grand.

CFNB

125 Hanwell Rd., P.O. Box 217
Fredericton, NB E3B 4Z4
(506) 459-5555
FAX (506) 458-1229
Frequency: 550 kHz (AM).
Format: Adult Contemporary.
Ownership: Radio Atlantic Ltd.
Station Manager: Ross Mathers.
Program Director: Dave Morell.

CIHI

206 Rockwood Ave.
Fredericton, NB E3B 2M2
(506) 453-0126
FAX (506) 453-9024
Frequency: 1260 kHz (AM).
Format: CHR.
Ownership: Radio One Ltd.
Program Director: Wayne Dion.

CKHJ

206 Rookwood Ave.
Fredericton, NB E3B 2M2
(506) 453-0093
FAX (506) 453-9024
Frequency: 93.1 MHz (FM).
Format: A/C.
Ownership: Radio One Ltd.
Program Director: Tom Blizzard.

CBA

250 Archibald St.
Moncton, NB E1C 8N8
(506) 853-6666
FAX (506) 853-6739
Frequency: 1070 kHz (AM).
Format: News and Information.
Station Manager: Mike Daigneault.
Program Director: Ray Rideout.

CBA

CBC
250 Archibald St.
Moncton, NB E1C 8N8
(506) 853-3061
Frequency: 95.5 MHz (FM).
Station Manager: Mike Daigneault.
Program Director: Ray Rideout.

CBAF

CBC
250 Archibald St.
Moncton, NB E1C 8N8
(506) 853-6666
Frequency: 1300 kHz (AM).
Format: Varied.
Ownership: Radio Canada.
Station Manager: C. Bourque.
Program Director: Laetitia Cyr.
Language: French.

CBAF

CBC
250 Archibald St.
Moncton, NB E1C 8N8
(506) 853-6666
FAX (506) 853-6739
Frequency: 98.3 MHz (FM).
Format: Varied.
Ownership: Radio Canada.
Station Manager: C. Bourque.
Program Director: Laetitia Cyr.

CFQM

1000 St. George Blvd.
Moncton, NB E1E 2E1
(506) 858-1039
FAX (506) 858-1209
Frequency: 103.9 MHz (FM).
Format: C&W.
Station Manager: Sandy Gillis.
Program Director: Dan Roman.

CJMO

27 Arsenault Ct.
Moncton, NB E1E 4J8
(506) 858-5525
FAX (506) 858-5539
Frequency: 103.1 MHz (FM).
Format: AOR.
Ownership: Radio Atlantic Ltd.
Station Manager: Rick Gordon.
Program Director: Eric Stafford.

CKCW

1000 St. George Blvd.
Moncton, NB E1E 2E1
(506) 858-1220
FAX (506) 858-1209
Frequency: 1220 kHz (AM).
Format: A/C.
Station Manager: Mr. Sandy Gillis.
Program Director: Doug Pond.

CFAN

245 Peasant St.
Newcastle, NB E1V 3M4
(506) 622-3311
FAX (506) 622-4792
Frequency: 790 kHz (AM).
Format: Varied.
Station Manager: Ian Byers.
Program Director: Ian Byers.

CBC

P.O. Box 2358
Saint John, NB E2L 3V6
(506) 632-7710
Frequency: 110 kHz (AM).
Format: News and Information.
Ownership: Canadian Broadcasting Corp.
Station Manager: M. Daigneault.
Program Director: A.P. Lumsden.

CBC

P.O. Box 2358
Saint John, NB E2L 3V6
(506) 632-7710
Frequency: 91.3 MHz (FM).
Format: News and Information.
Ownership: Canadian Broadcasting Corp.
Station Manager: M. Daigneault.
Program Director: Susan Lambert.

CFBC

68 Carleton St.
Saint John, NB E2L 4E2
(506) 658-2330
FAX (506) 634-0604
Frequency: 930 kHz (AM).
Format: CHR.
Ownership: Fundy Broadcasting Co. Ltd.
Station Manager: Dennis O'Neil.
Program Director: Dave Cochrane.

CHSJ

335 Union St.
P.O. Box 2000
Saint John, NB E2L 3T4
(506) 632-2222
FAX (506) 634-1727
Frequency: 700 kHz (AM).
Listening Area: Southern New Brunswick, Western Nova Scotia.
Cable: No.
Format: Country.
Program Director: Bob Henry.

CIOK

400 Main St.
Saint John, NB E2K 1J4
(506) 658-5100
FAX (506) 658-5116
Frequency: 101 MHz (FM).
Format: A/C.
Ownership: Maritime Broadcasting.
Station Manager: Art Noiles.
Program Director: Mark Lee.

CJYC

68 Carleton St.
P.O. Box 930
Saint John, NB E2L 4E2
(506) 658-2330
Frequency: 98.9 MHz (FM).
Listening Area: Southern New Brunswick, Northern Nova Scotia.
Cable: Yes.
Format: A/C.
Specialty Programming: *Fresh Fusion*, a two-hour Sunday morning jazz show.
Program Director: Bruce Weaver.

WQDY

P.O. Box 305
St. Stephen, NB E3L 2X2
(506) 466-4848
FAX (506) 454-3062
Frequency: 1230 kHz (AM).
Format: A/C.
Station Manager: Michael Goodine.
Program Director: Ron MacKechnie.

WQDY

P.O. Box 305
St. Stephen, NB E3L 2X2
(506) 466-4848
FAX (506) 454-3062
Frequency: 92.7 MHz (FM).
Format: A/C.
Station Manager: Michael Goodine.
Program Director: Ron MacKechnie.

CJCW
624 Main St.
Sussex, NB E0E 1P0
(506) 433-4522
Frequency: 590 kHz (AM).
Format: A/C.
Station Manager: Jim MacMullin.
Program Director: Kelli Young.

CJCJ
131 Queen St.
Woodstock, NB E0J 2B0
(506) 328-6661
FAX (506) 328-4648
Frequency: 920 kHz (AM).
Format: A/C.
Ownership: Radio Carleton Inc.
Station Manager: Charlie Russell.
Program Director: Rick McGuire.

NEWFOUNDLAND

CHVO
P.O. Box 1-850
Saddle Hill, CHVO Dr.
Carbonear, NF A0A 1T0
(709) 596-7144
Frequency: 850 kHz (AM).
Format: C&W.
Ownership: VOCM Radio Ltd.
Station Manager: Charlie Spurrell.
Program Director: Tom Ormsby.

CBY
162 Premier Dr.
Corner Brook, NF A2H 6N4
(709) 634-3141
FAX (709) 634-8506
Frequency: 990 kHz (AM).
Format: MOR.
Station Manager: W.S. Sheppard.
Program Director: Diane Humber.

CFCB
P.O. Box 570
Corner Brook, NF A2H 6H5
(709) 634-3111
FAX (709) 634-4081
Frequency: 570 kHz (AM).
Format: A/C.
Ownership: Humber Valley Broadcasting.
Station Manager: Roger Humber.
Program Director: Bill Bartlett.

CFLN
P.O. Box 570
Corner Brook, NF A2H 6H5
(709) 896-2969
FAX (709) 896-8708
Frequency: 1230 kHz.
Format: A/C.
Station Manager: Paul Sanders.

CFLW
P.O. Box 570
Corner Brook, NF A2H 6E6
(709) 282-3602
FAX (709) 282-5543
Frequency: 1340 kHz (AM).
Format: A/C.
Ownership: Humber Valley Broadcasting.
Station Manager: Joyce Simms.
Program Director: Bill Bartlett.

CBG
CBC
98 Sullivan Ave.
Gander, NF A1V 1W7
(709) 256-4321
Frequency: 1400 kHz (AM).
Format: Varied.
Ownership: Radio Canada.
Station Manager: Dennis Budgell.

CKXX
P.O. Box 1340
Corner Brook, NF A2H 7B2
(709) 634-1340
FAX (709) 634-6397
Frequency: 1340 kHz (AM).
Listening Area: Western Newfoundland.
Cable: Yes.
Format: Country.
Specialty Programming: *Newfoundland Sunday* (8:30 a.m. - 12 noon).
Program Director: Ron Combdon.
Affiliates: CRN - Star Country, Q-Radio Network.
Rebroadcasts: CKXX-Corner Brook, CKXX-1-Deer Lake.

CKGA
P.O. Box 650
Gander, NF A1V 1X2
(709) 651-3650
Frequency: 650 kHz (AM).
Format: MOR.
Ownership: VOCM Radio Ltd.
Station Manager: Fred Dixon.
Program Director: Jim Scharpegge.

CKYQ

P.O. Box 189
Grand Bank, NF A0E 1W0
(709) 832-2650
Frequency: 610 kHz (AM).
Format: C&W.
Station Manager: Robert Harris.
Program Director: Randy Strickland.

CBT

CBC
P.O. Box 218
Harris Ave.
Grand Falls, NF A2A 2J7
(709) 489-2102
Frequency: 540 kHz (AM).
Format: Varied.

CKCM

35 Grenfell Heights
P.O. Box 620
Grand Falls, NF A2A 2K2
(709) 489-2192
Frequency: 620 kHz (AM).
Listening Area: Central Newfoundland and
Eastern seaboard.
Cable: Yes.
Format: Top 40.
Specialty Programming: Irish Newfoundland
music and religious music.
Program Director: Jim Coady.
Affiliates: VOCM Radio Newfoundland.
Rebroadcasts: CKIM-Baie Verte, CKGA-
Gander.

CFGB

CBC
P.O. Box 3015, Stn. B
Happy Valley, NF A0P 1E0
(709) 896-2911
FAX (709) 896-8900
Frequency: 89.5 MHz (FM).
Format: News and Information.
Ownership: Radio Canada.
Station Manager: Charlie Veitch.

CHCM

P.O. Box 560
Marystown, NF A0E 2M0
(709) 279-2560
Frequency: 560 kHz (AM).
Format: C&W.
Ownership: VOCM Radio Ltd.
Station Manager: Russ Murphy.
Program Director: Gary Myles.

CFGN

High St.
Port Aux Basques, NF A0M 1C0
(709) 695-2183
Frequency: 1230 kHz (AM).
Format: C&W.
Ownership: Humber Valley Broadcasting.
Station Manager: G.N. Critchell.
Program Director: G.N. Critchell.

CBN

CBC
P.O. Box 12010
St. John's, NF A1B 3T8
(709) 737-4140
FAX (709) 737-4271
Frequency: 640 kHz (AM).
Format: Varied.
Station Manager: John O'Mara.
Program Director: Don Reynolds.

CFIQ

P.O. Box 6180
St. John's, NF A1C 5X8
(709) 753-4040
FAX (709) 753-4420
Frequency: 970 kHz (AM).
Format: Varied.
Ownership: CHUM Ltd.
Station Manager: Tom Hann.
Program Director: Roger Jamieson.

CFQZ

P.O. Box 2050
Logy Bay Rd.
St. John's, NF A1C 5R6
(709) 726-2922
FAX (709) 726-5107
Frequency: 109.3 MHz (FM).
Format: Varied.
Ownership: Newfoundland Broadcasting Co.
ltd.
Station Manager: Keith Soper.
Program Director: Keith Soper.

CFYQ

P.O. Box 6180
St. John's, NF A1C 5X8
(709) 753-4040
FAX (709) 753-4420
Frequency: 1010 kHz (AM).
Format: Varied.
Ownership: CHUM Ltd.
Station Manager: Tom Hann.
Program Director: Roger Jamieson.

CHOS

P.O. Box 2050
Logy Bay Rd.
St. John's, NF A1C 5R6
(709) 726-2922
FAX (709) 726-5107
Frequency: 95.9 MHz (FM).
Format: Varied.
Ownership: Newfoundland Broadcasting Co. Ltd.
Station Manager: Keith Soper.
Program Director: Keith Soper.

CHOZ

P.O. Box 2050, Logy Bay
St. John's, NF A1C 5R6
(709) 726-2922
FAX (709) 726-5107
Frequency: 95.7 MHz (FM).
Format: AOR.
Ownership: Newfoundland Broadcasting Co. Ltd.
Station Manager: Keith Soper.
Program Director: Keith Soper.

CHYQ

P.O. Box 6180
St. John's, NF A1C 5X8
(709) 753-4040
FAX (709) 753-4420
Frequency: 670 kHz (AM).
Format: MOR.
Ownership: CHUM Ltd.
Station Manager: Tom Hann.
Program Director: Roger Jamieson.

CIOS

P.O. Box 2050, Logy Bay
St. John's, NF A1C 5R6
(709) 726-2922
FAX (709) 726-5107
Frequency: 98.5 MHz (FM).
Ownership: Newfoundland Broadcasting Co. Ltd.
Station Manager: Keith Soper.
Program Director: Keith Soper.

CIOZ

P.O. Box 2050
Logy Bay Road
St. John's, NF AIC 5R6
(709) 726-2922
FAX (709) 726-5107
Frequency: 96.3 MHz (FM).
Format: Varied.
Ownership: Newfoundland Broadcasting Co. Ltd.
Station Manager: Keith Soper.
Program Director: Keith Soper.

CIYQ

P.O. Box 6180
St. John's, NF A1C 5X8
(709) 753-4040
FAX (709) 753-4420
Frequency: 680 kHz (AM).
Format: Varied.
Ownership: CHUM Ltd.
Program Director: Roger Jamieson.

CJOZ

P.O. Box 2050
Logy Bay Rd.
St. John's, NF A1C 5R6
(709) 726-2922
FAX (709) 726-5107
Frequency: 92.1 MHz (FM).
Format: AOR.
Ownership: Newfoundland Broadcasting Co. Ltd.
Station Manager: Keith Soper.
Program Director: Keith Soper.

CJYQ

P.O. Box 6180
St. John's, NF A1C 5X8
(709) 753-4040
FAX (709) 753-4420
Frequency: 930 kHz (AM).
Format: A/C.
Ownership: CHUM Ltd.
Station Manager: Tom Hann.
Program Director: Roger Jamieson.
CKCM
P.O. Box 8-590
St. John's, NF A1B 3P5
(709) 726-5590
FAX (709) 726-4633
Frequency: 1240 kHz.
Format: CHR.
Station Manager: John Murphy.
Program Director: John Murphy.
Ownership: VOCM Radio Ltd.

CKIX

P.O. Box 6180
St. John's, NF A1C 5X8
(709) 753-4040
FAX (709) 753-4420
Frequency: 99.1 MHz (FM).
Format: C&W.
Ownership: CHUM Ltd.
Station Manager: Tom Hann.
Program Director: Bob Banfield.

CKOZ

P.O. Box 2050, Logy Bay Rd.
St. John's, NF A1C 5R6
(709) 726-2922
FAX (709) 726-5107
Frequency: 92.3 MHz (FM).
Format: AOR.
Ownership: Newfoundland Broadcasting Co. Ltd.
Station Manager: Keith Soper.
Program Director: Keith Soper.

CKVO

P.O. Box 8-590
St. John's, NF A1B 3P5
(709) 726-5590
FAX (709) 726-4633
Frequency: 710 kHz (AM).
Format: C&W.
Ownership: VOCM Radio Ltd.
Station Manager: John Murphy.

CKYQ

P.O. Box 6180
St. John's, NF A1C 5X8
(709) 753-4040
FAX (709) 753-4420
Frequency: 610 kHz (AM).
Format: Varied.
Ownership: CHUM Ltd.
Station Manager: Tom Hann.
Program Director: Roger Jamieson.

VOAR

106 Freshwater Rd.
St. John's, NF A1C 2N8
(709) 579-2104
FAX (709) 576-4054
Frequency: 1230 kHz (AM).
Listening Area: St. John's - Mount Pearl, Newfoundland.
Cable: No.
Format: Christian Contemporary music and talk.
Specialty Programming: National and community news and information.
Program Director: Cameron Beierle.
Affiliates: ARN Network.

VOCM

P.O. Box 8-590
St. John's, NF A1B 3P5
(709) 726-5590
FAX (709) 726-4633
Frequency: 590 kHz (AM).
Format: A/C.
Ownership: VOCM Radio Ltd.
Station Manager: John Murphy.
Program Director: John Murphy.

VOCM

P.O. Box 8590
St. John's, NF A1B 3P5
(709) 726-5590
FAX (709) 726-4633
Frequency: 97.5 MHz (FM).
Format: A/C.
Ownership: VOCM Radio Ltd.
Station Manager: John Murphy.
Program Director: John Murphy.

VOWR

P.O. Box 7430
St. John's, NF A1E 3Y5
(709) 579-9233
Frequency: 800 kHz (AM).
Format: Varied.
Station Manager: Everett E. Hudson.
Program Director: Everett E. Hudson.

CFSX

30 Oregon Dr.
P.O. Box 276
Stephenville, NF A0N 1T0
(709) 643-2191
FAX (709) 643-5021
Frequency: 870 kHz (AM).
Listening Area: Stephenville - Bay St. George, Newfoundland.
Cable: Yes.
Format: MOR.
Program Director: Gerald Murphy.
Affiliates: CFCB - Corner Brook, Humber Valley Broadcasting Co. Ltd.

NORTHWEST TERRITORIES

CKHR

P.O. Box 949
Hay River, NT X0E 0R0
(403) 874-2278
Frequency: 107.3 MHz (FM).
Format: A/C.
Station Manager: B. Hynes.
Program Director: Rick Williams.

CHAK

CBC
Bag Service, No. 8
Inuvik, NT X0E 0T0
(403) 979-4411
FAX (403) 979-2411
Frequency: 860 kHz (AM).
Format: Varied.
Ownership: Radio Canada.
Station Manager: Anne Crossman.
Program Director: Dave McNaughton.

CFFB

CBC
P.O. Box 490
Iqaluit, NT X0A 0H0
(819) 979-5353
FAX (819) 979-4541
Frequency: 1230 kHz (AM).
Format: Varied.
Ownership: Radio Canada.
Station Manager: Simon Awa.
Program Director: Lynn MacDonald.

CBQR

CBC
P.O. Box 130
Rankin Inlet, NT X0C 0G0
(819) 645-2885
FAX (819) 645-2632
Frequency: 105.1 MHz (FM).
Ownership: Radio Canada.
Station Manager: Jose A. Kusugak.
Program Director: Elizabeth Kusugak.

CFYK

5002 Forrest Drive
P.O. Box 160
Yellowknife, NT X1A 2N2
(403) 920-5400
FAX (403) 920-5415
Format: 1340 kHz (AM).
Cable: Yes.
Format: CBC Information Programming.
Program Director: Craig MacKie.
Languages: English, Slavey, Dogrib,
Chipewyan.

CJCD

P.O. Box 218
Yellowknife, NT X1A 2N2
(403) 920-4636
FAX (403) 920-4033
Frequency: 1240 kHz (AM).
Format: A/C.
Ownership: CJCD Radio Ltd.
Station Manager: Charles Dent.
Program Director: Barry Sullivan.

CKNM

P.O. Box 1919
Yellowknife, NT X1A 2T4
(403) 920-2277
FAX (403) 920-4205
Frequency: 101.9 MHz (FM).
Format: C&W.
Ownership: Native Communications Society.
Station Manager: Percy Kinney.
Program Director: Percy Kinney.

NOVA SCOTIA

CKDH

32 Church St.
P.O. Box 670
Amherst, NS B4H 3V6
(902) 667-3875
FAX (902) 667-4490
Frequency: 900 kHz (AM).
Listening Area: Northwestern Nova Scotia,
Southeastern New Brunswick.
Cable: Yes.
Format: A/C.
Specialty Programming: Gold 50s and 60s.
Program Director: Michael Allard.
Affiliates: Maritime Broadcasting.

CKBW

215 Dominion St.
Bridgewater, NS B4V 2G8
(902) 543-2401
FAX (902) 543-1208
Frequency: 1000 kHz (AM).
Listening Area: Southern Nova Scotia.
Cable: Yes.
Format: Pop/Country.
Specialty Programming: Bluegrass,
Newfoundland and Maritime music.
Program Director: Gary Richards.
Affiliates: Broadcast News, Star Country
(overnight).
Program Director: CKBW FM-1-Liverpool, NS
(94.5 FM), CKBW FM2-Shelburne NS (93.1 FM).

CFDR

P.O. Box 1007
Dartmouth, NS B2Y 3Z7
(902) 469-9231
FAX (902) 469-1235
Frequency: 680 kHz (AM).
Format: MOR.
Ownership: Newcap Broadcasting Corp.
Program Director: Bruce Tinkham.

CFRQ

P.O. Box 1007
Dartmouth, NS B2Y 3Z7
(902) 469-9231
FAX (902) 469-9263
Frequency: 104.3 MHz (FM).
Format: MOR.
Ownership: Newcap Broadcasting Corp.
Station Manager: Bruce Tinkham.
Program Director: Kerri Loiselle.

CBH/CBH

5600 Sackville St.,
P.O. Box 3000
Halifax, NS B3J 3E9
(902) 420-8311 or 420-4422
FAX (902) 420-4429
Frequency: CBC Radio 90.5, CBC Stereo
102.7 MHz (FM).
Listening Area: CBC Radio-Mainland Nova
Scotia, CBC Stereo - Halifax and the Annapolis
Valley.
Format: CBC Radio - Information, CBC Stereo -
Performance.
Specialty Programming: Various including
radio drama, features, contemporary music, jazz
and other forms of music.
Director of Radio: Rick Alexander.
Affiliates: CBC.

CHFX

P.O. Box 400
1313 Barrington St.
Halifax, NS B3J 2R2
(902) 422-1651
FAX (902) 422-5330
Frequency: 101.9 MHz (FM).
Format: C&W.
Ownership: Maritime Broadcasting.
Station Manager: Dennis O'Neill.
Program Director: John Gold.

CHNS

P.O. Box 400
1313 Barrington St.
Halifax, NS B3J 2R2
(902) 422-1651
FAX (902) 422-5330
Frequency: 960 kHz (AM).
Format: A/C.
Ownership: Maritime Broadcasting.
Station Manager: Dennis O'Neill.
Program Director: Dan Roman.

CIOO

2885 Robie St.
Halifax, NS B3J 2Z4
(902) 453-2524
FAX (902) 453-3120
Frequency: 100 MHz (FM).
Format: A/C.
Ownership: CHUM Ltd.
Station Manager: Bill Bodnarchuk.
Program Director: Murray Brookshaw.

CJCH

2885 Robie St.
Halifax, NS B3J 2Z4
(902) 453-2524
FAX (902) 453-3120
Frequency: 920 kHz (AM).
Format: A/C.
Ownership: CHUM Ltd.
Station Manager: Bill Bodnarchuk.
Program Director: Murray Brookshaw.

CFAB

P.O. Box 310
Kentville, NS B4N 1H5
(902) 678-2111
FAX (902) 678-9894
Frequency: 1450 kHz (AM).
Format: Gold/Country.
Ownership: Annapolis Valley Radio Ltd.
Station Manager: Tom Fredericks.
Program Director: Dave Bannerman.

CKAD

P.O. Box 310
Kentville, NS B4N 1H5
(902) 825-3429
FAX (902) 678-9894
Frequency: 1350 kHz (AM).
Format: A/C.
Ownership: Annapolis Valley Radio Ltd.
Station Manager: Tom Fredericks.
Program Director: Dave Bannerman.

CKDY

P.O. Box 310
Kentville, NS B4N 1H5
(902) 678-2111
FAX (902) 678-9894
Frequency: 103.3 MHz (FM).
Format: A/C.
Ownership: Annapolis Valley Radio Ltd.
Station Manager: Tom Fredericks.
Program Director: Dave Bannerman.

CKEN

P.O. Box 310
Kentville, NS B4N 1H5
(902) 678-2111
FAX (902) 678-9894
Frequency: 1490 kHz (AM).
Format: Gold/Country.
Ownership: Annapolis Valley Radio Ltd.
Station Manager: Tom Fredericks.
Program Director: Dave Bannerman.

CKEC

84 Provost St.
P.O. Box 519
New Glasgow, NS B2H 5E7
(902) 752-4200
FAX (902) 755-2468
Frequency: 1320 kHz (AM).
Listening Area: Northern Nova Scotia, portions
of Prince Edward Island and Newfoundland.
Cable: Yes.
Format: Adult Contemporary and Country (day-
time and all night), Top 40 Rock (evenings).
Program Director: Scottish Traditional and
Celtic (two hours per week), Bluegrass (one hour
per week).
Program Director: Rod MacKey.

CIGO

MacIntosh Ave.
P.O. Bag 1410
Port Hawkesbury, NS B0E 2V0
(902) 625-1220
FAX (902) 625-2664
Frequency: 1410 kHz (AM).
Listening Area: Port Hawkesbury-Antigonish.
Format: A/C.
Program Director: Bob MacEachern.

CBI

CBC
P.O. Box 700
285 Alexandra St.
Sydney, NS B1P 6H7
(902) 539-5050
FAX (902) 562-7547
Frequency: 1140 kHz (AM).
Format: News and Information.
Ownership: Radio Canada.
Station Manager: Gordon Tizzard.
Program Director: Hal Doran.

CBI

CBC
P.O. Box 700
285 Alexandra St.
Sydney, NS B1P 6H7
(902) 539-5050
FAX (902) 562-7547
Frequency: 105.1 MHz (FM).
Format: Classics and Jazz.
Ownership: Radio Canada.
Station Manager: Gordon Tizzard.
Program Director: Gordon Tizzard.

CHER

500 Kings Rd., Suite 208
Sydney, NS B1S 1B1
(902) 539-8500
FAX (902) 562-5720
Frequency: 950 kHz (AM).
Format: A/C.
Ownership: Radio Cape Breton Ltd.
Station Manager: Eileen Oldford.
Program Director: Alan Leith.

CJCB

P.O. Box 1270
Radio Building
Sydney, NS B1P 6K2
(902) 564-5596
FAX (902) 595-1270
Frequency: 1270 kHz (AM).
Format: A/C.
Ownership: Celtic Investments Ltd.
Station Manager: J.M. Nathanson.
Program Director: Don Graham.

CKPE

P.O. Box 1270
Radio Building
Sydney, NS B1P 6K2
(902) 564-5596
FAX (902) 564-1057
Frequency: 94.9 MHz (FM).
Format: A/C.
Ownership: Celtic Investments Ltd.
Station Manager: N.L. Nathanson.
Program Director: Dave Reynolds.

CKCL

187 Industrial Ave.
P.O. Box 788
Truro, NS B2N 5E8
(902) 893-6060
FAX (902) 893-7771
Frequency: 600 kHz (AM).
Listening Area: Central Nova Scotia.
Cable: Yes.
Format: AOR.
Program Director: David Guy.
Affiliates: CKTO-FM (sister station).
Program Director: Re-broadcast on CKTO-FM, 100.9, midnight - 6 a.m.

CKTO

P.O. Box 788
187 Industrial Ave.
Truro, NS B2N 5E8
(902) 893-6060
FAX (902) 893-7771
Frequency: 100.9 MHz (FM).
Format: A/C.
Ownership: Radio Atlantic Ltd.
Station Manager: Dan Somers.
Program Director: D. Branscombe.

CJLS

328 Main St., Suite 201
Yarmouth, NS B5A 1E4
(902) 742-7175
FAX (902) 742-3143
Frequency: 1340 kHz (AM).
Format: Varied.
Station Manager: G.P. Wyman.
Program Director: Russ Le Blanc.

ONTARIO

CHOO
97 McMaster Ave.
Ajax, ON L1S 2E6
(416) 683-4131
FAX (416) 428-1390
Frequency: 1390 kHz (AM).
Listening Area: The Durham Region (including cottage country).
Cable: No.
Format: Country music and community oriented programming.
Program Director: Joe Frechette.

CKOA
1490 Short St.
Arnprior, ON K7S 3R2
(613) 623-7711
FAX (613) 623-3738
Frequency: 1490 kHz (AM).
Format: A/C.
Ownership: Ottawa Valley Radio Ltd.
Station Manager: Elizabeth Wall.
Program Director: Rick Wyman.
Specialty Programming: *The Valley at Noon.*

CJNH
P.O. Box 1240
Highway 28 E.
Bancroft, ON K0L 1C0
(613) 332-1423
Frequency: 1240 kHz (AM).
Format: MOR.
Station Manager: Nan Whitlaw.

CFJB
P.O. Box 95
400 Bayfield St., Suite 205
Barrie, ON L4M 5A1
(705) 721-1291
Frequency: 95.7 MHz (FM).
Format: AOR.
Station Manager: Doug Bingley.
Program Director: Rick Hallson.

CHAY
743 Bayfield St. N.
P.O. Box 937
Barrie, ON L4M 4Y6
(705) 737-3511
FAX (705) 722-3651
Frequency: 93.1 MHz (FM).
Listening Area: Huronia.
Cable: Yes.
Format: Easy Listening.
Specialty Programming: *Big Bands Saturday Night.*
Program Director: Vin Dittmer.

CKBB
P.O. Box 950
Barrie, ON L4M 4V1
(705) 726-9500
FAX (705) 726-0022
Frequency: 950 kHz (AM).
Format: A/C.
Station Manager: W.E. Bjorgan.
Program Director: Jeff Walther.

CIGL
10 Front St. S.
Belleville, ON K8N 5B2
(613) 969-5555
FAX (613) 969-0288
Frequency: 97.1 MHz (FM).
Format: MOR.
Ownership: Quinte Broadcasting Co.
Station Manager: William A. Morton.
Program Director: Bill Conlon.

CJBQ
10 Front St.
P.O. Box 488
Belleville, ON K8N 5B2
(613) 969-5555
FAX (613) 969-8122
Frequency: 800 kHz (AM).
Listening Area: Hastings and Prince Edward Counties in Eastern Ontario.
Cable: Yes.
Format: Full-Service A/C.
Specialty Programming: Daily open-line program, Expos Baseball Network, Local play-by-play OHL broadcasts.
Program Director: Peter Thompson.
Affiliates: Canadian Radio Networks (music radio).
Rebroadcasts: Part-time re-broadcast on CJNH-Bancroft, ON.

CFNY
83 Kennedy Rd. S.
Brampton, ON L6W 3P3
(416) 453-7452
FAX (416) 453-7711
Frequency: 102.1 MHz (FM).
Format: AOR.
Ownership: Selkirk Broadcasting Ltd.
Station Manager: Bill Hutton.
Program Director: Danny Kingsbury.

CIAO
50 Kennedy Rd. S.
Brampton, ON L6W 3R7
(416) 453-7111
FAX (416) 453-4788
Frequency: 790 kHz (AM).
Format: Ethnic/Multicultural.
Station Manager: A. Cremisio.
Program Director: G. Sarracini.

CKPC

571 West St.
Brantford, ON N3T 5P8
(519) 759-1000
FAX (519) 753-1470
Frequency: 1380 kHz (AM).
Format: A/C.
Ownership: Telephone City Broadcast Ltd.
Station Manager: Richard Buchanan.
Program Director: Gene Stevens.

CKPC

571 West St.
Brantford, ON N3T 5P8
(519) 759-1000
FAX (519) 753-1470
Frequency: 92.1 MHz (FM).
Format: MOR.
Ownership: Telephone City Broadcast Ltd.
Station Manager: Richard Buchanan.
Program Director: Gene Stevens.

CFJR

601 Stewart Blvd.
P.O. Box 666
Brockville, ON K6V 5V9
(613) 345-1666
FAX (613) 342-2438
Frequency: 830 kHz (AM)
Listening Area: Brockville and area.
Cable: Yes.
Format: Gold-Based Adult.
Program Director: Bruce Wylie.

CHXL

601 Stewart Blvd.
P.O. Box 666
Brockville, ON K6V 5V9
(613) 345-1666
FAX (613) 342-2438
Frequency: 103.7 MHz (FM).
Listening Area: Brockville-Prescott.
Cable: Yes.
Format: Jazz, New and Alternative Music.
Program Directors: Gord Watts.
Affiliated Stations: CFJR, CKLC, CFLY.

CING

4144 S. Service Rd.
Burlington, ON L7L 4X5
(416) 681-1079
FAX (416) 681-1758
Frequency: 107.9 MHz (FM).
Format: CHR.
Ownership: Burlington Broadcasting.
Station Manager: Con Chung.
Program Director: Norman Blakeley.

CIAM

46 Main St.
Cambridge, ON N1R 1V4
(519) 621-7510
FAX (519) 621-0165
Frequency: 960 kHz (AM).
Format: CHR.
Ownership: Kawartha Broadcasting.
Station Manager: Ray Norris.
Program Director: Ron Fitzpatrick.

CFCO

21 Keil Dr. S.
P.O. Box 630
Chatham, ON N7M 5K9
(519) 352-3000
FAX (519) 352-4801
Frequency: 630 kHz (AM).
Listening Area: Southwestern Ontario.
Cable: Yes.
Format: A/C.
Program Director: Mr. Robin Geoffery.

COSY/CKSY

117 Keil Dr.
P.O. Box 100
Chatham, ON N7M 5K1
(519) 354-2200
FAX (519) 354-2880
Frequency: 95.1 MHz (FM).
Listening Area: Chatham, Kent, Essex and
Lambton Counties.
Cable: Yes.
Program Director: Walter Ploegman.

CFMX

P.O. Box 1031
Cobourg, ON K9A 4W5
(416) 372-4366
FAX (416) 372-1625
Frequency: 103.1 MHz (FM).
Format: Classical and Jazz.
Ownership: Different Drummer Communications
Inc.
Station Manager: Jerry Good.
Program Director: Michael Compeau.

CHUC

Telephone Road, P.O. Box 520
Cobourg, ON K8N 4L3
(416) 372-5401
FAX (416) 372-6280
Frequency: 1450 kHz (AM).
Cable: Yes.
Format: Full Service, A/C.
Specialty Programming: Toronto Blue Jays
and Toronto Maple Leafs broadcasts.
Program Director: Paul Laing.
Affiliates: Broadcast News, TBS, Selltock.

CKCB

Highway 26 E.
P.O. Box 1400
Collingwood, ON L9Y 3Z3
(705) 444-1400
FAX (705) 444-6776
Frequency: 1400 kHz (AM).
Listening Area: Southern Georgian Bay.
Cable: Yes.
Format: A/C.
Program Director: John Nichols.
Affiliates: A Division of Power Broadcasting Inc.
Rebroadcasts: CKBB-Barrie, ON.

CFLG

237 Water St. E.
Cornwall, ON K6H 5V1
(613) 932-5180
FAX (613) 938-0355
Frequency: 104.5 MHz (FM).
Format: MOR.
Ownership: Tri-Co Broadcasting Ltd.
Station Manager: Keith Clingen.

CJSS

237 Water St. E.
Cornwall, ON K6H 5V1
(613) 932-5180
FAX (613) 938-0355
Frequency: 1220 kHz (AM).
Format: A/C.
Ownership: Tri-Co Broadcasting Ltd.
Station Manager: Keith Clingen.

CKDR

122 King St.
P.O. Box 580
Dryden, ON P8N 2Z3
(807) 223-2355
FAX (807) 223-5090
Frequency: 800 kHz (AM).
Listening Area: Dryden and area.
Cable: Yes.
Format: A/C.
Program Director: Howard G. Fawcett.
Rebroadcasts: CKEF-EAr FAlls, CKHD-Hudson, CKIG-Ignace, CKRE-Red Lake, CKSI- Sioux Lookout.

CKNR/CJNR

15 Charles Walk
Elliot Lake, ON P5A 2A2
(705) 848-3608
Frequency: 1340 and 730 kHz (AM).
Listening Area: Elliot Lake, Blind River, East Algoma.
Cable: Yes.
Format: Light CHR.
Specialty Programming: *Lunchtime at The Oldies, Hot 30 Countdown.*
Program Director: Mike Thurnell.
Affiliates: CRN, Mid Canada Radio.
Program Director: CJNR-Blind River, CKNS-Espanola.

CKNS

46 Mead Blvd.
Espanola, ON P0P 1C0
(705) 869-4930
Frequency: 930 kHz (AM).
Format: A/C Communications Corp.
Station Manager: Chuck Babcock.
Program Director: Jack Reid.

CFOB

242 Scott St.
P.O. Box 489
Fort Frances, ON P9A 3M8
(807) 274-5341
FAX (807) 274-2033
Frequency: 640 kHz (AM).
Listening Area: Fort Frances and area.
Cable: Yes.
Format: A/C.
Program Director: Howard G. Fawcett.
Rebroadcasts: CFOB-1 Atikokan, Ontario CFOB-1-Atikokan, ON.

CJOY

75 Speedvale Ave. E.
Guelph, ON N1E 6M3
(519) 824-7000
FAX (519) 824-4118
Frequency: 1460 kHz (AM).
Format: A/C.
Ownership: Guelph Broadcasting.
Station Manager: W.D. Dawkins.
Program Director: Guus Hazelaar.

CKLA

75 Speedvale Ave. E.
Guelph, ON N1E 6M3
(519) 824-7000
FAX (519) 824-4118
Frequency: 106.1 MHz (FM).
Format: MOR.
Ownership: Guelph Broadcasting.
Station Manager: Guus Hazelaar.
Program Director: Don Leblanc.
Specialty Programming: *Bandstand, Field of Jazz.*

CHAM

151 York Blvd.
Hamilton, ON L8R 3M2
(416) 526-8200
FAX (416) 525-1416
Frequency: 820 kHz (AM).
Listening Area: Southwestern Ontario.
Program Director: Gord Eno.

CHML

875 Main St. W.
Suite 900
Hamilton, ON L8S 4R1
(416) 521-9900
FAX (416) 521-2306
Frequency: 900 kHz (AM).
Format: A/C.
Ownership: CJOI Enterprise Ltd.
Program Director: John Keogh.

CKDS

875 Main St. W.
Hamilton, ON L8S 4R1
(416) 521-9900
FAX (416) 521-2306
Frequency: 95.3 MHz (FM).
Listening Area: Hamilton-Toronto.
Format: Light Rock.
Specialty Programming: Classical.
Program Director: Bill Osborn.
Affiliates: Westcom.

CKLH

73 Garfield Ave. S., P.O. Box 1150
Hamilton, ON L8N 3P5
(416) 545-5885
FAX (416) 545-1266
Frequency: 102.9 MHz (FM).
Listening Area: Southern Ontario.
Cable: Yes.
Format: A/C, Easy Listening.
Specialty Programming: *Gardening Show,*
plus Jazz, Big Band, Classical and Comedy.
Comedy.
Program Director: Nevin E. Grant.
Affiliates: CKOC-AM.

CKOC

73 Garfield Ave. S., P.O. Box 1150
Hamilton, ON L8N 3P5
(416) 545-5885
FAX (416) 545-1266
Frequency: 1150 kHz (AM).
Listening Area: Southern Ontario.
Cable: Yes.
Format: Top 40, CHR.
Specialty Programming: *90 Minutes Live
from Hamilton,* a talk show broadcast week-
days 9:00 a.m.-1030 a.m.
Program Director: Nevin E. Grant.
Affiliates: CKLH-FM - Hamilton.
Comments: CKOC is Canada's second-oldest
radio station and is Ontario's senior Top 40 radio
station (1959-1989).

CHPR

151 Principale E.
Suite 37
Hawkesbury, ON K6A 1A1
(613) 632-1119
Frequency: 102.1 MHz (FM).
Format: A/C.
Station Manager: Suzanne Turbide.
Program Director: Jean-Pierre Major.
Language: French.

CFBK

P.O. Box 1055
Huntsville, ON P0A 1K0
(705) 789-4461
FAX (705) 789-1269
Frequency: 105.5 MHz (FM).
Format: A/C.
Ownership: Muskoka/Parry Broadcasting.
Station Manager: Joe Duchesne.
Station Manager: Joe Duchesne.
Program Director: Craig Martin.

CKAP

24 Byng Ave.
Kapuskasing, ON P5N 1X5
(705) 335-2379
Frequency: 580 kHz (AM).
Format: CHR.
Ownership: Mid-Canada Communications Corp.
Station Manager: Dick Peplow.
Program Director: Dave Palmer.
Language: English, French.

CJRL

128 Main St. S.
P.O. Box 2490
Kenora, ON P9N 3N1
(807) 468-3181
FAX (807) 468-4188
Frequency: 1220 kHz (AM).
Listening Area: Kenora.
Cable: Yes.
Format: A/C.
Program Director: Howard G. Fawcett.

CFFX

479 Counter St.
Kingston, ON K7M 7J3
(613) 549-1911
FAX (613) 549-7974
Frequency: 960 kHz (AM).
Format: A/C.
Ownership: Frontenac Broadcasting Co.
Station Manager: Cam Shillington.
Program Director: Lee Sterry.

CFLY

99 Brock St.
Kingston, ON K7L 4Y5
(613) 544-1380
FAX (613) 546-9751
Frequency: 98.3 MHz (FM).
Format: A/C.
Ownership: St. Lawrence Broadcasting.
Station Manager: John Wright.
Program Director: Garry Barker.

CFMK

479 Counter St.
Kingston, ON K7M 7J3
(613) 549-1911
FAX (613) 549-7974
Frequency: 96.3 MHz (FM).
Format: C&W.
Ownership: Frontenac Broadcasting Co.
Station Manager: Cam Shillington.
Program Director: Dave Cunningham.

CFRC

Queen's University
Carruthers Hall
Kingston, ON K7L 3N6
(613) 545-2121
Frequency: 1490 kHz (AM).
Format: Varied.
Ownership: Radio Queen's University.
Station Manager: Steve Cutway.
Program Director: Peter Vamos.

CKLC

99 Brock St.
Kingston, ON K7L 4Y5
(613) 544-1380
FAX (613) 546-9751
Frequency: 1380 kHz (AM).
Format: CHR.
Ownership: St. Lawrence Broadcasting.
Station Manager: John P. Wright.
Program Director: Chris Ryan.

CJKL

CBC
P.O. Box 430
Kirkland Lake, ON P2N 3J4
(705) 567-3366
FAX (705) 567-6101
Frequency: 560 kHz (AM).
Format: A/C.
Ownership: Kirkland Lake Broadcasting Ltd.
Station Manager: Rob Connelly.
Program Director: Rob Connelly.
Specialty Programming: *Open Line.*

CFCA

864 King St. W.
Kitchener, ON N2G 4E9
(519) 576-1053
FAX (519) 578-8375
Frequency: 105.3 MHz (FM).
Format: A/C.
Ownership: Electrohome Ltd.
Station Manager: D. Macdonald.
Program Director: P. Scott.

CHYM

305 King St. W.
Kitchener, ON N2G 4E4
(519) 743-2611
FAX (519) 743-9025
Frequency: 570 kHz (AM).
Format: A/C.
Ownership: Key Radio Ltd.
Station Manager: Jim Webb.
Program Director: Paul Cugilari.

CKGL

305 King St. W.
Kitchener, ON N2G 4E4
(519) 743-2611
FAX (519) 743-9025
Frequency: 96.7 MHz (FM).
Listening Area: Waterloo Region.
Format: Contemporary Country.
Specialty Programming: Blue Jays.
Program Director: Vic Folliott.

CKKW

864 King St. W.
Kitchener, ON N26 4E9
(519) 579-1090
FAX (519) 578-8375
Frequency: 1090 kHz (AM).
Listening Area: Kitchener-Waterloo,
Cambridge.
Cable: Yes.
Specialty Programming: All-request Saturday
night.
Program Director: Brian J. Currie.
Affiliates: CFCA-FM, CKCO-TV.

CKWR

P.O. Box 2035, Stn. B
Kitchener, ON N2H 6K8
(519) 886-9870
Frequency: 98.7 MHz (FM).
Format: Varied.
Ownership: Wired World Inc.
Station Manager: Hans Gumz.
Program Director: Terry Parks.
Specialty Programming: *CKWR Magazine.*

CHYR

100 Talbot St. E.
Leamington, ON N8H 1L3
(519) 326-6171
FAX (519) 322-1110
Frequency: 710 kHz (AM).
Listening Area: Essex and Kent Counties.
Cable: Yes.
Format: A/C, Sports.
Specialty Programming: Blue Jays Baseball, Maple Leaf Hockey.
Program Director: Chuck Reynolds.
Affiliates: Bluewater Broadcasting, Maclean Hunter.

CKLY

249 Kent St. W.
Lindsay, ON K9V 2Z3
(705) 324-9103
FAX (705) 324-4149
Frequency: 910 kHz (AM).
Format: CHR.
Ownership: McNabb Broadcasting Ltd.
Station Manager: Andy McNabb.
Program Director: Nancy Stapleton.

CFPL

369 York St.
P.O. Box 2580
London, ON N6A 4H3
(519) 438-8391
FAX (519) 438-2415
Frequency: 980 kHz (AM).
Listening Area: Southwestern Ontario.
Cable: Yes.
Format: A/C.
Specialty Programming: Talk show, weekdays 9:00 a.m. - 11:00 a.m.
Program Director: Barry Rutledge.
Affiliates: CFPL-FM.

CFPL

369 York St.
P.O. Box 2580
London, ON N6A 4H3
(519) 438-8391
FAX (519) 438-2415
Frequency: 95.9 MHz (FM).
Listening Area: Southern Ontario - Erie, PA.
Cable: Yes.
Format: AOR.
Specialty Programming: Contemporary Christian Programming Sunday mornings, Jazz programming Sunday evenings.
Program Director: Barry Smith.
Affiliates: Some syndicated shows from Telemedia, Sound Source and Westwood One Canada.

CIQM

380 Wellington St.
London, ON N6A 5J2
(519) 661-2000
FAX (519) 673-4260
Frequency: 103.1 MHz (FM).
Format: A/C.
Ownership: London Broadcasters Ltd.
Station Manager: Gordon Hume.
Program Director: Braden Doerr.
Specialty Programming: *Midday Magazine.*

CIXX

1460 Oxford St.
London, ON N5V 1W2
(519) 453-2810
FAX (519) 452-3570
Frequency: 106.9 MHz (FM).
Format: A/C.
Ownership: Radio Fanshawe Inc.
Station Manager: G. O'Brien.
Program Director: Paul Vaneste.

CJBK

743 Wellington Rd. S., P.O. Box 1290, Stn. A
London, ON N6A 5A2
(519) 686-2525
FAX (519) 686-9067
Frequency: 1290 kHz (AM).
Listening Area: London and surrounding area.
Cable: Yes.
Format: A/C.
Program Director: Nelson Millman.
Affiliates: CJBX-London, CHOK-Sarnia.

CJBX

P.O. Box 5593
London, ON N6A 5H8
(519) 685-9393
FAX (519) 686-9067
Frequency: 92.7 MHz (FM).
Format: MOR
Ownership: Middlesex Broadcasting Ltd.
Station Manager: Warren Cosford.
Program Director: Dave Collins.

CKSL

380 Wellington St.
London, ON N6A 5J2
(519) 667-1410
FAX (519) 673-4260
Frequency: 1410 kHz (AM).
Format: CHR.
Ownership: London Broadcasters Ltd.
Station Manager: Gordon Hume.
Program Director: Braden Doer.

CIQM

380 Wellington St. Mezzanine Level
P.O. Box 1410
London, ON N6A 5J2
(519) 667-1410
FAX (519) 673-4260
Frequency: 103.1 MHz (FM).
Listening Area: London and area.
Cable: Yes.
Format: A/C.
Specialty Programming: Various foreground features.
Program Director: Braden Doerr.
Language: English.
Affiliates: Broadcast News.

CFNO

P.O. Box 1000
Marathon, ON P0T 2E0
(807) 229-1010
FAX (807) 229-1686
Frequency: 93.1 MHz (FM).
Format: A/C.
Ownership: North Superior Broadcasting.
Station Manager: S.S. Bell.
Program Director: S.S. Bell.

CKMP

490 Dominion Ave.
Midland, ON L4R 1P6
(705) 526-2268
FAX (705) 526-6522
Frequency: 1230 kHz (AM).
Format: A/C.
Ownership: Telemedia Communications.
Station Manager: Bob Bennett.
Program Director: Scott Warnock.
Specialty Programming: *Spotlight on Huronia.*

CJMR

P.O. Box 1190
Port Credit Station
Mississauga, ON L5G 4M3
(416) 279-1190
FAX (416) 338-1250
Frequency: 1190 kHz (AM).
Format: A/C.
Station Manager: Michael Caine.
Program Director: Michael Caine.
Specialty Programming: *Mississauga Magazine.*

CHMO

P.O. Box 400
Moosonee, ON P0L 1Y0
(705) 336-2301
FAX (705) 336-2186
Frequency: 1450 kHz (AM).
Format: C&W.
Ownership: James Bay Broadcasting Corp.
Station Manager: Bill Sleaver.
Program Director: Bill Sleaver.
Program Director: Enerst Hunter.
Language: English, French.

CJSB

1504 Merivale Rd.
Nepean, ON K2E 6Z5
(613) 226-5450
FAX (613) 226-8480
Frequency: 540 kHz (AM stereo).
Listening Area: Ottawa/Hull.
Cable: Yes.
Format: Top 40 (Car-based Rock).
Directors: Bob Mackowycz, Gord Taylor.
Affiliates: Standard Broadcasting.

CJTT

55 Whitewood Ave., E., P.O. Box 1058
New Liskeard, ON P0J 1P0
(705) 647-7334
FAX (705) 647-8660
Frequency: 1230 kHz (AM).
Listening Area: New Liskeard, Cobalt, Haileybury, Earlton, Englehart, Latchford.
Cable: Yes.
Format: Country, A/C.
Specialty Programming: *CBC Sunday Morning, CBC Cross Country Check-up, Quirks & Quarks, Air Farce, Dick Barley's Rock & Roll Oldies.*
Directors: Mike Perras (station manager), Rick Stow (program co-ordinator).
Language: English, plus one hour of French language programming per week.
Affiliates: CJKL-Kirkland Lake, Seltec, BN News, Westwood One, Telemedia Sports Network, The Sports Network (Radio), CNR Star Country.

CKAN

138 Davis Dr.
Newmarket, ON L3Y 2N1
(416) 898-1100
FAX (416) 853-4433
Frequency: 1480 kHz (AM).
Listening Area: York Region, Simcoe Country and the Northern reaches of Metro Toronto.
Cable: Yes.
Format: A/C, Classic Hits, (50s-80s).
Specialty Programming: Jazz programming on Sunday evenings.
Program Director: Terry Thomas.
Affiliates: Privately owned.
Comments: Peter Emmerson, formerly of CFTO and Global-TV, is the new owner.

CJRN

4668 St. Claire
Niagara Falls, ON L2E 6X7
(416)356-6710
FAX (416) 356-0696
Frequency: 710 kHz (AM).
Format: A/C.
Station Manager: Alan Magnacca.
Program Director: Bob Dancy.
Specialty Programming: *The John Gilbert Show.*

CFCH

743 Main St. E.
P.O. Box 3000
North Bay, ON P1B 8K8
(705) 474-2000
FAX (705) 474-7761
Frequency: 600 kHz (AM).
Listening Area: North Bay, Sturgeon Falls, Mattawa, Burks Falls.
Cable: Yes (FM 97.9).
Format: A/C, CHR.
Program Director: John Jacobs.
Affiliates: Telemedia Communications.

CHUR

245 Oak St. St. E.
North Bay, ON P1B 8P8
(705) 472-1110
FAX (705) 495-0922
Frequency: 840 kHz (AM).
Format: CHR.
Ownership: Gateway City Broadcasters Ltd.
Station Manager: Ron Smith.
Program Director: Andy Wilson.

CKAT

743 Main St.
P.O. Box 3000
North Bay, ON P1B 8K8
(416) 474-3693
Frequency: 101.9 MHz (FM).
Listening Area: North Bay and surrounding regions.
Cable: Yes.
Format: Country.
Specialty Programming: Telemedia Sports Network, Jazz, Bluegrass, Drama, Gospel.
Program Director: Mary Stillar.
Affiliates: Telemedia Radio Network, CFCH-AM.

CHWO

490 Wyecroft Rd.
Oakville, ON L6K 2M1
(416) 845-2821
FAX (416) 338-1250
Frequency: 1250 kHz (AM).
Format: MOR.
Station Manager: M.H. Caine.
Program Director: Michael Caine.

CIDC

287 Broadway Ave.
Orangeville, ON L9W 1L2
(519) 942-1030
FAX (519) 942-2550
Frequency: 103.5 MHz (FM).
Listening Area: Central and Southern Ontario.
Cable: Yes.
Format: Soft A/C.
Program Director: Bill Thomas.

CFOR

241 West Street N.
Orillia, ON
L3V 5C9
(705) 326-3511
Frequency: 1570 kHz (AM).
Format: A/C.
Ownership: Telemedia Communications.
Station Manager: Barry Norman.
Program Director: Jan Veitch.

CKAR

360 King St. W.
Oshawa, ON L1J 2K2
(416) 571-1350
FAX (416) 571-1150
Frequency: 1350 kHz (AM).
Format: CHR.
Ownership: Grant Broadcasting Ltd.
Station Manager: George Grant.
Program Director: George Grant.

CKQT

360 King St. W.
Oshawa, ON L1J 2K2
(416) 571-1350
FAX (416) 571-1150
Frequency: 94.9 MHz (FM).
Format: MOR.
Ownership: Grant Broadcasting Ltd.
Station Manager: George Grant.
Program Director: George Grant.

CBO

P.O. Box 3220, Stn. C
Ottawa, ON
K1Y 1E4
(613) 598-1200
FAX (613) 598-3430
Frequency: 920 MHz (FM).
Format: News and Information.
Ownership: Radio Canada.
Station Manager: Doug Ward.
Program Director: Doug Ward.

CBOF

C.P. 3220, Stn. C.
Ottawa, ON K1Y 1E4
(613) 724-1200
FAX (613) 724-5060
Frequency: 1250 kHz (AM).
Format: News and Information.
Ownership: Radio Canada.
Program Director: Sylvain LaFrance.

CBOF

P.O. Box 3220, Stn. C
Ottawa, ON K1Y 1E4
(613) 724-1200
FAX (613) 724-5060
Frequency: 102.5 MHz (FM).
Format: Classical and Jazz.
Ownership: Radio Canada.
Program Director: Sylvain LaFrance.
Language: French.

CFGO

1575 Carling Ave.
Ottawa, ON K1Z 7M3
(613) 729-1200
FAX (613) 729-9829
Frequency: 1200 kHz (AM).
Format: CHR.
Ownership: Rawlco Communications Ltd.
Station Manager: Dianne Wilson.
Program Director: Dianne Wilson.

CFMO

1900 Walkley Rd.
Ottawa, ON K1H 8P4
(613) 526-3279
FAX (613) 523-6423
Frequency: 93.9 MHz (FM).
Format: MOR.
Station Manager: Gord Atkinson.
Program Director: Bill Paton.

CFRA

1900 Walkley Rd.
Ottawa, ON K1H 8P4
(613) 738-2372
FAX (613) 523-6423
Frequency: 580 kHz (AM).
Format: A/C.
Ownership: CHUM Ltd.
Station Manager: Steve Madely.

CHEZ

126 York St.
Suite 509
Ottawa, ON K1N 5T5
(613) 563-1919
FAX (613) 563-3357
Frequency: 106.1 MHz (FM).
Ownership: CHEZ FM Inc.
Station Manager: Chuck Azzarello.
Program Director: Steve Colwill.

CIWW

112 Kent St., Tower B
Suite 1900
Ottawa, ON K1P 6J1
(613) 238-7482
FAX (613) 236-5382
Frequency: 1310 kHz (AM).
Format: CHR.
Ownership: Key Radio Ltd.
Station Manager: Hal Blackadar.
Program Director: Jerry Stevens.

CKBY

112 Kent St., Suite 1900
Ottawa, ON K1P 6J1
(613) 238-6862
FAX (613) 236-5382
Frequency: 105.3 MHz (FM).
Listening Area: Ottawa-Hull.
Cable: Yes.
Format: Country.
Program Director: Ted Daigle.

CFOS

270-9 St. E.
Owen Sound, ON N4K 5P5
(519) 376-2030
FAX (519) 371-9686
Frequency: 560 kHz (AM).
Format: CHR.
Ownership: Bayshore Broadcasting Corp.
Station Manager: Ross Kentner.
Program Director: Rick Moss.

CIXK

270-9 St. E.
Owen Sound, ON N4K 5P5
(519) 376-2030
FAX (519) 371-9683
Frequency: 106.6 MHz (FM).
Format: A/C.
Ownership: Bayshore Broadcasting Corp.
Station Manager: Ross Kentner.
Program Director: Rick Moss.

CKLP

4 Miller St.
Parry Sound, ON P2A 1S8
(705) 746-2163
FAX (705) 746-4292
Frequency: 103.3 MHz (FM).
Format: MOR.
Ownership: Playland Broadcasting Ltd.
Station Manager: Bob Bowland.
Program Director: Bob Bowland.

CFRH

CBC
63 Main St.
Penetang, ON L0K 1P0
(705) 549-3095
Frequency: 96.5 MHz (FM).
Format: A/C.
Station Manager: Claude Couillard.
Language: French.

CHRO

Forest Lea Rd., P.O. Box 1010
Pembroke, ON K8A 7T3
(613) 735-1036
FAX (613) 735-0022
Frequency: 1350 kHz (AM).
Listening Area: Pembroke and Renfrew
County.
Cable: 88.9 FM.
Format: Light CHR.
Specialty Programming: *Sunday Session*,
news magazine.
Program Director: Scott Jackson.
Affiliates: Affiliate of Mid Canada Radio
Communications.

CFMP

1825 Television Rd., P.O. Box 4150
Peterborough, ON K9H 5T8
(705) 748-6101
FAX (705) 742-7274
Frequency: 101.5 MHz (FM).
Listening Area: Peterborough, ON.
Cable: Yes.
Format: A/C.
Specialty Programming: Contemporary
Gospel, Jazz.
Program Director: Don Millar.

CHEX

340 George St. N.
Peterborough, ON K9J 6Y8
(705) 742-7708
FAX (705) 742-7274
Frequency: 980 kHz (AM).
Format: CHR.
Ownership: Kawartha Broadcasting.
Station Manager: Jack Ruttle.
Program Director: Kim Somers.

CKPT

340 George St. N.
Peterborough, ON K9J 6Y8
(705) 742-8844
FAX (705) 742-1417
Frequency: 1420 kHz (AM).
Format: A/C.
Ownership: CHUM Ltd.
Station Manager: J.J. Manol.
Program Director: Jack Roe.

CKQM

340 George St. N.
Peterborough, ON K9J 6Y8
(705) 742-8844
FAX (705) 742-1417
Frequency: 105.1 MHz (FM).
Format: C&W.
Ownership: CHUM Ltd.
Station Manager: J.J. Manol.
Program Director: Ric Johnson.

CKOA/CKOB

282 Raglan St. S.
P.O. Box 1400
Renfrew, ON K7V 4H9
(613) 432-6428
FAX (613) 432-8236
Frequency: CKOA-1490 kHz (AM), CKOB-
1400 kHz (AM).
Listening Area: Upper Ottawa Valley .
Cable: Yes.
Format: A/C days, CHR nights.
Specialty Programming: *Superadio Hot 30,
Superadio Open House Party*, plus a Comedy
Show and Sunday morning talk and religious
programming.
Program Director: Rick Wyman.
Rebroadcasts: CKOA-Arnprior, ON.

CFGM

10254 Yonge St.
Richmond Hill, ON L4C 3B7
(416) 921-6400
FAX (416) 883-9785
Frequency: 640 kHz (AM).
Listening Area: Southern Ontario.
Cable: Yes.
Format: Country.
Program Director: Tom Tompkins.
Affiliates: Westcom Radio Group Ltd.

CFGX

1415 London Rd.
Sarnia, ON N7G 1P6
(519) 322-5500
FAX (519) 542-1520
Frequency: 99.9 MHz (FM).
Format: A/C.
Ownership: Blue Water Broadcasting Ltd.
Station Manager: John Divinski.
Program Director: John Harada.

CHOK

148 North Front St.
Sarnia, ON N7T 7K5
(519) 336-1070
FAX (519) 336-7523
Frequency: 1070 kHz (AM).
Format: A/C.
Ownership: Middlesex/Lambton Communications Corp.
Station Manager: W. Steele.
Program Director: Paul Godfrey.
Specialty Programming: *AM Magazine, Midday Magazine.*

CKTY

1415 London Road
Sarnia, ON N7S 1P6
(519) 322-5500
FAX (519) 542-1520
Frequency: 1110 kHz (AM).
Format: C&W.
Ownership: Blue Water Broadcasting Ltd.
Station Manager: John Divinski.
Program Director: Mark Cartland.

CFYN

426 Bruce Street
Sault Ste-Marie, ON P6A 5N5
(705) 942-1050
FAX (705) 942-8246
Frequency: 1050 kHz (AM).
Format: A/C.
Ownership: Telemedia Communications.
Station Manager: Mike Prud'Homme.
Program Director: Darryl Mohamed.

CHAS

426 Bruce St.
Sault Ste. Marie, ON P6A 5N5
(705) 942-1050
FAX (705) 942-8246
Frequency: 100.5 MHz (FM).
Format: MOR.
Ownership: Telemedia Communications.
Station Manager: Mike Prud'Homme.
Program Director: Frank Holiday.

CJQM

111 Elgin St.
Suite 201
Sault Ste. Marie, ON P6A 6L6
(705) 759-9200
FAX (705) 942-6549
Frequency: 104.3 MHz (FM).
Format: C&W.
Ownership: Mid-Canada Communications Corp.
Program Director: Bruce Krause.

CKCY

111 Elgin St.
Suite 201
Sault Ste. Marie, ON P6A 6L6
(705) 759-9200
FAX (705) 942-6549
Frequency: 920 kHz (AM).
Format: CHR.
Ownership: Mid-Canada Communications Corp.
Station Manager: Gary Duguay.
Program Director: Scott Turnbull.

CHNR

600 Norfolk St., P.O. Box 1600
Simcoe, ON N3Y 4K8
(519) 426-7700
FAX (519) 426-8574
Frequency: 1600 kHz (AM).
Listening Area: Oxford-Haldimand-Norfolk and Brant Counties.
Cable: No.
Format: A/C.
Program Director: Ron Michaels.
Affiliates: CKRY-Calgary, CHSC/CHRE-St. Catharines, CJEZ-Toronto.

CHEQ/CJET

P.O. Box 1200, Jasper Highway
Smiths Falls, ON K7A 4T4
(613) 283-4630
FAX (613) 283-7243
Frequency: 630 AM - CJET, 101.1 FM-CHEQ.
Listening Area: CJET-Smiths Falls, Perth, Carleton Place, CHEQ-FM-Eastern Ontario/Ottaw-Hull/Northern New York State.
Cable: Yes.
Format: CJET-Easy listening. CHEQ Adult Contemporary.
Specialty Programming: CJET-Talk show/religion, CHEQ-FM-Jazz Show, Folk Show, Dance Show, Poetry.
Program Director: Brian Perkin.
Affiliates: CJET affiliated with CJET.

CHSC

36 Queenston St., P.O. Box 3020
St. Catharines, ON L2R 7C7
(416) 682-6691
FAX (416) 682-9434
Frequency: 1220 kHz (AM).
Listening Area: St. Catharines-Niagara.
Cable: No.
Format: Gold-based A/C.
Specialty Programming: *Live From The 60s,* Bob Fleming's Garden Show, Classic Express.
Program Director: Ted Yates.
Affiliates: CHRE-FM.

CHTZ

12 Yates St.
St. Catharines, ON L2R 6X7
(416) 684-1174
FAX (416) 684-4800
Frequency: 97.7 MHz (FM).
Format: AOR.
Ownership: Standard Radio Inc.
Station Manager: Greg Slaight.

CHRE

36 Queenston St.
P.O. Box 3020
St. Catharines, ON L2R 7C7
(416) 682-6691
FAX (416) 682-9434
Listening Area: St. Catharines - Niagara
Peninsula.
Cable: No.
Format: A/C.
Specialty Programming: *Images, Star
Performance, Entertainment Week, Nightcap,
CD Hour.*
Program Director: Ted Yates.

CKTB

12 Yates St.
St. Catharines, ON L2R 6X7
(416) 684-1174
Frequency: 610 kHz (AM).
Format: A/C.
Ownership: Standard Radio Inc.
Station Manager: Greg Slaight.

CHLO

133 Curtis St.
St. Thomas, ON N5P 3T8
(519) 631-3910
FAX (519) 631-3409
Frequency: 1570 kHz (AM).
Format: CHR.
Station Manager: Vern Furber.
Program Director: Warren Allen.

CJCS

178 Ontario St., P.O. Box 904
Stratford, ON N5A 6W3
(519) 271-2450
FAX (519) 271-3102
Frequency: 1240 kHz (AM).
Listening Area: Perth County.
Cable: Yes.
Format: Oldies.
Specialty Programming: *Music of Your Life.*
Program Director: Lynn Riddell.
Affiliates: Telemedia.

CBCS

CBC
15 MacKenzie St.
Sudbury, ON P3C 2A9
(705) 688-3200
FAX (705) 688-3236
Frequency: 99.9 MHz (FM).
Format: Varied.
Ownership: Radio Canada.
Station Manager: David Henley.
Program Director: David Henley.

CBON

CBC
15 MacKenzie St.
Sudbury, ON P3C 9H1
(705) 688-3200
FAX (705) 688-3236
Frequency: 98.1 MHz (FM).
Format: Contemporary.
Ownership: Radio Canada.
Station Manager: Robert Groulx.
Program Director: Robert Groulx.
Language: French.

CFBR

295 Victoria St.
Sudbury, ON P3C 1K5
(705) 674-6401
FAX (705) 674-8334
Frequency: 900 kHz (AM).
Format: Contemporary.
Ownership: Mid-Canada Communications Corp.
Program Director: F.B. Ricard.
Station Manager: Chuck Babcock.
Program Director: Gilles Lafortune.
Language: French.

CHNO

295 Victoria St.
Sudbury, ON P3C 1K5
(705) 674-6401
FAX (705) 674-8334
Frequency: 550 kHz (AM).
Format: CHR.
Ownership: Mid-Canada Communications Corp.
Station Manager: Chuck Babcock.
Program Director: Dave Sawyer.

CIGM

880 Lasalle Blvd.
Sudbury, ON P3A 5W7
(705) 566-4480
FAX (705) 560-7232
Frequency: 92.7 MHz (FM).
Format: C&W.
Ownership: Telemedia Communications.
Program Director: Greg Alexander.

CJMX

295 Victoria St.
Sudbury, ON P3C 1K5
(705) 674-6401
FAX (705) 674-8334
Frequency: 105.3 MHz (FM).
Format: A/C.
Ownership: Mid-Canada Communications Corp.
Program Director: Jim Hamm.

CKSO

880 Lasalle Blvd.
Sudbury, ON P3A 5W7
(705) 566-4480
FAX (705) 560-7232
Frequency: 790 kHz (AM).
Format: CHR.
Ownership: Telemedia Communications.
Station Manager: Paul Larche.
Program Director: Jim Hamm.

CBQ

CBC
213 Miles St. E.
Thunder Bay, ON P7C 1J5
(807) 625-5000
Frequency: 800 MHz (FM).
Format: News and information.
Ownership: Radio Canada.
Station Manager: Wilder Lewis.
Program Director: Wilder Lewis.

CJLB

P.O. Box 3448, Stn. P
Thunder Bay, ON P7B 5J9
(807) 345-5000
FAX (807) 345-6814
Frequency: 1230 kHz (AM).
Format: A/C.
Ownership: Leader Broadcasting Corp. Ltd.
Station Manager: John Turner.
Program Director: Gary Greer.

CJSD

87 North Hill St.
Thunder Bay, ON P7A 5V6
(807) 344-3526
FAX (807) 345-4671
Frequency: 94.3 MHz (FM).
Listening Area: Thunder Bay, Northwestern
Ontario.
Cable: Yes.
Format: A/C Soft Pop Rock.
Specialty Programming: Four hours of jazz
programming each week.
Program Director: Tim Goebel.

CKPR

87 North Hill St.
Thunder Bay, ON P7A 5V6
(807) 344-3526
FAX (807) 345-4671
Frequency: 580 kHz (AM).
Cable: Yes.
Format: A/C.
Program Director: Ray Dee.

CKOT

P.O. Box 10
77 Broadway
Tillsonburg, ON N4G 4H3
(519) 842-4381
FAX (519) 842-4284
Frequency: 101.3 MHz (FM).
Format: MOR.
Ownership: Tillsonburg Broadcasting Co.
Station Manager: John Lamers Jr.
Program Director: Doug Cooper.

CKOT

P.O. Box 10
77 Broadway
Tillsonburg, ON N4G 4H3
(519) 842-4381
FAX (519) 842-4284
Frequency: 1510 kHz (AM).
Format: CHR.
Ownership: Tillsonburg Broadcasting Co.
Station Manager: John Lamers, Jr.
Program Director: Doug Cooper.

CFCL

681 North Pine St.
Timmins, ON P4N 7G3
(705) 264-4211
FAX (705) 264-3266
Frequency: 620 MHz (FM).
Format: A/C.
Ownership: Mid-Canada Communications Corp.
Station Manager: Gerry Clifford.
Program Director: Laurier Roy.
Language: English, French.

CFTI

155 Pine St. S., P.O. Box 1046
Timmins, ON P4N 7H8
(705) 264-2351
FAX (705) 264-2984
Listening Area: Northeastern Ontario.
Cable: Yes.
Format: Country.
Specialty Programming: Jazz, German,
Classical.
Program Director: Art Pultz.
Affiliates: Telemedia.

CKGB

P.O. Box 046
Timmins, ON P4N 7H8
(705) 264-2351
FAX (705) 264-2984
Frequency: 750 kHz (AM).
Format: A/C.
Ownership: Telemedia Communications.
Station Manager: Chris Ruscica.
Program Director: Art Pultz.

CBL

CBC
509 Parliament St.
Toronto, ON M4X 1P3
(416) 975-7400
Frequency: 740 kHz (AM).
Format: News and Information.
Ownership: Radio Canada.
Station Manager: Gloria Bishop.
Program Director: Gloria Bishop.
Specialty Programming: *Radio Noon, Fresh Air.*
Rebroadcasts: On CBC affiliated throughout Southeastern Ontario.

CBL

CBC
509 Parliament St.
Toronto, ON M4X 1P3
(416) 975-7400
Frequency: 94.1 MHz (FM).
Format: Varied.
Ownership: Radio Canada.
Station Manager: Gloria Bishop.
Program Director: Susan Grant.

CFMX

468 Queen St. E., Suite 101
Toronto, ON M5A 1T7
(416) 367-5353
FAX (416) 367-1742
Frequency: 96.3 MHz (FM).
Format: Classics and Jazz.
Ownership: Different Drummer Communications Inc.
Station Manager: Jerry Good.
Program Director: Michael Compeau.

CFRB

2 St. Clair Ave. W.
Toronto, ON M4V 1L6
(416) 924-5711
FAX (416) 323-6830
Frequency: 1010 kHz (AM).
Format: News and Information.
Ownership: Standard Broadcasting Corp.
Station Manager: George Ferguson.
Program Director: George Ferguson.
Specialty Programming: A mix of quality news and information programming.

CFTR

25 Adelaide St. E.
Toronto, ON M5C 1H3
(416) 864-2000
FAX (416) 864-2002
Frequency: 680 kHz (AM).
Format: CHR.
Ownership: Rogers Broadcasting Ltd.
Station Manager: Anthony P. Viner.
Program Director: Sharon Taylor.

CHFI

25 Adelaide St. E.
Toronto, ON M5C 1H3
(416) 864-2070
FAX (416) 864-2002
Frequency: 98.1 MHz (FM).
Format: A/C.
Ownership: Rogers Broadcasting Ltd.
Station Manager: Tony Viner.
Program Director: Paul Fisher.

CHIN

637 College St.
Toronto, ON M6G 1B6
(416) 531-9991
FAX (416) 531-5274
Frequency: 1540 kHz (AM).
Format: Multicultural.
Station Manager: Robet Cullinton.
Program Director: Carl Redhead.

CHIN

637 College St.
Toronto, ON M6G 1B6
(416) 531-9991
FAX (416) 531-5274
Frequency: 100.7 MHz (FM).
Format: Multicultural, bilingual.
Station Manager: Robert Cullinton.
Program Director: Carl Redhead.

CHUM

1331 Yonge St.
Toronto, ON M4T 1Y1
(416) 925-6666
FAX (416) 926-4026
Frequency: 1050 kHz (AM).
Listening Area: Toronto and Ontario's Golden Horseshoe.
Cable: Yes.
Format: Oldies.
Program Director: Ross Davies.
Affiliates: The CHUM Group.

CHUM

1331 Yonge St.
Toronto, ON M4T 1Y1
(416) 925-6666
FAX (416) 926-4026
Frequency: 104.5 MHz (FM).
Listening Area: Toronto and Ontario's Golden Horseshoe.
Cable: Yes.
Format: A/C.
Program Director: Ross Davies.
Affiliates: The CHUM Group.

CILQ

2 Bloor St. E., Suite 3000
Toronto, ON M4W 1A8
(416) 967-3445
FAX (416) 924-2479
Frequency: 107 MHz (FM).
Listening Area: Southern Ontario, Northern U.S.
Cable: Yes.
Format: AOR.
Program Director: Gary Aube.
Affiliates: CFGM-AM .

CIRV

1087 Dundas St. W.
Toronto, ON M6J 1W9
(416) 537-1088
FAX (416) 537-2463
Frequency: 88.7 MHz (FM).
Format: Varied.
Station Manager: Frank Alvarez.
Program Director: Frank Alvarez.

CJBC

100 Carlton St., 2nd Floor
P.O. Box 500, Stn. A
Toronto, ON M5W 1E6
(416) 975-3566
FAX (416) 975-5622
Frequency: 860 kHz (AM).
Listening Area: Kingston, London, Toronto.
Format: Varied.
Specialty Programming: Election and press conference coverage.
Program Director: Jean Cois.
Language: French.

CJCL

40 Holly St., 7th Floor
Toronto, ON M4S 3C3
(416) 488-1430
FAX (416) 488-4381
Frequency: 1430 kHz (AM).
Listening Area: Metro Toronto and Southern Ontario.
Cable: Yes.
Format: Lite favorites.
Specialty Programming: Toronto Blue Jays and Maple Leaf Broadcasts, *Prime Time Sports, Out of the Blue (Jazz), Sock Hop* (Saturday and Sunday).
Program Director: Larry Green.
Ownership: Telemedia Communications.

CJEZ

40 Eglinton Ave. E.
Toronto, ON M4P 3B6
(416) 480-2097
FAX (416) 480-2724
Frequency: 97.3 MHz (FM).
Format: Varied.
Ownership: Redmond Communications.
Station Manager: Jay Jackson.
Program Director: Bill Ballentine.

CJRT

297 Victoria St.
Toronto, ON M5B 1W1
(416) 595-0404
Frequency: 91.1 MHz (FM).
Format: Classical and Jazz.
Station Manager: Cam Finley.
Program Director: Earle Toppings.

CKEY

1 Yonge St.
Toronto, ON M5E 1G1
(416) 361-1281
FAX (416) 361-9329
Frequency: 590 kHz (AM).
Format: A/C.
Ownership: Key Radio Ltd.
Station Manager: David Lyman.
Program Director: Terry Williams.

CKFM

24 St. Clair Ave. W.
Toronto, ON M4V 1L4
(416) 922-9999
FAX (416) 323-6800
Frequency: 99.9 MHz (FM).
Listening Area: Toronto.
Cable: Yes.
Format: A/C.
Station Manager: Weekend jazz specials.
Program Director: Marty Forbes.
Affiliates: CFRB-AM.

CJTN
31 Quinte St.
Trenton, ON K8V 5R1
(613) 392-1237
FAX (613) 394-6430
Frequency: 1270 kHz (AM).
Format: C&W.
Ownership: Quinte Broadcasting Co.
Station Manager: Robert S. Rowbotham.
Program Director: Sean Kelly.

CKMS
200 University Ave. W.
Waterloo, ON N2L 3G1
(519) 886-2567
Frequency: 94.5 MHz (FM).
Listening Area: Kitchener-Waterloo.
Cable: Yes.
Format: Alternative.
Specialty Programming: Reggae, Rap,
Rockabilly, Classical, Jazz, Folk, Children's.
Program Director: Jacqueline Bruner.
Language: English, Portuguese, Spanish,
Chinese, Turkish, Indian, Arabic.

CHOW
Regional Rd.
Welland, ON L3B 5R6
(416) 732-4433
FAX (416) 732-4780
Frequency: 1470 kHz (AM).
Format: C&W.
Ownership: Wellport Broadcasting Ltd.
Station Manager: G.W. Burnett.
Program Director: G.W. Burnett.

CBC
CBC
267 Pelissier
Windsor, ON N9A 4K5
(519) 255-3411
Frequency: 1550 kHz (AM).
Format: News and Information.
Ownership: Radio Canada.
Station Manager: Rick Alexander.
Program Director: Phil Peck.

CBC
CBC
267 Pelissier
Windsor, ON N9A 4K5
(519) 255-3411
Frequency: 89.9 MHz (FM).
Format: Varied.
Ownership: Radio Canada.
Station Manager: Rick Alexander.
Program Director: Phil Peck.

CBEF
267 Pelissier
Windsor, ON N9A 4K5
(519) 255-3411
FAX (519) 255-2403
Frequency: 540 kHz (AM).
Format: Varied.
Ownership: Radio Canada.
Program Director: Mina Grossman.

CJOM
300 Cabana Rd. E.
Windsor, ON N9G 1A3
(519) 966-7000
FAX (519) 966-1090
Frequency: 88.7 MHz (FM).
Format: CHR.
Ownership: CHUM Ltd.
Station Manager: Bill Timpson.
Program Director: Ian Davies.

CKLW
1640 Ouellette Ave.
Windsor, ON N9A 6M6
(519) 258-8888
FAX (519) 258-0182
Frequency: 800 kHz (AM).
Format: MOR.
Ownership: Amicus Communications.
Station Manager: Terry Cole.
Program Director: Dave Shafer.

CIMX
300 Cabana Rd. E.
Windsor, ON N9G 1A3
(519) 966-7000
FAX (519) 966-1090
Frequency: 88.7 MHz (FM).
Listening Area: Windsor, Essex and Kent
Counties.
Cable: Yes.
Format: CHR (adult).
Program Director: Ian Davies.

CKMR
1640 Ouellette Ave., P.O. Box 480
Windsor, ON M8X 1L1
(519) 258-8888
FAX (519) 258-0812
Frequency: 93.9 MHz (FM).
Listening Area: Windsor, Detroit, Toledo.
Cable: Yes.
Format: 50s-70s.
Specialty Programming: *Solid Gold
Saturday Night*, plus locally produced music
specials: *Archives* and *Lookin' Back*.
Program Director: Sandy Davis.
Affiliates: CKLW-AM.

CKWW

300 Cabana Rd. E.
Windsor, ON N9G 1A3
(519) 966-7000
FAX (519) 966-1090
Frequency: 580 kHz (AM).
Listening Area: Windsor and Essex Counties.
Cable: Yes.
Format: News, Talk, A/C.
Program Director: Al Pervin.
Affiliates: CHUM National News, BN.

CKNX

Carling Terrace
Wingham, ON N0G 2W0
(519) 357-1310
FAX (519) 357-1897
Frequency: 101.7 MHz (FM).
Format: A/C.
Station Manager: Jack Gillespie.
Program Director: Lisa Brandt.

CKDK

290 Dundas St.
Woodstock,ON N4S 7W7
(519) 539-7451
FAX (519) 539-7479
Frequency: 102.3 MHz (FM).
Format: A/C.
Ownership: Oxford Broadcasting Co. Ltd.
Station Manager: G. Marratto.
Program Director: David Sorrel.

CJWA

P.O. Box 1447
Wawa, ON P0S 1K0
(705) 856-4555
Frequency: 1240 kHz (AM).
Format: CHR.
Ownership: Mid-Canada Communications Corp.
Station Manager: Gary Duguay.
Program Director: John Huston.

P.E.I.

CBCT

CBC
P.O. Box 2230
Charlottetown, PE C1A 8B9
(902) 566-3591
FAX (902) 368-3118
Frequency: 96 MHz (FM).
Format: News and information.
Ownership: Radio Canada.
Station Manager: Barbara Trueman.
Program Director: John Brazill.

CFCY

141 Kent St., P.O. Box 1060
Charlottetown, PE C1A 7M7
(902) 892-1066
FAX (902) 566-1338
Frequency: 630 kHz (AM).
Listening Area: The Maritimes and parts of Quebec.
Cable: Yes.
Format: CHR, A/C.
Specialty Programming: Country music programming Saturdays 6:00 p.m.- 9:00 p.m., Saturday Evening Hoedown.
Program Director: Mike Brooks.
Affiliates: Maritime Broadcasting System.

CHLQ

141 Kent St.
Charlottetown, PE C1A 7M7
(902) 566-5550
FAX (902) 566-1338
Frequency: 93.1 MHz (FM).
Format: C&W.
Ownership: Eastern Broadcasting Co. Ltd.
Station Manager: Frank Lewis.
Program Director: Jim Ferguson.

CHTN

590 North River Rd.
P.O. Box 7200
Charlottetown, PE C1A 8V7
(902) 892-8591
FAX (902) 566-5904
Frequency: 720 kHz (AM).
Listening Area: Prince Edward Island, and parts of Nova Scotia and New Brunswick.
Cable: Yes.
Format: A/C.
Station Manager: Solid gold music programming.
Program Director: Paul Magee.
Affiliates: Newcap Broadcasting.

CJRW

218 Water ST.
Summerside, PE C1N 1B3
(902) 436-2201
FAX (902) 888-2926
Format: A/C.
Ownership: Gulf Broadcasting Co. Ltd.
Station Manager: P.H. Schurman.
Program Director: John Perry.

QUEBEC

CFVM

111 De L'Hopital
Amqui, PQ G0J 1B0
(418)629-2025
Frequency: 1220 kHz (AM).
Format: Contemporary.
Ownership: La Radio de la Matapedia Inc.
Program Director: Roger Quirion.

CJAN

185 Du Roi
Asbestos, PQ J1T 3M9
(819) 879-5430
Frequency: 1340 kHz (AM).
Format: MOR.
Ownership: Radio Victoriaville Ltee.
Station Manager: Marie-Paul Drouin.
Program Director: Denis Bourassa.

CFRP

399 De Puyjalon
Baie-Comeau, PQ G5C 2Z7
(418) 589-3771
FAX (418) 589-9086
Frequency: 640 kHz (AM).
Format: MOR.
Station Manager: Camille St-Pierre.
Program Director: Daniel Dionne.

CHLC

399 De Puyjalon
Baie-Comeau, PQ G5C 2Z7
(418) 589-3771
FAX (418) 589-9086
Frequency: 580 kHz (AM).
Format: MOR.
Station Manager: Camille St-Pierre.
Program Director: Daniel Dionne.

CHAI

25 Boul. St. Francis
Chateauguay, PQ J6J 1C8
(514) 692-6043
Frequency: 101.9 MHz (FM).
Format: A/C.
Station Manager: Jeanne D'Arc Germain.
Program Director: Mario Tremblay.

CFED

455-3 St.
Chibougamau, PQ G8P 1N6
(418) 748-7671
FAX (418) 748-7328
Frequency: 1340 kHz (AM).
Format: MOR.
Ownership: CJMD Chibougamau Inc.
Station Manager: Mario Loubier.
Program Director: Gaston Fournier.

CJMD

455-3 St.
Chibougamau, PQ G8P 1N6
(418) 748-7671
Frequency: 1240 kHz (AM).
Format: MOR.
Ownership: CJMD Chibougamau Inc.
Station Manager: Mario Loubier.
Program Director: Gaston Fournier.

CBJ

500 Des Sagueneen
Chicoutimi, PQ G7H 5E7
(418) 696-6600
FAX (418) 696-6689
Frequency: 1580 kHz (AM).
Format: MOR.
Ownership: Radio Canada.
Program Director: P. Tougas.

CBJ

CBC
500 Des Sagueneens
Chicoutimi, PQ G7H 5E7
(418) 696-6600
FAX (418) 696-6689
Frequency: 100.9 MHz (FM).
Format: Classical and Jazz.
Ownership: Radio Canada.
Station Manager: P. Tougas.
Program Director: P. Tougas.

CJAB

121 rue Racine, P.O. Box 1090
Chicoutimi, PQ G7H 5G4
(418) 545-8888
FAX (418) 545-9186
Frequency: 94.5 MHz (FM).
Listening Area: Saguenay-Lac St. Jean.
Cable: Yes.
Format: A/C.
Specialty Programming: New Age Music.
Program Director: Pierre Plante.
Language: French.

CJMT

1200 boul. du Royaume
Chicoutimi, PQ G7H 1T1
(418) 696-1420
FAX (418) 696-4164
Frequency: 1420 kHz (AM).
Format: MOR.
Ownership: Telemedia Communications.
Station Manager: Pierre Tremblay.
Program Director: Robert Boulay.

CHVD

1975 boul. Wallberg
Dolbeau, PQ G8L 1J5
(418) 276-3333
FAX (418) 276-0921
Frequency: 1230 kHz (AM).
Format: Contemporary.
Station Manager: Rosaire Leclerc.
Program Director: Michel Foprise.

CHRD

2070 St. Georges
Drummondville, PQ J2C 5G6
(819) 472-5458
FAX (819) 472-5672
Frequency: 1480 kHz (AM).
Format: MOR.
Station Manager: Radio Drummond Inc.
Program Director: Pierre Thibault.

CFGL

2830 boul. St. Martin e.
Duvernay, Laval, PQ H7E 5A9
(514) 664-1500
FAX (514) 664-1651
Frequency: 105.7 MHz (FM).
Format: MOR.
Ownership: Cogeco Group.
Station Manager: Yves Saucier.
Program Director: Jacques Charles Gilliot.

CFMF

P.O. Box 280
Fermont, PQ G0G 1J0
(418) 287-5147
Frequency: 103.1 MHz (FM).
Format: MOR.
Ownership: Radio Fermont Inc.
Station Manager: Carol Gagnon.
Program Director: Carol Gagnon.

CHIP

P.O. Box 820, Romain St.
Fort Coulonge, PQ J0X 1V0
(819) 683-3155
Frequency: 101.5 MHz (FM).
Format: Varied.
Ownership: La Radio du Pontiac Inc.
Station Manager: Jerry Berube.
Program Director: Wayne Adams.
Language: Bilingual.

CJRG

P.O. Box 380
Gaspe, PQ G0C 1R0
(418) 368-3511
FAX (418) 368-1663
Frequency: 94.5 MHz (FM).
Format: 94.5 MHz (FM).
Ownership: Radio Gaspesie Inc.
Station Manager: Mauril Minville.
Program Director: Daniel Henry.

CJMC

170 boul. Ste. Anne, P.O. Box 820
Gaspe Ouest, PQ G0E 2G0
(418) 763-5522
FAX (418) 763-7211
Frequency: 1490 kHz (AM).
Format: MOR.
Program Director: Gaston Fournier.
Language: French.

CJRC

22 rue St. Louis
Gatineau, PQ J8T 2R9
(819) 561-8801
FAX (819) 561-9439
Frequency: 1150 kHz (AM).
Format: MOR.
Ownership: Radiomutuel et Resau Nordique.
Station Manager: Charles Benoit.
Program Director: Marc Delorme.
Language: French.

CHEF

76 Dufferin
Granby, PQ J2G 9L4
(514) 372-1450
Frequency: 1450 kHz (AM).
Format: MOR.
Language: French.

CIMF

150 Edmonton St.
Hull, PQ J8Y 3S6
(819) 770-2463
FAX (819) 770-9338
Frequency: 94.9 MHz (FM).
Format: MOR.
Ownership: Telemedia Communications.
Program Director: Claude Gagne.
Language: French.

CKCH

72 rue Laval
Hull, PQ J8X 3H3
(819) 777-2771
FAX (819) 777-7724
Frequency: 970 kHz (AM).
Format: MOR.
Ownership: Telemedia Communications.
Station Manager: Francois Dunn.
Program Director: Maryo Bellemare.
Language: French.

CFIM

P.O. Box 490
Iles de Madeleine, PQ G0B 1B0
(418) 986-5233
FAX (418) 986-5205
Frequency: 92.7 MHz (FM).
Format: Varied.
Station Manager: Real Juteau.
Program Director: Pol Chantraine.
Language: English.

CJLM

854 Papineau
Joliette, PQ J6E 2L5
(514) 759-0772
FAX (514) 759-8751
Frequency: 1350 kHz (AM).
Ownership: Radio de Lanadiere Inc.
Station Manager: Pierre Cardin.
Program Director: Pierre Cardin.
Language: French.

CKRS

2455 Cantin
Jonquiere, PQ G7X 7V8
(418) 695-2577
FAX (418) 695-2654
Frequency: 590 kHz (AM).
Format: Contemporary.
Ownership: Radio Saguenay.
Station Manager: Huguette Arsenault.
Program Director: Huguette Arsenault.
Language: French.

CFLM

529 St. Louis
La Tuque, PQ G9X 3P6
(819) 523-4575
FAX (819) 676-8000
Frequency: 1240 kHz (AM).
Format: MOR.
Ownership: Radio Haute Mauricie Inc.
Station Manager: Rejean Leclerc.
Program Director: Rejean Leclerc.
Language: French.

CKBL

3852 Quebec Central
Lac Megantic, PQ G6B 2C6
(819) 583-0663
Frequency: 1400 kHz (AM).
Format: CHR.
Ownership: Radio Megantic Ltee.
Station Manager: Mme Lucie Fillion.
Program Director: Denis Bourassa.
Language: Bilingual.

CFGT

1441 Auger s.
Lac St. Jean, PQ G8B 5V2
(418) 662-6673
FAX (418) 662-9269
Frequency: 1270 kHz (AM).
Format: MOR.
Station Manager: Gilbert Pedneault.
Program Director: Mario Larouche.
Language: French.

CJLA

385 rue Principale
Lachute, PQ J8H 1Y1
(514) 562-8862
Frequency: 104.9 MHz (FM).
Listening Area: Territory between Montreal and Ottawa.
Cable: Yes.
Format: A/C.
Specialty Programming: Top 40.
Program Director: Pierre Tremblay.
Language: French.
Affiliates: Radio-Nord, CHPR-102.1.

CKLM

315 boul. Saint-Martin o.
Laval, PQ H7M 1Y7
(514) 662-2556
FAX (514) 662-8701
Frequency: 1570 kHz (AM).
Format: Varied.
Station Manager: Gerard Brunet.
Program Director: Pierre Leroux.

CFLS

5 Transcanada e.
Levis, PQ G6V 6P5
(418) 833-2151
Frequency: 920 kHz (AM).
Format: CHR.
Ownership: Radio Etchemin Inc.
Station Manager: Yves Lorrain.
Program Director: Yves Lorrain.

CHAA

240 rue St. Charles
Longueuil, PQ J4H 1E8
(514) 646-6800
Frequency: 103.1 MHz (FM).
Format: Varied.
Station Manager: Daniel Ouellette.
Program Director: Denis Dallaire.
Language: French.

CIEL

89 rue St. Charles o.
Longueuil, PQ J4H 1C5
(514) 527-8321
FAX (514) 522-9560
Frequency: 98.5 MHz (FM).
Format: Varied.
Station Manager: Pierre Paul Elie.
Program Director: Micheline Ricard.
Language: French.

CIMO

2056 rue Sherbrooke
Magog, PQ J1X 2T3
(819) 843-1414
FAX (819) 843-7769
Frequency: 106.1 MHz (FM).
Format: CHR.
Station Manager: Danielle Chagnon.
Program Director: Fernando Gasse.
Language: French.

CHGA

335 rue de Couvent
Maniwaki, PQ J9E 1H5
(819) 449-5590
FAX (819) 449-5132
Format: 97.3 MHz (FM).
Format: Varied.
Ownership: Radio Communautaine de la Haute
Gatineau.
Station Manager: Sylvie Geoffrion.
Program Director: Francois Laffond.
Language: French.

CKMG

P.O. Box 7
Maniwaki, PQ J9E 1P1
(819) 449-1211
FAX (819) 449-5132
Frequency: 1340 kHz (AM).
Format: Varied.
Ownership: Telemedia Communications.
Station Manager: Michel Riel.
Program Director: Michel Riel.
Language: French.

CHRM

800 Du Phare. o.
Matane, PQ 64W 1V7
(418) 562-4141
FAX (418) 562-0778
Frequency: 1290 kHz (AM).
Cable: No.
Format: MOR.
Specialty Programming: Country.
Program Director: Charles Lepage.
Language: French.
Affiliates: Radio Mutuel.

CBGA

CBC
155 St. Sacrement
Matane, PQ G4W 3P7
(418) 562-0290
Frequency: 1250 kHz (AM).
Format: MOR.
Ownership: Radio Canada
Station Manager: Louis Pelletier.
Program Director: Louis Pelletier.
Language: French.

CFEL

191 Chemin Des Poiriers
Montmagny, PQ G5V 4L2
(418) 248-1122
FAX (418) 248-1951
Frequency: 102.1 MHz (FM).
Format: MOR.
Ownership: Radio Montminy Inc.
Station Manager: Michel Montminy.

CBF

P.O. Box 6000
Montreal, PQ H3C 3A8
(514) 597-4779
FAX (514) 597-4710
Frequency: 690 kHz (AM).
Format: Varied.
Ownership: Radio Canada.
Station Manager: Jean Blais.
Program Director: Paul-Marie Lapointe.
Language: French.

CBF

P.O. Box 6000
Montreal, PQ H3C 3A8
(514) 597-4161
FAX (514) 597-4100
Frequency: 100.7 MHz (FM).
Format: Varied.
Ownership: Radio Canada.
Station Manager: Jean Blais.
Program Director: Paul-Marie Lapointe.
Language: French.

CBM

CBC
P.O. Box 6000
Montreal, PQ H3C 3A8
(514) 597-4444
Frequency: 940 kHz (AM).
Format: Varied.
Ownership: Radio Canada.
Station Manager: N. Belanger.
Language: English.

CBM

CBC
P.O. Box 6000
Montreal, PQ H3C 3A8
(514) 597-4444
FAX (514) 597-5551
Frequency: 93.5 MHz (FM).
Format: Varied.
Ownership: Radio Canada.
Station Manager: N. Belanger.
Program Director: Robert Blackwood.
Language: English.

CFMB

35 York St.
Montreal, PQ H3Z 2Z5
(514) 483-2362
FAX (514) 483-1362
Frequency: 1410 kHz (AM).
Listening Area: Montreal Metro.
Cable: Yes.
Format: MOR.
Specialty Programming: Multilingual (26 languages).
Program Director: Georges A. Sisto.
Languages: Italian, Greek, Portuguese, Spanish, Arabic, German, Yiddish, Hebrew, Armenian, Ukrainian, Polish, Hungarian, Persian, Yugoslav, Romanian, Chinese, Dutch, Flemish, Tamil, Creole, Vietnamese, Urdu, Hindi, French, English.

CFCF

1200 McGill College Ave., Suite 300
Montreal, PQ H3N 1M4
(514) 874-4040
FAX (514) 393-4659
Frequency: 600 kHz (AM).
Format: MOR.
Ownership: Mount Royal Broadcasting.
Station Manager: Pierre Arcand.
Program Director: Pierre Arcand.
Listening Area: English.

CFQR

1200 McGill College Ave., Suite 300
Montreal, PQ H3B 4G7
(514) 874-4040
FAX (514) 393-4659
Frequency: 92.5 MHz (FM).
Listening Area: Montreal area, Eastern Townships.
Cable: Yes.
Format: A/C.
Specialty Programming: Big Band and classical programming. (weekday evenings).
Program Director: Andre Chevalier.
Affiliates: CFCF-AM, Montreal.

CHCR

5899 Park Ave.
Montreal, PQ H2V 4H4
(514) 273-2481
Frequency: 89.9 MHz (FM).
Format: Varied.
Ownership: La Voix Hellenique du Canada.
Station Manager: Sophia Lappas.
Program Director: Marie Griffiths.

CIBL

1491 boul. Pie 1X
Local 406
Montreal, PQ H1V 2C3
(514) 526-2581
Frequency: 104.5 MHz (FM).
Format: Varied.
Ownership: Radio Communautaine de la Haute Gatineau.
Station Manager: Anne-Marie Pichette.
Program Director: Marc Thivierge.
Language: French.

CINQ

5212 boul. St. Laurent
Montreal, PQ H2T 1S1
(514) 495-2597
Frequency: 102.3 MHz (FM).
Listening Area: Central Montreal.
Cable: Yes.
Format: Community, Alternative.
Specialty Programming: Ethnic and alternative programming and music.
Language: French, English, Spanish, Greek, Creole, Portuguese, Chinese.
Comments: Address all correspondence to appropriate teams. e.g. send English promotional records to the music director for the English team.

CITE

1184 St. Catherine St. W.
Montreal, PQ H3B 1K1
(514) 866-3741
FAX (514) 393-9185
Frequency: 107.3 MHz (FM).
Format: MOR.
Ownership: Telemedia Communications.
Station Manager: Marc Blondeau.
Program Director: Yves Gagne.
Language: French.

CJAD

1411 Fort St.
Montreal, PQ H3H 2R1
(514) 989-2523
FAX (514) 989-2529
Frequency: 800 kHz (AM).
Format: A/C.
Ownership: Standard Radio Inc.
Station Manager: Rob Braide.
Program Director: Rob Braide.
Language: English.

CJFM

1411 Fort St.
Montreal, PQ H3H 2N6
(514) 989-2536
FAX (514) 989-2525
Frequency: 95.9 MHz (FM).
Listening Area: Montreal.
Cable: Yes.
Format: A/C.
Specialty Programming: Jazz programming,
plus *Saturday Night Dance Mix*.
Program Director: Jeff Vidier.
Language: English.
Affiliates: Standard Broadcasting.

CJMS

1717 Dorchester Blvd. E.
Montreal, PQ H2L 4T3
(514) 521-3732
FAX (514) 522-3127
Frequency: 1280 kHz (AM).
Format: MOR.
Ownership: Radiomutuel et Resau Nordique.
Station Manager: Paul-Emile Beaulne.
Program Director: Raynald Briere.
Language: English.

CKAC

1400 Metcalfe
Montreal, PQ H3A 1X4
(514) 845-5151
FAX (514) 845-2229
Frequency: 730 kHz (AM).
Format: News and Information.
Ownership: Telemedia Communications.
Station Manager: Richard Morency.
Program Director: Michel Charland.
Language: French.

CKMF

1717 Dorchester Blvd. E.
Montreal, PQ H2L 4T3
(514) 526-3732
FAX (514) 522-3127
Frequency: 94.3 MHz (FM).
Format: MOR.
Ownership: Radiomutuel et Resau Nordiq.
Station Manager: Danielle Chagnon.
Program Director: Luc Tremblay.
Language: English.

CRSG

1455 boul. de Maisonneuve o., Suite H-647
Montreal, PQ H3G 1M8
(514) 848-7401
Frequency: 89.1 MHz (FM).
Listening Area: West Montreal.
Cable: Yes.
Format: Alternative.
Specialty Programming: *Latin America
Today, Public Affairs, Common Ground*.
Program Director: Michael Prokaziuk.
Language: English.
Rebroadcasts: CKUT-Montreal, CINQ-Montreal.

CHNC

P.O. Box 610
New Carlisle, PQ G0C 1Z0
(418) 752-2215
FAX (418) 752-6939
Frequency: 610 kHz (AM).
Format: MOR.
Ownership: Telemedia Communications.
Station Manager: Reginald Poirier.
Program Director: Maxime Fillion.
Language: French.

CKTL

1646 ave. St. Laurent
Plessisville, PQ. G6L 2Y7
(819) 362-3737
Frequency: 1420 kHz (AM).
Format: Varied.
Ownership: Res Appalaches.
Station Manager: Johanne Talbot.
Program Director: Dennis Bourassa.
Language: French.

CIPC

8 boul. des Iles
Port-Cartier, PQ G5B 2J4
(418) 766-6868
FAX 766-6870
Frequency: 710 kHz (AM).
Format: CHR, A/C.
Specialty Programming: "Retro" music
programming.
Program Director: Mario Griffin.
Language: French.

CHIK

4 Parc Samuel Holland, Suite 200
Quebec, PQ G1S 3R3
(418) 687-9900
FAX (418) 687-3106
Frequency: 98.9 MHz (FM).
Format: CHR.
Ownership: Radiomutuel et Resau Nordiq.
Station Manager: Michel Audy.
Program Director: Martyne Rioux.
Language: French.

CIFT

580 Grande Alle e., Suite 250
Quebec, PQ G1R 2K2
(418) 525-4545
FAX (418) 525-6399
Frequency: 107.5 MHz (FM).
Format: MOR.
Ownership: Telemedia Communications.
Station Manager: Jacques Gauthier.
Program Director: Jean Emond.
Language: French, English.

CKCV

800 Place D'Youville, 21st Floor
Quebec, PQ G1R 4W7
(418) 694-1280
Frequency: 1280 kHz (AM).
Format: Nostalgia.
Ownership: Telemedia Communications.
Station Manager: Phil Germain.
Program Director: Phil Germain.
Language: French.

CKRL

47 rue Ste. Ursule
Quebec, PQ G1R 4E4
(418) 692-2575
Frequency: 89.1 MHz (FM).
Format: Varied.
Station Manager: Brigitte Duchesneau.
Program Director: Eric Etter.
Language: French.

CBVE

CBC
700 St. Cyrille Blvd.
Quebec City, PQ G1R 5A9
(418) 525-2120
Frequency: 104.7 MHz (FM).
Format: A/C.
Ownership: Radio Canada.
Station Manager: Robert Blackwood.
Language: French.

CJMF

600 Belvedere
Quebec City, PQ G1S 3E5
(418) 687-9330
FAX (418) 687-9718
Frequency: 93.3 MHz (FM).
Format: CHR.
Ownership: Cogeco Group.
Station Manager: Claude Thibodeau.
Program Director: Daniel Beaumont.

CFLP

875 blvd. St. Germain o.
Rimouski, PQ G5L 3T9
(418) 723-2323
FAX (418) 722-7508
Frequency: 1000 kHz (AM).
Format: MOR.
Station Manager: Gilles Rousseau.
Program Director: Lyse Bonenfant.

CJRB

273 St. Jean Baptiste
Rimouski, PQ G5L 4J8
(418) 723-2217
FAX (418) 722-7753
Frequency: 900 kHz (AM).
Format: News and Information.
Station Manager: Yvan Asselin.
Program Director: Yvan Asselin.

CJRB

273 St. Jean Baptiste
Rimouski, PQ G5L 4J8
(418) 723-2217
FAX (418) 722-7753
Frequency: 101.5 MHz (FM).
Format: Classical and Jazz.
Ownership: Radio Canada.
Station Manager: Yvan Asselin.
Program Director: Yvan Asselin.

CHRT

1 rue Frontenac
Riviere-Du-Loup, PQ G5R 1R7
(418) 862-8241
Frequency: 1450 kHz (AM).
Format: MOR.
Ownership: Telemedia Communications.
Station Manager: Guy Simard.
Program Director: Daniel St-Pierre.

CION

P.O. Box 1037
Riviere-Du-Loup, PQ
(418) 867-1037
FAX (418) 867-2829
Frequency: 103.7 MHz (FM).
Format: CHR.
Ownership: CION-FM Inc.
Station Manager: Ghislain Morisette.

CJAF

CBC
1 rue Frontenac
Riviere-Du-Loup, PQ G5R 1R7
(418) 862-8241
Frequency: 1240 kHz (AM).
Format: MOR.
Ownership: Telemedia Communications.
Station Manager: Guy Simard.
Program Director: Daniel St-Pierre.

CJFP

1 rue Frontenac
Riviere-Du-Loup, PQ G5R 1R7
(418) 862-8241
Frequency: 1400 kHz (AM).
Format: MOR.
Ownership: Telemedia Communications.
Station Manager: Guy Simard.
Program Director: Daniel St-Pierre.

CJTF

1 rue Frontenac
Riviere-Du-Loup, PQ G5R 1R7
(418) 862-8241
Frequency: 93.9 MHz (FM).
Format: Varied.
Ownership: Telemedia Communications.
Station Manager: Guy Simard.
Program Director: Daniel St-Pierre.

CHRL

568 boul. St. Joseph
Roberval, PQ G8H 2K6
(418) 275-1831
FAX (418) 275-2475
Frequency: 910 kHz (AM).
Format: A/C.
Ownership: Radio Roberval Inc.
Station Manager: Marc A. Levesque.
Program Director: Germain Gagnon.

CIRC

20 rue Reilly e.
Rouyn, PQ J9X 3N9
(819) 764-9505
Frequency: 88.7 MHz (FM).
Format: MOR.
Station Manager: Pierre Lapointe.
Program Director: Giorggio Cazzaro.

CHAD

380 Murdock Noranda
Rouyn-Noranda, PQ J9X 1G5
(819) 762-0740
FAX (819) 732-6310
Frequency: 1340 kHz (AM).
Format: Varied.
Ownership: Radio Nord Inc.
Station Manager: Michel Bolduc.
Program Director: Michel Bolduc.

CHLM

380 Murdock Noranda
Rouyn-Noranda, PQ J9X 1G5
(819) 762-0741
FAX (819) 762-2280
Frequency: 96.5 MHz (FM).
Format: MOR.
Ownership: Radio Nord Inc.
Station Manager: Darcy Kieran.
Program Director: Darcy Kieran.
Language: French.

CKLS

380 Murdock Noranda
Rouyn-Noranda, PQ J9X 1G5
(819) 762-0741
FAX (819) 333-2066
Frequency: 1240 kHz (AM).
Format: Varied.
Ownership: Radio Nord Inc.
Station Manager: Darcy Kieran.
Program Director: Darcy Kieran.
Language: French.

CKRN

380 Murdock Noranda
Rouyn-Noranda, PQ J9X 1G5
(819) 762-0741
FAX (819) 762-2280
Frequency: 1400 kHz (AM).
Format: Varied.
Ownership: Radio Nord Inc.
Station Manager: Rachel Martineau.
Program Director: Darcy Kieran.
Language: French.

CIBO

121 rue e Senneterre, P.O. Box 1150
Senneterre, PQ J0X 2M0
(819) 737-2222
FAX (819) 737-4352
Frequency: 100.5 MHz (FM).
Listening Area: Senneterre and surrounding area.
Cable: Yes.
Program Director: Francois Brazeau.
Language: French.

CBSI

350 rue Smith, Suite 30
Sept-Iles, PQ G4R 3X2
(418) 968-0720
FAX (418) 962-1344
Frequency: 98.1 MHz (FM).
Format: News and Information.
Ownership: Radio Nord Inc.
Station Manager: Pierre Lafreniere.

CKCN

437 Arnaud
Sept-Iles, PQ G4R 3B3
(418) 962-3838
Frequency: 560 kHz (AM).
Format: MOR.
Ownership: Radio Sept-Isles Inc.
Station Manager: Yvon Bergeron.
Program Director: Robert Savard.

CKSM

P.O. Box 695
Hotel De Ville
Shawinigan, PQ G9N 6V9
(819) 537-8824
FAX (819) 537-0465
Frequency: 1220 kHz (AM).
Format: MOR.
Station Manager: Pierre De Mondehare.
Program Director: P. De Mondehare/G. Forcier.

CFLX

244 Dufferin St., Suite 400
Sherbrooke, PQ J1H 4M4
(819)-566-2787
Frequency: 95.5 MHz (FM).
Station Manager: Real Bergeron.
Program Director: Gaetane Roy.
Language: French, English.

CHLT

25 rue Bryant
Sherbrooke, PQ J1J 3Z5
(819) 563-6363
FAX (819) 563-6363
Frequency: 630 kHz (AM).
Format: MOR.
Ownership: Telemedia Communications.
Station Manager: Michel Fortin.
Program Director: Mario Paquin.
Language: French.

CITE

25 Bryant
Sherbrooke, PQ J1J 3Z5
(819) 566-6655
FAX (819) 566-1011
Frequency: 102.7 MHz (FM).
Listening Area: Sherbrooke, Drummondville, Granby, Victoriaville.
Cable: Yes.
Format: MOR.
Program Director: Irenee Goulet.
Language: French.
Affiliates: Telemedia.

CJRS

3395 King o.
Sherbrooke, PQ J1L 1P8
(819) 567-8951
FAX (819) 567-2964
Frequency: 1510 kHz (AM).
Format: Varied.
Station Manager: Deny Grimard.
Program Director: Deny Grimard.

CKTS

901 Galt e.
Sherbrooke, PQ J1G 1Y6
(819) 563-9090
FAX (819) 563-9367
Frequency: 900 kHz (AM).
Format: CHR.
Ownership: Telemedia Communications.
Station Manager: Michel Fortin.
Program Director: Ted Silver.
Language: French.

CJRP

P.O. Box 4200
Sillery, PQ G1T 2S2
(418) 688-1060
FAX (418) 683-7058
Frequency: 1060 kHz (AM).
Format: Varied.
Station Manager: Andre Gagnon.
Program Director: Jacques Papin.
Language: French.

CIRB

P.O. Box 100, 170-12e rue
St. Georges, PQ G5Y 5C4
(418) 228-5535
Frequency: 1240 kHz (AM).
Format: Varied.
Ownership: Radio Beauce Inc.
Station Manager: Nelson Jalbert.
Program Director: Pierre Trottier.
Language: French.

CIRO

P.O. Box 100, 170-12e rue
St. Georges, PQ G5Y 5C4
(418) 228- 5535
Frequency: 99.7 MHz (FM).
Format: C&W.
Ownership: Radio Beauce Inc.
Station Manager: Nelson Jalbert.
Program Director: Pierre Trottier.
Language: French.

CKRB

P.O. Box 100, 170-12e rue
St-Georges, PQ G5Y 5C4
(418) 228-5535
Frequency: 1460 kHz (AM).
Format: Varied.
Ownership: Radio Beauce Inc.
Station Manager: Nelson Jalbert.
Program Director: Pierre Trottier.
Language: French.

CIHO

315 N. Cartier
St. Hilarion, PQ G0A 3V0
(418) 457-3333
Frequency: 96.3 MHz (FM).
Format: Radio Charlevoix Inc.
Station Manager: Guy Laprise.
Program Director: Martine Sauve.
Language: French.

CKBS

855 ave. St. Marie
St. Hyacinthe, PQ J2S 4R8
(514) 774-6486
Frequency: 1240 kHz (AM).
Format: MOR.
Ownership: Cogneco Group.
Station Manager: Richard Loiselle.
Program Director: Richard Loiselle.
Language: French.

CHRS

929 boul. Seminaire N.
St. Jean, PQ J3A 1B6
(514) 879-9046
Frequency: 1040 kHz (AM).
Format: CHR.
Program Director: Jim Welcher.

CIME

P.O. Box 1260
St. Adele, PQ J0R 1L0
(514) 430-3300
FAX (514) 229-7557
Frequency: 99.5 MHz (FM).
Format: A/C.
Ownership: Diffusion Laurentides Inc.
Station Manager: Pierre-Paul Elie.
Program Director: Julie Belanger.

CJSA

1-A rue St. Bruno
Ste-Agathe, PQ J8C 3K1
(819) 326-8182
Frequency: 1230 kHz (AM).
Format: MOR.
Station Manager: Pierre Donais.
Program Director: Michel Harnois.

CBV

2505 boul. Laurier
Ste. Foy, PQ G1V 2X2
(418) 654-1341
FAX (418) 654-3207
Frequency: 930 kHz (AM).
Format: Varied.
Ownership: Radio Canada.
Station Manager: Jacques D. Landry.
Program Director: Michel Gariepy.
Language: French.

CBV

2505 boul. Laurier
Ste Foy, PQ G1V 2X2
(418) 654-1341
FAX (418) 654-3207
Frequency: 95.3 MHz (FM).
Format: Varied.
Ownership: Radio Canada.
Station Manager: Michel Gariepy.
Program Director: Michel Gariepy.
Language: French.

CHOI

2136 chemin Ste. Foy
Ste. Foy, PQ G1V 1R8
(418) 687-9810
FAX (418) 682-8407
Frequency: 98.1 MHz (FM).
Format: A/C.
Station Manager: Jacques Duhamel.
Program Director: Paul O'Neill.
Language: French.

CHRC

2136 Chemin Ste. Foy
Ste. Foy, PQ G1V 1R8
(418) 688-8080
FAX (418) 682-8407
Frequency: 800 kHz (AM).
Format: News and Information.
Station Manager: Jacques Duhamel.
Program Director: Maurice Belanger.
Language: French.

CJVL

1360 Notre Dame s.
Ste. Marie, PQ G6E 3C4
(418) 387-1360
Frequency: 1360 kHz (AM).
Format: A/C.
Ownership: Clival Inc.
Station Manager: Richard J. Rheaume.
Program Director: Rene Nadeau.
Language: French.

CKVM

P.O. Box 3000
Temiscamingue, PQ J0Z 3W0
(819) 629-2710
FAX (819) 629-3131
Frequency: 710 kHz (AM).
Format: MOR.
Ownership: Radio Temiscamingue.
Station Manager: Yvon Lariviere.
Program Director: Yvon Lariviere.
Language: French.

CKVM

P.O. Box 3000
Temiscamingue, PQ J0Z 3W0
(819) 629-2710
FAX (819) 629-3131
Frequency: 89.3 MHz (FM).
Ownership: Radio Temiscamingue.
Station Manager: Yvon Lariviere.
Program Director: Yvon Lariviere.
Language: French.

CJLP

327 ave. Labbe
Thetford Mines, PQ G6G 5S3
(418) 335-7533
FAX (418) 338-0386
Frequency: 1230 kHz (AM).
Format: MOR.
Ownership: Radio Megantic Ltee.
Station Manager: Jeanne Martin.
Program Director: Denis Bourassa.
Language: French.

CKLD

327 ave. Labbe
P.O. Box 69
Thetford Mines, PQ G6G 5S3
(418) 335-7533
FAX (418) 338-0386
Frequency: 1330 kHz (AM).
Listening Area: Eastern Townships.
Cable: Yes.
Format: MOR.
Program Director: Raymond Cusson.
Language: French.
Affiliates: Telemedia.

CHLN

3550 boul. Royal
Trois Rivieres, PQ G9A 5G8
(819) 374-3556
Frequency: 550 kHz (AM).
Format: Varied.
Ownership: Telemedia Communications.
Station Manager: Michel Cloutier.
Program Director: Robert Montour.
Language: French.

CIGB

1675 boul. des Forges
Trois Rivieres, PQ G8Z 1T7
(819) 378-1023
FAX (819) 378-1360
Frequency: 102.3 MHz (FM).
Format: MOR.
Ownership: Legerbourg Inc.
Station Manager: Maurice Bourget.
Program Director: Francois Gauthier.
Language: French.

CJTR

1350 rue Royale
Trois Rivieres, PQ G9A 4J4
(819) 375-4855
FAX (819) 375-1233
Frequency: 1140 kHz (AM).
Format: Varied.
Station Manager: Rene Michaud.
Program Director: Richard Lachance.
Language: French.

CKVD

1729 - 3 Ave., P.O. Box 578
Val d'Or, PQ
Frequency: 900 kHz (AM).
Listening Area: Val D'Or and area.
Cable: Yes.
Format: MOR.
Program Director: Jean Gagnon.
Language: French.
Affiliates: Radio Nord.

CFLV

249 rue Victoria
Valleyfield, PQ J6T 1A9
(514) 373-1370
Frequency: 1370 kHz (AM).
Format: MOR.
Ownership: Radio Valleyfield Inc.
Station Manager: Jean-Guy Filiatrault.
Program Director: Jean-Guy Trudel.
Language: French.

CKOI

211 ave. Gordon
Verdun, PQ H4G 2R2
(514) 766-2311
FAX (514) 761-2122
Frequency: 96.9 MHz (FM).
Format: Adult Rock.
Ownership: Radio Futura Inc.
Station Manager: Malcom Scott.
Program Director: Bob Deboard.
Language: French.

CKVL

211 ave. Gordon
Verdun, PQ H4G 2R2
(514) 766-2311
FAX (514) 766-2122
Frequency: 850 kHz (AM).
Format: MOR.
Ownership: Radio Futura Inc.
Station Manager: Malcom Scott.
Program Director: Jean-Marie Menard.
Language: French.

CFDA

55 St. Jean Baptiste
Victoriaville, PQ G6P 6T3
(819) 752-5545
Frequency: 1380 kHz (AM).
Format: MOR.
Ownership: Radio Victoriaville Ltee.
Station Manager: Robert Daneau.
Program Director: Denis Bourassa.
Language: French.

CFMB

35 York St.
Westmount, PQ H3Z 2Z5
(514) 483-2362
FAX (514) 483-1362
Frequency: 1410 KHz.
Format: Varied.
Station Manager: Georges A. Sisto.
Program Director: Georges A. Sisto.
Language: Bilingual.

CFVD

6 rue Principale, Suite 654
Ville Degelis, PQ G0L 1H0
(418) 853-3370
Frequency: 1370 kHz (AM).
Format: CHR.
Ownership: Radio Degelis Inc.
Station Manager: Gilles Caron.
Program Director: Gilles Caron.
Language: French.

CHAL

1000-6 Ave.
Ville La Pocatiere, PQ G0R 1Z0
(418) 856-1310
FAX (418) 846-3747
Frequency: 1350 kHz (AM).
Format: Varied.
Ownership: Radio de la Pocaterie Ltd.
Station Manager: Jean-Marc Belzile.
Program Director: Jean-Marc Belzile.
Language: French.

CHGB

1000-6 Ave.
Ville La Pocatiere, PQ G0R 1Z0
(418) 856-1310
FAX (418) 846-3747
Frequency: 1310 kHz (AM).
Format: MOR.
Ownership: Radio de la Pocaterie Ltd.
Station Manager: Jean-Marc Belzile.
Program Director: Jean-Marc Belzile.
Language: French.

CHOM

1310 Greene Ave.
Westmount, PQ H3Z 2B5
(514) 935-2425
FAX (514) 935-8301
Frequency: 97.7 MHz (FM).
Format: AOR.
Ownership: CHUM Ltd.
Station Manager: Lee Hambleton.
Program Director: Ian Maclean.
Language: English.

CHTX

1310 Greene Ave.
Westmount, PQ H3Z 2B5
(514) 931-4487
FAX (514) 935-8301
Frequency: 980 kHz (AM).
Format: AOR.
Station Manager: Lee Hambleton.
Program Director: Susan Davis.
Language: English.

SASKATCHEWAN

CJSL

1134-5 St.
Estevan, SK S4A 2H8
(306) 634-1280
FAX (306) 634-6464
Frequency: 1280 kHz (AM).
Format: C&W.
Ownership: Soo Line Broadcasting.
Station Manager: John Empey.
Program Director: Matt Bradley.

CJNS

P.O. Box 1660
Meadow Lake, SK S0M 1V0
(306) 236-6494
FAX (306) 236-6141
Frequency: 1240 kHz (AM).
Format: C&W.
Ownership: Northwestern Radio Partnership.
Station Manager: H.G. Dekker.
Program Director: Ken Schiller.

CJVR

611 Main St.
P.O. Box 1420
Melfort, SK S0E 1E0
(306) 752-2867
FAX (306) 752-5932
Frequency: 1420 kHz (AM).
Listening Area: Northeast Saskatchewan.
Cable: No.
Format: Country, A/C.
Program Director: Bill Wood.

CHAB

116 Main St. N.
Moosejaw, SK S6H 3J7
(306) 694-0800
FAX (306) 693-3058
Frequency: 800 kHz (AM).
Listening Area: Southern Saskatchewan.
Cable: Yes.
Format: Favorites of yesterday and today.
Specialty Programming: Warriors Hockey (WHL).
Program Director: Gavin Tucker.
Language: English.
Affiliates: Moffat Communications.

CJNB

1711-100 St.
P.O. Box 1460
North Battleford, SK S9A 2Z5
(306) 445-2477
FAX (306) 445-4599
Frequency: 1050 kHz (AM).
Listening Area: Northwest-Central Saskatchewan.
Cable: Yes.
Format: Contemporary Country.
Program Director: Doug Harrison.
Affiliates: CJNS-Meadow Lake, SK.
Rebroadcasts: 1240 CJNS-Meadow Lake, SK

CFMM

1316 Central Ave.
Prince Albert, SK S6V 5R4
(306) 922-6936
FAX (306) 764-1850
Frequency: 99.1 MHz (FM).
Format: AOR.
Ownership: Central Broadcasting.
Station Manager: J.V. Scarrow.
Program Director: Garth Kalin.

CKBI

1316 Central Ave.
Prince Albert, SK S6V 7R4
(306) 763-7421
FAX (306) 764-1850
Frequency: 900 kHz (AM).
Format: A/C.
Ownership: Central Broadcasting.
Station Manager: Jim Scarrow.
Program Director: John Wessel.

CBK

CBC
2440 Broad St.
Regina, SK S4P 4A1
(306) 347-9540
FAX (306) 347-9490
Frequency: 96.9 MHz (FM).
Format: Varied.
Ownership: Canadian Broadcasting Corp.
Station Manager: Ron Smith.
Program Director: Jan Carter.

CBKF

CBC
2440 Broad St.
Regina, SK S4P 4A1
(306) 347-9540
FAX (306) 347-9490
Frequency: 860 kHz (AM).
Format: Varied.
Ownership: Radio Canada.
Station Manager: Lionel Bonneville.
Program Director: Richard Marcotte.
Language: French.

CMFQ

2060 Halifax St., P.O. Box 9800
Regina, SK S4P 3J4
(306) 525-9195
FAX (306) 781-7338
Frequency: 92.1 MHz (FM).
Listening Area: Regina, Moose Jaw and surrounding areas.
Format: A/C (Gold-based).
Specialty Programming: *The Canadian Connection* (Mondays at 10 p.m.) features Canadian music, both new and classic, with new Regina artists a priority. *Society Jazz* (Sunday nights at 6 p.m.) co-hosted by members of the Regina Jazz Society.
Program Director: David Jones.
Language: English.
Affiliates: CKRM-AM.

CIZL

2401 Saskatchewan Dr., Suite 210
Regina, SK S4P 4H8
(306) 359-9936
FAX (306) 347-8557
Frequency: 98.9 MHz (FM).
Format: AOR.
Ownership: Rawlco Communications Ltd.
Program Director: Shannon Cooke.

CKRM

2060 Halifax St.
Regina, SK S4P 1T7
(306) 566-9800
FAX (306) 781-7338
Frequency: 980 kHz (AM).
Format: A&W.
Ownership: Harvard Communications.
Station Manager: John Huschi.
Program Director: Willy Cole.

CBK

2440 Broad St.
Regina, SK S4P 4A1
(306) 347-9540
FAX (306) 347-9490
Frequency: 540 kHz (AM).
Format: Varied.
Ownership: Radio Canada.
Station Manager: Ron Smith.
Program Director: Michael Snook.

CBKF

2440 Broad St.
Regina, SK S4P 4A1
(306) 347-9540
FAX (306) 347-9490
Frequency: 97.7 MHz (FM).
Format: Varied.
Ownership: Radio Canada.
Station Manager: Lionel Bonneville.
Program Director: Richard Marcotte.

CJME

2401 Saskatchewan Dr.
Regina, SK S4P 3B9
(306) 569-1300
FAX (306) 347-8557
Frequency: 1300 kHz (AM).
Format: A/C.
Ownership: Rawlco Communications Ltd.
Station Manager: Michael Zaplitny.
Program Director: Rob Alexander.

CKCK

P.O. Box 6200
Regina, SK S4P 3H7
(306) 569-6200
FAX (306) 347-7920
Frequency: 620 kHz (AM).
Format: A/C.
Ownership: Armadale Communications Ltd.
Station Manager: Mr. Gayle Robinson.
Program Director: Allan Mitchell.

CKIT

P.O. Box 1049
Regina, SK S4P 3B2
(306) 924-1049
FAX (306) 347-7920
Frequency: 104.9 MHz (FM).
Format: A/C.
Ownership: Armadale Communications Ltd.
Station Manager: Gayle Robinson.
Program Director: Ken Singer.

CFYM

P.O. Box 490
Rosetown, SK S0L 2V0
(306) 882-2686
FAX (306) 882-3037
Frequency: 1210 kHz (AM).
Format: A/C.
Ownership: Dace Broadcasting Co.
Station Manager: Dennis Dyck.
Program Director: Earl Harris.

CJYM

P.O. Box 490
Rosetown, SK S0L 2V0
(306) 882-2686
FAX (306) 882-3037
Frequency: 1330 kHz (AM).
Format: A/C.
Ownership: Dace Broadcasting Co.
Station Manager: Dennis Dyck.
Program Director: Earl Harris.

CFMC

3333-8 St. E.
Saskatoon, SK S7H 0W3
(306) 955-9500
FAX (306) 373-7587
Frequency: 95.1 MHz (FM).
Format: A/C.
Ownership: Rawlco Communications Ltd.
Station Manager: Pam Carley.
Program Director: Kent Newson.

CFQC

216-1 Ave. N.
Saskatoon, SK S7K 3W3
(306) 665-8600
FAX (306) 665-0450
Frequency: 600 kHz (AM).
Format: A/C.
Ownership: Baton Broadcasting.
Station Manager: Dennis Fisher.
Program Director: Lee Friesen.

CJWW

345-4 Ave. S.
Saskatoon, SK S7K 5S5
(306) 244-1975
FAX (306) 665-7730
Frequency: 750 kHz (AM).
Listening Area: Central and Northern
Saskatchewan.
Cable: Yes.
Format: Country.
Specialty Programming: Gospel show and
Old Tyme Dance Party.
Program Director: Vic Dubois.
Affiliates: CHMG-Edmonton, CKST-Vancouver.

CKOM

3333-8 St. E.
Saskatoon, SK S7H 0W3
(306) 955-6595
FAX (306) 373-7587
Frequency: 650 kHz (AM).
Format: CHR.
Ownership: Rawlco Communications Ltd.
Station Manager: Pam Carley.
Program Director: Greg Harrison.

CJSN

90-3 Ave. E.
Shaunavon, SK S0N 2M0
(306) 297-2671
Frequency: 1490 kHz (AM).
Format: MOR.
Ownership: Frontier City Broadcasting.
Station Manager: Joe Gregoire.
Program Director: Joe Gregoire.

CIMG

P.O. Box 1590
28-4 Ave. N.W.
Swift Current, SK S9H 4G5
(306) 773-1505
FAX (306) 778-3737
Frequency: 94.1 MHz (FM).
Format: A/C.
Ownership: Grasslands Broadcasting.
Station Manager: Dale Redmond.
Program Director: Kelly Evjen.

CKSW

134 Central Ave. N.
Swift Current, SK S9H 3W2
(306) 773-4605
FAX (306) 773-6390
Frequency: 570 kHz (AM).
Format: C&W.
Ownership: Frontier City Broadcasting.
Station Manager: Len Enns.
Program Director: Len Enns.

CFSL

305 Souris Ave., P.O. Box 340
Weyburn, SK S4H 2K2
(306) 842-4666
FAX (306) 842-2720
Frequency: 1190 kHz (AM).
Listening Area: Southeastern Saskatchewan.
Cable: Yes.
Format: Country.
Program Director: Jay Hitchen.
Affiliates: CJSL-Estevan, Star Country.
Rebroadcasts: CJSL-Estevan, SK.

CJGX

120 Smith St. E., 4th Floor
Broadcast Place
Yorkton, SK S3N 3V3
(306) 782-2256
FAX (306) 783-4994
Frequency: 940 kHz (AM).
Format: A/C.
Ownership: Yorkton Broadcasting Co. Ltd.
Station Manager: G.G. Gallagher.
Program Director: Doug Anderson.

YUKON

CFWH

CBC
3103-3 Ave.
Whitehorse, YT Y1A 1E5
(403) 668-8400
FAX (403) 668-8408
Frequency: 570 kHz (AM).
Format: Varied.
Ownership: Radio Canada.
Station Manager: James A. Boyles.
Program Director: Charles Gregersen.

CHON

4228A-4 Ave.
Whitehorse, YT Y1A 1K1
(403) 668-6629
FAX (403) 668-6612
Frequency: 98.1 MHz (FM).
Format: C&W.
Ownership: Northern Native Broadcasting.
Station Manager: M. Telep.
Program Director: B. Charlie.

CKRW

4103-4 Ave., Suite 203
Whitehorse, YT Y1A 1H6
(403) 668-6100
FAX (403) 668-4209
Frequency: 610 MHz (FM).
Format: A/C.
Ownership: Klondike Broadcasting Co. Ltd.
Station Manager: Glen Darling.
Program Director: Glen Darling.
Rebroadcasts: On stations througout the Yukon.

RADIO STATIONS (CAMPUS)

ALBERTA

CJSW
University of Calgary
MacEwan Hall, Room 127
Calgary, AB T2N 1N4
(403) 220-3904
Frequency: 90.9 MHz (FM).
Listening Area: Calgary and surrounding communities.
Cable: Yes.
Format: Alternative Rock, Jazz, Blues, World Music and Spoken Word.
Specialty Programs: Women's and literary arts programs.
Program Director: Kerry Clarke.
Languages: Primarily English. Also: French, German, Spanish, Croatian, Tagalog and Chinese.
Affiliated Stations or Networks: NCRA.
Comments: Winner of *The Record's* Campus Radio Station of the Year Award (l989).

CMRC
Mount Royal College
4825 Richard St. S.W.
Calgary, AB T3E 6K6
(403) 240-6909
Frequency: Closed circuit.
Listening Area: Calgary.
Format: Light Rock.
Program Director: Paul Dunthy.
Languages: English.

CLCR
Camrose Lutheran College
4901-46 Ave.
Camrose, AB T4V 2R3
(403) 672-2999
Frequency: 101.5 MHz (FM).
Cable: Yes
Listening Area: Campus.
Format: Open.

401

CJSR
University of Alberta
Students Union Building, Room 224
Edmonton, AB T6G 2J7
(403) 492-5244
FAX (403) 492-4643
Frequency: 88.5 MHz (FM).
Listening Area: Metropolitan Edmonton.
Cable: Yes.
Format: Varied programming.
Specialty Programs: Jazz, Blues, Folk, Country, Classical, Roots, Rock, Metal, Chinese, Polish, Spanish, Experimental, etc.
Program Director: Richard Thornley.
Languages: French, Chinese, Spanish, Polish, English.
Affiliated Stations or Networks: NCRA.
Comments: CJSR offers a very wide variety of programming, and is Edmonton's only campus and community radio station. CJSR has a very active news and public affairs department that complements the eclectic programming of the station.

CKUL
University of Lethbridge
4401 University Dr.
Lethbridge, AB T1K 3M4
(403) 329-2335
Frequency: 99.7 MHz (FM).
Listening Area: Lethbridge.
Cable: Yes.
Format: Variable.
Station Manager: Brian Heinrich.
Languages: English.

CLCC
Lethbridge Community College
3000 College Dr.
Lethbridge, AB T1K 1L6
(403) 320-3254
Frequency: Closed circuit.
Listening Area: Campus.
Cable: No.
Format: CHR and Country.
Program Director: Tom Gilespy.
Languages: English.

BRITISH COLUMBIA

CFML
B.C.I.T. Radio
3700 Willingdon Ave.
Burnaby, BC V5G 3H2
(604) 432-8414
Frequency: 940 kHz (AM).
Listening Area: Greater Vancouver and the lower Fraser Valley.
Cable: Yes.
Format: A/C and information.
Specialty Programs: 60 minute daily talk show, weekly children's show, weekly sports magazine.
Languages: English.

CJIV
Simon Fraser University
TC 216
Burnaby, BC V5A 1S6
(604) 291-3727
FAX (604) 291-4455
Frequency: 940 kHz (AM), 93.9 MHz (FM).
Listening Area: Greater Vancouver.
Cable: Yes.
Format: Alternative music and information.
Specialty Programs: Blues, Classical, Comedy, Hardcore, Metal, Folk, Latin, Rap, Dance, Jazz, New Age, Radioart.
Program Director: Nadia Chivilo.
Languages: Mostly English.
Affiliated Stations or Networks: NCRA.

CMMD
Caribou College
900 College Rd.
P.O. Box 3010
Kamloops, BC V2C 5N3
(604) 828-5080 or 828-5081
FAX (604) 828-5086
Frequency: Closed circuit.
Listening Area: Local.
Cable: No.
Format: Rock (18-25 age group).
Specialty Programs: Some music features.
Program Director: Changes each fall.
Languages: English.

CITR

University of British Columbia
6138 SUB Blvd.
Vancouver, BC V6T 2A5
(604) 228-3017
FAX (604) 228-6093
Frequency: 101.9 MHz (FM).
Listening Area: Vancouver and surrounding area.
Cable: Yes.
Format: Alternative with focus on local and independent artists.
Specialty Programs: Jazz, Native, Industrial, African, Bebop, Punk, Funk, Metal, Folk, Classical, Reggae, C&W.
Program Director: Randy Iwata.
Languages: English.
Affiliated Stations or Networks: NCRA.

CNBC

Vancouver Community College, Langara Campus
100 W. 49 Ave.
Vancouver, BC V5Y 2Z6
(604) 324-5340
Frequency: Closed circuit.
Cable: Yes.

CAMO

Camosun College
3100 Foul Bay Rd.
Victoria, BC V8P 4X8
(604) 592-1113
Frequency: Closed circuit.
Listening Area: Camosun College, Lansdowne campus.
Cable: No.
Format: Rock, Variety.
Specialty Programs: Artist features.
Languages: English.
Comments: Radio training vehicle for students in the applied communication program.

CFUV

University of Victoria
Student Union Building
P.O. Box 1700
Victoria, BC V9B 1M8
(604) 721-8702
FAX (604) 721-8653
Frequency: 101.9 MHz (FM).
Listening Area: Greater Victoria plus Vancouver Island on cable.
Cable: Yes.
Format: Rock, Folk, Jazz, Classical, Public Affairs.
Specialty Programs: Spoken Word, Reggae, Rap, Public Affairs.
Program Director: Magnus Thyvold.
Languages: English.

MANITOBA

CKUW

University of Winnipeg
224 Lockhart Hall
515 Portage Ave.
Winnipeg, MB R3B 2E9
(204) 786-9782
FAX (204) 786-1824
Frequency: Closed circuit.
Listening Area: On campus.
Cable: No.
Format: Alternative music including Rock, Jazz, Classical, Blues, Reggae and Folk.
Specialty Programs: University of Winnipeg, Wesman basketball broadcasts (starting September 1990).
Program Director: Mick Humphreys.
Languages: English.
Affiliated Stations or Networks: NCRA.
Comments: CKUW is pursuing a distribution deal that should take effect September 1990. The station also publishes *Stylus*, a quarterly program guide and magazine.

CMOR

Red River Community College
2055 Notre Dame Ave., Room DM20
Winnipeg, MB R3H 9J9
(204) 632-2475
Listening Area: Campus.
Cable: No.
Format: Rock, (old, new and Top 40).
Program Director: Derek Rawlins.
Languages: English.

NEW BRUNSWICK

CHSR

University of New Brunswick
P.O. Box 4400
Fredericton, NB E3B 5A3
(506) 453-4985
FAX (506) 453-4599
Frequency: 97.9 MHz (FM).
Listening Area: Fredericton.
Cable: Yes.
Format: Alternative Rock.
Specialty Programs: Current Affairs, Classical, Jazz, Folk, Blues, Reggae, Dance, Experimental, Cultural.
Languages: English, French.
Affiliated Stations or Networks: NCRA.

CKUM

Les Media Acadiens Universitaires Inc.
Universite de Moncton
159 Massey Ave.
Moncton, NB E1A 3E9
(506) 858-4485
Frequency: 105.7 MHz (FM).
Listening Area: Moncton and surrounding areas.
Cable: Yes.
Format: 65% French.
Specialty Programs: Heavy Metal, Alternative, Jazz, etc.
Program Director: Michel Godbout.
Languages: French.

CHMA

Mount Allison University
303 University Centre
Sackville, NB E0A 3C0
(506) 364-2221
FAX (506) 536-4230
Frequency: 106.9 MHz (FM).
Listening Area: Sackville, New Brunswick; Amherst, Nova Scotia.
Cable: No.
Format: Community braodcasting.
Specialty Programs: Eclectic.
Program Director: Verna MacPhee.
Languages: English (with French specialty shows).

CRSJ

Campus Radio Saint John
SUB UNBSJ, Tucker Park
Saint John, NB E2L 4L5
(506) 648-5667
Frequency: 104.1 MHz (FM).
Listening Area: Saint John and vicinity.
Cable: Yes.
Format: Alternative, Rock, Pop, Rap.
Program Director: Fernand Comeau.
Languages: English, French.

NEWFOUNDLAND

CHMR

Memorial University
Elizabeth Ave. P.O. Box A-119
St. John's, NF A1C 5S7
(709) 737-4777
FAX (709) 737-4569
Frequency: 93.5 MHz (FM).
Listening Area: St. John's and surrounding areas.
Cable: Yes.
Format: Alternative, campus radio.
Specialty Programs: Various including Classical, Jazz, Folk, Blues, News Specials, etc.
Program Director: Mike Hickey.
Languages: English, French.
Affiliated Stations or Networks: NCRA.

NOVA SCOTIA

CFXU

St. Francis Xavier University
P.O. Box 948
Antigonish, NS B2G 1C0
(902) 867-2410
Frequency: 700 kHz (AM).
Listening Area: Campus.
Cable: Yes.
Format: Alternative, Rock, Top 40, Classical.
Program Director: Bill Dawe.
Languages: English.

CFSM

Saint Mary's University
920 Robie St.
Halifax, NS B3H 3C3
(902) 423-1739
Frequency: 550 kHz (AM).
Cable: No.
Format: Community-oriented radio.
Specialty Programs: Alternative, Blues, Reggae, Heavy Metal, Human Interest, Golden Oldies.
Languages: English.
Comments: CFSM combines musical and spoken word programming to fulfill the interests of the university community.

CKDU

Dalhousie University
Student Union Building
Halifax, NS B3H 4J2
(902) 424-2585
FAX (902) 424-2319
Frequency: 97.5 MHz (FM).
Languages: Halifax-Dartmouth.
Cable: Yes.
Format: Alternative and community radio.
Specialty Programs: Multi-cultural.
Program Director: Jane Farrow.
Languages: English, Indian, Chinese and
others.

CKIC

Acadia University
Acadia Students' Centre
P.O. Box 1269
Wolfville, NS B0P 1X0
(902) 542-2287, ext. 37
Frequency: 790 kHz (AM).
Listening Area: On campus.
Cable: Yes.
Format: Alternative, AOR.
Specialty Programs: Jazz, Folk, Classical.
Listening Area: English, French.

ONTARIO

CBLC

Loyalist College
P.O. Box 4200
Belleville, ON K8N 5B9
(613) 962-9501, ext. 327
Frequency: Closed circuit.
Listening Area: Campus area only.

CFRU

University of Guelph
Level 2, UC
Guelph, ON N1G 2W1
(519) 824-4120, ext. 8341
Frequency: 93.3 MHz (FM).
Listening Area: Guelph (10-mile radius).
Cable: Yes.
Format: Open, block and alternative
programming.
Specialty Programs: Classical, Jazz, Reggae,
Hip Hop, Soul, Funk, Bluegrass, Country, Folk,
Blues.
Program Director: John Stevenson.
Languages: English, French, Spanish,
Portuguese, Polish.

CFMU

McMaster University
1280 Main St. W.
Hamilton Hall, Suite 319
Hamilton, ON L8S 4K1
(416) 525-9140, ext. 2053
FAX (416) 529-3208
Frequency: 93.3 MHz (FM).
Listening Area: Hamilton and surrounding
area.
Cable: Yes.
Format: New Music, Rock, Jazz, Classical, Folk,
Blues.
Program Director: Brian Johnson.
Languages: Mostly English with the exception
of ethnic programs.

CHMR

Mohawk College
135 Fennell Ave. W.
Hamilton, ON L8N 3T2
(416) 575-2175
FAX (416) 575-2378
Listening Area: Hamilton.
Cable: Yes.
Format: Alternative.
Specialty Programs: British, Country,
Canadian Jazz, Psychedelic, Heavy Metal,
House, Dance.

CFRC

Queen's University
Carruthers Hall
Kingston, ON K7L 3N6
(613) 545-2121
FAX (613) 545-6300
Frequency: 101.9 MHz (FM).
Listening Area: Belleville to Brockville and
north to Smith's Falls.
Cable: Yes.
Format: Alternative.
Program Director: Peter Vamos.
Languages: English with some French and
Chinese.

CRSL

St. Lawrence College
King and Portsmouth Ave.
Kingston, ON K7L 5A6
(613) 544-5400, ext. 1271
Listening Area: Campus.
Cable: No.
Format: Rock, Top 40.
Program Director: Wayne Furlotte.
Languages: English.

CXLR
Conestoga College
299 Doon Valley Dr.
Kitchener, ON N2G 4M4
(519) 748-5220
Frequency: Closed circuit.
Listening Area: Campus.
Cable: No.
Format: AOR.
Languages: English.

CFRL
Fanshawe College
1460 Oxford St. E.
London, ON N5W 5H1
(519) 453-2810
Frequency: Closed circuit.
Listening Area: Campus.
Cable: No.
Format: CHR.
Program Director: Deedee Russell.
Languages: English.

CHRW
University of Western Ontario
Room 222, UCC
University of Western Ontario
London, ON N6A 3K7
(519) 661-3601
Format: Rock, Jazz, Folk, Blues, and more.

CFRE
Erindale College
3359 Mississauga Rd.
Mississauga, ON L5L 1C6
(416) 828-5310
Frequency: 91.9 Maclean-Hunter Cable FM.
Listening Area: Erindale College and area via cable.
Cable: Yes.
Format: Moderately alternative Pop, Rock.
Specialty Programs: Classical, Jazz, Rock.
Program Director: Todd Kyle.
Languages: English.

CBRT
Algonquin College
1385 Woodroffe Ave.
Nepean, ON K2G 1V8
(613) 727-7740
Frequency: Closed circuit.
Listening Area: Woodroffe campus.
Cable: No.
Format: Album Rock.
Specialty Programs: News, current affairs, sports.
Program Director: Various.
Languages: English, French.
Affiliated Stations or Networks: BN wire.

CRTV
Canadore College
Gormanville Rd., P.O. Box 5001
North Bay, ON P1B 8K9
(705) 474-7600
FAX (705) 474-2384
Frequency: 89.9 MHz (FM).
Listening Area: North Bay.
Cable: Yes.
Format: A/C (days), Rock (nights).
Specialty Programs: Features, Classical, some Country. All types of music throughout the day.
Program Director: Bruce Ruggles.
Languages: English.

CORS
Sheridan College
1430 Trafalgar Rd.
Oakville, ON L6H 2L1
(416) 845-3311
Frequency: Closed circuit.
Listening Area: Oakville campus of Sheridan College.
Cable: No.
Format: Pop, Alternative.
Program Director: Curtis Lessels.
Languages: English.

CHUO
University of Ottawa
85 Hastey, Suite 227
Ottawa, ON K1N 6N5
(613) 564-2903
Frequency: 89.1 MHz (FM).
Listening Area: Ottawa-Hull region.
Cable: Yes.
Format: French; AOR, wide variety.
Specialty Programs: Classical, Jazz, Blues, Reggae, frequent remote broadcasts for festivals.
Program Director: Tom Metuzals.
Languages: 50% English, 50% French.
Affiliated Stations or Networks: NCRA.
Comments: CHUO is a university-based, community radio station.

CKCU
Carleton University
Unicentre, 5th Floor
Ottawa, ON K1S 5B6
(613) 788-2898
Frequency: 93.1 MHz (FM).
Listening Area: 100-km radius.
Cable: Yes.
Format: Community, alternative.
Specialty Programs: Multi-cultural.
Program Director: Dave Dejongh.
Languages: English, French.

CFFF
Trent University
715 George St. N.
Peterborough, ON K9J 7B8
(705) 748-1777
Frequency: 96.3 MHz (FM).
Listening Area: Peterborough and surrounding area.
Cable: Yes.
Format: Community-oriented, cultural and educational radio.
Program Director: Peter Rukacina.
Languages: English.

CFLR
Laurentian University
935 Ramsay Lake Rd.
Sudbury, ON P3E 2C6
(705) 675-8492
Cable: Yes.
Format: Multi-format.
Specialty Programs: Ethnic programs.
Languages: English, Polish, German.

CBFM
George Brown College
St. James Campus
P.O. Box 1015, Stn. B
Toronto, ON M5T 2T9
(416) 867-2000
Frequency: Closed circuit.
Program Director: Laura McGowan.
Languages: English.

CFHC
Humber College
P.O. Box 1900
Toronto, ON M9V 2B3
(416) 675-3111
Frequency: Closed circuit.
Listening Area: Campus only.
Format: AOR.
Program Director: Craig Venn.
Languages: English.

CHRY
York University
4700 Keele St.
Toronto, ON M3J 1P3
(416) 736-5293
Frequency: 105.5 MHz (FM).
Listening Area: North York.
Cable: Yes.
Format: Alternative music and community affairs.
Specialty Programs: Musical emphasis on Folk, Traditional, Reggae, Caribbean, African.
Program Director: Lisa Roosen-Runge.
Languages: English, French.

CKCC
Centennial College
651 Warden Ave.
Toronto, ON M1L 3Z6
(416) 694-3033
Frequency: Closed circuit.
Cable: No.
Format: Varied.
Program Director: Kara Daley.
Languages: English.

CKLN
Ryerson Polytechnical Institute
380 Victoria St.
Toronto, ON M5B 1W7
(416) 595-1477
Frequency: 88.1 MHz (FM).
Listening Area: Toronto and surrounding region.
Cable: Yes.
Format: Non-commercial alternative.
Specialty Programs: Jazz, R&B, Soul, Reggae, Calypso, Soca, Blues, African, Hip Hop, Dance.
Program Director: David Barnard.
Languages: English, French, Spanish.
Comments: CKLN plays a wide variety of music in both open format and specialty programming. The station also conducts an annual public fundraising drive which raises over $130,000.

CIUT
University of Toronto
91 St. George St.
Toronto, ON M5S 2E8
(416) 595-0909
Frequency: 89.5 MHz (FM).
Listening Area: Toronto and area.
Format: Alternative, non-commercial.
Cable: Yes.
Specialty Programming: Jazz, Current Affairs, Feminist.
Languages English, French.
Comments: 15,000 watts (strongest non-commercial radio signal in Canada).

CKRG
York University
Glendon College
2275 Bayview Ave.
Toronto, ON M4N 3M6
(416) 487-6739
Frequency: 800 kHz (AM).
Listening Area: Campus residences, pubs and common areas.
Cable: No.
Format: Alternative, Jazz, Roots Rock. Emphasis on new Canadian artists.
Specialty Programs: Music for campus pub-nights and dances programmed live from studios.
Languages: French, English.

CRSC
Seneca College
1750 Finch Ave. E.
Toronto, ON M2N 5T7
(416) 491-5050, ext. 2560
Frequency: Closed circuit.
Listening Area: Seneca College, Newnham Campus.
Cable: No.
Format: Christian, Pop, Ethnic, Folk, Punk.
Languages: English.

CSCR
University of Toronto, Scarborough Campus
1265 Military Tr.
Toronto, ON M1C 2A4
(416) 284-3356
Frequency: 90.5 (Cable-FM)
Listening Area: Scarborough and Pickering.
Cable: Yes.
Format: Alternative community programming.
Specialty Programs: Ethnic, Women's, Classical, New Age, Heavy Metal, Community News, Reggae.
Program Director: Bill Elman.
Languages: English, Polish, Spanish.

CKMS
University of Waterloo
200 University Ave. W.
Waterloo, ON N2L 3G1
(519) 886-2567
Frequency: 94.5 MHz (FM).
Listening Area: Kitchener-Waterloo and parts of Cambridge and Stratford.
Cable: Yes.
Format: Alternative Rock and contemporary non-Top 40.
Specialty Programs: Jazz, Blues, Reggae, Classical, WorldBeat, Rap.
Program Director: Jacqueline Bruner.
Languages: English, German, Portuguese, Greek, Chinese, Indian, Arabic, Spanish, Croatian.

CRNC
Niagara College
Woodlawn Rd., P.O. Box 1005
Welland, ON L3B 5S2
(416) 735-2211
Frequency: Closed circuit.
Cable: No.
Format: CHR, AOR.
Specialty Programs: Magazine shows and remotes.

CJAM
University of Windsor
401 Sunset
Windsor, ON N9B 3P4
(519) 258-8786
FAX (519) 253-8871
Frequency: 91.5 MHz (FM).
Listening Area: Windsor-Metro Detroit, Michigan.
Cable: Yes (91.9 FM).
Format: Alternative music, with an emphasis on new releases from independent artists.
Specialty Programs: Special interest music and information.
Program Director: Marc Fedak.
Languages: Primarily English.
Affiliated Stations or Networks: NCRA.

PRINCE EDWARD ISLAND

CIMN
University of Prince Edward Island
550 University Ave.
Charlottetown, PE C1A 4P3
(902) 892-8980
Frequency: 102.3 MHz (FM), 700 kHz (AM).
Listening Area: Closed circuit available on campus and throughout Charlottetown.
Format: New Music, Rock, Pop, Reggae, Jazz.
Specialty Programs: Open format during evenings.
Languages: English.

HCFM
Holland College
Charlottetown Centre, Weymouth St.
Charlottetown, PE C1A 4Z1
(902) 566-4191
Frequency: Closed circuit.

QUEBEC

CJMQ
Bishop's University
Mountain House, Room 111, P.O. Box 2135
Lennoxville, PQ J1M 1Z7
(819) 822-0887
Frequency: Closed circuit.
Listening Area: Campus, Lennoxville, Sherbrooke.
Cable: Yes.
Format: Rock, Alternative, Variety, Reggae.
Languages: 90% English, 10% French.

CIRL

Concordia University
6931 Sherbrooke St. W.
Montreal, PQ H4B 1R6
(514) 848-7470
Frequency: 88.5 MHz (FM), 650 kHz (AM).
Listening Area: Greater Montreal.
Cable: Yes.
Program Director: Jamie Ross.
Languages: English, French.
Comments: CIRL welcomes correspondence
from other college radio stations. Writers will
receive CIRL-FM Top 40 playlist.

CKUT

McGill University
3480 McTavish St.
Montreal, PQ H3A 1X9
(514) 398-6787
FAX (519) 398-3594
Frequency: 90.3 MHz (FM).
Listening Area: Montreal and surrounding area.
Cable: Yes.
Format: Non-commercial.
Specialty Programs: Jazz, Gay and Lesbian,
Salsa, African, Reggae, Theatre, Hip Hop, Electro-
acoustic.
Program Director: Bryan Zuraw (music
program director), Ian Pringle (spoken word
program director).
Affiliated Stations or Networks: NCRA.
Comments: 5,700 watts, 24-hour programming.

CKVR

Vanier College CEGEP
821 Ste. Croix Blvd., Room B-132
Montreal, PQ H4L 3X9
(514) 744-7060
Listening Area: Campus.
Cable: No.
Format: Varied (Top 40, Alternative, Reggae,
Funk).
Specialty Programs: Classical hour, Reggae
specials, Ska hour.
Languages: English, French.

CRSG

Concordia University
1455 de Maisonneuve, Room H647
Montreal, PQ H3G 1M8
(514) 848-7401
Frequency: 88.9 MHz (FM).
Cable: Yes.
Format: Alternative.
Specialty Programs: Jazz, Classical, Reggae,
Blues, Public Affairs, etc.
Program Director: Michael Prokaziuk.
Languages: English, French.
Affiliated Stations or Networks: NCRA.

CKRL

Laval University
47 Ste. Ursule
Quebec, PQ G1R 4E4
(418) 692-2575
Frequency: 89.1 MHz (FM).
Listening Area: Quebec City and surrounding
area.
Cable: Yes.
Format: General.
Program Director: Eric Etter.
Languages: French.

CAJT

College de Rimouski
60 Eveche o.
Rimouski, PQ G5L 4H6
(418) 723-1880, ext. 2265
Frequency: Closed circuit.
Listening Area: On campus.
Program Director: Alain Pelletier.
Languages: French.

SASKATCHEWAN

CKUR

University of Regina
University of Regina, SUB
Regina, SK S4S 0A4
(306) 584-7600
Frequency: 760 kHz (AM).
Listening Area: On campus.
Format: Alternative.
Program Director: Terry Wazelainka.
Languages: English, Native, Chinese, French.

RECORD COMPANIES

A&M Records of Canada Ltd.

939 Warden Ave.
Scarborough, ON M1L 4C5
(416) 752-7191
FAX (416) 752-0059
Acts Handled: Pop, MOR, Rock, C&W, Metal, Jazz, Classical, New Age.
Subsidiary Labels: Virgin Records, Attic Records, Windham Hill, Troubadour, Spy Records, Vendetta, Antones, Chameleon Records, Current Records, Elephant, Concord Jazz. Fantasy, American Gramaphone, Nimbus, Delos, Rykodisc, Lullaby Lady, Oak Street, Hug Bug, Sernyk, Smarty Pants.
Canadian Artists: Bryan Adams, Paul Janz, Veronique Beliveau, The Works, David Gibson, Indio, Nancy Martinez, Silver & Degazio, Syre, Craig Jacks, Madeleine Morris.
Distributed By: A&M Records.
Contact: Max Hutchinson (A&R), James Monaco, Nicole Duchesne (PR), Randy Wells (promotion).
Branch Offices:
167 Merizzi St.
St. Laurent, PQ H4T 1Y3
(514) 733-5358/5359/5350
FAX (514) 733-3608

6020 2 St. S.E., Suite 22B
Calgary, AB T2H 2L8
(403) 253-8411
FAX (403) 255-5450

1334 W. 6 Ave., Suite 100
Vancouver, BC V6H 1A7
(604) 734-7443
FAX (604) 738-0496

2308 Maynard St., Suite 5
Halifax, NS B3K 3T7
(902) 423-1413
FAX (902) 423-0508

32C Forester Cr.
Bells Corner, ON K2H 8Y2
(613) 596-6447
FAX (613) 596-6447

274 Dundas St., Suite 408
London, ON N6B 1T6
(519) 642-7167
FAX (519) 642-7167

Winnipeg, MB
(204) 788-4555
FAX (204) 423-0580

Edmonton, AB
(403) 488-7453
FAX (403) 488-1028

411

A-Frame Records

3491 Ouellette Ave.
Windsor, ON N9E 3M1
(519) 969-6585
FAX (519) 945-8146
Acts Handled: Pop, Alternative, plus novelty and comedy.
Subsidiary Labels: Warped Records.
Canadian Artists: Sufferin' Catfish, Richard Janik exclusively. Various artists on compilation releases.
Distributed By: Independent.
Contact: Richard Janik.

A Major Record Label

148 Hoover Cr.
Hamilton, ON L9A 3H3
(416) 389-6244
Acts Handled: Pop, Rock, New Music.
Canadian Artists: Various.
Distributed By: Fringe, independent.
Contact: Michael Allan Guild.

Alert Records

41 Britain St., Suite 305
Toronto, ON M5A 1R7
(416) 364-4200
Canadian Artists: Michael Breen, Kim Mitchell, The Box.
Distributed By: PolyGram.

Ambiances Magnetiques

P.O. Box 263, Stn. E.
Montreal, PQ H2T 3A7
(514) 842-7479
Acts Handled: New Music.
Canadian Artists: Various.
Distributed By: Ambiances Magnetiques, other independents.
Contact: Rene Lussier (A&R).

Amok Records Inc.

10715 Guelph Line
Campbellville, ON L0P 1B0
(416) 854-0826
FAX (416) 854-0825
Acts Handled: New Music, Alternative, World Beat.
Canadian Artists: Courage of Lassie, Condition, The Whirleygigs, Psyche, Tupac Amaru, Dario, Domingues, Teknakuller Raincoats, Sturm Group, Nevermen, Weather Permitting, Eugene Ripper and The North, The Randypeters, Kinga, Look People, Third Waffle, FAT, Whitenoise,
Celebrity Drinks.

Anthem Records

189 Carlton St.
Toronto, ON M5A 2K7
(416) 923-5855
Acts Handled: Rock.
Canadian Artists: Rush, Images in Vogue.
Distributed By: Capitol/EMI (Canada), PolyGram (U.S.).

Apricot Records

(A Division of Apricot Talent & Recording Industries Inc.)
1449 Ridgebrook Dr., Suite 120
Gloucester, ON K1B 4T1
(613) 749-1116
FAX (613) 238-1687
Acts Handled: Top 40 Rock, MOR, Rock, Metal.
Canadian Artists: Gleneagle.
Distributed By: Apricot.
Contact: Gord Kent.

Aquarius Records Ltd.

4060 St. Catherine St. W., 6th Floor
Montreal, PQ H3Z 2Z3
(514) 939-3775
FAX (514) 939-2778
Acts Handled: Pop, Rock, Metal.
Canadian Artists: Corey Hart, Myles Goodwyn, Sass Jordan, Sword, others.
Distributed By: Capitol Records of Canada.
Contact: Rene Leblanc (A&R), Noni Resitz (PR).

Aquitaine Records

P.O. Box 130, Stn. Z
Toronto, ON M5N 2Z3
(416) 226-9608

Les Ateliers Saint-Gregoire

Saint-Benoit-du-Lac, PQ J0B 2M0
(819) 843-4080
Styles Handled: Gregorian chant, organ and harpsichord music.
Subsidiary Labels: SBL.
Canadian Artists: Choeur des Moines de Saint-Benoit-du-Lac.
Distributed By: Interdisc Distribution Inc.

Atlast Records

General Delivery
Huntsville, ON P0A 1K0
(705) 789-6024
Acts Handled: New Age.
Subsidiary Labels: Atlast Records is a subsidiary of Atlast Productions Inc., and Kids' Atlast Records.
Canadian Artists: Beverley Glenn-Copeland.
Distributed By: Moss Music Group (Canada).
Contact: Evelyn Wolf (promotion).

Attic Music Group

624 King St. W.
Toronto, ON M5V 1M7
(416) 862-0352
FAX (416) 862-0915
Acts Handled: Pop, MOR, Rock, Metal, New Music.
Canadian Artists: Lee Aaron, The Nylons, Roman Grey, John James, Haywire, Joey DeSimone.
Distributed By: A&M Records of Canada Limited.
Contact: Brian Allen (A&R), Steve Waxman (PR), Steve Waxman (promotion).

BFish Records Ltd.

192 Augusta Ave.
Toronto, ON M5T 2L6
(416) 977-6509
Acts Handled: New Jazz, Metafunk.
Canadian Artists: Whitenoise, Nat King Fudge, Rainer Wiens and Silk Stockings.
Distributed By: Electric Distribution.
Contact: Bill Grove.

Service de Musique B.M.

3465 Ontario St. E.
Montreal, PQ H1W 1R4
(514) 526-2464
Acts Handled: Pop, C&W, Folk.
Canadian Artists: Various.
Distributed By: Distribution Select.

BMG Music Canada Inc.

2245 Markham Rd.
Toronto, ON M1B 2W3
(416) 299-9000
Branch Offices:
2070 Oxford St.
Halifax, NS B3L 2T2

5460 ave. Mont-Royal, Suite 101
Montreal, PQ H4P 1H7

1625 Dublin Ave., Suite 120
Winnipeg, MB R3H 0W3

2880 Glenmore Tr. S.E.
Glenmore Commerce Ct.
Calgary, AB T2C 2E7

4894 Fraser St., Suite 201
Vancouver, BC V5V 4H5

Banzai Records

1238 Crescent St.
Montreal, PQ H3G 2A9
(514) 878-1648
Acts Handled: Rock, Metal.
Canadian Artists: VoiVod, Exciter.
Distributed By: PolyGram Records.

Berandol Records

110A Sackville St.
Toronto, ON M5A 3E7
(416) 869-1872
FAX (416) 869-1873
Acts Handled: Top 40, New Music, Dance, Soul and Instrumental.
Canadian Artists: Cosmic Orchestra, Rob Liddell, CYAN.
Distributed By: Berandol Major (relative to product).
Contact: Tony Procewiat.

Big Peach Records

P.O. Box 1177, Stn. F
Toronto, ON M4Y 2T8
(705) 424-6176
Acts Handled: C&W.
Canadian Artists: Debbie Bay-Shaw.
Contact: Peter Komisar (PR).

Black Market Records/ Domenic Troiano

357 Ormont Dr.
Weston, ON M9L 1N8
(416) 743-9979
Acts Handled: Pop, Rock, R&B.
Canadian Artists: David Gibson, Johnny R.

Boomtalk Musical Production

406 River Ave.
Winnipeg, MB R3L 0L5
(204) 453-8972
Acts Handled: All.
Canadian Artists: Trig Anderson, Joan Hanton.
Distributed By: National.

Boomtown Music

296 Richmond St. W., Suite 305
Toronto, ON M5V 1X2
(416) 979-8455
FAX (416) 979-8766
Acts Handled: Rock, Pop.
Canadian Artists: Big House.

Boot Records

1343 Matheson Blvd. E.
Mississauga, ON L4H 1K1
(416) 625-2676
Acts Handled: Reggae, Country, Folk, Esoteric.

Botany Park Records
361 Walter Dr.
Keswick, ON L4P 3A8
(416) 476-6605
Acts Handled: Pop, MOR, Rock, New Music.
Canadian Artists: Lioness, Marlaine Rennocks.
Distributed By: Botany Park Records and Music Publishing Co.
Contact: Marlaine Rennocks.

Boulevard Records
3447 Kennedy Rd.
Scarborough, ON M1V 3S1
(416) 496-1707
FAX (416) 496-0182
Subsidiary Labels: Subsidiary of Power Records Inc.
Contact: Vincent Degiorgio (A&R).

Bovine International Record Co.
3665 Arista Way, Suite 1910
Mississauga, ON L5A 4A3
(416) 277-3908
Acts Handled: Pop, MOR, C&W.
Subsidiary Labels: Bovine Records.
Canadian Artists: John Moorhouse, The Keynotes, Solid Ivory Brothers' Band.
Distributed By: Solid Ivory Music.
Contact: John Moorhouse.

Brandywine Enterprises Ltd./Pancake Records
18504-85 Ave.
Edmonton, AB T5T 1G7
(403) 487-7597
Acts Handled: Folk.
Canadian Artists: Brandywine.
Distributed By: Brandywine Enterprises Ltd., Red Deer College Press (University of Toronto Press).
Contact: David Spalding.

Brickhouse of Canada
P.O. Box 467, Stn. Z
Toronto, ON M5N 2Z6
(416) 633-5474
Acts Handled: Pop, MOR Reggae, R&B, New Music.
Canadian Artists: Arawak, Rainbow.

Bullseye Records
4352 Kingston Road, P.O. Box 11
Scarborough, ON M1E 2M8
(416) 428-2461
Acts Handled: Pop, Rock, Punk, Alternative, Post-Modern.
Subsidiary Labels: Snide Records, Capitol Records.
Canadian Artists: Moving Targetz, Swedish Fish, Swindled.
Distributed By: Bullseye Records.
Contact: Jaimie Vernon.

CBC Enterprises
P.O. Box 500, Stn. A
Toronto, ON M5W 1E6
(416) 975-3502
FAX (416) 975-3482
Acts Handled: Classical music and jazz.
Subsidiary Labels: SM5000 series, Musica Viva and Jazzimage.
Distributed By: CBC Enterprises.
Contact: Joelle Turgeon (514) 597-7857.

CBS Records Canada Ltd.
1121 Leslie St.
Don Mills, ON M3C 2J9
(416) 447-3311
Distributed By: Columbia, Epic, Portrait, CBS Associated, Pasha, T-Neck, Tabu, Carrere, Kiddin' Around, Caribou, Nemperor, PIR, Scott Bros., Silver Blue, Full Moon, Masterworks, True North, Parc, Def Jam, MTM, Austin.
Branch Offices:
610G-70 Ave. S.E.
Glenmore Centre
Calgary, AB T2H 2G2
(403) 253-8719

1847 W. Broadway, Suite 101
Vancouver, BC V6J 1Y6
(604) 734-5151

3550 Ashby Rd.
Ville St. Laurent, PQ H4R 2C1
(514) 337-6896

602 Blythwood Ave.
Riverview, NB E1B 2H5
(506) 386-1515

Calliope Music

71 Pembroke St.
Kingston, ON K7L 4N6
(613) 544-3910 or 549-5600
Acts Handled: Contemporary Folk, Children's Music.
Canadian Artists: Tom Mawhinney, Zucchini Alley.
Distributed By: Festival Records.
Contact: Tom Mawhinney.

Capitol Records/ EMI of Canada Ltd.

3109 American Dr.
Mississauga, ON L4V 1B2
(416) 677-5050
Acts Handled: All.
Distributed By: Anthem, Aquarius, Nettwerk, Enigma.
Canadian Artists: Tom Cochrane & Red Rider, Dalbello, Glass Tiger, Grapes of Wrath, Corey Hart, Helix, The Jitters, Luba, Frank Mills, Anne Murray, The Partland Brothers, Rock and Hyde, Strange Advance, David Wilcox, Burton Cummings, Paul Shaffer.
Branch Offices:
9924 Cote-de-Liesse Rd.
Lachine, PQ H8T 1A1
(514) 631-9072

7180-11 St. S.E., Suite 103
Calgary, AB T2H 2S9
(403) 258-2336

2182 W. 12 Ave.
Vancouver, BC V6K 2N4
(604) 736-6691

Centrediscs/ Centredisques

20 St. Joseph St.
Toronto, ON M4Y 1J9
(416) 961-6601
FAX (416) 961-7198
Acts Handled: Contemporary Canadian concert music by associate composers of the Canadian Music Centre.
Distributed By: Canadian Music Centre Distribution Service, Electric Distribution, Select Distribution, Fusion III.
Contact: Richard Truhlar.

Cesspool of Lust Records

2245 Markham Rd.
Tornto, ON M1B 2W3
(416) 299-9000
Acts Handled: Various.
Canadian Artists: Picture Comes to Life.
Distributed By: BMG Music Canada Inc.

Cherry Beach

16 Munition St.
Toronto, ON M5A 3M2
(416) 461-4224

Children's Hour Productions Ltd.

81 MacDonald Ave.
Weston, ON M9N 2E5
(416) 241-1233
Acts Handled: Children's entertainment.
Distributed By: Independent.
Contact: Jim Aquano (A&R), George Szabo (PR).

Circle "M" Records

P.O. Box 972
Mount Forest, ON N0G 2L0
(519) 323-2810
Acts Handled: C&W.
Subsidiary Labels: CBA Records.
Canadian Artists: Clare Adlam, Alfie Fromager, David Fromager.
Distributed By: Clare Adlam Enterprises.
Contact: Clare Adlam.

Citation Records.

191A Wolseley St., Suite 200
Thunder Bay, ON P7A 3G5
(807) 345-2448
Acts Handled: Country, Country Rock.
Comments: Production and artist direction.

Cityspeak

20 Fairford Ave.
Toronto, ON M4L 2J7
(416) 461-9538
Canadian Artists: Cityspeak.
Distributed By: Cityspeak.
Contact: Ian Gregory Wright.

Classified Records

510 Stiles St.
Winnipeg, MB R3G 3A4
(204) 774-0788
Acts Handled: New Music, Rap.
Canadian Artists: Class Info, Boy O Boy, J Jay W.
Distributed By: Classified Records.
Contact: Jay Willman.

Contagious Records

P.O. Box 183, Stn. C
Winnipeg, MB R3M 3S7
(204) 942-2123
Acts Handled: Dance, New Music, Electronic, Coldwave, Industrial.
Canadian Artists: They Never Sleep, Jon Krocker, Joe Silva, Too Cold to Sin.
Distributed By: Impulse Records.

Current Records/ Management

366 Adelaide St. E., Suite 437
Toronto, ON M5A 3X9
(416) 361-1101
FAX (416) 867-9501
Acts Handled: Pop, Dance, MOR, Rock, Alternative.
Canadian Artists: Mystery Romance, M+M (Martha and the Muffins), Alta Moda, Double Dare, The Parachute Club, Strange Advance.
Contact: Trevor G. Shelton (A&R), Judy Torti (PR), Shelley-Lynn Pybus (promotion).

Productions Diadem Inc.

P.O. Box 33
Pointe-Gatineau, PQ J8T 4Y8
(819) 561-4114
Subsidiary Labels: Diadem.
Canadian Artists: Diane, Denise and Marie Marleau.
Distributed By: Interdisc.

Diffusion i Media

4487 rue Adam
Montreal, PQ H1V 1T9
(514) 254-7794
FAX (514) 844-6263
Styles of Acts Handled: New Music, Media Art and Electro-Acoustic.
Subsidiary Label: empreintes DIGITALes.
Canadian Artists: Christian Calon, Robert Normandeau, Alain Thibault.
Distributed By: Diffusion i Media, Canadian Music Centre.
Contact: Jean-Francois Denis, Claude Schryer.

Direction Four Management

(A Division of The Paquin Entertainment Group)
140 Bannatyne Ave., Suite 301
Winnipeg, MB R3B 3C5
(204) 947-9200
FAX (204) 943-3588
Acts Handled: Family, Rock.
Canadian Artists: Fred Penner, Al Simmons, Jeffrey Hatcher and The Big Beat, Norman Foote.

Dirty Little Nipper Records

253 College St., Suite 340
Toronto, ON M2J 2B7
(416) 922-6297
FAX (416) 285-7104
Acts Handled: Roots related New Music.
Canadian Artists: Dr. Limbo and His Fabulous Off-Whites.
Contact: James MacLean (A&R), Sheldon Jafine (PR), Jim Duncan (promotion).

Distribution Select

500 Ste. Catherine e.
Montreal, PQ H2L 2C6
(514) 849-6201
Canadian Artists: Richard Seguin, others.
Distributed By: Distribution Select.

Downs Record Co. Ltd.

3740 Portage Ave., Suite 220
Winnipeg, MB R3K 0Z9
(204) 889-9371
Acts Handled: MOR, C&W.

Duke Street Records

204 King St. E.
Toronto, ON M5A 1J7
Acts Handled: Pop, New Music, Jazz, Instrumental.
Canadian Artists: NEO A4 Jane Siberry, Moe Koffman, Eye Eye, Manteca, Scott Merritt, Chalk Circle, Mark Korven, Hugh Marsh, Hagood Hardy.
Distributed By: MCA Records Canada Inc.

EMC Records of Canada

189 Scugog St.
Bowmanville, ON
(416) 723-8916
Acts Handled: Pop, Classical, Jazz, Country.
Comments: An independent record label specializing in Canadian music and its promotion.
Contact: Paul Andrew Smith (president), Randy Begg (A&R), Linda Begg (secretary).

E.M.O. Records Ltd.

P.O. Box 8, Site 8, R.R. 1
Shediac, NB E0A 3G0
Acts Handled: Pop, MOR, New Music, Christian, Gospel.
Canadian Artists: Myles Anderson.
Distributed By: E.M.O. Records.

Earth Records

1105 Cadboro Rd., Suite 6
Gloucester, ON K1J 7T8
(613) 747-8960
FAX (613) 745-2761
Acts Handled: Rock, New Music.
Canadian Artists: Cheetah and The Adopted.
Distributed By: Record Peddler and
independents.
Contact: Johnny Cinanni.

Elephant Records

24 Ryerson Ave., 4th floor
Toronto, ON M5T 2P3
(416) 364-3387
FAX (416) 364-1324
Acts Handled: Children's.
Canadian Artists: Sharon, Lois & Bram,
Eric Nagler.
Distributed By: A&M Records.
Contact: Alan Nagel.

Embrace Records

342 Jarvis St.
Toronto, ON M4Y 2G6
(416) 920-6969
Canadian Artists: Rain.

Empress Records/ Les Disques Empress

P.O. Box 687, Stn. NDG
Montreal, PQ H4A 3R1
(514) 735-3061

Enigma Canada Ltd.

2183 Dunwin Dr.
Mississauga, ON L5L 3S3
(416) 828-6121
Acts Handled: Pop, MOR, Rock, Metal, Jazz,
Hardcore, Dance, New Music.
Subsidiary Labels: Intima, Restless, Sytheside,
Medusa.
Distributed By: Capitol Records/EMI of
Canada.

Expression Records

4824 Cote-des-Neiges Rd., Suite 38
Montreal, PQ H3V 1G4
(514) 739-4774
Acts Handled: Soft Rock.

Fanfare Records Ltd.

467 Church St.
Toronto, ON M4Y 2C5
(416) 966-5107
Acts Handled: Classical.
Subsidiary Labels: Encore.
Canadian Artists: Maureen Forrester, Ofra
Harnoy, Andrew Davis, Riki Turofsky, Erich
Kunzel.
Distributed By: Fanfare Records, Distribution
Fusion.

Firmus Records Inc.

156 Woburn Ave.
Toronto, ON M5M 1K7
(416) 484-1728
Acts Handled: Pop, MOR.
Canadian Artists: Betty Richardson,
Milan Kymlicka.
Distributed By: Independent.

Flyin' High Records

P.O. Box 1217, R.R. 2
Odessa, ON K0H 2H0
(613) 386-3582
FAX (613) 386-3582
Acts Handled: Country.
Canadian Artists: Dieter Boehme, Anne Banks,
Dan Kennedy.
Comments: Tree Stump Publishing is an affili-
ated company.

Fogarty's Cove/ Cole Harbour Music Ltd.

23 Hillside Ave. S.
Dundas, ON L9H 4H7
(416) 627-9808
Acts Handled: Folk.
Canadian Artists: Stan Rogers, Grit Laskin,
David Parry, Friends of Fiddler's Green.
Contact: Ariel Peart.

Freedom Records

377 Ridelle Ave., Suite 1220
Toronto, ON M6B 1K2
(416) 783-5166
Acts Handled: Pop, MOR, Rock, C&W.
Canadian Artists: James Gordon, John Lewis,
Neil Merryweather, Ceedees, Tim Roland, Rick
Curtis, Diane Young.
Distributed By: Independent.

Fringe Product

P.O. Box 670, Stn. A
Toronto, ON M5W 1G2
(416) 365-7878
FAX (416) 869-0017
Acts Handled: Rock, Metal, New Music.
Subsidiary Labels: Lone Wolf Records,
Diabolic Force, Fist Fight Records.
Canadian Artists: Sacrifice, Sudden Impact,
Guilt Parade, Dayglo Abortions, Corpus Vile,
Death Sentence, Razor, Breeding Ground.
Distributed By: Electric Distribution,
Record Peddler, Groovy Times.
Contact: Angus MacKay.

Gamma Records (Quebec) Ltd.

300 Leo Pariseau, Suite 701
P.O. Box 1010, Place du Parc
Montreal, PQ H2W 2S2
(514) 842-4666
FAX (514) 843-4135
Acts Handled: Pop, MOR, Rock.
Subsidiary Labels: Gamma Publishing Co.
Canadian Artists: Robert Charlebois,
Tex Lecor, Pauline Julien, Claude Gauthier.
Distributed By: Trans-Canada.
Contact: Dan Lazare.

Goldrush Records

1234 W. 6 Ave.
Vancouver, BC V6H 1A5
(604) 733-4012
Canadian Artists: Joelle Rabu, Six Cylinder,
Dan Smith, Richard Newman.
Distributed By: Festival Records.

Great Pacific Records

1450 Johnson Rd., Suite 244
White Rock, BC V4B 1J6
FAX (604) 538-5848
Canadian Artists: Trooper, Vogen.
Distributed By: WEA.
Contact: R.A. McGuire.

Hammerhead Records

134 Peter St., Suite 314
Toronto, ON M5V 2H2
(416) 581-0198
Acts Handled: Rock, Pop, Alternative, Metal,
Jazz, Folk.
Canadian Artists: A.K.A., Wipeout Beach,
Sara Craig, Stop Screaming, Paul Wild.
Distributed By: Independent.
Contact: Paul Irvine.
Comments: New label (first release January
1990).

Happy Onion Music

P.O. Box 86183
N. Vancouver, BC V7L 4J8
(604) 986-2826
Acts Handled: New Age, Classical.
Canadian Artists: Marcia Meyer.
Distributed By: Happy Onion, various others.

Harvestholm

P.O. Box 37
Nobel, ON P0G 1G0
(705) 342-9304
Acts Handled: MOR, C&W.
Canadian Artists: Terry Christenson.
Distributed By: BGM Music.

Haute Rock Records

220-12A St. N.E.
Calgary, AB T2E 4R7
(403) 269-1356
Acts Handled: All.

Highland Records

1464 Beckworth Ave.
London, ON N5V 2K7
(519) 453-0892
FAX (519) 453-6303
Acts Handled: Scottish Traditional, Popular,
Folk.
Canadian Artists: Cromdale, 78th Fraser
Highlanders, MacNish Distillery.
Distributed By: Scott's Highland Services Ltd.
Contact: C. James Scott.

I.R.S. Records Canada

99 Sudbury St., Suite 3
Toronto, ON M6J 3S7
(416) 533-0671
FAX (416) 533-4590
Acts Handled: Rock, Pop, New Music, Metal,
Reggae, Instrumental.
Canadian Artists: Candi.
Distributed By: MCA Records Canada.
Contact: Paul Orescan (A&R), Christina
Scazighino (PR), Paul Orescan (promotion).

Icedrum Records Inc.

P.O. Box 2310, Stn. A
Sudbury, ON P3A 4S8
(705) 560-3769
FAX (705) 560-1702
Acts Handled: Pop, Rock, Funk, Rap, House,
Alternative.
Canadian Artists: John Hartman, E.T.P.,
Now We Lustre.
Contact: Cindy Olivier (PR).

Innovation Records

2145 Lakeshore Blvd. W.
Toronto, ON M8V 2Z6
(416) 255-5340
Canadian Artists: Joy Steele, Eugene Amaro,
The Brass Connection, Ed Bickert, Joe Sealy,
Rob McConnell and the Boss Brass,
Sara Hamilton & David.
Distributed By: Distribution Fusion III
(in Canada).

Intermodal Productions

P.O. Box 2199
Vancouver, BC V6B 3V7
(604) 669-4399
Acts Handled: Pop, MOR, C&W, Jazz,
Classical.
Subsidiary Labels: IPL, Rada, VLM,
Ranch House, Resurgam.
Distributed By: Independent.

ISBA Records Inc.

1327 St. Joseph St. E.
Montreal, PQ H2J 1M1
(514) 522-ISBA
Acts Handled: Pop, Rock, Dance, Alternative,
New Music.
Canadian Artists: Mitsou, Paris Black, Les
B.B., Les Taches, Nuance.
Distributed By: CBS Records Canada.
Contact: Maurice Velenosi (president).
Branch Office:
18 The Donway E., Suite 607
Don Mills, ON M3C 1X9
(416) 461-0895
Contact: Steve Sechi.

Island Records of Canada Ltd.

96 Granby St.
Toronto, ON M5B 1J1
(416) 596-8055
FAX (416) 596-1239
Acts Handled: Pop, MOR, Rock, Metal, New
Music.
Canadian Artists: Andrew Cash.
Distributed By: MCA Records Canada.
Contact: William "Skinny" Tenn (A&R), Barbara
Fraser (PR), Doug Caldwell
(promotion).

Jennie Records/Jennie Music Publishing Co.

21 Cutler Ct., P.O. Box 421
Schomberg, ON L0G 1T0
(416) 939-7900
Acts Handled: Country, MOR, Easy Listening,
A/C.
Acts Handled: Ross Allen, Ray St. Germain,
Sherisse Laurence, Razzy Bailey (U.S.).

Jewel Records

220 Browndale Cr.
Richmond Hill, ON L4C 3J1
(416) 883-4127
Acts Handled: Pop, MOR, Rock.
Canadian Artists: Neil Donell, Matt Segriff,
Louise Lambert, Craig Davidson.
Distributed By: Jewel Records.
Contact: Dalton Kehoe (A&R).

Justice Records

80 Oriole Ave.
Mississauga, ON L5G 1V2
(416) 271-0951
Canadian Artists: Kumari.
Distributed By: Independent.
Contact: Paul Gandhi (A&R).

Justin Time Records Inc./Les Disques Justin Time

5455 rue Pare, Suite 101
Montreal, PQ H4P 1P7
(514) 738-9533
FAX (514) 738-9780
Acts Handled: Pop, Comedy, French Pop,
Instrumental, Gospel, Jazz.
Canadian Artists: Oliver Jones, Oliver
Whitehead, Jon Ballantyne, Montreal Jubilation
Gospel Choir, Bowser & Blue, Dave Turner,
Ranee Lee, Marie Andree
Ostiguy, Alain Lamontagne, Young/Donato,
Sonny Greenwich, Paul Bley, Jean Beaudet.
Distributed By: Distribution Fusion III Inc.
Contact: Jim West and Caroline Lagueux.

Key Records of Canada

(A Division of Lant-International)
569 Lynwood Dr., P.O. Box 1085
Cornwall, ON K6H 5V2
(613) 938-1532
Acts Handled: Pop, MOR, C&W.
Contact: Charles W.B. Lant, CEO.

Kids' Atlast Records

General Delivery
Huntsville, ON P0A 1K0
(705) 789-6024
Acts Handled: Children's Music.
Subsidiary Labels: Kids' Atlast Records is a
subsidiary of Atlast Productions Inc., and Atlast
Records.
Canadian Artists: Beverley Glenn-Copeland.
Contact: Evelyn Wolf.

Kids' Records

68 Broadview Ave., Suite 303
Toronto, ON M4M 2E6
(416) 461-0268
Acts Handled: Children's.
Distributed By: Independent.
Contact: Bill Usher.

John Lennon Records

1801 Eglinton Ave. W.
Toronto, ON M6E 2H8
(416) 785-5669
Subsidiary Labels: Musicline International.
Canadian Artists: Mona Carrie, Carl Ellison, Hylton Cohen, J.D. Lennon.
Distributed By: Independent.
Contact: Headley Lennon (PR).

Lick 'N' Stick Records

208 Indian Grove
Toronto, ON M6P 2H2
(416) 767-6816
Canadian Artists: Paul James Band.
Distributed By: Roblan, A&A, Records on Wheels.

Lone Wolf Records

1235 Lambeth Rd.
Oakville, ON L6H 2E2
(416) 849-0244
Acts Handled: Varied.
Distributed By: The Record Peddler (Canada).

Love Productions Limited/Daffodil Records

P.O. Box 615
Don Mills, ON M3C 2T6
(416) 923-7369
FAX (416) 923-4821
Acts Handled: All.
Subsidiary Labels: Daffodil.
Canadian Artists: Crowbar, Klaatu, A Foot In Coldwater, King Biscuit Boy, Fludd, etc.
Contact: F. Davies (A&R), Lynda Squires (PR), William Ballard (promotion).

MCA Records of Canada

2450 Victoria Park Ave.
Toronto, ON M2J 4A2
(416) 491-3000
Acts Handled: All styles.
Subsidiary Labels: Chess, Chrysalis, Constellation, Crusaders, Curb, Duke St., I.R.S., Island, Motown, Zebra.
Canadian Artists: Triumph, Boulevard, Skywalk.
Contact: Dave Watt (A&R).

MCG Records

70 Yorkville Ave.
Toronto, ON M5R 1B9
(416) 922-1361

MRV Records

P.O. Box 224
Allan, SK S0K 0C0
(306) 257-3588
Acts Handled: C&W.
Canadian Artists: Madeleine.
Distributed By: Independent.

Magnum Opus Records

P.O. Box 91, Stn. T
Toronto, ON M6B 3Z9
(416) 783-0087
Acts Handled: Reggae, Pop, R&B, New Age.
Canadian Artists: Syren.
Distributed By: Independent.
Contact: Lyn Harper (A&R).

Magnum Records

8607-128 Ave.
Edmonton, AB T5E 0G3
(403) 476-8230
Acts Handled: Country.
Canadian Artists: Catheryne Greenly, Billy Jay Legere, Cormier Country (Gordon & Loretta Cormier), Nolan Murray.
Distributed By: Independent.
Contact: Bill Maxim.

Mainroads Productions Inc.

310 Judson St., Unit 14
Toronto, ON M8Z 1V3
(416) 252-9146
Acts Handled: Gospel, Contemporary Christian.
Subsidiary Labels: Jim Records.
Canadian Artists: Eye Witness, Stacey Band, Ginny Ambrose, Briddle.
Distributed By: Independent.

Manville Records

127 Manville Rd., Unit 9
Scarborough, ON M1L 4J7
(416) 288-9967
Acts Handled: All styles.
Subsidiary Labels: Sunbird.

Marigold Records Ltd.

P.O. Box 141, Stn. S
Toronto, ON M5M 4L6
(416) 484-8789
Acts Handled: Pop, MOR, Rock, C&W.
Canadian Artists: Rick Dodson, Debbie Johnson, Gloria Kaye, Fortunato, Brian Tyrrell.
Distributed By: The Moss Music Group Inc.

Marquis Records

144 Front St. W., Suite 460
Toronto, ON M5J 2L7
(416) 595-5498
Acts Handled: Classical.
Canadian Artists: Various, including Vancouver
Chamber Choir, Mark Dubois, York Winds,
Andrew Davis, Elmer Iseler, Anton Kuerti,
Catherine Robbin.
Distributed By: Electric Distribution.

Carmen Martin Productions

49 Yonge Blvd.
Toronto, ON M5M 3G7
(416) 485-2056
Acts Handled: Flamenco, Dance, Classical,
MOR.
Canadian Artists: Juan Tomas, Cuadre
Flamenco.
Distributed By: New Music, CKQT Radio,
C. Martin Productions.

Matador Records

466 Dovercourt Rd., Suite 3
Toronto, ON M6H 2W4
(416) 533-9311

Materials and Processes

3 Belvedere Blvd.
Toronto, ON M8X 1J9
(416) 231-4337
Acts Handled: Rock, New Age.

Maze Records

2373 Bloor St. W., Suite 17
Toronto, ON M6S 1P6
(416) 273-3662
Canadian Artists: Frank Marino, Saga,
Killer Dwarfs, Exciter, Virgin Steel.
Distributed By: A&M Records.

McGill Records

555 Sherbrooke St. W.
Montreal, PQ H3A 1E3
(514) 398-4537
FAX (514) 398-8061
Acts Handled: Classical.
Distributed By: Distribution Fusion III.
Contact: Dr. Paul Pederson.

Micah Records

43 Applemore Rd.
Scarborough, ON M1B 1R7
(416) 298-3108
Acts Handled: Gospel, Children's.
Canadian Artists: Sweet Sound, Toronto
AGMM Mass Choir. The Trinity Singers.
Distributed By: Micah Distribution.
Contact: Oswald Burke (A&R), Karen Burke
(PR), Courtney Williams (promotion).

Muffin Record Co.

238 Davenport Rd., Suite 348
Toronto, ON M5R 1J6
(416) 591-7785
Acts Handled: Children's, French.
Canadian Artists: Matt Maxwell.
Distributed By: Independent.

Music Machine Records

P.O. Box 541
Regina, SK S4P 3A2
Acts Handled: Pop, MOR, Rock, C&W.
Canadian Artists: Donald LeBlanc.
Distributed By: Independent.

Musica Viva Records

P.O. Box 500, Stn. A.
Toronto, ON M5W 1E6
(416) 975-3502
Acts Handled: Classical.
Canadian Artists: Quartango.
Comments: Affiliated with CBC Enterprises.

Mystery Records

19 Nealon Ave.
Toronto, ON M4K 1Y8
(416) 429-6570
Acts Handled: New Age, Pop.
Canadian Artists: Polar Life, Alan Douglas,
Dada, The Graham Thomas Band.

Nettwerk Productions

1755 Robson St., P.O. Box 330
Vancouver, BC V6G 1C9
(604) 687-8649
Acts Handled: Music with artistic and
commercial viability.
Canadian Artists: Grapes of Wrath, Skinny
Puppy, Moev, The Water Walk, Pretty Green,
The Tea Garden, Sarah McLachlan.

Newsflash Sounds
P.O. Box 333
Grand Falls, NF A2A 2J7
(709) 489-9496
Acts Handled: Country, Country Gospel, MOR.
Canadian Artists: John Lane, Doug Lane, Wally White, Sandra Burt, Keith Whittall.
Distributed By: Newsflash Distributing.

Nightlife Records Inc.
4091 Pheasant Run
Mississauga, ON L5L 2C2
(416) 820-6400
FAX (416) 820-9512
Subsidiary Labels: Advent Records, JCO Records.
Canadian Artists: Peter Foldy, Joey Cee, Task Force, Power Patrol, Camilleri, Elay Orchestra, Stars On Steel, Endless Wave, Keith Fromm.
Distributed By: Nightlife Records.
Contact: Joey Cee.

Les Disques Nobel
2328 Sherbrooke St. E., Suite 3
Montreal, PQ H2H 1E5
Acts Handled: Pop, MOR, Rock.
Subsidiary Labels: Les Disques No. 1.
Canadian Artists: Rene Simard, Nathalie Simard, Alain Barriere.
Distributed By: Distribution Trans-Canada.

Nosferatu Records
P.O. Box 304, Stn. S
Montreal, PQ H4E 4J8
(514) 769-9096
Acts Handled: Pop, Rock, Metal.
Canadian Artists: Trop Feross.
Distributed By: Independent.

Og Music
P.O. Box 182, Stn. F
Montreal, PQ H3J 2L1
(514) 937-9425
Acts Handled: Punk, Rockabilly, Psychedelic, Country.
Canadian Artists: Deja Voodoo, others.
Distributed By: The Record Peddler, Bonaparte, Zulu.

ohama records/ midnite news
P.O. Box 90
Rainer, AB T0J 2M0
(403) 362-5601
Acts Handled: New Music.
Canadian Artists: 21 Hundrez, ohama, Lola.
Distributed By: Record Peddler, Bonaparte, Beaches.

One-Eyed Duck Recording and Publishing
49 Rainsford Rd.
Toronto, ON M4L 3N7
(416) 694-6900
Acts Handled: Children's.
Canadian Artists: Sphere Clown Band.
Distributed By: Independent.

Pacific Wave Records
68 Water St., Suite 203
Vancouver, BC V6B 1A4
(604) 681-1193
Acts Handled: Pop, Rock, C&W.
Canadian Artists: Sue Medley, Baby Face.
Distributed By: Electric Distribution.

Paradise Records
205A Lakeshore Rd. E.
Mississauga, ON L5G 1G2
(416) 891-0336
FAX (416) 278-1799
Acts Handled: Metal, Commercial Rock, New Music, MOR, Blues, Jazz, Progressive Rock-Fusion.
Canadian Artists: Ancient Tribe, Ginzia, The Call.
Distributed By: Independent.
Contact: Mark McLay (A&R), B. Reck (PR), Bernadine Reck (promotion).

Parallel One Records
1622 W. 7 Ave., Suite 301
Vancouver, BC V6J 1S5
(604) 736-0434
Acts Handled: Pop, Rock.
Canadian Artists: Body Electric, Jato.

Disques Patrimoine
273 rue Principale, P.O. Box 148
Charlevoix, PQ G0A 2M0
(418) 635-2466
Acts Handled: Folk.
Distributed By: Independent.

Penta Entertainment Inc.
68 Water St., Suite 406
Vancouver, BC V6B 1A4
(604) 688-7274

Polaris Productions Ltd.
1151 Drouillard Rd.
Windsor, ON N8Y 2R2
(519) 973-4944
Comments: Recording company.

PolyGram Inc.
6000 Cote-de-Liesse
St. Laurent, PQ H4T 1E3
(514) 739-2701
Labels Owned or Distributed: Abkco, Airea, Alm. O.R., Alert, Apprentice, Atlantic Artists, Baby Boomers, Banzai, Barclay, Beggars Banquet, Big Time, Capricorn, Casablanca, Coda, De-Lite, Deram, Deutsche Grammophon (Galleria Signature, Resonance, Favorit, Focus, Imago, Walkman, Pocket Music, Panorama Classics, Musikfest, DG Special, Super Concerts, Archiv Produktion), Drefus, ECM, Emarcy, Erdenklang, 4 A.D., Factory, Fontana, G-Discs!, GRP Ice, Kent, Kid Stuff, Landscape, London (Pop; Classical — Oiseau Lyre, Argo, Argo Spoken Word, Jubilee, Ovation, Viva, World Of, Weekend Classics, Opera Gala, Cinema Gala), Limelight, Mercury, Metal Beat, MMC, MPS. Parrot, Philips (Pop; Classical - Silver Line, Classics on Tour, Festivo, Sequenza, Living Baroque, Musica Da Camera, Mercury), Polydor, Polydor/Oyster, Polytel, Profile, Riva, RSO, Smash, Telarc, Teldec, (Telefunken, Noblesse), Threshold, U.R.T.I., Vertigo, Verve, WAA, Wing. Wonderland, DJM, Strange Fruit, Gold Castle. Roulette, Bludgeon Riffola/Vertigo.
Canadian Artists: Gino Vannelli, Baron Longfellow, Pierre Bertrand, Diane Tell, Montreal Symphony Orchestra, Angela Hewitt, Eight Seconds, Marie-Michelle Desrosiers, Refugee, Zamfir, Deaf Dealer, Cindy Valentine, Men Without Hats.
Contact: Bob Ansell (PR, promotion).
Branch Offices:
Airway Centre
5945 Airport Rd., Suite 155
Mississauga, ON L4V 1R9
(416) 677-2500 or 677-1641

16 Berkshire Bay
Winnipeg, MB R2J 2M1
(204) 233-0192 or 235-1667

7220 Fisher St. S.E., Suite 320
Calgary, AB T2H 2H8
(403) 253-7665

805 W. Broadway, Mezzanine
Vancouver, BC V5Z 1K1
(604) 873-2466

Power Records
3447 Kennedy Rd., Unit 4
Scarborough, ON M1V 3S1
(416) 754-2653
Acts Handled: Pop, Dance.
Subsidiary Labels: Boulevard, Chateau, Blackout.
Canadian Artists: Never...But Always.
Distributed By: Electric Distribution.
Contact: Vincent Degiorgio (A&R), Music Brokers (PR).

Pure Pacific Music
31905 Woodcock Cr.
Mission, BC V2V 4K2
(604) 826-4946
FAX (604) 826-4355
Acts Handled: Light Country.
Canadian Artists: Laurie Thain, John Arpin.
Distributed By: Festival Records, Vancouver.

Quantum Records
170A Baldwin St.
Toronto, ON M5T 1L8
(416) 593-9547
FAX (416) 593-0461
Acts Handled: Pop, Rock, MOR.
Canadian Artists: Mad About Plaid, Steve Fox, Look People, Jay W. McGee, Harlow.
Distributed By: Electric Distribution.
Contact: Mike Alyanak (A&R), Jane Harbury (PR), Anya Wilson (promotion).

Radioactive Records
11160-136 St.
Surrey, BC V3R 3B6
(604) 584-6350
Acts Handled: Rock.
Canadian Artists: Sparkling Apple.

Raging Records
P.O. Box 7473, Stn. E
Calgary, AB T3C 3M3
(403) 228-9980
FAX (403) 292-3555
Acts Handled: Rock.
Canadian Artists: Forbidden Dimension, Color Me Psycho, Enemy Mind Feel.
Contact: Greg Dinwoodie.

Rana Records
2475 Dunbar St.
Vancouver, BC V6R 3N1
(604) 734-4617
Acts Handled: Pop, MOR, Rock, C&W.
Canadian Artists: Various.

Random Records
209A Madison Ave.
Toronto, ON M5R 2S6
(416) 538-2666
FAX (416) 538-0583
Acts Handled: Pop, Rock, MOR, Country.
Canadian Artists: Timeline, Peter Randall,
Shaun Firth.
Contact: Peter Randall.

Regal Recordings Ltd.
2421 Hammond Rd.
Mississauga, ON L5K 1T3
(416) 855-2370
FAX (416) 855-1773
Acts Handled: Jazz.
Canadian Artists: Oscar Peterson.
Distributed By: Fantasy, Polydor.

Reveal Productions Ltd.
4322 Cleroux Blvd.
Laval, PQ H7T 2E3
(514) 687-8966
Acts Handled: Rock, Classical.
Subsidiary Labels: Reveal.
Canadian Artists: Ted Paul and Gary
Barnet, Gaetan Amos, Ron Cash, Henry
Dermer, Mike Walker.
Distributed By: Independent.
Branch Offices:
4738 Beatrice
Vancouver, BC V5N 4J3

Revolving Records
190 Don Park Rd., Unit 16
Markham, ON L3R 2V8
(416) 470-7730
FAX (416) 470-7739
Acts Handled: Dance music.
Canadian Artists: Kon Kan.
Distributed By: Starsound Records (416)
470-7730.
Contact: Sepehr Azari.

Riptide Records
18 The Donway E, Suite 607
Don Mills, ON M3C 1X9
(416) 445-0678
Acts Handled: Pop, Commercial, A/C.
Canadian Artists: Joe Vincent.
Contact: Steve Sechi (A&R).

Riser Records
5045 Sidley St.
Burnaby, BC V5J 1T6
Acts Handled: Pop, MOR, Rock, New
Music.
Subsidiary Labels: Colly Records.
Canadian Artists: Dorian, Medd & Shaw,
Menage a Trois.
Distributed By: Independent.

Rising Records
23 Lascelles Blvd., Suite 1802
Toronto, ON M4V 2B9
(416) 483-4473
Acts Handled: Children's.
Subsidiary Labels: Cubbyhole Records.

Risque Disque Inc.
25 Draper St.
Toronto, ON M5V 2M3
(416) 596-0353
FAX (416) 596-8120
Acts Handled: Pop, MOR, Rock, Reggae.
Canadian Artists: Basic English, Blue
Rodeo, Crash Vegas, The Sattalites, Bob
Wiseman.
Contact: Tonni Nielsen and Terry Brown
(A&R), Peter Vitols (PR and promotion).

Roto-Noto Records
148 Erin Ave.
Hamilton, ON L8K 4W3
(416) 572-7474
Acts Handled: Pop, MOR, Rock, C&W.
Canadian Artists: Various.
Distributed By: Various.

Rumenal Records of Canada
P.O. Box 730, Stn. C
Toronto, ON M6J 3S1
(416) 367-0925
Acts Handled: Pop, MOR, Rock, C&W,
New Music.
Subsidiary Labels: Barron Records, Try
Me Records.
Canadian Artists: Six Gun Justice, Sam
Spada, Frank Carlone and the Good Things,
A.B. Trail, The Nomen Rumenals, Afterimage.
Distributed By: Rumenal Records Canada.
Contact: J.M. Pedrow and Bill Culp (A&R),
R. Van Langen (promotion).

SGB Records
P.O. Box 714
Guelph, ON N1H 6L3
(519) 767-0142
Acts Handled: Folk, Kids', New Folk.
Canadian Artists: Tamarack, James
Gordon.
Distributed By: Record Peddler.
Contact: Sue Richards.

Sackville Records
64 Dundas St. E.
Toronto, ON M5B 1C7
(416) 593-7320

Savannah Music Inc.
5409 Eglinton Ave. W., Suite 104
Etobicoke, ON M9C 5K6
(416) 620-0396
FAX (416) 620-0398
Acts Handled: Country.
Canadian Artists: Terry Carisse, Gary
Fjellgaard, The Good Brothers, Matt
Minglewood, Anita Perras.
Distributed By: WEA Music of Canada Ltd.
Contact: Sylvia Witkowski (A&R), Deborah
Wood (PR and promotions).

Schoolhouse
P.O. Box 8004, Stn. F
Calgary, AB T2J 4V2
(403) 293-2700
Acts Handled: Children's.
Canadian Artists: Lee and Sandy Paley.
Distributed By: Independent.

Scone Records
R.R.1 Fulford Harbour
Salt Spring Island, BC V0S 1C0
(604) 653-4563
Canadian Artists: Susan Cogan.

Scratch Records
P.O. Box 5381
Whitehorse, YK Y1A 4Z2
(403) 668-4046
Acts Handled: Jazz, Contemporary, New
Music.

Second Avenue Records
472 Dupont St.
Toronto, ON M5R 1W6
(416) 967-5721

Sensible Records
20 Shudell Ave.
Toronto, ON M4J 1C6
(416) 466-4534
Acts Handled: New Music.
Canadian Artists: Ten Commandments,
Los Pops, L'etranger.
Distributed By: Independent.

721 Records
P.O. Box 296, Stn. J
Toronto, ON M4J 4Y1
(416) 425-3692
Acts Handled: Pop, Funk, Hip Hop, House,
Rap.
Canadian Artists: Sisi & The Beat.
Distributed By: Roblan, Record Peddler,
Independent.

Seventh Sword Productions
312 Adelaide St. W., Suite 415
Toronto, ON M5V 1R2
(416) 960-3123
Acts Handled: Rock.
Canadian Artists: City Speak, Those Guys.
Distributed By: Seventh Sword
Productions.
Contact: Ian Gregory Wright.

Shaky Records
P.O. Box 71, Stn. C
Winnipeg, MB R3M 3S3
(204) 474-2956
Acts Handled: Hard Rock.
Canadian Artists: Lawsuit.
Distributed By: Record Peddler, Roblan,
Sound Insight.
Contact: Shaky.

Shaman Records
1578 Erin St.
Winnipeg, MB R3E 2T1
(204) 774-3715
Acts Handled: New Age, New Music, Pop,
Rock.

Shotgun Music Corp.
1242 Colborne St. E.
Brantford, ON N3T 5L4
(519) 752-0839
Acts Handled: Pop, MOR, Rock, C&W,
Gospel.
Subsidiary Labels: Shotgun, Empire, Solid
State, Listen.
Canadian Artists: Danny Thompson, Linda
Lee, The Breeze, Lisa McCrory, Ron Martin,
Jim Windle, Charlie Clemens.
Distributed By: Independent.

Signature Records
500 Newbold St.
London, ON N6E 1K6
(519) 686-5060
Acts Handled: Country, Pop, MOR, Rock.
Contact: Geoff Keymer.

Slak Records
214 St. George St., Suite 608
Toronto, ON M5R 2N8
(416) 964-0695
Acts Handled: R&B, Pop, Dance.
Canadian Artists: Lorraine Scott.
Contact: Al Kussin (A&R).

Snocan Enterprises Limited
2415 Holly Lane
Ottawa, ON K1V 7P2
(613) 731-4668
Acts Handled: All styles.
Subsidiary Labels: Icicle Records.
Distributed By: Pose Distribution.

Snowy River Records
P.O. Box 459, Stn. J
Toronto, ON M4J 4Z2
(416) 461-5083
Canadian Artists: Alex Sinclair, Donna Streen, The Fabulous Cowbelles.
Distributed By: Independent.

Soffwin Records
4990 Fulton St.
Montreal, PQ H3W 1V4
(514) 737-2470 or (416) 594-0701
Acts Handled: Contemporary Acoustic.
Canadian Artists: Noah Zacharin.
Distributed By: Soffwin Records.
Contact: Noah Zacharin.

Somersault Records
431 Queen St. E.
Toronto, ON M5A 1T5
(416) 365-1509
Acts Handled: Pop, Rock.
Canadian Artists: The New Buildings, Vis-a-Vis, Nebula, Rita Johns, Candid.
Distributed By: Electric Distribution.

Sometimes We Do This...Musical Productions
P.O. Box 805, Stn. P
Toronto, ON M5S 2Z1
(416) 921-3806
Acts Handled: New Celtic Music, Bagpipe, Jazz, Funk, Fusion.
Canadian Artists: Rare Air.
Distributed By: Independent.

Sound Source Productions
24 St. Clair Ave. W.
Toronto, ON M4V 1L4
Acts Handled: Progressive Rock, Top 40.
Canadian Artists: Emergency Task Force, Grim Reaper, Glammatron, Zero One, Magnum Prodigy.

Spin Records
300 Trillium Dr.
Kitchener, ON N2E 2K6
(519) 893-1172
Acts Handled: Pop, MOR, C&W.
Canadian Artists: James Warren, Madonna Tassi, Nikki, Terry Odette, Random Access, Mary Anne.
Distributed By: Independent.

Star Records
148 Simcoe St.
Oshawa, ON L1H 4G7
(416) 723-0040
Acts Handled: Rock.
Canadian Artists: The Forgotten Rebels, others.
Distributed By: Independent.

Stony Plain Recording Co. Ltd.
P.O. Box 861
Edmonton, AB T5J 2L8
(403) 468-6423
FAX (403) 465-8491
Acts Handled: Country, Roots, Traditional, Blues, Jazz, R&B.
Canadian Artists: Ian Tyson, Sylvia Tyson, Downchild Blues Band, Paul James Band, Long John Baldry, Big Miller, Shuffle Demons, Amos Garrett, King Biscuit Boy.
Distributed By: WEA Canada.
Contact: Holger Petersen.

Stubby Records
401 Richmond St. W., Suite 219
Toronto, ON M5V 1X3
(416) 340-9245
FAX (416) 340-9951
Acts Handled: Jazz, Bop Rap, Dense Music.
Canadian Artists: The Shuffle Demons, Vector.
Contact: Richard Underhill.

Sun-Scape Records
(A Division of Sun-Scape Enterprises Limited.)
P.O. Box 793, Stn. F
Toronto, ON M4Y 2N7
(416) 221-2461
FAX (416) 881-8119
Acts Handled: Classical, New Music.
Canadian Artists: The Star-Scape Singers, The Earthstage Actors. (spoken word dramatic presentation with original music).
Distributed By: Sun-Scape Records.
Contact: Linda Roedl (A&R), Valerie Webster (PR), Susan Alberghini (promotion).

Sunset Records
508 Queen St. W., Suite 200
Toronto, ON M5V 2B3
(416) 361-3266
Acts Handled: Rock, Reggae, R&B, Classical, Pop.
Subsidiary Labels: Version Records.
Canadian Artists: Messenjah, Lazy Jane, Peter Mathers, Rique Franks, No Choice, Stesha.
Distributed By: Electric, Fusion.

Sunshine Records
228 Selkirk Ave.
Winnipeg, MB R2W 2L6
(204) 586-8057
Acts Handled: Pop, MOR, C&W, Old Time Country, Ethnic.
Subsidiary Labels: Charish Records, Hot Wax, Baba Records.
Distributed By: Independent.

Tandem Records Inc.
5231 MacMahon St.
Montreal, PQ H4V 2B8
(514) 482-9836
FAX (514) 738-9256
Acts Handled: Pop, Rock.
Canadian Artists: Moral Support, Durante, Wolfe, The Buzz Band, George Hills.
Distributed By: Looking for a new distributor.
Contact: John Morin (A&R), Anya Wilson (PR and promotion).

Tembo Music Canada Inc.
225 Mutual St.
Toronto, ON M5B 2B4
(416) 593-5450
FAX (416) 977-7147
Acts Handled: Pop, MOR, C&W.
Canadian Artists: Carroll Baker, Louisa Florio.
Distributed By: BMG.
Contact: J. Edward Preston (A&R), Sharyn (Sam) Patsas (PR).

The Theory Works
2004 Fernwood Ave.
Victoria, BC V8T 2V9
(604) 389-0252
Canadian Artists: Various.

Together Records
R.R. 1
Claremont, ON L0H 1E0
(416) 294-9488.
FAX (416) 649-2951
Acts Handled: All styles.
Subsidiary Labels: Chalet Studio.
Canadian Artists: Chester, accepting new acts.
Contact: Everett Ravestein and David Chester.

Tower Town Tunes
19 Sandford Ave.
Toronto, ON M4L 2E6
(416) 463-0110
Acts Handled: Various.
Canadian Artists: Perfect World.
Distributed By: Various.

Transmission Records
1180 St. Antoine W., Suite 407
Montreal, PQ H3C 1B4
(514) 866-6091
Canadian Artists: Roland Gagnon, E.J. Brule, M.A.D.
Distributed By: RCA, Bonaparte Transmission.

Trebas Records
451 St. Jean St.
Montreal, PQ H2Y 2R5
(514) 845-4141
Acts Handled: Pop, MOR, Rock, New Music.
Distributed By: Trebas Institute.
Contact: Dave Leonard.

Troubadour Records
6043 Yonge St.
Willowdale, ON M2M 3W3
(416) 222-2592

True North Records
151 St. John St., Suite 301
Toronto, ON M5V 2T2
(416) 596-8696
Canadian Artists: Bruce Cockburn.

Ugly Dog Records

P.O. Box 1583
Brantford, ON N3T 5V6
(519) 753-2081
Acts Handled: Rock & Roll, New Jazz.
Canadian Artists: The Children, Stu
Broomer and John Mars, The Recognitions,
The Popp Tarts, The Martians.
Distributed By: Ugly Dog (Canada), Bomp
(U.S.), Move (U.K.).
Contact: Marilyn Guest (A&R), John Mars
(PR).

Umbrella

c/o Trend Records & Tapes Ltd.
47 Racine Rd.
Toronto, ON M9W 6B2
(416) 749-6601
FAX (416) 749-3918
Acts Handled: Canadian talent.
Canadian Artists: Boss Brass, Canadian
Brass, Toronto Chamber Orchestra, Rough
Trade.
Distributed By: Trend Ltd.
Contact: Jeff Bolter (A&R), Abby Sholzberg
(PR and promotion).

Uptown Records/ Glen A. Fraser Ent.

10751-63 St.
Edmonton, AB T6A 2N2
Acts Handled: Country.
Canadian Artists: Brian Sklar.

VOT Records

P.O. Box 5395, Stn. B
Montreal, PQ H3B 4P1
(514) 457-3691
Acts Handled: Pop, Rock, New Music.
Canadian Artists: Weather Permitting, Se-
cret Act.
Distributed By: Fusion III.

Vibration Records/Roy Jourdan Publishing

P.O. Box 245, Stn. Place du Parc
Montreal, PQ H2W 2N8
(514) 987-1198
FAX (514) 987-1204
Canadian Artists: Michael Roy, Roger
Gravel.
Distributed By: Musidisc (Europe).

Vice Records

68 Water St., Suite 303
Vancouver, BC V6B 1A4
(604) 684-5115
Acts Handled: Pop, Rock.
Canadian Artists: Brian Trudeau, Urban
Heat.
Distributed By: Independent.

Vilnius Records of Canada

5400 Louis Badaillac
Carignan, PQ J3L 4A7
(514) 376-3261
Acts Handled: Lithuanian Folk Music.
Canadian Artists: Lithuanian groups and
choirs.
Distributed By: Fusion III.

Virgin Records Canada Inc.

167 Merizzi St.
St. Laurent, PQ H4T 1Y3
(514) 733-5358
FAX (514) 733-3608
Acts Handled: Pop, MOR, Rock, C&W,
Metal, New Music.
Subsidiary Labels: Lupins Records.
Canadian Artists: Rita MacNeil, Northern
Pikes, Colin James, Sway, G N P, Mary
Margaret O'Hara, Handsome Ned.
Distributed By: A&M Records Canada.
Contact: Yves Lamarche.

WEA Music of Canada Ltd.

1810 Birchmount Rd.
Scarborough, ON M1P 2J1
(416) 291-2515
FAX (416) 291-6044
Acts Handled: All styles.
Subsidiary Labels: Canadian affiliates
include Bonair, Penta, Stony Plain, Savannah.
Canadian Artists: Honeymoon Suite, Blue
Rodeo, Brighton Rock, Frozen Ghost, George
Fox, Spirit of The West, Alannah Myles.
Distributed By: WEA.
Contact: Bob Roper (A&R), Nigel Best (PR),
Kevin Shea (promotion).
Branch Offices:
1792 Birchmount Rd.
Scarborough, ON
(416) 754-7861
FAX (416) 754-7865
Contact: Herb Forgie.

68 Water St., Suite 400
Vancouver, BC V6B 1A4
(604) 684-7417
FAX (604) 684-2839
Contact: Randy Stark.

6325-12 St. S.E., Unit #12
Calgary, AB T2H 2K1
Contact: Alex Clark.

24 Northview Ave.
Moncton, NB E1C 8Z1
(506) 389-2538
FAX (506) 389-9141
Contact: John Poirier.

184 Merizzi St.
St. Laurent, PQ H4T 1E7
(514) 731-6401
FAX (514) 738-3051
Contact: Ken Dion.

12204-144 Ave.
Edmonton, AB T5X 2M4
(403) 456-1685
FAX (403) 457-6579
Contact: Lina Botto.

906 Meadowlands Dr. E.
Ottawa, ON K2C 0K3
(613) 723-8201
FAX (613) 723-7984
Contact: Mary Armstrong.

2115-118 St., Suite 17
Edmonton, AB T6J 5N1
(403) 438-3993
FAX (403) 436-0957
Contact: Marilyn Brodeur.

465 Castle Grove Boul., Suite 402
London, ON N6G 3R8
(519) 473-1456
FAX (519) 473-2189
Contact: Dale Kotyk.

1625 Dublin Ave., Suite 124
Winnipeg, MB R3H 0W3
(204) 783-2346
FAX (204) 772-4041.
Contact: Jeff Storry.

6301 Quinpool Rd.
Halifax, NS B3L 1A4
(902) 852-4278
FAX (902) 852-3739
Contact: Wendy Salsman.

7537 Place des Grebes
Charny, PQ G6X 2C1
(418) 832-7011
FAX (418) 832-7028
Contact: Luc Laroche.

3344 Dawson Cr.
Regina, SK S4R 6K7
(306) 545-5905
FAX (306) 775-3315
Contact: Kevin Korchinski.

187 Robinson Ave., 1st Floor
Hamilton, ON L8P 1Z7
(416) 529-9186
Contact: Connie Stefanson.

Wave Records
40 Stewart Blvd.
Brockville, ON K6V 4W1
(613) 345-2879
Acts Handled: Rock, New Music.
Canadian Artists: Moral Panic.
Distributed By: Independent.

Westar Records
502-45 St. W., Suite 3
Saskatoon, SK S7L 6H2
(306) 244-2815
FAX (306) 242-3301
Acts Handled: Pop, MOR, Rock, C&W,
Metal, New Music.
Canadian Artists: May Run, The Johner
Brothers, Glen Stace, Against the Grain, Lori
Van.
Distributed By: Electric Distribution.
Contact: Blaine Wilkins.

Windchime Records
99 Ivy Ave.
Toronto, ON M4L 2H8
(416) 465-7688
Acts Handled: Jazz, Pop, Rock, Folk.
Canadian Artists: Terry Watada, Night's
Disgrace, Roy Miya.
Distributed By: Windchime Records.
Contact: T. Watada.

Zonik Records
P.O. Box 223, Sub 11
Edmonton, AB T6G 2E0
(403) 432-0430
Acts Handled: Pop, Rock, Electric.
Distributed By: Independent.
Contact: Wilfred Kozub (PR).

Zulu Records
1869 W. 4 Ave.
Vancouver, BC V6J 1M4
(604) 738-3232
Acts Handled: Pop, Psychedelia, Rock,
New Music.
Canadian Artists: Enigmas, Go For Three,
Phil Smith, The Actionauts, Slow, Brilliant
Orange.
Distributed By: Record Peddler,
Independent.

A & M Records of Canada Limited

939 Warden Ave.
Scarborough, ON M1L 4C5
(416) 752-7191
FAX (416) 752-0059
Lines Carried: Various.
Accounts: Rackjobbers, sub-distributors, one-stops and retailers.
New Lines Accepted: Yes.
Coverage: Canada.
Comments: Offices in Toronto, Vancouver, Calgary, Montreal, Edmonton, Winnipeg, Ottawa, Halifax and London (see Record Companies).

AMOK Import & Distribution

P.O. Box 7309, Vanier Terminal
Ottawa, ON K1L 8E4
(613) 746-5572
Lines Carried: AMOK Records, EXIL Musik, JARO/FUEGO, Temporary Music, Biber Records, Schreckschuss Platten, IndepenDance.
Accounts: Record stores, mail orders, exports.
New Lines Accepted: Yes.
Coverage: Canada.

AMS Records & Tapes

(A Divsion of Climax Industries Ltd.)
635 Main St. E.
Milton, ON L9T 3J2
(416) 878-8803
FAX (416) 878-8805
Lines Carried: Pro-Arte, Pro-Jazz, Cinedisc, Maxi-Play, Quintessence, Critic's Choice, Halpern Sound, Feels So Good, Nova, Fanfare, Maximus, Sheffield Lab, Mobile Fidelity.
Accounts: Record retailers, chains, independents, audio retailers, mail order.
New Lines Accepted: Yes.
Coverage: Canada.
Comments: Most labels are either owned or licensed. Canadian artists looking for Canadian or international manufacturing and distribution are invited to call. Preference is given to classical, new age and jazz artists.

Alta Record Distributors Ltd.

5326-1A St. S.E.
Calgary, AB T2H 1J2
(403) 252-7322
Lines Carried: The Emeralds, Era International, K5, Country Records, R. Steinhoff Wholesale, Royalty Records, Haney Old Time Fiddlers, Snow Goose, Cole Harbour, Fogarty's Cove.
Accounts: Rackjobbers and retailers.
New Lines Accepted: Yes.
Coverage: Western Canada.

Anderson Impex Enr.
65 Hillcrest Ave.
Ville St. Pierre, PQ H8R 1J3
(514) 484-4587
FAX (514) 484-3592
Lines Carried: Importing and distribution of all Brazilian labels.
Accounts: A&A, Sam the Record Man, specialty retail stores.
New Lines Accepted: No.
Coverage: Canada and the Northeastern U.S.

Atlantica Music
1800 Argyle St., Suite 507
Halifax, NS B3J 3N8
(902) 422-7000
FAX (902) 422-2929
Lines Carried: Distribution of music products from Atlantic Canada.

Audio Market Sales
633 Main St. E.
Milton, ON L9T 3J2
(416) 878-8803
FAX (416) 878-8805
Lines Carried: CDs, records, tapes.

Auracle Records/ Here Records
10808-82 Ave.
Edmonton, AB T6E 2B3
(403) 439-6564
FAX (403) 457-0292
Lines Carried: Art of Mix, Hot Tracks, Ultimix, Disconet, NRG Mixx, Prime Cuts, Rhythm Stick, Clubtrax, Mixx-It, T-Dance, On The Beat, Razormaid, Intense.
Accounts: DJs, nightclubs, record company personnel and radio stations.
New Lines Accepted: Yes.
Coverage: Canada.

BMG Music Canada Inc.
151 John St., Suite 109
Toronto, ON M5V 2T2
(416) 586-0454
FAX (416) 586-0022
Lines Carried: RCA, Arista, Eureka, Bookshop, Camden, Oriola, Damon, Tembo.
Accounts: Retail stores and wholesale jobbers.
Branches:
2245 Markham Rd.
Scarborough, ON M1B 2W3

2070 Oxford St.
Halifax, NS B3L 2T2

5460 ave. Mont-Royal, Suite 101
Montreal, PQ H4P 1H7

1625 Dublin Ave., Suite 120
Winnipeg, MB R3H 0W3

4849 Fraser St., Suite 103
Vancouver, BC V5V 4H5

2880 Glenmore Tr. S.E., Suite 145
Calgary, AB T2C 2E7

Beam 103 Audio-Arts
155 Libery Ave., Basement
Toronto, ON
(416) 531-5443
Lines Carried: Various experimental progressive bands e.g., Abstract Gallery, Dreaming of Beauty, Alstress, Syntax Error.
New Lines Accepted: Yes.
Coverage: Canada, North America, Europe.
Comments: This distribution service is strictly involved with experimental bands and labels. All recording, dubbing and distribution is done in-house.

CBC Enterprises/ Les Entreprises Radio-Canada
P.O. Box 500, Stn. A
Toronto, ON M5W 1E6
(416) 975-3500
FAX (416) 975-3482
Lines Carried: SM5000, Musicaviva, Jazzimage, RCI, WRC.
Coverage: International.
Branch:
P.O. Box 6440, Stn. A
Montreal, PQ H3C 3L4
(514) 285-2687

CBS Records Canada Ltd.

1121 Leslie St.
Don Mills, ON M3C 2J9
(416) 447-3311
FAX (416) 447-6973
Lines Carried: Columbia, Epic, Anthem, CBS Associated, Pasha, T-Neck, Tabu, Carrere, Kiddin' Round, Caribou, Nemperor, PIQ, Scotti Bors, Private T, Silver Blue, Full Moon, Masterworks, True North, Def Jam, WTG.
Branches:
610G-70 Ave. S.E.
Glenmore Centre
Calgary, AB T2H 2G2
(403) 253-8719

1847 W. Broadway, Suite 101
Vancouver, BC V6J 1Y6
(604) 734-5151

3550 Ashby Rd.
St. Laurent, PQ H4R 2C1
(514) 337-6896

602 Blythwood Ave.
Riverview, NB E1B 2H5
(506) 386-1515

Canadian Music Centre Distribution Service

20 St. Joseph St.
Toronto, ON M4Y 1J9
(416) 961-6601
FAX (416) 961-7198
Lines Carried: Centrediscs, Melbourne, SNE, McGill University, Music Gallery Editions, independents.
Accounts: Record chains, independent stores, universities, libraries, schools, mail order.
New Lines Accepted: Yes.
Coverage: International.

Capitol Records/ EMI of Canada Ltd.

3109 American Dr.
Mississauga, ON L4V 1B2
(416) 677-5050
FAX (416) 677-1651
Lines Carried: Anthem, Aquarius.
Coverage: Canada.
Branches:
9924 Cote-de-Liesse Rd.
Montreal, PQ H8T 1A1
(514) 631-9072

7180-11 St. S.E., Suite 103
Calgary, AB T2H 5S9
(403) 258-2336

2182 W. 12 Ave., Suite 103
Vancouver, BC V6K 2N4
(604) 736-6691

Cargo Records

747A Guy St.
Montreal, PQ H3J 1T6
(514) 939-7186
FAX (514) 939-7185
Lines Carried: SST, WaxTrax, Cruz, Cargo, Dischord, Bondage.
Accounts: Retail stores, sub-distributors.
New Lines Accepted: Yes.
Coverage: Canada, U.S., U.K.
Branch:
2243 North Clybourn
Chicago, IL 60614
(312) 935-5683
FAX (312) 935-6218

Celtic Distributors Ltd.

15016-62 St.
Edmonton, AB
(403) 478-6417
Lines Carried: Highway, Lismor, Topic, Temple, Iona, REL, Vunkeld Klub.
Accounts: Chains, independents, libraries.
New Lines Accepted: Yes.
Coverage: National.

Circle "M" Records

P.O. Box 972
Mount Forest, ON N0G 2L0
(519) 323-2810
Lines Carried: Country music.
Accounts: Any and all.
New Lines Accepted: No.
Coverage: Canada.

Claymar Record Sales

P.O. Box 112
Weymouth, NS B0W 3T0
(902) 837-4338
Lines Carried: County, Boot, Candor, Gusto, independents.
Accounts: Retail, small businesses, wholesale.
New Lines Accepted: Yes.
Coverage: International.
Comments: Deals only with country and bluegrass. Basically a mail order business (both wholesale and retail) selling country and bluegrass product from a variety of labels.

Dancin' Fast Independent Record Distributors

14 Tullamore Dr.
Willowdale, ON M2L 2E8
(416) 445-3414
Lines Carried: Numerous independently-owned U.S. and U.K. record labels.
Accounts: Retailers dealing with specialty, imported, collectable, and independently-released records.
New Lines Accepted: Yes.
Coverage: Ontario and Quebec.
Comments: Specializing in distribution of independently-released domestic and imported recordings.

Distribution Fusion III Inc.

5455 rue Pare, Suite 101
Montreal, PQ H4P 1P7
(514) 738-4600
FAX (514) 737-9780
Lines Carried: Charly, Ace, Demon, Blacksaint/ Soul Note, Celestial Harmonies, Parkwood, Unity, McGill, Vergo, Koch, Innovation, Justin Time, Pierre Verany, Enja, Avan-Guard, Lyrichord, OMD, OWL, Fortuna, DRG, DEJA-VU.
Accounts: All types of accounts, nationwide.
New Lines Accepted: Yes.
Coverage: National.

Distribution Jonction

11500 Ovide Clermont
Montreal, PQ H1G 3Y8
(514) 325-4500
FAX (514) 325-0170
Lines Carried: Amical, Ami-Son, Contact, Budgetel, Routiers du Quebec.
Accounts: Sub-distributors, record chains, radio stations, record stores and rackjobbers.
New Lines Accepted: Yes.
Coverage: Eastern Canada.

Distribution Select

500 rue Ste. Catherine e.
Montreal, PQ H2L 2C6
(514) 849-6201
FAX (514) 849-0764
Lines Carried: Audiogram, Star, Paroles & Musiques, Axion, ADM, Laser, CBC, Hungaratran.
Accounts: Rackjobbers.
New Lines Accepted: Yes.
Coverage: Canada.

Electric Distribution

3447 Kennedy Rd., Unit 4
Scarborough, ON M1V 3S1
(416) 297-2752
FAX (416) 297-6532
Lines Carried: Power, Boulevard, Somersault, Shanachie, Unidisc, Blackout, S.E.X., Version, P.O.T., Fringe Products, Green Linnet, Pigeon.
Accounts: Chain stores, one-stops, rackjobbers.
New Lines Accepted: Yes.
Coverage: National.

Exile International

31 Leading Rd.
Toronto, ON M9V 4B7
(416) 234-9199
Lines Carried: Various.

Handleman Company of Canada Ltd.

10 Newgale Gate, Units 1-3
Scarborough, ON M1X 1C5
(416) 298-0411
FAX (416) 291-5324
Accounts: Department stores.
New Lines Accepted: No.
Coverage: Canada.
Comments: Products include computer software, music videos, movie videos, LPs, cassettes and CDs.
Branches:
140 Barr St., Bldg. 605
St. Laurent, PQ H4T 1W6
(514) 341-1822

7408-40 St. S.E., Suite 5
Calgary, AB T2C 2H5
(403) 236-3868

450 Edinburgh Dr.
P.O. Box 2158
Moncton, NB E1C 3B2
(506) 857-8590

Interdisc Distribution Inc.

27 Louis-Joseph Doucet
Lanoraie, PQ J0K 1E0
(514) 887-2384
FAX (514) 887-7561
Lines Carried: Over 25 different labels from France, Italy, Germany and Switzerland.
Accounts: Retail stores, libraries.
Coverage: Canada.

Iroqcrafts Ltd.
R.R. 2 Oshweken
Six Nations Reserve, ON N0A 1M0
(416) 765-4206
FAX (416) 765-5633
Lines Carried: Three different recordings of Iroquois social dance songs in both disc and cassette form. Handled by mail order.
Accounts: Museum gift shops, Canadian outlets, Indian craft stores.
Coverage: North America, Europe, Japan.

Kareena Services
4330 Halifax St.
Burnaby, BC V5C 3X5
(604) 294-3101
FAX (604) 298-2452
Lines Carried: All major labels including WEA, CBS, Capitol, BMG, PolyGram, MCA, A&M.
Accounts: Retail music stores.
New Lines Accepted: Yes.
Coverage: British Columbia, Alberta, Yukon Territory, Ontario.

Kops Record Shop
436 Queen St. W.
Toronto, ON M5V 2A8
(416) 363-3844
Lines Carried: Full-line of reissued 45s and LPs from the 50s to the 80s.
Accounts: Distributors, retail stores, juke box operators and DJ services.
New Lines Accepted: Yes.
Coverage: Canada.
Comments: Canada's leading distributor of vintage 45s.

Ky-Cam International Limited
1750 Plummer St., Unit 18
Pickering, ON L1W 3L7
(416) 420-8685
FAX (416) 420-8790
Musical Styles Carried: Classical, Jazz, C&W, New Age, Relaxation, Environmental Sound Recordings, Language Tapes and Self-Improvement Cassettes.
Accounts: Record stores, wholesalers and rackjobbers.
New Lines Accepted: Yes.
Coverage: Nationwide.

MCA Records
2450 Victoria Park Ave.
Willowdale, ON M2J 4A2
(416) 491-3000
FAX (416) 490-8206
Lines Carried: Island, Motown, Chrysalis, IRS, Curb, Constellation, Duke Street.
Coverage: Canada.

Maritime Express
157 Sussex Ave.
Riverview, NB E1B 3A8
(506) 386-2996
Lines Carried: Old-time fiddling records.
Accounts: Wholesalers, retailers.
New Lines Accepted: Yes.
Coverage: Predominantly the maritimes with limited distribution across Canada and the U.S.

Marvin Melnyk Associates Ltd.
P.O. Box 220
Queenston, ON L0S 1L0
(416) 262-4964
FAX (416) 262-5303
Lines Carried: Educational materials including records, cassettes and video tapes.
Accounts: Educational institutions.
New Lines Accepted: Yes.
Coverage: Canada.
Comments: Have sales reps in all major population areas.

Millbank Music Distribution Ltd.
245 Montee-de-Liesse
St. Laurent, PQ H4T 1P5
(514) 341-4511
FAX (514) 341-1717
Lines Carried: All majors, plus cut-outs.
Accounts: Major and independents.
New Lines Accepted: Yes.
Coverage: Canada.

Money-Talks Productions Inc.
P.O. Box 88, Stn. H
Montreal, PQ H3G 2K5
(514) 935-9089
Lines Carried: Musicworks Records, Street Level Records, AM-FM Records.
New Lines Accepted: Yes.
Coverage: U.S., Canada.

Numuzik Inc.

6838 Bombardier
St. Leonard, PQ H1P 3K5
(514) 329-0940
FAX (514) 349-0942
Lines Carried: Warner Bros., PolyGram, all dance music labels.
Accounts: Retail stores, DJs.
New Lines Accepted: Yes.
Coverage: Quebec, Ottawa region.
Comments: Exclusively dance music.

One Stop Recording Supplies

336 Harbour Ave.
North Vancouver, BC V7J 2E9
(604) 985-0475
FAX (604) 255-7355
Lines Carried: 7- and 12-inch singles, cassette singles.
Accounts: HMV Canada, A&B Sound, Sight & Sound, Kelly's, Big K and other record store chains.
Coverage: Nationwide, predominantly British Columbia and Alberta.

Ottawa Record Pool

207 Dalhousie
Ottawa, ON K1N 7C9
(613) 237-6466
FAX (613) 237-0477
Lines Carried: Dance records, Disco, Funk.
Accounts: Clubs, DJ services.
New Lines Accepted: Yes.
Coverage: Ottawa-Hull.

Les Promotions Patribec

273 rue Principale, P.O. Box 148
Les Eboulements en Charlevoix, PQ G0A 2M0
(418) 635-2466
Lines Carried: Disques Patrimoine.
Accounts: Schools, commercial arts centres, record stores.
New Lines Accepted: Yes.
Coverage: Quebec, Canada, U.S.
Comments: Specialization in folk music.

Pe-Ko International

1555 Dudemaine
Montreal, PQ H3M 1R2
(514) 337-5718
FAX (514) 337-2074
Lines Carried: Pe-Ko.
Accounts: Retail record and grocery stores.
New Lines Accepted: No.
Coverage: North America.

Pindoff Record Sales Ltee.

277A Brunswick
Pointe-Claire, PQ H9R 5A1
(514) 694-6231
FAX (514) 694-0429
Lines Carried: WEA, CBS, PolyGram, BMG, Select.
Accounts: Retail stores, department stores.
Coverage: Canada.

Plum Music

157 Bestview Dr.
Toronto, ON M2M 2Y4
(416) 222-8845
FAX (416) 733-2247
Lines Carried: Exclusive labels on CD. Labels include Duet, Ditto, Lyric, Claque, Christophorous, Fonit Cetera, Gothic, Legato, Delphon, Mode, Standing Room Only, Jecklin, Grammont, Great Opera Performances, Preiser. Specializing in opera and classical music.
Accounts: Independent stores and major chains such as Sam the Record Man and A&A.
New Lines Accepted: Yes.
Coverage: Canada.

PolyGram Distribution

600 ch. Cote-de-Liesse
St. Laurent, PQ H4T 1E3
(514) 739-2701
FAX (514) 739-4556
Lines Carried: Beggar's Banquet, Deutsche Grammophone, Fontana, London, Mercury, Phillips, Polydor, Phonogram, Vertigo, ECM, and others.
Accounts: Retail stores, audio stores, magazine stores, libraries.
New Lines Accepted: Yes.
Coverage: Canada.

Quality Special Products

480 Tapscott Rd., Suite 1
Scarborough, ON M1B 1W3
(416) 291-5590
FAX (416) 291-7537
Lines Carried: Quality record and video products.
Accounts: Retail stores and rackjobbers.
New Lines Accepted: Yes.
Coverage: Canada.

RMP Record Sales Co. Ltd.

300 Bates Rd.
Montreal, PQ H3S 1A3
(514) 739-5662 or 739-8988
FAX (514) 735-9252
Lines Carried: Major and minor labels in all formats.
Accounts: Music stores.
New Lines Accepted: Yes.
Coverage: Quebec, Ottawa Valley.
Comments: Also carries accessories.

R.O.W. Entertainment

255 Sheilds Ct.
Markham, ON L3R 8V2
(416) 475-3550
FAX (416) 475-4163
Lines Carried: All labels distributed by A&M, BMG, Capitol, CBS, MCA, PolyGram and WEA. Also a small number of independent labels.
New Lines Accepted: Yes.
Coverage: Franchises nationwide and independent retailers throughout Canada.

Record Peddler

12 Brant St.
Toronto, ON M5V 2M1
(416) 364-5507
FAX (416) 869-0017
Lines Carried: American and European labels.
Accounts: Independent and chain record stores.
New Lines Accepted: Yes.
Coverage: Canada.
Comments: Specialist in new alternative Rock, also, reissues and nostalgic material. No classical or country.

Roblan Distributors Inc.

274 Church St.
Toronto, ON M5B 1Z5
(416) 977-6490
FAX (416) 977-7565
Lines Carried: Full catalog of CDs, albums, tapes and accessories.
Accounts: Sam the Record Man.
New Lines Accepted: Yes.
Coverage: Canada.
Comments: Full import division, special requests, full selection.

Saturn Distributing

70 Esna Park, Unit 14
Markham, ON L3R 6E7
(416) 470-2666
FAX (416) 470-2672
Lines Carried: Current and vintage CDs, LPs and cassettes.
Accounts: Retail record outlets.
New Lines Accepted: Yes.
Coverage: Canada.
Branches:
9916 Cote-de-Liesse
Montreal, PQ H8T 1A1
(514) 636-0801

550-42 Ave. S.E.
Calgary, AB T2G 1Y6
(403) 287-2712

Scott's Highland Services Ltd.

1464 Beckworth Ave.
London, ON N5V 2K7
(519) 453-0892
FAX (519) 453-6303
Lines Carried: Scott's Highland Records plus other independent Scottish Tattoo fiddle recordings.
Accounts: Scottish specialty stores, chain stores, record libraries, mail orders.
New Lines Accepted: Yes.
Coverage: North America, U.K., Australia, New Zealand.

Serenity Sound

88 Woodmount Ave.
Toronto, ON M4C 3Y2
(416) 467-8820
FAX (416) 463-2488
Lines Carried: Independent new age labels.
Accounts: Retail stores.
New Lines Accepted: Yes.
Coverage: Canada.

Starsound

427 Yonge St.
Toronto, ON M4S 1T4
(416) 977-0525
FAX (416) 977-2422
Musical Styles Carried: Dance, Rap, R&B, Reggae, NRG, Alternative. 12-inch records, LPs, CDs and cassettes.
Accounts: Clubs, DJs and DJ services.
New Lines Accepted: Yes.
Coverage: Canada, U.S.
Comments: Starsound is a large importer and exporter of dance music which handles mail order and wholesale accounts.

Summit Sound SIAD Inc.
P.O. Box 333
Westport, ON K0G 1X0
(613) 273-2818
Lines Carried: Specialize in Christian music production for gospel artists. Three in-house labels: Summit, Mello-D and Brick Street.
Accounts: Complete custom record and tape manufacturing and distribution.
New Lines Accepted: Yes.
Coverage: Canada, U.S.
Comments: All aspects of custom record and tape production. Complete in-house production and design services, plus a 16-track studio.

Sunshine Records Ltd.
228 Selkirk Ave.
Winnipeg, MB R2W 2L6
(204) 586-8057
FAX (204) 582-8397
Lines Carried: Madacy, specialty lines.
Accounts: Department stores, rackjobbers, one-stops.
New Lines Accepted: Yes.
Coverage: Canada.

The Sunsweat & Moontears Music
1124 Lonsdale Ave., Suite 1149
North Vancouver, BC V7M 2H1
(604) 986-5949
FAX (604) 986-5949
Lines Carried: Independent singles and albums in all formats.
Accounts: Radio stations in Canada, the U.S. and Europe.
New Lines Accepted: Yes.
Coverage: International.

Total Sound Ltd.
10333-174 St.
Edmonton, AB T5S 1H1
(403) 483-3217
FAX (403) 486-0589
Lines Carried: All major manufacturers.
Accounts: Rock record stores.
New Lines Accepted: Yes.
Coverage: Western Canada.

Group de Musique Trans-Canada
2620 Trans-Canada Highway
Pointe-Claire, PQ H9R 1B1
(514) 426-2500
FAX (514) 426-2424
Accounts: Record and chain stores.
New Lines Accepted: Yes.
Coverage: Eastern Canada.

Trend Records & Tapes Ltd.
47 Racine Rd., Unit 6
Toronto, ON M9W 6B2
(416) 749-6601
FAX (416) 749-3918
Lines Carried: Various (please contact for details).
Accounts: All major record stores across Canada.
New Lines Accepted: Yes.
Coverage: Canada.

Unity Gain Records Ltd.
6216 Seaforth St.
Halifax, NS B3L 1P9
(902) 455-7588
Lines Carried: Labels which focus on Celtic, Acoustic Music, R&B, Blues, Bluegrass.
Accounts: Retail and wholesale, craft shops, department stores, etc.
New Lines Accepted: Yes.
Coverage: International: U.S., Canada, Scotland, Ireland, England, Europe, Australia.
Comments: Record and music production, advertising.

WEA Music of Canada Ltd.
1810 Birchmount Rd.
Scarborough, ON M1P 2J1
(416) 291-2515
FAX (416) 291-6044
Lines Carried: Various.
Accounts: All.
New Lines Accepted: Yes.
Coverage: Canada.
Branches:
17 Donovan Terrace, Townhouse 6
Moncton, NB E1A 4N9

184 Merizzi St.
St. Laurent, PQ H4T 1E7

6325-12 St. S.E., Unit 12
Calgary, AB T2H 2K1

68 Water St., Suite 400
Vancouver, BC V6B 1A4

6 Lansing Sq., Suite 211
Willowdale, ON M2J 1T1

Western Imperial Magnetics Ltd.
12840 Bathgate Way, Suite 7
Richmond, BC V6V 1Z4
(604) 270-8682
FAX (604) 270-2745
Lines Carried: Era, K-Tel, Dominion, Arrival, Headfirst.
Accounts: Government and education plus the studio, broadcast, medical, retail and church markets.
New Lines Accepted: Yes.
Coverage: Canada.

Word Communications Ltd.
7720 Alderbridge Way
Vancouver, BC V6X 2A2
(604) 270-7231
FAX (604) 270-0821
Musical Styles Carried: Contemporary Christian music including Pop, MOR, Rock, C&W and Gospel.

Zulu Records
1292 W. Georgia St., Suite 202
Vancouver, BC V6E 3J3
(604) 662-7846
Lines Carried: Og Records, Fringe Product, MoDaMu, Better Youth Organization, plus many independent releases.
New Lines Accepted: Yes.
Coverage: National.

RECORD MANUFACTURERS

Ambience Records
220 Rideau St.
Ottawa, ON K1N 5Y1
(613) 236-5282
FAX (613) 235-5473
Lines Carried: Vinyl, CDs.
New Lines Accepted: Yes.
Coverage: North America.
Comments: In-house graphic design and production facility.
Estimates available on request.

Americ Disc
2525 le Canadien
Drummondville, ON J2B 6V4
(819) 474-2655
FAX (819) 474-2870
Lines Carried: CD manufacturer.
New Lines Accepted: No.
Coverage: Canada, U.S., International.
80% outside Quebec.

ART-TEC Records & Tapes
323 Talbot St., 2nd Floor
St. Thomas, ON N5P 1B5
(519) 633-6518
FAX (519) 633-6518
Accounts: Blank cassette retailers, recording studios, and record and cassette wholesalers.
New Lines Accepted: Yes.
Coverage: International.
Comments: Complete in-house manufacturing, duplication and packaging. In-house graphic art department plus analog and digital mastering capabilities.
Personnel: Don Baker, Toronto rep
(416) 924-2386; Tony Mariano,
S.W. Ontario rep (519) 676-8939.

441

Astro Custom Records Ltd.

510 Coronation Dr., Suite 21
West Hill, ON M1E 4X6
(416) 284-3501
FAX (416) 281-8579
Lines Carried: Records, cassettes, CDs.
New Lines Accepted: Yes.
Coverage: Canada.

Audiobec Recording Canada/Enregistrements Audiobec Canada Inc.

600 Port Royal o.
St. Laurent, PQ H3L 2C5
(514) 384-6667
FAX (514) 388-1488
Lines Carried: Complete cassette manufacturing, disc mastering and printing services offered.

CBS Records Canada Ltd.

1121 Leslie St.
Don Mills, ON M3C 2J9
(416) 447-3311
FAX (416) 447-6973
Lines Carried: Columbia, Epic, CBS Associated, WTG.
Lines Distributed: Anthem, ISBA, True Blue.
New Lines Accepted: Yes.
Coverage: Canada.

Capitol Records/ EMI of Canada Ltd.

3109 American Dr.
Mississauga, ON L4V 1B2
(416) 677-5050
FAX (416) 677-1651
Lines Carried: Audio cassettes.
Accounts: Rackjobbers, retail distributors.
New Lines Accepted: No.
Coverage: Canada.
Comments: CDs and LPs by Americ Disc.

Cinram

2255 Markham Rd.
Scarborough, ON M1B 2W3
(416) 298-8190
FAX (416) 298-9307
Coverage: Canada, U.S.

Circle "M" Records

P.O. Box 972
Mount Forest, ON N0G 2L0
(519) 323-2810
Lines Carried: Country Music.
Accounts: Various.
New Lines Accepted: No.
Coverage: Canada.

Cod Oil Productions Limited

P.O. Box 8568
St. John's, NF A1B 3P2
(709) 745-3304
Comments: Promotion and marketing of recorded music published with Cod Oil Productions only.

Distribution Jonction

11500 Ovide Clermont
Montreal, PQ H1G 3Y8
(514) 325-4500
FAX (514) 325-0170
Lines Carried: Amical, Ami-Son, Contact, Budgetel, Routiers du Quebec.
Accounts: Sub-distributors, record chains, radio stations, record stores and rackjobbers.
New Lines Accepted: Yes.
Coverage: Eastern Canada.

Dynapak Music Services Ltd.

3121 Universal Dr.
Mississauga, ON L4X 2E2
(416) 625-8311
FAX (416) 625-5209
Lines Carried: Audio cassettes.
Accounts: Musicians and record companies.
New Lines Accepted: No.
Coverage: Canada, U.S.

ERA International Limited

10 Grenoble Dr., Apt. 1516
Don Mills, ON M3C 1C7
(416) 423-0210
FAX (416) 423-0210
Lines Carried: K-Tel, Dominion, Headfirst, Nouveau Crush Music, MA Music, Arrival, ERA, AJK Music.
Accounts: Rackjobbers, retailers, wholesalers, sub-distributors.
New Lines Accepted: Yes.
Coverage: Seven sales reps cover all of Canada. Parent company is K-Tel International.
Comments: ERA has warehousing/shipping facilities in Winnipeg.

Gamma Records (Quebec) Ltd.

300 Leo Pariseau, Suite 701
P.O. Box 1010, Place du Parc
Montreal, PQ H2W 2S2
(514) 842-4666
FAX (514) 843-4135
New Lines Accepted: Yes.
Coverage: Quebec and Eastern Canada.

Iroqrafts Ltd.

R.R. 2
Ohsweken, ON N0A 1M0
(416) 765-4206
FAX (416) 765-5633
Lines Carried: A set of Iroquois social dance songs (records and cassettes).
Accounts: Canadiana stores and museum gift shops.
New Lines Accepted: No.
Coverage: International.

Precision Sound Corp.

5614 Goring St.
Burnaby, BC V5B 3A3
FAX (604) 299-4146
Lines Carried: Manufacturing, packaging and duplicating of audio cassettes.
Accounts: Musicians, music distribution houses and studios.
Coverage: Mostly Western Canada.
Comments: Distributor for TDK products.

RDR Promotions

P.O. Box 2294, Stn. B
Scarborough, ON M1N 2E9
(416) 267-3276
FAX (416) 267-1963
Lines Carried: Tapes, CDs, 7- and 12-inch records.
New Lines Accepted: Yes.
Coverage: Canada, Europe.
Comments: Broker for Cinram.

Disques RSB Inc.

8400 Cote-de-Liesse
St. Laurent, PQ H4T 1G7
(514) 342-8511
FAX (514) 342-0401
Services: Mastering, record pressings, CD and high-speed cassette duplication.
Coverage: Canada, U.S.

Sackville Recordings

P.O. Box 87, Stn. J
Toronto, ON M4J 4X8
(416) 593-7230
Lines Carried: Sackville

T.D.C. Tape Duplicating Centre

2182 W. 12 Ave., Suite 109
Vancouver, BC V6K 2N4
(604) 734-4546
Lines Carried: Blank tape manufacturing.

3M Canada Inc.
(Magnetic Media Division)
P.O. Box 5757
London, ON N6A 4T1
(519) 451-2500
FAX (519) 452-6298
Lines Carried: Professional audio/video and specialty products and accessories.
Accounts: Professional broadcasting and production companies; industrial, educational and government accounts; recording studios.
Coverage: Canada.
Comments: Manufacturer of audio/video tape and cassettes.

World Records
1712 Baseline Rd. W., P.O. Box 2000
Bowmanville, ON L1C 3Z3
(416) 686-2828
(416) 433-0250 (Oshawa)
FAX (416) 433-1868
Lines Carried: Complete record, cassette and CD manufacturing and packaging services.
Coverage: North America.
Comments: 45 and LP mailers in stock.

RECORD PRODUCERS

Clare Adlam
289 Fergus St. S.
Mount Forest, ON N0G 2L0
(519) 323-2810
Category: Independent producer.
Area of Expertise: C&W.

Air In Motion Productions
72 Beaconsfield Ave.
Toronto, ON M6J 3H9
(416) 536-3266
Category: Independent producer.
Area of Expertise: All styles.
Artists Produced: Various independent artists.

Brian Allen
Attic Records Ltd.
624 King St. W.
Toronto, ON M5V 1M7
(416) 862-0352
FAX (416) 862-0915
Category: Independent producer.
Area of Expertise: Rock, Pop.
Artists Produced: Haywire, Toronto, Lee Aaron.
Comments: Produces Attic artists only.

Mike Alyanak
Quantum Records
170A Baldwin St.
Toronto, ON M5T 1L8
(416) 593-9547
FAX (416) 593-0461
Category: Independent producer.
Area of Expertise: Pop, Rock, MOR.
Artists Produced: Mad About Plaid, Look People, Belinda Metz, Harlow, Rex Chainbelt.

445

Ambassador Records

185 Oshawa Blvd. S.
Oshawa, ON L1H 5R6
(416) 579-7476
Category: Independent producer.
Area of Expertise: Ambassador records a variety of musical styles but the majority of clients are Gospel and Country artists.
Comments: Ambassador Records is a 16-track, full-service recording facility. Additional services include cassette manufacturing and duplicating.

Warren Anderson

Century City Recording Studios
2207 Halifax Cr. N.W.
Calgary, AB T2M 4E1
(403) 282-2555
Category: Independent producer.
Area of Expertise: Rock & Roll, Country Rock, Pop and New Age material.
Artists Produced: Rattle Snake Kane, Thieves of Silence, various artists.
Comments: Please send no more than four songs on cassette. Include a S.A.S.E. for return of your material. Also interested in quality demos for video and film scores. All strong submissions are kept on file.

Morris Apelbaum

3880 Clark St.
Montreal, PQ H2W 1W6
(514) 842-1303
Category: Independent Producer.
Area of Expertise: Jazz, Pop, Folk, Roots.
Artists Produced: Oliver Jones (Juno), Ranee Lee, The Darned, Rachel Green, Penny Lang, Bowser & Blue.
Comments: Apelbaum has received two Felix nominations, two Juno nominations and one Juno award (Best Jazz Album of The Year).

Audio Plus Productions

409 King St. W. Suite 508
Toronto, ON M5V 1K1
(416) 340-9871
Category: Independent producer.
Area of Expertise: Commercials, audio for video, jingles, music production for any format.
Artists Produced: The Bourbon Tabernacle Choir, Wish One Wish.
Comments: Audio Plus offers independent engineers and producers, artist management and music consultation services. Clients include: Royal Bank of Canada, CBS Records of Canada, Exclusive Communications, Canadian Association of Broadcasters, Maclean Hunter, Ontario Hydro, Actors' Equity, Nelvana Productions, CIRPA, Wizard Productions, Steve's Music Stores, Consumers Distributing, Norstar Entertainment.

George Axon

1117 Mississauga Valley Blvd.
Mississauga, ON L5A 2A1
(416) 566-1567
Category: Independent producer.
Area of Expertise: Pop, Jazz, Folk.
Comments: 10 years of experience, 24-track studio.

Eric R. Baragar/ John C. Collins

B & C Productions
12 Riverside Dr., P.O. Box 1012
Trenton, ON K8V 6E6
(613) 392-5144 or 392-6296
Category: Production house.
Area of Expertise: Country, Pop, Rock, Dance.
Artists Produced: The Haggarty's, Brentwood Rocker, D.J. Thompson, Colin Amey, Laser, The Press, Sands of Time, Jackie Findlay.

Carmon Barry

Emmanuel Productions
31B Industrial St.
Toronto, ON M4G 1Z2
(416) 423-7131
FAX (416) 467-6805
Category: Independent producer.
Area of Expertise: Pop, Crossover Country, Contemporary Gospel.
Artists Produced: A range of independent artists.

Brian Bell

BFHB Audio Inc.
168 Empress Ave.
North York, ON M2N 3T8
(416) 221-7445
Category: Independent producer.
Area of Expertise: Pop, New Age, Jazz, Easy Listening.
Artists Produced: Gary O, Terry and Laurel Black, Jordana, Ron Lasalle, Sail Cats, JBB, George Randall.
Comments: Specializing in computer-based MIDI production.

Jocelyn Bournival

Son-Art Studio
5230 Begin
St. Hubert, PQ J3Y 2P9
(514) 676-0636
Category: Independent producer.
Area of Expertise: Pop, Classical, Jazz.
Artists Produced: Claude Gauthier, Claude Garden, Lise Delbec, Philippe Noireaut, Jacques Antonin.

Phil Bova

Ambience Recorders
220 Rideau St.
Ottawa, ON K1N 5Y1
(613) 236-5282
FAX (613) 235-5473
Category: Production house.
Area of Expertise: Pop, Rock, Classical, Jazz, Country, New Age, World Beat, etc.
Artists Produced: Ian Tamblyn, Dario Dominques, George Stryker & the Bandits, Marc Stern & the Big Umbrella, Dennis Whittey, etc.

Peter Brennan

Auto Records
36 Silverdale Place
London, ON N5Z 4A7
(519) 686-0711
Category: Independent producer.
Area of Expertise: All musical styles. Full arrangements and orchestrations.
Artists Produced: Monkey See, Guilded Cage, Twice Shy, Michael Dee, Equus, Suffermachine.

Rene Brossard

Boss Productions Inc.
1220 Shaw St.
Toronto, ON M6G 3N6
(416) 538-6761
Category: Production house.
Area of Expertise: Pop albums.
Artists Produced: Nana, Richard Nattress, Rick McLarnon, Martin Barret, Edwin Chan and Michelle Glover.

Ira Brown

10 Muirhead Rd., Suite 405
Willowdale, ON M2J 4P9
(416) 499-8088
Category: Independent producer.
Area of Expertise: Pop, Rock, jingles.

Terry Brown

Risque Disque Inc.
25 Draper St.
Toronto, ON M5V 2M3
(416) 596-0353
FAX (416) 596-8120
Category: Independent producer.
Area of Expertise: Rock.
Artists Produced: Cutting Crew, Rush, Roman Grey, Blue Rodeo, Basic English, Watertown Trio.

Saby Buccella Productions

8943 Maritain
Montreal, PQ H1R 3J4
(514) 328-3622
Category: Independent producer.
Area of Expertise: Pop.
Artists Produced: The Erotic Drum Band, Sonia Benezra, MTL Express, Claude Barzotti, Dutch Robinson, Martin Bee.

Larry Campbell

570 Redwood Ave.
Winnipeg, MB R2S 1T1
(204) 586-4536
Category: Independent producer.
Area of Expertise: Country.
Artists Produced: Rhonda Hart, Cyndi Cain, Donna Henry.

Peter Cardinali

Peter Cardinali Productions Inc.
12 Ecclesfield Dr.
Scarborough, ON M1W 3J6
(416) 494-2000
Category: Independent producer.
Area of Expertise: Pop, Funk, R&B, Jazz.
Artists Produced: Hugh Marsh, Rick James, Teena Marie, John James. Also arrangments for Anne Murray. The Temptations, Brecker Brothers.
Comments: Juno nomination for Producer of The Year, 1985.

Joey Cee

4091 Pheasant Run
Mississauga, ON L5L 2C2
(416) 820-6400
FAX (416) 820-9512
Category: Independent producer.
Area of Expertise: All formats and music categories. Specializing in A/C and dance music.
Artists Produced: Ron Victors, Task Force, Endless Wave, Stars On Steel, Elay Orchestra, The Puppies, Artsy, Joey Cee, Jive Bombers, Tiger Tiger, Champion V, Astrid Young, etc.

Wayne Chaulk

Ambassador Music
P.O. Box 8386, Stn. F
Calgary, AB T2J 2V5
(403) 271-3897
Category: Production house and independent producer.
Area of Expertise: Pop, Instrumental, Soft Rock, Easy Listening, MOR, Gospel.
Artists Produced: Terry Anthony (multilingual artist, debut CD and debut Italian album), Heather Hovannes, plus various other artists and commercial productions.
Comments: Complete productions including arranging and playing of keyboards, synthesizers, programming, composing, theme music, LPs and demos. MIDI and analog recording capabilities.

Angelo Civiero Productions

1461 Hurontario St.
Mississauga, ON L5G 3H5
(416) 278-6835
FAX (416) 891-2558
Category: Independent producer.
Area of Expertise: New music production and pre-production for new talent. Recording and shopping demos to major labels.
Artists Produced: Frost In June, Jeff Steven, Richard Janik.

Les Productions Guy Cloutier Inc.

2322 rue Sherbrooke e.
Montreal, PQ H2K 1E5
(514) 598-5877
FAX (514) 525-2548
Category: Independent producer.
Area of Expertise: Pop, Pop Rock, Rock, MOR, Instrumental.
Artists Produced: Rene Simard, Nathalie Simard, Johanne Blouin.

Robbert Cobban

Keytrax Productions
51 Harcourt Ave.
Toronto, ON M4J 1J3
(416) 463-8332
Category: Independent producer.
Area of Expertise: Mainly Pop, will work with all styles.
Artists Produced: Michael Jones.
Comments: Audio post-production.

Randall Cousins

Roto-Noto Records
148 Erin Ave.
Hamilton, ON L8K 4W3
(416) 572-7474
Category: Independent producer.
Area of Expertise: Rock, Pop, R&B, Country, Country Rock.
Artists Produced: Lynne Wilson and the Rebels, Jack Diamond, Diane Raeside, Michael Terry, Bobby McGee, Frequency.

Spencer Critchley

62-12 St.
Toronto, ON M8V 3G7
(416) 252-0775
FAX (416) 251-7834
Category: Production house.
Area of Expertise: Film music plus jingle and album production.
Clients: Bermuda Department of Tourism, General Motors of Canada.

David Daw

Summit Sound Inc.
40 Main St. Unit 1B, P.O. Box 333
Westport, ON K0G 1X0
(613) 273-2818
FAX (613) 273-7320
Category: Production house and independent producer.
Area of Expertise: Independent Christian and jingle music production.
Artists Produced: Over 300 Canadian and U.S. gospel artists including Proverbs, Selah, The Sniders, Urgency, Promise, Torchmen, and Nations.
Comments: Covenant award winner, best gospel album production for 1986, '87 '88, '89.

Gerry Dere

c/o IMS and DMT
11714-113 Ave.
Edmonton, AB T5G 0J8
(403) 454-6848 or 454-9291
Category: Independent producer.
Area of Expertise: All.
Artists Produced: Jenson Interceptor, Mary Lou Sonmor, P.J. McDonald, Miriam Kidd Country, Five Wheel Drive, Good Friends, Garry Lee & Showdown, Sassy Donna Lee, Pam Henry, Lynne Donavan, Brian Ault, Mile Zero, China White
Comments: Also engineered Trooper's platinum album *Flying Colors*.

Martin Dibbs

I.V.M. Recording Studio
P.O. Box 405
Rodney, ON M0L 2C0
(519) 785-2180
Category: Independent producer.
Area of Expertise: Pop, Dance, Rock, Country.
Artists Produced: Xpertise, Denise Pelley, Chevy Blue, RAM, Albans.

Robert Doidge

Grant Avenue Studio (1985) Inc.
38 Grant Ave.
Hamilton, ON L8N 2X5
(416) 522-5227
Category: Independent producer.
Area of Expertise: Pop, Country.
Artists Produced: Sherry Kean, Smith & Smith's Comedy Mill, Mark Laforme, Ray Materick, Lynne & The Rebels, Tia Hofgraff, Jack Diamond Band, Doug Reansbury.
Comments: Robert Doidge is also a TV musical director.

Daniel Donahue

327 Kingston Cr.
Winnipeg, MB R2M 0T5
(204) 233-8502
Category: Independent producer.
Area of Expertise: Albums, commercials, film scores and special effects.
Artists Produced: Connie Kaldor, Fred Penner, Hart Rouge, Heather Bishop, Jeff Hatcher.
Comments: Two-time Juno finalist and winner in 1988 children's category (Connie Kaldor and Carmine Campagne).

Jody Ellis

Triton Sound Studios
3886 Chesswood Dr.
Downsview, ON M3J 2W6
(416) 638-3869
Category: Independent producer.
Area of Expertise: Pop, Rock.

Richard Bruce Ellis

Waxworks Productions
P.O. Box 299
St. Jacobs, ON N0B 2N0
(519) 664-3762
Category: Independent producer.
Area of Expertise: Pop Rock, Country, Gospel.

Gregory English

Harlow Sound
31 Harlow Cr.
Rexdale, ON M9V 2Y6
(416) 741-0165
Category: Production house and independent producer.
Area of Expertise: Classical as well as Pop Rock.
Artists Produced: Cerafim, Marc James Fortin, Images in Vogue, Culture Industry, Norbert Kraft, East West, Donkey.

Exclusive Management

55 Wynford Heights, Apt. 1910
Don Mills, On M3C 1L4
(416) 449-9612
FAX (416) 792-1059
Category: Independent Producer.

Karl R. Falkenham

2060 Elm St.
Halifax, NS B3L 2Y3
(902) 422-3275 or 455-7588 or
(902) 420-4470 (CBC)
Category: Independent producer.
Area of Expertise: All types of music, live and studio. Direct to stereo and multitrack.
Artists Produced: Various.
Comments: Recording engineer and music producer.

Craig Fotheringham

1492 Lincoln Ave.
Winnipeg, MB R3E 0Z1
(204) 774-7770
Category: Independent producer.
Area of Expertise: Pop, Country.
Artists Produced: Against the Grain, C-Weed Band, Freebird.

Mike Francis

1399 Shadowa Rd.
Mississauga, ON L5H 2N6
(416) 278-2975
Category: Independent producer.
Area of Expertise: Country, Pop.
Artists Produced: Carroll Baker, Robert Armes, Terry Carrisse, Joan Kennedy, Matt Minglewood, The Good Brothers.

Norah Fraser

Pavanne Audio
P.O. Box 7, Place du Parc
Montreal, PQ H2W 2M9
(514) 485-7955
Category: Independent producer.
Area of Expertise: Classical.
Comments: Norah Fraser worked for several years as a professional musician, has three years technical training in McGill's "tonmeister" program and works as an independent recording engineer/producer of cassettes and CDs. Extensive experience with digital recording.

Bob Fuhr

1253 Clarence Ave., Suite 3
Winnipeg, MB R3T 1T4
(204) 543-8484
Category: Production house.
Area of Expertise: Pop, Rock, Jazz, Blues, Country.
Artists Produced: The Guess Who, Graham Shaw, Rex Bartlett, Double Eagle Band, CKIS-FM Homegrown Album (1989).

G.S. Productions

90 Rabbit Lane
Islington, ON M9B 5S9
(416) 622-4568
Category: Record production and engineering.
Area of Expertise: R&B, Blues, Reggae, Country.

Ian Guenther

Three Hats Productions
84 Mavety St.
Toronto, ON M6P 2L6
(416) 766-1029
Category: Independent producer.
Area of Expertise: All styles.

Morley R. Halsmith

986 Vanier Dr.
Mississauga, ON L5H 3T7
(416) 274-0471
Category: Independent producer.
Area of Expertise: Pop, Country, Gospel, plus classical and contemporary scoring. Experienced with both MIDI and acoustical arranging.
Comments: Producer, arranger and orchestrator on more than 30 record albums and cassettes for indepent releases. Affiliated with excellent 2-inch and digital facilities.

Hara Musical Productions Inc.

46 Dearbourne Blvd., Suite 50
Brampton, ON L6T 1J6
(416) 458-0349
Category: Production house.
Area of Expertise: MIDI production.
Comments: Composition for TV and radio. French language production.

John J. Hartman

Icedrum Records Inc.
P.O. Box 2310, Stn. A
Sudbury, ON P3A 4S8
(705) 560-3769
FAX (705) 560-1702
Category: Production house and independent producer.
Area of Expertise: Pop, Rock, Rap, House, Funk, Alternative, Dance.
Artists Produced: Self-produced album *Million, E.T.P.* (Rap) and *Now We Lustre* (Alternative). Arranged, performed and produced the Remembrance Day theme, *In Flanders Fields*, as well as *My Canada*.
Comments: Pre-production and full recording facilities available. Specialize in composition, production and arrangements employing computer-based MIDI and sequence technology in harmony with any acoustic orchestration.

Andrew Henderson

690 Graham
Dorval, PQ H9P 2B5
(514) 631-1272
FAX (819) 687-9893
Category: Production house.
Area of Expertise: Pop, Rock, R&B, Country, Reggae.
Artists Produced: Town Hounds, 88's, Skipper Dean, Dr. Sax, 2 Men Laughing, John Phillip Bruney, Kenny Hamilton.
Comments: Willing to work at any studio in Montreal area (can get good rates and quality production).

Rob Hewes

Studio West
502-45 St. W., Suite 3
Saskatoon, SK S7L 6H2
(306) 244-2815
FAX (306) 242-3301
Category: Independent producer.
Area of Expertise: Pop, Country.
Artists Produced: The Johner Brothers, Lori Van, John Lindsay, Ian Eaton.

Harry Hinde

325 Walmer Rd.
Toronto, ON M5R 2Y3
(416) 968-7337
Category: Independent producer.
Area of Expertise: Pop, Country.

Peter Hudson

108 Hallam St.
Toronto, ON M6H 1W8
(416) 588-6075
Category: Independent producer.
Area of Expertise: Contemporary Rock, Country, Alternative Jazz.
Artists Produced: Fifth Column, Rocktopus, Shadowy Men, Central People, Joe Hall.

Hutt-Biggs Productions

300 Trillium Dr., Suite 9
Kitchener, ON N2E 2K6
(519) 893-1115
Category: Production house.
Area of Expertise: All types.
Artists Produced: Jamie Warren, Madonna Tassi, Terry Odette, Random Access, Picture Comes to Life, Mary Anne, Tom Cochrane and Red Rider.

Les Productions l'Idee Inc.

Simon Carpentier
43 cote de la Canoterie
Quebec, PQ G1K 3X5
(418) 694-0111
FAX (418) 694-1594
Category: Independent producer.
Area of Expertise: All styles.
Artists Produced: Fashion Passion, Bertrand Gosselin, General Frank, Christian Thomas, Hans Reveille, Geddes Thurton, Charles Brieres, Pastel.

Industrial Art Music Productions

26 Boustead Ave., Suite A
Toronto, ON M6R 1Y4
(416) 769-4256 or 348-8718
FAX (416) 348-9668
Category: Independent producer.
Area of Expertise: All styles, but originality a must.
Artists Produced: Various Toronto bands.
Comments: We specialize in the establishment and development of original music groups in both live and studio situations. Engineering and computer programming also available.

Paul Irvine

Pi Music Productions
134 Peter St., Suite 314
Toronto, ON M5V 2H2
(416) 581-0198
Category: Independent producer.
Area of Expertise: All styles.
Artists Produced: Mark James Fortin, Sara Craig, A.K.A., Wipeout Beach, Sandi Currie, Paul Wild.
Comments: Expertise in arranging, composition and recording techniques.

Paul James

208 Indian Grove
Toronto, ON M6P 2H2
(416) 767-6816
Category: Independent producer.
Area of Expertise: Rock & Roll, R&B, Blues, Rockabilly.
Artists Produced: Paul James, Rita Chirelli.

Richard Janik

A-Frame Records
3491 Ouellette Ave.
Windsor, ON N9E 3M1
(519) 969-6585
FAX (519) 945-8146
Category: Independent producer.
Area of Expertise: Pop, Country and Alternative. Also novelty projects.
Artists Produced: Sufferin' Catfish, Richard Janik.
Comments: Mainly interested in producing theme and topical material for radio and television.

Gregory Johnston

Tanis Productions
4160 Dundas St. W.
Etobicoke, ON M8X 1X3
(416) 233-7029
FAX (416) 445-5145
Category: Production house.
Area of Expertise: Pop, Rock, R&B, Jazz.
Artists Produced: Various.
Comments: Complete production services: writing, arranging, talent, recording and publishing.

Keytrax Productions

51 Harcourt Ave., Lower Level
Toronto, ON M4J 1N2
(416) 463-8332
FAX (416) 968-3219
Category: Independent producer.
Area of Expertise: Pop.
Artists Produced: Various local acts.
Comments: Eight years' engineering experience and access to 24-track recording facility.

Peter Kilgour

3125 Yukon St.
Vancouver, BC V5Y 3R6
(604) 873-3306
Category: Production house.
Area of Expertise: Pop, Jazz, Country plus jingles and film work.
Artists Produced: Roge Belanger, Bill Legere, Cecille Larochelle.
Comments: Experience as a musician and engineer. Access to studio.

Mitchell Kitz

2 Bloor St. W., Suite 100-379
Toronto, ON M4W 3E2
(416) 534-5233
FAX (416) 968-9417
Category: Independent producer.
Area of Expertise: Pop, Dance, Alternative.
Artists Produced: Primitive Fire, Sandra Caldwell, Wellington Lambert, Christina, Kevin Fallerty.

Andy Krehm

Silverbirch Productions
680 Queens Quay W., Suite 600
Toronto, ON M5V 2Y9
(416) 596-0266
FAX (416) 593-8651
Category: Independent producer.
Area of Expertise: Pop, Rock, R&B, Dance.
Artists Produced: Vivienne Williams, Clazz, Ruth Powell, Rosanne Baker Thornley, and many others.
Comments: Krehm also does musical arrangements for theatre. Credits include *Jacob Two Two Meets The Hooded Fang, The Fabulous Kelley* and *Thin Ice.*

Al Kussin

Slak Records
214 St. George St., Suite 608
Toronto, ON M5R 2N8
(416) 964-0695
FAX (416) 348-9668
Category: Independent producer.
Area of Expertise: R&B, Pop, A/C.
Artists Produced: Lorraine Scott, Sounds Caribbean.
Comments: Received Juno nomination 1988 for best R&B recording.

LTM Productions

7305 Woodbine Ave., Suite 467
Markham, ON L3R 3V7
(416) 449-4035
Category: Production house.
Area of Expertise: All types of music, with the exception of Classical.
Artists Produced: Ben E. King, James Brown, Patti Labelle, Bo Diddley, Mary Wells, The Drifters, The Young Rascals, Peter-Best (ex Beatle), Jackson Hawk, Bond, Zon, Lydia Taylor, Patricia Dalquist, The Nylons.
Comments: Produced 12 international number-one hits and two Juno winners.

Yvan Labelle

100 High Park Ave., Suite 317
Toronto, ON M6P 2S2
(416) 763-0103
Category: Independent producer.
Area of Expertise: Background music for films, industrials and commercials. Has also produced music in the following genres: Heavy Metal, New Age, Rock, Pop, Choral and Gospel.
Artists Produced: Dimitrius.
Comments: Tailor-made music.

Bobby Lalonde

P.O. Box 21
Fournier, ON K0B 1G0
(613) 524-2838
FAX (613) 524-3315
Category: Production house.
Area of Expertise: Country, plus educational music and jingles.
Artists Produced: Bobby Lalonde Band, Francois Viau.
Comments: In-house 64-track MIDI sequencer recording studio.

Tom Lavin

Blue Wave
34 W. 8 Ave.
Vancouver, BC V5Y 1M7
(604) 873-3388
FAX (604) 873-0674
Category: Independent producer.
Area of Expertise: Pop, Rock, Blues, Country, Jazz.
Artists Produced: Powder Blues, Jim Byrnes, Susan Jacks, Amos Garrett, Long John Baldry.

Steven Long

1527 Chiddingstone Circle
Mississauga, ON L5M 3P8
(416) 567-4272
Category: Independent producer.
Area of Expertise: Pop, Rock and some Country.
Comments: Access to 24-track, fully automated facilities. Can also assist artists in lyric writing and vocals.

Anand Maharajh

P.O. Box 88, Stn. H
Montreal, PQ H3G 2K5
(514) 935-9089
Category: Production house and independent producer.
Area of Expertise: Pop, Dance, R&B.
Artists Produced: Mac Thornhill, Suzanne Riches, Ty Benskin.

John Mars
Ugly Dog Records
P.O. Box 1583
Brantford, ON N3T 5V6
(519) 753-2081
Category: Independent producer.
Area of Expertise: Rock & Roll, New Jazz.
Artists Produced: The Children, The Martians, The Popp Tarts, The Recognitions, Stu Broomer and John Mars.
Comments: Creative direction provided. Send cassette demo. Fees negotiable.

Christopher P. Mayo
Good Egg Productions
71 Bank St., Suite 507
Ottawa, ON K1P 5N2
(613) 233-7698
Category: Production house.
Area of Expertise: Pop, Rock, Country.
Artists Produced: Available on request.

Tim McCauley
Red Line Recorders
612 Yonge St.
Toronto, ON M4Y 1Z3
(416) 963-8000

Mark McLay
Pyramid Productions
205A Lakeshore Rd. E.
Mississauga, ON L5G 1G2
(416) 891-0336
FAX (416) 278-1799
Category: Production house and independent producer.
Area of Expertise: Heavy Metal, Commercial Rock, Blues, Jazz, Christian Music plus jingles, TV and movie soundtracks. Live and multitrack recording.
Artists Produced: Black Glamma, Terraced Garden, The Call, Ancient Tribe, Toronto Male Choir, Ginzia (U.S.), Vision (international).
Comments: Music and video productions plus in-house writing, arranging and producing. Albums, CDs, ambience and theme music for film and TV. Also electronic music, jingle production and artist promotion.

Stan Meissner
644 Christie St.
Toronto, ON M6G 3E7
(416) 651-1260
Category: Independent producer.
Area of Expertise: Rock, Pop.
Artists Produced: Stan Meissner, Livingroom, David Quinton, Barry Hagarty.
Comments: Records, plus extensive film and TV credits.

Larry Mercey Productions
590 Hunters Place
Waterloo, ON N2K 3L1
(519) 746-8488
Category: Independent producer.
Area of Expertise: Country.
Artists Produced: Marie Bottrell, Terry Carisse, Susan Tyler, Nicole Hartt.

Merlin Productions
Main P.O. Box 5087
Vancouver, BC V6B 4A9
(604) 525-9194
Category: Independent producer.
Area of Expertise: Pop, Dance, Metal.
Artists Produced: Various.
Comments: Active with GAS (Germany, Austria, Switzerland) since 1982 through EMI Publishing, Germany.

Metropolitan Productions
343 Richmond St., Suite 301
London, ON N6A 3C2
(519) 667-3622
FAX (519) 642-7453
Category: Production house.
Area of Expertise: Pop, Country, Easy Listening, Metal, jingles.
Artists Produced: Monkee See, Media Maria, Michael Dee, Equus, Twice Shy, Glenn Bennett, Keith Barrie, The Waiting, Dave Hoy.
Comments: Peter Brennan, Blaine Selkirk (staff producers).

Micah Production
P.O. Box 608, Adelaide St. Stn.
Toronto, ON M5C 2J8
(416) 298-3108
Category: Independent producer.
Area of Expertise: Gospel, Children's.
Artists Produced: Sweet Sound, Toronto A.G.M.M. Mass Choir.

Paul Mills
153 Glenmount Park Rd.
Toronto, ON M4E 2N3
(416) 690-5729

Paul Milner
7808 Yonge St.
Thornhill, ON L4J 1W3
(416) 889-7264
Category: Independent producer.
Area of Expertise: All styles.
Comments: Record engineering background.

Peter Mitchell

Fluid Sound Studios
198 W. Hastings St.
Vancouver, BC V6B 1H2
(604) 683-5843
Area of Expertise: Everything including Pop,
Country, Jazz, Folk, Blues, Modern Dance.
Artists Produced: John Beatty (Rubber Biscuit,
Big Medecin), Sandy Scofield, (Crimpolines, Hot
Tamale Twisters), Mark Shelan (Folk), The
Zealots, The Love Weasel, The Sign, The Jaunting
Car, The Hard Rock Miners, Nelson Ross, John
Dowler. Music for CBC special, *Knowledge
Network* and many industrials.
Comments: Writer, arranger, engineer,
producer, multi-instrumentalist, studio builder
and owner.

John Moorhouse

Bovine Int'l Record Co.
3665 Arista Way, Suite 1910
Mississauga, ON L5A 4A3
(416) 277-3908
Category: Independent producer.
Area of Expertise: Pop, R&B, Country.
Artists Produced: John Moorhouse, Solid Ivory
Brothers' Band, The Keynotes.

Ross Munro

c/o Random Entertainment Inc.
3100 Ridgeway Dr., Suite 26
Mississauga, ON L5L 5M5
(416) 569-3100
FAX (416) 569-1221
Category: Independent producer.
Area of Expertise: Rock, Pop, Country.
Artists Produced: Danny Brooks, Simon
Chase, Jannetta, Triumph, Reckless, Ronnie Haw-
kins, Uranus, Mardels.

Musicline International Inc. - John Lennon

1801 Eglinton Ave. W., Unit 1797D
Toronto, ON M6E 2H8
Area of Expertise: R&B, Pop. Also studio and
pre-production recordings.
Artists Produced: Errol Starr, Yvonne Moore,
Hylton Cohen, Elizabeth Klyeman.
Comments: Open to songs from outside
writers. Submit two-four pop-oriented songs and
include lyrics and lead sheets. Cassettes only.
S.A.S.E. for returns.

Nephilim Records/ Mario Rubnikowich

Studio Works
404 St. Henri
Montreal, PQ H3C 2P5
(514) 871-8481
Category: Production house.
Area of Expertise: Pop, Rock.
Comments: Engineered works by Sam Ma,
Mario Rubnikowich.

Paul Northfield

Worlds End Management
183 Martel Ave., Suite 270
Los Angeles, CA 90036
(213) 965-1540
Category: Independent producer.
Area of Expertise: Pop, Rock.
Artists Produced: Vain (Island Records),
8 Seconds (PolyGram Records), Paul Piche
(Audiogram Records).
Comments: Producer of the year - ADISO for
Paul Piche *Nouvelles d'Europe*. Engineered for
over 15 years. (Credits include. Glass Tiger,
Rush, Kim Mitchell, Asia, Men Without Hats,
Luba, and others).

Paroles et Musique

3815 St. Denis
Montreal, PQ H2W 2M4
(514) 282-1811
FAX (514) 282-1828
Category: Production house.
Area of Expertise: New Age.
Artists Produced: Joan Robitalle, UZEB.

Hayward Parrott

McClear Place Recording Studios.
225 Mutual St.
Toronto, ON M5B 2B4
(416) 977-9740
FAX (416) 977-7147.
Category: Independent producer.
Area of Expertise: Pop, Classical, Jazz, Coun-
try, Albums, plus jingles and film scores.
Artists Produced: Liona Boyd, Frank Mills,
Roger Whittaker, Bill King, Kenny MacLean, Matt
Segriff, Kamal, The Front.
Comments: Numerous Juno, Gemini and
Ampac nominations and awards.

William Petrie

Studio "B"
983 Victoria Park Ave.
Toronto, ON M4B 2J4
(416) 757-4891
Category: Independent producer.
Area of Expertise: Pop, Country, Children's.
Artists Produced: Andy Curran, Soho 69,
Valerie Shearman, Cheyenne, Stumblin' Blind,
Mach IV, And so We Go, Shari and Jerry, Kideo.

Stefan Podgrabinski

Sound Proofs
37 Scarborough Rd.
Toronto, ON M4E 3M4
(416) 690-3888
Category: Production house.
Area of Expertise: Pop, film music.
Artists Produced: Popular Front, David Storey,
Napoleon Solo, Kyro, Alfred Schall, Kids in the
Lab.
Comments: Finished digital masters produced
in-house.

Peter Probst

P.O. Box 112
Inglewood, ON L0N 1K0
(416) 838-3686
FAX (416) 890-0873
Category: Independent producer.
Area of Expertise: Pop.
Artists Produced: Mankind.
Comments: MIDI studio experience.

Peter Randall

SC Entertainment
99 Sudbury St.
Toronto, ON M6J 3S7
(416) 538-2666
FAX (416) 538-0583
Category: Independent producer.
Area of Expertise: Pop, Rock, Country.
Artists Produced: Timeline, Peter Randall, The
Fact, Quadra, The Phantom A's.

Reaction Productions

Reaction Studios
72 Stafford St., Rear
Toronto, ON M6J 2R9
(416) 865-9468
Category: Production house.
Area of Expertise: Rock, Pop, Dance, New
Age, World Beat.
Artists Produced: Various local artists and
bands.
Comments: Live and MIDI, 24-track studio.
Producers: O. Jobin, J. Stewart, M. Dematteo.

Regal Recordings Limited

2421 Hammond Rd.
Mississauga, ON L5K 1T3
(416) 855-2370
FAX (416) 855-1773
Category: Independent producer.
Area of Expertise: Jazz.
Artists Produced: Oscar Peterson, Clark Terry,
Lorne Lofsky, Phil Nimmons, Norman Simons,
Ella Fitzgerald.

Al Rodger

Seraphim Sound Studios
266 E. 1 St.
North Vancouver, BC V7L 1B3
(604) 985-0177
Category: Production house.
Area of Expertise: Pop, Rock.
Artists Produced: Al Rodger, Under Rain, John
Gray, Daryl Burgess And The Rhythm Snakes,
The Pride.

Michael Roy

P.O. Box 245, Stn. Place du Parc.
Montreal, PQ H2W 2N8
(514) 987-1198 or 289-9001
FAX (514) 987-1204
Category: Independent producer.
Area of Expertise: MOR.
Artists Produced: Michael Roy.

SCI Productions/ Bill Szawlowski and Gary Moffet

P.O. Box 941, N.D.G.
Montreal, PQ H4A 3S3
(514) 487-4551
Category: Independent producer.
Area of Expertise: Rock.
Artists Produced: Ray Lyell and the Storm,
Marjo, Mindstorm.
Comments: Production and engineering team
specializing in artist development.

S and S/Mike Sepe and Bruno Sepe

134 Pleasant Ave.
Willowdale, ON M2M 1M1
(416) 221-9332
Category: Independent producer.
Area of Expertise: Dance-oriented pop.
Artists Produced: Catch 22.

Roy Salmond

Whitewater Productions
3900 Steveston Highway, Suite 190
Richmond, BC V7E 2P7
(604) 277-3189
Category: Independent producer.
Area of Expertise: Pop, Hard Rock, Country,
Contemporary Christian.
Artists Produced: Morgan Cryar, Connie Scott,
Mercury Festival, Justus, Sean Garrett, Arlan
Salte.
Comments: Extensive MIDI programming
experience and gear. Own independent 16-track
pre-production facility.

Sim Savory/Sim's Studio

Sim's Studio
P.O. Box 10
Belleoram, NF A0H 1B0
(709) 881-6181 or 881-4576
FAX (709) 881-6391
Category: Independent producer.
Area of Expertise: Country, Folk.
Artists Produced: 50 local bands.

Jim Scott

1464 Beckworth Ave.
London, ON N5V 2K7
(519) 453-0892
FAX (519) 453-6303
Category: Independent producer.
Area of Expertise: Scottish Folk, Traditional, Pipe Bands.
Artists Produced: Cromdale, Stuart Anderson, Grant Fraser, MacNish Distillery Pipe Band.

Jon-E-Shakka

176B Woodridge Cr.
Nepean, ON K2B 7S9
(613) 596-5918
Category: Production house and independent producer.
Area of Expertise: Funk, Rap, House, Pop, Rock, R&B.
Artists Produced: August Skyy, J.T. Flash.
Comments: Also specialize in film scores.

Shemac Entertainment Group Inc.

Clarence St.
Woodbridge, ON L4L 1L4
(416) 850-3630
FAX (416) 850-2830
Area of Expertise: Pop, Rock.
Artists Produced: Dorian Gray, Benjamin's Kite.

Productions Pierre Simard

P.O. Box 25, Stn. E
Montreal, PQ H2T 3A5
(514) 521-3013
FAX (514) 521-3432
Category: Independent producer.
Area of Expertise: Pop, Rock.
Artists Produced: Madame, Philipe Lafontaine.

Sound Source Productions

67 Mowat Ave., Suite 031
Toronto, ON M6K 3E3
(416) 531-1390
FAX (416) 531-7439
Category: Production house.
Area of Expertise: Pop, MOR, Progressive Rock, Top 40, New Music.
Artists Produced: Prodigy, Grim Reaper, Tony Springer, Zero One, Titan (U.S.), Emergency Task Force, Magnum, Glamatron, NRG.
Comments: Complete music production. Specialize in producing, arranging, writing LPs, singles, demos and CDs. Also music for film, TV and radio. MIDI production available.

Spiral Sky Music

58 Phoebe St.
Toronto, ON M5T 1A9
(416) 591-6891
Area of Expertise: Pop, Rock, New Age, Ambient.
Artists Produced: The Trees, La Marche, Richard Samuels.
Comments: Music production and MIDI recording facility plus film and TV sound design and music composition.

Glen Stace

Studio West
502-45 St. W., Suite 3
Saskatoon, SK S7L 6H2
(306) 244-2815
FAX (306) 242-3301
Category: Independent producer.
Area of Expertise: Pop, Country.
Artists Produced: Casey Stone, May Run, Brian Sklar.

Dennis Stevenson

331 E. 19 St.
Hamilton, ON L9A 4S9
(416) 574-6878
Category: Independent producer.
Area of Expertise: Calypso, Soca, Reggae, Soul.
Artists Produced: Derrick Seales.
Comments: Dennis Stevenson is the first Western calypso composer to have received air-play in the U.S.S.R.

Paul Stillo

Steele Breeze Productions
17 Atkins Ave.
Toronto, ON M6K 1V9
(416) 532-3209
Category: Production house.
Area of Expertise: Demo production for artists and songwriters in the Pop Rock field.

D. Craig Strong

Mid-Ocean Recording Studio
1578 Erin St.
Winnipeg, MB R3E 2T1
(204) 774-3715
Category: Independent producer.
Area of Expertise: All styles.
Comments: Strong works out of Mid-Ocean
Recording Studios in Winnipeg and has prod-
uced for Attic Records, Shaman Records, and
others. Produces all types of music.

Studio West Productions

Studio West
502-45 St. W., Suite 3
Saskatoon, SK S7L 6H2
(306) 244-2815
FAX (306) 242-3301
Category: Independent producer.
Area of Expertise: All styles.
Artists Produced: Brian Plummer, May Run,
Glen Stace, Northern Pikes, Roxanne.

Sunshine Records Ltd.

228 Selkirk Ave.
Winnipeg, MB R2W 2L6
(204) 586-8057
FAX (204) 582-8397
Category: Production house and independent
producer.
Area of Expertise: Country, Ethnic, Old Tyme,
Gospel, Bluegrass.
Artists Produced: C-Weed, Brian Sklar, Tom
Jackson, Nestor Pistor, Reg Bonvette.

John Switzer

49 Pears Ave.
Toronto, ON M5R 1S9
(416) 964-6005
Category: Independent producer.
Area of Expertise: Pop, Folk, Rock, Country.
Artists Produced: Jane Siberry, Andrew Cash,
Mark Korven, Don Freed, Images In Vogue, Daisy
Debolt, Bratty, Bamff, Suffer Machine. Also: film
music production for *I've Heard The Mermaids
Singing* and *White Room* by Patricia Rozema.
Comments: Interested in all styles of popular
music with strong emphasis on lyrical content.
Primary goal is to capture the most committed
performances, and create a unique and commu-
nicative sonic landscape.

T.O.C. Talent Agency/ Deidre Sam

1155 West Georgia St., Suite 800
Vancouver, BC V6E 3H4
(604) 683-4230
FAX (604) 687-5519
Category: Independent producer.
Area of Expertise: Traditional Native Songs,
C&W, Contemporary, and Classical. All types of
music and song performed by Native and some
non-Native artists.
Artists Produced: Rick Patterson.
Comments: Sponsored Chief Len George:
Storytelling and Mythology.

Tambre Productions

550 Queen E. 205, Suite 205
Toronto, ON M5A 1V2
(416) 367-9797
FAX (416) 367-8356
Area of Expertise: All styles of music.
Specializing in music for film, TV and advertising.
Artists Produced: The Frantics.

Kevin Taylor

ART-TEC Production and Recording Studios
323 Talbot St., 2nd Floor
St. Thomas, ON N5P 1B5
(519) 633-6518
FAX (519) 633-6518
Category: Production house and independent
producer.
Area of Expertise: Pop, Metal, Rock, Classical,
Jazz, Country, Christian, Instrumental plus A/V
marketing.

Vezi Tayyeb

Quantum Records
170A Baldwin St.
Toronto, ON M5T 1L8
(416) 593-9547
FAX (416) 593-0461
Category: Independent producer.
Area of Expertise: Pop, Rock, MOR.
Artists Produced: Steve Fox, Jay W. McGee,
Keith McKie.

Ken Tobias

Reaction Studios
P.O. Box 609, Stn. F
Toronto, ON M4Y 2L8
(416) 922-1600 or 360-5288
Category: Independent producer.
Area of Expertise: R&B, Pop, Rock, New Age,
World Beat, plus documentary soundtracks.
Artists Produced: Cory Hart (demos), Ken
Tobias, Syren, Dan Clancy.
Comments: Experienced songwriter.

Domenic Troiano/ Black Market Records.

Round Sound
357 Ormont Dr.
Weston, ON M9L 1N8
(416) 743-9979
Category: Production house and independent producer.
Area of Expertise: Pop, R&B, Rock.
Artists Produced: David Gibson, Johnny R.
Comments: TV and film scoring for Night Heat, Airwaves, Hot Shots, True Blue.

John Tucker

Keen Communication Systems Inc.
11 Soho St., Suite 203
Toronto, ON M5T 1Z6
(416) 977-9845
FAX (416) 599-9714
Category: Production house.
Area of Expertise: Pop, Rock, plus music for theatre, dance and performance art.
Artists Produced: Kenny MacLean, Boys Brigade, KLO, Meryn Cadell, Bengt Jorgen.
Comments: Contact: John Tucker or Thomas Neuspiel.

Richard Underhill

Shuffle Demon Productions
401 Richmond St. W., Suite 219
Toronto, ON M5V 1X3
(416) 340-9245
FAX (416) 340-9951
Category: Independent producer.
Area of Expertise: Jazz, various.
Artists Produced: The Shuffle Demons, Walsh/ Underhill Duo.
Comments: Also produced videos for Shuffle Demons.

Bill Usher

BamBoom Productions
87 Dearbourne Ave.
Toronto, ON M4K 1H6
(416) 465-8749
FAX (416) 461-0810
Category: Independent producer.
Area of Expertise: Pop, Family, World Beat.
Artists Produced: The Horseflies, Bob McGrath, Big Bird & Oscar The Grouch, The Spaceheaters.
Comments: Winner of three Juno awards.

Gilles Valiquette

MIDI Musique
3868 Hochelaga
Montreal, PQ H1W 1J6
(514) 259-6434
FAX (514) 259-4044
Category: Production house.
Area of Expertise: Records, Ice Capades, film/ video, fireworks, festivals, and documentaries.
Artists Produced: Daniel Lemire, Richard Seguin, Festival Benson & Hedges International, Ice Capades '89, Flash Varicelle, Montreal ce soir.
Comments: French and English music production.

Ron "Rocko" Vaugeois

Diversified Music Group c/o Brian Wadsworth.
1969 Pandora St.
Vancouver, BC V5L 5B2
(604) 255-3536
FAX (604) 255-8711
Category: Independent producer.
Area of Expertise: Country, Country Rock, Rock.
Artists Produced: One Horse Blue, Bear Mountain Boys.

Jaimie Vernon

Nonrev Productions
4352 Kingston Rd., P.O. Box 11
Scarborough, ON M1E 2M8
(416) 428-2461
Category: Independent producer.
Area of Expertise: Any acts in the Rock, Pop, Alternative, Punk, or Post- Modern vein.
Artists Produced: Moving Targetz, Swindled.
Comments: Will work on charge basis depending on enthusiasm of project. Included in price is also a vast store-house of musicians such as backing singers, guitarists, drummers, etc.

Douglas Virgin

Mediaplex/Yonge Street Records
397 Donlands Ave.
Toronto, ON M4J 3S2
(416) 467-1488
FAX (416) 467-1492
Category: Independent producer.
Area of Expertise: All styles.
Artists Produced: Brett McNaul, Main Street, Johnny Lovesin.

W.E.T. Productions

3336 Mainway
Burlington, ON L7M 1A7
(416) 332-4424
FAX (416) 847-0308
Category: Production house and independent producer.
Area of Expertise: Pop, Dance, R&B.
Artists Produced: Tagg, Never...But Always, Self Serve, Kon Kan.
Comments: Complete in-house production facilities.

Joel Wade/Billy Osborne

c/o Tayko Music House
387 Bloor St. E., 5th Floor
Toronto, ON M4G 2H2
(416) 924-8566
FAX (416) 962-6805
Category: Production house and independent producer.
Area of Expertise: Pop, R&B.
Artists Produced: Joel Wade, Vesta, Linda Clifford, Samona Cooke.

Terry Watada

Windchime Records
99 Ivy Ave.
Toronto, ON M4L 2H8
(416) 465-7688
Category: Independent producer.
Area of Expertise: Rock, Folk, Jazz.
Artists Produced: Terry Watada, Night's Disgrace, Roy Miya.

Chuck Williams

Citation Records
191A Wolseley St.
Thunder Bay, ON P7A 3G5
(807) 345-2448
Category: Independent producer.
Area of Expertise: Country, Country Rock.
Artists Produced: Co-produced: Carroll Baker, Myrna Lorrie, David Thompson, Chris Krienke, Jerry Palmer, Lynn Larabie, Grace Miller, 49th Parallel, The Plague.

Jay C. Willman

510 Stiles St.
Winnipeg, MB R3G 3A4
(204) 774-0788
Category: Independent producer.
Area of Expertise: Wave, Rap, Rock, Country.
Artists Produced: Class Info, J Jay W.
Comments: 16-track studio facilities.

Michael Phillip Wojewoda

36 Wright Ave.
Toronto, ON M6R 1K8
(416) 531-2185 or 534-0524
FAX (416) 869-0017
Category: Independent producer.
Area of Expertise: Pop, Jazz, Rock
Artists Produced: Chalk Circle, Shuffle Demons, Plasterscene Replicas, Change of Heart, Vital Sines, NoMind, Jellyfishbabies, Pig Farm, The Nevermen, Itsa Skitsa, Fifth Column.
Comments: Available as a music recording engineer and composer.

Ian Gregory Wright

312 Adelaide St. W., Suite 415
Toronto, ON M5V 1R2
(416) 960-3123
Category: Production house.
Area of Expertise: Rock.
Artists Produced: Brass Soldier, City Speak, Those Guys.

ZoRo Productions/ George Rondina and Jim Zolis

Number Nine Sound Studios Inc.
314 Jarvis St., Suite 101
Toronto, ON M5B 2C5
(416) 348-8718
FAX (416) 348-9668
Category: Independent producer.
Area of Expertise: Pop, Dance, etc.
Artists Produced: Figures At Dawn, Rave Reviews, May Day Parade.

RECORDING STUDIO EQUIPMENT SUPPLIERS

ASC Acoustic Sciences Corporation

P.O. Box 1179
Kaslo, BC V0G 1M0
(604) 353-2626
FAX (604) 353-7370
Type of Company: Licensed Canadian manufacturer of Tube Traps.
Special Services: Applied acoustics research design and development.
Product Specialty: Portable, retrofit and broadband acoustic systems for studio, broadcast, performing and playback environments.

Acoustic Design Group Inc.

2465 Cawthra Rd., Suite 128
Mississauga, ON L5A 3P2
(416) 272-4495
FAX (416) 273-9756
Type of Company: Loudspeaker manufacturer.
Special Services: Will custom build.

Adamson Acoustic Design Corporation

850 Brock Rd., Unit 1
Pickering, ON L1W 1Z8
(416) 420-6279
FAX (416) 420-0813
Type of Company: Manufacturer and distributor of commercial sound reinforcement systems and associated electronics.
Top Brands: Adamson Acoustic (manufacture), McCauley loudspeakers (distribute).

Adcom Electronics Ltd.

310 Judson St., Unit 1
Toronto, ON M8Z 5T6
(416) 251-3355
FAX (416) 251-3977
Type of Company: Sales agency and distributor.
Top Brands: Quantec, Sound Master, Sony, Pro Audio, Calrec, Evertz.
Product Specialty: System house for audio post-production of film and video.

Amber Electro Design Ltd.
6969 Trans-Canada Highway
St. Laurent, PQ H4T 1V8
(514) 333-8748
FAX (514) 333-1388
Type of Company: Manufacturer and distributor.
Top Brands: Amber
Product Specialty: Audio test equipment for noise and distortion.

Ampex of Canada
1770 Argentia Rd.
Mississauga, ON L5N 3S7
(416) 858-1056
Type of Company: Manufacturer.
Top Brands: Ampex.
Product Specialty: Tape and equipment (audio and video).

Analogue Industries
6902 Park Ave.
Montreal, PQ H3N 1W9
(514) 278-8273
FAX (514) 273-8883
Type of Company: Audio tape manufacturer.
Special Services: Real-time duplication, blank cassettes, recording supplies.
Top Brands: BASF, Ampex, Scotch.

Atlas Electronics Ltd.
50 Wingold Ave.
Toronto, ON M6B 1P7
(416) 789-7761
FAX (416) 789-3053
Type of Company: Distributor.
Top Brands: Amprobe, VNK, Atlas Soundalier.
Product Specialty: Components, instrumentation, sound.

Audio Hardware
869 Connor Dr.
Toronto, ON M4B 2S7
(416) 288-1458
Type of Company: Manufacturer and sales agency.
Top Brands: TBL, Electro-Voice, Crest, Rane.
Product Specialty: Audio products, cabinets, enclosures.

Audionova Inc.
2083 Chartier Ave.
Dorval, PQ H9P 1H3
(514) 631-5787
FAX (514) 631-5789
Type of Company: Pro audio and lighting supplier.
Top Brands: NSI, EAW, SCS.

Audio Products International
3641 McNicoll Ave.
Scarborough, ON M1X 1GS
(416) 321-1800
FAX (416) 321-1500
Top Brands: Mirage, Energy, Image, Audio Pulse.
Product Specialty: Stereo Speakers.

Audio Video Specialists
2134 Trans-Canada Highway S.
Montreal, PQ H9P 2N4
(514) 683-1771
FAX (514) 683-5307
Top Brands: Audio Technica, GE video and audio, Klipsch.
Product Specialty: Cartridges, microphones, video cassette recorders, loudspeaker systems, stereo equipment.

Avalanche Effects
P.O. Box 582, Stn. C
Toronto, ON MJ6 3R9
(416) 864-0306
Type of Company: Manufacturer.
Product Specialty: Brianizer (Leslie emulator effects box).

B & J Music
469 King St. W.
Toronto, ON M5V 1K4
(416) 596-8361
FAX (416) 596-8822
Type of Company: Distributor of musical instruments and accessories.
Special Services: Complete repair services.
Top Brands: Ross electronics.
Product Specialty: Music electronics.

Bose Limited
35 East Beaver Creek Rd., Suite 8
Richmond Hill, ON L4B 1B3
(416) 886-9123
FAX (416) 886-9134
Type of Company: Loudspeaker manufacturer.
Special Services: Sound system design (CAD).
Top Brands: Bose.

Bryston Marketing Limited
57 Westmore Dr.
Rexdale, ON M9V 3Y6
(416) 746-0300
Type of Company: Amplifier manufacturer.

C.M.S. Music Inc.
8660 Jeanne-Mance
Montreal, PQ H2P 2S6
(514) 387-7331
FAX (514) 383-3576
Type of Company: Supplier of musical instruments and sound equipment.

Cerwin-Vega Canada Ltd.
2360 Midland Ave., Unit 21
Scarborough, ON M1S 4A9
(416) 292-6645
FAX (416) 292-4330
Type of Company: Loudspeaker distributor.
Product Specialty: Speakers.

Classe Audio
9414 Cote-de-Liesse Rd.
Lachine, PQ H8T 1A1
(514) 636-6384
FAX (514) 636-1428
Type of Company: Manufacturer and distributor.
Top Brands: Classe.
Product Specialty: Amplifiers and pre-amplifiers.

Contact Distribution
60 Venture Dr., Suite 6
Scarborough, On M1B 1S4
(416) 287-1144
FAX (416) 287-1204
Type of Company: Distributor.
Top Brands: Rane, Crest, Technical Projects, BSS.
Product Specialty: Pro audio products, amplifiers, crossover, mixers.

Doyle Custom Enclosures
53 Budworth Dr.
West Hill, ON M1E 3H8
(416) 755-9101
Type of Company: Manufacturer of custom electronic components.
Special Services: Rentals, installations.
Product Specialty: Crossovers, pre-amps, ERS, Doyle custom enclosures, PA stage and studio monitors.

Elnova Professional Electronics Ltd.
325 rue Clement o.
Lasalle, PQ H8R 4B4
(514) 364-2118
FAX (514) 364-0791
Type of Company: Distributor of professional audio products.
Top Brands: Beyer Dynamic, Schoeps, Klein & Hummel, ASL.
Product Specialty: Microphones, headphones, headsets, amplifiers, intercom equipment.

Equity Sound Investments
629 Eastern Ave., Unit 2
Toronto, ON M4M 1E4
(416) 465-4888
FAX (416) 465-3919
Type of Company: Loudspeaker manufacturer.
Special Services: Custom design and analysis.
Top Brands: Intersonics ServoDrive, BOND, Gane.

Erikson
(A Division of JAM Industries)
378 Isabey
St. Laurent, PQ H4T 1W1
(514) 738-3000
FAX (514) 737-5069
Type of Company: Canadian supplier.
Special Services: Exclusive Canadian distribution.
Top Brands: Fostex, Valley, DIC, KMD, Biamp.
Branches:
111 Granton Dr., Units 404 & 406
Richmond Hill, ON L4B 1L5
(416) 764-6350
FAX (416) 764-6799

3496 Vanness Ave.
Vancouver, BC V5K 5A9
(604) 438-9212
FAX (604) 438-7911.

Evolution Audio Inc.
1131 South Service Rd. W.
Oakville, ON L6L 6K4
(416) 847-8888
FAX (416) 847-7408
Type of Company: Importer and distributor.
Top Brands: Carver, Polk Audio, Monster Cable, Audio Control.
Product Specialty: Amplifiers, speakers, cable, sound adjustment products.

GERR Electro-Acoustics Ltd.
363 Adelaide St. E.
Toronto, ON M5A 1N3
(416) 868-0528
FAX (416) 868-6419
Type of Company: Retailer of quality pro audio equipment.
Special Services: Custom design and manufacturing of specialized audio equipment.
Top Brands: Synclavier, Sound Workshop, Timeline, GEM.

Gould Marketing Inc.
6445 Cote-de-Liesse
Montreal, PQ H4T 1E5
(514) 342-4441
FAX (514) 342-5597
Type of Company: Distributor of professional and consumer audio electronics.
Special Services: Custom home automation systems.
Top Brands: JBL, AKG Acoustics, Otari, Aphex.

H.D.S. Industries
P.O. Box 4374, Stn. E.
Ottawa, ON K1V 8P1
(613) 733-6892
Type of Company: Manufacturer.
Top Brands: Combat loudspeakers.

Head-Water Imports
635 Caron Ave.
Windsor, ON N9A 5B8
(519) 256-5665
FAX (519) 256-2522
Type of Company: Manufacturer and distributor of audio products.
Special Services: Custom electronics and manufacturing.
Top Brands: Drawmer, Hill Audio, OHM Ind.
Product Specialty: Noise gates, dynamic processors, power amplifiers, mixing consoles.

The Russ Heinl Group
41 Industrial Park Place S.
Aurora, ON L4G 3Y5
(416) 727-1951
FAX (416) 841-1312
Type of Company: Distribution agency.
Top Brands: DOD Electronics, Gallien Krueger, AB Systems amps, Trace Elliott.
Product Specialty: Amplifiers, signal processing, sound reinforcement.

Hemisphere Speaker Systems
10 Muirhead Rd., Suite 405
Willowdale, ON M2J 4P9
(416) 499-8088
Type of Company: Loudspeaker manufacturer.
Top Brands: Hemisphere.
Product Specialty: Close field reference monitors.

The Imaginative Marketing Group
1444 Hymus Blvd.
Dorval, PQ H9P 1J6
(514) 685-2046
FAX (514) 685-2094
Type of Company: Distributor.
Special Services: Automation installation (Twister).
Top Brands: Focusrite, Twister Automation, CAD.
Product Specialty: Quality recording equipment.

Mark IV Audio
345 Herbert St., P.O. Box 520
Gananoque, ON K7G 2V1
(613) 382-2141
FAX (613) 382-7466
Type of Company: Manufacturer.
Top Brands: Electro-Voice.
Product Specialty: Loudspeakers and microphones.

Omnimedia Corporation Ltd.
9653 Cote-de-Liesse Rd.
Dorval, PQ H9P 1A3
(514) 636-9971
FAX (514) 636-5347
Type of Company: Distributor.
Special Services: Servicing of audio products.
Top Brands: Crown, Klark-Technik, Samson, Soundtracs, Turbosound, Whirlwind, U.S. Audio.
Product Specialty: Equipment for the pro audio, recording and broadcast markets.

Paco Electronics

20 Steelcase Rd. W., Unit 10
Markham, ON L3R 1B2
(416) 475-0740
FAX (416) 475-0464
Type of Company: Distributor.
Top Brands: Paco, Paso, Fuji.
Product Specialty: Microphones, accessories, sound columns, amplifiers, audio and video cassettes.

Precision Sound Corporation

5614 Goring St.
Burnaby, BC V5B 3A3
(604) 299-4141
Type of Company: Manufacturer and distributor of audio and video tape.
Special Services: Real-time duplication, cassette packaging.
Top Brands: TDK (audio and video tape).
Product Specialty: Music duplication on TDK custom wound tape.

Rodam Manufacturing (Canada) Ltd.

91 Pelham Ave.
Toronto, ON M6N 1A5
(416) 656-8462
FAX (416) 656-8695
Type of Company: Manufacturer of audio cables and direct boxes.
Top Brands: Rodam, Rimshot.
Product Specialty: Cables, drum sticks.

Roland Canada Music Ltd.

13880 Mayfield Place
Richmond, BC V6V 2E4
(604) 270-6626
FAX (604) 270-6552
Type of Company: Manufacturer of electronic musical instruments.
Branches:
346 Watline Ave.
Mississauga, ON L4Z 1X2

9425 Trans-Canada Service Rd. N.
St. Laurent, PQ H4S 1V3

S.F. Marketing Inc.

3254 Griffith St.
St. Laurent, PQ H4T 1A7
(514) 733-5344
FAX (514) 733-7140
Type of Company: Manufacturer, distributor.
Product Specialty: Cables.

Sennheiser Canada

221 Labrosse Ave.
Pointe Claire, PQ H9R 1A3
(514) 426-3010
FAX (514) 426-2979
Type of Company: Distributor of microphones, wireless microphones and infrared equipment.
Special Services: Theatre installations and equipment for the hard of hearing.

A.C. Simmonds and Sons Ltd.

975 Dillingham Rd.
Pickering, ON L1W 3B2
(416) 839-8041
FAX (416) 839-2667
Type of Company: Distributor.
Top Brands: Shure.
Product Specialty: Microphones (wireless and wired), broadcast and microphone mixers.
Branch Offices:
4259 Canada Way, Suite 203
Burnaby, BC V5G 1H1
(604) 438-5267
FAX (604) 438-5269
Branch Manager: Martin Topp.

5963-103A St.
Edmonton, AB T6H 2J7
(403) 438-4044
FAX (403) 437-4308
Office Manager: Jim Letkeman.

1700 boul. Taschereau, Suite 200
Ville Lemoyne, PQ J4P 3M9
(514) 466-5250
FAX (514) 466-5252
Regional Manager: Pierre Laliberte.

P.O. Box 815
Lower Sackville, NS B4C 3V3
(902) 865-1889
FAX (902) 865-5120
Sales Representative: David Orser.

Sony of Canada Ltd.

405 Gordon Baker Rd.
Toronto, ON M2H 2S6
(416) 499-1414
Type of Company: Manufacturer and distributor of pro hardware, microphones, mixers, DAT.
Special Services: Pro audio system configuration.
Top Brands: Sony.

Soundcraft Canada Inc.

1444 Hymus Blvd.
Dorval, PQ H9P 1J6
(514) 685-1610
FAX (514) 685-2094
Type of Company: Sales and service of Soundcraft consoles.
Special Services: Maintenance and service.
Top Brands: Soundcraft mixing consoles.
Product Specialty: PA (recording and video).

Studer Revox Canada

14 Banigan Dr.
Toronto, ON M4H 1E9
(416) 423-2831
FAX (416) 425-6906
Type of Company: Manufacturer and distributor.
Top Brands: Studer, Revox.
Product Specialty: Consumer and professional audio products, sales and service.

StudioLab Audio Inc.

29 Bermondsey Rd.
Toronto, ON M4B 1Z7
(416) 757-3265
Type of Company: Loudspeaker manufacturer (consumer and pro audio).
Special Services: Custom speakers.
Top Brands: StudioLab.

TC Electronics

221 Labrosse Ave.
Pointe Claire, PQ H9R 1A3
(514) 426-3010
FAX (514) 426-2979
Type of Company: Distributor.
Top Brands: Sennheiser, Marantz, Final Technology.
Product Specialty: Microphones, headphones, wireless microphones.

TMI

2530 Davies Ave., P.O. Box 279
Port Coquitlam, BC V3C 3V7
(604) 464-1341
FAX (604) 464-9275
Type of Company: Distributor.
Special Services: Product specialists and clinicians. Inventory finance plans.
Top Brands: Fender, Akai, Alesis, Sunn, Audix, Casio.
Product Specialty: Recording, stage lighting, PA systems, amplification.

TOA Electronics Inc.

1351 Matheson Blvd. E., Unit 3
Mississauga, ON L4W 2A1
(416) 624-2317
FAX (416) 624-7348
Type of Company: Manufacturer of professional sound system equipment.
Special Services: Sales, service, cross-Canada distribution.
Product Specialty: Mixers, amps, speakers, home recording systems.
Branches:
1396 Saint Patrick St.
Montreal, PQ H3K 1A6
(514) 931-5888
FAX (514) 931-2359

10712-181 St.
Edmonton, AB T5S 1K8
(403) 489-5511
FAX (403) 489-7038

19691 Shellbridge Way, Suite 130
Richmond, BC V6X 2W8
(604) 273-5212
FAX (604) 270-3644

Tannoy/TGI North America Inc.

300 Gage Ave. Unit 1
Kitchener, ON N2M 2C8
(519) 745-1158
FAX (519) 745-2364
Type of Company: North American distributor.
Top Brands: Tannoy
Product Specialty: Dual concentric reference monitors.

TEAC Canada Ltd. (TASCAM)

340 Brunel Rd.
Mississauga, ON L4Z 2C2
(416) 890-8008
FAX (416) 890-9888
Type of Company: Manufacturer and distributor of TASCAM audio production equipment.

Tele-Tech Electronics Ltd.

920 Denison St., Unit 11
Markham, ON L3R 3K5
(416) 475-5646
FAX (416) 475-5684
Type of Company: Pro audio equipment supplier.
Special Services: Pro audio sales, rental and service.
Top Brands: TASCAM, Fostex, Sony.
Branches:
931 Leathorne St.
London, ON N5Z 3M7
(519) 685-6561

134 Peter St.
Toronto, ON M5V 2H2
(416) 598-3456

Thorvin Electronics Inc.

720 Burnhamthorpe Rd. W. Units 15-16
Mississauga, ON L5C 2R9
(416) 276-7271
FAX (416) 276-4196
Type of Company: Distributor of commercial and industrial sound equipment.
Special Services: Rental of spectrum analyzer to dealer base.
Top Brands: Soundsphere, Anchor Audio, Williams Sound.

3M Canada Inc.

P.O. Box 5757
London, ON N6A 4T1
(519) 451-2500
FAX (519) 452-6262
Type of Company: Manufacturer.
Top Brands: Scotch, 3M.
Product Specialty: Open reel audio tape, open reel video tape, video cassettes.
Branches:
1001-53 Ave. N.E., P.O. Box 3954, Stn. B
Calgary, AB T2M 4M5
(403) 275-7330

4808-87 St., Unit 120
Edmonton, AB T6E 5W3
(403) 275-7330

680 Lepine Blvd.
Dorval, PQ H9P 2S5
(514) 631-7600

1155 Lola St.
Ottawa, ON K1K 4C1
(613) 741-2007

155 Lesmill Rd., P.O. Box 1500
North York, ON M3C 2V3
(416) 449-8010
(800) 268-7770

7100 River Rd.
Richmond, BC V6X 1X5
(604) 273-2211

Western Imperial Magnetics Ltd.

12840 Bathgate Way, Suite 7
Richmond, BC V6V 1Z4
(604) 270-8682
FAX (604) 270-2745
Type of Company: Manufacturer and distributor of audio and video magnetic tape.
Special Services: Service department.
Top Brands: Adtec, DMC, Ampex, Scotch.
Product Specialty: Cassettes.

Yamaha Canada Music Ltd.

135 Milner Ave.
Toronto, ON M1S 3R1
(416) 298-1311
FAX (416) 292-0732
Type of Company: Manufacturer and wholesaler of musical instruments, sound equipment.

RECORDING STUDIOS

ALBERTA

Ambassador Music Studios

P.O. Box 8386, Stn. F
Calgary, AB T2J 2V5
(403) 271-3897
Owner: Wayne Chaulk.
Manager: Wayne Chaulk.
No. of Studios: One.
Services Offered: Demos, LPs, CDs, arranging, videos, soundtracks.
Rates: Varies by project.
Mixing Consoles: TASCAM 24.
Tape Machines: TASCAM 38.
Special Equipment: Complete MIDI set-up, sequencers, etc.
Accommodations: No.
Comments: Small studio designed for personalized attention.

Banana Belt Recording Studio

P.O. Box 1800
High Prairie, AB T0G 1E0
(403) 523-2455
Owner: Rick Perry.
Manager: Rick Perry.
No. of Tracks: 32.
No. of Studios: One.
Rates: $50 per hour.
Rehearsal Space: No.
Mixing Consoles: Soundcraft 200B.
Tape Machines: Fostex B-16.
Special Equipment: Lexicon, Valley People, Audiologic, A.T.& T., Emulator.
Accommodations: No.

Century City Recording Studios

2207 Halifax Cr. N.W.
Calgary, AB T2M 4E1
(403) 282-2555
Owners: Warren and Deb Anderson.
Manager: Warren Anderson.
No. of Tracks: 16.
No. of Studios: One.
Services Offered: Tape duplication, post-video, albums, jingles, live sound truck (location recording).
Rates: Negotiable on a per project basis.
Rehearsal Space: No.
Mixing Consoles: Studiomaster.
Tape Machines: TASCAM 8-track analog.
Special Equipment: Roland W-30 workstation, DX7, Eventide Harmonizer,
Symetrix, Delta Lab, Yamaha, Lexicon, JBL monitoring. Good selection of microphones including Neumann, EV, AKG and Shure.
Accommodations: No.
Comments: Currently working with artists for possible soundtrack work. Prefer rock, and rock with country touches.

Gerry Dere's Master Factory

11714-113 Ave.
Edmonton, AB T5G 0J8
(403) 454-6848 or 454-9291
Owners: Gerry Dere and Danny Makarus.
Manager: Danny Makarus.
No. of Tracks: 8 (tape), 16 (MIDI).
No. of Studios: One.
Services Offered: Record production, stageshows, video production.
Rates: $40 per hour.
Rehearsal Space: Can be arranged.
Mixing Consoles: Yamaha.
Tape Machines: TEAC, TASCAM.
Special Equipment: MIDI patch bay, V110 Roland samplers, SPX 90, SPX 50D, Yamaha REV5, Roland MC500 computer, R8 Roland drums, SYMTE, Song Pointer, FSK Sinc., Yamaha DX7 and DX100, Roland Juno 60.
Accommodations: Can be arranged.
Comments: Composed new stage shows for Raveen and produced the 1990 Canadian All Girl Showcase Tour.

E.K. Sound

2848-19 St. N.E.
Calgary, AB T2E 6Y9
(403) 291-9112
FAX (403) 250-2698
Owner: Ernest Klumpp.
Managers: Ernest Klumpp and Darcy Klumpp.
No. of Tracks: 24.
No. of Studios: Two.
Services Offered: Multitrack recording, audio-to-video synchronization, cassette duplication, extensive MIDI set-up.
Rates: $80 per hour (24-track).
Rehearsal Space: No.
Mixing Consoles: MCI JH-600 with CM4400.
Tape Machines: Sony JH-24, Otari MX-80/24, Otari MTR-12, Mitsubishi X-86.
Special Equipment: AMS RMX-16, Roland R-880, Dolby Sr, Audio Kinetics Q-Lock with Eclipse Editor. Neumann and AKG tube microphones.
Accommodations: No.

Final Take Studio

13 Moseley Close
Red Deer, AB T4N 5S8
(403) 347-5785
Owner: Cal Maier Musical Instruments.
Manager: Cal Maier.
No. of Tracks: 16.
No. of Studios: One.
Rates: $35 per hour.
Rehearsal Space: No.
Mixing Consoles: PA:CE (16x8x16x2).
Tape Machines: TASCAM MSR-16, TASCAM MTR-Z, Fostex A-2.
Accommodations: No.

Homestead Recorders (1985) Ltd.
14522-118 Ave.
Edmonton, AB T5L 2M8
(403) 454-8434
FAX (403) 452-6829
Owners: Keith James and Barry Allen.
Manager: Keith James.
No. of Tracks: 16.
No. of Studios: One.
Services Offered: Audio for video, radio and TV. Also, music, jingles and tape duplication.
Rates: $75 per hour.
Rehearsal Space: No.
Mixing Consoles: Soundcraft (16x24)
Tape Machines: Otari MX70, Otari MTR12, MX50/50 BII.
Special Equipment: Mega 4 Atari w/SMPTE track PRG, ADAP 1
Sound Rack, JVC BR7700U, Korg M1,JBL4435 monitors, plus full outboard assortment.
Accommodations: No.
Comments: Second control room for edit-dub-assembly. Green room (bring your own darts).

InEar Sounds
116 Forge Rd. S.E.
Calgary, AB T2H 0S8
(403) 255-6673
Owners: Gary Bruckner and Shane Connelly.
Managers: Gary Bruckner and Shane Connelly.
No. of Tracks: 24.
No. of Studios: One.
Services Offered: Video production.
Rates: $45 per hour.
Rehearsal Space: No.
Mixing Consoles: TAC Scorpion.
Tape Machines: Soundcraft 2".
Accommodations: No.

Premier Recordings Ltd.
8530-190 St.
Edmonton, AB T5T 4Z8
(403) 487-3083
Owner: Mel Gargus.
Manager: Mel Gargus.
No. of Tracks: 16.
No. of Studios: One.
Services Offered: Production music.
Rates: $45 per hour.
Rehearsal Space: No.
Mixing Consoles: Trident Trimix.
Accommodations: No.

Sound Shadow Studios
9336-49 St.
Edmonton, AB T6B 2L7
(403) 468-1748
FAX (403) 465-9825
Owners: Darryl and Nancy Goede.
Manager: David Teha.
No. of Tracks: 24.
No. of Studios: Three.
Services Offered: Audio lay back to video.
Rates: On request.
Rehearsal Space: No.
Tape Machines: Lyrec 24-Track, Otari MTR1O-11, ATR100.
Special Equipment: Advanced Music System (AMS).
Accommodations: No.

The Sundae Sound Studio Ltd.
3516-1 St. N.E.
Calgary, AB T2E 3C9
(403) 230-2331
FAX (403) 276-8187
Owners: Doug Wong, Ken Bird, Nigel Blagborne, Robert Bartlett.
Manager: Doug Wong.
No. of Tracks: 24.
No. of Studios: One.
Services Offered: Music recording, jingles, A/V and video soundtracks, audio for video post-production.
Rates: $80 per hour.
Rehearsal Space: No.
Mixing Consoles: Soundcraft 2400 (28 x 24 x 2 with automation).
Tape Machines: Otari MTR-90, Otari MTR-12, Otari MX-5050 (2).
Accommodations: No.
Comments: Clients include Ian Tyson, Mystery Romance, Adventures in Paradise, Sailcats, CFCN-TV, NFL Films, Rocky Mountain Auto Tours.

West 11th Audio

822-11 Ave. S.W., Suite 306
Calgary, AB T2R 0E5
(403) 265-0258
FAX (403) 265-4012
Owner: Lanny Williamson.
Manager: Chris McIntosh.
No. of Tracks: 24.
No. of Studios: Two.
Services Offered: Audio production for radio, TV, video and film.
Rates: $60-105 per hour.
Rehearsal Space: No.
Mixing Consoles: Remix 40 Channel.
Tape Machines: Studer A-80, Studer B-67, ISV-3500 R-DAT.
Special Equipment: Zeta Three Synchronizer, Atari 1040ST, Lexicon, Digitech, Urei, Neumann, Drawmer.
Accommodations: No.
Comments: Part of West 11th communications group.

BRITISH COLUMBIA

Andromeda Sound Studios

1304 Seymour St.
Vancouver, BC V6B 3P3
(604) 669-7900
Owner: Paul McCarthy.
Manager: Paul McCarthy.
No. of Tracks: 16.
No. of Studios: One.
Rates: $50 per hour.
Rehearsal Space: Yes.
Comments: An established studio, professionally equipped and staffed, offering a number of professional services.

B.C. Recording

3760 Departure Bay Rd.
Nanaimo, BC V9T 1C4
(604) 758-3424
Owner: Scott Littlejohn.
Manager: Scott Littlejohn.
No. of Tracks: 16.
No. of Studios: One.
Services Offered: Real-time cassette duplication, three-camera video.
Rates: $30 per hour.
Rehearsal Space: Yes.
Mixing Consoles: Dynamix.
Tape Machines: Fostex B-16, Sony Beta Hi-Fi, Pioneer half-track.
Accommodations: No.
Comments: Mobile recording studio.

Bastion City Mobile Recording Ltd.

3760 Departure Bay Rd.
Nanaimo, BC V9T 1C4
(604) 758-3424
Comments: Studio or location multitrack recording.

Beat Productions

3125 Yukon St.
Vancouver, BC V5Y 3R6
(604) 873-3306
Owner: Peter Kilgour.
Manager: Peter Kilgour.
No. of Tracks: 8 (analog), 30 (digital).
No. of Studios: One.
Services Offered: Synchronization.
Rates: $25-100 per hour.
Rehearsal Space: No.
Mixing Consoles: Roland Custom (56x4).
Tape Machines: TASCAM, Fostex.
Special Equipment: MIDI sampling facility.
Comments: Efficient layout and computer mixing makes for an accurate finished product.

Blue Wave Studios

34 W. 8 Ave.
Vancouver, BC V5Y 1M7
(604) 873-3388
FAX (604) 873-0674
Owner: T. Lavin.
Manager: M. Duperreault.
No. of Tracks: 2 x 24.
No. of Studios: Two.
Services Offered: Audio, A/V post-production, voiceovers, production.
Rates: On request.
Rehearsal Space: No.
Mixing Consoles: API.
Tape Machines: MCI.
Special Equipment: Tube mics, all types of outboard gear, concert grand, Hammond, drums, etc.
Accommodations: No.

Breakthrough Recording Studios

P.O. Box 962, Stn. A
Kelowna, BC V1Y 7P7
(604) 861-4144
Owner: J. Keith Hunter.
No. of Tracks: 8 (analog), 28 (digital).
No. of Studios: One.
Services Offered: Studio recording, mobile recording, tape duplication, music copying, arranging and composing.
Rates: $30 per hour.
Rehearsal Space: No.
Mixing Consoles: Yamaha 1608.
Tape Machines: Otari (50/50).
Comments: Write and produce video soundtracks, film scores and TV commercials.
Accommodations: No.

Creation Studios Inc.

2925 Fromme Rd.
North Vancouver, BC V7K 2C6
(604) 984-2448
FAX (604) 980-9161
Owners: Ian MacLellan and Barry Henderson.
Manager: Barry Henderson.
No. of Tracks: 24.
No. of Studios: One.
Services Offered: Audio post-production, MIDI
production, production staff.
Rates: On request.
Rehearsal Space: Yes.
Mixing Consoles: Sound Workshop 34.
Tape Machines: Studer A80/MK1V 24-track,
A80/2-Track, A807 2-Track.
Special Equipment: Neumann, AKG,
Sennheiser microphones. Also, R-DAT, Macintosh
computers and a layback machine.
Accommodations: No.

Ferocious Fish Productions

2115 Inglewood Ave.
West Vancouver, BC V7V 1Z6
(604) 922-9594
Owner: James Guttridge, Daryl Bennett, Erika
Florian.
Manager: Erika Florian.
No. of Tracks: 24.
No. of Studios: One.
Services Offered: Film, video and TV scoring
and original sound design. Mix to picture
capabilities.
Rates: On request.
Mixing Consoles: AKAI MG1214, AKAI MPX
820.
Tape Machines: AKAI MG1214.
Special Equipment: Lots of samplers, synths
and outboard gear. Also, video editing equipment.
Accommodations: No.
Comments: TV and film credits.

Fine Eye Productions

603 E. 26 Ave.
Vancouver, BC V5V 2H6
(604) 877-0350
Owners: Matt Singh and Eric Adams.
Manager: Matt Singh.
No. of Tracks: 12 (plus MIDI).
No. of Studios: One.
Services Offered: In-house and remote
recording, tape duplication.
Rates: Call for quote.
Rehearsal Space: No.
Mixing Consoles: Akai 1212 (plus Yamaha
sub-mixer).
Tape Machines: Akai, TEAC, Sony.
Special Equipment: Fostex 4010, Atari, Urei,
Yamaha, AKG, Shure, Roland, SMPTE
track, etc.
Accommodations: No.

Fluid Sound Studios Ltd.

198 West Hastings St.
Vancouver, BC V6B 1H2
(604) 683-5843
Manager: Peter Mitchell.
No. of Tracks: 24.
No. of Studios: Two.
Services Offered: A quality recording studio
for music and film (post-audio).
Rates: Negotiable (rates for all budgets).
Mixing Console: TASCAM Pro Series (62 in-
put).
Tape Machines: Ampex 2″ 24-track, Panasonic
DAT, Studer-Revox 2-track, Fostex 1/2 track with
SMPTE centre stripe, and TASCAM 8-track.
Accommodations: Yes.
Comments: A charming state-of-the-art studio
in an elegant heritage building in downtown
Vancouver.

Inside Trak Studios Ltd.

7490 Edmonds St.
Burnaby, BC V3N 1B4
(604) 525-3422
Owners: Gordon Ross and Rick Picard.
Manager: Lisa Barton.
No. of Tracks: 24.
No. of Studios: One.
Rates: On request.
Rehearsal Space: No.
Mixing Consoles: MCI JH-636.
Tape Machines: MCI JH 24-track, MCI
JH110B 2-track with 1/2″ Heastack.
Special Equipment: AMS DMX15-80S, AMS
RMX, AMS Keyboard Controller, Lexicon 224,
Valley People Kepex II noise gates and
gainbrains, Yamaha, REV7, DDL D1500, SPX90,
SPX9011, (2) Roland SRV2000, compressor/
limiter Urei 1178 stereo, Symetrix Stereo,
Parametric, Pultec EQ-P1A, Dolby SR, R-DAT.
Accommodations: Yes.
Comments: Projects: Paul Janz, Connie Scott,
Kick Axe, Sue Medley, Alibi. Engineers: Dave
Slagter, Gary Tole, Bill Buckingham, Steve Smith.

The Little Mountain Sound Studios Ltd.

201 W. 7 Ave.
Vancouver, BC V5Y 1L9
(604) 873-4711
FAX (604) 873-4718
Owner: Bob Brooks.
Manager: Alison Glass.
No. of Tracks: 48.
No. of Studios: Four.
Services Offered: Full recording, audio post-production, film scoring.
Rates: On request.
Rehearsal Space: No.
Mixing Consoles: Solid State Logic G Series.
Tape Machines: Studer.
Special Equipment: 2-track Sony Dash for mixdown, full range of outboard gear.
Accommodations: No.
Comments: Projects: Bon Jovi, Aerosmith, The Cult, Motley Crue, Colin James, Little Caesar, Make A Difference Album (Anti Drug), etc.

Mushroom Studios

1234 W. 6 Ave.
Vancouver, BC V6H 1A5
(604) 734-1217
FAX (604) 734-3901
Owner: Charlie Richmond.
Manager: Linda Nicol.
No. of Tracks: 40.
No. of Studios: Three.
Services Offered: Complete MIDI production facility.
Rates: Call for rates.
Rehearsal Space: Yes.
Mixing Consoles: 48-channel, 24 buss output custom-built by Richmond Sound Design Ltd.
Tape Machines: Studer A80 MKII 16-track and MKIII 24-track.
Special Equipment: Neve 1081 EQ, Q-Lock video synchronization, DBX Lexicon, Yamaha, Korg, Drawmer processing equipment.
Accommodations: Yes.
Comments: Five minutes from downtown, beaches, hotels, etc.

Ocean Studios

1758 W. 2 Ave.
Vancouver, BC V6J 1H6
(604) 733-3146
FAX (604) 738-5959
Owner: The Ocean Sound Corporation.
Manager: Ken Morrison.
No. of Tracks: 24.
No. of Studios: Two.
Services Offered: Video production.

Profile Sound Studios

3448 Commercial St.
Vancouver, BC V5N 4E9
(604) 875-6821
Owner: Profile Sound Studios Ltd.
Manager: Don Ramos.
No. of Tracks: 24.
Services Offered: Album production, MIDI programming.
Rates: Negotiable.
Rehearsal Space: No.
Mixing Consoles: Harrison 3232-C.
Tape Machines: MCI JH24.
Special Equipment: Direct to disc, 3402 2-track, digital, Mac-based MIDI system.
Accommodations: No.

Seacoast Sound

825 Broughton St.
Victoria, BC V8W 1E5
(604) 386-1131
Owner: Mel Cooper.
Manager: Geoff Bate.
No. of Tracks: 24.
No. of Studios: Two.
Rates: $60-90 per hour.
Rehearsal Space: No.
Mixing Consoles: Auditronics.
Tape Machines: Sony PCM digital 24-track, MCI mastering machines, Ampex mono machines.
Special Equipment: Lexicon digital reverb, Prime Time digital delay, Keplex 11, (4) DBX 166 compressors, LA4 compressor/limiter, Yamaha SPX 90, Yamaha REV7, Korg sampling digital 2DD2000, Roland SRV 2000, Urei peak limiter, Aphex 602 aural exciter, Studer 710 cassette deck, Urei 813 Yamaha NS10M monitors.
Accommodations: Yes.
Comments: Specialists in commercial jingles, audio/visual production, soundtracks, spoken word commercial writing and production, syndicated radio programs.

Seraphim Sound Studios

266 E. 1 St.
N. Vancouver, BC V7L 1B3
(604) 985-0177
Owner: Soren Lonnqvist.
Manager: Al Rodger.
No. of Tracks: 24.
No. of Studios: One.
Services Offered: Recording.
Rates: $60 per hour.
Rehearsal Space: No.
Mixing Consoles: MCI JH652 52 input.
Tape Machines: Otari MX-80 24-track.
Special Equipment: SU3500 R-DAT, Tube Tech, PEIB EQ.
Accommodations: No.

Soundwerks Rehearsal and Production Studios

1969 Pandora St.
Vancouver, BC V5L 5B2
(604) 255-3536
FAX (604) 255-8711
Owner: Diversified Music Group.
Managers: Brian Wadsworth and Jai Allan.
No. of Tracks: 16.
No. of Studios: One.
Services Offered: Sound recording.
Rates: $10 per hour.
Rehearsal Space: Yes.

Studioplex Production Services

4429 Juneau St.
Burnaby, BC V5C 4C4
(604) 294-6887
FAX (604) 294-6887
Managers: Terry Gray, Ian Warner, Dan Cowan.
No. of Tracks: 16 (analog), 30 (MIDI).
No. of Studios: Two.
Services Offered: 1/2" video production suite, tape duplication, stage gear and prop rental and storage, plus sound lights and monitor rentals.
Rates: $25 per hour.
Rehearsal Space: Yes.
Mixing Consoles: Aries (16x8x16).
Tape Machines: Fostex with MIDI and SMPTE E16 multitrack/Fostex E2 2-track TASCAM 22-2 1/2 track, Nakamichi MRI cassette deck.
Special Equipment: SPX digital EFX, SRV 2000 digital reverb, Atari 1040 computer w/SMPTE track pro sequencing and various software.
Accommodations: Can be arranged.

Trebas Recording Studios

112 E. 3 Ave., Suite 305
Vancouver, BC V5T 1C8
(604) 872-2666
FAX (604) 872-3001
President: David P. Leonard
Manager: Kirk.
No. of Tracks: 24.
No. of Studios: Two (24-track and MIDI).
Services Offered: MIDI, audio post-production, jingle and music productions.
Rates: On request.
Rehearsal Space: No.
Mixing Consoles: Amek/Mozart (32-channel, fully-automated).
Tape Machines: Otari MX-80 24-track, Otari MX-55TM 2-track with SMPTE, Mitsubishi digital 2-track.
Special Equipment: Full range of signal processing, MIDI and synchronization equipment.
Accommodations: No.
Comments: Creative and technical specialists in jingle and music productions. Audio post-production for video and film.

MANITOBA

Century 21

1085 Salter St.
Winnipeg, MB R2V 2E7
(204) 334-4304
FAX (204) 334-7931
Owners: John and Harry Hildebrand.
Manager: John Hildebrand.
No. of Tracks: 24.
No. of Studios: Two, plus one remote.
Rates: $90 per hour.
Rehearsal Space: No.
Mixing Consoles: Neve 8068 VCA control, Soundcraft.
Tape Machines: MTR 90, JH24 MCI.
Special Equipment: Digital delays, reverbs, limiters, compressors and various effects.
Accommodations: No.

Wayne Finucan Productions Ltd.

697 Sargent Ave.
Winnipeg, MB R3E 0A8
(204) 786-5578
Owner: Wayne Finucan.
Manager: Shirley Schritt.
No. of Tracks: 16, 24.
No. of Studios: Two.
Services Offered: Video post-production and tape duplication.
Rates: $45-150 per hour.
Rehearsal Space: Yes.
Mixing Consoles: MCI.
Tape Machines: MCI, Otari, Ampex.
Special Equipment: SMPTE Q-Lock, assorted outboard gear, reverb, Otari centre-track for 35mm stereo sound transfers, DAT machines.
Accommodations: No.
Comments: CD sound effects library.

Maddock Studio

331 Maddock Ave.
Winnipeg, MB R3C 4A2
(204) 338-1538
Owner: Dave Roman.
Manager: Dave Roman.
No. of Tracks: 24.
No. of Studios: One.
Services Offered: Complete album, CD and cassette fabrication.
Rates: $60 per hour.
Rehearsal Space: No.
Mixing Consoles: Soundcraft 2400 (28x24).
Tape Machines: Soundcraft, Otari.
Special Equipment: Sony DAT.
Accommodations: No.

Moon Tango Studios

234 Sydney Ave.
Winnipeg, MB R2K 1B6
(204) 668-1002
No. of Tracks: 24.

Perry Audio and Recording

115 Quincy Bay
Winnipeg, MB R3T 4K2
(204) 269-4340
Owner: Clive Perry.
Manager: Clive Perry.
No. of Tracks: 8.
No. of Studios: One.
Services Offered: On-location music recording, computer-based sound editing and audio post-production.
Rates: On request.
Rehearsal Space: No.
Mixing Consoles: Soundcraft.
Tape Machines: Sony, Fostex R-8.
Special Equipment: AKG and B&K mics, Fostex, Studio 3 MIDI/SMPTE synchronizers, samplers, effects, processors, Macintosh edit system.
Comments: Professional services include music and film mixing.

Sunshine Sound Studios

228 Selkirk Ave.
Winnipeg, MB R2W 2L6
(204) 586-8057
FAX (204) 582-8397
Owner: Ness Michaels.
Manager: Adam Salamandyk.
No. of Tracks: 16.
No. of Studios: One.
Services Offered: Tape duplication.
Rates: $40 per hour.
Rehearsal Space: No.
Mixing Consoles: Aries 16.
Tape Machines: Fostex.
Accommodations: No.

Trillium Recording Centre Inc.

1253 Clarence Ave., Unit 3
Winnipeg, MB R3T 1T4
(204) 453-8484
Owner: Bob Fuhr (part-owner).
Manager: Bob Fuhr.
No. of Tracks: 24.
No. of Studios: One.
Services Offered: Video production, tape duplication, MIDI.
Rates: $75 per hour for 24-track recording, $125 per hour for film/video, $60 per hour for MIDI, $85 per hour for lock between MIDI and 24-track.
Rehearsal Space: Yes.
Mixing Consoles: Soundcraft Series 600: 60 inputs, 24 tracks of twister automation.
Tape Machines: Atari MX-80 2″ 24-track.
Special Equipment: MIDI, in-house samplers and synthesizers.
Accommodations: No.
Comments: May have accommodations in the future.

NEW BRUNSWICK

C.M.S. Studios

151 Mountain Rd.
Moncton, NB E1C 2K8
(506) 858-0073
FAX (506) 859-7406
Owner: Nando Speranza.
Manager: Simon Marchant Gauvin.
No. of Tracks: 24.
No. of Studios: One.
Services Offered: Fully equipped 24-track studio with post-video production and computer animation.
Rates: $100 per hour.
Rehearsal Space: Yes.
Mixing Consoles: AMEK Angela (56x28x24).
Tape Machines: Soundcraft (equipped with noise reduction).
Special Equipment: Quantec room simulator, (2) Lexicon 70, Tube-Tech, Aphex Exciter, (4) Aphex 612 noise gates, Eventide H-3000.
Accommodations: No.
Comments: MIDI system includes Linn 9000, Akai S-1000, Mac II with lots of music software and various sound sources.

Studio Madouess

45 Savoie, R.R. 4
Edmundston, NB E3V 3V7
(506) 735-7258
Owner: Daniel Violette.
Manager: Daniel Violette.
No. of Tracks: 24.
No. of Studios: Two.
Services Offered: Jingle video production and tape duplication.
Rates: $50-70 per hour.
Rehearsal Space: Yes.
Mixing Consoles: Soundcraft.
Tape Machines: Soundcraft, TASCAM, Otari.
Special Equipment: Lexicon, Yamaha, Valley People, BBE, Neumann, AKG, Beyer, Electro-Voice.
Accommodations: No.
Comments: Completely MIDI equipped including sequencers, controllers and sound modules. Various instruments: Pearl, Sabian, Fender, Selmer and Norman.

NEWFOUNDLAND

Sims Studio

P.O. Box 10
Belleoram, NF A0H 1B0
(709) 881-6181 or 881-4576
FAX (709) 881-6391
Owner: Sim Savory.
Manager: Sim Savory.
No. of Tracks: 16 (analog), 100 (digital).
No. of Studios: One.
Rates: $30 per hour.
Rehearsal Space: Yes.
Mixing Consoles: TASCAM.
Tape Machines: Fostex, Revox, TASCAM.
Accommodations: Yes.
Comments: Cabins for rent nightly, weekly or monthly.

NOVA SCOTIA

ABS Productions Ltd.

196 Joseph Zatzman Dr.
Dartmouth, NS B3B 1N4
(902) 463-2335
Owner: R.G. Sandoz.
Manager: R.G. Sandoz.
No. of Tracks: 8.
No. of Studios: One audio, one video.
Services Offered: Video production, video-lock, audio and video cassette duplication.
Rates: Varies according to services and equipment required.
Rehearsal Space: Yes.
Mixing Consoles: Soundcraft.
Tape Machines: Nagra, Scully, TASCAM.
Special Equipment: Orban de-essing, reverb, Urei filters, Allison noise gates, DBX, Evertz chasers for lock to video, 16mm and 35mm motion picture recorders and more.
Accommodations: No.
Comments: Specialize in audio track building and sweetening for film and video productions.

db Sound Productions

100 Maple Ave., Suite 92
New Glasgow, NS B2H 2B4
(902) 752-7712
FAX (902) 755-2468
Owner: Hector Broadcasting Co. Ltd.
Manager: D.B. Freeman.
No. of Tracks: 24.
No. of Studios: Three.
Rates: $65 per hour.
Rehearsal Space: Yes.
Mixing Consoles: Soundcraft 6000.
Tape Machines: Soundcraft Saturn 2" 24-track, Studer A807 2-track, (3) Revox PR99 MK-111 2-track.
Special Equipment: Lexicon 200 and 97 Rev, REV7, Yamaha D-1500, (2) Alesis Quadraverb, (2) dbx Comp/Lim/Gte.
Accommodations: No.
Comments: Yamaha grand piano C7F, Yamaha upright, Yamaha GS-2 MIDI, Yamaha DX7, Yamaha TX-7 SynthMod, Yamaha RX-11 drum machine, Yamaha CS5M 128 music computer, Roland MKS-20 piano module, Roland Octapad, Prophet 600, Korg M-1 and M-1R, Solina string machine, 8-piece Tama drum kit, wide variety of microphones, and other interesting gadgets.

Reel Time Recorders Ltd.

1489 Hollis St.
Halifax, NS B3J 3H5
(902) 422-8567
Owner: Chuck O'Hara.
Manager: Chuck O'Hara.
No. of Tracks: AMS audiophile.
No. of Studios: One.
Services Offered: Audio-video link and post-production audio for video.
Rates: $60-100 depending on services.
Rehearsal Space: No.
Mixing Consoles: TASCAM.
Tape Machines: Sony R-DAT, Otari.
Special Equipment: EMT-plate, Roland SDE 1000, DDL, Orban de-esser, Urei limiters.
Accommodations: No.

ONTARIO

A Flat Minor Productions

174 Winter Gardens Tr.
West Hill, ON M1C 3N2
(416) 287-1967
Owner: Tony Giverin.
Manager: Tony Giverin.
No. of Tracks: Unlimited MIDI.
No. of Studios: One.
Services Offered: Sound engineering and original music for film, TV and radio.
Rates: Negotiable.
Rehearsal Space: Yes.
Mixing Consoles: Fostex 450-16.
Tape Machines: TEAC, Panasonic DAT machine.
Special Equipment: Bryston amps, Yamaha reverb and monitors, Prophet T8, Roland D50, Korg DDD1.
Accommodations: No.
Comments: Other services include sound engineering for broadcast.

A.R.P. Track Productions

28 Valrose Dr.
Stoney Creek, ON L8E 3T4
(416) 662-2666
FAX (416) 662-7295
Owner: Nick Keca.
Manager: John Keca.
No. of Tracks: 24.
No. of Studios: Two.
Services Offered: Video post-production.
Rates: $75 per hour.
Rehearsal Space: No.
Mixing Consoles: Soundtracs, TAC Scorpion.
Tape Machines: Sony, MCI.
Special Equipment: E-11, Mac II Plus, SP-12, FX rack, Shadow sync units, Lexicon, Softouch controller.
Accommodations: Yes.
Comments: Call for quotes and production co-ordination.

Airwaves Audio Inc. Recording Studios

15 Toronto St., Lower Level.
Toronto, ON M5C 2E3
(416) 863-6881
FAX (416) 867-9107.
Owner: A. Staruch.
Manager: C. Onyskiw.
No. of Tracks: 16,24.
No. of Studios: Two.
Rates: $90-110 per hour.
Rehearsal Space: No.
Tape Machines: MCI JH-24, Otari 16-track, Studer 2-track, JVC 3/4" video machine.
Accommodations: No.
Comments: Specialize in radio commercial recording, TV soundtrack and A/V post-production.

Ambassador Records

185 Oshawa Blvd. S.
Oshawa, ON L1H 5R6
(416) 579-7476
Owner: Paul Evans.
Manager: Linda Evans.
No. of Tracks: 16.
No. of Studios: One.
Services Offered: Custom cassette manufacturing and duplicating.
Rates: $35 per hour.
Rehearsal Space: No.
Mixing Consoles: Audio Trac.
Tape Machines: TASCAM 90-16, TEAC 3440, TEAC 3300 SX.
Special Equipment: Baby grand piano, 7-piece set of Tama Drums, REV7, SPX 90, Imager-Exciter, Neumann U-87 microphone.
Accommodations: No.

Ambience Recorders

220 Rideau St.
Ottawa, ON K1N 5Y1
(613) 236-5282
FAX (613) 235-5473
Owner: Phil Bova.
Manager: Janet Kirby.
No. of Tracks: 24.
No. of Studios: Two.
Services Offered: In-house graphic design, production and manufacturing division.
Rates: On request.
Rehearsal Space: No.
Mixing Consoles: Soundcraft 2400 Series, TAC Magnum.
Tape Machines: Studer A820 with Dolby SR, Soundcraft 760.
Special Equipment: Studio A: Dolby SR on all tracks including 2-track mastering deck, B: MIDI facility.
Accommodations: No.
Comments: Broad selection of signal processing gear included in hourly rental in either studio. Studio A boasts three isolation rooms, a collection of over 450 instruments (including a Baldwin nine-foot grand piano) and a large selection of mics including 14 Bruel & Kjaer microphones.

ART-TEC Production & Recording Studios

323 Talbot St. 2nd Floor
St. Thomas, ON N5P 1B5
(519) 633-6518
FAX (519) 633-6518
Owner: Kevin Taylor
Manager: Michelle Butler.
No. of Tracks: 16 w/computer lock.
No. of Studios: One.
Services Offered: Full in-house production, musicians and artist development.
Rates: Per project.
Rehearsal Space: No.
Mixing Consoles: Fostex 2440.
Tape Machines: Fostex E-16, Fostex E-Z, Sony DAT, TASCAM 122.
Special Equipment: Full MIDI capability with Macintosh lock-up. Large selection of instruments.
Accommodations: No.

Audio Trax Digital Performance Concepts

15 Towns Rd.
Toronto, ON M8Z 1A2
(416) 255-8284
Owner: Don Sklepowich.
Manager: Don Sklepowich.
No. of Tracks: 8.
Services Offered: Pre- and post-production, mobile recording and composition and arranging.
Rates: $25 per hour.
Rehearsal Space: No.
Mixing Consoles: (4) Yamaha DMP-7 Digital Consoles.
Tape Machines: TASCAM 8-track 1/2".
Special Equipment: Computer-based MIDI, digital sound, (5) samplers, Synth racks, 30-piece MIDI drums, various special effects.
Accommodations: No.
Comments: An ambitious 8-track studio.

Arnyard Studios

155 Toryork Dr., Unit 15
Weston, ON M9L 1X9
(416) 740-0423
FAX (416) 738-9779
Owner: Arnold Lanni.
Manager: Mike Saricini.
No. of Tracks: 24.
No. of Studios: One.
Rates: On request.
Rehearsal Space: Yes.
Mixing Consoles: Amek Mozart.
Tape Machines: MCI.
Special Equipment: Various effects and MIDI equipment.
Accommodations: No.

Axon Music Productions Inc.

375 Fairlawn Ave.
Toronto, ON M5M 1T7
(416) 781-4065
Owner: George Axon.
Manager: George Axon.
No. of Tracks: 24.
No. of Studios: One.
Services Offered: Video lock, custom music and jingles, production services.
Rates: $75 per hour, $100 per with video lock.
Rehearsal Space: No.
Mixing Consoles: TAC Matchless 24/26.
Tape Machines: SONY MCI JH 24, SONY APR 5003, JVC 8250.
Special Equipment: Adams Smith Synchronizer, complete MIDI set-up.
Accommodations: No.
Comments: 10 years experience, award-winning jingles.

B&C Sound Studio

12 Riverside Dr., Unit 1, P.O. Box 1012
Trenton, ON K8V 6E6
(613) 392-5144 or 392-6296
Owners: Eric Baragar and John Collins.
Manager: Bruno Biasini.
No. of Tracks: 16.
No. of Studios: One.
Services Offered: Audio recording and custom musical creative for video.
Rates: $50 per hour.
Rehearsal Space: No.
Mixing Consoles: Studiomaster Series 11 (MIDI automation).
Tape Machines: Fostex B-16, TEAC A-33005.
Special Equipment: Complete MIDI studio, analog and digital synths and samplers.
Accommodations: Yes.
Comments: Custom record label, complete in-house production and promotion package, songwriter assistance available.

Brock Sound Post Audio

576 Manning Ave.
Toronto, ON M6G 2V9
(416) 534-7464
FAX (416) 538-2563
Owner: Brock Fricker.
Manager: Brock Fricker.
No. of Tracks: 16.
No. of Studios: One.
Services Offered: Voiceovers, sound effects, music creation for film and TV, corporate video post-audio.
Rates: $50 per hour minimum, $70 per hour voiceovers, $110 per hour tape-lock to video.
Rehearsal Space: No.
Mixing Consoles: Trident Trimix w/ computerized mixdown.
Tape Machines: (2) Studer 16-track, Studer 1" video layback, Sony 2-track w/T.C.
Special Equipment: Sony BVW-75 Betacam S.P., Soundmaster tapelock system, Dolby SR, computerized sound effects layup, MIDI system.
Accommodations: No.
Comments: MIDI system has over 3,000 sounds.

Cedar-tree Studio

300 Trillium Dr., Suite 9
Kitchener, ON N2E 2K6
(519) 748-5810
Owner: Rick Hutt and Doug Biggs.
Manager: Doug Biggs.
No. of Tracks: 24, MIDI post-production.
No. of Studios: Two.
Services Offered: Video production.
Rates: $80 per hour.
Rehearsal Space: No.
Mixing Consoles: Soundcraft, Lexicon 480L.
Tape Machines: Sony.
Special Equipment: Wide variety of digital processing equipment as well as complete MIDI studio.
Accommodations: No.
Comments: Full arrangement and production.

Chalet Studio

R.R. 1
Claremont, ON L0H 1E0
(416) 649-1360
FAX (416) 649-2951
Owner: David Chester.
Manager: Everett Ravertein.
No. of Tracks: 24-track.
No. of Studios: One.
Services Offered: Residential studio with a 24-hour block rate.
Rates: $975 per day (24-hour block rate plus ten hours of engineering services).
Mixing Consoles: Sony MTX 3036 (hard disk automation).
Tape Machines: Sony Apr 24-track, Sony DAT, TASCAM 122.
Special Equipment: Lexicon 480L, FocusRite EQ, Tube-Tech pre-amps, Valley noise gates, Urei compressors, Mac ST.
Accommodations: Yes. Includes maid service, chef, sauna, etc.
Comments: Recent clients include Rush, Liona Boyd, Watertown, Clean Slate, Blue Rodeo, ARTFX: Rupert Hines, Terry Brown.

Cherry Beach Sound

16 Munition St.
Toronto, ON M5A 3M2
(416) 461-4224
Owners: Carman Guerrieri and Robert Natale.
Manager: Tracy Callahan.
No. of Tracks: 24.
No. of Studios: One.
Services Offered: 24-track recording, mixing, video lock and MIDI.
Rates: On request.
Rehearsal Space: No.
Mixing Consoles: Sony, MCI.
Tape Machines: Studer 24-track.
Accommodations: No.
Comments: Easy highway access.

Comfort Sound Recording Studio

26 Soho St., Suite 390
Toronto, ON M5T 1Z7
(416) 593-7992
Owner: Doug McClement.
Manager: Doug McClement.
No. of Tracks: 24.
No. of Studios: Two (plus a mobile studio).
Services Offered: Foley, audio post for video, real-time cassette duplication, 24-track mobile.
Rates: $135 per hour.
Rehearsal Space: No.
Mixing Consoles: MCI (studio), Neotek (mobile).
Tape Machines: Otari (studio), AMPEX (mobile).
Special Equipment: Soundmaster Synchronizer, four-machine video lock, 16-track 1/2" studio with video lock for voiceovers.
Accommodations: No.
Comments: Well equipped mobile studio (over 700 remote recordings during the past 12 years).

Creative Sound Studio

134 Peter St., 3rd Floor
Toronto, ON M5V 2H2
(416) 598-3456
FAX (416) 598-5216
Manager: Rick Noel.
No. of Tracks: 24, 48.
No. of Studios: Two.
Services Offered: Lock synchronizers for post-audio production, digital editing for DAT, and disk-based automation.
Rates: From $45-100 per hour.
Rehearsal Space: No.
Mixing Consoles: MCI.
Tape Machines: Sony APR 24, MCI JH24.
Special Equipment: Focus Rites, 480L, Neve.
Accommodations: No.

Deschamps Recording Studios Ltd.

314 Dundas St. W.
Toronto, ON M5T 1G5
(416) 977-5050
FAX (416) 977-6945
Owner: Claude Deschamps.
Manager: Claude Deschamps.
No. of Tracks: 8, 16, 24.
No. of Studios: Three (includes audiofile suite).
Services Offered: Sound recording and audio for video.
Rates: Audiofile $175, 16 and 24-track ($120 audio, $160 video), 8-track ($100 audio, $140 video).
Mixing Consoles: Sound Workshop, Neve, Neotek Essence.
Tape Machines: Studer.
Special Equipment: Soundmaster, Brooke Sirens.
Accommodations: No.

Digital Ears Music Productions

24 Erindale Ave.
Toronto, ON M4K 1R9
(416) 463-5830
Owner: David Miller.
Manager: David Miller.
No. of Tracks: 16 (analog), 24 (MIDI).
No. of Studios: One.
Services Offered: Music composition and special effects.
Rates: $30-60 per hour.
Rehearsal Space: No.
Mixing Consoles: Akai, Aries.
Tape Machines: Fostex, Sony, Nagra.
Special Equipment: Sony digital mixdown, Atari 1040, Steinberg Pro-24 w/SMPTE code lock to multitrack or video.
Accommodations: No.

Don Valley Sound

210 Don Park Rd., Unit 5
Markham, ON L3R 2V2
(416) 470-9477
Owners: William and Patricia Wainwright.
No. of Tracks: 24.
No. of Studios: One.
Services Offered: Adam Smith 2600 video sync, full MIDI facilities.
Rates: $80 per hour.
Rehearsal Space: Yes.
Mixing Consoles: Sony/MCI 636 (automated).
Tape Machines: Sony/MCI JH24-2" Revox B77, Otari 50/50-1/2 track 1/4".
Special Equipment: Panasonic SV3500 digital mix.
Accommodations: No.
Comments: 1,200 square foot studio in an industrial complex. Free parking.

E.M.A.C. Sound Recording Studios

432 Rectory St.
London, ON
(519) 667-3622
FAX (519) 642-7453
Owner: Electronic Media Arts Corporation.
Manager: Robert Nation.
No. of Tracks: 24.
No. of Studios: Two.
Services Offered: Records, audio post-production, tape duplication, jingles.
Rates: $75 per hour.
Rehearsal Space: No.
Mixing Consoles: D&R 4000.
Tape Machines: MCI, ATR 102.
Special Equipment: Adam Smith synchronizer.
Accommodations: No.

Eastern Sound

48 Yorkville Ave.
Toronto, ON M4W 1L4
(416) 968-1855
FAX (416) 924-9973
Owner: A Division of Standard Broadcasting.
Manager: Kevin Evans.
No. of Studios: Three.
Rates: On request.

E-Norm-Us Sound Studios

28B Howden Rd.
Scarborough, ON M1R 3E4
(416) 757-8775
Owner: The E-Norm-Us Corp.
Manager: Lynne Moore.
No. of Tracks: 24.
No. of Studios: One.
Rates: $50 per hour.
Rehearsal Space: No.
Mixing Consoles: Neve.
Tape Machines: Studer.
Accommodations: No.

Emmanuel Productions

31B Industrial St.
Toronto, ON M4G 1Z2
(416) 423-7131
FAX (416) 467-6805
Owner: Carmon Barry.
Manager: Carmon Barry.
No. of Tracks: 8, 24.
No. of Studios: Two.
Services Offered: Cassette tape duplication, post-production audio for video, MIDI music cassette tape duplication, post-production, music recording.
Rates: 24-track ($90 per hour); 8 track ($55 per hour).
Rehearsal Space: No.
Mixing Consoles: D&R.
Tape Machines: Otari.
Special Equipment: Neumann, AKG, Yamaha baby grand piano.
Accommodations: No.
Comments: Large, well-maintained facility.

Escarpment Sound Studio

210 Main St. N.
Acton, ON L7J 1W9
(519) 853-4010
Owner: Brian Hewson.
Manager: Brian Hewson.
No. of Tracks: 16.
No. of Studios: One.
Services Offered: Recording and mixing.
Rates: $32 per hour.
Rehearsal Space: No.
Mixing Consoles: Soundcraft 600 series.
Tape Machines: Fostex B16, TASCAM 52 2-track, Tandberg TD-20 2-track.
Special Equipment: Lexicon PCM 70, Yamaha SPX 90 and RX 11 DBX 166, BBE 402, JBL 4425 studio monitors.
Accommodations: No.
Comments: Pre-production and demo studio which offers a relaxed atmosphere.

Experiment IV Recording Studios

133 Lawson Rd.
Scarborough, ON
M1C 2J3
(416) 284-3794
Owner and Manager: Edward Agabeg
No. of Tracks: 16
No. of Studiod: One, MIDI
Rates: $35/hr., block rates available.
Mixing Consoles: Fostex 2440, Yamaha DMP7.
Tape Machines: Fostex G16, Sony DTC1000 DAT, Yamaha KX-500U cassette.
Special Equipment: Lexicon, Yamaha REV7, Quadraverb, others.
Accommodations: No.

Good Egg Productions

71 Bank St., Suite 507
Ottawa, ON K1P 5N2
(613) 233-7698
Owner: Christopher P. Mayo.
Manager: Karen Temple.
No. of Tracks: 12.
No. of Studios: One.
Services Offered: Multitrack recording, soundtracks, tape duplication (audio and video), tape editing, audio post and sweetening, digital mastering graphic layout and design.
Rehearsal Space: Yes.
Mixing Consoles: Akai.
Tape Machines: Akai, Revox.
Special Equipment: 16-channel MIDI production facility using Apple Macintosh w/Performer sequencing software.
Accommodations: No.

Grant Avenue Studio (1985) Inc.

38 Grant Ave.
Hamilton, ON L8N 2X5
(416) 522-5227
Owners: Robert Doidge and Maureen Doidge.
Manager: Maureen Doidge.
No. of Tracks: 24.
No. of Studios: One.
Rates: $80 per hour.
Rehearsal Space: No.
Mixing Consoles: MCI 500C.
Tape Machines: MCI JH24, MCI 1/2", (3) MCI 1/4".
Special Equipment: (6) Neve 1068, AMS Delay, EMT 250, plus an assortment of vintage tube microphones.
Accommodations: No.

Greenledge Studios

5551 Joella Cr.
Osgoode, ON K0A 2W0
(613) 826-3057
Owner: Ward Green.
Manager: Ward Green.
No. of Tracks: 16.
No. of Studios: One.
Services Offered: 16-track recording, 1/4" EIA mastering, high-quality one-off cassette copies.
Rates: $30 per hour.
Rehearsal Space: No.
Mixing Consoles: TASCAM M-520.
Tape Machines: TASCAM MS-16, TASCAM 122 MK II.
Special Equipment: Beyer MC 74ON (C) P48 microphone.
Accommodations: No.
Comments: Greenledge specializes in presenting demo packages to record companies. Production services are available.

The Groove

172 Toryork Dr., Unit 10
North York, ON M9L 1X8
(416) 742-5693
Comments: Analogue and MIDI recording systems, rehearsal space, promotional packages. A complete production facility.

Harlow Sound

31 Harlow Cr.
Rexdale, ON M9V 2Y6
(416) 741-0165
Owner: Greg English.
Manager: Greg English.
No. of Tracks: 16.
Services Offered: Video and film production, voiceovers.
Rates: $45 per hour (block rates available).
Rehearsal Space: No.
Mixing Consoles: Soundtracs.
Tape Machines: Fostex B-16.
Special Equipment: Keyboards, special effects, drum machines.
Accommodations: No.
Comments: Talent and producers available.

Hopewell Sound Studios

391 Hopewell Ave.
Toronto, ON M6E 2S1
(416) 785-5621
FAX (416) 782-8574
Owner: Tony Paniccia, Angelo Petraglia, Sandro Coretti.
Manager: Tony Paniccia.
No. of Tracks: 24.
No. of Studios: Two.
Services Offered: MIDI studio, tracking, mixing, tape duplication.
Rates: $75 per hour.
Rehearsal Space: No.
Mixing Consoles: TASCAM M-600.
Tape Machines: TASCAM ATR-80 24-track,, ATR-60 2-track.
Accommodations: No.
Comments: Special rates on eight-hour sessions.

Hypnotic Sound Studios

96 Spadina Ave. 9th Floor
Toronto, ON
(416) 362-8839
FAX (416) 847-9379
Owner: Tom Truemuth.
Manager: Duncan Lindsay.
No. of Tracks: 24.
No. of Studios: One.
Services Offered: Video lock.
Rates: $90 per hour.
Rehearsal Space: No.
Mixing Consoles: Sound workshop.
Tape Machines: Sony-DAT, MCI 24-track.
Special Equipment: Focus Rite EQ, PCM-70, SPX-90, API EQ, Pultec EQ, Yamaha and Tannoy speakers, Drawmer noise gates and compressers, AMS reverb and delay, BBE Aural Exciter, Casio Fz1 16-bit sampler with Atari 1040 computer and software, Tube 447 microphone.

I.V.M. Recording Studio

P.O. Box 405
Rodney, ON N0L 2C0
(519) 785-2180
Owner: Inverted vision music.
Manager: Martin Didds.
No. of Tracks: 8.
No. of Studios: One.
Services Offered: Complete recording packages and remote recording.
Rates: $20 per hour, $35 per hour remote.
Rehearsal Space: No.
Mixing Consoles: Fostex.
Tape Machines: Fostex.
Special Equipment: AKAI X7000 sampler with CD sound library, Roland and Casio synths.
Accommodations: No.
Comments: Fully MIDI-compatible with Atari 520 ST computer and Dr. T's, K.C.S. MIDI sequencing.

Inception Sound Studio

3876 Chesswood Dr.
Downsview, ON M3J 2W6
(416) 630-7150
Owners: Harold Kiliansky, Chad Irschick, Jeffrey Wolpert.
No. of Tracks: 24.
No. of Studios: Two.
Services Offered: Video production, post-production.
Rates: $115-135 per hour.
Rehearsal Space: No.
Mixing Consoles: (2) MCI-500s.
Tape Machines: Sony DAT, (2) MCI 24-track, Sony PCM-701, Otari 4-track.
Special Equipment: AMS, digital delay, harmonizer, compressors.
Accommodations: No.

Keen Communication Systems Inc.

11 Soho St., Suite 203
Toronto, ON M5T 1Z6
(416) 977-9845
FAX (416) 599-9714
Owner: John Tucker, Fred Gaysek, Rod Robbie, Angus Robbie.
Manager: Thomas Neuspiel.
No. of Tracks: 16, 24.
No. of Studios: Two.
Services Offered: Music production, sound design, audio post-production, jingle production.
Rates: $60-230 per hour.
Rehearsal Space: No.
Mixing Consoles: Soundcraft TS-12, Soundcraft Series 800.
Tape Machines: MCI JH-24, Otari MTR-12, PCM 701/601, B-16.
Special Equipment: Fairlight CMI Series III, Apple Mac w/Performer software, synths from Oberhiem, Roland, Korg, Prophet and outboard from Lexicon and Klark Tecnik.
Accommodations: No.

Kensington Sound

170A Baldwin St.
Toronto, ON M5T 1L8
(416) 593-9607
FAX (416) 593-0461
Owner: Mike Alyanak.
Manager: Berge Alyanak.
No. of Tracks: 24.
No. of Studios: One.
Rates: $70 per hour.
Rehearsal Space: No.
Mixing Consoles: Midas.
Tape Machines: MCI.
Special Equipment: Lexicon 224 reverb, Eventide H3000 harmonizer, Roland DEP-5 effects unit, Yamaha REV7, Alesis Midiverb, and DBX Ashley and ADR compressors.
Accommodations: No.

Kirkland Sound Recording

11 Summit Ave.
Kirkland Lake, ON P2N 1M6
(705) 567-3847
Owner: B. May.
Manager: B. May.
No. of Tracks: 16.
No. of Studios: One.
Services Offered: Recording studio and real-time tape duplication.
Rates: $29 per hour.
Rehearsal Space: No.
Mixing Consoles: Fostex 450-16.
Tape Machines: Fostex B16, TASCAM 32.
Special Equipment: Yamaha SPX 90, Ashley SC50 compressor.
Accommodations: No.

Lakeshore Sound

P.O. Box 2917
Sarnia, ON N7T 7W2
(519) 542-3878
Owner: Allan D. Hill.
Manager: Allan D. Hill.
No. of Tracks: 16.
No. of Studios: One.
Rates: $45 per hour (block rates available).
Rehearsal Space: No.
Mixing Consoles: TASCAM M520 (20 x 8 x 16).
Tape Machines: Fostex B16, Tandberg TD20A, Technics SV 100 digital.
Special Equipment: Lexicon DCM-60, Roland SRV-2000 digital reverbs, (2) Alesis quadraverbs, Neumann U87, Sony ECM-S6F, Crown PCM, Sennheiser 421 and 441 microphones, SDE-3000, Delta Lab Effectron, DBX 166 Over Easy, MIDI sequencing, DBX de-esser.

Madison Avenue Recording Studio

70 Silver Star Blvd., Unit 125
Scarborough, ON
(416) 299-6474
Owners: Frank La Magna, John Mizzi, Guy Broncatto.
No. of Tracks: 24.
No. of Studios: One.
Services Offered: Audio post-production, jingle production, film scoring, album projects.
Rehearsal Space: No.
Mixing Consoles: TADCAM M600.
Tape Machines: TASCAM ATR-80.
Special Equipment: Various.
Accommodations: No.

Manta Sound Co.

311 Adelaide St. E.
Toronto, ON M5A 1N2
(416) 863-9316
FAX (416) 863-1448
Owner: Paja Company Ltd.
Manager: LuAnn Leonard.
No. of Tracks: 24, 32, 48.
No. of Studios: Five.
Services Offered: Audio recording, post-production, and duplication.
Rehearsal Space: No.
Mixing Consoles: Neve, Amek, Westar.
Tape Machines: 24/32 Studer and Mitsubishi.
Accommodations: No.
Comments: Manta specializes in digital audio formats.

Marigold Productions Ltd.

P.O. Box 141, Stn. S
Toronto, ON M5M 4L6
(416) 484-8789
Owner: Rich Dodson.
Manager: M.L. Dodson.
No. of Tracks: 24.
No. of Studios: One.
Services Offered: None.
Rehearsal Space: No.
Mixing Consoles: Custom console with Neve API components.
Tape Machines: MCI, Studer.
Accommodations: No.

Master's Workshop

306 Rexdale Blvd., Units 1-9
Rexdale, ON M9W 1R6
(416) 741-1312
FAX (416) 741-1894
Owner: Maclean Hunter.
Manager: Jim Frank.
No. of Tracks: 72.
No. of Studios: Nine.
Services Offered: Audio post-production for feature films, TV, music recording and mixing.
Rates: On request.
Rehearsal Space: No.
Mixing Consoles: Neotek.
Tape Machines: Sony (analog and digital).
Special Equipment: A wide variety of outboard gear.
Accommodations: No.
Comments: Specialists in digital and analog sound design, mixing, editing, and music scoring for film using Soundmaster audio control systems.

Mastertrack

35A Hazelton Ave.
Toronto, ON M5R 2E3
(416) 922-4004
FAX (416) 922-8634
Owner: Ken Burgess.
Manager: Andy Condon.
No. of Tracks: 24 plus.
No. of Studios: Three.
Services Offered: Audio post-production.
Rehearsal Space: No.
Accommodations: No.

McClear Place Recording and Mastering Studios

225 Mutual St.
Toronto, ON M5B 2B4
(416) 977-9740
FAX (416) 977-7147
Owner: Bob Richards.
President: Hayward Parrott.
Manager: Jane Rowan.
No. of Tracks: 24, 48 analog, 32 digital.
No. of Studios: Three .
Services Offered: Recording, post-production, mixing, disc mastering, CD pre-mastering and digital editing.
Rates: On request.
Rehearsal Space: No.
Mixing Consoles: SSL 6000 E Series, Sony 3000 (automated).
Tape Machines: Studer A-820, MCI JH-24, Mitsubishi X-850, Sony.
Special Equipment: Full digital and analog recording equipment with time code-based automation and video lock. 24 channels of Dolby SR, and Yamaha C7E MIDI grand piano.
Accommodations: No.
Comments: World-class studio in downtown Toronto. Three outstanding resident engineers with international credits: Hayward Parrott, Steve Ibelshauser, Peter Lee.

McLean Hannah

154 Sanford Ave.
Hamilton, ON L8L 5Z5
(416) 587-9113
FAX (416) 528-1018
Owners: Paul Hannah and Dam McLean.
Manager: Y.L. Hannah.
No. of Tracks: 16.
No. of Studios: One.
Services Offered: Voiceover recording.
Rates: $60 per hour.
Rehearsal Space: No.
Mixing Consoles: TAC Scorpion.
Tape Machines: TASCAM 85-16B.
Accommodations: No.

Metalworks Recording Studios Inc.

3611 Mavis Rd., Unit 5
Mississauga, ON L5C 1T7
(416) 279-4008
FAX (416) 279-4006
Owner: Gil Moore.
Manager: Alex Andronache.
No. of Tracks: 24, 48.
No. of Studios: Two.
Rates: $125-235 per hour.
Rehearsal Space: No.
Mixing Consoles: SSL 4056 G Series, Neve Spitfire.
Tape Machines: Studer A800s, Studer A820s, Otari MTR-90 II, Sony PCM 2500A.
Special Equipment: Dolby As and SRs, Eventide H3000 harmonizer, Focusrite ISA 110 EQs, Lexicon 480L reverb, outboard Neve EQs and limiters, Hammond organ w/Leslie.
Accommodations: No.
Comments: Just 20 minutes from downtown Toronto and only 10 minutes from the international airport. First-class hotels, night clubs and restaurants are all within minutes of the studio.

Montclair Sound

91 Montclair Ave.
Toronto, ON M5P 1P5
(416) 488-0603
Owner: B. McVicker.
Manager: K. Pleming.
No. of Tracks: 48.
No. of Studios: Two.
Services Offered: Music production, duplication and post-sound for TV, video and industrials.
Rates: $75-135 per hour.
Mixing Consoles: BWM, Neve, Chilton.
Tape Machines: Studer A80.
Special Equipment: Wide assortment of outboard gear for audio and video production.
Accommodations: No.

Moondog Recording Studios

Mendips House, 189 Scugog St.
Bowmanville, ON
(416) 723-8916
Owner: Paul Andrew Smith.
No. of Tracks: 16.
No. of Studios: One.
Services Offered: Audio recording, tape duplication.
Rehearsal Space: No.
Mixing Consoles: D&R 4000 Series.
Tape Machines: Fostex B16, TASCAM.
Special Equipment: Full selection of effects.
Accommodations: No.

Number Nine Sound Studios Inc.

314 Jarvis St., Suite 101
Toronto, ON M5B 2C5
(416) 348-8718
FAX (416) 348-9668
Owners: George Rondina and Jim Zolis.
Manager: George Rondina.
No. of Tracks: 24.
No. of Studios: Two.
Services Offered: Equipment rentals, tape duplication and MIDI studio.
Rates: On request.
Rehearsal Space: No.
Mixing Consoles: Amek Angela (36 x 24 automated).
Tape Machines: Sony, JH-24.
Special Equipment: Focusrites, Neve EQs, (2) Lexicon 480, digital reverbs, Eventide, Urei, Studer, Sony digital.
Accommodations: No.
Comments: Clients include: Jane Siberry, Andrew Cash, Rita MacNeil, The Northern Pikes, Glass Tiger, Lorraine Scott, CBS Records, Virgin Records, Capitol Records, etc.

Palindrome Recording Services

200 University Ave. W.
Waterloo, ON N2L 3G1
(519) 886-2567
Owner: CKMS-FM.
Manager: Bill Wharrie.
No. of Tracks: 8.
No. of Studios: One.
Rates: $25 per hour.
Rehearsal Space: No.
Mixing Consoles: TASCAM.
Tape Machines: TASCAM, Revox.
Accommodations: No.

Perception Media

591 Annette St.
Toronto, ON M6S 2C2
(416) 769-1300
FAX (416) 769-9774
Owner: Roger St-Denis.
Manager: Roger St-Denis.
No. of Tracks: 24.
No. of Studios: One.
Services Offered: Audio post-production, real-time cassette duplication, MIDI music production.
Rates: $95 per hour.
Rehearsal Space: No.
Mixing Consoles: TASCAM M600.
Tape Machines: TASCAM ATR-80, Otari MTR-10, Otari 5050.
Special Equipment: Sony DRE 2000 digital reverb, Klark Teknik effects, Megamix automated system, Sony PCM 601 digital processor.
Accommodations: No.
Comments: Custom music production and sound effects library on CD also available.

Personal Recording Services

79 Garden Ave.
Toronto, ON M6R 1H8
(416) 533-0704
Owners: Gad Foltys and John Stokes.
Manager: John Stokes.
No. of Tracks: 16.
No. of Studios: One.
Services Offered: Audio post-production and music composition.
Rates: $30-60.
Rehearsal Space: No.
Mixing Consoles: D&R 4000 Series 24-track.
Tape Machines: TASCAM MS 16-1".
Special Equipment: Macintosh with Performer software.
Accommodations: No.

Phase One Recording Studios Ltd.

3015 Kennedy Rd., Unit 10
Scarborough, ON M1V 1E7
(416) 291-9553
FAX (416) 299-1398
Owners: Paul Gross and Doug Hill.
Manager: Robin Brouwer.
No. of Tracks: 24, 48.
No. of Studios: Three.
Services Offered: Video production, film work.
Rates: A room: $85-130 per hour (eight-hour block rate available) $950 for eight-hour block; B room: $170 per hour, $1,200 for eight hours: C room: $85 per hour, $600 for eight hours.
Rehearsal Space: No.
Mixing Consoles: SSL G Series, Neve.
Tape Machines: Studer A 80s, Mitsubishi 32-track digital.
Special Equipment: DAT machine.

Pizazzudio

1063 Spadina Rd.
Toronto, ON M5N 2M7
(416) 489-9555
Owner: Barry Lubotta.
Manager: Barry Lubotta.
No. of Tracks: 16.
No. of Studios: One.
Services Offered: Special projects, video and record production.
Rates: $30 per hour.
Rehearsal Space: No.
Mixing Consoles: Hill Audio Remix (24 x 16), Roland M-16E.
Tape Machines: TASCAM MSR 16, Fostex E22, Fostex M20.
Special Equipment: Panasonic SU3500 DAT machine, JVC HR-S10000 VCR, Lexicon PCM 70, Lexicon PCM 60, Neumann U87, Korg T2, Drawmer M500.
Accommodations: No.

Polaris Recording Studios

1151 Drouillard Rd.
Windsor, ON N8Y 2R2
(519) 973-4944
No. of Tracks: 24.
Services Offered: Digital to analog. Interlock capability.

Powerlines Recording Studios

51 Kingspark Blvd.
Toronto, ON M4J 2B9
(416) 466-6517
Owner: Fred Duval.
Manager: Fred Duval.
No. of Tracks: 16.
No. of Studios: One.
Services Offered: Various recording-related services.
Rates: $25 per hour.
Rehearsal Space: Yes.
Mixing Consoles: D&R 24-channel.
Tape Machines: B-16 Fostex 16-track.
Special Equipment: PCM digital mix, S-900 sampler, Neumann microphones, JBL and Tannoy monitors plus lots of outboard gear.
Accommodations: No.

Pyramid Productions

205A Lakeshore Rd. E.
Mississauga, ON L5G 1G2
(416) 891-0336
FAX (416) 278-1799
Owner: Mark McLay.
Manager: Mark McLay.
No. of Tracks: 16.
No. of Studios: Two.
Services Offered: Digital multitrack recording, mobile recording, lock to video and computer animation.
Rates: $45 per hour, $90 per hour for tape lock to video.
Rehearsal Space: Yes.
Mixing Consoles: Yamaha 2408.
Tape Machines: TASCAM 85-16B 1", JVC 6650 3/4", Sony PCM 701 digital mixdown.
Special Equipment: Fostex video lock with two cameras, Atari notator 64-track MIDI recorder and publisher, DX5, RX5, D110, 550 with large sound library, Lexicon PCM 70, 60 and Primetime, Dep5, Klark Teknik, Korg A3, DBX 166, Rocktron, JBL, Bryston, Yamaha, Urei, Sennheiser, AKG414, Computer animation.
Accommodations: Yes.

Quest Recording Studio

215 Toronto Ave.
Oshawa, ON L1H 3C2
(416) 576-1279
Owner: Paul Lachapelle.
Manager: Paul Lachapelle.
No. of Tracks: 24.
No. of Studios: One.
Services Offered: 24-track record and demo productions, 36-input automated mixing, Mitsubishi digital 2-track.
Rates: $75 per hour.
Rehearsal Space: No.
Mixing Consoles: Mitsubishi Westar.
Tape Machines: Studer 24- and 2-track, Mitsubishi X86 digital 2-track.
Special Equipment: Lexicon PCM 70 and 200 digital reverb, AMS DDL Drawmer gates and compressors, Aphex, BBE, Alesis Quadraverb, Akai S1000, Korg M1 Yamaha six-foot grand piano.
Accommodations: No.

Rainbow Recording Studios

8407 Stanley Ave., Unit 5
Niagara Falls, ON L2E 6X8
(416) 356-2234
Owner: Warren Parker.
Manager: Brad Murphy.
No. of Tracks: 16.
No. of Studios: One.
Services Offered: Tape duplication.
Rates: $45 per hour.
Rehearsal Space: Yes.
Mixing Consoles: Auditronics.
Tape Machines: Scully 100.
Special Equipment: Sony DAT for digital mixdown.
Accommodations: No.

Reaction Studios

72 Stafford St., Rear
Toronto, ON M6J 2R9
(416) 865-9468
Owner: Ormond Jobin.
Manager: Ormond Jobin.
No. of Tracks: 42.
No. of Studios: One.
Services Offered: Specialize in album and demo projects.
Rates: $45-55 per hour.
Rehearsal Space: No.
Mixing Consoles: Soundcraft 1600 Series.
Tape Machines: Studer A80 MK1V 24-track, MCI JH110B 2-track.
Special Equipment: Neve Prism Rack, Lexicon 480L.
Accommodations: No.

Round Sound Studios

357 Ormont Dr.
Weston, ON M9L 1N8
(416) 743-9979
Owner: Round Sound Studios Inc.
Manager: Victor J. Rivera.
No. of Tracks: 24.
No. of Studios: One.
Services Offered: Video production.
Rates: On request.
Rehearsal Space: No.
Mixing Consoles: Mitsubishi Westar (36x24x24 hard disk-automated).
Tape Machines: Otari MTR-90, MTR-10 and MX5050B II.
Special Equipment: Lexicon 224 reverb, AMMS 1S-805 delay, Emulator II digital synth, Akai S-900 sampler, Q-lock 310 synchronizer.
Accommodations: No.
Comments: In-house musicians and creative production services.

Rumenal Records Recording Studios

P.O. Box 730, Stn. C
Toronto, ON M6J 3S1
(416) 367-0925
Owner: J.M. Pedrow.
Managers: R. Van Langen and W.B. Culp.
No. of Tracks: 2, 8, 16.
No. of Studios: Two.
Services Offered: Tape duplication (available for studio customers only).
Rates: $15-25 per hour.
Rehearsal Space: Yes.
Mixing Consoles: (2) Studiomaster.
Tape Machines: TASCAM MS 16, Fostex H8.
Special Equipment: TASCAM half track M32, 20 cassette decks, 16 soundgates, compressors, Premier drums, Peavey amps, Gibson electric and acoustic guitars, keyboards, AKG mics and headphones.
Accommodations: No.

SRS - Sound Recording Studio

500 Newbold St.
London, ON N6E 1K6
(519) 686-5060
Owner: Paul Steenhuis.
Manager: Geoff Keymer.
No. of Tracks: 24 plus.
No. of Studios: Three.
Services Offered: Full service music production and video post-production interlock services.
Rates: $60 per hour.
Rehearsal Space: Yes.
Mixing Consoles: Mitsubishi Westar 8000.
Tape Machines: Studer A80.
Special Equipment: Digital mastering, Adam-Smith synchronizer, full MIDI production, DX5, d50s, S50, S1000, MI, MPC60, Lexicon, grand piano.
Accommodations: No.
Comments: Studio musicians, staff producers, entertainment law and music business consultants.

Satellite Sound

648 Queen St., Rear
Sault Ste. Marie, ON P6A 2A4
(705) 759-0585
Owner: Bob McLeod.
Manager: Barbara McLeod.
No. of Tracks: 8.
No. of Studios: One.
Services Offered: Real-time tape duplication and jingle production.
Rates: $30 per hour, $175 per day.
Rehearsal Space: No.
Mixing Consoles: Soundcraft 500 Series.
Tape Machines: Otari 8-track, Revox 2-track.
Special Equipment: REV5 DDL, Proverb DDL, Effectron DDL, Gatex noise gates, Urei compressors, vocal enhancer, Valley d-esser.
Accommodations: Yes.

Saved by Technology Productions

10 Breadalbane St.
Toronto, ON M4Y 1C3
(416) 928-5957
Contact: Kim Devine.
Comments: Pre-production and post-production only.

Skyhawk Studio

301 Bridge St. E.
Belleville, ON K8N 1P5
(613) 966-4218
Owner: Eric Baragar.
Manager: Eric Baragar.
No. of Tracks: 32.
No. of Studios: One.
Services Offered: MIDI studio.
Rates: $45 per hour.
Rehearsal Space: No.
Special Equipment: ESP, IFX, Octapad.
Comments: Professional MIDI studio specializing in musical arrangements and pre-production for songwriters, producers and soundtrack recordings.

Snocan Recording Studio

2415 Holly Lane
Ottawa, ON K1V 7P2
(613) 731-4668
Owner: Ralph Carlson, David Dennison, Stewart Dennison.
Manager: David Dennison.
No. of Tracks: 16.
No. of Studios: One.
Services Offered: Full recording for tape, record and CD production.
Rates: $35 per hour.
Rehearsal Space: Yes.
Mixing Consoles: Midas (16 x 16).
Tape Machines: Studer A80 16-track, Tanberg 2-track, Revox 77 2-track.
Special Equipment: EMT plate stereo reverb, REV7, Urei and Pandora limiters and compressors, and Lexicon digital delay.
Accommodations: No.

Solid State Recording Studio

1242 Colborne St. E.
Brantford, ON N3T 5L4
(519) 752-0839
Owner: Len Wilde.
Manager: Harry Serabian.
No. of Tracks: 16.
No. of Studios: One.
Rates: $45 per hour.
Rehearsal Space: No.
Mixing Consoles: TEAC.
Tape Machines: MCI, Otari.
Special Equipment: Standard microphones and outboard gear.
Accommodations: No.
Comments: Home of four labels, three publishing firms, jingle company, management, record and cassette packages, one hour from most major centres. Accommodations and restaurants close by.

Sound Art Music Productions

7181 Delmonte Cr.
Mississauga, ON L4T 3L4
(416) 677-8478
Owner: Arthur H.B. Atkinson.
Manager: Arthur H.B. Atkinson.
No. of Tracks: 16.
No. of Studios: One.
Rates: On request.
Rehearsal Space: No.
Mixing Consoles: Soundcraft Series II.
Tape Machines: TASCAM MS 16, TEAC 25-2.
Special Equipment: Digital delay, reverb, exciter, harmonizer, noise gates, compressor.
Accommodations: No.

Sound Design Studios

397 Donlands Ave.
Toronto, ON M4J 3S2
(416) 467-1488
FAX (416) 467-1492
Owner: SMB Communications Group Inc.
Manager: Doug Virgin.
No. of Tracks: 16.
No. of Studios: Three.
Services Offered: Original and stock music and effects, voiceovers and production.
Rates: $60-175 per hour.
Rehearsal Space: Yes.
Mixing Consoles: Sound Workshop.
Tape Machines: Otari X3, Fostex B-16, MCI-16.
Special Equipment: Sound Master tape lock, Lexicon reverb, Neumann, AKG, Sennheizer, Telefunken.
Accommodations: No.
Comments: Unique auditorium for live acoustic and classical recordings.

Sound Ideas

105 West Beaver Creek Rd., Unit 4
Richmond Hill, ON L4B 1C6
(416) 977-0512
FAX (416) 886-6800
Owner: Brian Nimens.
Manager: Brian Nimens.
No. of Tracks: 24.
No. of Studios: One.
Services Offered: Video production.
Rates: $100 per hour, $135 per hour with tape lock.
Rehearsal Space: No.
Mixing Consoles: Westar, (automated with disk mix).
Tape Machines: (2) Studer A20, Studer A80.
Special Equipment: Sony DAT2500, Mitsubishi X-86 digital 2-track, (2) Akai 5-1000.
Accommodations: No.
Comments: Sound Ideas sound effects library series 1000-4000, available on CD. Sound Ideas sampler and production music library also available.

Sound Path Productions Ltd.

1100 Invicta Dr., Unit 20
Oakville, ON L6H 2K9
(416) 842-1743
FAX (416) 849-3886
Owner: Bill Drew.
Manager: Bill Drew.
No. of Tracks: 16.
No. of Studios: One.
Services Offered: Video and A/V production, graphic design for promo and albums, logo design.
Rates: $45-55 per hour depending on length of block booking.
Rehearsal Space: No.
Mixing Consoles: MCI 600 Series.
Tape Machines: MCI JH-16 Multitrack, MCIJH-110B mastering, TEAC.
Special Equipment: Neumann, AKG, Sennheiser and Shure microphones, - extensive outboard gear.
Accommodations: No.
Comments: Drum kit, pianos and in-house talent available.

Sound Proofs/ Echosphere Production

37 Scarborough Rd.
Toronto, ON M4E 3M4
(416) 690-3888
Owner: Stefan Podgrabinski.
Manager: Stefan Podgrabinski.
No. of Tracks: 16, 48.
No. of Studios: Two.
Services Offered: Video production.
Rates: $40 per hour music production and voiceovers, $50 per hour with tape lock.
Mixing Consoles: Seck (18x8x2), Yamaha DMP 7.
Tape Machines: Fostex B-16, Sony PCM Digital 2-track.
Special Equipment: Full Mac-based MIDI system including samplers, also analog and digital synths, digital effects, and automated mixdown.
Accommodations: No.
Comments: Original music for jingles, film, TV, etc. Priority and special consideration given to peace, environmental, and educational projects.

Sound Stage Niagara

7040 Thorold Stone Rd.
Niagara Falls, ON L2J 1B6
(416) 358-6592
Owner: Dave Hall.

Sounds Interchange Ltd.
506 Adelaide St. E.
Toronto, ON M5A 1N6
(416) 364-8512
FAX (416) 866-7968
Services Offered: Album, film, TV and jingle music; Post-Audio for film and TV (SFX, ADR, etc.).
Comments: Phone P. Mann (GM) for specific information.

The Source Recording
402 Huron St.
Toronto, ON M5S 2G6
(416) 979-1901
Owner: Bob Read.
Manager: Bob Read.
No. of Tracks: 16.
No. of Studios: One.
Services Offered: Full MIDI and live recording.
Rates: $35 per hour (block rates available).
Rehearsal Space: No.
Mixing Consoles: Yamaha 1608
Tape Machines: Fostex B16, Otari 5050 2-track, Nakamichi cassette deck.
Special Equipment: (2) DBX 160X compressor/limiters, Lexicon PCM60 reverb, Midiverb II reverb, Orban parametric equalizer, Korg M-1, Yamaha D110, PC computer with Textures software.
Accommodations: No.
Comments: Three separate sound rooms.

The Source Recording Studio Inc.
67 Mowat Ave., Suite 031
Toronto, ON M6K 3E3
(416) 531-1390
FAX (416) 531-7439
Owner: Greg G. Baker.
Manager: Greg G. Baker.
No. of Tracks: 16.
No. of Studios: One.
Services Offered: Full MIDI production recording studio.
Rates: $30 per hour.
Rehearsal Space: No.
Mixing Consoles: Neve, Sound Workshop.
Tape Machines: TASCAM 16-track.
Special Equipment: Instruments supplied at no charge: Milestone drums.
Comments: Specialize in music for film, TV, radio jingles.

Straightwire
22 Linden St.
Toronto, ON M4Y 1V6
(416) 922-9922
FAX (416) 960-6166
Owner: Hoffert Music Inc. and Concertmasters Inc.
Manager: Ruth Taylor.
No. of Tracks: 2.
No. of Studios: One.
Services Offered: Digital editing, dubbing and transferring, remote digital recording, rental of digital audio equipment.
Rates: First two hours: $125 per hour, additional hours $85 (includes operator).
Rehearsal Space: No.
Tape Machines: (2) Sony DMR 4000, Sony 2500A & B DAT.
Special Equipment: Sony 1100A editor, Sony 1630 processor, Sony 601 digital processor, Sony 701 digital processor (modified for digital transfers).
Accommodations: No.
Comments: Sound-proof listening room with live-end/dead-end acoustics; read after write and read after read capability for maximum security at remotes and to read marginal tapes with a minimum of errors.

Studio A Recording Studio
190 Highway 7 W., Unit 6
Brampton, ON L7A 1A2
(416) 455-1043
Owner: Bill Hughes and Archy Hachey.
Manager: Archy Hachey.
No. of Tracks: 16.
No. of Studios: One.
Services Offered: Audio production, tape duplication, music arrangement and production, keyboard drum programming.
Rates: $32 per hour.
Rehearsal Space: Yes.
Mixing Consoles: Studiomaster.
Tape Machines: TASCAM.
Special Equipment: Full MIDI, tape interlock and MIDI suite, Beta and VHS facilities.
Accommodations: No.

Studio "B"

983 Victoria Park Ave.
Toronto, ON M4B 2J4
(416) 757-4891
Owner: William Petrie.
Manager: William Petrie.
No. of Tracks: 24.
No. of Studios: One.
Services Offered: Digital and multitrack
recording services.
Rates: $80 per hour.
Rehearsal Space: No.
Mixing Consoles: Soundcraft.
Tape Machines: Otari, Sony.
Special Equipment: Atari, MIDI/SMPTE se-
quencing and synchronizing.
Accommodations: No.

Studio Depot Inc.

3 Ontario St.
Grimsby, ON L3M 3G8
(416) 945-2821
Owner: David Buckley.
Manager: David Buckley.
No. of Tracks: 32.
No. of Studios: One.
Services Offered: Video production.
Rehearsal Space: No.
Mixing Consoles: Stephenson Interface.
Tape Machines: Sony F-1 digital.
Special Equipment: Nine-foot concert grand
piano, effects on request.
Accommodations: No.
Comments: Production house - no outside
bands.

Studio 423 West

423 West St.
Dunnville, ON N1A 2V4
(416) 774-5515
Owners: Bill and James Verutis.
Manager: Bill Verutis.
No. of Tracks: 16.
No. of Studios: One.
Rates: On request.
Rehearsal Space: No.
Mixing Consoles: Biamp 2016 bimix.
Tape Machines: Fostex B16, Tandberg TD20A,
Nikko and TASCAM cassettes.
Special Equipment: Symetrix, C/L and
parametric EQ, Ibanez and Fostex DDLs, Biamp
and Ulissus reverb.
Accommodations: No.

Studio 92

92 Cadorna Ave.
Toronto, ON M4J 3X2
(416) 467-9597
Owner: Norm Barker.
Manager: Ruth Barker.
No. of Tracks: 16.
No. of Studios: One.
Services Offered: 16-track and complete MIDI
studio.
Rates: $25 per hour (block rates available).
Rehearsal Space: No.
Mixing Consoles: Seck 1882, Roland M-160.
Tape Machines: TASCAM MSR 16 16-track,
TASCAM 32 2-track.
Special Equipment: AKGs including C414,
Sennheiser, Shure, Emulator library, EMAX, Lexi-
con, Alesis, Peavey, Ibanez and Fostex outboard
gear, SMPTE, Roland S-330, Roland U110,
HUSH IIC.
Accommodations: No.
Comments: Broadcast quality production: from
demo to complete LP. Studio musicians available
on request.

Summit Sound Inc.

40 Main St., P.O. Box 333
Westport, ON K0G 1X0
(613) 273-2818
FAX (613) 273-7325
Owner: David Daw.
Manager: David Daw.
No. of Tracks: 16.
No. of Studios: One.
Services Offered: Tape duplication.
Rates: $35 per hour and up.
Rehearsal Space: No.
Mixing Consoles: TASCAM (20 x 20 x 4 x 1).
Accommodations: Yes.
Comments: Complete custom production
services, arranging, musicians at $12.50 per
hour. More than 300 album projects produced.

Tanis Productions

4160 Dundas St. W.
Islington, ONn M8X 1X3
(416) 233-7029
FAX (416) 445-5145
Owner: Gregory Johnston.
Manager: Gregory Johnston.
No. of Tracks: 24 plus MIDI.
No. of Studios: One.
Services Offered: Commercial productions,
jingles, original music, corporate A/V, artist
recordings.
Rates: $75 per hour.
Rehearsal Space: No.
Mixing Consoles: Sound Workshop Series 30.
Tape Machines: MCI, Otari.
Special Equipment: Akai and Roland
samplers, Lexicon, Yamaha and Alesis
processors.
Accommodations: No.
Comments: A comfortable and spacious studio.

Tenthline Productions

General Delivery
Calabogie, ON K0J 1H0
(613) 752-2201
Owner: William Griffiths.
Manager: William Griffiths.
No. of Tracks: 8.
No. of Studios: One.
Rates: $40 per hour.
Rehearsal Space: Yes.
Mixing Consoles: TASCAM 520.
Tape Machines: TASCAM, TEAC 80-8.
Special Equipment: Lexicon, Alesis.
Accommodations: Yes.

This is it Recording Studio

37 Dormington Dr.
Scarborough, ON M1G 3N1
(416) 438-3137
Owners: Mike Cicciarella and Salvatore Cicciarella.
No. of Tracks: 16.
No. of Studios: One.
Services Offered: Recording of master tapes and limited duplication.
Rates: $30 per hour.
Rehearsal Space: No.
Mixing Consoles: Soundcraft 1600 Series.
Tape Machines: TASCAM ATR 60 1".
Special Equipment: Panasonic 18-bit DAT records at 44.1 kHz, Hybrid Arts SMPTE track (Atari forat), Lexicon PCM 70 reverb.
Accommodations: No.
Comments: Available for albums, demos jingles. Specializing in reggae, rap, soul and R&B. Arranging done on request.

Triton Sound Studios

3886 Chesswood Dr.
Downsview, ON M3J 2W6
(416) 638-3869
Owners: Jody Ellis and Steven Dell'Angelo.
Manager: Steven Dell'Angelo.
No. of Tracks: 24.
No. of Studios: One.
Services Offered: Audio/video post-production, in-house production, jingle production, MIDI pre-production.
Rates: $80 per hour, $110 per hour for video interlock.
Mixing Consoles: MCI 600 Series.
Tape Machines: Sony JH-24.
Special Equipment: Emulator, Macintosh.
Accommodations: No.
Comments: Excellent block rates available.

Venture Sound Productions

45 Playter Cr.
Toronto, ON M4K 1S4
(416) 461-1566
Owner: William Culp.
Manager: William Culp.
No. of Tracks: 8.
No. of Studios: One.
Services Offered: VSP is a multitrack recording facility specializing in mobile recordings.
Rates: Negotiable.
Rehearsal Space: No.
Mixing Consoles: Fostex 1240.
Tape Machines: TASCAM 38 1/2".
Special Equipment: DBX noise reduction, Yamaha NS-10M monitors, Yamaha R100 reverb, Alesis microverb, Valley micro compressor/limiter.
Accommodations: No.
Comments: VSP offers a complete package including recording, mastering, cassette duplication, artwork and packaging at a very competitive price. Also offers a unique fundraising program for schools and churches.

Waxworks Recording Studio Inc.

P.O. Box 299
St. Jacobs, ON N0B 2N0
(519) 664-3762
FAX (519) 664-3554
Owner: Jim Evans.
Manager: Stephen Morris.
No. of Tracks: 24.
No. of Studios: One.
Services Offered: Complete video production, jingle house, scoring for TV and film.
Rates: Negotiable.
Rehearsal Space: No.
Mixing Consoles: MCI 636.
Tape Machines: Stephens 24-track, Ampex 2-track.
Special Equipment: Adam Smith Zeta Three synchronizer, assorted outboard gear.
Accommodations: Yes.

Wellesley Sound Studios

106 Ontario St.
Toronto, ON M5A 2V4
(416) 364-9533
Owner: Jeff McCulloch, Roger Slemin.
Manager: Cindy Campol.
Services Offered: Real-time duplication.
Rates: Upon request.
Mixing Consoles: SoundTracs 8 CM4400 (23x24x2 with automation), TASCAM M16(24x16x2).
Tape Machines: Sony 24-track JH110, Studer A80 2-track, TASCAM 52 2-track, Sony 701E digital 2-track.
Special Equipment: Monitor amplifiers, Dyaxis digital audio workstation hard-disk recorder, Crown AB, Studer, Monitor speakers Urei 813, Yamaha NS10-Ms, Aura Tones, Rogers LS35A, Echo reverb and delays, Lexicon 200, Sony DRE 2000, Lexicon PCM60, 42, 41, 70, Super Prime Time, Yamaha REV7, SPX90, AMS dual sampler, compueffectron, Roland DP5, other outboard gear Kepex II, Valley People 610, DBX 160X, Orban parametric EQ 662B, Orban de-esser, Symetrix 522, Roland SBX80 sync box, Omni Craft GT-4, Orange County compressor/limiter/expander, Ward Beck EQ. Microphones: AKG, Tube 414, 451, D12, Sennheiser 421, 441, Sony ECM 56, P2M. Instruments: full set of Ludwig drums, guitars, basses, Prophet 5, Drumtracs, percussion, DX7, TX816, Prophet 2002, Yamaha piano. Any additional equipment can be arranged.

Winfield Sound Studio

3805 Weston Rd.
Weston, ON M9L 2S8
(416) 748-2969

The Wychwood Studio

644 Christie St.
Toronto, ON M6G 3E7
Owner: Stan Meissner.
Manager: Rags Schnauzer (canine).
No. of Tracks: 24.
No. of Studios: One.
Services Offered: Video production.
Rates: On request.
Rehearsal Space: No.
Mixing Consoles: MCI JH-636 (automated).
Tape Machines: MCI 24-track and MCI 2-track, TEAC 2-track.
Special Equipment: Lexicon and Yamaha digital reverbs, Lexicon DDL, DBX compressor, Kepex, sundry other EQs and special effects.
Accommodations: No.
Comments: Yamaha grand piano, Ludwig drum kit, large microphone selection, various guitars and extensive MIDI equipment.

Zaza Sound Productions Limited

322 Dufferin St.
Toronto, ON M6K 1Z6
(416) 534-4211
FAX (416) 534-9520
Owner: Paul T. Zaza.
Manager: Paul T. Zaza.
No. of Tracks: 24.
No. of Studios: One, plus three editing suites.
Services Offered: Video production.
Rates: Upon request.
Rehearsal Space: No.
Mixing Consoles: MCI JH-600, Yamaha boards for editing suites.
Tape Machines: MCI.
Special Equipment: DX7, Emulator IIs, various video equipment, screening facilities.
Accommodations: No.

QUEBEC

CRSG Recording Studios

1455 boul. de Maisonneuve o.
Montreal, PQ H3G 1M8
(514) 848-7401
Owner: Concordia University Students' Association.
Manager: Simon Minshall.
No. of Tracks: 8.
No. of Studios: Two.
Services Offered: Music and sound recordings.
Rates: $15 per hour.
Rehearsal Space: No.
Mixing Consoles: TASCAM M-35, TASCAM M-30.
Tape Machines: TASCAM 38.
Special Equipment: Yamaha SPX 90 II, Yamaha REV7 Roland digital delay SDE 3000, Symetrix compressor, Yamaha graphic EQ.
Accommodations: No.
Comments: CRSG Radio, through its recording studio, has played a major part in the development of underground music in Montreal.

Decibel

2143 rue de Champlain
Montreal, PQ H2L 2T1
(514) 525-5975
Owner: Christian Montmarquette.
Manager: Christian Montmarquette.
No. of Tracks: 8.
No. of Studios: One.
Rates: $25 per hour.
Rehearsal Space: No.
Mixing Consoles: Trident.
Tape Machines: TASCAM.
Special Equipment: Drumulator, Yamaha RX-15.
Accommodations: No.
Comments: Can obtain subventions for SOCAN members to record demos. Composition and recording services for jingles and theatre.

Honey Music Productions

10 Waverley Rd.
Pointe Claire, PQ H9S 4W3
(514) 694-0310
Owner: Wayne Prue.
Manager: Wayne Prue.
No. of Tracks: 8 (analog), 64 (MIDI).
No. of Studios: One.
Services Offered: Tape demos and pre-production.
Rates: $15 per hour.
Rehearsal Space: No.
Mixing Consoles: Fostex.
Tape Machines: Fostex.
Special Equipment: Atari 1040 computer with Notator sequencing and printing program.
Accommodations: No.
Comments: 25 years of musical experience.

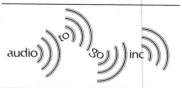
Inspiration Recording Studio

P.O. Box 220
LaPrairie, PQ J5R 3Y2
(514) 659-1772
Owner: Richard Loder.
Manager: Carole Vincent.
No. of Tracks: 16.
No. of Studios: One.
Services Offered: Record and cassette production (gospel music only).
Rates: On request.
Rehearsal Space: No.
Mixing Consoles: Neptune.
Tape Machines: TASCAM MS-16, TASCAM 32, TASCAM 122 MKII.
Special Equipment: Yamaha REV7, Yamaha SPX 90 II, Neumann U-67, Delta Lab Effectron, DBX 263 de-esser, Roland MK2 20 piano, Alesis HR-16.
Accommodations: No.
Comments: 28 gospel album credits. Special package for soloists and bands at very affordable rates. Write or call for a brochure.

Inter-Session Recording Studio

990 Salaberry, Suite 200
Chomedey, PQ H7S 2J1
(514) 662-2311
Owner: Roland Lefebvre and Gilles Collin.
No. of Tracks: 24 (analog), 48 (digital).
No. of Studios: One.
Rates: $80 per hour.
Rehearsal Space: Yes.
Mixing Consoles: Neotek Elite.
Tape Machines: Otari MTR-90, Sony Dash-48.
Special Equipment: Dolby SR., DAT and various types of microphones.
Accommodations: Yes.
Comments: Monitoring system by state-of-the-art CF-2000 with four QSC amplifiers.

Listen! Audio Productions Limited

308 Place d'Youville
Montreal, PQ H2Y 2B6
(514) 842-9725
FAX (514) 844-7736
Owner: George Morris.
Manager: Carole Akazawa.
No. of Tracks: 2,4,8,16,24,40 compatible.
No. of Studios: Two.
Rates: $80-150 per hour.
Rehearsal Space: Yes.
Mixing Consoles: Neil Mancy, Roger Mayer Customized Neve/API, Neve 5305.
Tape Machines: Studer A80 MKIII 24-track, MCI JH-10 16-track, various others.
Accommodations: No.
Comments: Complete creative and technical staff available for production of jingles, radio programs and album jackets.

MIDI II

3284 Edgar
Fabreville, PQ H7P 2E2
(514) 628-MIDI
Owners: Louise Paradis and Guy Desjardins.
No. of Tracks: 16.
No. of Studios: One.
Services Offered: Record production, audio for video post-production.
Rates: $35 per hour.
Rehearsal Space: No.
Mixing Consoles: Studiomaster Series II (40x8x2).
Tape Machines: TASCAM 85-16 with DBX.
Special Equipment: SMPTE-based sequencing, S-1000 (8 Megs), MPC-60, TX-816, D- 50, IBM at with Voyetra Seq + Mark III.
Accommodations: No.

Marko Studios

910 de la Gauchetiere e.
Montreal, PQ H2L 2N4
(514) 282-0961
FAX (514) 499-1227
Owner: Cliff Balson.
No. of Tracks: 24.
No. of Studios: Four.

Mecart

110 de Rotterdam
St. Augustin, PQ G3A 1T3
(418) 878-3584
FAX (418) 878-4877

Montreal Sound Studios

5000 Buchan, Suite 601
Montreal, PQ H4P 1T2
(514) 738-1300.
FAX (514) 733-9932.
Owner: GCH Productions.
Manager: Don Richards.
No. of Tracks: 16, 24.
No. of Studios: Two.
Services Offered: Analog recording, audio/video interlock, production.
Rates: $55 per hour.
Rehearsal Space: Yes.
Mixing Consoles: Harrison.
Tape Machines: MCI 24-track, Studer 2-track, Fostex 16-track.
Special Equipment: AMS, Lexicon, etc.
Accommodations: No.

Neptune

690 Graham
Dorval, PQ H9P 2B5
(514) 631-1272
FAX (819) 687-9893
Owner: Andrew Henderson.
Manager: Andrew Henderson.
No. of Tracks: 16.
No. of Studios: One.
Services Offered: Recording analog masters.
Rates: $30 per hour.
Rehearsal Space: Yes.
Mixing Consoles: Chilton.
Tape Machines: MCI.
Special Equipment: 16-track 2″ tape format, (3) 2-track machines, Urei aligned monitors.
Accommodations: No.

PGV Studio

2452 Bourbonniere, Rear
Montreal, PQ H1W 3P3
(514) 254-2497
FAX (514) 259-4044
Owner: Gilles Valiquette.
Manager: Luc Beaugrand.
No. of Tracks: 24 (analog), 24 (digital).
No. of Studios: One.
Services Offered: MIDI with IBM, Mac and Atari environments, video and sync.
Rates: $125 per hour.
Rehearsal Space: No.
Mixing Consoles: Amek, Scorpion.
Tape Machines: Studer A80, Akai, A-DAM.
Special Equipment: Akai digital patch bay, Twister with Steinberg software, Casio DAT, Urei monitoring.
Accommodations: No.
Comments: Recording booth for overdubs.

P.S.M. Studios

115 rue St. Pierre
Quebec, PQ G1K 4A6
(418) 692-1571
FAX (418) 692-1745
Manager: Jean-Marc Payer.
No. of Tracks: 24.
No. of Studios: One.
Services Offered: Video production, post-production.
Rates: $140 per hour.
Rehearsal Space: No.
Mixing Consoles: Trident TSM (32x24x24).
Tape Machines: Studer A800, Sony PCM 1610.
Special Equipment: Eclipse controller, Q-lock.
Accommodations: No.

Pavanne Audio Recording

P.O. Box 7, Place du Parc
Montreal, PQ H2W 2M9
(514) 485-7955
Owner: N. Fraser.
No. of Tracks: 2 (digital).
No. of Studios: Remote recording only.
Services Offered: Will record classical music and jazz on location or in- concert. Edit to cassette master, 1/4" or digital. Consultation on editing, mastering and budgets for CD production.
Rates: $300 per day (inquire about packages).
Mixing Consoles: Furman.
Tape Machines: Nakamichi DMT100 digital PCM, Betamax SLHF-300, Harmon Kardon and AIWA cassette decks.
Special Equipment: Schoeps microphones, Canare cables.
Comments: Experienced and highly-trained (technically and musically).

Saint-Charles

85 Grant
Longueuil, PQ J4H 3H4
(514) 674-4927
FAX (514) 674-6929
Owner: Tele Metropole Inc.
Manager: Yves E. Senecal.
No. of Tracks: 32.
No. of Studios: Two.
Services Offered: Video post-production and tape duplication.
Rates: $150 per hour.
Rehearsal Space: Yes.
Mixing Consoles: Trident TSM-PSM Modules.
Tape Machines: Studer A-800.
Special Equipment: Quested monitoring system, Dolby SR, large floating recording room (50-musician capacity.)
Accommodations: Yes.

Sequence

43 cote de la Canoterie
Quebec City, PQ G1K 3X5
(418) 694-0111
FAX (418) 694-1594
President: Simon Carpentier.
Manager: Marie-Pierre Lapointe.
No. of Tracks: 16, 24.
No. of Studios: Two, plus a MIDI studio.
Services Offered: Post-sync audio for video and film.
Rates: $50-125 per hour.
Rehearsal Space: No.
Mixing Consoles: Harrisson MR-4 with automation.
Tape Machines: TASCAM, Otari.
Special Equipment: Keyboards and samplers: S-SSO, EMAX HD, S-1000, S-900, TX- 816, MKS-80, M-1. Cass 1 (post-sync).
Accommodations: Yes.

Silent Sound

3880 Clark St.
Montreal, PQ H2W 1W6
(514) 842-1303
Owner: Morris Apelbaum.
Manager: Morris Apelbaum.
No. of Tracks: 24.
No. of Studios: Two.
Services Offered: CD, LP and tape duplication and manufacturing.
Rehearsal Space: Yes.
Mixing Consoles: Trident.
Tape Machines: Soundcraft Saturn 24-track, Studer 2-track, Sony PCM digital 2- track.
Accommodations: Yes.

Son-Art

5230 Begin
St. Hubert, PQ J3Y 2P9
(514) 676-0636
Owner: Jocelyn Bournival.
Manager: Jocelyn Bournival.
No. of Tracks: 16.
Services Offered: Album, demo and video post-production.
Rehearsal Space: Yes.
Mixing Consoles: Soundcraft.
Tape Machines: TASCAM, Technics, Sony R-DAT.
Special Equipment: Lexicon, Audio Logic, Kurzweil, Roland.
Accommodations: No.

Studio Centre-Ville

1168 rue Bishop
Montreal, PQ H3G 2E3
(514) 878-3456
FAX (514) 866-0331
Manager: Jean-Raymond Bourque.
No. of Tracks: 24.
No. of Studios: One.
Services Offered: Video Production.
Rehearsal Space: No.
Mixing Consoles: Neotek Series 2 (28x8x2).
Tape Machines: Otari MTR-10, Otari MX-70, Sony JH-24, JL Cooper automation, Cypher Digital synchronization system.
Accommodations: No.

Studio de Son Albatros Enr.

870 Jean-Masse St., Suite 11
Montreal, PQ H4J 1S3
(514) 332-1317
Owner: Richard Murray.
Manager: Richard Murray.
No. of Tracks: 8.
No. of Studios: One.
Rates: Upon request.
Rehearsal Space: No.
Mixing Consoles: TASCAM.
Tape Machines: TASCAM 80-8, Otari MX5050, Otari MX5050B, Revox 377, (3) cassette decks.
Special Equipment: Lexicon prime time, PCM-60, Korg digital delay, MicMix XL- 305, Yamaha baby grand, AKG and Neumann microphones, Atari 1040 computer, Emax sampler.
Accommodations: No.

Les Studios Jacasson Inc.

4450 rue St. Denis, Suite 200
Montreal, PQ H2J 2L1
(514) 844-6667
Owner: Jean-Jacques Bourdeau.
No. of Tracks: 16.
No. of Studios: One.
Rates: $50 per hour.
Rehearsal Space: Yes.
Mixing Consoles: Dynamix (32x16).
Tape Machines: TASCAM 858-16B.
Special Equipment: SMPL control.
Accommodations: No.
Comments: Sound effects on CD.

Studio La Majeure Inc.

1110 rue Bleury, 4th Floor
Montreal, PQ H2Z 1N4
(514) 871-9585
Owners: Luc Fontaine and Sylvain Lefebvre.
Manager: Luc Fontaine.
No. of Tracks: 24 (analog).
No. of Studios: One.
Services Offered: Stock music and effects library, tape duplication, sync to video.
Rates: $125 per hour.
Rehearsal Space: No.
Mixing Consoles: Neve Melbourne (34 inputs).
Tape Machines: Otari MTR-9011, MTR-10 2CT, Ampex ATR-100, AG-440.
Special Equipment: State-of-the-art monitoring, processing gear by Lexicon, Eventide, Yamaha, DBX, BSS and ADR. Also, AKG, Neumann and Sennheiser, microphones.
Accommodations: No.

Le Studio Mobile

P.O. Box 367, Outremont Stn.
Montreal, PQ H2V 4N3
(514) 273-6861
FAX (514) 273-4605
Owner: Guillaume Bengle.
Manager: Guillaume Bengle.
No. of Tracks: 24.
No. of Studios: One.
Services Offered: 24-track remote recording available in Toronto and Montreal.
Rates: Please call.
Rehearsal Space: No.
Mixing Consoles: Soundcraft (64 inputs).
Tape Machines: Studer.
Special Equipment: Complete recording studio in 25-foot truck.
Accommodations: No.

Le Studio Morin-Heights

201 Perry Rd.
Morin-Heights, PQ J0R 1H0
(514) 226-2419
FAX (514) 226-5409
Owner: Groupe Andre Perry Inc.
Manager: Richard Ealey.
No. of Tracks: 48.
No. of Studios: One.
Rates: On request.
Rehearsal Space: No.
Mixing Consoles: SSL 4056 G Series (total recall).
Tape Machines: Studer A800, MTR90, AB0 1/2″ 2-track.
Special Equipment: Quested monitor system 412, Focus Rite ISA 110 EQ, Le Studio custom tube EQ, JVC Digital BP90.
Accommodations: Yes.
Comments: Residential studio with a six-bed-room guest house on 225 acres, with a private lake. Album credits includes: The Police, David Bowie, Keith Richards, Rush, Kim Mitchell, Glass Tiger, and many more.

Studio Multisons Inc.

1208 Beaubien St. E., Suite 107-108
Montreal, PQ H2S 1T7
(514) 272-7641
FAX (514) 272-3191
Owners: Jacques Bigras, Raymond du Berger.
Manager: Raymond du Berger.
No. of Tracks: 16, 24.
No. of Studios: Two.
Services Offered: Video production and post-production.
Rates: $75-100 per hour depending on requirements.
Rehearsal Space: No.
Mixing Consoles: Soundcraft 1600.
Tape Machines: Otari MTR 90 II 24-track.
Special Equipment: Ursa Major 8X32B digital reverb.
Accommodations: No.
Comments: Korg M-1, Yamaha C3D piano.

Les Studios Productions Parametres Inc.

1070 Bleury, Suite 301
Montreal, PQ H2Z 1N3
(514) 272-7634
Owner: Guy Delisle.
Manager: Guy Delisle.
No. of Tracks: 16.
No. of Studios: One.
Services Offered: Cassette and tape duplication. Video production starting September 1990.
Rates: $25-35 per hour.
Rehearsal Space: No.
Mixing Consoles: Soundcraft.
Tape Machines: TASCAM 90-16 1", Phillips Pro 51 1/4".
Special Equipment: Reverb: Lexicon PCM 70, PCM 42, LXP-1+MRC, Yamaha SPX 90 II, REV7. Exiter BBE 402. Compresser/limiter: DBX 166, 161, 119, Sampler: Akai S-1000 and many other synthesizers.
Accommodations: No.
Comments: High-speed cassette duplication and creative services available for film, jingle and record productions. Downtown location.

Studio Sonscript

910 rue de la Gauchetiere e.
Montreal, PQ H2L 2N4
(514) 499-1427
FAX (514) 499-1227
Owner: Barry Lucking.
Manager: Barry Lucking.
No. of Tracks: 8.
No. of Studios: Two.
Rates: $90-150 per hour.
Rehearsal Space: No.
Mixing Consoles: Studer.
Tape Machines: Studer, MCI.
Accommodations: No.

Studio Tempo Inc.

0707 Charlevoix
Montreal, PQ H3K 3Y1
(514) 937-9571
FAX (514) 937-8201
Owner: Yves Lapierre.
Manager: Dawn Corbett.
No. of Tracks: 2, 4, 8, (2) 24.
No. of Studios: Two.
Services Offered: Audio post-production.
Rates: $110 per hour ($50 extra for interlock).
Mixing Consoles: Helios 32, Amek G2520, Studer A827 and A800 III.
Tape Machines: Studer, Superanalog dolby and dolby A, Studer and Otari stereo and mono.
Special Equipment: CMX Cass 1.
Accommodations: No.

Studio Works

404 St. Henri
Montreal, PQ H3C 2P5
(514) 871-8481
FAX (514) 866-0147
Owners: Mario Rubnikowich and Mitch Knowles.
Manager: Mario Rubnikowich.
No. of Tracks: 8, 16, 24.
No. of Studios: One.
Services Offered: Tape duplication, soundtracks, jingles and albums. Also arrangement and production.
Rates: $20-75 per hour.
Rehearsal Space: No.
Special Equipment: Digital, Dolby SR, DBX.
Accommodations: No.
Comments: Engineers: John Klepko, Mario Rubnikowich, Gerry Bribosia.

Trebas Recording Studios

451 St. Jean St.
Montreal, PQ H2Y 2R5
(514) 845-4141
FAX (514) 845-2581
President: David P. Leonard.
Manager: Mike Matlin.
No. of Tracks: 24.
No. of Studios: Two (1 MIDI, 1 analog).
Services Offered: MIDI, audio post-production, jingle and music productions.
Rates: On request.
Rehearsal Space: No.
Mixing Consoles: Amek Mozart (32-channel, fully automated).
Tape Machines: Otari MX-80 24-track, Otari MX-55 TM 2-track with SMPTE, Mitsubishi digital 2-track.
Special Equipment: Full range of signal processing, MIDI, and synchronization equipment.
Accommodations: No.
Comments: Creative and technical specialists in jingle and music productions, audio post-production for video and film, and MIDI.

SASKATCHEWAN

Right Tracks Productions Ltd.
226B Portage Ave., Sub P.O. 18
Saskatoon, SK S7H 0Y0
(306) 933-4949
Owners: Lyndon Smith and Tim Wachowicz.
Manager: Lyndon Smith.
No. of Tracks: 8.
No. of Studios: One.
Services Offered: Video production.
Rates: On request.
Rehearsal Space: No.
Mixing Consoles: Soundtracs T Series.
Tape Machines: TASCAM, Sony.
Special Equipment: Sony PCM 601 digital 2-track, Roland SBX80 SMPTE synchronizer, Sony and JVC VCRs, DBX noise reduction.
Accommodations: No.

Studio West Pike Lake Recording Retreat
502-45 St. W.
Saskatoon, SK S7L 6H2
(306) 244-2815
FAX (306) 242-3301
Owners: Wayne Wilkins and Blaine Wilkins.
Manager: Blaine Wilkins.
No. of Tracks: 8, 24.
No. of Studios: Two.
Services Offered: Video production, record label, recording courses.
Rates: On request.
Rehearsal Space: No.
Mixing Consoles: MCI JH-636 (automated).
Tape Machines: MCI JH-24, Sony PCM F1.
Special Equipment: AMS RMX-16 digital reverb, AMS DMX 15-80 digital delay, Klark Teknik DN780 digital reverb, (8) Valley People 610 dual compressor expanders, Urei 4-band stereo parametric equalizer, Barcus Berry 802 processor, (2) AMCROM Microtech 1000, Bryston 2B and 3B pro amplifiers, Sony SL2700 Beta HiFi, Electrohome HQ VHS VCRs, Sony KV 2064 video monitor.

REHEARSAL STUDIOS

The Band Factory
4544 Dufferin St., Suite 24
Downsview, ON M3H 5X2
(416) 665-5844
Rooms: One.
Preferred Musical Styles: All styles.
Services Offered: Short- and long-term rehearsal space and storage.
Special Projects: On-site video studio.

Equity Showcase Theatre
221 Dufferin St., Suite 308A
Toronto, ON M6K 1Y9
(416) 533-6100
FAX (416) 534-9087
Rooms: Three.
Equipment Storage: Yes (summer only).
Rental Rates: Negotiable.
Comments: Evening bookings are more readily available. Facility highlights include hardwood floors, kitchen, washroom, air-conditioning and ample parking. Rentals by the hour, day or week.

The Jam Factory
50 Carroll St.
Toronto, ON M4M 3G3
(416) 463-2279
Rooms: One, 30' x 30'.
Rental Rates: $10-30/hour.
Comments: Used for video and large band rehearsal.

Oh! Studio
1331A rue Ste. Catherine e.
Montreal, PQ H2L 2H4
(514) 274-3114
Rooms: One.
Equipment Storage: Yes.

Preston Rehearsal Space

184 Preston
Ottawa, ON K1R 7P9
(613) 236-9899
Rooms: Two.
Equipment Storage: No.
Rental Rates: $160-176 per band, per month.

Regency/The House of Music Inc.

16 Phipps St.
Toronto, ON M4Y 1J8
(416) 924-3677

Rehearsal ah' Studio

6 Ossington Ave.
Toronto, ON M6J 2Y7
(416) 534-2480
Rooms: Two.
Equipment Storage: No.
Rental Rates: $8-11/hour.

Rising Star Rehearsal Studios

267 Bering Ave.
Toronto, ON M8Z 3A5
(416) 236-1257
FAX (416) 236-1255
Rooms: Seven.
Equipment Storage: No.
Rental Rates: Hourly, weekly.
Comments: New building with fully equipped, air-conditioned studios.

Street Brothers Productions

80 Parklawn, Suite 215
Toronto, ON M8Y 3H8
(416) 252-5129
Rooms: Five.
Equipment Storage: Yes.
Rental Rates: $250-300/week.
Comments: Two 600 square foot studios, three 400 square foot studios.

Take 5 Studios

222 King St. E., Suite 220
Hamilton, ON L8N 1B5
(416) 521-8001
Rooms: Five.
Equipment Storage: Yes.
Rental Rates: $250-300/month.
Comments: Fully equipped, air-conditioned.

World Group Productions

3080 Lenworth Dr.
Mississauga, ON L4X 2G1
(416) 625-3865
FAX (416) 277-1356
Rooms: Three.
Equipment Storage: Yes.
Rental Rates: $800/month.
Comments: Open 24 hours a day, seven days a week. Fully carpeted, acoustically insulated, large rooms. Loading bay. All on one level.

York Theatre Ltd.

639 Commercial Dr.
Vancouver, BC V5L 3W3
(604) 254-5934
Rooms: Six.
Equipment Storage: No.
Rental Rates: Daily, weekly, monthly.

Zack's Rehearsal Studios

172 Toryork Dr., Suite 10
Weston, ON M9L 1X8
(416) 742-5693
Rooms: Two.
Equipment Storage: Yes.
Rental Rates: Daily, weekly, monthly.

ALBERTA

Allstar Sound Equipment Ltd.
11212-143 St.
Edmonton, AB T5M 1V5
(403) 452-2546
Type of Company: Sales and rental agency.
Top Brands: Soundcraft, QSC, ASD.
Product Specialty: Nightclub systems, professional recording equipment.

Axe Music
11931-72 St.
Edmonton, AB T5B 1Y4
(403) 471-2001
FAX (403) 479-1443
Type of Company: Manufacturer, sales and rental agency, installer.
Special Services Offered: Servicing.
Top Brands: TOA, JBL, QSC.
Product Specialty: Sound and lighting for nightclubs and theatres.

Force Majeure Systems
11616-154 St.
Edmonton, AB T5M 3N8
(403) 451-1353
Type of Company: Rental agency.
Product Specialty: Sound reinforcement and stage lighting.

Kapers Kustom Entertainment
12835-106 St.
Edmonton, AB T5E 4T5
(403) 475-2659
Product Specialty: Custom entertainment service. DJs, video, limos, photography, flowers, sound and lighting for weddings, tours and other functions.

Lighting By Monty Ltd.
9170 Yellowhead Tr.
Edmonton, AB T5B 1G2
(403) 477-5077
FAX (403) 477-8247
Type of Company: Distributor, sales and rental agency.
Top Brands: Strand, Altman, Leprecon.

Pro-Lite Productions Ltd.
550-42 Ave. S.E.
Calgary, AB T2G 1Y6
(403) 243-2688
FAX 243-2689
Type of Company: Sales, rental and service of quality lighting equipment.
Special Services Offered: Support to the music and theatre industry plus churches and corporations.
Top Brands: Leprecon, Tomcat, Lycian, Genie.
Product Specialty: Lighting, DJ systems and special effects.

Pyramid Sound Ltd.
1530A-9 Ave., S.E.
Calgary, AB T2G 0T7
(403) 269-4054
Type of Company: Rental agency.
Top Brands: Crest, Hill, T.A.C.
Product Specialty: PA and bar systems for concerts and trade shows.

RCA Inc.
12855-141 St.
Edmonton, AB T5L 4N1
(403) 452-9831
Top Brands: Altec, Electro-Voice, Bryston.
Product Specialty: Sound system installations, sales and service.

BRITISH COLUMBIA

Commercial Electronics Ltd.
1335 Burrard St.
Vancouver, BC V6Z 1Z7
(604) 669-5525
Type of Company: Distributor, sales and rental agency.
Special Services Offered: System design and consulting.
Top Brands: Atari, TASCAM, JBL, Altec.

D.L. Sound Production Ltd.
3708 Casey Dr.
Victoria, BC V8Z 4J5
(604) 479-0607 or 383-1605
Type of Company: Rentals of sound reinforcement and lighting equipment.

Deyong Sound Services Ltd.
271 E. 2 Ave.
Vancouver, BC V5T 1B8
(604) 873-3841
Type of Company: Concert sound services and equipment rentals.
Special Services Offered: Mobile multitrack recording services.

Electrosound Entertainment Services Ltd.
680 Sumas St.
Victoria, BC V8T 4S6
(604) 389-0005
FAX (604) 389-0808
Type of Company: Sound and lighting equipment rentals.
Special Services Offered: Sales and repairs.
Top Brands: Electro-Voice, Peavey, Yamaha.

Goldrush Sound Studios Ltd.
1234 W. 6 Ave.
Vancouver, BC V6H 1A5
(604) 733-4012
Special Services Offered: Live sound mixing for concert venues.
Product Specialty: Sound system design consultants.

Jason Sound Industries Ltd.
1709 Welch St.
North Vancouver, BC V7P 3G9
(604) 986-2367
FAX (604) 988-1036
Type of Company: Concert sound contracting.

Kian Concert Sound Services Ltd.

2195 W. 13 Ave.
Vancouver, BC V6K 2S2
(604) 733-5728
FAX (604) 732-8525 (on request)
Type of Company: Concert sound services.
Special Services Offered: Tour support.
Top Brands: Meyer, Yamaha PM3000, Ramsa 840F.

Frank McKnight Ltd.

269 Charlotte St.
Sydney, NS B1P 6K3
(902) 539-5030
Type of Company: Service, sales and rental agency.
Special Services Offered: Warranty and non-warranty repairs to, JBL speakers.
Top Brands: JBL, Shure, Urei, Crown, PZM, Sennheiser, Otari, Roland.

Huyghe Meakes Illuminations Ltd.

3612 W. 4 Ave., Suite 9
Vancouver, BC V6R 1P1
(604) 736-4977
Pager: (604) 253-7596 (Page 2040)
Type of Company: Sound and lighting contractor.
Special Services Offered: Film and video lighting services and equipment rentals.

Mountain Music Ltd.

P.O. Box 989
Rossland, BC V0G 1Y0
(604) 362-7795
Type of Company: Sales and rentals.
Top Brands: Sunn, Alexis, Roland, Fender, Akai.

Rocky Mountain Sound Ltd.

1113 Union St.
Vancouver, BC V6A 2C7
Type of Company: Sound services, sales and rentals.
Branch Offices:
544-38A Ave. S.E.
Calgary, AB T2G 1X4

1060 Stacey Ct. Unit 2
Mississauga, ON L4W 2X8

Skana Sound and Light Systems

254 Ellis St.
Penticton, BC V2A 4L6
(604) 492-4710
Type of Company: Sound and lighting company and retailer.
Special Services Offered: Electronic supplies and repairs.

Tommy Tune Ltd.

315 W. 1 St., Suite 101
North Vancouver, BC V7M 1B5
(604) 986-7160
FAX (604) 980-8199
Type of Company: Sales and installation of sound and video equipment.
Special Services Offered: Service and custom-design (commercial, residential).
Top Brands: Pioneer, Toshiba, Tannoy.

West Coast Stage Lighting Ltd.

1111 Union St.
Vancouver, BC V6A 2C7
(604) 255-0211
FAX (604) 255-9899
Type of Company: Lighting, sales and rentals.
Branch Office:
Alberta Stage Lighting Ltd.
11210-143 St.
Edmonton, AB T5M 1V5
(403) 452-5483

Western Sound Limited

3711 E. 1 Ave.
Burnaby, BC V5C 3V6
(604) 299-9341
FAX (604) 299-8340
Type of Company: Sound, lighting, video and A/V sales and rentals.
Special Services Offered: System design, TEF analysis of acoustics.
Top Brands: Electro-Voice, Meyer, Altec.
Product Specialty: High-performance sound systems.

MANITOBA

Banquox Sound Ltd.
438 Dufferin Ave.
Winnipeg, MB R2W 2Y5
(204) 589-8351
FAX (204) 944-0457
Type of Company: Sound system rentals, sales and installation.
Special Services Offered: Production for concerts, festivals and fairs.

Hallcraft Electronics
1760 Sargent Ave.
Winnipeg, MB R3H 0C7
(204) 786-5846
Type of Company: Distributor, sales and rental agency.
Special Services Offered: Installation and service.

Westsun Media Ltd.
120 James Ave.
Winnipeg, MB R3B 0N8
(204) 943-1690
FAX (204) 943-1081
Type of Company: Manufacturer, distributor, sales and rental agency.
Special Services Offered: Tour support.
Product Specialty: Theatrical, TV and entertainment lighting systems.

NEW BRUNSWICK

Max Technique et Musique
45 Savoie St.
Edmunston NB E3V 3V7
(506) 735-4700
Type of Company: Sales, rentals, service and commercial installations of sound and light systems.
Top Brands: JBL, Soundcraft, Lexicon, Roland.

NEWFOUNDLAND

Petrivision Ltd.
P.O. Box 9056, Stn. B
St. John's, NF A1A 2X3
(709) 739-9502
FAX (709) 739-9502
Type of Company: Film and TV lighting and production.
Special Services Offered: Music video production.

NOVA SCOTIA

Atlantic Illumination
23 Sheridan St.
Dartmouth, NS B3A 2C9
(902) 463-7418
FAX (902) 469-3255
Type of Company: Rentals and club installations.
Special Services Offered: Major warranty repairs.
Top Brands: Altman, Celco, Leprecon.
Product Specialty: Lights and dimming for tours and theatre.

Musicstop Ltd.
6065 Cunard St.
Halifax, NS B3K 1E6
(902) 422-6571
Special Services Offered: Sound reinforcement sales and service.
Top Brands: Yamaha, Peavey, Roland.
Product Specialty: Electronic and acoustic musical instruments.

Standard Sound Systems
3091 Oxford St.
Halifax, NS B3L 2W8
(902) 423-8421
Type of Company: Service, sales and rental agency.
Top Brands: Roland, Airphone, Shure.
Product Specialty: Permanent PAs, installation and service.

Tour Tech East Ltd.

200B Wyse Rd.
Dartmouth, NS B3A 1M9
(902) 466-6850
FAX (902) 466-3173
Type of Company: Sound and lighting rentals.
Special Services Offered: Custom touring packages including transportation and technicians.
Top Brands: Rosco, Strand Century, Great Performance Products.

ONTARIO

AOT Pro Audio

(A Division of Handsome Dan Music Inc.)
500 Trillium Dr., Unit 8
Kitchener, ON N2R 1A7
(519) 748-2780
FAX (519) 748-2781
Type of Company: Sound reinforcement sales, leasing, rentals and repair.
Top Brands: Soundcraft, JBL, Yorkville.

Ainsworth Productions

120 Bermondsey Rd.
Scarborough, ON M4A 1X6
(416) 585-8500
Type of Company: Distributor, installer, sales and rental agency.
Product Specialty: Complete staging and design services for music, video, trade shows and industrials.

Armor Pro Audio

R.R. 6
Woodstock, ON N4S 7W1
(519) 462-2882
Type of Company: Pro sound contractor.
Special Services Offered: Sales, service, installations, rentals, tour support.
Top Brands: Electro-Voice, OSC, TAC.
Comments: Manufacturer of Armor flight cases.

Audio Concept Toronto

1951 Denison St., Unit 16
Markham, ON L3R 3W9
(416) 940-1820
FAX (416) 940-1382
Type of Company: Sound reinforcement sales and distribution.
Special Services Offered: Pro audio rentals.
Top Brands: Australian Monitor (power amplifiers), Ramsa, Meyer.
Branch:
2229 rue Ste. Catherine e.
Montreal, PQ H2K 2J3
(514) 527-8366
FAX (514) 525-5949

BCB Sound & Lighting Productions

1535 Meyerside Dr., Unit 8
Mississauga, ON L5T 1M9
(416) 672-3444
Type of Company: Distributor and sales agency.
Special Services Offered: Repairs.
Top Brands: JBL, Sennheiser, SF Marketing.
Product Specialty: Complete disco lighting and aluminum lighting fixtures.

Band Aid Services

371A Danforth Rd.
Scarborough, ON M1L 3X8
(416) 690-3343
FAX (416) 690-3363
Type of Company: Sound and stage production.

Bandworld Inc.

1250B Reid St.
Richmond Hill, ON L4B 1G3
(416) 886-4040
FAX (416) 886-4041
Type of Company: Sound and lighting sales and repairs.
Special Services Offered: Event co-ordination (decor and special effects).
Installations and support for concerts and conventions.
Top Brands: Adamson Acoustics, Soundcraft, Yorkville Sound.

Canadian Staging Projects

571 Adelaide St. E.
Toronto, ON M5A 1N8
(416) 947-9400
FAX (416) 367-8708
Type of Company: Distributor.
Top Brands: Strand, Altman, Rosco.
Product Specialty: Fibre optics; rentals, sales and service.

Concord Sound

1594 Dundas St. W.
Toronto, ON M6K 1T8
(416) 534-2605
Type of Company: Distributor, service, sales and rental agency.
Special Services Offered: Sound consultation.
Top Brands: Electro-Voice, Shure, TOA.

Cosmo Sound
9201 Yonge St.
Richmond Hill, ON L4C 6Z2
(416) 889-6382
Type of Company: Sales and rental agency, installations.
Top Brands: King, Tama.
Product Specialty: Nightclubs, touring, outdoor concerts.

E.T.I.
150 McLevin Ave., Unit 8
Scarborough, ON M1B 4Z7
(416) 754-7747
FAX (416) 291-0666
Type of Company: Manufacturer, sales and rental agency.
Special Services Offered: Lighting equipment and special effects for concerts, theatres and discotheques.

Ear Music Company
526 Brentwood Ave.
Oshawa, ON L1G 2T1
(416) 723-8916
Product Specialty: Sound reinforcement.

Entertainment Media Corporation
513 Broadway Ave.
Toronto, ON M4K 2N5
(416) 469-8300
Type of Company: Design and sales for nightclubs and discotheques.
Special Services Offered: Background music systems for restaurants.
Top Brands: JBL, Bose, Cerwin-Vega.
Product Specialty: Recorded music reproduction.

Entertainment Technology
90 Thorncliffe Park Dr.
Toronto, ON M4H 1M5
(416) 422-4940
FAX (416) 425-6196
Type of Company: Supplier of sound and lighting equipment to nightclubs and restaurants.
Special Services Offered: Design and installation of lasers and special effect lighting.

Explosive Design Inc.
18 Automatic Dr., Unit 18
Brampton, ON L6S 5N4
(416) 791-PYRO
FAX (416) 792-1059
Type of Company: Sales and rental agency, service centre.
Special Services Offered: Sales and rental of custom-designed effects and indoor and outdoor fireworks.

Jack A. Frost Ltd.
3245 Wharton Way
Mississauga, ON L4X 2R9
(416) 624-5344
FAX (416) 624-2386
Type of Company: Distributor and sales of motion picture and theatrical lighting.
Special Services Offered: Custom-built power distribution equipment.
Type of Company: Strand, Altman, Ushio.
Product Specialty: Specialty lamps.

GERR Electro-Acoustics Ltd.
363 Adelaide St. E.
Toronto, ON M5A 1N3
(416) 868-0528
FAX (416) 868-6419
Type of Company: Sales of quality PA and post-production audio equipment.
Top Brands: Synclavier, Sound Workshop, Timeline, GEM.

Half Nelson Systems Inc.
253 Regent St.
Sudbury, ON P3C 4C6
(705) 674-1450
Type of Company: Professional touring company.
Special Services Offered: Complete production services.
Top Brands: Meyer, Martin, Midas, Soundcraft, LMI.
Client Specialty: Institutions, theatres, bands, festivals, etc.

Lammert Entertainment Enterprises Inc.
47 Fieldgate Dr.
Nepean, ON K2J 1V3
(613) 825-3111
Type of Company: Supplier of staging, lighting, PA systems, background music and DJ services.
Clients: Theme, fashion and variety shows.

Light Concert Services
2 Vanbrugh Ave.
Scarborough, ON M1N 3S7
(416) 261-4522
Type of Company: Technical support.
Special Services Offered: Transportation and road crews.
Top Brands: JBL, Soundcraft, Yamaha.
Product Specialty: Technical services and specialized sound and lighting equipment for concert and convention functions.

N.M.E. Sound Design
1156-1/2 Queen St. E., Suite 8
Toronto, ON M4M 1L2
(416) 466-7785
Type of Company: Production company.
Specialty: Show design and engineering.
Special Services Offered: Special effects consultant.

National Show Systems
36 Malley Rd.
Toronto, ON M1L 2E2
(416) 755-8666
FAX (416) 752-1382
Type of Company: Show services.
Special Services Offered: Sound, lighting, staging, outdoor roofs.

Necessity Sound Production
18 Earlington Ave.
Toronto, ON M8X 2N5
(416) 248-9925
Special Services Offered: Production, service and installation.

Niagara Sound Systems
2756 Wedgewood Cr.
Niagara Falls, ON L2J 2B7
(416) 354-1349
Type of Company: Sale of pro sound equipment.
Special Services Offered: Complete staging and operator-included rentals.
Top Brands: Apogee, Atlas, Shure.
Product Specialty: Automatic microphone systems.

P.A. Plus Sound Productions Inc.
555 Eastern Ave., Suite 2
Toronto, ON M4M 1C8
(416) 466-4420
FAX (416) 466-4699
Type of Company: Sound reinforcement for tours and clubs.
Special Services Offered: Installations.
Top Brands: Electro-Voice, Crest, Carver.

Peak Productions
P.O. Box 433
Westport, ON K0G 1X0
(613) 273-2818
Type of Company: Sales agency.
Top Brands: Most major lines.
Product Specialty: Pro audio sales and installations.

Pierce Sound Equipment
411 Industrial Rd., Unit 6
London, ON N5V 3L3
(519) 455-7041
FAX (519) 455-6506
Type of Company: Sound and lighting equipment contractors and suppliers.
Special Services Offered: Roof and stage systems.
Top Brands: Meyer, Thomas-Avokite, Soundcraft Series 4.
Product Specialty: Tours, TV broadcasts, main events, trade shows.

Professional Sound & Lighting
1392 Star Top Rd.
Ottawa, ON K1B 4V7
(613) 744-0990
FAX (613) 744-8787
Type of Company: Pro PA and stagelighting sales, rentals, installations and service.
Special Services Offered: Special effects distributor (Pyropak "Pyro" systems and powders).
Top Brands: JBL (speakers), QSC (amplifiers), Strand (dimmers and controls).
Product Specialty: JBL concert sound dealer.

Progressive Lighting Concepts
272 Eglinton Ave. W., Unit 7
Toronto, ON M4R 1B2
(416) 483-5442
Type of Company: Lighting design and consultation.
Client Specialty: Music, trade, industrial, fashion, TV and video.

Pyrotek Special Effects

617 Pharmacy Ave.
Scarborough, ON M1L 3H1
(416) 288-9938
FAX (416) 288-9483
Type of Company: Distributor, designer and supplier of special effects for theatre and concerts.
Special Services Offered: Indoor and outdoor fireworks.
Top Brands: Pyro Pak, Rosco, Le Maitre.
Product Specialty: Pyrotechnics.

R.I.B. Systems

384-1/2 George St. N., Suite 2
Peterborough, ON K9H 3R3
(705) 749-9565
Type of Company: Audio and lighting support for music, theatre and other live productions.
Special Services Offered: Remote recording, audio and lighting installation consultation, recording project production services and performance facility management.

Reel Time Productions/ Straight Line Designs

851 Richmond St. W.
Toronto, ON M6J 1E2
(416) 368-0851
FAX (416) 368-1839
Type of Company: Technical production and set design.
Special Services Offered: Support for theatre, conventions industrials and music.

Rent-a-Rig Touring Systems Inc.

41 River Rd. E., Unit 8
Kitchener, ON N2B 2G3
(519) 745-8423
Type of Company: Rental agency.
Special Services Offered: Total production for tours, etc.
Top Brands: Meyer, Martin, Midas, Klark Teknik, Brook Siren.
Product Specialty: Equipment and operation.

Rocky Bridges Lighting

112 Homestead Rd.
West Hill, ON M1E 3S2
(416) 282-2089
Type of Company: Rental agency.

Rocky Mountain Sound and Lighting

1060 Stacey Ct.
Mississauga, ON L4X 2X8
(416) 629-1525
FAX (416) 629-4124
Type of Company: Sound and lighting reinforcement, sales and rentals.
Comments: Offices in Calgary and Vancouver.
Top Brands: Adamson, Acoustic Design, Soundcraft.
Branch:
544-38A Ave. S.E.
Calgary, AB T2G 1X4
(403) 262-9964
FAX (403) 243-5162

Rosebank Audio/ Video Services

128 Manville Rd., Unit 7
Scarborough, ON M1L 4JS
(416) 757-4229
Type of Company: Sales and rental agency.
Top Brands: Sony, JVC, Bell & Howell, Shure, Telex, FSR, Nisel.
Product Specialty: Audio/Video production and staging.

Show Pro

(A Division of Rock Velocity Sound Incorporated)
2005 Danforth Ave.
Toronto, ON M4C 1J7
(416) 699-9699
Type of Company: Sound and lighting for live shows.
Special Services Offered: Customized service.
Top Brands: JBL, AKG, DBX.

Showtek Productions Inc.

70 Hickson Ave.
Kingston, ON K7K 2N6
(613) 542-4905
FAX (613) 542-4906
Type of Company: Retail sales and rental of lighting and sound equipment.
Special Services Offered: Installations, service, rentals and convention services.
Top Brands: Adamson, Crest, Leprecon.

Solid Sound Systems

33 O'Donnell
Toronto, ON M8Z 3Y1
(416) 255-5457
Type of Company: Sales agency.
Top Brands: Nikko, Audox.
Product Specialty: Sound systems, dance systems, installations and service.

The Sound Company

1423 Queen St. E.
Sault Ste. Marie, ON P6A 2G1
(705) 942-8687
FAX (705) 942-3649
Type of Company: Production company and supplier of PA systems, lighting and techs.
Special Services Offered: Custom road cases and service work on audio equipment.

Stagetech Inc.

275 Berkeley St.
Toronto, ON M5A 2X3
(416) 368-0839
FAX (416) 368-6856
Type of Company: Manufacturer, distributor and sales agency.
Special Services Offered: Rentals and installations.
Top Brands: Rosco, Times Square, Philips.
Product Specialty: Lighting systems and special effects for trade shows, fashion shows, touring and theatre productions.

Superior Communications

251 Canarctic Dr.
Toronto, ON M3J 2N7
(416) 667-1611
Type of Company: Sound system sales, installation and service.
Top Brands: Wired-in background music.

Technical Production Management

86 Barrington Ave.
Toronto, ON M4C 4Z1
(416) 699-3394
Type of Company: Product design and management.
Product Specialty: Technical/administrative design and management for any live entertainment format.

3L Sound Reinforcement and Lighting

1200 Aerowood Dr., Unit 9
Mississauga, ON L4W 2S7
(416) 238-8949
FAX (416) 625-2165
Type of Company: Live production support (audio and lighting), sales and rental.
Special Services Offered: Rehearsal studios, technicians, transport.
Top Brands: Adamson, Soundcraft, Carver.
Specialty: Fashion shows, industrials and convention production.

Touch Technologies Inc.

363 Adelaide St. E.
Toronto, ON M5A 1N3
(416) 865-1877
Type of Company: Manufacturer.

Ultrastage Inc.

4917 Bridge St.
Niagara Falls, ON L2E 2S2
(416) 356-0499
FAX (416) 356-9187
Type of Company: Sales and rentals of theatrical sound and lighting.
Special Services Offered: Show production.

Video Concert Productions

73 Roywood Dr.
Don Mills, ON M3A 2C9
(416) 444-8880
Type of Company: Rental agency.
Special Services Offered: Video production.
Product Specialty: Sound and lighting for video productions, dances, conventions and live music.

Wall Sound

1640 Woodward Dr.
Ottawa, ON K2L 3R8
(613) 225-2190
Type of Company: Sound installations, rentals and service.
Top Brands: Martin, JBL, Avolite, Strand.
Product Specialty: Fashion, trade shows, nightclubs, touring systems.

Westbury/National Show Systems

36 Malley Rd.
Scarborough, ON M1L 2E2
(416) 752-1371
FAX (416) 752-1382
Type of Company: Sales, service, and rentals of sound and lighting equipment.
Special Services Offered: Full audio, lighting, staging and production services.
Top Brands: Electro-Voice, Yamaha, Adamson.
Product Specialty: Concert sound and lighting equipment.

QUEBEC

Ateliers Albert Inc.

2222 Ontario St. E.
Montreal, PQ H2K 1V8
(514) 521-2225
FAX (514) 521-2806
Special Services Offered: Rentals, installations and service.
Top Brands: Altman, Lee.

Audesco Electronics Ltd.

1396 St. Patrick
Montreal, PQ H3K 1A6
(514) 931-5888
FAX (514) 931-2359
Type of Company: Distributor and sales agency.
Top Brands: Discomotion, Miralum, Crystaline.
Product Specialty: Custom-designed sound systems.

Conception Audio/ Visuels Projecson Inc.

176-13 St.
Rouyn-Noranda, PQ J9X 2H8
(819) 762-1404
FAX (819) 762-5532
Type of Company: Manufacturer and sales agency.
Special Services Offered: Rentals and service.
Product Specialty: Sound and lighting rentals for shows and full design for clubs and discotheques. Also a manufacturer of road cases and sound and lighting equipment.

Darkhorse Musical Productions Reg'd.

P.O. Box 137, Stn. NDG
Montreal, PQ H4A 3P5
(514) 484-3478
Type of Company: Rental agency.
Product Specialty: Sound reinforcement equipment.

Duoson Inc.

P.O. Box 1568
Shawinigan, PQ G9N 6W8
(819) 537-1828
FAX (819) 537-3188
Type of Company: Sales, installation and servicing of professional sound and lighting gear.

Kitsch Audio Ltd.

1565 Iberville
Montreal, PQ H2K 3B8
(514) 527-2323
FAX (514) 527-2326
Type of Company: Sound and lighting services.
Special Services Offered: Support for tours, shows and conventions.
Top Brands: Hill, Soundcraft, Yamaha.

Kostar Sound

7345 St. Hubert
Montreal, PQ H2R 2N4
(514) 271-1564
FAX (514) 271-8489
Type of Company: Sales and rentals of sound and lighting products.
Special Services Offered: Tour production and club installations.
Top Brands: Adamson, Soundcraft, QSC.
Product Specialty: Martin Disco Lighting Effects.

Lumibec

3609 Ste. Catherine e.
Montreal, PQ H2K 3B8
(514) 525-0616
Type of Company: Sales and rental agency.
Top Brands: Strand, Sylvania, Lee.

Richard Audio Inc.

6078 Sherbrooke St. W.
Montreal, PQ H4A 1Y1
(514) 487-9950

Solotech

4235 Iberville
Montreal, PQ H2H 2L5
(514) 526-7721
Type of Company: Rental agency.
Top Brands: JBL, Strand, Crown, Celco.
Product Specialty: Sound and lights.

Sonotechnique PJL Inc.

2585 Bates, Suite 304
Montreal, PQ H3S 1A9
(514) 739-3368
Type of Company: Distributor, sales agency
and contractor.
Top Brands: Chilton, Neotek, Neve, Sonosax.

Audio Service Stephane Inc.

12042 Lachappelle St.
Montreal, PQ H4J 2M4
(514) 332-5261
Type of Company: Sound installer.
Special Services Offered: Installation and
sales.
Top Brands: Altec Lansing, TOA, TASCAM.
Product Specialty: PA systems and broadcast
and recording equipment.

Strad Service Son Lumiere Ltee

373 Sir Wilfrid Laurier
St. Basil-Le-Grand, PQ J0L 1S0
(514) 441-4141
FAX (514) 441-4444
Type of Company: Lighting, sound reinforce-
ment and recording equipment sales, rentals and
installation.
Special Services Offered: Emergency service
(anytime).
Top Brands: Turbosound, TASCAM,
Soundtracs.
Product Specialty: Custom service for special
projects.

SASKATCHEWAN

Gould Vibrations

1405 Lorne St.
Regina, SK S4R 2K3
(306) 565-3111
FAX (306) 565-8772
Type of Company: Production services, rentals
and sales.
Top Brands: Adamson, Bose, Yamaha.

Independent Canadian Staging, Sound and Lighting

1014-4 St. E.
Saskatoon, SK S7H 1K5
(306) 363-9314
Type of Company: Rental agency.
Product Specialty: Staging and draperies.

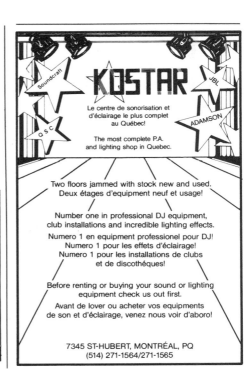
515

Production Lighting Ltd.

615-10 St. E.
Saskatoon, SK S7H 0G8
(306) 664-0011
FAX (306) 664-6423
Type of Company: Stage lighting services, rental and sales.
Special Services Offered: Design and custom fabrication.
Branch Office:
1405 Lorne St.
Regina, SK S4R 2K3

Show Sound Lighting and Staging Inc.

3830-13 Ave.
Regina, SK S4T 7J4
(306) 586-2992
FAX (306) 584-1187
Type of Company: Rental and sales agency.
Special Services Offered: Supplier of concert services to arenas, auditoriums, outdoor events.
Product Specialty: JBL, Electro-Voice, Gladiator (spotlights).

State of the Art Productions

3830 Argyle Rd.
Regina, SK S4S 2B4
(306) 586-2992
FAX (306) 584-1187
Type of Company: Rentals.
Product Specialty: Mobile vision screens, truck mounted mobile or containerized portable units. Programming opportunities for corporate sponsors.

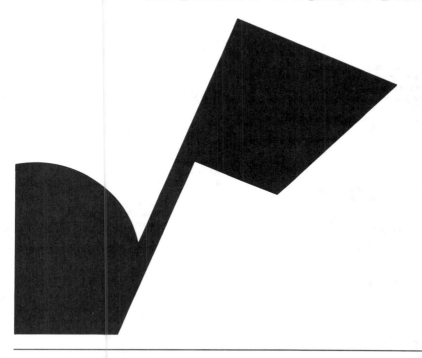

This new category lists the major, multi-outlet offices as well as the smaller, single-location agencies. For those of the former type, only the main offices are listed; information as to their respective sub-outlets can be obtained from them. Entries are organized first by province, then alphabetically.

ALBERTA

Bass Ticket Services
Sun Life Building
10123-9 Ave.
Edmonton, AB T5J 3H1
(403) 451-8000
No. of Regional Outlets: 13.
Region Served: Edmonton, Red Deer.
Charge by Phone: Yes.
Events Handled: Everything.
Venues Represented: Northlands Coliseum, Jubilee Auditorium, Commonwealth Stadium, Convention Centre.
Other Services: Booking ads for media.

Ticket Exchange
10010-107A Ave.
Edmonton, AB T5H 4H8
(403) 493-8120
No. of Regional Outlets: One.
Region Served: National.
Charge by Phone: Yes.
Events Handled: Concerts, all styles of music.
Venues Represented: Various stadiums, arenas, theatres.
Other Services: In-house advertising.

BRITISH COLUMBIA

Ticketmaster

1304 Hornby
Vancouver, BC V6Z 1W6
(604) 682-8455
No. of Regional Outlets: 34.
Region Served: All of British Columbia.
Charge by Phone: Yes.
Events Handled: All kinds.
Venues Represented: B.C. Place Stadium,
Pacific Coliseum, Queen Elizabeth Playhouse,
Queen Elizabeth Theatre, Vancouver Trade
Convention Centre.
Other Services: In-house advertising and
promotion services.

MANITOBA

Ticketmaster

305 Broadway, Suite 202
Winnipeg, MB R3C 0R9
(204) 985-6801
No. of Regional Outlets: Seven.
Region Served: Winnipeg.
Charge by Phone: Yes.
Events Handled: Rock concerts, ballet, opera,
theatre.
Venues Represented: All except the Arena
and the Stadium.
Other Services: Advertising department.

QUEBEC

Billetech

Grand Theatre
269 boul. St. Agrille e.
Quebec, PQ G1R 2B3
(418) 643-8131
No. of Regional Outlets: 15
Region Served: Quebec City.
Charge by Phone: Yes.

Teletron

300 Leo-Parizeau
Montreal, PQ H2W 2N1
(514) 288-2525
No. of Regional Outlets: One.
Region Served: Montreal, Ottawa, Sherbrooke,
Granby.
Charge by Phone: Yes.
Events Handled: All kinds.
Venues Represented: Most major venues.

Ticketron

300 Leo-Parizeau
Montreal, PQ H2W 2N1
(514) 288-3652
No. of Regional Outlets: 35
Region Served: Montreal, Ottawa, Sherbrooke,
Granby.
Charge by Phone: No.
Events Handled: All kinds.
Venues Represented: Most major venues.

ONTARIO

Brant Ticket Agency

920 Brant, Suite 12
Burlington, ON L7R 2J1
(416) 639-1304
No. of Regional Outlets: One.
Region Served: Hamilton, Burlington, Niagara,
Toronto.
Charge by Phone: Yes.
Events Handled: Theatre, concerts.
Venues Represented: Copps Coliseum, The
Auditorium, Rich Stadium, Sky Dome, Maple Leaf
Gardens, Ivor Wynne Stadium.

Five Star Tickets

Kiosk at Yonge and Dundas St.
Toronto, ON M5S 2C6
(416) 596-8211
No. of Regional Outlets: Two.
Region Served: Toronto.
Events Handled: Music, theatre, dance, opera,
Shaw and Stratford festivals.
Venues Represented: Various.

Maple Leaf Ticket Agency

594 Main St. E.
Hamilton, ON L8M 1J4
(416) 521-0817
No. of Regional Outlets: One.
Region Served: Southern Ontario.
Charge by Phone: No.
Events Handled: All concerts, all styles.
Venues Represented: Hamilton Place, Copps
Coliseum, Ivor Wynne Stadium, Maple Leaf
Gardens, SkyDome, Massey Hall, others.

Ticket Time Inc.

27 Carlton St., Suite 204
Toronto, ON M5B 1L2
(416) 340-9999
No. of Regional Outlets: One.
Region Served: North America.
Charge by Phone: Yes.
Events Handled: All.
Venues Represented: SkyDome, Maple Leaf
Gardens, O'Keefe Centre, Massey Hall, Roy
Thomson Hall, Royal Alexandra Theatre.
Other Services: Tickets for major events
throughout North America; sports, concerts,
theatre.

Ticketmaster

100 Metcalfe St., Suite 201
Ottawa, ON K1P 5M1
(613) 755-1111
No. of Regional Outlets: Nine.
Region Served: Ottawa-Hull.
Charge by Phone: Yes.
Events Handled: All kinds.

Ticketmaster

250 Dundas St. W., Suite 200
Toronto, ON M5T 2Z5
(416) 872-1111
No. of Regional Outlets: 52.
Region Served: All of Ontario, Buffalo.
Charge by Phone: Yes.
Events Handled: All kinds.
Venues Represented: Most major venues.

Ticketron

284 King St.
Toronto, ON M5V 1J2
(416) 593-5499
No. of Regional Outlets: 16.
Region Served: Ontario.
Charge by Phone: Yes.
Events Handled: Live theatre, sports and
entertainment, Stratford Festival.
Venues Represented: Royal Alexandra
Theatre, Bathurst St. Theatre, Music Hall Theatre,
Roy Thomson Hall.

Alta Record Distributors Ltd.

5326-1A St. S.E.
Calgary, AB T2H 1J2
(403) 252-7322
Lines Carried: The Emeralds, Era International, K5, Country Records, R. Steinhoff Wholesale, Royalty Records, Haney Old Time Fiddlers, Snow Goose, Cole Harbour, Fogarty's Cove.
Accounts: Rackjobbers, retailers.
New Lines Accepted: Yes.
Coverage: Western Canada.

Cavis Marketing Incorporated/ World Wide Video

35 Church St. Suite 604
Toronto, ON M5E 1T3
(416) 863-6863
FAX (416) 365-0277
Lines Carried: General, documentaries, music, fashion, adventure, action, comedy.
Accounts: Wholesalers.
New Lines Accepted: Yes.
Coverage: Canada.

Charles S. Chaplin Enterprises Inc.

318 Hillhurst Blvd.
Toronto, ON M6B 1N2
(416) 781-0131
FAX (416) 366-6503
Lines Carried: Diversified product line.
Accounts: Video distributors worldwide.
New Lines Accepted: Yes.
Coverage: International.

ERA International Limited

10 Grenoble Dr., Apt. 1516
Don Mills, On M3C 1C7
(416) 423-0210
FAX (416) 423-0210
Lines Carried: Simitar, K-5.
Accounts: Rackjobbers, retailers, wholesalers, sub-distributors.
New Lines Accepted: Yes.
Coverage: Seven sales reps covering all of Canada. Parent company is K-Tel International Inc.
Comments: ERA is a full-line record distributor with Canadian warehousing/shipping facilities in Winnipeg, MB.

Filmoption Internationale Inc.

4060 Ste. Catherine o., Suite 315
Montreal, PQ H3Z 2Z3
(514) 931-6180
FAX (514) 939-2034

521

Handleman Company of Canada Limited
10 Newgale Gate, Units 1-3
Scarborough, ON M1X 1C5
(416) 298-0411
FAX (416) 291-5324
Lines Carried: Computer software, music videos, movie videos, LPs cassettes, CDs.
Accounts: Department stores.
New Lines Accepted: No.
Coverage: Canada.

Thomas Howe Associates
1100 Homer St.
Vancouver, BC V6B 2X6
(604) 687-4215
FAX (604) 688-8349
Lines Carried: Sony (CBS Records), Warner Home Video, MCA Home Video Canada, MPI, HBO.
Accounts: Canadian libraries.
New Lines Accepted: Yes.
Coverage: Canada.
Branch Office:
39 Baywood Rd.
Rexdale, ON M9V 3Y8
(416) 745-0708
FAX (416) 745-7179

Kinetic Inc.
408 Dundas St. E.
Toronto, ON M5A 2A5
(416) 963-5979
Lines Carried: 16mm films and video tapes on the subject of music.
Accounts: All public libraries, school boards.
New Lines Accepted: Yes.
Coverage: Canada, U.S., Australia.

Montevideo Entertainment
4012 Cote Vertu
St. Laurent, PQ H4R 1V4
(514) 333-7635
FAX (514) 333-7639
Lines Carried: Night Magic Video, KidCartoons, Triangle Films.
New Lines Accepted: Yes.
Coverage: Canada.

Quality Special Products
480 Tapscott Rd., Suite 1
Scarborough, ON M1B 1W3
(416) 291-5590
FAX (416) 291-7537
Lines Carried: Quality special products.
Accounts: Rackjobbers, retailers.
New Lines Accepted: Yes.
Coverage: Canada.

Rumark Video Inc.
P.O. Box 8, Stn. S
Toronto, ON M5M 4L6
(416) 789-7881
Lines Carried: Most leading brands of video music lessons including Rumark Video, Atkins Video Society, DCI Music Video, Home Spun Video, Star Licks, Hot Licks, Video Conservatory.
New Lines Accepted: Yes.
Coverage: Canada.

The Shannock Corporation
4222 Manor St.
Burnaby, BC V5G 1B2
(604) 433-3331
FAX (604) 433-4815
Lines Carried: Records, cassettes, CDs, accessories (all major labels), video movies (all major studios).
Accounts: Video stores, record stores, department stores, grocery chains.
New Lines Accepted: Yes.
Coverage: Canada.

Trend Records & Tapes Ltd.
47 Racine Rd., Unit 6
Toronto, ON M9W 6B2
(416) 749-6601
FAX (416) 749-3918
Lines Carried: Various.
Accounts: Major record stores.
New Lines Accepted: Yes.
Coverage: Canada.

VIDEO PRODUCTION COMPANIES

ABS Productions Ltd.
196 Joseph Zatzman Dr.
Dartmouth, NS B3B 1N4
(902) 463-2335
Services Provided: All types of video, film and A/V production, plus video editing and sound recording.
Specialization: Corporate videos, commercials and programs.
Clients: Petro Canada, Northern Telecom, CAT.
Comments: Established 1971.

A M Video Productions
255A E. 1 Ave.
Vancouver, BC V5T 1A7
(604) 875-9927
FAX (604) 875-9230
Services Provided: Video productions.
Specialization: Corporate videos, educational videos, how-to videos.
Clients: Bob Bernier, Flakt, Arthritis Society.

(ab'-er-a'-shan) Pictures
(Aberration Pictures)
474 Bathurst St., Suite 401
Toronto, ON M5T 2S6
(416) 924-4883
Services Provided: From story board to broadcast tape. 16mm transfer to Betacam or will shoot Betacam.

Air Manouvres
1461 Hurontario St.
Mississauga, ON L5G 3H5
(416) 278-6835
FAX (416) 891-2558
Services Provided: Music, voice-overs and sound effects, plus production for presentations, industrials, videos and commercials.
Specialization: Creative music for motivational sales meetings. Music written to picture.
Clients: Lawrence Marshall Productions Ltd., Multi Images Inc., M&M Film Productions.
Comments: Complete production services.

523

Black Tiger Productions

264 rue Ste. Catherine o.
Montreal, PQ H2X 2A1
(514) 954-1221
Services Provided: Record and video
production.

Broadcast Productions Inc.

77 Huntley St. Suite 2522
Toronto, ON M4Y 2P3
(416) 961-1776
Services Provided: Production and direction
for film, video tape and computer animation.
Specialization: Commercials, corporate videos,
programming.
Clients: Foster Advertising, Goodyear Canada,
SkyDome.

The Caber Film and Video Company Limited

18 Automatic Rd., Unit 18
Brampton, ON L6S 5N5
(416) 792-1060
FAX 792-1059
Services Provided: Full film and video produc-
tion services.
Clients: New Hollywood, Doug Cameron.
Comments: Bryon Patchett (video producer).

Cambium Film and Video Productions Ltd.

141 Gerrard St. E.
Toronto, ON M5A 2E3
(416) 964-8750
FAX (416) 964-1980
Services Provided: Television and feature
films, music specials.

Champagne Motion Picture Company

437 Sherbourne St.
Toronto, ON M4K 1K5
(416) 928-3001
FAX (416) 928-3496
Services Provided: Commercial and industrial
film production and music videos.
Comments: Directors: Stephen Amini, Steven
Chase, Kari Skagland, Jeff Butler. Director
cameraman: Paul Cameron.

Cooke Communications/ Video Plus

95 Railsmoke Cr.
Toronto, ON M9C 1L9
(416) 621-2565
FAX (416) 621-4939
Services Provided: Film and video production
(from script to screen). Also A/V slides,
soundtracks and computer graphics.
Specialization: Video production.

Corvideocom

383 Parkdale Ave., Suite 105
Ottawa, ON K1Y 4R4
(613) 722-2553
FAX (613) 722-3918
Services Provided: Video production.
Specialization: Commercial productions and
sales productions as well as educational,
broadcast and music videos.

Creative Media Productions

1035 Richards St., Suite 31
Vancouver, BC V6B 3E4
(604) 684-0602
FAX (604) 681-4355
Services Provided: Full video production from
concept to completion in all formats (Betacam,
3/4", VHS); off-line editing suite.
Specialization: Corporate videos for marketing
and raising investor dollars. Plus, commercials
and videos for performing artists.
Clients: MacMillan Bloedel, Crown Forest, CBC.
Comments: Services include post-production
work on material that has already been shot
(assembly, scripting, narration and music).

Disada Productions Ltd.

5788 Notre Dame de Grace Ave.
Montreal, PQ H4A 1M4
(514) 489-0527
Services Provided: Film and video production,
live-action and full animation.
Specialization: Can provide live-action,
animation and effects under one roof. Full
creative services and production.
Clients: Polydor Records, K-Tel Records,
Schweppes Albums.
Comments: Animation department has also
produced album graphics.

Echosphere Productions

37 Scarborough Rd.
Toronto, ON M4E 3M4
(416) 690-3888
Services Provided: Production and post-production for film, video, audio and multimedia.
Specialization: Complete in-house graphics, audio production and original music services.
Clients: Cine Video Productions, S. Ippolito Society, Cornice Entertainment, Mako Films, First Choice.
Comments: Priority and special consideration given to peace, environmental and educational projects.

Editcomm Inc.

100 Lombard St., Suite 104
Toronto, ON M5C 1M3
(416) 664-1780
FAX (416) 864-1664
Services Provided: Complete video post-production service including editing and dupication. 3M and Sony tape dealer.
Specialization: Digital video effects.
Contact: Bob Chuter.

ElectricImages

67 Lombard St.
Toronto, ON M5C 1M2
(416) 366-1662
FAX (416) 366-4488
Services Provided: Post-production computer graphics. TV mobile unit.
Specialization: Multi-camera concert coverage and music video editing.
Clients: MuchMusic, TSN, City-TV.
Comments: Three on-line edit suites as well as a 38-foot TV mobile unit. Equipment rentals available.

Frame 30 Productions Ltd.

10816A-82 Ave., Suite 202
Edmonton, AB T6E 2B3
(403) 439-5322
FAX (403) 431-1905
Services Provided: Film, video and commercial production, plus some music videos.
Specialization: TV Commercials, film productions.
Clients: Mostly advertising agencies.

Gastown Post and Transfer

50 W. 2 Ave.
Vancouver, BC V5Y 1B3
(604) 872-7000
FAX (604) 872-2106
Services Provided: Complete post-production facilities and services for the broadcast, advertising and film industries.
Specialization: Digital effects, film transfer to tape, computer animation.
Clients: Circle Productions, Stephen J. Cannell, Polaris.

Go Video Productions

R.R. 1
Gowanstown, ON N0G 1Y0
(519) 335-6173
Services Provided: Production and post-production of music and sports videos, plus tape duplication.
Specialization: Sports and video commercials.
Comments: North American sports video distributor.

Grattan Communications Int'l Ltd.

P.O. Box 181, Victoria Stn.
Westmount, PQ H3Z 2V5
(514) 932-1463
Services Provided: Full-service production capabilities for A/V, film and video productions.
Specialization: Corporate productions, documentaries, sports and events coverage.
Clients: CBC, NBC, CBS.
Contact: James D. Grattan.

Hulen Enterprises

2447 Falcon Ave., Suite 2
Ottawa, ON K1V 8C8
(613) 738-2373
FAX (613) 521-2673
Services Provided: Consultation and video pre- and post-production services.

ITV Productions

5325-104 St.
Edmonton, AB T6H 5B8
(403) 436-1250
FAX (403) 438-8448
Services Provided: Commercial and music video production.
Specialization: Movie and industrial film production.
Clients: Various ad agencies throughout Canada and the U.S.
Comments: Subsidiary of Allarcom Ltd.

The Imaginators Inc.

P.O. Box 1061, Stn. F
Toronto, ON M4Y 2T7
(416) 922-1600
FAX (416) 922-0799
Services Provided: Full film and video production services (video, 35mm, 16mm).
Specialization: Music videos, music documentaries and corporate TV for the international market.
Clients: Attic, Capitol-EMI, CBS, WEA, Duke St.
Comments: Videos shot for: Perfect World, Anvil, Manteca, Haywire, Helix, Honeymoon Suite, The Nylons, Killer Dwarfs. Chris Terry (director), Tony Tobias (producer).

Inframe Productions

1157 Wellington St.
Montreal, PQ H3C 1V9
(514) 935-7025
FAX (514) 935-9238
Services Provided: Writing, directing, conceptualization, producing, shooting and editing.
Specialization: Effective visual concepts and talent direction, stylized lighting and sharp editing.
Comments: Experienced in commercials, dramatic television, feature film, and music video production. Call for demo reel.

KP Productions

276 Carlaw Ave., Studio 302
Toronto, ON M4M 3L1
(416) 778-7763
Services Provided: Motion picture, video and 16mm productions, plus music videos and TV commercials.
Specialization: Film productions (concept to final production). Independent artists.
Clients: Tint King, Buddy's Reaviews.
Comments: Can accommodate modest budgets.

LTM Pro Video

7305 Woodbine Ave., Suite 467
Markham, ON L3R 3V7
(416) 449-4035
Services Provided: Promotional videos for musicians and people in the arts.

Lightbox Studios Inc.

31 Mercer St.
Toronto, ON M5V 1H2
(416) 596-7086
FAX (416) 348-9567
Services Provided: Animated film production.
Specialization: Traditional cel animation and special effects. Also cel animation combined with cel animation.
Clients: Dare Foods, Kellogg's, Salada and Canadian Tire.

Lobzun Visuals

2341 Highland Ave.
Windsor, ON N8X 3S6
(519) 973-7516
Services Provided: 16mm film and Betacam SP productions. Script to screen services.
Specialization: Location shoots where angels fear to tread.
Clients: CBC, PBS, YTV.
Comments: 1989 Emmy award for *Jimmy Cliff in Jamaica* (PBS). Broadcast and corporate clients in Canada, the U.S., and abroad.

MH Communications

154 Sanford Ave. N.
Hamilton, ON L8L 5Z5
(416) 577-9113
FAX (416) 528-1018
Services Provided: Corporate video productions.
Clients: Hamilton Airport, Safer Canada, Hamilton Street Railway.

Music Video Productions

1140 Castle Cr.
Port Coquitlam, BC V3C 5M3
(604) 942-9288
Services Provided: Rock and concert videos plus television specials and films.
Specialization: Affordable, quality productions.
Clients: Chilliwack, Headpins, Prism.
Comments: Over 30 major music and video awards including two Juno awards.

Network Video

461 North Service Rd. W. Unit 8B
Oakville, ON L6M 2V5
(416) 847-7999
FAX (416) 847-0231
Services Provided: Music video pool and retail video.
Specialization: Music videos programmed to suit individual needs.
Comments: Branch office in British Columbia.

Clark Nikolai

P.O. Box 8943
Saskatoon, SK S7K 6S7
(306) 665-7250
Services Provided: Freelance video production
(3/4" production and post-production equipment).
Specialization: Alternative and avant-garde
bands.
Clients: Border, the MolePeople, Ley Ward.

Off'n Online Video and Audio Post Production

511 King St. W., Suite 301
Toronto, ON M5V 1K4
(416) 591-1143
FAX (416) 591-6661
Services Provided: Multi-format video tape
editing (VHS, 3/4", Betacam SP, 1"). Also,
24-track audio mixing and video tape duplication
and transfers.
Specialization: On-line and off-line video tape
editing plus audio editing and mixing.
Clients: Eureka Records, CTV, CBC.
Comments: Shoot facilities available on request.

O'Mara & Ryan Ltd.

2897 Bellevue Ave.
West Vancouver, BC V7V 1E7
(604) 926-9155
FAX (604) 926-9152
Services Provided: Complete marketing
services including photography, graphic design
and art direction. Music video production and
direction also available.
Clients: A&M Records, MCA Records, Bruce
Allen Talent, S.L. Feldman.
Comments: A unique service in Canada which
provides a full spectrum of creative and
marketing services for various music clients.

Les productions l'Ombre Magique

6887 Mazarin
Montreal, PQ H4E 2X8
(514) 769-2330
Services Provided: 16mm and video production from concept to final copy.
Specialization: Experimental and avant-garde
art.
Clients: Universite de Montreal, Regroupement
des Maisons de Jeunes du Quebec.

Omni Media Productions Limited

Martindale Business Centre
235 Martindale Rd., Suite 6
St. Catharines, ON L2W 1A5
(416) 684-9455
FAX (416) 682-4555
Services Provided: Location Betacam and
16mm shooting. Also off-line video editing.
Specialization: Corporate presentations, live to
tape shoots of entertainers.
Clients: Magic Of The Nelsons, Stom Dance
Foundation, CHCH-TV.

Panvideo Productions

45 Bastion Sq., Suite 204
Victoria, BC V8W 1J1
(604) 381-6822
FAX (604) 383-6514
Services Provided: Established in 1986,
Panvideo Productions offers complete broadcast
quality television and video production capability
utilizing a state-of-the-art Sony Betacam 3CCD
SP camera and full support gear. They specialize
in tourism, corporate, promotional and training
videos, as well as documentaries and television
commercials. The company provides consultation
and script-writing services, a video field
production crew, video tape editing, tape
duplication, still photography, custom music
soundtracks, print and graphics.
Clients: Government of British Columbia, Drivers
Seat, Pacific Rim Media.
Comments: Panvideo also has researchers
available to research any project prior to
production. Key personnel: David Malysheff
(director of photography),
Russ Lindsay (producer).

Paradise Audio-Visual Inc.

296 Brunswick Ave., Suite 208
Toronto, ON M5S 2M7
(416) 960-1258 or 925-7557
Services Provided: Music video production.
Clients: Ray Lyell and the Storm,
Jack De Keyzer, Big Bang.

Paradise Media Corporation

204 Caribou St., Suite 302
P.O. Box 1057
Banff, AB T0L 0C0
(403) 762-5119
FAX (403) 762-5118
Services Provided: Video production and
distribution, A/V rentals, staging and sales.
Clients: The Banff Centre, Chedd-Angier
Production Company (New York), CTV (I988
Winter Olympics).

Parklane Productions Ltd.

10305-65 Ave.
Edmonton, AB T6H 1V1
(403) 435-4508
FAX (403) 435-4606
Services Provided: Complete in-house video production services.
Specialization: Industrial, training, corporate and product-presentation videos.
Clients: Esso Petroleum, Shell Canada, Sheritt Gordon.
Comments: Betacam 1" editing. Branch offices in Edmonton and Calgary.

Polaris Entertainment Corporation

134 Abbott St., 6 Floor
Vancouver, BC V6B 2K6
(604) 688-9561
FAX (604) 688-2810
Services Provided: Rock video and commercial productions in 16mm and 35mm film formats. Also, production management and consultation.
Specialization: Concept, art direction and design.
Clients: Spotlight '86 winner. *Twentieth Century*.
Contacts: Geoff Halton, (rock video marketing rep.), Greg Marquette (director), Carolyn Carr, (producer).

Pretty Pictures Inc.

14 Neville Park Blvd.
Toronto, ON M4E 3P6
(416) 699-8889
Services Provided: Production of music videos, documentaries, dramas, short films and commercials.
Comments: Sharon Lee Chapelle (producer), Robert Fresco, (director).

Promptvision Productions

39 Pardee Ave.
Toronto, ON M6K 3H1
(416) 533-4477
FAX (416) 533-5064
Services Provided: Film and video productions.
Specialization: Creative, high-quality videos and films.
Clients: 20th Century Fox, General Arts Management, Eliakyui Fausaig.
Comments: Principals each have over 25 years of experience in film and video, and have won many international awards for their work.

Pyramid Productions

205A Lakeshore Rd. E.
Mississauga, ON L5G 1G2
(416) 891-0336
FAX (416) 278-1799
Services Provided: Production of music videos, plus corporate, industrial, sales and educational films. Additional services include computer animation and sound design.
Clients: Ancient Tribe, Golden Screen Films, Ginzia.
Comments: Post-audio and video production services available.

Pyrate Films (The Pyrate Group)

451 St. Sulpice, Studio L
Montreal, PQ H2Y 2V9
(514) 284-0761
FAX (514) 284-1838
Services Provided: Conception, production and post-production.
Specialization: Film production.
Clients: VoiVod, Ajo & The Hungry Boys, Madame.
Comments: Integrated production service with Pyrate Animation (computer generated animation).

The Reel Network

1491 Yonge St., Suite 201
Toronto, ON M4T 1Z4
(416) 964-7539
FAX (416) 964-5920
Services Provided: Duplication, distribution and production of English and French commercials. Plus radio, TV, promo, PSAs and trailers.
Clients: Warner Brothers, Academy of Canadian Cinema and TV, Dairy Queen.

Rock 'n' Reel Motion Pictures Inc.

14 Bulwer St.
Toronto, ON M5T 2V3
(416) 597-0404
FAX (416) 375-8674
Services Provided: Music videos, concerts, industrials, commercials and feature films.
Specialization: Music videos.
Clients: Island Records, IRS, Foster McCann.

Shalites Entertainment Inc.
120 McGill St.
Montreal, PQ H2Y 2E5
(514) 878-3662
FAX (514) 878-4342
Comments: Film and music video production company.

Shooters Eureka and Hay
95 Berkeley St.
Toronto, ON M5A 2W8
(416) 862-1955
FAX (416) 862-7189
Services Provided: Commercial production for television.

Skerrett Communications
165 Portland St.
Dartmouth, NS B2Y 1J2
(902) 463-8822
FAX (902) 464-7980
Services Provided: Advertising video and A/V services.

Smooth Rock Studios
624 Beaver Dam Rd. N.E., Suite 1-D
Calgary, AB T2K 4W6
(403) 275-6110
Services Provided: Audio-for-video synchronization using Q-lock 4.10 with Eclipse Editor. Also scoring to picture.
Comments: Well-equipped 24-track facilities for quality recording, mixing and synching.

Spectra Video Productions Ltd.
1253 Clarence Ave., Bay 3
Winnipeg, MB R3T 1T4
(204) 452-9832
FAX (204) 453-6437
Services Provided: Broadcast quality, full-facility video production, from concept through to post-production and duplication. Production of documentaries, training tapes, point of purchase videos and commercials.

Spectrum Productions
1160 Bellamy Rd. N.
Toronto, ON M1H 1H2
(416) 438-5046
Services Provided: Educational A/V productions.
Specialization: Slide/music and slide/video/music productions.
Users: Public and separate school systems and university student councils.
Comments: Spectrum is a non-profit organization offering educational media resources.

Straiton Films
360A Dundas St. E.
Toronto, ON M5A 2A3
(416) 323-9679
Services Provided: Music videos, ski films, etc.
Clients: The Pleasure Toys, Moving Targetz, Small Town Preachers.

Studio West Productions
502-45 St. W., Suite 3
Saskatoon, SK S7L 6H2
(306) 244-2815
FAX (306) 242-3301
Services Provided: Music videos, commercials, industrials and documentaries. Also, jingles (creative to production).
Clients: Video: Big Valley Jamboree, Saskatchewan Energy, Saskatchewan Roughriders. Jingle: Elder's Grain, Federated Co-Ops, Saskatchewan Tourism.

Sunrise Studios
1110 Edmonton Tr. N.E.
Calgary, AB T2E 3K4
(403) 283-7777
FAX (403) 283-9562
Specialization: News productions.
Comments: Will accept work for music video production.

Supertel Productions
350 boul. Montpellier
Montreal, PQ H4N 2G7
(514) 748-1371
FAX (514) 748-1256
Services Provided: Concept creation, scriptwriting, ENG, EFP, studio production, editing, special effects.
Specialization: Broadcast quality corporate video productions.
Clients: LPS, CN, Scepter.

TDE Pictures

980 Yonge St.
Toronto, ON M4W 2J9
(416) 924-3371
FAX (416) 924-7001
Services Provided: Broadcast and non-broadcast production.
Specialization: Aerial and underwater shoots.

Tango Productions Inc.

7428-49 Ave., Suite 14
Red Deer, AB T4P 1M2
(403) 346-8881
FAX (403) 343-2431
Services Provided: Total production facility (Betacam to 1" format).
Specialization: TV commercials and corporate videos.
Clients: Alberta Wheat Pool, Drummond Beer, Travelaire Canada.

Topix Computer Graphics And Animation Inc.

217 Richmond St. W.
Toronto, ON M5V 1W2
(416) 971-7711
FAX (416) 971-6188
Services Provided: On- and off-line video special effects and two-and three- dimensional animation.
Specialization: Producing computer graphics and animation for TV.
Comments: Largest computer graphics and animation house in Canada.
Clients: CBC, Vickers & Benson, Sears Canada.

Total Eclipse A Film Group Ltd.

3 Carlaw Ave., 2nd Floor
Toronto, ON M4M 2R6
(416) 462-1400
FAX (416) 469-4453
Services Provided: Music video production including creative through post-production. Also produces TV commercials.
Clients: BMG Music, Capitol Records, Virgin Records.

Ultra Violet Energy Inc.

518 Beatty St., Suite 203
Vancouver, BC V6B 2L3
(604) 685-1199
FAX (604) 669-6968
Services Provided: Full-service advertising agency, and film and video production company.
Specialization: International award-winning director and technical crews for 16mm and 35mm film production. Consultation, concept to completion.
Clients: CBS Records (Vancouver), Knowledge Network, Westcoast Musicians Aid for Africa (director).
Comments: Progressive, innovative film techniques with global appeal. Versatile director/producer team with fashion, music and dance backgrounds.

Vast Productions

67 Mowat Ave.
Toronto, ON M6K 1W4
(416) 534-9914
FAX (416) 534-5726
Services Provided: Film and music video production.

Videotron Communications Ltd.

10450-178 St.
Edmonton, AB T5S 1S2
(403) 486-6560
FAX (403) 486-6555
Services Provided: Weekly television/coverage: interviews and videos showcasing Canadian talent.
Specialization: Professional television promotion of Canadian artists.

Visualeyes Productions Ltd.

1493 Merivale Rd., Lower Level
Ottawa, ON K2E 5P3
(613) 723-5933
FAX (613) 723-8583
Services Provided: Video production services (concept through to post- production).
Specialization: Corporate, commercial and broadcast productions.
Clients: CARE Canada, The Glenview Corporation, Newbridge.

Waxworks Productions

Albert St., P.O. Box 299
St. Jacobs ON N0B 2N0
(519) 664-3311
Services Provided: 3/4" post-production with
SMPTE interlock.
Contact: Jim Evans.
Comments: 24-track audio studio. Talent
available on request.

Western Visions Productions Ltd.

1112 Winnipeg St., Suite 103
Regina, SK S4R 1J6
(306) 569-8711
FAX (306) 352-8099
Services Provided: Film and video production.
Specialization: Variety specials, documentaries,
dramas, short films and corporate videos.
Contact: Murray MacDonald.

Wharf Rat Productions

P.O. Box 8202, Stn. A
Halifax, NS B3K 5L9
(902) 835-4404
Services Provided: Music video production.

William S. Eldridge Communications

12 Lynwood Ave.
Toronto, ON M4V 1K2
(416) 960-1258
Services Provided: Production of music
videos.
Clients: Paul James, Liberty Silver,
The Canadian Aces.
Comments: The company is a partnership
between Joe Fried and Scott Eldridge.

Yaletown Productions

990 Homer St., Suite 304
Vancouver, BC V6B 2W7
(604) 669-3543
FAX (604) 669-5149
Services Provided: Film and video scripting,
production and post-production.
Specialization: Corporate, educational and
promotional videos.
Clients: National Film Board, CBC.

Zap Video

197 Queen St. E.
Toronto, ON M5A 1S2
(416) 860-1265
FAX (416) 860-1293
Services Provided: Production of music
videos.
Specialization: Rock music videos.
Clients: National Velvet, Robert Priest, Murray
McLauchlan.
Comments: Zap Video is a partnership between
Barry Stone and Roger Larry. Zap features its
own grip, lighting, and camera packages, as well
as its own studio.

ARTIST CONTACTS

A.K.A
Style of Music: Rock, Pop
Record Company: Hammerhead Records

Lee Aaron
Style of Music: Rock, Metal
Management Company: Propas Management
Record Company: Attic Records
Music Publisher: Attic Music
Booking Agency: The Agency

Abraxas Trio
Style of Music: Classical
Management Company: Brookes Diamond Productions
Booking Agency: Michael Ardenne

Gayle Ackroyd
Style of Music: R&B, Rock
Management Company: Jerry Knight
Record Company: Reba Records
Music Publisher: Calabogie Music (SOCAN, ASCAP)
Booking Agency: Progressive Talent

Bryan Adams
Style of Music: Rock
Management Company: Bruce Allen Talent
Record Company: A&M

Clare Adlam
Style of Music: C&W
Record Company: Circle "M" Records
Music Publisher: Clar-Don Publishing (SOCAN)

Adventures in Paradise
Style of Music: Rock
Management Company: Doug Wong Music

Against The Grain
Style of Music: C&W, Rock
Management Company: Platinum Productions
Record Company: Westar
Booking Agency: Platinum Productions

Bob Alexander
Style of Music: MOR
Record Company: DMT Records
Booking Agency: Bob Alexander

533

Alibi
Style of Music: Contemporary Country
Management Company: Cloana Music Group
Record Company: Comstock/Cloana
Music Publisher: Cloana Publishing/Diclo Publishing
Booking Agency: ITS Inc.

Lillian Allen
Style of Music: Reggae
Record Company: Verse to Vinyl

Ross Allen
Style of Music: Pop
Record Company: Jennie Records
Music Publisher: Jennie Music Publishing

Alta Moda
Style of Music: Pop, Dance
Management Company: Current
Record Company: Current Records
Music Publisher: Current Sounds
Booking Agency: The Agency

Vicki Alynn
Style of Music: Country
Management Company: Barry's Pro Music Agency Ltd.
Record Company: Replay Records
Booking Agency: Barry's Pro Music Agency Ltd.

Anagnoson & Kinton
Style of Music: Classical
Management Company: Hart/Murdock
Record Company: Fanfare/Pro-Arte & CBC
Booking Agency: Brandon Bayer, Hart/Murdock

Bob Anderson
Style of Music: Duo
Management Company: Danny Makarus Musical Services
Record Company: DMT Records
Music Publisher: Seldom Tunes (SOCAN)
Booking Agency: International Musical Services

Annihilator
Style of Music: Rock
Management Company: T.K.O. Entertainment Inc.
Record Company: MCA

Antix
Style of Music: Hard Rock
Management Company: Unistar Productions
Record Company: Unistar Productions
Music Publisher: Four Guys From Canada
Booking Agency: Apricot Talent & Recording

Peter Appleyard
Style of Music: Jazz, Big Band Swing, Easy Listening
Management Company: Jim Ford & Associates
Booking Agency: Jim Ford & Associates

Nancy Argenta
Style of Music: Classical
Management Company: Hart/Murdock
Record Company: Philips, Archiv, Deutschgramophone
Booking Agency: Anne Murdock

Armour/Woytiuk Duo
Style of Music: Classical
Management Company: Marie Rakos Concert Management
Booking Agency: Marie Rakos Concert Management

John Arpin
Style of Music: Jazz, Easy, Ragtime, Broadway
Record Company: Pro Arte/Fanfare Records
Music Publisher: Pure Pacific Music
Booking Agency: Jim Ford & Associates

Brian Ault
Style of Music: Country, Pop
Record Company: DMT Records
Music Publisher: Danny Makarus Music/La Nash Music
Booking Agency: International Musical Services

The Backstreet Boys
Style of Music: Rock, Variety
Management Company: Talent Source Entertainment
Booking Agency: Talent Source Entertainment

Brenda Baker
Style of Music: Pop, Folk
Record Company: Independent

Carroll Baker
Style of Music: C&W
Record Company: Tembo Music Canada Inc.

Jon Ballantyne
Style of Music: Jazz
Management Company: Clark Agency
Record Company: Justin Time Records Inc.
Music Publisher: Janijam Music (SOCAN)
Booking Agency: Clark Agency

Ballroom Sounds
Style of Music: Big Band Swing
Management Company: Bob Carlisle
Productions Inc.
Booking Agency: Bob Carlisle Productions Inc.

Bambi
Style of Music: Rock
Management Company: Azumuve Management

Anne Banks
Style of Music: Country
Record Company: Flyin' High Records
Music Publisher: Tree Stump Publishing

Basic English
Style of Music: Rock
Management Company: The Artist Consulting
Team Inc.
Record Company: Risque Disque Inc.
Music Publisher: Risque Disque Music
Booking Agency: Trick or Treat Entertainment
Booking

Debbie Bay-Shaw
Style of Music: Country
Record Company: Big Peach Records
Music Publisher: Big Peach Publishing Co.

Bear Mountain Boys
Style of Music: Country-Rock
Management Company: Rockin' Horse
Management
Record Company: Rockin' Horse Music
Booking Agency: Noteable Entertainment
Limited

The Beards
Style of Music: Contemporary Electric Jazz
Management Company: Gina Brown Management
Music Publisher: Bloc-Notes Notation
Booking Agency: Gina Brown Management

Beatlemania
Style of Music: Tribute
Management Company: M&G Promotions
Booking Agency: M&G Promotions

Jean Beaudet
Style of Music: Jazz
Management Company: Fleming Artists'
Management
Record Company: Justin Time
Music Publisher: VU Music/ETC Music
Booking Agency: Fleming Artists' Management

Martin Beaver
Style of Music: Classical
Management Company: Great World Artists
Management Inc.
Booking Agency: Great World Artists
Management Inc.

Bel-Combo
Style of Music: Quebec Folklore
Management Company: Bob Carlisle
Productions Inc.
Booking Agency: Bob Carlisle Productions Inc.

Veronique Beliveau
Style of Music: Pop
Management Company: Showbiz
International
Record Company: A&M

Benjamin's Kite
Style of Music: Rock
Management Company: Shemac
Entertainment Group Inc.
Record Company: SEG Productions
Music Publisher: MacAttack Music

Willie P. Bennett
Style of Music: Country, Folk
Management Company: Joanne Smale Productions
Record Company: Duke Street Records/MCA
Music Publisher: Top Side Charlie
Booking Agency: Joanne Smale Productions

Barney Bentall
Style of Music: Pop
Record Company: CBS

Art Bergman
Style of Music: Rock
Management Company: S.L. Feldman &
Associates
Record Company: Duke Street Records
Booking Agency: S.L. Feldman & Associates

Louise Bessette
Style of Music: Contemporary
Management Company: Latitude 45/Arts
Promotion

Salome Bey
Style of Music: Blues
Management Company: Great World Artists
Management Inc.
Booking Agency: Great World Artists
Management Inc.

Big Bam Boo
Style of Music: Pop
Record Company: UNI Records
Music Publisher: UNI Records

Big Bang
Style of Music: Rock
Management Company: William Seip Management Incorporated
Record Company: Spy Records
Music Publisher: Spy Publishing
Booking Agency: Frontline Attractions Inc.

Big House
Style of Music: Rock
Management Company: Head Office Management
Record Company: Boomtown
Music Publisher: Town Songs/Boom Songs

Heather Bishop
Style of Music: Folk, Children's
Management Company: Joan Miller
Record Company: Mother of Pearl Records
Booking Agency: Joan Miller

Bitchin'
Style of Music: Rock
Booking Agency: The Shoe String Booking Agency

The Black Diamond Band
Style of Music: MOR, Rock, Country
Management Company: Lizard Mountain Music
Record Company: Lizard Mountain Records
Music Publisher: Lizard Mountain Music
Booking Agency: Lizard Mountain Music

Blackboard Jungle
Style of Music: Rock
Booking Agency: Fisher and Associates

Errol Blackwood
Style of Music: Reggae
Record Company: Wax Works Productions

Daniel Blanchet
Style of Music: New Age
Management Company: Les Productions Rubicon Inc.
Music Publisher: Les Editions Daniel Blanchet
Booking Agency: Les Productions Rubicon Inc.

Blazing Apostles
Style of Music: Rock
Management Company: Blazing Management
Booking Agency: Blazing Management

Johanne Blouin
Style of Music: Pop, Pop-Rock
Management Company: Les Productions Guy Cloutier Inc.
Record Company: Les Productions Guy Cloutier Inc.
Music Publisher: Editions Cloutier
Booking Agency: Guy Cloutier

Blue Rodeo
Style of Music: Pop,Rock
Management Company: The Artist Consulting Team Inc.
Record Company: Risque Disque Inc.
Music Publisher: Risque Disque Music
Booking Agency: Trick or Treat Entertainment

Blushing Brides
Style of Music: Tribute
Booking Agency: Canadian Talent International

Body Electric
Management Company: Parallel One Artists Inc.
Record Company: Parallel One

Dieter Boehme
Style of Music: Country
Management Company: Anita Boehme
Record Company: Flyin' High Records
Music Publisher: Tree Stump Publishing
Booking Agency: Evergreen Talent Agency

Stu Boomer & John Mars
Style of Music: Pop
Management Company: John Mars
Record Company: Ugly Dog Records
Music Publisher: Utter Nonsense Publishing

La Bottine Souriante
Style of Music: Folk
Management Company: Productions Paul Tanguay
Record Company: Bouleau Noir
Music Publisher: Editions de la Bottine Souriante
Booking Agency: Productions Paul Tanguay

The Bourbon Tabernacle Choir
Style of Music: R&B
Management Company: Audio Plus Productions
Booking Agency: Audio Plus Productions

Bowser & Blue
Management Company: Trick or Treat
Agency
Record Company: Justin Time
Music Publisher: Janijam Music
Booking Agency: Trick or Treat Agency

The Box
Style of Music: Rock, Pop
Management Company: Alert Management

Liona Boyd
Style of Music: Classical Guitar.
Management Company: John Telfer, 1841
Broadway, New York, NY 10023 (212) 265-
6549.
Record Company: A&M
Booking Agency: ITG, 729-7 Ave., New York,
NY 10019 (212) 221-7878.
Music Publisher: Mid-Continental Music.

The Business
Style of Music: Rock/Country
Booking Agency: Canadian Talent International

Rude Boyz
Style of Music: Rock
Management Company: Media &
Entertainment Development

Kim Boz
Style of Music: Pop, MOR
Management Company: Brass Ring
Productions Ltd.
Record Company: Brass Ring Records
Music Publisher: Brass Ring Productions Ltd.
(SOCAN)
Booking Agency: Brass Ring Productions Ltd.

Brandywine
Style of Music: Folk, Childrens
Management Company: Brandywine
Enterprises Ltd.
Record Company: Brandywine Enterprises Ltd.
Music Publisher: Brandywine Enterprises Ltd.
Booking Agency: Brandywine Enterprises Ltd.

Gerry Brannagan Orchestra
Management Company: Ray Douglas
Promotions
Booking Agency: Ray Douglas Promotions

Larry Branson
Style of Music: Tribute
Management Company: Jaguar Entertainment

Michael Breen
Style of Music: Original
Record Company: Alert

Alistair Brereton
Style of Music: Gospel
Music Publisher: Micah Music

Bob Brew Orchestra and Clown Band
Management Company: Ray Douglas
Promotions
Booking Agency: Ray Douglas Promotions

Brighton Rock
Style of Music: Rock
Management Company: Head Office
Management
Record Company: WEA
Music Publisher: Healer Music/Fraze Songs

Claude Brisson
Style of Music: Classical Saxophone
Management Company: Productions
Musicales Cibe
Record Company: Cibe
Booking Agency: Irene Brisson

Alma Fay Brooks
Style of Music: Top 40
Booking Agency: Brian Pombiere Productions

Danny Brooks
Style of Music: Rock
Management Company: Random Entertain-
ment Inc.
Record Company: Duke Street Records
Music Publisher: Toon Town Music
Booking Agency: The Agency

Denis Brott
Style of Music: Classical
Management Company: Great World Artists
Management Inc.
Booking Agency: Great World Artists
Management Inc.

Val Browne
Management Company: Ray Douglas
Promotions
Booking Agency: Ray Douglas Promotions

Bruno Gerussi's Medallion
Style of Music: Rock, Alternative
Record Company: BMG
Music Publisher: BMG

Buddy Wasisname and the Other Fellers
Style of Music: Newfoundland Traditional, Comedy.
Record Company: Third Wave Productions
Booking Agency: Jim Ford & Associates

Jane Bunnett
Style of Music: Jazz
Management Company: Jane Bunnett
Record Company: Dark Light Records
Music Publisher: In Due Time
Booking Agency: Jane Bunnett

Karen Burke
Style of Music: Gospel
Music Publisher: Micah Music

Burnin' Bad
Style of Music: Rock
Booking Agency: The Fox Agency

Sandra Burt
Style of Music: Gospel
Record Company: Newsflash Sounds
Music Publisher: Newsflash Publishers

Edith Butler
Style of Music: Pop, Folk
Management Company: Superstrat Inc.
Record Company: Kappa Inc.
Music Publisher: Trictrac Inc.
Booking Agency: Lise Aubut

Howard Cable
Style of Music: Classical
Management Company: Great World Artists Management Inc.
Booking Agency: Great World Artists Management Inc.

Cactus Cats
Style of Music: C&W.
Booking Agency: Music Unlimited Ltd.

Christian Calon
Style of Music: Electronic Music
Record Company: Diffusion I Media
Music Publisher: YUL Media (SOCAN)

John Allan Cameron
Style of Music: Folk, Celtic
Management Company: Brookes Diamond Productions
Record Company: Freedom Records Inc.
Booking Agency: Michael Ardenne

Camilleri
Style of Music: Spoken Word, Easy Listening
Management Company: JCO Artists Management
Record Company: Nightflite Records
Music Publisher: Nightflite Music

Canadian Brass
Style of Music: Classical, Contemporary, Jazz
Management Company: Bernie Fiedler
Record Company: CBS.

Canadian Country Fever
Style of Music: C&W
Management Company: M&G Promotions
Booking Agency: M&G Promotions

Philip Dent Candelaria
Style of Music: Classical, Light Classical, Contemporary, Avant-Garde
Management Company: Canadent Concerts Management
Record Company: Canadian Music Centre
Booking Agency: June Baxter

Candi
Style of Music: Dance, Pop
Record Company: I.R.S./MCA
Booking Agency: The Agency

Captain Skullsauce and the Schlonkhonkers
Style of Music: Rock
Booking Agency: Secret Agency

Terry Carisse
Style of Music: Country
Management Company: Supervision
Record Company: Savannah Music
Music Publisher: Carisse Rawlins Publishing Co.
Booking Agency: Canadian Talent International

Carmen Carozza
Style of Music: Original
Management Company: Ray Douglas Promotions
Booking Agency: Ray Douglas Promotions

Frank Carroll
Style of Music: Reggae
Management Company: Conch Rock Productions
Record Company: Little Train Records
Booking Agency: Image Control Productions Ltd.

Andrew Cash
Style of Music: Rock
Management Company: William Tenn Management
Record Company: Island Records
Music Publisher: Positively Music/B.M.G. Songs
Booking Agency: Boomtown Artists

Catch 22
Style of Music: Pop, Dance
Management Company: Spinners Promotions
Record Company: MSB Records
Booking Agency: Spinners Promotions

Joey Cee
Style of Music: Top 40, Contemporary
Management Company: JCO Artists Management
Record Company: Nightflite Records
Music Publisher: Nightflite Music

Chalk Circle
Style of Music: Rock
Management Company: Victory Artist Management
Record Company: Duke Street Records

Change Of Heart
Style of Music: Rock
Management Company: Change Of Heart
Record Company: Primitive Records
Music Publisher: Taylor/Blurton Duffy
Booking Agency: Ian Blurton

Jim Chapman
Style of Music: Comedy, Satire, Original
Management Company: Tom Johnson Marketing
Music Publisher: Jimsongs

Dennis Charney
Style of Music: All
Record Company: DMT Records
Music Publisher: Top Rail Publishing (SOCAN)

Simon Chase
Style of Music: Rock
Management Company: Random Entertainment Inc.
Music Publisher: Toon Town Music

The Children
Style of Music: Rock
Management Company: John Mars
Record Company: Ugly Dog Records
Music Publisher: Utter Nonsense Publishing

China White
Style of Music: Rock
Management Company: Danny Makarus Musical Services
Record Company: DMT Records
Music Publisher: Danny Makarus Music
Booking Agency: Network Entertainment

Pat Ciccone Strollers
Style of Music: Original
Management Company: Ray Douglas Promotions
Booking Agency: Ray Douglas Promotions

Dominique Cimon
Style of Music: Classical, Soprano
Management Company: Productions Musicales Cibe
Booking Agency: Irene Brisson

Cinder - Alley
Style of Music: Country
Management Company: Danny Makarus Musical Services
Music Publisher: La Nash Music
Booking Agency: International Musical Services

Cindy & The Slammers
Style of Music: Rock
Management Company: 20/20 Management

Cinema V
Style of Music: Rock
Booking Agency: Brian Pombiere Productions

City Speak
Style of Music: Rock
Management Company: Seventh Sword Productions
Record Company: Seventh Sword Productions
Music Publisher: Seventh Sword Productions
Booking Agency: Seventh Sword Productions

Clazz
Style of Music: Classical
Management Company: Elwood Saracuse Productions
Record Company: Clazz Records
Booking Agency: Elwood Saracuse Productions

Clearlight
Style of Music: Tribute
Management Company: The Agency
Booking Agency: The Agency

Charlie Clements and the Justice Band
Style of Music: Rock
Booking Agency: Evergreen Talent Agency

Tom Cochrane and Red Rider
Style of Music: Rock
Management Company: Sky Is Falling Inc.
Record Company: Capitol
Music Publisher: Sky Is Falling Inc.
Booking Agency: The Agency

Bruce Cockburn
Style of Music: Folk, Rock
Management Company: Bernie Finklestein
Record Company: True North

Susan Cogan
Style of Music: Folk, Jazz
Management Company: Susan Cogan
Record Company: Scone Records
Music Publisher: Batyona Music
Booking Agency: Prestige Entertainment

Leonard Cohen
Style of Music: Original
Record Company: CBS

Color Me Psycho
Style of Music: Rock
Management Company: Greg Dinwoodie Repulsive Artists
Music Publisher: Crawling Eye Music (SOCAN)

Condition
Style of Music: Alternative
Record Company: AMOK Records Inc.

Jim Corcoran
Style of Music: Pop
Management Company: Spectra Scene

Cormier Country
Style of Music: Country
Management Company: Magnum Music Corporation Ltd.
Record Company: Magnum Records
Music Publisher: Ramblin' Man Music Publishing
Booking Agency: Magnum Music Corp.

Courage Of Lassie
Style of Music: New Age Folk
Record Company: AMOK Records Inc.
Music Publisher: KOMA Publishing
Booking Agency: Lorenz Eppinger

Randall Cousins & Frequency
Style of Music: Rock
Management Company: Secret Agency
Record Company: Roto-Noto Music
Music Publisher: Secret Agency Music/Alleged Iguana Music
Booking Agency: Secret Agency

Cowboy Junkies
Style of Music: C&W, Blues
Management Company: BMG Music
Record Company: BMG Records

Sara Craig
Style of Music: Alternative Folk Rock
Record Company: Hammerhead Records

Paul Cram Orchestra
Style of Music: Jazz
Record Company: Apparition

Crash Vegas
Style of Music: Pop, Rock
Management Company: The Artist Consulting Team Inc.
Record Company: Risque Disque Inc.
Music Publisher: Risque Disque Music
Booking Agency: Trick Or Treat Entertainment Booking

Kenny Crone Jazz Ensemble
Style of Music: Jazz
Management Company: Ray Douglas Promotions
Booking Agency: Ray Douglas Promotions

Crossection
Style of Music: Gospel Rock
Record Company: Image 7 Records
Music Publisher: Image 7 Music Inc. (SOCAN)
Booking Agency: Crossection

Crossfire
Style of Music: Pop
Booking Agency: Eastern Talent International

Burton Cummings
Style of Music: MOR
Record Company: Capitol/EMI

Boby Curtola
Style of Music: Country, Rock & Roll
Management Company: Mr. "C" Productions
Record Company: RBI Records
Music Publisher: Wheel in Wheel Music Publishing
Booking Agency: Mr. "C" Productions

DMT All Stars
Style of Music: Country, Country-Rock
Management Company: Danny Makarus Musical Services
Booking Agency: International Musical Services

D.O.A.
Style of Music: Rock
Management Company: Laurie Mercer
Record Company: Enigma Records
Music Publisher: La Rana Music
Booking Agency: The Agency

Dalbello
Style of Music: Pop, Rock
Record Company: Capitol/EMI
Music Publisher: Capitol/EMI

Dalhousie Street Paraders
Management Company: Ray Douglas Promotions
Booking Agency: Ray Douglas Promotions

Dano Domingues
Style of Music: World Beat
Record Company: AMOK Records Inc.
Music Publisher: KOMA Publishing
Booking Agency: Lorenz Eppinger

The Debenhams
Style of Music: Country
Record Company: Altair Four Records
Booking Agency: Phil's Entertainment Agency Ltd.

Jack De Keyzer
Style of Music: Country, Blues, Rock & Roll
Management Company: Blue Train
Record Company: Blue Train Records
Music Publisher: Blue Train Music
Booking Agency: The Agency

Jean-Francois Denis
Style of Music: Electroacoustic Music
Record Company: Diffusion i Media
Music Publisher: YMX Media (SOCAN)

Jean Derome
Style of Music: Satyrical Avant-Jazz
Management Company: Latitude 45/Arts Promotion
Record Company: Ambiences Magnetiques
Booking Agency: Kevin Myers

Dezire
Style of Music: Pop, Rock
Management Company: Tony Paniccia Management
Record Company: TGO Records
Music Publisher: Angel Eyes Music
Booking Agency: Tony Paniccia Management

Jack Diamond
Style of Music: Rock
Booking Agency: Secret Agency

Susan Dibbon
Style of Music: Pop
Booking Agency: Eastern Talent International.

Diodati
Music Publisher: Isba Music Publishing

Celine Dion
Management Company: Rene Angelil
Record Company: CBS

The Dobson Brothers
Style of Music: Pop, Rock
Booking Agency: Talent Source Entertainment

Doc the Doo-Wops
Style of Music: MOR
Booking Agency: Music Unlimited

Dr. Henry
Style of Music: Pop, MOR
Booking Agency: John Goodwin Entertainment Agency

Dr. Jazz
Style of Music: Jazz
Booking Agency: Portimari Productions

Dr. Limbo
Style of Music: Rock
Management Company: OHM Music International (OMI)
Record Company: Dirty Little Nipper Records
Booking Agency: OHM Music International (OMI)

Lynne Donavan
Style of Music: Country
Management Company: Glenco Management
Record Company: DMT Records
Booking Agency: Lyle Boe

Dorion & The Freeriders
Style of Music: Rock
Management Company: Out Of The Blue Management
Music Publisher: Freeride Music

The Dots
Style of Music: Rockabilly, Country
Record Company: East Side Records
Music Publisher: East Side Records

Double Dare
Style of Music: Rock
Management Company: Current Management
Record Company: Current Records

Ray Douglas International Big Band
Style of Music: Big Band
Management Company: Ray Douglas Promotions
Booking Agency: Ray Douglas Promotions

Downchild Blues Band
Style of Music: R&B
Management Company: The Agency
Record Company: Stony Plain
Music Publisher: Stony Plain
Booking Agency: The Agency

Teresa Doyle
Style of Music: Traditional
Record Company: Bedlam Records
Music Publisher: Bedlam Publishing

Driver
Style of Music: Rock
Management Company: Media & Entertainment Development

Annette Ducharme
Style of Music: Pop
Record Company: Capitol

Wilf Ducharme & Angus
Style of Music: C&W
Booking Agency: Barry's Pro Music Agency

Raoul Duguay & Michel Robidoux
Style of Music: New Age
Management Company: Les Productions Rubicon Inc.
Record Company: Les Disque Trente-Trois
Music Publisher: Les Productions Mirahuse
Booking Agency: Les Productions Rubicon Inc.

Duo Don Juan
Style of Music: Czardas
Management Company: C.D.C.B. Production Inc.
Booking Agency: J-R Slight

The Duo Pach
Style of Music: Classical
Management Company: A. Couturier & Company Inc.
Booking Agency: A. Couturier & Company Inc.

John Eastman and the Music Makers
Style of Music: Band
Management Company: Ray Douglas Promotions
Booking Agency: Ray Douglas Promotions

Ken Edge
Style of Music: Pop, MOR, Dixieland
Booking Agency: Crossroads Entertainment

Dee Edwards
Style of Music: Original
Management Company: Ray Douglas Promotions
Booking Agency: Ray Douglas Promotions

Shirley Eikhard
Style of Music: Pop
Management Company: Lynn Johnston Management
Record Company: EIKA Records
Music Publisher: Canvee Music

Elay Orchestra
Style of Music: A/C, Easy Listening
Management Company: JCO Artists Management
Record Company: Nightflite Records
Music Publisher: Nightflite Music

Elora Festival Singers
Style of Music: Classical, Choral
Management Company: Colwell Arts Management

Rik Emmett
Style of Music: Rock
Management Company: Random Entertainment Inc.
Booking Agency: The Agency

The Entertainers
Style of Music: MOR, 50s - 80s
Management Company: Bob Carlisle Productions Inc.
Booking Agency: Bob Carlisle Productions Inc.

Kevin Erwin
Style of Music: Country, Rock
Management Company: Music Unlimited (1978) Ltd.
Record Company: Steamboat Records
Booking Agency: Music Unlimited (1979) Ltd.

Evergreen Club Gamelan
Style of Music: Contemporary
Management Company: Great World Artists Management Inc.
Booking Agency: Great World Artists Management Inc.

Eye Eye
Style of Music: Pop, Rock
Management Company: P.R.E.S. Management Services Inc.
Record Company: Duke Street Records

The Fact
Style of Music: Rock
Music Publisher: Random Image Music

Johnnie Fagan Zedco Band
Style of Music: Band
Management Company: Ray Douglas Promotions
Booking Agency: Ray Douglas Promotions

Leslie Fagan
Style of Music: Classical
Management Company: Colwell Arts Management.

Mary Lou Fallis
Style of Music: Classical
Management Company: Great World Artists Management Inc.
Booking Agency: Great World Artists Management Inc.

Family Brown
Style of Music: C&W
Management Company: CTI
Record Company: BMG
Booking Agency: CTI

Famous Blue Raincoat
Style of Music: Rock
Booking Agency: Fisher and Associates

Fantastix
Style of Music: Rock
Booking Agency: The Fox Agency

Fantasy
Style of Music: Pop, MOR
Record Company: T.B.A.
Music Publisher: T.B.A.
Booking Agency: John Goodwin Entertainment

James Fast
Style of Music: Classical
Management Company: Colwell Arts Management

Favorite Nation
Style of Music: Rock
Management Company: Hendrica Verheyden Artist Management
Music Publisher: One Nation Music
Booking Agency: FN Productions

Fax
Style of Music: Rock
Management Company: Media & Entertainment Development

Fifth Avenue
Style of Music: Pop, MOR
Management Company: Crossroads Entertainment
Booking Agency: Crossroads Entertainment

54-40
Style of Music: Rock
Management Company: Gangland Artists
Record Company: Reprise Records
Music Publisher: 54-40 Songs Inc.
Booking Agency: S.L. Feldman & Associates

Shaun Firth
Style of Music: Pop, Rock
Record Company: Random Records
Music Publisher: Random Image Music

John Fisher
Style of Music: Pop
Record Company: DMT Records
Music Publisher: Danny Makarus Music/La Nash Music

R.D. Fisher
Style of Music: Country, Rock
Booking Agency: Frank Pollard Entertainment Agency

Five Wheel Drive
Style of Music: Country
Management Company: Danny Makarus Musical Services
Record Company: DMT Records
Music Publisher: Danny Makarus Music/La Nash Music (SOCAN)
Booking Agency: International Musical Services

Gary Fjellgaard
Style of Music: Country, Folk
Management Company: Supervision
Record Company: Savannah Music
Music Publisher: Silversongs/Slim Creek Music
Booking Agency: Prestige Entertainment

Flatland
Style of Music: Rock
Management Company: Complete Control
Record Company: Complete Control
Music Publisher: Exall/Myers Sternberg
Booking Agency: Covert Communications

Flipside
Style of Music: Original
Management Company: Artistic Canadian Entertainers Management Association

Louisa Florio
Style of Music: Pop
Record Company: Tembo Music Canada Inc.

Claude Foisy
Style of Music: Classical, Contemporary, Jazz
Management Company: Bob Carlisle Productions Inc.
Booking Agency: Bob Carlisle Productions Inc.

Norman Foote
Style of Music: Children's
Management Company: Direction Four Management
Record Company: Oak Street Music
Music Publisher: Branch Group Music
Booking Agency: Direction Four Management

Forbidden Dimension
Style of Music: Rock
Management Company: Repulsive Artists
Record Company: Raging Records
Music Publisher: Crawling Eye Music (SOCAN)
Booking Agency: Repulsive Artists

Louise Forestier
Style of Music: Pop
Management Company: Spectra Scene

Forgotten Rebels
Style of Music: Rock
Record Company: Restless
Music Publisher: Restless

George Fox
Style of Music: Country
Management Company: Balmur Ltd.
Record Company: WEA Music of Canada/Warner Bros.
Music Publisher: Balmur Music/Warner Chappell
Booking Agency: Canadian Talent International

Steve Fox
Style of Music: Pop, Rock
Management Company: Quantum Records
Record Company: Quantum Records
Music Publisher: Longjohn Music

Lucien Francoeur
Style of Music: Pop
Management Company: Showbiz International

Hugh Fraser Quintet
Style of Music: Jazz
Record Company: CBC Enterprises

Alfie Fromager
Style of Music: C&W
Record Company: Circle "M" Records

Front Page
Style of Music: MOR
Booking Agency: Ace International Entertainment Agency

Frozen Ghost
Style of Music: Rock
Management Company: 20/20 Management Limited
Record Company: WEA Music Of Canada Ltd.
Music Publisher: Bananaree Publishing
Booking Agency: The Agency

544

Andre Gagnon
Style of Music: Pop, Classical
Management Company: Great Artists Management

Claude Garden
Style of Music: Classical, Pop
Management Company: Productions Paul Tanguay
Music Publisher: Editions Calins
Booking Agency: Productions Paul Tanguay

Andre-Philippe Gagnon
Style of Music: Comedy, Satire
Management Company: Pierre Gravel - Impresario
Booking Agency: Pierre Gravel - Impresario

Rena Gaile Band
Style of Music: Pop, Rock, C&W
Booking Agency: Cornerstone Entertainment Concepts Inc.

Amos Garrett
Style of Music: Roots, Blues
Management Company: Stony Plain Management
Record Company: Stony Plain Records
Music Publisher: Stony Plain Records
Booking Agency: Stony Plain

Marty Gillan
Style of Music: Country
Management Company: Prestige Entertainment
Record Company: Book Shop
Music Publisher: Hello Again Productions (SOCAN)
Booking Agency: Prestige Entertainment

Glass Tiger
Style of Music: Pop, Rock
Management Company: Management West International
Record Company: Capitol
Booking Agency: The Agency

The Good Brothers
Style of Music: Country
Management Company: Supervision
Record Company: Savannah Music
Music Publisher: Hat Trick Publishing
Booking Agency: Canadian Talent International

Good Friends
Style of Music: Pop
Management Company: Danny Makarus Musical Services
Record Company: DMT Records
Music Publisher: Danny Makarus Music/La Nash Music (SOCAN)
Booking Agency: International Musical Services

James Gordon
Style of Music: Newfolk, Kids
Management Company: SGB Productions
Record Company: SGB Records
Music Publisher: SGB Productions
Booking Agency: SGB Productions

Robb Gott and Hyrd Help
Style of Music: Country, Rock
Management Company: Image Control Management
Record Company: DMT/Royalty
Booking Agency: Image Control Productions

Gowan
Style of Music: Rock
Management Company: S.R.O. Productions
Booking Agency: The Agency

Grace Under Pressure
Style of Music: Original
Booking Agency: Fisher and Associates

John Gracie
Style of Music: MOR
Management Company: Virgo Promotions
Record Company: World Records
Booking Agency: Talent Source Entertainment

The Grapes of Wrath
Style of Music: Rock
Record Company: Capitol

Dorian Gray
Style of Music: Rock
Management Company: Shemac Entertainment Group Inc.
Music Publisher: DGE Songs
Great Western Orchestra
Style of Music: C&W
Record Company: CBS

Green River
Style of Music: Rock
Management Company: Management West International

Catheryne Greenly
Style of Music: Country
Management Company: Magnum Music Corporation Ltd.
Record Company: Magnum Records
Music Publisher: Ramblin' Man Music Publishing
Booking Agency: Magnum Music

Ted Greer
Style of Music: Duo
Management Company: Danny Makarus Musical Services
Record Company: DMT Records
Music Publisher: Seldom Tunes (SOCAN)
Booking Agency: International Musical Services

Paul Gregory
Style of Music: Rock
Management Company: Ted Mansfield Talent Management

The Grunions
Style of Music: Pop, Rock
Booking Agency: Talent Source Entertainment Coordinators Ltd.

Wilfrand Guillemette
Style of Music: Classical
Management Company: Productions Musicales Cibe
Booking Agency: Irene Brisson

Al Guaraliuk and the Champagne Orchestra
Style of Music: Big Band, Pop
Management Company: Total Entertainment Network

Gwar
Style of Music: Alternative
Booking Agency: Paizley Productions

Warren Halstrom
Style of Music: Gospel, Pop
Record Company: Image & Records
Music Publisher: Skyliner Music (SOCAN)

Handsome Ned
Style of Music: C&W
Record Company: Virgin

Bill Hanson
Style of Music: Country, Country-Rock
Management Company: Danny Makarus Musical Services
Record Company: DMT Records
Music Publisher: Danny Makarus Music/La Nash Music
Booking Agency: International Musical Services

Michael Hanson
Style of Music: Rock
Management Company: Head Office Management

Hagood Hardy
Style of Music: Easy Listening
Record Company: Duke Street Records
Music Publisher: Big Boy Music

Harlequin
Style of Music: Rock
Record Company: CBS
Booking Agency: Hungry I Agency

Neil James Harnett
Style of Music: Original
Record Company: Penta
Music Publisher: Pentachord Ipentarch/Rock Headquarters

Jeffrey Hatcher and the Big Beat
Style of Music: Rock
Management Company: Direction Four Management
Record Company: CBS
Music Publisher: 3 Amp Fuse
Booking Agency: The Agency

Havana
Style of Music: Latin
Booking Agency: Portinari Productions

Haven
Style of Music: Pop
Record Company: DMT Records
Booking Agency: International Musical Services

Ronnie Hawkins
Style of Music: C&W
Management Company: Backstage Productions International

Howard Hayes and the Country Drifters
Style of Music: C&W
Management Company: Reynolds Agency Reg'd
Booking Agency: Reynolds Agency Reg'd

Jeff Healey Band
Style of Music: Blues, Rock
Record Company: BMG
Booking Agency: The Agency

Helix
Style of Music: Hard Rock
Management Company: William Seip Management Incorporated
Record Company: Capitol Records-EMI of Canada Ltd.
Music Publisher: William Seip Music Incorporated
Booking Agency: The Agency

George Hellow Band
Management Company: Ray Douglas Promotions
Booking Agency: Ray Douglas Promotions

Pam Henry
Style of Music: Pop
Record Company: DMT Records

The Heretics
Style of Music: Rock
Booking Agency: Pat Jeffries

Angela Hewitt
Style of Music: Classical
Management Company: Great World Artists Management Inc.
Booking Agency: Great World Artists Management Inc.

Dan Hill
Style of Music: MOR
Management Company: B.C. Fiedler Management
Record Company: CBS
Booking Agency: The Agency
Music Publisher: SBK Publishing

Desmond Hoebig
Style of Music: Classical
Management Company: Hart/Murdock
Record Company: CBC
Booking Agency: Hart/Murdock

Honeymoon Suite
Style of Music: Rock
Record Company: WEA
Music Publisher: Dee Songs/Autotunes Publishing
Booking Agency: The Agency

Hook & Ladder Jazz Band
Style of Music: Jazz
Booking Agency: Ace International Entertainment Agency

Kelly Hoppe and the Windsor Dukes Blues Band
Management Company: Ray Douglas Promotions
Booking Agency: Ray Douglas Promotions

Paul Horn
Style of Music: Jazz, New Age
Management Company: Inside Music Inc.
Record Company: Celestial Harmonies
Music Publisher: Samadhi Music Procan

John Horrocks
Style of Music: MOR, Folk
Management Company: Les Productions Musicales Darkhorse Enr.
Record Company: Empress Records
Music Publisher: Les Editions Wingspirit Enr.

Hot Pepper
Style of Music: Pop, MOR
Booking Agency: Crossroads Entertainment

Hourglass
Style of Music: Pop, MOR
Booking Agency: Crossroads Entertainment

Tommy Hunter
Style of Music: Country
Record Company: BMG
Music Publisher: BMG

Roy Hurlbert
Style of Music: Country, Country-Rock
Management Company: Danny Makarus Musical Services
Record Company: DMT Records
Music Publisher: Danny Makarus Music/La Nash Music
Booking Agency: International Musical Services

Images In Vogue
Style of Music: Rock
Management Company: S.R.O. Productions
Record Company: Anthem Records
Music Publisher: Brandy Publishing

In & Out
Style of Music: Rock
Booking Agency: Apricot Talent and Recording Agency

Indecent Xposure
Style of Music: Rock
Booking Agency: Brian Pombiere Productions

Indio
Style of Music: Original
Record Company: A&M

Elmer Iseler Singers
Style of Music: Classical
Management Company: Great World Artists Managament Inc.
Booking Agency: Great World Artists Management Inc.

J Jay W
Style of Music: Rapadelic
Record Company: Classified Records
Music Publisher: Classified Records

Colin James
Style of Music: Pop
Management Company: Homestead Productions
Record Company: Virgin
Music Publisher: Instead Publishing

Elsworth James
Style of Music: Reggae
Record Company: Crash

Paul James Band
Style of Music: Rock, Blues
Management Company: Paul James
Record Company: Lick 'N' Stick Records
Music Publisher: Mar Sol Music (SOCAN)
Booking Agency: The Agency

Richard Janik
Style of Music: Pop
Record Company: A-Frame Records
Music Publisher: Mundi Music (SOCAN)
Booking Agency: Brookes Diamond Production

Jannetta
Style of Music: Pop, Top 40
Management Company: Backstage Productions International
Record Company: Trilogy
Booking Agency: Backstage Productions

Paul Janz
Style of Music: Rock
Management Company: Michael Godin Management Inc.
Record Company: A&M
Music Publisher: Almo/Irving/Rondor Music of Canada

Jellyfishbabies
Style of Music: Rock
Management Company: Covert Communications
Record Company: Pathetic Romantic
Music Publisher: Scott Kendall
Booking Agency: Covert Communications

Jenson Interceptor
Style of Music: Pop, Rock
Management Company: Danny Makarus Musical Services
Record Company: DMT Records
Booking Agency: International Musical Services

Kennedy Jenson
Style of Music: MOR
Record Company: DMT Records
Booking Agency: Network Entertainment

The Jitters
Style of Music: Pop, Rock
Management Company: Adelman/O' Connell Enterprises
Record Company: Capitol Records - EMI of Canada Ltd.
Music Publisher: Nervous Noise (SOCAN)
Booking Agency: The Agency

The Johner Brothers
Style of Music: Country Rock
Management Company: Studio West Productions
Record Company: Westar Records

Johnny the Fox
Style of Music: Rock
Booking Agency: Apricot Talent and Recording Agency

Debbie Johnson
Style of Music: Pop
Management Company: Tony Paniccia Management Inc.
Record Company: Marigold Records
Music Publisher: Sleepoat Music
Booking Agency: Tony Paniccia Management Inc.

Joker's Wild
Style of Music: Rock
Booking Agency: Talent Source Entertainment Coordinators Ltd.

Jon-E-Shakka
Style of Music: Dance
Management Company: Lammert Entertainment Enterprises
Booking Agency: Lammert Entertainment Enterprises

Floyd Jones Band
Style of Music: Band
Management Company: Ray Douglas Promotions
Booking Agency: Ray Douglas Promotions

Lexy Jones
Style of Music: Rock
Booking Agency: Apricot Talent and Recording Industries Inc.

Oliver Jones
Style of Music: Jazz
Management Company: Janijam Music (SOCAN)
Record Company: Justin Time Records Inc.
Booking Agency: Clark Agency

Lori Jordan
Style of Music: Country Rock
Management Company: Rockin' Horse Management
Record Company: Rockin' Horse Music
Music Publisher: Brainchild Music
Booking Agency: Noteable Entertainment Limited

Joyride
Style of Music: Original
Management Company: Artistic Canadian Entertainers Management Association

Just For Mom
Style of Music: Rock
Management Company: In Motion Productions
Booking Agency: In Motion Productions

Sheldon Kagan Band
Style of Music: Pop
Management Company: Sheldon Kagan Productions
Booking Agency: Sheldon Kagan Productions

Katherine van Kampen
Style of Music: Classical
Management Company: Colwell Arts Management

Diane Kauffman
Style of Music: Country
Management Company: Cloana Music Group
Record Company: Cloana Records
Music Publisher: Cloana Publishing
Booking Agency: Cloana Promotions

Sherry Kean
Style of Music: C&W, Rock, Pop
Management Company: Canadian Talent International
Record Company: A&M

Terry Kelly
Style of Music: Contemporary
Management Company: T. K. Productions Ltd.
Record Company: Attic Records
Music Publisher: Attic Publishing
Booking Agency: Tony Kelly

Dan Kennedy
Style of Music: Country
Record Company: Flyin' High Records
Music Publisher: Tree Stump Publishing

Joan Kennedy
Style of Music: Country, Pop
Management Company: Brookes Diamond Productions
Booking Agent: Michael Ardenne

Laurie Kerr
Style of Music: Country Rock
Management Company: Danny Makarus Musical Services
Record Company: DMT Records
Music Publisher: Danny Makarus Music
Booking Agency: International Musical Services

The Keynotes
Style of Music: 50s, 60s, C&W
Management Company: The John Moorehouse Agency
Booking Agency: The John Moorehouse Agency

Kick Axe
Style of Music: Rock
Management Company: Gillstrom Management
Record Company: C.B.S./Pasha
Music Publisher: I Told You So
Booking Agency: S.L. Feldman (Canada)

Kidd Country
Style of Music: Country
Management Company: Danny Makarus Musical Services
Record Company: DMT Records
Music Publisher: Danny Makarus Music/La Nash Music (SOCAN)
Booking Agency: International Musical Services

Kidd Wicked
Style of Music: Rock
Booking Agency: Talent Source Entertainment Coordinators Ltd.

Kimberley & New Wine
Style of Music: Contemporary Christian
Record Company: Roadside Records Nashville
Music Publisher: To Want It Music Publishing
Booking Agency: Harold Wainwright

Bill King
Style of Music: Jazz
Management Company: E.M.C.
Record Company: Gimesushi Records
Music Publisher: William James Music
Booking Agency: G.A.M.I.

King Apparatus
Style of Music: Rock
Management Company: Top Sound Management
Record Company: Raw Energy Records
Booking Agency: CTI

The King's Singers
Style of Music: Choral, Classical
Management Company: Hart/Murdock Artists Management
Booking Agency: Hart/Murdock Artists Management

The Kings
Style of Music: Rock
Management Company: Management West International

Valerie Kinslow
Style of Music: Classical
Management Company: Colwell Arts Management

Franz Paul Klassen
Style of Music: Orchestral, Opera, Choral
Management Company: Colwell Arts Management

Kon Kan
Style of Music: Dance
Record Company: Revolving Records

Robert Kortgaard
Style of Music: Classical
Management Company: Renee Simmons Artists Management
Booking Agency: Renee Simmons Artists Management

Norbert Kraft
Style of Music: Classical
Management Company: Renee Simmons Artists Management
Record Company: Chandos Records
Booking Agency: Renee Simmons Artists Management

Chris Krienke
Style of Music: Country, Country Rock
Management Company: Citation Management
Record Company: Citation Records
Music Publisher: Lincoln Park Music (SOCAN)

Kumari
Style of Music: Pop
Management Company: Gandhi Management
Record Company: Justice Records
Music Publisher: Stanton Music
Booking Agency: Gandhi Management

Pat Labarbera
Style of Music: Jazz
Management Company: Clark Agency
Record Company: Justin Time Records Inc.
Music Publisher: Batlab Publishing
Booking Agency: Clark Agency

Denis Lacombe
Style of Music: Comedy
Management Company: Pierre Gravel - Impresario
Booking Agency: Pierre Gravel - Impresario

The Bobby Lalonde Band
Style of Music: Country
Management Company: Bolab Productions
Record Company: Bookshop Records (BMG)
Music Publisher: Bolab Publishing (SOCAN)
Booking Agency: Bolab Productions

Wellington Lambert
Style of Music: Pop
Management Company: Presence Of Mind

Claude Landre
Style of Music: Comedy
Management Company: Bob Carlisle Productions Inc.
Booking Agency: Bob Carlisle Productions Inc.

Doug Lane
Style of Music: Country Gospel
Record Company: Newsflash Sounds
Music Publisher: Newsflash Publishing

John Lane
Style of Music: Country
Record Company: Newsflash Sounds
Music Publisher: Newsflash Publishing

Robbie Lane & The Disciples
Style of Music: Pop, MOR
Booking Agency: Crossroads Entertainment

k.d. lang
Style of Music: C&W
Management Company: Bumstead Productions
Record Company: WEA

Daniel Lanois
Style of Music: Roots
Record Company: Opal/Warner Bros.

Dennis Larabie
Style of Music: Country
Management Company: Danny Makarus Music
Record Company: DMT Records
Music Publisher: Danny Makarus Music/La Nash Music
Booking Agency: International Musical Services

Michael Laucke Group
Style of Music: Flamenco, Classical
Record Company: Intermede Musique Media Inc.
Music Publisher: Waterloo Music Co. Ltd.
Booking Agency: Michael Laucke and Company

Laughton & Humphries
Style of Music: Classical
Management Company: Great World Artists Management Inc.
Booking Agency: Great World Artists Management Inc.

Bolero Lava
Style of Music: Pop, Rock
Management Company: Gangland Artists

Paul Lawson
Style of Music: Rock
Record Company: Top Hat
Music Publisher: Summer Songs
Booking Agency: Talent Source Entertainment Coordinators Ltd.

Lawsuit
Style of Music: Hard Rock
Record Company: Shaky Records
Music Publisher: Shaky Publishing Co.
Booking Agency: Hungry I Agency

Garry Lee & Showdown
Style of Music: Country
Management Company: Danny Makarus Musical Services
Record Company: DMT Records
Music Publisher: Danny Makarus Music/La Nash Music (SOCAN)
Booking Agency: International Musical Services

Jess Lee
Style of Music: C&W
Management Company: Jaguar Entertainment

Alain Lefevre
Style of Music: Classical
Management Company: Great World Artists Management Inc.
Booking Agency: Great World Artists Management Inc.

Bill Jay Legere
Style of Music: Country
Management Company: Magnum Music Corporation Ltd.
Record Company: Magnum Records
Music Publisher: Ramblin' Man Music Publishing
Booking Agency: Magnum Music

Stephane Lemelin
Style of Music: Classical
Management Company: Marie Rakos Concert Management
Booking Agency: Marie Rakos Concert Management

Daniel Lichti
Style of Music: Classical
Management Company: Colwell Arts Management
Record Company: Dorian

Gordon Lightfoot
Style of Music: Folk-Rock
Management Company: Early Morning Productions

John Lindsay
Style of Music: Pop
Record Company: Comstock Records

Liquid Light
Style of Music: Rock
Booking Agency: Frank Pollard Entertainment Agency

Long John Baldry
Style of Music: Rock, Blues
Management Company: Roy Young
Booking Agency: CTI/Eastern Canada

Steven Long
Style of Music: Pop
Management Company: Zonneveld Enterprises
Record Company: Random Records
Music Publisher: Random Music Publishing

Anne Lord
Style of Music: Pop
Record Company: Comstock Records

Loverboy
Style of Music: Rock
Management Company: Lou Blair Management Inc.
Record Company: CBS Records
Music Publisher: April/Blackwood Music
Booking Agency: S.L. Feldman & Associates

Luba
Style of Music: Rock
Record Company: Capitol

Rene Lussier
Style of Music: Satyrical Avant Jazz
Management Company: Latitude 45/Arts Promotion
Record Company: Ambiences Magnetiques
Booking Agency: Kevin Myers

Ray Lyell and The Storm
Style of Music: Commercial Rock
Management Company: William Seip Management Incorporated
Record Company: Spy Records
Music Publisher: Lyell Communications/Skarrat Promotions Publishing Inc.
Booking Agency: Boomtown Artists

M + M
Style of Music: Pop, Dance
Management Company: Current Management
Record Company: Current Records
Music Publisher: Mystery Song
Booking Agency: The Agency

Danny Mack
Style of Music: Original
Management Company: Rockin' Horse Management
Record Company: Rockin' Horse Music
Booking Agency: Noteable Entertainment Limited

Rita MacNeil
Style of Music: Pop
Management Company: Brookes Diamond Productions
Record Company: Virgin
Music Publisher: Morning Music Ltd.
Booking Agency: Brookes Diamond Productions

Fraser MacPherson
Style of Music: Jazz
Management Company: Clark Agency
Record Company: Justin Time Records Inc.
Music Publisher: Janijam Music (SOCAN)
Booking Agency: Clark Agency

Mad About Plaid
Style of Music: Pop
Management Company: Quantum Records
Record Company: Quantum Records
Music Publisher: Kensingtunes Publishing
Booking Agency: C.T.I.

Magazine
Style of Music: Pop
Booking Agency: Eastern Talent International

Magenta
Style of Music: Rock
Booking Agency: Wildrose Entertainment

Manfred Trio
Style of Music: Classical
Management Company: Marie Rakos Concert Management
Booking Agency: Marie Rakos Concert Management

Mankind
Style of Music: Pop, Rock
Record Company: MCR
Music Publisher: Propet Music

552

Eric Mannering and the Imperial Jazz Band
Style of Music: Jazz
Management Company: Ray Douglas Promotions
Booking Agency: Ray Douglas Promotions

Manteca
Style of Music: Jazz, Funk, Salsa
Management Company: MZM Productions
Record Company: Duke Street Records

Ray Manzerolle Jazz Group
Style of Music: Jazz
Management Company: Ray Douglas Promotions
Booking Agency: Ray Douglas Promotions

Juliette Marczuk
Style of Music: Classical
Management Company: Marie Rakos Concert Management
Booking Agency: Marie Rakos Concert Management

Tanya Marie
Style of Music: Pop
Record Company: Comstock Records

Frank Marino
Style of Music: Rock
Management Company: Propas Management Corp.

Mark & The Sharks
Style of Music: Rock
Booking Agency: Secret Agency

The Marlaine Sisters
Style of Music: C&W
Management Company: International Talent Services Inc.
Booking Agency: International Talent Services Inc.

Hugh Marsh
Style of Music: Pop, Jazz
Management Company: Resource One
Record Company: Duke Street Records

Duo Martini
Style of Music: Light Classical
Management Company: C.D.C.B. Productions Inc.
Booking Agency: J.R. Slight

Tom Mawhinney
Style of Music: Contemporary Folk
Record Company: Calliope Music
Booking Agency: Calliope Music

May Run
Style of Music: Pop
Management Company: Studio West Productions
Record Company: Westar Records
Booking Agency: Music City Promotions

P.J. McDonald
Style of Music: Country
Record Company: DMT Records
Booking Agency: International Musical Services

Bobby McGee
Style of Music: Country
Record Company: Roto-Noto Music
Music Publisher: Gold Alliance Music
Booking Agency: Various

Sarah McLachlan
Style of Music: Alternative, Pop
Record Company: Nettwerk

Rob McLane
Style of Music: C&W
Management Company: Platinum Productions
Record Company: Westar
Booking Agency: Platinum Productions

Murray McLauchlan
Style of Music: Country
Management Company: Joanne Smale Productions
Record Company: Capitol Records Canada
Music Publisher: Thompson Music Publishing
Booking Agency: S.L. Feldman & Associates

Carolyne McNabb
Style of Music: Original
Management Company: Ray Douglas Promotions
Booking Agency: Ray Douglas Promotions

Melodies On Canvas
Style of Music: New-Age Performance
Management Company: Les Productions Musicales Darkhorse Enr.
Record Company: Empress Records
Music Publisher: Les Editions Soft C Enterprises/Les Editions Wingspirit Enr.

Men Without Hats
Style of Music: Rock, Alternative
Record Company: Mercury/Polygram
Music Publisher: Polygram Music Publishing Companies

Larry Mercey
Style of Music: MOR & C&W
Management Company: Larry Mercey Productions
Record Company: MBS Records
Music Publisher: Larry Mercey Music/Shandon Music
Booking Agency: Larry Mercey Productions

Messenjah
Style of Music: Reggae
Booking Agency: Trick or Treat Agency

Martine Michaud
Style of Music: New Age
Management Company: Productions RAM-16
Record Company: Saga Disques
Music Publisher: Editions Flash Cube
Booking Agency: Lynn Briand

Mile Zero
Style of Music: Country
Record Company: DMT Records

Cathy Miller
Style of Music: Folk, Jazz
Management Company: Marie Rakos Concert Management
Record Company: Sealed With A Kiss Records
Booking Agency: Marie Rakos Concert Management

Chester Miller
Style of Music: Reggae
Record Company: Metro Sounds

Darby Mills
Style of Music: Rock
Management Company: Top Drawer Management
Booking Agency: Noteable Entertainment Ltd.

Frank Mills
Style of Music: AOR
Management Company: Balmur Ltd.
Record Company: Capitol Records
Music Publisher: Peter Piper Music
Booking Agency: Prestige Entertainment

Robert Minden Ensemble
Style of Music: Varied
Record Company: Otter Bay Recordings
Music Publisher: Common Editions (SOCAN)

Matt Minglewood
Style of Music: Country
Management Company: Supervision
Record Company: Savannah Music
Music Publisher: South Harbour Music
Booking Agency: The Good Brothers

Miriam
Style of Music: Pop
Management Company: Danny Makarus Musical Services
Record Company: DMT Records
Music Publisher: Danny Makarus Music (SOCAN)
Booking Agency: International Musical Services

Kim Mitchell
Style of Music: Rock
Management Company: Alert Management
Record Company: Alert Records
Booking Agency: The Agency

Michael Mitchell
Style of Music: Folk
Management Company: MKM Music Productions Ltd.
Record Company: MKM
Music Publisher: MKM
Booking Agency: MKM

Mitsou
Style of Music: Pop, Dance
Record Company: ISBA
Music Publisher: Isba Music Publishing Inc.

Moev
Style of Music: Rock
Record Company: Nettwerk

MollyBelle & Dax
Style of Music: Pop, Rock
Management Company: Bernardo Carrara Management
Record Company: Venus Landing Records
Music Publisher: MollyBelle & Dax
Booking Agency: Bernardo Carrara Management

Montreal Symphony Orchestra
Style of Music: Classical, Orchestral
Record Company: London

Monuments Galore
Style of Music: Pop, Rock
Record Company: Eureka Records
Booking Agency: CTI/Eastern Canada

Amie Moore
Style of Music: Rock
Management Company: Ted Mansfield Talent Management

John Moorehouse
Style of Music: Pop, MOR, R&B, C&W
Management Company: The John Moorehouse Agency
Record Company: Bovine Int'l Record Company
Music Publisher: Solid Ivory Music Co.
Booking Agency: The John Moorehouse Agency

Priscilla Morin
Style of Music: Country
Management Company: Danny Makarus Musical Services
Record Company: DMT Records
Music Publisher: Art International (SOCAN)
Booking Agency: International Musical Services

Moving Targetz
Style of Music: Rock
Record Company: Bullseye Records
Music Publisher: Barking At The Ants Music/ Anti-Conscious Music

Anne Murray
Style of Music: Pop, Country
Management Company: Blamur Ltd.
Record Company: Capitol-EMI
Booking Agency: Fred Lawrence & Associates

Music Machine
Style of Music: Pop, MOR
Management Company: Crossroads Entertainment Consultants
Booking Agency: Crossroads Entertainment Consultants

Alannah Myles
Style of Music: Rock
Management Company: Trick Or Treat
Record Company: WEA
Booking Agency: Trick Or Treat

Mystery Romance
Style of Music: Pop
Management Company: Current
Record Company: Current Records
Music Publisher: Today's Tunes
Booking Agency: The Agency

Eric Nagler
Style of Music: Family
Management Company: Kitchen Music
Record Company: Elephant Records
Music Publisher: Snagglepuss Music
Booking Agency: Kitchen Music

Nasty Klass
Style of Music: Rock
Management Company: EKG Music

NEO A4
Style of Music: Rock
Management Company: Wagers and Co.
Record Company: Duke Street Records
Music Publisher: A4 Publishing

Niky Nero
Style of Music: Pop
Management Company: Josie Productions

Never...But Always
Style of Music: Pop, Dance, Top 40
Management Company: Stars Management Group
Music Publisher: Potion Music
Booking Agency: Stars Inc.

Nexus
Style of Music: Contemporary
Management Company: Great World Artists Management Inc.
Booking Agency: Great World Artists Management Inc.

Night's Disgrace
Style of Music: Rock
Management Company: Windchime Records
Record Company: Windchime Records
Booking Agency: Terry Watada

Nite Life
Style of Music: Pop, MOR
Management Company: Crossroads Entertainment Consultants
Booking Agency: Crossroads Entertainment

Dalyn Norgard
Style of Music: Pop, MOR
Management Company: Brass Ring Productions Ltd.
Record Company: Brass Ring Records
Music Publisher: Brass Ring Productions Ltd.
Booking Agency: Brass Ring Productions Ltd.

Patrick Norman
Style of Music: C&W
Record Company: Star

Robert Normandeau
Style of Music: Electroacoustic Music
Record Company: Diffusion I Media
Music Publisher: YMX Media (SOCAN)

The Northern Pikes
Style of Music: Pop, Rock
Management Company: The Agency
Record Company: Virgin
Booking Agency: The Agency

Mary Margaret O'Hara
Style of Music: Pop
Management Company: The Agency
Record Company: Virgin
Booking Agency: The Agency

One Eyed Wendy
Style of Music: Rock
Management Company: Image Control Management
Record Company: Churchyard Group
Music Publisher: Churchyard Publishing
Booking Agency: Image Control Productions Ltd.

One Horse Blue
Style of Music: Country Rock
Management Company: Rockin' Horse Management
Record Company: Rockin' Horse Music
Music Publisher: Wadsongs/One Horse Blue Music
Booking Agency: Noteable Entertainment Limited

The Orford String Quartet
Style of Music: Classical, Chamber
Record Company: Delos

Over the Garden Wall
Style of Music: Tribute
Management Company: The Agency
Booking Agency: The Agency

Ozark Mountain Daredevils
Style of Music: Country, Rock
Booking Agency: Frank Pollard Entertainment Agency

Pacific
Style of Music: Rock
Management Company: In Motion Productions
Booking Agency: In Motion Productions

Page One
Style of Music: Pop, MOR
Booking Agency: Crossroads Entertainment Consultants

Elio Palazzi Group
Style of Music: Band
Management Company: Ray Douglas Promotions
Booking Agency: Ray Douglas Promotions

Parachute Club
Style of Music: Rock
Management Company: Current Management
Record Company: Current Records

Paradise
Style of Music: Rock
Management Company: Gillstrom Management
Music Publisher: Handsome Two
Booking Agency: S.L. Feldman

Paradox
Style of Music: Rock
Management Company: Paul Levesque Management
Record Company: MCA
Booking Agency: Les Productions C.R. Inc.

Paris Black
Style of Music: Original
Music Publisher: Isba Music Publishing

Jamie Parker
Style of Music: Classical
Record Company: CBC
Booking Agency: Hart/Murdock

Jon Kimura Parker
Style of Music: Classical
Management Company: Hart/Murdock
Record Company: Telarc
Booking Agency: Hart/Murdock

Fred Penner
Style of Music: Family & Children's
Management Company: Direction Four Management
Record Company: Oak Street Music Inc.
Music Publisher: Branch Group Music
Booking Agency: Direction Four Management

Anita Perras
Style of Music: Country
Management Company: Supervision
Record Company: Savannah Music
Music Publisher: Prehensile Publishing Co.
Booking Agency: Canadian Music International

Oscar Peterson
Style of Music: Jazz
Management Company: Regal Recording Limited
Record Company: Regal Recording Limited
Music Publisher: Tomi Music Company
Booking Agency: Regal Recordings Limited

The Phantoms
Style of Music: New Age, Funk, Blues, Rock
Management Company: Blue Train Management
Music Publisher: Phantoons Music
Booking Agency: The Agency

Pharazon Dance Company
Style of Music: Dance
Management Company: Elwood Saracuse Productions
Booking Agency: Elwood Saracuse Productions

Phase IV
Style of Music: Rock
Management Company: Adelman/O'Connell Enterprises

The Phillcos
Style of Music: Pop, MOR
Booking Agency: Crossroads Entertainment Consultants

Marina Piccinini
Style of Music: Classical
Management Company: Renee Simmons Artists Management
Booking Agency: Renne Simmons Artists Management

Paul Piche
Style of Music: Pop
Management Company: Spectra Scene

Picture Comes To Life
Style of Music: Pop
Record Company: Cesspool of Lust
Music Publisher: Cesspool of Lust

Pig Farm
Style of Music: Rock
Management Company: Joanne Smale Productions Ltd.
Booking Agency: Joanne Smale Productions Ltd.

Robin Pitre
Style of Music: Jazz,New Age
Management Company: Marie Rakos Concert Management
Booking Agency: Marie Rakos Concert Management

Plasterscene Replicas
Style of Music: Rock
Record Company: Raining Records
Music Publisher: Raining Records

Donald Poliquin
Style of Music: Children's
Management Company: Productions Paul Tanguay
Record Company: Bokasse
Music Publisher: Editions Bokasse
Booking Agency: Paul Tanguay Productions

The Popp Tarts
Style of Music: Pop
Management Company: John Mars
Record Company: Ugly Dog Records
Music Publisher: Utter Nonsense Publishing

Powder Blues
Style of Music: Blues, Rock
Management Company: Blue Wave Management
Record Company: Penta Records
Music Publisher: Uncut Music
Booking Agency: Blue Wave

Power Patrol
Style of Music: Dance, Contemporary
Management Company: JCO Artists Management
Record Company: Nightflite Records
Music Publisher: Nightflite Music

Powerhouse
Style of Music: Rock
Booking Agency: Vehicle Entertainment Agency

The Prisoners
Style of Music: C&W
Booking Agency: Barry's Pro Music Agency

Peter Michael Probst
Style of Music: Pop, New Age
Music Publisher: Sound Proof Creations

Prodigy
Style of Music: Progressive Rock, Technical
Management Company: Sound Source Productions
Music Publisher: Sonic Laser Music

Laura Pudwell

Style of Music: Classical
Management Company: Colwell Arts Management

The Pursuit Of Happiness

Style of Music: Rock
Management Company: Swell Inc.
Record Company: Chrysalis/MCA Canada
Music Publisher: SBK Publishing
Booking Agency: The Agency

Barbara Ann Quigley

Style of Music: Traditional Folk
Management Company: A. Couturier & Company Inc.
Booking Agency: A. Couturier & Company Inc.

Tony Quinn

Style of Music: Pop, Traditional, Comedy
Management Company: Brookes Diamond Productions
Booking Agency: Jeannine Huczel

Diane Raeside

Style of Music: Country-Pop
Management Company: Roto-Noto Music
Record Company: Roto-Noto Music
Music Publisher: Alleged Iguana Music
Booking Agency: Randall Cousins

Randy Raine-Reusch

Style of Music: Multi-Instrumental, World Beat
Booking Agency: Latitude 45/Arts Promotion

Peter Randall

Style of Music: Pop, Rock
Record Company: Random Records
Music Publisher: Random Image Music

Ranee Lee

Style of Music: Jazz
Management Company: Clark Agency
Record Company: Justin Time Records Inc.
Booking Agency: Clark Agency

Rare Air

Style of Music: Jazz
Management Company: SKU Productions

Razor

Style of Music: Thrash Metal
Management Company: Dave Carlo
Record Company: Fist Fight Records
Music Publisher: Big Fist Music (SOCAN)
Booking Agency: Dave Carlo

Razorbacks

Style of Music: Rockabilly
Booking Agency: The Agency

Red Rum

Style of Music: Rock
Management Company: Image Control Management
Booking Agency: David Wave

Regatta

Style of Music: Rock
Management Company: Double A Entertainment Inc.

Al Reid

Style of Music: C&W, Pop
Management Company: Ray Douglas Promotions
Record Company: Polaris Recording Co.
Music Publisher: Hel-Low Publishing Co./Hel-Luk Publishing
Booking Agency: Ray Douglas Promotions

Remember

Style of Music: R&B
Management Company: Bob Carlisle Productions Inc.
Booking Agency: Bob Carlisle Productions Inc.

Rembrandt Trio

Style of Music: Classical
Management Company: Great World Artists Management Inc.
Booking Agency: Great World Artists Management Inc.

Renegade

Style of Music: Rock
Management Company: Renegade Productions Inc.
Music Publisher: Arpieye Music
Booking Agency: Renegade Productions Inc.

Mary Lynn Renn

Style of Music: Country Music
Management Company: Wren Management

Lou Restivo

Style of Music: Original
Management Company: Ray Douglas Promotions
Booking Agency: Ray Douglas Promotions

Riopel

Style of Music: Rock
Management Company: Out Of The Blue Management
Music Publisher: Spin Music

Michel Rivard
Style of Music: Pop
Management Company: Spectra Scene

Catherine Robbin
Style of Music: Classical
Management Company: Hart/Murdock
Record Company: Marquis/Philips/Archiv/
Deutschgramophone
Booking Agency: Anne Murdock

Robbie Robertson
Style of Music: Pop
Record Company: WEA

Rockafellas
Style of Music: 50s & 60s
Booking Agency: Bob Carlisle Productions Inc.

The Rockin' Rollers
Style of Music: Rock
Booking Agency: Shoe String Booking Agency

The Romaniacs
Style of Music: Ethno-Fusion
Management Company: Roadside Attractions
Record Company: Ethnic Fringe Music
Music Publisher: Ethnic Fringe Music
Booking Agency: Roadside Attractions Inc.

Rocky Rosnovan
Style of Music: Original
Management Company: Ray Douglas Promotions
Booking Agency: Ray Douglas Promotions

Rough Trade
Style of Music: Rock
Record Company: Umbrella

Michael Roy
Style of Music: MOR
Record Company: Vibrations Records
Music Publisher: Roy Sourdan
Booking Agency: Alain Williams/Nadine Thomas

Andy Rox
Style of Music: Pop
Management Company: Image Control Management
Record Company: Churchyard Group
Music Publisher: Churchyard Publishing
Booking Agency: Image Control Productions Ltd.

The Rubels
Style of Music: Rock
Booking Agency: The Fox Agency

Craig Ruhnke
Style of Music: Pop, MOR
Management Company: Crossroads Entertainment Consultants
Booking Agency: Crossroads Entertainment

Rush
Style of Music: Progressive Rock
Management Company: S.R.O. Productions
Record Company: Anthem Records
Booking Agency: The Agency

Brett Ryan
Style of Music: Folk, Rock
Management Company: Brookes Diamond
Booking Agency: Talent Source Entertainment Coordinators Ltd.

Terilyn Ryan
Style of Music: Country
Record Company: High Falutin' Records
Music Publisher: Terilyn Spooner

Sab
Style of Music: Rock
Booking Agency: The Shoe String Booking Agency

Saint Eves
Style of Music: Rock
Management Company: B&E Records
Record Company: B&E Records
Music Publisher: B&E Records

Ray St. Germain
Style of Music: Pop
Record Company: Jennie Records
Music Publisher: Jennie Music Publishing

Arlen Salte
Style of Music: Gospel Rock
Management Company: New Creation Ministries
Record Company: Image 7 Records
Music Publisher: Image 7 Music
Booking Agency: New Creation Ministries

Sass Jordan
Style of Music: Rock
Record Company: Aquarius

Sassy Donna Lee
Style of Music: Country, Country-Rock
Management Company: Danny Makarus Musical Services
Record Company: DMT Records
Music Publisher: Danny Makarus Music/La Nash Music (SOCAN)
Booking Agency: International Musical Services

The Sattalites
Style of Music: Reggae
Management Company: The Artists Consulting Team Inc.
Record Company: Risque Disque Inc.
Music Publisher: Risque Disque Inc.
Booking Agency: Trick Or Treat Entertainment Booking

Daniel Scheidt
Style of Music: Electroacoustic
Record Company: Diffusion i Media
Music Publisher: YMX Media (SOCAN)

Henriette Schellenberg
Style of Music: Classical
Record Company: Dorian

Claude Schryer
Style of Music: Electroacoustic
Record Company: Diffusion i Media
Music Publisher: YMX Media (SOCAN)

Connie Scott
Style of Music: Gospel, Pop, Rock
Management Company: Heartbeat Ministries
Record Company: Image 7 Records
Music Publisher: Image 7 Music
Booking Agency: Wayne Coombs Artists

Lorraine Scott
Style of Music: R&B, Pop
Management Company: Big Picture International
Record Company: Slak Records
Music Publisher: Clotille Publishing

Rick Scott
Style of Music: Folk, Pop, Children's
Management Company: Great Scott! Productions
Record Company: Jester Records
Music Publisher: Grand Poobah Music
Booking Agency: Valley Hennell

The Scramblers
Style of Music: Rock
Management Company: Laurie Mercer
Record Company: Penta Records
Music Publisher: Pentarch Music
Booking Agency: The Agency

Derrick Seales
Style of Music: Calypso, Reggae, Soul
Management Company: Den Special Records
Record Company: Den Special Records
Music Publisher: Dennis Stevenson
Booking Agency: Kenrick Seow

Stephanie Sebastian
Style of Music: Classical
Management Company: Renee Simmons Artists Management
Booking Agency: Renee Simmons Artists Management

Matt Segriff
Style of Music: Pop
Management Company: E.M.C.
Record Company: Gimesushi Records
Music Publisher: Mayo Tayo Music
Booking Agency: G.A.M.I.

Richard Seguin
Style of Music: Pop
Record Company: Distribution Select
Music Publisher: Musi-Art

Self Serve
Style of Music: Pop, Dance, Top 40
Management Company: Stars Management Group
Record Company: Prime Time Records
Music Publisher: Potion Music/Vlev Music
Booking Agency: Prime Time Records/Stars Inc.

7th Veil
Style of Music: Rock
Booking Agency: Vehicle Entertainment Agency

Paul Shaffer
Style of Music: Fusion
Record Company: Capitol-EMI
Music Publisher: Capitol-EMI

Shaky
Style of Music: Rock
Record Company: Shaky Records
Music Publisher: Shaky Publishing Co.
Booking Agency: Hungry I Agency

Herb Sharman
Style of Music: Country
Record Company: Sno Can Records
Booking Agency: Phil's Entertainment Agency
Ltd.

Kenny Shaw
Style of Music: Country, Comedy
Management Company: Rockin' Horse Management
Record Company: Rockin' Horse Music
Booking Agency: Noteable Entertainment
Limited

Sheree
Style of Music: Rock
Record Company: RCA
Music Publisher: Strait Life/O'Brien/
Sold For A Song

Kenny Shields Band
Style of Music: Rock
Booking Agency: Hungry I Agency

Rick Shirmack
Style of Music: Rock
Management Company: Danny Makarus Musical Services
Record Company: DMT Records
Music Publisher: Danny Makarus Music
Booking Agency: Network Entertainment

Showcase
Style of Music: Pop, MOR
Booking Agency: Crossroads Entertainment

The Shuffle Demons
Style of Music: Bop, Rap, Jazz
Management Company: Shuffle Demon
Productions
Record Company: Stubby Records/Stony
Plane Records
Music Publisher: Wild Moose Publishing/
Roach House Music
Booking Agency: Shuffle Demon Productions

Silver & Degazio
Style of Music: C&W
Record Company: A&M

Bonnie Silver
Style of Music: Classical
Management Company: Renee Simmons Artists Management
Booking Agency: Renee Simmons Artists Management

Silver City
Style of Music: C&W
Management Company: International Talent
Services Inc.
Booking Agency: International Talent Services
Inc.

Rene & Nathalie Simard
Style of Music: Pop, Rock
Management Company: Les Productions Guy
Cloutier Inc.
Record Company: Les Productions Guy
Cloutier Inc.
Music Publisher: Editions Cloutier
Booking Agency: Guy Cloutier

Al Simmons
Style of Music: Variety
Management Company: Direction Four Management
Record Company: Oak Street Music
Music Publisher: Nicely Done Entertainment
Booking Agency: Direction Four Management

Alex Sinclair
Style of Music: Folk, Satire
Management Company: Marie Rakos Concert
Management
Record Company: Snowy River Records
Booking Agency: Marie Rakos Concert Management

Sisi & The Beat
Style of Music: Dance
Management Company: Music Brokers
Record Company: 721 Records

Skywalk
Style of Music: Jazz, Fusion
Management Company: Susanne Worst
Record Company: Zebra
Music Publisher: Graeme Coleman Music
Booking Agency: Scott Southard Talent

Mary Lou Sonmor
Style of Music: Country
Management Company: Danny Makarus
Musical Services
Record Company: DMT Records
Music Publisher: Danny Makarus Music/La
Nash Music (SOCAN)
Booking Agency: International Musical Services

Sons Of Freedom
Style of Music: Rock
Management Company: Gangland Artists
Record Company: WEA
Music Publisher: Love Mao Music Ltd.
Booking Agency: S.L. Feldman & Associates

Sounds Dixie
Style of Music: Dixieland
Management Company: Bob Carlisle Productions Inc.
Booking Agency: Bob Carlisle Productions Inc.

Southeast Movement
Style of Music: C&W, Rock
Booking Agency: Wildrose Entertainment

Speck Jennings
Style of Music: Rock
Booking Agency: Vehicle Entertainment Agency

Sphere
Style of Music: Pop
Management Company: Sphere
Record Company: Sphere
Booking Agency: Sphere

Sphere Clown Band
Style of Music: Children's
Management Company: R.H. Entertainment
Record Company: One-Eyed Duck
Music Publisher: One-Eyed Duck
Booking Agency: Sphere

Spirit Of The West
Style of Music: Original
Record Company: Stony Plain

The Tony Springer Band
Style of Music: Blues, Rock
Management Company: 20/20 Management Limited

Erroll Starr
Style of Music: R&B, Soul
Record Company: A&M
Booking Agency: The Agency

Stiletto
Style of Music: Rock
Management Company: Lapointe-Dubay Inc.
Booking Agency: Lapointe-Dubay Inc.

Stoker Brothers
Style of Music: C&W
Record Company: North Star

Fred Stoltzfus
Style of Music: Conductor
Management Company: Colwell Arts Management
Record Company: McGill University Records

Stompin' Tom Connors
Style of Music: C&W
Music Publisher: Morning Music Ltd.

Strange Advance
Style of Music: Rock
Record Company: Current Records

Sufferin' Catfish
Style of Music: Progressive
Record Company: Warped Records
Music Publisher: Mundi Music (SOCAN)
Booking Agency: A-Frame Records

Sunforce
Style of Music: Reggae
Management Company: Cyrus Sundar Singh
Music Publisher: Sun Songs
Booking Agency: Cyrus Sundar Singh

Tom Suthers
Style of Music: Original
Management Company: Ray Douglas Promotions
Booking Agency: Ray Douglas Promotions

Rocky Swanson
Style of Music: Pop
Management Company: T.K.O. Entertainment Ink
Record Company: Musicline

Sway
Record Company: Virgin
Style of Music: Pop

Swedish Fish
Style of Music: Alternative
Record Company: Bullseye Records

Sweet Sound
Style of Music: Gospel
Management Company: Sweet Sound Ministries
Record Company: Micah Records
Music Publisher: Micah Music
Booking Agency: Sweet Sound Ministries

Syncona
Style of Music: Caribbean
Booking Agency: Ace International Entertainment Agency

Syre
Style of Music: Rock
Management Company: EKG Management Incorporated
Record Company: A&M Records
Music Publisher: EKG Music Incorporated
Booking Agency: Frontline Attractions

Tafelmusik Baroque Chamber Orchestra
Style of Music: Classical, Baroque
Management Company: Collegium Arts Management
Record Company: BMG

Tamarack
Style of Music: Folk
Management Company: SGB Productions
Record Company: SGB Records
Music Publisher: SGB Productions
Booking Agency: SGB Productions

Ron Tarrant Band
Style of Music: C&W
Management Company: International Talent Services Inc.
Booking Agency: International Talent Services Inc.

Tim Taylor
Style of Music: Country
Record Company: Tailspin Records
Music Publisher: Prehensile Publishing Co.
Booking Agency: C.T.I.

Laurie Thain
Style of Music: Country
Record Company: Pure Pacific Music
Music Publisher: Pure Pacific Music

Alain Thibault
Style of Music: Electroacoustic
Record Company: Diffusion i Media
Music Publisher: YMX Media (SOCAN)

Ian Thomas
Style of Music: Pop, Rock
Record Company: WEA

David Thompson
Style of Music: Country, Country-Rock
Management Company: Citation Management
Record Company: Citation Records
Music Publisher: Lincoln Park Music (SOCAN)

Those Guys
Style of Music: Rock
Management Company: Seventh Sword Productions
Record Company: Seventh Sword Productions
Music Publisher: Seventh Sword Productions
Booking Agency: Seventh Sword Productions

Ken Tobias
Style of Music: Pop
Management Company: The Pangaea Music House
Music Publisher: Gloosecap Music

Alan Torok
Style of Music: Classical
Management Company: BGS Music Promotions
Booking Agency: Deborah Pape

Toronto AGMM Mass Choir
Style of Music: Gospel
Management Company: Association Of Gospel Music Ministries
Record Company: Micah Records
Music Publisher: Micah Music
Booking Agency: Association Of Gospel Music Ministries

Touchstones
Style of Music: Rock
Management Company: Victory Artist Management

The Tourists
Style of Music: Rock, Pop
Booking Agency: Cornerstone Entertainment Concepts

Toxic Reasons
Style of Music: Metal
Booking Agency: Paizley Productions

Tragically Hip
Style of Music: Rock
Management Company: Jacob J. Gold & Associates

Tristan
Style of Music: Rock
Booking Agency: Wildrose Entertainment

Triumph
Style of Music: Rock
Management Company: Musicon Management Inc.
Record Company: MCA
Music Publisher: Triumphsongs
Booking Agency: The Agency

Trooper
Style of Music: Pop, Rock
Record Company: Great Pacific
Music Publisher: Great Pacific

Alain Trudel
Style of Music: Solo Trombonist
Management Company: Latitude 45 Arts/Promotion
Booking Agency: Latitude 45

Tumo
Style of Music: New Age
Booking Agency: Cornerstone Entertainment Concepts

Dave Turner
Style of Music: Jazz
Management Company: Clark Agency
Record Company: Justin Time Records Inc.
Music Publisher: Janijam (SOCAN)
Booking Agency: Clark Agency

Stanley Turner
Style of Music: Original
Management Company: Ray Douglas Promotions
Booking Agency: Ray Douglas Promotions

Tuyo
Style of Music: Original
Management Company: Latitude 45 Arts/Promotion
Booking Agency: Latitude 45 Arts/Promotion

Tyra
Style of Music: Original
Management Company: Artistic Canadian Entertainment Management Inc.

Ian Tyson
Style of Music: C&W
Record Company: Stony Plain
Music Publisher: Stony Plain

Sylvia Tyson
Style of Music: Country
Management Company: AMK Management
Record Company: Stony Plain Records
Music Publisher: Salt Music/Stony Plain
Booking Agency: Canadian Talent International

U.K. Subs
Style of Music: Alternative
Booking Agency: Paizley Productions

Shari Ulrich
Style of Music: Pop
Management Company: Ulrich Productions
Record Company: Doremus
Music Publisher: Doremus Music

Unison
Style of Music: Calypso, Pop
Management Company: Bob Carlisle Productions Inc.
Booking Agency: Bob Carlisle Productions Inc.

Venus
Style of Music: Pop, MOR
Booking Agency: John Goodwin Entertainment Agency

Roch Voisine
Style of Music: Pop
Record Company: Star

Elvis Wade & The Jordainnaires
Style of Music: Pop
Management Company: M&G Promotions
Booking Agency: M&G Promotions

Rufus Wainwright
Style of Music: Original
Record Company: Les Productions La Fete

Walsh/Underhill Duo
Style of Music: Jazz
Management Company: Shuttle Demon Productions
Music Publisher: Wild Moose Publishing/Contextural Music
Booking Agency: Shuffle Demon Productions

The Warning
Style of Music: Rock
Management Company: EKG Management
Music Publisher: EKG Management

Terry Watada
Style of Music: Rock, Pop, Folk
Management Company: Windchime Records
Record Company: Windchime Records

The Watchmen
Style of Music: Rock
Booking Agency: Hungry I Agency

564

Watertown Trio
Style of Music: Acoustic Rock
Management Company: The Artist Consulting Team Inc.
Record Company: WEA Music Of Canada Ltd.
Music Publisher: Watertown Music Inc.
Booking Agency: Trick Or Treat Entertainment Booking

Doc Watson
Style of Music: Band
Management Company: Ray Douglas Promotions
Booking Agency: Ray Douglas Promotions

Daniel Weaver
Style of Music: Rock
Management Company: Hendica Verheyden Artist Management
Music Publisher: One Nation Music
Booking Agency: FN Productions

Gordie West
Style of Music: Country
Management Company: Pat Rowley
Booking Agency: Barry's Pro Music Agency Ltd.

White Heat
Style of Music: Rock
Management Company: Chart Toppers
Record Company: The Record Company
Music Publisher: Most Requested Music
Booking Agency: The Agency

Wally White
Style of Music: Gospel
Record Company: Newsflash Sounds
Music Publisher: Newsflash Publishing

Keith Whittall
Style of Music: Christmas
Record Company: Newsflash Sounds
Music Publisher: Newsflash Publishing

Charlotte Wiebe
Style of Music: Pop, Rock
Management Company: Danny Makarus Musical Services
Record Company: DMT Records
Music Publisher: Danny Makarus Music/La Nash Music
Booking Agency: International Music Services

David Wilcox
Style of Music: Rock
Record Company: Capitol
Booking Agency: The Agency

Paul Wild
Style of Music: Rock
Record Company: Hammerhead Records

Wild Rose
Style of Music: Rock
Booking Agency: The Fox Agency

Wilfred N And The Grown Men
Style of Music: Pop, Rock
Management Company: Zonik Music Productions
Record Company: Zonik Records
Music Publisher: Zonik Music Productions

Jimmy Wilkins Orchestra
Style of Music: Band
Management Company: Ray Douglas Promotions
Booking Agency: Ray Douglas Promotions

Melissa Williams
Style of Music: Original
Management Company: Ray Douglas Promotions
Booking Agency: Ray Douglas Promotions

Vivienne Williams
Style of Music: R&B, Dance, Pop
Management Company: Silverbirch Productions

Lynn Wilson And The Rebels
Style of Music: Country-Rock
Management Company: Roto-Noto Music
Record Company: Roto-Noto Music
Music Publisher: Alleged Iguana Music
Booking Agency: David Peever

Jesse Winchester
Style of Music: C&W
Record Company: Attic

Wipeout Beach
Style of Music: Psycho-Rock
Record Company: Hammerhead Records

Colette Wise
Style of Music: Country
Management Company: Cloana Music Group
Record Company: Cloana Records
Music Publisher: Cloana Publishing
Booking Agency: Cloana Promotions

Bob Wiseman

Style of Music: Alternative, Modern Jazz
Management Company: The Artist Consulting Team Inc.
Record Company: Risque Disque Inc.
Music Publisher: Carpe Diem Music Inc.
Booking Agency: Trick Or Treat Entertainment Booking

The Works

Style of Music: Pop, Rock
Record Company: A&M Records
Music Publisher: A&M

Worrall Brothers

Style of Music: Rock
Booking Agency: Brian Pombiere Productions

Carlton Wright

Style of Music: Gospel
Music Publisher: Micah Music

Michelle Wright

Style of Music: C&W
Management Company: Supervision
Record Company: Arista Records
Music Publisher: Silversongs
Booking Agency: Canadian Talent International

Lori Yates

Style of Music: C&W
Management Company: Carbine Management
Record Company: CBS

Karen Young/Michel Donato

Style of Music: Jazz
Management Company: Fleming Artists' Management
Record Company: Justin Time Records
Music Publisher: Sablo, Ursh, Young/Latins
Booking Agency: Fleming Artists' Management

Neil Young

Style of Music: Rock
Record Company: WEA

Noah Zacharin

Style of Music: Contemporary Acoustic
Record Company: Soffwin Records
Music Publisher: Soffwin Music

Zappacosta

Style of Music: Pop, Rock
Management Company: Lou Blair Management Inc.
Record Company: Penta Records
Music Publisher: The Music Publisher/EMI Music Publishing
Booking Agency: S.L. Feldman & Associates

Doug Zimmerman

Style of Music: Pop, MOR
Booking Agency: Crossroads Entertainment

Zombox

Style of Music: Rock
Management Company: Ted Mansfield Talent Management

Zucchini Alley

Style of Music: Children's
Record Company: Calliope Music
Booking Agency: Calliope Music

AWARD WINNERS

GALA DE L'ADISQ

Album Of The Year (Pop/Rock)

1988 - Journee d'Amerique, Richard
Seguin
1989 - Helene, Roch Voisine

Album Of The Year (Pop)

1980 - Je ne suis qu'une chanson,
Ginette Reno
1981 - Fabienne Thibault, Fabienne
Thibault
1982 - Turbulences, Diane Dufresne
1983 - Tellement j'ai d'amour, Celine
Dion
1984 - Transit, Veronique Bellveau
1985 - Il y a de l'amour dans l'air,
Martine St. Clair
1986 - Ce soir l'amour est dans tes
yeux, Martine St. Clair
1987 - Un trou dans les nuages,
Michel Rivard
1988 - Merci Felix, Johanne Blouin
1989 - Ne m'en veux pas, Ginette
Reno

Album Of The Year (Rock)

1979 - Traversion, Offenbach
1980 - Offenbach en fusion,
Offenbach
1981 - Starmania Made in Quebec,
Starmania
1982 - Illegal, Corbeau
1983 - Rhythm of Youth, Men Without
Hats
1984 - First Offense, Corey Hart
1985 - Nouvelles d'Europe, Paul Piche
1986 - Double vie, Richard Seguin
1987 - Celle qui va, Marjo
1988 - Le parfum du hasard, Pierre
Flynn
1989 - Rendez-vous doux, Gerry
Boulet

Album Of The Year (Country/Folk)

1979 - Julie et ses musiciens, Julie et Paul Daraiche
1980 - Mon Sourine, Bobby Hachey
1981 - La musique de Tennessee, Denis Champoux
1982 - Jerry et Jo'Anne, Jerry et Jo'Anne
1983 - C'est mon histoire, Renee Martel
1984 - Aujourd'hui, Jerry et Jo'Anne
1985 - Cadeau, Renee Martel
1986 - Un jour a la fois, Andre Breton
1987 - En amour, Gilles Godard
1988 - None
1989 - Soyons heureux, Patrick Norman

Album Of The Year (Folk/Traditional)

1979 - Garolou, Garolou
1980 - Romancero, Garolou
1981 - Tetu, Jim Corcoran
1982 - Le reve du diable, Le reve du diable

Album Of The Year (Instrumental)

1979 - Le Saint Laurent, Andre Gagnon
1980 - Concerto pour piano et orchestre, Francois Dompierre et O.S.M.
1981 - Virage a gauche, Andre Gagnon
1982 - Hors d'oeuvres, Francois Dompierre
1983 - Souffle, Alain Lamontagne
1984 - Impressions, Andre Gagnon
1985 - Verseau, Claude Sirois
1986 - None
1987 - Comme dans un film, Andre Gagnon
1988 - Le cirque du soleil, Le cirque du soleil
1989 - Des dames de coeurs, Andre Gagnon

Best-Selling 45

1982 - Call Girl, Nanette Workman
1983 - Safety Dance, Men Without Hats
1984 - Comment ca va, Rene Simard
1985 - Une Colombe, Celine Dion
1986 - Ce soir l'amour est dans tes yeux, Martine St. Clair
1987 - Vivre dans la muit, Nuance
1988 - Tourne la page, Nathalie and Rene Simard

Best Children's Record

1981 - Passe-Partout, vol. 1 & II, Passe-Partout
1982 - Passe-Partout, vol. III, Passe-Partout
1983 - Passe-Partout, vol. IV, Passe-Partout
1984 - Mai et Fafouin, Clair Pimpare
1985 - La guerre des tuques, Nathalie Simard
1986 - Noel de Pruneau et Canelle, Passe-Partout
1987 - Trame sonore du film, Bach et Bottines
1988 - Joyeux Noel a tous les enfants, Nathalie Simard

English Record Of The Year

1986 - Between The Earth And Sky, Luba
1987 - Closer Together, The Box
1988 - Pop Goes The World, Men Without Hats

Classical Recording Of The Year

1983 - Ravel, Bolero, Montreal Symphony Orchestra
1984 - Montreal Symphony Orchestra
1985 - Stravinsky, Le Sacre du Printemps, Montreal Symphony Orchestra
1986 - None
1987 - Tchaikovski, 1812 Overture, Montreal Symphony Orchestra

Dance Record Of The Year

1979 - Taxi pour une nuit blanche, Toulouse
1980 - Dangerous Ladies, Toulouse
1981 - Closer, Gino Soccio
1982 - Lime 2, Lime
1983 - Lime 3, Lime
1984 - Message on the Radio, Trans X
1985 - Let It Go, Luba

Composer-Record Of The Year

1979 - Deux cents nuits a l'heure, Fiori/Seguin
1980 - Entre Nous, Diane Tell
1981 - En Fleche, Diane Tell
1982 - Sortie, Claude Dubois
1983 - Robert Charlebois, Robert Charlebois
1984 - Tension Attention, Daniel Lavoie
1985 - Boy In The Box, Corey Hart

Album Of The Year (Jazz)

1983 - Fast Emotion, Uzeb
1984 - You Be Easy, Uzeb
1985 - Le trio Lorraine Desmarais, Lorraine Desmarais
1986 - Between The Lines, Uzeb
1987 - Live a l'Olympia, Uzeb
1988 - Contredanse, Karen Young et Michael Donato
1989 - Just Friends, Oliver Jones

Best-Selling Record

1979 - Libre, Angele Arsenault
1980 - Je ne suis qu'une chanson, Ginette Reno
1981 - Passe-Partout, Passe-Partout
1982 - J'suis ton amie, Chantal Pary
1983 - La danse des canards, Nathalie Simard
1984 - Les chemins de ma maison, Celine Dion
1985 - Melanie, Celine Dion
1986 - Le Party d'Edith, Edith Butler
1987 - Quand on est en amour, Patrick Norman
1988 - Celle qui va, Marjo
1989 - Ne m'en veux pas, Ginette Reno

Best Debut Album

1989 - El Mundo, Mitsou

Video Of The Year

1983 - Gilles Becaud a la Baie James
1984 - Neige et Graffiti
1985 - Rumeurs sur la ville, Michel Rivard
1986 - Le feu sauvage de l'amour, Rock et belle oreilles
1987 - Closer Together, The Box
1988 - Tourne la page, Nathalie et Rene Simard
1989 - Amere America, Luc De Larochelliere

Peformance Of The Year (Comedy)

1981 - Clemence Desrochers
1982 - None
1983 - Les lundis des Ha! Ha!
1984 - Les lundis des Ha! Ha!
1985 - Ding et Dong
1986 - Andre Philippe Gagnon
1987 - Jean-Guy Moreau
1988 - Ding et Dong
1989 - Andre Philippe Gagnon

AWARD WINNERS

Performance Of The Year (Pop/Rock)

1989 - Vos plaisirs et le mal, Joe Bocan

Performance Of The Year (Pop)

1980 - Offenbach au Forum, Offenbach
1981 - Starmania, Starmania
1982 - Sortie, Claude Dubois
1983 - Hollywood/Halloween, Diane Dufresne
1984 - Je t'aime comme un fou, Robert Charlebois
1985 - Un million de fois que je t'aime, Edith Butler
1986 - Paradoxale, Joe Bocan
1987 - Top Secret, Diane Dufresne
1988 - Un trou dans les nuages, Michel Rivard
1989 - La prochaine fois qu'j'aurai vingt ans, Ginette Reno

Performance Of The Year (Rock)

1985 - Solid Salad, Michel Lemieux
1986 - Le dernier show, Offenbach
1987 - Celle qui va, Marjo
1988 - Un trou dans les nuages, Michel Rivard
1989 - Rendez-vous doux, Gerry Boulet

Pop Song Of The Year

1979 - Le Blues du Businessman, Luc Plamondon
1980 - Je ne suis qu'une chanson, Diane Juster
1981 - Si j'etais un homme, Diane Tell
1982 - Plein de tendresse, Claude Dubois
1983 - Je t'aime comme un fou, L. Plamondon et R. Charlebois
1984 - Tension Attention, Daniel Lavoie
1985 - Une Colombe, Celine Dion
1986 - Ce soir l'amour est dans tes yeux, Martine St. Clair
1987 - Quand on est en amour, Patrick Norman
1988 - Incognito, Celine Dion
1989 - Helene, Roch Voisine

Discovery Of The Year

1979 - Fabienne Thibault
1980 - Diane Tell
1981 - Martine St. Clair
1982 - Groupe Pied de Poule
1983 - Celine Dion
1984 - Martine Chevrier
1985 - Rock et Belles oreilles
1986 - Nuance
1987 - Marc Drouin
1988 - Mitsou
1989 - Roch Voisine

Female Artist Of The Year

1979 - Fabienne Thibault
1980 - Ginette Reno
1981 - Diane Tell
1982 - Diane Dufresne
1983 - Celine Dion
1984 - Celine Dion
1985 - Celine Dion
1986 - Martine St. Clair
1987 - Marjo
1988 - Celine Dion
1989 - Johanne Blouin

Male Artist Of The Year

1979 - Claude Dubois
1980 - Daniel Lavoie
1981 - Daniel Lavoie
1982 - Claude Dubois
1983 - Claude Dubois
1984 - Daniel Lavoie
1985 - Corey Hart
1986 - Claude Dubois
1987 - Patrick Norman
1988 - Michel Rivard
1989 - Roch Voisine

Group Of The Year

1979 - Fiori/Seguin
1980 - Offenbach
1981 - Corbeau
1982 - Corbeau
1983 - Men Without Hats
1984 - Uzeb
1985 - The Box
1986 - Madame
1987 - Nuance
1988 - Madame
1989 - Uzeb

French Artist Most Celebrated In Quebec

1985 - A. Morisod et S. People
1986 - Francis Cabrel
1987 - Herbert Leonard
1988 - La Compagnie Creole
1989 - Francis Cabrel

Best English Band Or Artist

1985 - Corey Hart
1986 - Luba
1987 - The Box
1988 - None
1989 - Sass Jordan

Best Classical Artist Or Group

1989 - Joseph Rouleau

Quebec Artist Most Celebrated Outside Quebec

1980 - Diane Dufresne
1981 - April Wine
1982 - April Wine
1983 - Celine Dion
1984 - Men Without Hats
1985 - Daniel Lavoie
1986 - Edith Butler
1987 - Danial Lavoie
1988 - Celine Dion
1989 - Marc Drouin, Andre Gagnon, tie

Author/Composer Of The Year

1985 - Corey Hart
1986 - Richard Seguin
1987 - L. Forestier
1988 - Daniel Deshaime
1989 - Luc De Larochelliere

Tribute Award/Academy Award

1979 - Felix Leclerc
1980 - Raymond Levesque
1981 - Willie Lamothe
1982 - Gilles Talbot
1983 - Rose Ouellet
1984 - Beau Dommage
1985 - Gilles Vigneault
1986 - Andre Perry
1987 - Yvon Deschamps
1988 - Guy Latraverse
1989 - Luc Plamondon

Manager Of The Year

1989 - Guy Cloutier

Record Producer Of The Year

1989 - Star Records

Record Company Of The Year

1989 - Audiogram

AWARD WINNERS

AWARD WINNERS

Record Distributer Of The Year

1989 - Distribution Select

Publisher Of The Year

1989 - Janvier/Kennebec

Producer Of The Year

1989 - Pierre Bazinet

Arranger Of The Year

1989 - Marc Perusse

Sound Engineer Of The Year

1989 - Glen Robinson

Record Promotion Team Of The Year

1989 - Martine Berube and Nick Carbone

Concert Promoter Of The Year

1989 - Fogel/Sabourin Productions

Agency Of The Year

1989 - Avanti Plus Productions

Lighting Concert Of The Year

1989 - Francois Doyon

Tour Promoter Of The Year

1989 - Roland Janelle

Stage Producer Of The Year

1989 - Martine Michaud

Venue Of The Year

1989 - Salle J. Antonio Thompson, Trois-Rivieres

Soundman Of The Year

1989 - Stephane Morency

Concert Promotion Team Of The Year

1989 - Therese David Publicity

Music Television Show Of The Year

1989 - Rendez-vous avec Gerry

Comedy Television Show Of The Year

1989 - La Grande Liquidation des fetes de Rock et Belles Oreilles

Television Producer Of The Year

1989 - Pram Productions

Video Production House Of The Year

1989 - Public Camera

CFGL Mozart Award

1989 - Roch Voisine

Miscellaneous Past Awards

1979 - Fiori/Seguin, Deux cents nuits
a l'heure (Album of the Year)
Starmania, Starmania (Album
Co-Production of the Year)
1981 - Diane Tell, En Fleche (Album
of the Year)
1982 - Claude Dubois, Sortie (Album
of the Year)
Groupe Pied de Poule (Performance of the Year, Words
and Music)
1985 - Montreal International Jazz
Festival (Special Event of the
Year)
Celine Dion, Melanie (Journal de
Quebec Trophy)
1988 - Celine Dion (Best Stage Performance)
Spectel Video (Television Variety Show)

Black Music Association of Canada (BMAC) Awards

No awards presented in 1988 or
1989. To resume in 1990 after
a reconstruction and redirection of
the association's goals.

Top Single

1985 - Hit And Run Lover, Yvonne
Moore
1986 - The Key, Erroll Starr
1987 - Peek-a-Boo, Kim Richardson

Top Album

1985 - Strength In Numbers, Manteca
1986 - Love Is A Contact Sport, Billy
Newton-Davis
1987 - Meanwhile, Leroy Sibbles

Top Male Performer

1985 - Gino Soccio
1986 - Billy Newton-Davis
1987 - Erroll Starr

Top Female Performer

1985 - Luba
1986 - Liberty Silver
1987 - Kim Richardson

Top Group

1985 - Tapps
1986 - Tapps
1987 - Manteca

Top Producer

1985 - Peter Frost
1986 - David Bendeth
1987 - Carl Harvey/Carl Otway (C&C)

Top Label

1985 - Power Records
1986 - CBS
1987 - A&M

Hall Of Fame

1985 - Claudja Barry, Quality
Records, Jackie Valasek
1986 - Calypsonian Lord Protector,
Trade Winds Group,
Club Blue Note
1987 - The Lincolns, Kensington
Sound Studios, Dick
Syncona-Smith

Friends Of BMAC Award

1987 - CARAS

CAPAC Composition Awards

Sir Ernest MacMillan Award (Orchestral Music)

1970 - Alexina Louie
1972 - Myra Grimley-Dahl
1973 - Christian Lecuyer
1974 - Dennis Patrick
1975 - Tomas Dusatko
1976 - Myke Roy
1977 - Marjan Mozetich, Patrick Cardy, Tomas Dusatko
1978 - Patrick Cardy, Robin Minard
1979 - Stephen Klein, Claude Frenette, Pierre-M Bedard
1980 - Alain Lalonde, Alan Salvin, John Armstrong
1981 - Serge Arcuri, Robin Minard, Elma Miller
1982 - Brian Sexton, Francois Tousignant, Rodney W. Sharman
1983 - Timothy Brady, James Harley, Denis Dion
1984 - Andrew P. MacDonald, James Rolfe, Linda Schwartz
1985 - Martin van de Ven, Denis Dion, Tom Hajdu
1986 - Robert C. May, Andrew P. MacDonald, William Peltier
1987 - Isabelle Marcoux
1988 - Andrew P. MacDonald, James Harley, Robert Lemay
1989 - Alain Perron, Melissa Hui, Stephen Sung Chi Ho

William St. Clair Low Award (Chamber Music)

1970 - Clifford Ford
1972 - Edward Dawson
1973 - Bruce Pennycook
1974 - David Alan Tanner
1975 - Patric Cardy
1976 - Not Awarded
1977 - Gilles Bellemare, Tomas Dusatko, Claude Caron, Denis Gougeon
1978 - Michael Maquire, Alexina Louie, John Armstrong
1979 - Hope Lee, Jacques Gouin, David Eagle
1980 - Claude Caron, Henry Kucharzyk, Pierre-M Bedard
1981 - Denis Gougeon, Timothy Brady, Tomas Dusatko
1982 - Hope Lee-Eagle, Wendy Prezament, Claude Schryer
1983 - Michelle Boudreau, Timothy Brady, James Harley
1984 - Matthew Patton, David B. Colwell, Rodney Sharman
1985 - Michelle Boudreau, Sylvaine Martin, Robert C. May
1986 - Denis Dion, Peter Hatch, James Rolfe
1987 - Robert C. May, Brent Lee, Richard Desilets
1988 - Melissa Hui, Stephen Sung Chi Ho, Andrew P. MacDonald
1989 - James Rolfe, Robert Lemay

Hugh Le Caine Award (Electronic Music)

1981 - Bernard Gagnon, Henry Kucharzyk
1982 - Paul Dolden
1983 - Daniel Toussaint, Mychael Danna
1984 - Paul Dolden, Jean Lesage
1985 - Mychael Danna, Roxanne Turcotte
1986 - Brent Lee, Jamie Bonk
1987 - Not Awarded
1988 - Elliot E. Freedman
1989 - Roxanne Turcotte, Hem Advani

Rodolphe Mathieu Award
(Solo Or Duet)

1985 - Robert C. May, Timothy Brady, Denis Dion, James Harley, Andrew P. MacDonald
1986 - Reid N. Robins, Richard Desilets, Peter Hatch
1987 - Michael Bussiere, Jean Lesage, Andrew P. MacDonald
1988 - Brent Lee, Robert Lemay, Marc Hyland
1989 - James Rolfe, Elliot E. Freedman, Jeff Ryan

Godfrey Ridout Award
(Choral Music)

1986 - Denis Dion, James Harley
1987 - Michael Bussiere, James Rolfe
1988 - Jeff Ryan, Mark Mitchell
1989 - Veronika Krausas, Brent Lee

CASBYs
(Formerly the U-Knows)

Album

1981 - Teenage Head, Frantic City
1982 - Bruce Cockburn, Inner City Front
1983 - Rough Trade, Shaking The Foundations
1984 - Parachute Club, Parachute Club
1985 - Parachute Club, Feet Of The Moon
1986 - Jane Siberry, Speckless Sky
1987 - Parachute Club, Small Victories
1988 - Robbie Robertson, Robbie Robertson
1989 - Jeff Healey Band, See The Light

Group

1981 - Teenage Head
1982 - Martha & The Muffins
1983 - The Spoons
1984 - Parachute Club
1985 - Parachute Club
1986 - Images In Vogue
1987 - Parachute Club
1988 - Blue Rodeo
1989 - Blue Rodeo

Female Vocalist

1981 - Carole Pope
1982 - Carole Pope
1983 - Carole Pope
1984 - Lorraine Segato, Parachute Club
1985 - Jane Siberry
1986 - Luba
1987 - Luba
1988 - k.d. lang
1989 - k.d. lang

Male Vocalist

1981 - B.B. Gabor
1982 - B.B. Gabor
1983 - Leroy Sibbles
1984 - Paul Humphries, Blue Peter
1985 - Bruce Cockburn
1986 - Bruce Cockburn
1987 - Corey Hart
1988 - Robbie Robertson
1989 - Jeff Healey

Most Promising Group

1981 - Blue Peter
1982 - The Spoons
1983 - L'Etranger
1984 - 20th Century Rebels, Images In Vogue
1985 - Pukka Orchestra
1986 - Chalk Circle
1987 - Pursuit Of Happiness
1988 - The Razorbacks
1989 - Sons Of Freedom

Blues Album

1981 - Powder Blues, Uncut

Single

1981 - Echo Beach, Martha & The Muffins
1982 - Chinese Graffiti, Blue Peter
1983 - Eyes Of A Stranger, Payola$
1984 - Safety Dance, Men Without Hats
1985 - Tell No Lies, The Spoons
1986 - In The House, Images In Vogue
1987 - How Many (Rivers To Cross), Luba
1988 - Try, Blue Rodeo
1989 - Angel Eyes, Jeff Healey Band

Instrumental Album

1982 - Nash The Slash, Decomposing

Most Promising Male Vocalist

1981 - Paul Humphries, Blue Peter
1982 - John Paul Young
1983 - Ivan, Men Without Hats
1984 - Dale Martindale, Images In Vogue
1985 - Gowan
1986 - Michel Lemieux

Most Promising Female Vocalist

1981 - Michaele Jordana
1982 - Shari Ulrich
1983 - Lorraine Segato
1984 - Sherry Kean
1985 - Luba
1986 - Diane Boss, Perfect World

Most Promising Artist

1987 - Colin James
1988 - Andrew Cash
1989 - Alannah Myles

Most Promising Non-Recording Act

1982 - Boys Brigade
1983 - Current Situation
1984 - Maja Bannerman
1986 - Monuments Galore
1987 - Basic English
1988 - Bratty And The Baby-Sisters

Comedy Album

1982 - Bob & Doug McKenzie, The Great White North

Album Artwork

1982 - Moving Pictures, Rush, Deborah Samuel/Hugh Syme
1983 - Arias & Symphonies, The Spoons, Mark Krawczynski/ Peter Noble
1984 - Talkback, The Spoons, Noble/ Heslip
1985 - Dean Motter
1986 - Gane/Johnson/Safari/Syme, M+M
1987 - Mind: The Perpetual Inter- course, Skinny Puppy
1988 - Treehouse, Grapes Of Wrath
1989 - Touch, Sara McLachlan

Engineer/Producer

1981 - Stacey Heydon
1982 - Daniel Lanois, This Is The Iceage, Martha & The Muffins
1983 - Marc Durand, Men Without Hats
1984 - Daniel Lanois, Parachute Club
1985 - Daniel Lanois
1986 - Siberry/Switzer/Naslen, Jane Siberry
1987 - Bruce Fairbairn, Rock & Hyde, Dirty Water
1988 - Daniel Lanois/Robbie Robertson
1989 - Malcolm Burn, Diamond Mine

International Album

1982 - Human League, Dare
1983 - Simple Minds, New Gold Dream
1984 - Tears For Fears, The Hurting
1985 - U2, The Unforgettable Fire
1986 - Peter Gabriel, So
1987 - Paul Simon, Graceland
1988 - INXS, Kick
1989 - Fine Young Cannibals, The Raw And The Cooked

NOW Humanitarian Award

1982 - Bernie Finklestein
1983 - Billy Bryans

Most Promising Independent

1983 - Messenjah
1984 - 20th Century Rebels
1986 - Vis A Vis
1987 - Breeding Ground
1988 - The Shuffle Demons
1989 - Skinny Puppy

Video

1983 - Nova Heart, The Spoons
1984 - Safety Dance, Men Without Hats
1986 - Call It Democracy, Bruce Cockburn
1987 - Dirty Water, Rock And Hyde
1988 - Try, Blue Rodeo
1989 - Misguided Angel, Cowboy Junkies

Best Independent Video

1987 - Pursuit Of Happiness
1988 - Out Of My House, Roach, The Shuffle Demons
1989 - 68 Hours, National Velvet

Best Jazz Recording

1987 - Shuffle Demons
1988 - Fire Me Up, Manteca
1989 - Bop Rap, The Shuffle Demons

Best R&B/Reggae Recording

1987 - Billy Newton-Davis
1988 - Show Me Some Kind Of Sign, Sattelites

Best Reggae Act

1989 - Messenjah

Canadian Country Music Awards

Entertainer

1982 - Family Brown
1983 - Family Brown
1984 - Ronnie Prophet
1985 - Dick Damron
1986 - Family Brown
1987 - k.d. lang
1988 - k.d. lang
1989 - k.d. lang

Females Vocalist

1982 - Carroll Baker
1983 - Marie Bottrell
1984 - Marie Bottrell
1985 - Carroll Baker
1986 - Anita Perras
1987 - Anita Perras
1988 - k.d. lang
1989 - k.d. lang

Male Vocalist

1982 - Terry Carisse
1983 - Dick Damron
1984 - Terry Carisse
1985 - Terry Carisse
1986 - Terry Carisse
1987 - Ian Tyson
1988 - Ian Tyson
1989 - Gary Fjellgaard

Group

1982 - Family Brown
1983 - Family Brown
1984 - Family Brown
1985 - Mercey Brothers
1986 - Family Brown
1987 - Family Brown
1988 - Family Brown
1989 - Family Brown

Duo

1984 - Glory Anne Carriere and Ronnie Prophet
1985 - Anita Perras and Tim Taylor
1986 - Anita Perras and Tim Taylor
1987 - Anita Perras and Tim Taylor
1988 - Anita Perras and Tim Taylor
1989 - Gary Fjellgaard and Linda Kidder

Single

1982 - Some Never Stand A Chance, Family Brown
1983 - Raised On Country Music, Family Brown
1984 - A Little Good News, Anne Murray
1985 - Riding On The Wind, Gary Fjellgaard
1986 - Now And Forever, Anne Murray
1987 - Navajo Rug, Ian Tyson
1988 - One Smokey Rose, Anita Perras
1989 - Town Of Tears, Family Brown

Album

1982 - Family Brown, Raised On Country Music
1983 - Family Brown, Raised On Country Music
1984 - Family Brown, Repeat After Me
1985 - Terry Carisse, The Closest Thing To You
1986 - Family Brown, Feel The Fire
1987 - Ian Tyson, Cowboyography
1988 - k.d. lang, Shadowland
1989 - k.d. lang, Shadowland

Song

1982 - Some Never Stand A Chance, Family Brown
1983 - Raised On Country Music, Family Brown
1984 - Jesus It's Me Again, Dick Damron
1985 - Counting The I Love Yous, Terry Charisse/Bruce Rawlins
1986 - Now And Forever, Anne Murray
1987 - Heroes, Gary Fjellgaard, The Mercey Brothers
1988 - One Smokey Rose, Tim Taylor
1989 - Town Of Tears, Barry Brown, Randall Prescott and Bruce Campbell

Vista (Rising Star)

1982 - Ruth Ann
1983 - Kelita Haverland
1984 - Roni Sommers
1985 - Ginny Mitchell
1986 - J.K. Gulley
1987 - k.d. lang
1988 - Blue Rodeo
1989 - George Fox

International Album

1986 - Carroll Baker, Hymns Of Gold
1987 - Randy Travis, Storms Of Life
1988 - Randy Travis, Always And Forever
1989 - Randy Travis, Old 8x10

Hall Of Honour Inductees

1988 - Jack Feeney
1989 - Ian Tyson, Don Grashey

JUNOS

Canadian Entertainer
Of The Year

1987 - Bryan Adams
1988 - Glass Tiger
1989 - The Jeff Healey Band

Best Selling Album

1974 - Bachman-Turner Overdrive,
Not Fragile
1975 - Bachman-Turner Overdrive,
Four Wheel Drive
1976 - Andre Gagnon, Neiges
1977 - Dan Hill, Fuse
1978 - Burton Cummings, Dream Of
A Child

Best Selling Single

1974 - Terry Jacks, Seasons In The
Sun
1975 - Bachman-Turner Overdrive,
You Ain't Seen Nothing Yet
1976 - Sweeney Todd, Roxy Roller
1977 - Patsy Gallant, Sugar Daddy
1978 - Nick Gilder, Hot Child In The
City

Album Of The Year
(Formerly Best Selling Album)

1979 - Anne Murray, New Kind Of
Feeling
1980 - Anne Murray, Greatest Hits
1981 - Loverboy, Loverboy
1982 - Loverboy, Get Lucky
1983-84 - Bryan Adams, Cuts Like A
Knife
1985 - Bryan Adams, Reckless
1986 - Glass Tiger, Thin Red Line
1987 - Kim Mitchell, Shakin' Like A
Human Being
1989 - Robbie Robertson, Robbie
Robertson
1990 - Alannah Myles, Alannah Myles

Single Of The Year
(Formerly Best Selling Single)

1979 - Anne Murray, I Just Fall In
Love Again
1980 - Anne Murray, Could I Have
This Dance; Martha & The Muffins, Echo Beach
1981 - Loverboy, Turn Me Loose
1982 - Payola$, Eyes Of A Stranger
1983-84 - Parachute Club, Rise Up
1985 - Corey Hart, Never Surrender
1986 - Glass Tiger, Don't Forget Me
(When I'm Gone)
1987 - Glass Tiger, Someday
1989 - Blue Rodeo, Try
1990 - Alannah Myles - Black Velvet

Female Vocalist Of The Year

1974 - Anne Murray
1975 - Joni Mitchell
1976 - Patsy Gallant
1977 - Patsy Gallant
1978 - Anne Murray
1979 - Anne Murray
1980 - Anne Murray
1981 - Anne Murray
1982 - Carole Pope
1983-84 - Carole Pope
1985 - Luba
1986 - Luba
1987 - Luba
1989 - k.d. lang
1990 - Rita MacNeil

Male Vocalist Of The Year

1974 - Gordon Lightfoot
1975 - Gino Vannelli
1976 - Burton Cummings
1977 - Dan Hill
1978 - Gino Vannelli
1979 - Burton Cummings
1980 - Bruce Cockburn
1981 - Bruce Cockburn
1982 - Bryan Adams
1983-84 - Bryan Adams
1985 - Bryan Adams
1986 - Bryan Adams
1987 - Bryan Adams
1989 - Robbie Robertson
1990 - Kim Mitchell

Group Of The Year

1974 - Bachman-Turner Overdrive
1975 - Bachman-Turner Overdrive
1976 - Heart
1977 - Rush
1978 - Rush
1979 - Trooper
1980 - Prism
1981 - Loverboy
1982 - Loverboy
1983-84 - Loverboy
1985 - The Parachute Club
1986 - Honeymoon Suite
1987 - Red Rider
1989 - Blue Rodeo
1990 - Blue Rodeo

Composer Of The Year

1974 - Paul Anka
1975 - Hagood Hardy,
The Homecoming
1976 - Gordon Lightfoot, Wreck Of
The Edmund Fitzgerald
1977 - Dan Hill, Sometimes When We
Touch
1978 - Dan Hill, Sometimes When We
Touch
1979 - Frank Mills, Peter Piper
1980 - Eddie Schwartz, Hit Me With
Your Best Shot - Pat Benatar
1981 - Mike Reno & Paul Dean, Turn
Me Loose - Loverboy
1982 - Bob Rock & Paul Hyde, Eyes
Of A Stranger - Payola$
1983-84 - Bryan Adams & Jim
Vallance, Cuts Like A Knife
- Bryan Adams
1985 - Bryan Adams & Jim Vallance
1986 - Jim Vallance
1987 - Jim Vallance
1989 - Tom Cochrane
1990 - David Tyson and Christopher
Ward

Country Female Vocalist Of The Year

1974 - Anne Murray
1975 - Anne Murray
1976 - Carroll Baker
1977 - Carroll Baker
1978 - Carroll Baker
1979 - Anne Murray
1980 - Anne Murray
1981 - Anne Murray
1982 - Anne Murray
1983-84 - Anne Murray
1985 - Anne Murray
1986 - Anne Murray
1987 - k.d. lang
1989 - k.d. lang
1990 - k.d. lang

Country Male Vocalist Of The Year

1974 - Stompin' Tom Connors
1975 - Murray McLauchlan
1976 - Murray McLauchlan
1977 - Ronnie Prophet
1978 - Ronnie Prophet
1979 - Murray McLauchlan
1980 - Eddie Eastman
1981 - Ronnie Hawkins
1982 - Eddie Eastman
1983-84 - Murray McLauchlan
1985 - Murray McLauchlan
1986 - Murray McLauchlan
1987 - Ian Tyson
1989 - Murray Mclauchlan
1990 - George Fox

Country Group Of The Year

1974 - Carlton Showband
1975 - Mercey Brothers
1976 - Good Brothers
1977 - Good Brothers
1978 - Good Brothers
1979 - Good Brothers
1980 - Good Brothers
1981 - Good Brothers
1982 - Good Brothers
1983-84 - Good Brothers
1985 - The Family Brown
1986 - Prairie Oyster
1987 - Prairie Oyster
1989 - The Family Brown
1990 - The Family Brown

Most Promising Female Vocalist Of The Year

1974 - Suzanne Stevens
1975 - Patricia Dahlquist
1976 - Colleen Peterson
1977 - Lisa Dal Bello
1978 - Claudja Barry
1979 - France Joli
1980 - Carole Pope
1981 - Shari Ulrich
1982 - Lydia Taylor
1983-84 - Sherry Kean
1985 - k.d. lang
1986 - Kim Richardson
1987 - Rita MacNeil
1989 - Sass Jordan
1990 - Alannah Myles

Most Promising Male Vocalist Of The Year

1974 - Gino Vannelli
1975 - Dan Hill
1976 - Burton Cummings
1977 - David Bradstreet
1978 - Nick Gilder
1979 - Walter Rossi
1980 - Graham Shaw
1981 - Eddie Schwartz
1982 - Kim Mitchell
1983-84 - Zappacosta
1985 - Paul Janz
1986 - Billy Newton-Davis
1987 - Tim Feehan
1989 - Colin James
1990 - Daniel Lanois

Most Promising Group Of The Year

1974 - Rush
1975 - Myles & Lenny
1976 - T.H.P. Orchestra
1977 - Hometown Band
1978 - Doucette
1979 - Streetheart
1980 - Powder Blue
1981 - Saga
1982 - Payola$
1983-84 - Parachute Club
1985 - Idle Eyes
1986 - Glass Tiger
1987 - Frozen Ghost
1989 - Barney Bentall &
        The Legendary Hearts
1990 - The Tragically Hip

Instrumental Artist Of The Year

1975 - Hagood Hardy
1976 - Hagood Hardy
1977 - Andre Gagnon
1978 - Liona Boyd
1979 - Frank Mills
1980 - Frank Mills
1981 - Liona Boyd
1982 - Liona Boyd
1983-84 - Liona Boyd
1985 - The Canadian Brass
1986 - David Foster
1987 - David Foster
1989 - David Foster
1990 - Manteca

Folksinger Of The Year

1974 - Gordon Lightfoot
1975 - Gordon Lightfoot
1976 - Gordon Lightfoot
1977 - Gordon Lightfoot
1978 - Murray McLauchlan
1979 - Bruce Cockburn
1980 - Bruce Cockburn
1981 - Bruce Cockburn

Children's Album Of The Year

1978 - Anne Murray, There's A Hippo
        In My Tub
1979 - Sharon Lois & Bram,
        Smorgasbord
1980 - Sharon Lois & Bram, Singing
        'n' Swinging
1981 - Sandra Beech, Inch By Inch
1982 - Bob Schneider, When You
        Dream A Dream
1983-84 - The Rugrats, Rugrat Rock
1985 - Robert Munsch, Murmel
        Murmel Munsch
1986 - Charlotte Diamond, 10 Carrot
        Diamond
1987 - Bill Usher, Drums!
1989 - Fred Penner, Fred Penner's
        Place and Connie Kaldor &
        Carmen Champagne, Lullaby
        Berceuse
1990 - Susan Hammond and Barbara
        Nichol, Beethoven Lives
        Upstairs

Comedy Album Of The Year

1978 - The Air Farce, The Air Farce Album
1979 - Rich Little, A Christmas Carol
1980 - No Category
1981 - Bob & Doug McKenzie, The Great White North
1982 - No Category
1983-84 - Bob & Doug McKenzie, Strange Brew

Best Selling International Album

1974 - Paul McCartney, Band On The Run
1975 - Elton John, Greatest Hits
1976 - Peter Frampton, Frampton Comes Alive
1977 - Fleetwood Mac, Rumours
1978 - Bee Gees, Saturday Night Fever

International Album Of The Year (Formerly Best Selling International Album)

1979 - Supertramp, Breakfast In America
1980 - Pink Floyd, The Wall
1981 - John Lennon, Double Fantasy
1982 - Men At Work - Business As Usual
1983-84 - The Police, Synchronicity
1985 - Bruce Springsteen, Born In The U.S.A.
1986 - Dire Straits, Brothers In Arms
1987 - Madonna, True Blue
1989 - Various, Dirty Dancing
1990 - Milli Vanilli, Girl You Know It's True

Best Selling International Single

1974 - Paper Lace, The Night Chicago Died
1975 - The Captain and Tenille, Love Will Keep Us Together
1976 - Tina Charles, I Love To Love
1977 - Leo Sayer, When I Need You
1978 - John Travolta/Olivia Newton-John, You're The One That I Want

International Single Of The Year (Formerly Best Selling International Single)

1979 - Blondie - Heart Of Glass
1980 - Pink Floyd, Another Brick In The Wall
1981 - Kim Carnes, Bette Davis Eyes
1982 - Survivor, Eye Of The Tiger
1983-84 - Michael Jackson, Billie Jean
1985 - Foreigner, I Want To Know What Love Is
1986 - Opus - Live Is Life
1987 - Bananarama, Venus
1989 - M.A.R.R.S., Pump Up The Volume
1990 - Jive Bunny and The Mixmasters, Swing The Mood

International Entertainer Of The Year

1989 - U2
1990 - Melissa Etheridge

Producer Of The Year

1974 - Randy Bachman
1975 - Peter Anastasoff, The Home-
coming - Hagood Hardy
1976 - M. Flicker, Dreamboat Annie -
Heart
1977 - (Single) McCauley/Mollin,
Sometimes When We Touch -
Dan Hill. (Album) McCauley/
Mollin, Longer Fuse - Dan Hill
1978 - Gino/Joe/Ross Vannelli,
Brother To Brother -
Gino Vannelli
1979 - Bruce Fairbairn, Armageddon -
Prism
1980 - Gene Martynec, Tokyo - Bruce
Cockburn and High School
Confidential - Rough Trade
1981 - Paul Dean/Bruce Fairbairn,
Working For The Weekend
and It's Over - Loverboy
1982 - Bill Henderson/Brian McLeod,
Watcha Gonna Do, Secret
Information - Chilliwack
1983-84 - Bryan Adams, Cuts Like A
Knife - Bryan Adams
1985 - David Foster, Chicago 17 -
Chicago
1986 - David Foster, St. Elmo's Fire
Soundtrack
1987 - Daniel Lanois, So, Peter
Gabriel
1989 - Daniel Lanois and Robbie
Robertson
1990 - Bruce Fairbairn

Recording Engineer Of The Year

1975 - Michel Ethier, Dompierre
1976 - Paul Page, Are You Ready For
Love
1977 - Terry Brown, Hope - Klaatu
1977 - David Green, Big Band Jazz -
Rob McConnell & The Boss
Brass
1978 - Ken Friesen, Let's Keep It That
Way - Anne Murray
1979 - David Greene, Hoffert: Concerto For Contemporary Violin -
Paul Hoffert
1980 - Mike Jones, Factory, We're OK
- Instructions
1981 - Gary Gray, Attitude, For Those
Who Think Young - Rough
Trade, Keith Stein/Bob Rock,
When It's Over, It's Your Life -
Loverboy
1982 - Bob Rock, No Stranger To
Danger - Payola$
1983-84 - John Naslen, Stealing Fire -
Bruce Cockburn
1985 - Hayward Parrott, Underworld -
The Front
1986 - Joe and Gino Vannelli,
Black Cars
1987 - Joe and Gino Vannelli, Wild
Horses
1989 - Mike Fraser
1990 - Kevin Doyle

Best Classical Composition/ Composer

1987 - Malcolm Forsyth/Atayoskewin,
Forsyth - Freedman
1989 - Alexina Louie, Songs Of
Paradise
1990 - Oskar Morawetz, Concerto For
Harp and Chamber Orchestra

Best Classical Recording

1976 - Anton Kuerti, Beethoven - Vols. 1, 2 & 3
1977 - Toronto Symphony Orchestra, Three Borodin Symphonies
1978 - Glenn Gould & Roxolana Roslak, Hindemith: Das Marienleben (CBS)
1979 - Judy Loman, The Crown Of Ariadne: R. Murray Schafer, Composer
1980 - Arthur Ozolins, Stravinsky - Chopin Ballads
1981 - l'Orchestra Symphonique de Montreal, conducted by Charles Dutoit, Ravel: Daphnis et Chloe (Complete ballet)
1982 - Glenn Gould, Bach: The Goldberg Variations
1983-84 - Glenn Gould, Brahms Op. 10, Raphsodies Op. 79
1985 - (Solo or Chamber Ensemble) The Orford String Quartet, W.A. Mozart - String Quartets
1985 - (Large Ensemble) l'Orchestra Symphonique de Montreal/ Charles Dutoit, Ravel: Ma Mere l'Oye/Pavane pour un infante defunte/Tombeau de Couperin and Valses nobles et sentimentales
1986 - (Solo or Chamber Ensemble) James Campbell, Eric Robertson, Stolen Gems
1986 - (Large Ensemble) Toronto Symphony Orchestra/Andrew Davis (Conductor), Holst: The Planets
1987 - (Solo or Chamber Ensemble) Orford String Quartet/Ofra Harnoy, Schubert, Quintet in C
1987 - (Large Ensemble) Orchestre Symphonique de Montreal, Charles Dutoit Conductor, Holst: The Planets
1989 - (Large Ensemble) Orchestra Symphonique de Montreal, Charles Dutoit, cunductor; Bartok - Concerto for Orchestra, and Music For Strings, Percussion and Celeste

1989 - (Solo or Chamber Ensemble) Ofra Harnoy; Schubert - Arpeggione Sonata
1990 - (Large Ensemble) Tafelmusik Baroque Orchestra, Boccherini, Cello Concertos and Symphonies
1990 - (Solo or Chamber Ensemble) Louis Lortie, 20th Century Original Piano Transcriptions

Best Album Graphics

1974 - Bart Schoales, Night Vision - Bruce Cockburn
1975 - Bart Schoales, Joy Will Find A Way - Bruce Cockburn
1976 - Michael Bowness, Ian Tamblyn - Ian Tamblyn
1977 - Dave Anderson, Short Turn - Short Turn
1978 - Alan Gee/Greg Lawson, Madcats
1979 - Rodney Bowes, Cigarettes - The Wives
1980 - Jeanette Hanna, We Deliver - Downchild Blues Band
1981 - Hugh Syme/Deborah Samuel, Moving Pictures - Rush
1982 - Dean Motter, Metal On Metal
1983-84 - Dean Motter/JeffJackson/ Deborah Samuel, Seamless - The Nylons
1985 - rob macintyre/Dimo Safari, Strange Animal - Gowan
1986 - Hugh Syme/Dimo Safari, Power Windows - Rush
1987 - Jamie Bennet/Shari Spier, Small Victories, The Parachute Club
1989 - Hugh Syme, Levity, Ian Thomas
1990 - Hugh Syme, Presto, Rush

Best Video Of The Year

1983-84 - Rob Quartly, Sunglasses At
Night - Cory Hart
1985 - Rob Quartly, A Criminal Mind -
Gowan
1986 - Greg Masauk, How Many
(Rivers To Cross) - Luba
1987 - Ron Berti, Love Is Fire - The
Parachute Club
1989 - Michael Buckley, Try - Blue
Rodeo
1990 - Cosimo Cavallaro, Boomtown -
Andrew Cash

R&B/Soul Recording
Of The Year

1985 - Lost Somewhere Inside Your
Love, Liberty Silver
1986 - Love Is A Contact Sport, Billy
Newton-Davis
1987 - Peek-A-Boo, Kim Richardson
1989 - Angel, Erroll Starr
1990 - Spellbound, Billy Newton-Davis

Reggae/Calypso Recording

1985 - Heaven Must Have Sent You,
Liberty Silver, Otis Gayle
1986 - Revolutionary Tea Party, Lillian
Allen
1987 - Meanwhile, Leroy Sibbles
1989 - Conditions Critical, Lillian Allen
1990 - It's Too Late To Turn Back
Now, The Satallites

Best Jazz Album

1980 - Present Perfect, Rob McConnell
and The Boss Brass
1981 - The Brass Connection, The
Brass Connection
1982 - I Didn't Know About You,
Fraser MacPherson/Oliver
Grannon
1983-84 - All In Good Time, Rob
MacConnell and The Boss
Brass
1985-86 - Lights Of Burgundy, Oliver
Jones
1987 - If You Could See Me Now, The
Oscar Peterson Four
1989 - Looking Up, The Hugh Fraser
Quintet
1990 - Skydance, John Ballantynes
Trio Featuring Joe Henderson

Walt Grealis
Special Achievement Award

1984 - J. Lyman Potts
1985 - A. Hugh Joseph
1986 - Jack Richardson
1987 - Bruce Allen
1989 - Sam Sniderman, C.M.
1990 - Raffi

Hall Of Fame Award

1978 - Guy Lombardo,
Oscar Peterson
1979 - Hank Snow
1980 - Paul Anka
1981 - Joni Mitchell
1982 - Neil Young
1983 - Glenn Gould
1984 - Crewcuts, Diamonds,
Four Lads
1985 - Wilf Carter
1986 - Gordon Lightfoot
1987 - The Guess Who
1989 - The Band
1990 - Maureen Forrester

Best Dance Album

1990 - I Beg Your Pardon, Kon Kan

Leslie Bell Prize
(Choral Conducting)

1973 - Edward Moroney
1974 - Robert Cooper
1975 - David Christiani
1976 - Carol E. Boyle
1977 - Jean Ashworth-Bartle
1978 - Gerald Neufeld
1981 - Brainerd Blyden-Taylor
1983 - Richard Dacey
1984 - Daniel Hanson
1985 - David Fallis
1986 - Karen Price-Wallace
1988 - Laurence Ewashko

Toronto Music Awards

Best Toronto Guitarist

1987 - Rik Emmett
1988 - Jeff Healey
1989 - Jeff Healey

Best Toronto Bassist

1987 - Geddy Lee
1988 - Geddy Lee
1989 - Geddy Lee

Best Toronto Drummer

1987 - Neil Peart
1988 - Neil Peart
1989 - Neil Peart

Best Toronto Keyboard Player

1987 - Gowan
1988 - Gowan
1989 - Greg Wells

Best Toronto Group/Artist (Local Success)

1987 - Chalk Circle
1988 - Blue Rodeo
1989 - Kim Mitchell

Best Toronto Group/Artist (International Success)

1987 - Rush
1988 - Blue Rodeo
1989 - Jeff Healey

Best Toronto Female Vocalist

1987 - Lee Aaron
1988 - Lee Aaron
1989 - Alannah Myles

Best Toronto Male Vocalist

1987 - Kim Mitchell
1988 - Jim Cuddy
1989 - Kim Mitchell

Best Toronto Club Band

1987 - Paul James Band
1988 - Razorbacks
1989 - L.A.

Best Toronto Pop/Dance Group/Artist

1989 - Candi

Best Toronto Reggae Group/Artist

1987 - Messenjah
1988 - Errol Blackwood
1989 - Messenjah

Best Toronto Country Group/Artist

1987 - Blue Rodeo
1988 - Blue Rodeo
1989 - Murray McLauchlan

Best Toronto R&B/Soul/Rap Group/Artist

1987 - Billy Newton-Davis
1988 - Erroll Starr
1989 - Liberty Silver

Best Toronto "Rising Star" Band/Artist

1988 - Eye Eye
1989 - The Razorbacks

Best Toronto Blues Group/Artist

1987 - Jeff Healey
1988 - Jeff Healey
1989 - Downchild Blues Band

Best Toronto Jazz Instrumental Group/Artist

1987 - Manteca
1988 - Shuffle Demons
1989 - Shuffle Demons

Best Toronto Folk/Traditional Artist

1987 - Bruce Cockburn
1988 - Bruce Cockburn
1989 - Bruce Cockburn

Best Toronto Club

1987 - The Diamond
1988 - The Diamond
1989 - The Diamond

Toronto Sun's Cutting Edge Award/Career Achievement

1987 - Domenic Troiano
1988 - Blue Rodeo
1989 - Cowboy Junkies

The Mayor's Music Award

1987 - Bruce Cockburn
1988 - Rush
1989 - Jeff Healey

Labatt's Blue Harmony Award

1988 - Bruce Cockburn
1989 - Gordon Lightfoot

Toronto's "Rising Star" Guitarist

1987 - Jeff Healey
1988 - Greg Fraser

Toronto's "Rising Star" Bassist

1987 - Wolf Hassell
1988 - Stevie Skreebs

Toronto's "Rising Star" Drummer

1987 - Paul DeLong
1988 - Greg Loates

Toronto's "Rising Star" Keyboard Player

1987 - Arnold Lanni
1988 - John Rogers

Toronto's "Rising Star" Female Vocalist

1987 - Sharon Lee Williams
1988 - Rita Chiarelli

Toronto's "Rising Star" Male Vocalist

1987 - Zappacosta
1988 - Andrew Cash

Best Rock Journalist

1987 - Bob Thompson

Concert Of The Year

1987 - Bon Jovi

Local Band Most Deserving of a Record Contract

1987 - Rita Chiarelli

Tribute To West Coast Music

Group

1981 - Loverboy
1982 - Loverboy
1983 - Chilliwack
1984 - Payola$
1985 - Doug & The Slugs
1986 - Idle Eyes
1987 - Idle Eyes
1988 - Paul Janz
1989 - Colin James

Album/EP

1981 - Loverboy, Loverboy
1982 - Loverboy, Get Lucky
1983 - Chilliwack, Opus X
1984 - Payola$, Hammer On A Drum
1985 - Doug And The Slugs, Propaganda
1986 - Idle Eyes, Idle Eyes
1987 - Skywalk, The Bohemians
1988 - Paul Janz, Electricity
1989 - Colin James, Colin James

Song Of The Year

1981 - The Kid Is Hot Tonight, Loverboy
1982 - My Girl, Chilliwack
1983 - Eyes Of A Stranger, Payola$
1984 - Where Is This Love, Payola$
1985 - Day By Day, Doug & The Slugs
1986 - Tokyo Rose, Idle Eyes
1987 - X-Ray Eyes, Jim Foster
1988 - Believe In Me, Paul Janz
1989 - Five Long Years, Colin James

Independent Album/EP

1981 - Too Bad, Doug & The Slugs
1982 - In The Mood, Wildroot Orchestra
1983 - Silverlode, Silverlode
1984 - Bloodied But Unbowed, D.O.A.
1985 - Propaganda - Doug & The Slugs
1986 - You Better Dancing, Rick Scott
1987 - Hook, Line and Single, Colin James
1988 - Walking Through Walls, Body Electric
1989 - No Doubts, Alibi

Club Performer

1981 - D.O.A.
1982 - Headpins
1983 - b-Sides
1984 - Jim Byrnes
1985 - Jim Byrnes
1986 - Rick Scott/Spirit Of The West
1987 - Jim Byrnes
1988 - D.O.A.

Most Promising Act

1981 - Loverboy
1982 - Bryan Adams
1983 - Bryan Adams (major), French
       Letters (independent)
1984 - H.B. Concept
1985 - Annette Ducharme
1986 - Fabulon
1987 - Colin James
1988 - Barney Bentall &
       The Legendary Hearts

Country Act

1981 - Blue Northern
1982 - Midnite Rodeo Band
1983 - Midnite Rodeo Band
1984 - Midnite Rodeo Band
1985 - Midnite Rodeo Band
1986 - Lone Star Cattle Co.
1987 - Spirit Of The West
1988 - Alibi
1989 - Alibi

Jazz Performer

1981 - Claire Lawrence Band
1982 - Skywalk
1983 - Tom Keenlyside
1984 - Skywalk
1985 - Skywalk
1986 - Graham Boyle
1987 - Skywalk
1988 - June Katz
1989 - Skywalk

Classical Performer

1981 - Vancouver Symphony
1988 - Sal Ferreras
1989 - John Kimura Parker

Folk/Bluegrass Act

1981 - Valdy
1982 - Bim
1983 - Valdy

Traditional/Ethnic Act

1985 - The Rovers
1989 - Spirit Of The West

Female Vocalist

1981 - Shari Ulrich
1982 - Shari Ulrich
1983 - Shari Ulrich
1984 - Darby Mills, Headpins
1985 - Anne Mortifee
1986 - Darby Mills
1987 - Nancy Nash
1988 - Sue Medley
1989 - k.d. lang

Male Vocalist

1981 - Ra MaGuire, Trooper
1982 - Bill Henderson, Chilliwack
1983 - Bryan Adams
1984 - Paul Hyde, Payola$
1985 - Doug Bennett, Doug &
       The Slugs
1986 - Paul Hyde
1987 - Jim Byrnes
1988 - Paul Janz
1989 - Colin James

Guitarist

1981 - Tom Lavin, Powder Blues
1982 - Bill Henderson, Chilliwack
1983 - Brian MacLeod, Chilliwack/
       Headpins
1984 - Brian MacLeod, Headpins
1985 - Keith Scott
1986 - Harris Van Berkel
1987 - Harris Van Berkel
1988 - Colin James
1989 - Colin James

Bassist

1981 - Jack Lavin, Powder Blues
1982 - Ab Bryant, Chilliwack/
       Headpins
1983 - Ab Bryant, Chilliwack/
       Headpins
1984 - Ab Bryant, Headpins
1985 - Ab Bryant, Headpins
1986 - Rene Worst
1987 - Rene Worst
1988 - Brian Newcombe
1989 - Rene Worst

Percussionist

1981 - Duris Maxwell, Powder Blues
1982 - Matt Frenette, Loverboy
1983 - Matt Frenette, Loverboy
1984 - Chris Taylor, Payola$
1985 - Pat Steward
1986 - Chris Taylor
1987 - Daryl Burgess
1988 - Jerry Adolphe
1989 - Jerry Adolphe

Reed/Brass Player

1981 - Duris Maxwell, Powder Blue
1982 - Tom Keenlyside
1983 - Tom Keenlyside
1984 - Tom Keenlyside
1985 - Tom Keenlyside
1986 - Mark Hasselbach
1987 - Tom Keenlyside
1988 - Kirstin Nash
1989 - Tom Colclough

Keyboardist

1981 - Robbie King
1982 - Robbie King
1983 - Dave Pickell
1984 - Graeme Coleman, Skywalk
1985 - Graeme Coleman
1986 - Dave Pickell
1987 - Graeme Coleman
1988 - Paul Janz
1989 - Dave Pickell

Songwriter

1981 - Tom Lavin, Powder Blues
1982 - Bryan Adams/Jim Vallance,
       Bryan Adams
1983 - Bill Henderson/Brian MacLeod,
       Chilliwack
1984 - Paul Hyde/Bob Rock, Payola$
1985 - Paul Hyde/Bob Rock, Payola$
1986 - Tad Campbell
1987 - Jim Foster
1988 - Bob Rock/Paul Hyde
1989 - Sarah McLachlan

Producer

1981 - Tom Lavin
1982 - Tom Lavin
1983 - Bill Henderson/Brian MacLeod
1984 - Bob Rock
1985 - Brian MacLeod
1986 - Bill Henderson
1987 - Graeme Coleman
1988 - Bob Buckley/David Sinclair
1989 - Bruce McLeod

Engineer

1981 - Rolf Henneman
1982 - Brian Campbell, Blue Wave
       Sound Recorders
1983 - Bob Rock, Little Mountain
       Sound
1984 - Bob Rock, Little Mountain
       Sound
1985 - Bob Rock
1986 - Bob Rock
1987 - Ron Obvious
1988 - Roger Monk
1989 - Howard Rissin

Graphics

1981 - Cognac and Bologna, Doug &
       The Slugs
1982 - Wrap It!, Doug & The Slugs
1983 - Worlds Away, Strange
       Advance
1984 - Cuts Like A Knife, Bryan
       Adams (James O'Mara)
1985 - Propoganda, Doug & The
       Slugs (D. Bennett)
1986 - Steve Gilmore, Grapes Of
       Wrath
1987 - Doug Bennett
1988 - O'Mara & Ryan, Talk To Me
1989 - Sarah McLachlan/Greg Sykes,
       Touch

Video

1984 - Lust For Love, Images In
       Vogue (Doug Bennett)
1985 - Day By Day, Doug & The
       Slugs (D. Bennett)
1986 - James O'Mara
1987 - Rob Quartly
1988 - Mark Jowett, Talk To Me
1989 - Keith Porteous/Allen May,
       One Thing

International Achievement

1984 - Bryan Adams, Chilliwack,
       Loverboy
1985 - David Foster
1986 - Bryan Adams, Jim Vallance
1987 - Bryan Adams

Special Merit Award

1981 - Tom Harrison
1982 - Bruce Allen
1983 - Dan McLeod, Georgia Straight
1984 - Drew Burns
1985 - Dan Tolan
1986 - Janet Forsyth
1987 - Lynn Partridge
1988 - Fraser McPherson
1989 - Terry David Mulligan

Independent Group

1988 - Body Electric
1989 - Alibi

Song Of The Year (Independent)

1988 - Walking In The Rain Tonight,
       Gary Fjellgaard
1989 - Do You Have Any Doubts, Alibi

Video Of The Year (Independent)

1988 - Matthew O'Connor/Michael
       Rosati, Isn't Love Crazy
1989 - Cloane Music Group/
       Optdesign, Do You Have Any
       Doubts

Children's Performer Of The Year

1988 - Charlotte Diamond
1989 - Charlotte Diamond

Country Male Vocalist

1988 - Gary Fjellgaard
1989 - Gary Fjellgaard

Country Female Vocalist

1988 - Sue Medley
1989 - k.d. lang

Live Sound Engineer

1988 - Bill Buckingham
1989 - Bill Buckingham

CARAS BC Citation

1988 - Les Vogt
1989 - Terry Jacks

Inspirational Performer

1988 - Connie Scott

Country Record Of The Year

1988 - Crying Over You, Sue Medley

Most Promising Club Performer

1988 - Sons Of Freedom

Best Debut Recording

1989 - Colin James, Colin James

Live Performer (Recorded)

1989 - k.d. lang

Live Performer (Non-Recorded)

1989 - Scramblers

Best Live Performance

1989 - Colin James

Gospel Performer Of The Year

1989 - Connie Scott

Heavy Metal Performer Of The Year

1989 - Young Gun

Rock Band Of The Year

1981 - Loverboy

Acoustic Act

1984 - Bim

SCHEDULE OF EVENTS

1990

JUNE

Dundalk Square Dance Competition

Date: TBA.
Location: Dundalk, ON.
Sponsoring Organization: Dundalk Herald (see Competitions).

Mariposa: The Festival of Roots Music

Date: June 22-24.
Location: Molson Park, Barrie, ON.
Sponsoring Organization: Mariposa Folk Foundation (see Associations).

Jazzfest International Victoria BC

Date: June 22-July 1.
Location: Market Square Courtyard, Victoria, BC.
Sponsoring Organization: Victoria Jazz Society.

Earthsong

Location: Dundurn Park, Hamilton, ON.
Date: June 29-July 2, 1990.
Sponsoring Organization: Creative Arts Inc.

Festival International de Jazz de Montreal

Date: June 29-July 8, 1990.
Location: Downtown Montreal, PQ.
Sponsoring Organization: Festival International de Jazz de Montreal.

JULY

Teen Choir Camp '90, St. Peter's Abbey

Date: July 1-7, 1990.
Location: Muenster, SK.
Sponsoring Organization: Saskatchewan Choral Federation (see Associations).

Maritime Old Time Fiddling Contest

Date: July 6-7.
Location: Prince Andrew High School Auditorium, Dartmouth, NS.
Sponsoring Organization: Saint Thomas More Council of Catholic Men.

Canadian Open Country Singing Contest

Date: July 6-8.
Location: Simcoe, ON.
Sponsoring Organization: Board of Directors (see Competitions).

Northern Lights Festival Boreal

Date: July 6-8.
Location: Bell Park Amphitheatre, Sudbury, ON.
Sponsoring Organization: Northern Lights Festival Boreal.

Quinte Summer Music Festival

Date: July 6-22.
Location: Various sites, Picton, ON.
Sponsoring Organization: Quinte Summer Music.

Maritime Old Time Jamboree

Date: July 8.
Location: Beazley Sport Field, Dartmouth, NS.
Sponsoring Organization: Saint Thomas More Council of Catholic Men.

International Symphony Summer Strings

Date: July 9-13.
Location: Sarnia, ON.

Academy of Advanced Study

Date: July 13-August 5.
Location: Parry Sound, ON.

Festival of the Sound

Date: July 13-August 5.
Location: Festival Hall, Parry Sound, ON.
Sponsoring Organization: Festival of the Sound (see Music Festivals).

Harmony Intensive Training School

Date: July 18-21.
Location: Geneseo State College, Geneseo, NY.
Sponsoring Organization: Harmony, Inc.

Shawnigan Lake Music Holiday

Date: July 22-29.
Location: Shawnigan Lake, BC.
Sponsoring Organization: West Coast Amateur Musicians Society.

Ontario Open Fiddle and Stepdance Competition

Date: July 27-28.
Location: Arena, Bobcaygeon, ON.

The Elora Festival

Date: July 27-August 12.
Location: Elora, ON.
Sponsoring Organization: The Elora Festival (see Music Festivals).

Acadia Summer Workshop

Date: July 28-August 4.
Location: Anapolis Valley, NS.
Sponsoring Organization: Acadia University (see Music Camps).

Saskatchewan Sings '90

Date: July 29-August 4.
Location: University of Saskatchewan, Music Department, Saskatoon, SK.
Sponsoring Organization: Saskatchewan Choral Federation.

Scarborough Arts Council Songwriting Competition

Date: TBA.
Location: Scarborough, ON.
Sponsoring Organization: Scarborough Arts Council (see Financial Aid).

AUGUST

Les Arcadiades

Date: August 3-11.
Location: Saint-Antoine, NB.
Sponsoring Organization: A Coeur Joie, NB.

Hornby Island Festival

Date: August 8-12.
Location: Hornby Island, BC.
Sponsoring Organization: Hornby Island Festival.

Canadian Open Championship Old Time Fiddler's Contest

Date: August 10-11.
Location: Shelburne Sports Complex, Shelburne, ON.
Sponsoring Organization: Shelburne Rotary Club.

Festival of Friends
Date: August 10-12.
Location: Gage Park, Hamilton, ON.
Sponsoring Organization: Creative Arts Inc.

Adventures in Summer Music
Date: August 13-17.
Location: Red Deer, AB.
Sponsoring Organization: Red Deer College (see Music Camps).

RCCO National Convention
Date: August 14-17.
Location: Inn on 7th, Edmonton, AB.
Sponsoring Organization: RCCO Edmonton Centre.

Sunfest
Date: August 17-19.
Location: Victoria, BC.
Sponsoring Organization: Victoria Jazz Society.

Music Camp '90
Date: August 19-25.
Location: Newfoundland.
Sponsoring Organization: Memorial University of Newfoundland (see Music Camps).

41st Annual Conference and General Meeting
Date: August 24-26.
Location: University of Regina, Regina, SK.
Sponsoring Organization: Federation of Canadian Music Festivals (see Music Festivals).

Festival Musical 1990
Date: August 25.
Location: Universite of Montreal, Montreal, PQ.
Sponsoring Organization: Federation des Associations Musicales du Quebec (F.A.M.Q. - see Associations)

Inter-Provincial Music Camp
Date: August 25-September 2.
Location: (see Music Camps).

CIBC National Music Festival
Date: August 27-29.
Location: University of Regina, Regina, SK.
Sponsoring Organization: Federation of Canadian Music Festivals (see Music Festivals).

SEPTEMBER

Algoma Fall Festival
Date: TBA.
Location: Algoma, ON.
Sponsoring Organization: Algoma Arts Festival Association (see Associations).

CASBY Music Awards
Date: TBA
Location: Unconfirmed.
Sponsoring Organization: CFNY-FM (see Awards).

Toronto Arts Awards
Date: TBA
Location: Toronto, ON.
Sponsoring Organization: Toronto Arts Awards Foundation (see Awards).

Country Music Week '90
Date: September 3-9.
Location: Edmonton, AB.
Sponsoring Organization: Canadian Country Music Association (see Associations).

Canadian Country Music Awards
Date: September 8.
Location: Edmonton, AB.
Sponsoring Organization: CCMA (see Awards).

Mariposa In The Park
Date: September 8.
Location: Christie Pits, Toronto, ON.
Sponsoring Organization: Mariposa Folk Foundation (see Associations).

The CE-EX Show
Date: September 8-10.
Location: Toronto Airport Hilton, Toronto, ON.
Sponsoring Organization: C.A.E.M. (See Consumer and Trade Shows).

Focus On Video '90.
Date: September 13-19.
Location: Canadian Exposition Conference Centre, Toronto, ON.
Sponsoring Organization: Premiere Magazine/Promex Productions.

Congres annuel des directeurs musicaux des harmonies du Quebec

Date: September 21-23.
Location: Camp Musical d'Asbestos, Asbestos, PQ.
Sponsoring Organization: Federation des Harmonies du Quebec.

SRMTA Convention

Date: September 21-23.
Location: Regina, SK.
Sponsoring Organization: SRMTA, Regina Branch.

Toronto Arts Week

Date: September 22-30.
Location: Toronto, ON.
Sponsoring Organization: Toronto Arts Award Foundation (see Awards).

OCTOBER

Dimensions '90

Date: October 2-4.
Location: Metro Toronto Convention Centre, Toronto, ON.
Sponsoring Organization: A/V Shows Canada Ltd. (See Consumer and Trade).

K-W Oktoberfest Thanksgiving Day Parade

Date: October 8.
Location: Kitchener, ON.
Sponsoring Organization: K-W Oktoberfest Inc. (see Festivals).

Gala de l'ADISQ

Date: October 21.
Location: Place des Arts, Montreal, PQ.
Sponsoring Organization: ADISQ (see Awards).

CBC Radio Competition for Young Composers

Date: TBA.
Location: Quebec, PQ.
Sponsoring Organization: CBC (see Competitions).

Canadian Dream Festival

Date: TBA.
Location: Toronto, ON.
Sponsoring Organization: JCO Communications (see Competitions).

Showcase Canada in Los Angeles

Date: TBA.
Location: Hollywood, CA.
Sponsoring Organization: The Joey Cee Organization.

NOVEMBER

Alberta Music Conference

Date: November 8-10.
Location: Calgary, AB.
Sponsoring Organization: Alberta Choral Federation.

Saskatchewan Talent Showcase

Date: November 9-11.
Location: Saskatoon, SK.
Sponsoring Organization: Saskatchewan Recording Industry Association. (see Associations).

1990 International Annual Convention and Contests

Date: November 14-18.
Location: Inn On The Park, Toronto, ON.
Sponsoring Organization: Harmony, Inc.

World of Commodore

Date: November 29 - December 2.
Location: Toronto International Centre, Toronto, ON.
Sponsoring Organization: Hunter-Nichols Inc. (see Consumer and Trade Shows).

Francofolies de Montreal

Date: November 30 - December 9.
Location: Spectrum de Montreal, Place des Arts, Montreal, PQ.
Sponsoring Organization: Les Francofolies de Montreal.

DECEMBER

Toronto Music Awards
Date: TBA.
Location: Toronto, ON.
Sponsoring Organization: CILQ-FM107 (see Awards).

1991

JANUARY

OSM Concours
Date: January, TBA.
Location: Montreal, PQ.
Sponsoring Organization: Orchestre Symphonique de Montreal.

World Music - Staro Selo
Date: TBA.
Location: Music Gallery, 1087 Queen St. W., Toronto ON.
Sponsoring Organization: CCMC Music Gallery (see Associations).

Demo Listen Derby
Date: January, TBA.
Location: Various live music venues, Vancouver, BC.
Sponsoring Organization: Pacific Music Industry Association.

FEBRUARY

A Celebration of Drums
Date: TBA.
Location: Faculty of Music, University of Western Ontario, London, ON.
Sponsoring Organization: Ontario Percussive Arts Society (see Associations).

Sunderland Lions Music Festival
Date: TBA.
Location: Sunderland Town Hall and Sunderland United Church, Sunderland, ON.
Sponsoring Organization: Sunderland Lions Club (see Music Festivals).

Purcell Quartet at Hycroft
Date: TBA.
Location: Hycroft Manor, Vancouver, BC.
Sponsoring Organization: Purcell Concert Society (see Associations).

Downtowners Optimist Band and Vocal Jazz Festival
Date: TBA.
Location: Saskatchewan Centre of the Arts, Regina, SK.
Sponsoring Organization: Downtowners Optimist Club of Regina (see Music Festivals).

Porcupine Music Festival
Date: February-March
Location: Timmins, ON.
Sponsoring Organization: (see Competitions).

Cariboo (Art) Festival
Date: February-March
Location: Williams Lake (various schools and churches) Williams Lake, BC.
Sponsoring Organization: Cariboo Festival Society (see Music Festivals).

MARCH

Saskatchewan Music Festival Association Concerto Competition
Date: TBA.
Location: Regina, SK.
Sponsoring Organization: Saskatchewan Music Festival Association (see Music Festivals).

l'International Montreal
Date: TBA.
Location: Complexe Sportif Claude Robillard, Montreal, PQ.
Sponsoring Organization: F.A.M.Q. et Les Sonnor de la Prairie (see Music Festivals).

Scotia Festival Winter Series
(Shostakovich String Quartet)
Date: TBA.
Location: Canadian Martyrs Parish Church, Halifax, NS.
Sponsoring Organization: Scotia Chamber Players.

Dreaming of Beauty
Date: TBA.
Location: Music Gallery, Toronto, ON.
Sponsoring Organization: CCMC Music Gallery.

Pacific Northwest Music Festival
Date: TBA.
Location: Terrace, BC.

Musicfest
Date: TBA.
Location: West Point Grey United Church, Vancouver, BC.
Sponsoring Organization: West Coast Amateur Musicians Society (see Associations).

Juno Awards Show
Date: TBA.
Location: O'Keefe Centre, Toronto, ON.
Sponsoring Organization: Canadian Academy of Recording Arts and Sciences (see Associations).

Inde
Date: TBA.
Location: Harbourfront, Toronto, ON.
Sponsoring Organization: Dance Umbrella of Ontario.

Lethbridge and District Kiwanis Music Festival
Date: March - April.
Location: Lethbridge, AB.
Sponsoring Organization: Kiwanis Club of Lethbridge (see Music Festivals).

Festival of Canadian Choral Music
Date: TBA.
Location: First Presbyterian Church, Regina SK.
Sponsoring Organization: Saskatchewan Choral Federation (see Associations).

APRIL

Oshawa-Whitby Kiwanis Music Festival
Date: TBA.
Location: Oshawa.
Sponsoring Organization: Kiwanis Club of Oshawa-Whitby.

Sackville Music Festival
Date: TBA.
Location: Sackville, NB and Amherst, NS.
Sponsoring Organization: Sackville Music Festival Association.

Okanagan Valley Music Festival
Date: TBA.
Location: Okanagan Valley Music Festival, Penticton, BC.
Sponsoring Organization: Okanagan Valley Music Festival Society of Penticton.

Canadian Festival of Youth Orchestras
Date: TBA.
Location: The Banff Centre, Banff, AB.
Sponsoring Organization: Canadian Association of Youth Orchestras (see Associations and Orchestras).

New Glasgow Folk Song Competition
Date: TBA.
Location: New Glasgow, ON.
Sponsoring Organization: New Glasgow Music Festival Association.

Dance Highlights Concert
Date: TBA.
Location: Community Centre Theatre, Penticton, BC.
Sponsoring Organization: Okanagan Valley Music Festival Society.

Music Highlights Concert
Date: TBA.
Location: Penticton Secondary School Auditorium, Penticton, BC.
Sponsoring Organization: Okanagan Valley Music Festival Society.

Six Pianos
Date: TBA.
Location: Premiere Dance Theatre, Toronto, ON.
Sponsoring Organization: ARRAYMUSIC (see Orchestras).

New Brunswick Competitive Festival of Music
Date: TBA.
Location: Local high schools and churches, Saint John, NB.
Sponsoring Organization: New Brunswick Competitive Festival of Music.

Computer Expo
Date: TBA.
Location: Toronto International Centre, Toronto, ON.
Sponsoring Organization: Task Corp. (See Consumer and Trade Shows).

Canadian Collector's Congress
Date: TBA.
Location: Ramada Inn, Toronto, ON.
Sponsoring Organization: West Mississauga Jazz Muddies.

The Montreal Classical Music Festival
Date: TBA.
Location: Marianopolis College, Montreal, PQ.
Sponsoring Organization: The Montreal Classical Music Festival.

Calgary Kiwanis Music Festival
Date: April - May.
Location: Calgary, AB.
Sponsoring Organization: Calgary Kiwanis Music Club (see Competitions).

Midwestern Ontario Rotary Music Festival
Date: April - May.
Location: Walkerton, ON.
Sponsoring Organization: Walkerton Rotary Club (see Competitions).

Guelph Spring Festival
Date: April - May.
Location: Guelph Churches and auditoriums, Guelph, ON.
Sponsoring Organization: Edward Johnson Music Foundation.

Kiwanis Music Festival of Stratford
Date: TBA.
Location: Stratford, ON.
Sponsoring Organization: Kiwanis Club of Stratford.

MAY

Spring At The Arboretum
Date: TBA.
Location: The Arboretum Centre, University of Guelph, Guelph, ON.
Sponsoring Organization: Department of Music and The Arboretum. (see Music Education).

Make Music Expo
Date: TBA.
Location: Automotive Building, Exhibition Place, Toronto, ON.
Sponsoring Organization: MIAC (see Associations).

MUSICANADA '90
Date: TBA.
Location: Automotive Building, Exhibition Place, Toronto, ON.
Sponsoring Organization: MIAC (see Associations).

Scotia Festival of Music
Date: TBA.
Location: Dalhousie Arts Centre, Halifax, NS.
Sponsoring Organization: Scotia Chamber Players.

CMEA Conference '91: Canada And The Pacific Rim
Date: May 8-11.
Location: University of British Columbia, Vancouver, BC.
Sponsoring Organization: CMEA.

From the Floating World
Date: TBA.
Location: DuMaurier Theatre Centre, Toronto, ON.
Sponsoring Organization: ARRAYMUSIC (see Orchestras).

Association of Canadian Orchestras National Conference
Date: TBA.
Location: Victoria Conference Centre and Empress Hotel, Victoria, BC.
Sponsoring Organization: Association of Canadian Orchestras (see Associations).

WorldMusic - Cymbali
Date: TBA.
Location: Music Gallery, Toronto, ON.
Sponsoring Organization: CCMC Music Gallery.

Edward Johnson Music Competition
Date: TBA.
Location: University of Guelph, Guelph, ON.
Sponsoring Organization: Edward Johnson Music Foundation (see Competitions).

MusicFest Canada
Date: May.
Location: TBA.
Sponsoring Organization: MusicFest Canada.

Festival annuel des Harmonies du Quebec
Date: TBA.
Location: University de Sherbrooke, Sherbrooke, PQ.
Sponsoring Organization: Federation des Harmonies du Quebec.

Hyack Festival Pops Concert
Date: TBA.
Location: New Westminster, BC.
Sponsoring Organization: (see Music Festivals).

CBC National Radio Competition for Amateur Choirs
Date: TBA.
Location: Montreal, PQ.
Sponsoring Organization: CBC (see Competitions).

22nd Montreal International Music Competition
Date: May 22-June 5.
Location: Montreal, PQ.
Sponsoring Organization: Montreal International Music Competition.
Featured Instrument: Violin.

Busking Fest
Date: TBA.
Location: City Hall, Hamilton, ON.
Sponsoring Organization: Creative Arts Inc.

SEPTEMBER

Canadian Country Music Awards
Date: September 14, 1991
Location: Calgary, AB.
Sponsoring Organization: CCMA (see Awards).

Country Music Week '91
Date: Sept. 9-15.
Location: Hamilton, ON.
Sponsoring Organization: Canadian Country Music Association (see Associations).

AMNAQ Annual Conference
Date: September.
Location: Montreal, PQ.
Sponsoring Organization: AMNAQ (see Associations).

NOVEMBER

1991 International Annual Convention and Contests
Date: November 6-10.
Location: Halifax, NS.
Sponsoring Organization: Harmony, Inc. (ScotianAires - Hostess Chapter).

1992

APRIL

Banff International String Quartet Competition
Date: April 19-25.
Location: Banff, AB.
Sponsoring Organization: Banff Centre for the Arts (see Associations).

MAY

23rd Montreal International Music Competition
Date: May 27 - June 5.
Location: Place des Arts, Montreal, PQ.
Sponsoring Organization: Montreal International Music Competition.
Featured Instrument: Piano

SEPTEMBER

Country Music Week '92
Date: September 14-20.
Location: Calgary, AB.
Sponsoring Organization: CCMA (see Associations).

NOVEMBER

1992 International Annual Convention and Contests
Date: November 4-8.
Location: Rochester, NY.
Sponsoring Organization: Harmony, Inc.

This section is a selective listing of recordings by Canadian pop, jazz, country, folk and French artists. The names of groups and artists have been arranged alphabetically within each subsection, as have the titles of their respective LPs and EPs (45 rpm singles are not included). The right-hand column under each group or artist's name lists the record label and/or distributor of the corresponding recording.

The listings are not comprehensive, but selective, based on titles from the last 10-20 years by artists and groups who are still actively recording, or who have been recording until quite recently.

POP/ROCK

Artist & Recording   Label/Distributor

Lee Aaron

Bodyrock	Attic
Call of the Wild	A&M
Lee Aaron	A&M
Lee Aaron(1987)	A&M
Metal Queen	A&M

Bryan Adams

Bryan Adams	A&M
Bryan Adams Collection	A&M
Cuts Like a Knife	A&M
Cuts Like a Knife/You Want It	A&M
Diana	A&M
Heaven	A&M
Into the Fire	A&M
Reckless	A&M
Run to You	A&M
You Want It, You Got It	A&M

Adventures in Paradise
It's Just a Matter of Time .... Quality

After All
How High the Moon.............................Nettwerk

Alta Moda
Alta Moda....................................... Current

Animal Slaves
Dog Eat Dog ....Zulu

Annihilator
Alice in Hell.. MCA

Anvil
Backwaxed...A&M
Forged in Fire...A&M
Forged in Fire/Metal on Metal ....A&M
Hard 'n' Heavy..A&M
Metal on Metal.......................................A&M
Past and Present .... Enigma
Pound for Pound.................................. Enigma
Strength of Steel ....Capitol-EMI

April Wine
Animal Grace................................... Capitol
April Wine .... Capitol
Best of Rock Ballads........................ Capitol
Electric Jewels .... Capitol
First Glance...................................... Capitol
Forever For Now .... Capitol
Greatest Hits.................................... Capitol
Harder...Faster................................. Capitol
Live.. Capitol
Live at the El Mocambo..................... Capitol
Nature of the Beast .... Capitol
On Record.. Capitol
One for the Road.............................. Capitol
Power Play....................................... Capitol
Stand Back...................................... Capitol
Whole World's Going Crazy .... Capitol

The Arrows
Stand Back...A&M
Talk Talk ....A&M
The Lines Are Open...............................A&M

Long John Baldry
Baldry's Out..................................... Capitol
Best of.. Capitol
It Ain't Easy... WEA
Silent Treatment..................................Music Line

The Band
Anthology, Vol.1 .... Capitol
Anthology, Vol.2......................... Capitol
Basement Tapes(with Dylan)......................CBS
Best of(Mid Line) .... Capitol
Last Waltz .... WEA
Moon Dog Matinee................................ Capitol
Music from the Big Pink........................ Capitol
Northern Lights/Southern Cross.......... Capitol
Rock of Ages, Vol.1............................. Capitol
Rock of Ages, Vol.2............................. Capitol
Stage Fright....................................... Capitol
The Band.. Capitol
To Kingdom Come .... Capitol

Willie P. Bennett
The Lucky One....................................Duke St.

Art Bergmann
Crawl With Me....................................Duke St.
Sexual Roulette...................................Duke St.

Big Bam Boo
Faith and Fairplay............................... MCA

Blue Rodeo
Diamond Mine............................. Risque Disque
Outskirts...................................... Risque Disque

Body Electric
Body Electric ....A&M
Two Worlds..A&M
Walking Through Walls .... Parallel One

Boulevard
Blvd... MCA
Into the Street .... MCA

The Box
All the Time, All the Time, All the Time...........Alert
Closer Together................................... Alert
The Pleasure and the Pain.......................... Alert

The Breit Bros.
The Breit Bros......................................RCA

Brighton Rock
Brighton Rock .... WEA
Take a Deep Breath .... WEA
Young, Wild and Free.......................... WEA

Danny Brooks
After The Storm ....Duke St.

Bruno Gerussi's Medallion
In Search of the Fourth Chord .... WEA

Candi
Candi .... IRS

Andrew Cash
Boomtown .... Island
Time and Place .... Island

Chalk Circle
Mending Wall .... Duke St.
The Great Lake .... Duke St.

Richard Clapton
Solidarity .... Duke St.

Clean Slate
Clean Slate .... Anthem

Tom Cochrane and Red Rider
As Far as Siam .... Capitol
Breaking Curfew .... Capitol
Don't Fight It .... Capitol
Neruda .... Capitol
The Symphony Sessions .... Capitol
Tom Cochrane & Red Rider .... Capitol
Victory Day .... Capitol

Bruce Cockburn
Big Circumstance .... CBS
Bruce Cockburn .... CBS
Circles in the Stream
.... The Master's Collection
Circles in the Stream Live .... CBS
Dancing in Dragon's Jaws .... CBS
Further Adventures of .... CBS
High Winds White Sky .... CBS
Humans .... CBS
In the Falling Dark .... CBS
Inner City Front .... CBS
Joy Will Find a Way .... CBS
Mommy Dust .... CBS
Night Vision .... CBS
Salt, Sun & Time .... CBS
Stealing Fire .... CBS
Sunwheel Dance .... CBS
Trouble with Normal .... CBS
World of Wonders .... CBS
Waiting for a Miracle .... CBS

Leonard Cohen
Best of .... CBS
Leonard Cohen .... CBS
Songs from a Room .... CBS
Songs of Love & Hate .... CBS
Various Positions .... CBS

Cowboy Junkies
Trinity Session .... BMG
The Caution Horses .... BMG

Crash Vegas
Red Earth .... Risque Disque

Terry Crawford
Total Loss of Control .... Attic

Burton Cummings
Burton Cummings .... CBS
Dream of a Child .... CBS
Heart .... CBS
My Own Way to Rock .... CBS
Plus Signs .... Capitol
The Best of .... CBS

Dalbello
Whomanfoursays .... Capitol
She .... Capitol

Deja Voodoo
Cemetary .... Zulu
Too Cool to Live .... Zulu

D.O.A.
Don't Turn Your Back .... Zulu
Let's Wreck The Party .... Zulu
Murder .... Enigma
War on 45 .... Zulu

Aaron Davis
Neon Blue .... Duke St.

A Diamond in the Rough
A Diamond in the Rough .... Virgin

Celine Dion
Unison .... CBS

Double Dare
Double Dare .... Current

Doug & The Slugs

10 Big Ones .... RCA
Cognac & Bologna .... RCA
Music for the Hard of Thinking .... RCA
Popaganda .... A&M
Wrap It .... RCA

Doughboys

Home Again .... Enigma

Annette Ducharme

Blue Girl .... Capitol

Bobby Edwards

Twilight Drive .... Duke St.

Eight Seconds

Almacanter .... PolyGram
Kiss You When it's Dangerous .... PolyGram

William Ellwood

Openings .... Narada
Renaissance .... Narada
Vista .... Narada

Eye Eye

Common Ground .... Duke St.
Just in Time to be Late .... Duke St.

FM

Black Noise .... A&M
Contest .... Duke St.
Tonight .... Duke St.

Maynard Ferguson

High Voltage .... Enigma
High Voltage II .... Enigma

54.40

54.40 .... WEA
Fight for Love .... WEA
Set the Fire .... Mo-Da-Mu
Show Me .... WEA

Louisa Florio

Louisa Florio .... Tembo

Forgotten Rebels

Surfin' on Heroin .... Enigma
Untitled .... Enigma

David Foster

David Foster .... WEA
The Best of .... WEA
The Symphony Sessions .... WEA

Steve Fox

Where the Blue Moon Rises .... Quantum

The Front

Gina's at a Party .... A&M
Underworld .... A&M

Frozen Ghost

Frozen Ghost .... WEA
Nice Place to Visit .... WEA

GNP

Safety Zone .... Virgin

David Gibson

David Gibson .... A&M

Glass Tiger

Diamond Sun .... Capitol
Thin Red Line .... Capitol

Goddo

An Act of Goddo .... PolyGram
Live-Best Seat in the House .... A&M
Pretty Bad Boys .... A&M
Who Cares .... PolyGram

Myles Goodwyn

Myles Goodwyn .... Aquarius

Gowan

Gowan .... CBS
Great Dirty World .... CBS
Strange Animal .... CBS

Grapes of Wrath

Now and Again .... Nettwerk
September Bowl of Green .... Nettwerk
Treehouse .... Nettwerk

Greenway

Serious Business .... WEA

Roman Grey

Edge of the Shadow .... Attic

Hagood Hardy

All My Best.................................Duke St.
All My Best, Vol II,....................Duke St.
As Time Goes By........................A&M
Chasing a Dream ....Duke St.
Christmas Album.........................A&M
Collections...................................A&M
Hagood Hardy.........................Duke St.
Homecoming/Time Goes By.....................A&M
Love Me Closer...........................A&M
Maybe Tomorrow.......................A&M
Night Magic.............................Duke St.
Reflections.................................A&M
Tell Me My Name.......................A&M
The Homecoming.......................A&M

Harlequin

Harlequin IV.................................CBS
Love Crimes.................................CBS
One False Move............................CBS
Radio Romances..........................CBS
Victim of a Song...........................CBS

Corey Hart

Bang.......................................Aquarius
Boy in the Box.........................Aquarius
Fields of Fire ....Aquarius
First Offence...........................Aquarius
Young Man Running ....Aquarius

Haywire

Bad Boys ....Attic
Don't Just Stand There.....................Attic

Jeff Healey Band

See the Light...................................BMG

Helix

Breaking Loose............................. H&S
Long Way to Heaven...............Capitol
No Rest for the Wicked...........Capitol
Over 60 Minutes With..............Capitol
Walkin' The Razor's Edge ......Capitol
White Lace & Black Leather.......... H&S
Wild in the Streets ....Capitol

Dan Hill

Love in the Shadows.........................PolyGram

Honeymoon Suite

Big Prize...................................... WEA
Honeymoon Suite .... WEA
Racing After Midnight.................. WEA
The Singles.................................. WEA

Paul Hyde (& the Payola$)

Here's the World for Ya...................A&M
Turtle Island .... Capitol

Idle Eyes

Idle Eyes...................................... WEA
Love's Imperfection .... WEA

Images in Vogue

Call It Love.................................. WEA
Images In Vogue........................... WEA
In the House............................... Quality
Rituals....................................... WEA
The Spell ....Anthem

Indio

Big Harvest.................................A&M

Terry & Susan Jacks

Into the Past ....A&M
The Poppy Family's Greatest Hits.............A&M

Paul Janz

Electricity....................................A&M
High Strung..................................A&M
Renegade Romantic ....A&M

Colin James

Colin James .... Virgin

Paul James

Rockin' the Blues .... WEA

The Jitters

The Jitters .... Capitol

Michael Jones

Seascapes....................................Narada
Sunscapes ....Narada
After the Rain ....Narada

Sass Jordan

Tell Somebody.........................Aquarius

Sherry Kean

Maverick Heart...........................A&M
People Talk .... Capitol

Kick Axe

Rock the World .... CBS
Vices.. CBS
Welcome to the Club.................... CBS

Killer Dwarfs
Stand Tall.. Maze

Bill King
Magnolia Nights .... WEA

Kings
Are Here .... WEA

Kon Kan
Move to Move... WEA

Mark Korven
Ordinary Man .... Duke St.
Passengers .... Independent

Krokus
Hardware.. PolyGram
Hardware... RCA
Headhunter.. RCA
Metal Rendezvous............................... PolyGram
Metal Rendezvous....................................... RCA
One Vice at a Time...................................... RCA
One Vice at a Time.............................. PolyGram
The Blitz.. RCA

Jim LaMarche
Lamarche.. A&M
Searching for the Sunrise........................... A&M

Daniel Lanois
Acadie.. WEA

Michel Lemieux
Taming the Power Inside................... PolyGram

Robert Leroux
Leroux 79-84.. CBS

Gordon Lightfoot
Back Here on Earth .... Capitol
Best of... Capitol
Cold on the Shoulder .... WEA
Collection.. Fusion
Did She Mention My Name.................... Capitol
Don Quixote.. WEA
Dream Sweet Rose .... WEA
East of Midnight... WEA
Endless Wire.. WEA
Gord's Gold.. WEA
Lightfoot .... Capitol
Old Dan's Records .... WEA
Salute .... WEA
Shadows... WEA
Sit Down Young Stranger .... WEA
Summer Side of Life.................................... WEA
Summertime Dream .... WEA
Sunday Concert...................................... Capitol
Sundown... WEA
The Way I Feel .... Capitol

Colin Linden
The Immortals.. WEA
When the Spirit Comes .... A&M

Baron Longfellow
Prisoner by Design .... PolyGram

Loverboy
Get Lucky .... CBS
Keep it Up .... CBS
Loverboy... CBS
Lovin' Every Minutes of it............................ CBS
Wildside .... CBS

Luba
All or Northing.. Capitol
Between the Earth and Sky.................... Capitol
Luba.. Capitol
Over 60 Minutes With.............................. Capitol
Secrets and Sins .... Capitol

Ray Lyell and the Storm
Ray Lyell and the Storm .... A&M

M+M
Cooling the Medium...................................... RCA
Danseparc... RCA
Metro Music... RCA
Mystery Walk.. RCA
This Is the Ice Age....................................... RCA
Trance and Dance.. RCA

Kenny MacLean
Don't Look Back ....*Justin*

Rita MacNeil
Born a Woman ....*Canadian Folk*
Flying on Your Own ....*Virgin*
Now the Bells Ring ....*Virgin*
Rita ....*Virgin*

Frank Marino
Fall Circle ....*Maze*

Hugh Marsh
The Bear Walks ....*Duke St.*
Shaking the Pumpkin ....*Duke St.*

Nancy Martinez
For Tonight ....*WEA*
Move Out ....*WEA*
Not Just the Girl ....*WEA*
Unpredictable ....*A&M*

Max Webster
The Best of Max Webster ....*Anthem*
Diamonds Diamonds ....*Capitol*
High Class in Borrowed Shoes ....*Capitol*
Live Magnetic Air ....*Capitol*
Max Webster ....*Capitol*
Million Vacations ....*Capitol*
Mutiny Up My Sleeve ....*Capitol*
Universal Juveniles ....*Capitol*

Raymond May
Unadulterated Addiction ....*WEA*

Kate & Anna McGarrigle
Dancer With Bruised Knees ....*WEA*
Kate & Anna McGarrigle ....*WEA*
Love Over and Over ....*PolyGram*
Pronto Monto ....*WEA*

Ellen McIlwaine
Looking for Trouble ....*WEA*

Sarah McLachlan
Touch ....*Nettwerk*

Men Without Hats
Adventures of Women and Men Without Hate in the 21st Century ....*PolyGram*
Freeways ....*WEA*
Moonbeams ....*PolyGram*
Pop Goes the World ....*PolyGram*
Rhythm of Youth ....*WEA*
Where do Boys Go ....*WEA*

Mendelson Joe
Born to Cuddle ....*Anthem*
Some of the Best of ....*WEA*

Scott Merritt
Desperate Cosmetics ....*Little Jona*
Gravity Is Mutual ....*Duke St.*
Serious Interference ....*Duke St.*
Violet & Black ....*Duke St.*

Messenjah
Session ....*WEA*

Frank Mills
A Special Christmas ....*Capitol*
Look at Me Real ....*PolyGram*
Music Box Dancer ....*Capitol*
My Piano ....*Capitol*
Prelude to Romance ....*Capitol*
Rondo ....*Capitol*
Sunday Morning Suite ....*Capitol*
The Traveller ....*Capitol*

Mindstorm
Mindstorm ....*Aquarius*

The Minglewood Band
Me & The Boys ....*Quality*
Minglewood Band ....*RCA*

Bruce Mitchell
Dancing on the Edge ....*Narada*
Hidden Pathways ....*Narada*

Joni Mitchell

Blue.. WEA
Chalk Mark in a Rainstorm...................... WEA
Clouds .... WEA
Court & Spark .... WEA
Dog Eat Dog .... WEA
Don Juan's Reckless Daughter............... WEA
For the Roses...................................... WEA
Hejira... WEA
Hissing of Summer Lawns .... WEA
Joni Mitchell....................................... WEA
Ladies of the Canyon .... WEA
Miles of Aisles..................................... WEA
Mingus... WEA
Shadows & Light .... WEA
Wild Things Run Fast............................ WEA

Kim Mitchell

Akimbo Alogo......................................PolyGram
Kim Mitchell .... Capitol
Rockland... Alert
Shakin'like a Human Being....................... Alert

Modern Man

Modern Man ....Aquarius

Moev

Dusk & Desire......................................Nettwerk
Yeah, Whatever....................................Nettwerk

Monuments Galore

Monuments Galore................................. Eureka

Rick Moranis

You, Me,the Music and Me............................ IRS

Ann Mortifee

Baptism .... Capitol
Born To Live .... WEA
Bright Encounter.................................. WEA
Ecstacy of Rita Joe .... WEA
Journey to Kairos .... WEA
Reflections.. WEA

Anne Murray

A Country Collection .... Capitol
A Little Good News................................ Capitol
A Love Song... Capitol
Anne Murray Country............................ Capitol
Annie .... Capitol
As I Am... Capitol
Christmas Wishes................................. Capitol
Country Collection(Mid Line)................. Capitol
Danny's Song .... Capitol
Greatest Hits....................................... Capitol
Greatest Hits, Vol. 2 .... Capitol
Heart Over Mind .... Capitol
Highly Prized Possession...................... Capitol
Hippo in my Tub................................... Capitol
Honey, Wheat & Laughter...................... Capitol
Hottest Night....................................... Capitol
I'll Always Love You .... Capitol
Keeping in Touch.................................. Capitol
Let's Keep it That Way .... Capitol
Reason to Believe .... Capitol
Snowbird... Capitol
Somebody's Waiting.............................. Capitol
Something to Talk About........................ Capitol
Straight, Clean & Simple .... Capitol
Talk it over in the Morning..................... Capitol
Together .... Capitol
Where Do You Go When You Dream .. Capitol

Alannah Myles

Alannah Myles..................................... WEA

Mystery Romance

Human Sexuality .... Current

National Velvet

National Velvet..................................... Capitol
Courage .... Capitol

Neo A4

Desire...Duke St.
The Hard Way.......................................Duke St.
NEO A4 ....Duke St.
The Warmer Side of You............... Independent

New Regime

New Regime .... RCA
Play to Win.. RCA

The Northern Pikes

Big Blue Sky .... Virgin
The Northern Pikes............................... Virgin
Snow in June .... Virgin

The Nylons
Happy Together .... Attic
The Nylons .... Attic
One Size Fits All................................... Attic
Rockapella .... Attic
Seamless .... Attic

Mary Margaret O'Hara
Miss America................................... Virgin

One to One
Forward Your Emotions............................... WEA
1-2-1 .... WEA

The Parachute Club
At The Feet of the Moon .... RCA
Moving Thru Moonlight .... RCA
The Parachute Club.................................... RCA
Small Victories....................................... RCA

Paradox
Paradox .... MCA

Partland Brothers
Electric Honey.................................. Capitol
Between Worlds .... Capitol

Picture Comes to Life
Picture Comes to Life.................................BMG

Rob Piltch
Rob Piltch .... Duke St.

Plastercine Replicas
Glow .... Raining Records

Platinum Blonde
Alien Shores..................................... CBS
Contact.. CBS
Crying Over You .... CBS
Standing in the Dark............................. CBS
Platinum Blonde.................................. CBS

Brian Plummer
And the Suspects.................................... Duke St.

Pretty Green
Pretty Green.......................................Nettwerk

Peter Pringle
Noel Coward - A Portrait .... Aquarius

The Pursuit of Happiness
I'm an Adult Now .... WEA
Love Junk..................................... Chrysalis

Rare Air
Hard to Beat.................................. WEA

Rational Youth
Cite Phosphore/Power Zone..................... CBS
Heredity....................................... Capitol
I Want to See/Coboloid Race................... CBS
In Your Eyes/Hot Streets....................... Capitol
Rational Youth .... Capitol
Saturday in Silesia/Pile ou face .... CBS

The Razorbacks
Live a Little.................................. WEA
The Razorbacks Go to Town .... WEA

Refugee
Burning from the Inside Out .... PolyGram
Survival in the Western World .... PolyGram

Regatta
Regatta..BMG

Robbie Robertson
Robbie Robertson.. WEA

Rock & Hyde
Under the Volcano .... Capitol

Don Ross
Bearing Straight.................................... Duke St.

Walter Rossi
All the Best..Aquarius
Six Strings Nine Lives.........................Aquarius

Rush

All the World's a Stage .... Capitol
Archives .... Capitol
Caress of steel .... Capitol
Exit Stage Left .... Capitol
A Farewell to Kings .... Capitol
Fly by Night .... Capitol
Grace Under Pressure .... Capitol
Hemispheres .... Capitol
Hold Your Fire .... Anthem
Moving Pictures .... Capitol
Permanent Waves .... Capitol
Power Windows .... Capitol
Presto .... Anthem
Rush .... Capitol
A Show of Hands .... Capitol
Signals .... Capitol
2112 .... Capitol

Tim Ryan

On Purpose .... Duke St.

Saga

Behaviour .... Maze
Heads or Tales .... A&M
Images at Twilight .... A&M
Images/Silent Knight .... A&M
In Transit .... A&M
Saga .... A&M
Saga/World's Apart .... A&M
Silent Knight .... A&M
Wildest Dream .... A&M
World's Apart .... A&M

Buffy Sainte-Marie

Best of .... Quality
Country Girl Again .... Quality
Fire and Fleet .... Quality
Illuminations .... Quality
Little Wheel .... Quality
Native Child-Odyssey .... Quality
Wanna Be A Ballerina .... Quality
Best of, Vol.2 .... Quality

Eddie Schwartz

No Refuge .... A&M
Public Life .... WEA
Schwartz .... A&M

Lorraine Segato

Pheonix .... WEA

Sheree

Sheree .... BMG

Jane Siberry

Bound by the Beauty .... Duke St.
Jane Siberry .... Fusion
No Borders Here .... Duke St.
The Speckless Sky .... Duke St.
The Walking .... Duke St.

Silver & Degazio

Just Between Us .... A&M

Skinny Puppy

Bites .... Nettwerk
Cleanse, Fold and Manipulate .... Nettwerk
MindTPI .... Nettwerk
VIVI sect VI .... Nettwerk

Skydiggers

Skydiggers .... Capitol

Spirit of the West

Tripping up the Stairs .... WEA
Labour Day .... WEA
Old Material .... WEA
Save This House .... WEA

The Spoons

Arias & Symphonies .... WEA
Bridges Over Borders .... Anthem
Listen to the City .... Ready
Nova Heart .... WEA
Stick Figure Neighbourhood .... WEA
Talk Back .... WEA
Tell No Lies .... WEA
Vertigo Tango .... Anthem

Strange Advance

The Distance Between .... Current
IV .... A&M
2WO .... Capitol
Worlds Away .... Capitol

Terry Sumsion

Midnight Invitation .... WEA
Our Lovin' Place .... WEA

Strangeways

Strangeways .... WEA

Sword

Sweet Dreams .... Aquarius

Tchukon

Here & Now .... Aquarius

The Tear Garden
Tired Eyes, Slowly Burning ....Nettwerk

Teenage Head
Endless Party... WEA
Frantic City ....PolyGram
Some Kinda Fun.....................................PolyGram

Ian Thomas
Glider... Capitol
Greatest Hits.. Capitol
Levity... WEA
Riders on Dark Horses............................ Capitol
The Runner.. Capitol

Ken Tobias
Dream No.2...Attic
Every Bit of Love.....................................Attic
Friends.. CBS
Gallery..CBC
The Magic's in the Music.........................Attic
Siren Spell ....Attic
So Far So Good ....Attic
Street Ballet..Attic

The Tragically Hip
The Tragically Hip.. MCA
Up to Here.. MCA

Triumph
Allied Forces ....PolyGram
Classics.. MCA
Just a Game..PolyGram
Never Surrender ....PolyGram
Progressions of Power ....PolyGram
Rock 'n' Roll Machine.......................PolyGram
Sport of Kings... MCA
Stages... MCA
Surveillance.. MCA
Thunder 7 .... MCA
Triumph...PolyGram

Trooper
Flying Colours... MCA
Hot Shots.. MCA
The Last of the Gypsies........................... WEA
Two for the Show.................................... MCA

Tu
Siamese Kiss...RCA

Cindy Valentine
Secret Rendezvous ....PolyGram

Gino Vannelli
Big Dreamers Never Sleep...............PolyGram
Black Cars...PolyGram
Brother to Brother ....A&M
Brother/Powerful People ....A&M
Crazy Life..A&M
Gist of the Gemini...................................A&M
Money..PolyGram
Nightwalker... RCA
A Pauper in Paradise...............................A&M
Powerful People......................................A&M
Storm at Sunup ....A&M
The Best of ....A&M
Wild Horses...PolyGram

The Viletones
Saturday Night, Sunday Morning..............Zulu

Virgin Steel
Virgin Steel .... Maze
Burn The Sun... Maze
Noble Savage.. Maze

Vogen
Berlin Wall... WEA

Voivod
Nothingface... MCA

The Wardells
The Wardells..Zulu

Watertown
No Singing At The Dinner Table............... WEA

The Waterwalk
The Waterwalk ....Nettwerk

David Wilcox
Bad Reputation.. Capitol
Best of... Capitol
My Eyes Keep Me In .... Capitol
The Natural Edge .... Capitol
Out of the Woods .... Capitol

Bob Wiseman
In Her Dream............................... Risque Disque

The Works
From Out of Nowhere ....A&M

SELECTED DISCOGRAPHY

Neil Young

After the Goldrush .... WEA
American Stars 'n' Bars .... WEA
Comes a Time .... WEA
Decade .... WEA
Everybody Knows .... WEA
Everybody's Rock .... WEA
Freedom .... WEA
Harvest .... WEA
Hawks & Doves .... WEA
Journey Through the Past .... WEA
Landing .... WEA
Life .... WEA
Live Rust .... WEA
Neil Young .... WEA
Old Ways .... WEA
On the Beach .... WEA
Re-Ac-Tor .... WEA
Rust Never Sleeps .... WEA
This Note's for You .... WEA
Time Fades Away .... WEA
Tonight's the Night .... WEA
Trans .... WEA
Zuma .... WEA

Zappacosta

Zappacosta .... Capitol

COUNTRY/FOLK/ TRADITIONAL

Carroll Baker

A Step in the Right Direction .... Tembo
All for the Love of a Song .... RCA
At Home in the Country .... Tembo
Carroll Baker .... RCA
Greatest Hits .... K-Tel
Greatest Hits .... RCA
Heartbreak to Happiness .... Tembo
Hollywood Love .... RCA
I'd Go Thru It All Again .... RCA
If it Wasn't for You .... RCA
Sweet Sensation .... RCA
20 Country Classics .... TeeVee

Gary Buck

Blossom/I'm Glad You Finally
Got Around to Me .... Tembo

Terry Carisse

A Gospel Gathering .... Savannah
The Closest Thing to You .... Savannah
None of the Feeling is Gone .... Savannah
That Was A Long Time Ago .... WEA

The Carter Family

Breaking Tradition .... ARC Sound
Green Fields of Virginia .... RCA
On Border Radio .... Fusion
Vol.I 1928-34 .... Hillcan
Vol.II 1935-36 .... Hillcan
Vol.III 1936-40 .... Hillcan
Vol.IV 1934-41 .... Hillcan

Stompin' Tom Connors

The Hockey Song .... Pose
60 More Old Time Favorites .... Pose
At the Gumboot Cloggeroo .... Pose
Bringing Them Back .... Pose
Bud the Spud .... Pose
Live at the Horseshoe .... Pose
Meets Big Joe Mufferaw .... Pose
Meets Muk Tuk Annie .... Pose
Merry Christmas Everybody .... Pose
My Stompin' Grounds .... Pose
North Atlantic Squadron .... Pose
Northlands Zone .... Pose
Pistol Packin' Mama .... Pose
The Unpopular .... Pose
To It & At It .... Pose
Fiddle and Song .... Capitol

The Corndogs

Tell Your Friends There's Friends
Around .... BMG

Dick Damron

The Legend & the Legacy .... RCA

Family Brown

Best of .... RCA
Feel the Fire .... RCA
Life & Times .... BMG
Raised on Country Music .... RCA
Repeat After Me .... RCA
These Days .... BMG

Gary Fjellgaard

Ballads and Beer .... Royalty
Heart of a Dream .... WEA
Me and the Martin .... Royalty
No Time to Lose .... Savannah
Time and Innocence .... Slim Creek

George Fox

George Fox .... WEA
With All My Might .... WEA

616

The Good Brothers
Deliverin' the Goods............................Savannah

Ronnie Hawkins
A Legend in His Spare Time ....CBS
Making it Again ....CBS
Hello Again Mary-Lou ....Epic
Sold Out..Quality

Audie Henry
Heart of the Country.......................................RCA

Kelita
Kelita...Boot
Too Hot to Handle..RCA

k.d. lang
Absolute Torch and Twang.........................WEA
Angel With a Lariat.......................................WEA
Shadowland...WEA
Truly Western Experience ....WEA

Murray McLauchlan
Boulevard ....CBS
Day to Day Dust..CBS
Greatest Hits...CBS
Hard Rock Town ....CBS
Heroes ....CBS
Into a Mystery...CBS
Live at the Orpheum ....CBS
Midnight Break ....CBS
Murray McLauchlan ....CBS
Only the Silence Remains ....CBS
Song From the Street......................................CBS
Storm Warning..CBS
Sweep the Spotlight Away..............................CBS
Swinging on a Star.....................................Capitol
Timberline...CBS
Whispering Rain..CBS
Windows..CBS

Don Messer
And His Islanders.............................Moss Music
Canadian Gold..MCA
Don Messer Family.........................Moss Music
Down East.......................................Moss Music
The Good Old Days.........................ARC Sound
The Very Best of...MCA

Matt Minglewood
Me and the Boys....................................Savannah
The Promise..Savannah

Anita Perras
Anita & Tim...Savannah
Touch my Heart......................................Savannah

Prairie Oyster
Oyster Tracks ....BMG
Prairie Oyster.. WEA

Stan Rogers
Between the Breaks-Live..........Canadian Folk
Fogarty's Cove ....Canadian Folk
For the Family ....VAL/CFM
From Fresh Water......................Canadian Folk
Northwest Passage ....Canadian Folk
The Complete.............................Canadian Folk
Turnaround ....Canadian Folk

Hank Snow
Best of (Vol.1-2)...RCA
Collector's Series ....RCA
The Highest Bidder..RCA
Hits of..RCA
Hits of (Vol.2)...RCA
I'm Movin' On..RCA
I've Been Everywhere ....RCA
My Early Country Favorites.............................RCA
My Nova Scotia Home......................................RCA
The One and Only Hank Snow.................RCA
Tales of the Yukon ....RCA

Ian Tyson
Irving Berlin is 100 Years .... WEA
Cowboyography.. WEA
Corrals and Sagebrush...............................WEA
Ian Tyson.. WEA
Ol' Eon...A&M
One Jump Ahead of the Devil....................Pose
The Big Spotlight.. WEA
You Were On My Mind ....WEA

Ian & Sylvia Tyson
Best of..Quality
Early Morning Rain ....Quality
Folk Songs..Quality
Four Strong Winds.......................................Quality
Greatest Hits..Quality
Greatest Hits, Vol.2 ....Quality
Northern Journey ....Quality
Play One More ....Quality

Valdy

Country..A&M
Family Gathering ....A&M
Hot Rocks...A&M
Landscapes ....A&M
Notes from Places.........................Duke St.
Passport..A&M
Valdy & The Hometown Band....................A&M

Diamond Joe White

Branded .... WEA
High River.. WEA

Michelle Wright

Do Right By Me................................ WEA

JAZZ AND BLUES

The Canadian Brass

A Touch of Brass...................... Moss Music
Baroque Music.................................... RCA
Best of the Brass .... Moss Music
Canadian Brass ....Trend
Christmas With .... RCA
Greatest Hits...................................... RCA
High, Bright, Light & Clear .... RCA
Mostly Flats .... RCA
Pachelbel Canon .... RCA
The Village Band .... RCA
Unexplored Territory...................... Moss Music

Downchild

Been so Long .... WEA
Gone Fishing .... WEA

Paul Horn

China...Attic
Inside the Cathedral ....Attic
Heart to Heart ....Attic
Inside the Magic of Findhorn................Attic
Jupiter-8...Attic
Live From Russia (With Love)...............Attic
In Concert...Attic
Traveler..Attic
Sketches ....Attic
Live at Palm Beach Casino,
Cannes 1980 ....Attic

Oliver Jones

Lights of Burgundy.........................Fusion
Live at Biddles Jazz & Ribs ....Fusion
Many Moods of................................Fusion
Pianist ....Fusion

Moe Koffman

Back to Back .... Capitol
Best of.. Capitol
Best of (Vol.2)................................... Capitol
If You Don't Know Me........................... WEA
Moe-Mentum...................................Duke St.
One Moe Time..................................Duke St.
Oop Pop a Da ....Duke St.

Ranee Lee

Deep Song ....JustinTime

Liberty Silver

Private Property .... Eureka

Manteca

Fire Me Up ....Duke St.
Manteca ....Duke St.
No Heroes..Duke St.
Perfect Foot ....Duke St.

Rob McConnell & The Boss Brass

Again, Vol.1 .... Trend
Again, Vol.2 .... Trend
All in Good Time .... RCA
Big Band Jazz,Vol.1 .... Trend
Big Band Jazz,Vol.2 .... Trend
Jazz Album...A&M
The Jazz Album .... Trend
The Boss of the Boss Brass................Duke St.

Oscar Peterson

Carioca .... Select
Night Train ....PolyGram
Oscar Peterson.................................. Select
Rarest Performances ....Fusion
Respect to Nat King Cole ....PolyGram
Tristeza ....PolyGram
We Get Requests ....PolyGram
West Side Story ....PolyGram

The Sattalites

Miracles.................................. Risque Disque

Paul Shaffer

Coast to Coast.. Capitol

The Shuffle Demons

Bop Rap .... WEA
Streetniks.. WEA

Skywalk

The Bohemians .... MCA
Silent Witness .... MCA

The Spitfire Band

A Sentimental Journey .... CBS
Flight II .... RCA
Home for the Holidays .... RCA
In Flight .... CBS
The Spitfire Band .... RCA

Uzeb

Between the Lines .... Select
Fast Emotion .... Select
Live in Europe .... Select
Noisy Nights .... Select
Uzeb Club .... Select
You Be Easy .... A&M

FRENCH CANADIAN

Pier Beland

Chante l'amour .... Select
Seduction .... Select

Veronique Beliveau

Borderline .... A&M
Cover Girl .... A&M
Transit .... A&M
Veronique Beliveau .... RCA

Jano Bergeron

Feline .... CBS
Jano Bergeron .... CBS

Pierre Bertrand

Ciel variable .... PolyGram
Esperance .... PolyGram
Pierre Bertrand .... PolyGram

Johanne Blouin

Johanne Blouin .... Select
Merci Felix .... Select

Gerry Boulet

Rendez-vous doux .... Select

Edith Butler

Et le party continue .... Select
Le party d'Edith .... Select
Party pour danser .... Select

Robert Charlebois

Couchemar .... Diskade
Disque d'or Vol.1 .... Diskade
Disque d'or Vol 2 .... Diskade
Nouveaux en amour .... Diskade
Les Grands succes Barclay .... PolyGram
Live in Paris .... Diskade
Longue distance .... Diskade
R. Charlebois .... Diskade
Solide .... Diskade
Super Position .... Diskade
Swing Charlebois swing .... Diskade

Julien Clerc

Aime moi .... A&M
Ce n'est rien .... Select
Disque d'or .... Select
Disque d'or,Vol.2 .... Select
Fommes,Indiscretion,Blaspheme .... A&M
Jaloux .... Diskade
Julien .... Select
Julien Clerc .... Select
Pleurer le bon Dieu .... Select
Preferences .... A&M
Profil,Vol.1 .... Diskade
Si on chantait .... Select
This Melody .... Select

Claude Dubois

Cadeau .... Select
Dubois .... Select
Fable d'espace .... Select
Face a la musique .... Select
Manitou .... Select
Profil,Vol.1 .... Select
Profil,Vol.2 .... Select
Sortie .... Select

Yves Duteil

La langue de chez-nous .... Select
Profil .... Select
Ton Absence .... Select

Lucien Francoeur

Aut' chose .... MTL Gamma
Le Cauchemar American .... CBS
Chaud comme un juke-box .... CBS
Encore .... CBS
Les Gitans reviennent toujours .... A&M
Jour et nuit .... Pelo
Prends une chance avec moe .... CBS
Le retour de Johnny Frisson .... Kebec-Disque
Le rock a l'ecole .... Hasard
Une nuit comme une autre .... CBS

Daniel Lavoie

Aigre doux .... WEA
Nirvana bleu .... MCA
Tension attention .... Diskade
Tips .... Capitol

Herbert Leonard

Disque d'or .... Select
Je suis un grand sentimental .... Select
Laissez-nous rever .... Select

Patrick Norman

12 grands success .... Select
Il pleut a mourir................................ Select
Only Love Sets You Free..................... Select
Quand on est en amour....................... Select
Soyons heureux.................................. Select

Nuance

Vivre dans la nuit .... ISBA

Offenbach

Gaite parisienne............................ Moss Music
Le dernier show .... CBS
Never Too Tender................................A&M
Offenbach..A&M
Offenbach—1972 a 1985..................... Select
Rockorama... CBS
Traversion .... CBS

Michel Pagliaro

Sous peine d'amour .... Select

Paul Piche

A qui appartient le beau temps .... Select
Integral.. Select
Nouvelles d'Europe .... Select
Sur le chemin des incendies.................. Select

Ginette Reno

Ce que j'ai de plus beau........................ Select
Ginette Reno...................................... Select
Je ne suis qu'une chanson...................... Select
Ne m'en veux pas............................... Select
Si ca vous chante .... Select
Souvenirs tendres .... Select

Michel Rivard

Michel Rivard...................................... Select
Sauvage .... Select
Un trou dans les nuages....................... Select

Richard Seguin

Double vie.. Select
En attendant...................................... WEA
Journee d'Amerique .... Select
Recolte de reve .... Capitol
Seguin.. WEA
Trace et contraste...............................PolyGram

Rene & Nathalie Simard

Rene & Nathalie Simard .... Select
Tourne la page.................................... Select
Tout si tu m'aimes............................... Select

Nathalie Simard

Joyeux Noel a tous les enfants .... Select
Village de Nathalie .... Select

Diane Tell

Chimeres..PolyGram
Diane Tell...PolyGram
En flesche..PolyGram
Entre nous ....PolyGram
Faire a nouveau connaissance ....PolyGram
Greatest Hits......................................PolyGram
On a besoin d'amour...........................PolyGram

Top Sonart

Pas de panique .... RCA
Top Sonart .... RCA

Roch Voisine

Helene... Select
Roch Voisine....................................... Select

Doughboys

Home Again .... Enigma

Annette Ducharme

Blue Girl.. Capitol

SUGGESTED READING

REFERENCE

Baker's Biographical Dictionary of Musicians, 6th Edition
Nicholas Slonimsky
(Schirmer Books)

Book of Classical Music Lists
Herbert Kuperberg
(Penguin)

The Canadian Jazz Discography 1916-1980
Jack Litchfield
(University of Toronto Press)

Canadian Music: A Selected Checklist 1950-73
Lynne Jarman
(University of Toronto Press)

Dictionary of Music
Alan Isaacs
(Penguin)

A Dictionary of Musical Quotations
Ian Crofton and Donald Fraser
(Collier MacMillan)

A Dictionary of Musical Terms
Theodore Baker
(Schirmer Books)

Directory of Musical Canada
Wayne Gilpin, ed.
(GLC)

Directory of the Arts
Jocelyne Rouleau
(Canadian Conference of the Arts)

The Electronic Music Dictionary
Craig Anderton
(Music Sales Corp.)

Encyclopedia of Music in Canada
Helmut Kallman, Gilles Potvin and Kenneth Winters, eds.
(University of Toronto Press)

Gigging: The Musician's Underground Touring Directory
Michael Dorf and Robert Appel
(Prentice Hall)

Made In Canada
Martin Melhuish
(Sound And Vision)

Million Selling Records from the 1900s to the 1980s: An Illustrated Directory
Joseph Murrells
(Arco)

Music Directory Canada
Andrew Charron and Richard Allen, eds.
(CM Books)

A Musician's Dictionary
David W. Barber
(Sound And Vision)

The National Radio Guide
Catherine Robertson, ed.
(Core Group)

New College Encyclopedia of Music
J.A. Westrup and F.L. Harrison
(Penguin)

The New Harvard Dictionary of Music
Don Randel
(Belknap Press)

The Performing Arts Handbook
Janice Papolos
(Writer's Digest)

Song Writer's Market 1990
Mark Garvey, ed.
(Prentice Hall)

Who Teaches What
Jocelyne Rouleau
(Canadian Conference of the Arts)

HISTORICAL

Bach, Beethoven and the Boys
David W. Barber and Dave Donald
(Sound and Vision)

Boogie Pete & The Senator: Canadian Musicians in Jazz, the Eighties
Mark Miller
(Nightwood Editions)

Canadian Music of the Twentieth Century
George A. Proctor
(University of Toronto Press)

Closing the Circle: A Cultural History of the Rock Revolution
Herbert I. London
(Nelson-Hall)

Grand Tradition: Seventy Years of Singing on Record (1900-1970)
J. Steane
(Ronald P. Frye and Co.)

The Guitar: The History, the Music, the Players
Gene Santoro
(Musson)

A History of Music In Canada 1534-1914
Helmut Kallman
(University of Toronto Press)

History of Song
Denis Stevens
(Penguin)

The History of the Guitar in Jazz
Norman Mongan
(Music Sales Corp.)

Hymns and the Christian Myth
Lionel Adey
(University of British Columbia Press)

Jazz in Canada
Mark Miller
(University of Toronto Press)

Medieval and Renaissance Music: A Performers Guide
Timothy McGee
(University of Toronto Press)

Music of Canada
Timothy McGee
(Penguin)

Pelican History of Music, Vol. III
Steven Robertson
(Penguin)

Percussion Instruments and Their History
James Blades
(Penguin)

Roll Back the Years: History of Canadian Recorded Sound and its Legacy
(Canadian Government)

A Selected Biography of Musical Canada
Ian L. Bradley
(GLC)

Swinging In Paradise: The Story of Jazz in Montreal
John Gilmore
(Vehicule Press)

Twentieth Century Music
Richard Burbank
(Facts on File)

Yesterday's Popular Song in America
Charles Hanna
(Penguin)

INSTRUCTIONAL

Basics of Ear Training
Boris Berlin and Warren Mould
(Gordon V. Thompson)

Bluegrass Guitar
Happy Traum
(Music Sales Corp.)

Complete Course in Professional Piano Tuning, Repair and Re-building
Floyd A. Stevens
(Nelson-Hall)

Complete Handbook of Songwriting
Mark Liggett
(Penguin)

The Complete Rock & Pop Keyboard Player
Kenneth Baker
(Music Sales Corp.)

Creative Guitar: A Guide to Finger-Style Playing
Eric West
(Jesperson Press)

Elementary Rudiments of Music
Barbara Wharram
(Irwin Publishing)

Everything About Guitar Chords
Wilbur M. Savidge
(Music Sales Corp.)

For All Piano Teachers
Cora Aherns and G.D. Atkinson
(Frederick Harris)

Form and Analysis
Arthur Creighton
(Waterloo)

Heavy Metal Riffs for Bass
David C. Gross
(Music Sales Corp.)

Heavy Metal Riffs for Guitar
Mark Michaels
(Music Sales Corp.)

Home Recording for Musicians
Craig Anderton
(Amsco)

How to Play Saxophone
John Robert Brown
(Penguin)

How to Play the Flute
Howard Harrison
(Penguin)

How to Play Trumpet
Digby Fairweather
(Penguin)

How to Prepare for and take a Practical Music Examination
Daryl Irvine & R.G. Condie
(Frederick Harris)

How to Sing Better
Al Lewis
(New Generation)

Improvising Rock Guitar
Artie Traum and Arti Funaro
(Music Sales Corp.)

Improvising Rock Piano
Jeff Gutcheon
(Music Sales Corp.)

Jazz Riffs for Bass
Rick Laird
(Music Sales Corp.)

Make Your own Music
Peter K. Alfaenger
(Douglas & MacIntyre)

Making Music
George Martin, ed.
(Pan Books)

Materials of Western Music
Andrews and Sclater
(Gordon V. Thompson)

A New Guide to Good Singing
Glenda Nielsen
(The Avondale Press)

Play Rock Keyboards
Dewi Evans
(Music Sales Corp.)

Pop Basslines
Joe Hubbard
(Music Sales Corp.)

Slide Guitar
Arlen Roth
(Music Sales Corp.)

Sound and Symbol:The Rudiments of Music
David Paul
(Irwin Publishing)

The Spectrum of Music
Mary Val Marsh, Caroll Rinehart, Edith Savage
(Collier-MacMillan)

Teach Yourself Drums
Mike Finklestein
(Music Sales Corp.)

What to Listen for in Music
Aaron Copeland
(Penguin)

Writing Music
James Lawless and Tela Podoliak
(Waterloo Music)

You Can Write Great Lyrics
Pamela Phillips Gland
(Prentice-Hall)

BIOGRAPHY/ AUTOBIOGRAPHY

Andrew Lloyd Webber: His life and works
Michael Walsh
(Prentice-Hall)

Barbara Pentland
Sheila Eastman and Timothy McGee
(University of Toronto Press)

Birds of a Different Feather ... My Musical Colleagues
Rivka Golani
(Mosaic)

Born to Run: The Bruce Springsteen Story
Dave Marsh
(Dell)

Bowie
Jerry Hopkins
(Penguin)

Elvis and the Colonel
Dirk Vellenga with Mick Farren
(Dell)

Elvis Costello: A Man out of Time
David Gouldstone
(McClelland & Stewart)

Geza Kresz and Norma Drewett Kresz: An Illustrated Biography
Peter Kivoli and Maria Kresz
(Canadian Stage & Arts Publications)

Glenn Gould: A Life in Variations
Otto Friedrich
(Lester & Orpen Dennys)

The Glenn Gould Reader
Tim Page, ed.
(Lester & Orpen Dennys)

Harry Somers
Brian Cherney
(University of Toronto Press)

Healey Willan: Life and Music
F.R.C. Clarke
(University of Toronto Press)

Lives/John Lennon
Albert Goldman
(Bantam Books)

Lotfi Mansouri: An Operatic Life
Lotfi Mansouri and Aviva Layton
(Mosaic)

Maureen Forrester: Out of Character
Maureen Forrester
(McClelland & Stewart)

Memories and Melodies of World War II
W. Ray Stevens
(Boston Mills Press)

Music from Within: A Memoir from the Composer S.C. Eckhardt-Gramatte
Ferdinand Eckhardt
(University of Manitoba Press)

Musical Canada: Words and Music Honouring Helmut Kallman
John Beckwith and Frederick A. Hall
(University of Toronto Press)

The Musical World of Frances James and Murray Adaskin
Gordana Lazarevich
(University of Toronto Press)

My Orchestras and Other Adventures: The Memories of Boyd Neel
David J. Finch
(University of Toronto Press)

No Direction Home: The life and music of Bob Dylan
Robert Shelton
(Penguin)

Oscar Peterson: The Will to Swing
Gene Lees
(Lester & Orpen Dennys)

R. Murray Shafer
Stephen Adams
(University of Toronto Press)

Recollections of a Violinist
Maurice Solway
(Mosaic)

Unforgettable Fire: The Story of U2
Eamon Dunphy
(Penguin)

BUSINESS/ INDUSTRY

Careers in Music
Thomas Green, Patricia Sauerbrei and Don Sedgwick, eds.
(Irwin Publishing)

Careers in Music: A guide for Canadian Students
Henri Brossard et al.
(Frederick Harris Music)

How to Make and Sell Your Own Record
Diane Rapaport
(Headlands Press)

How to Make Money in Music
Gerby Harris and Lucien Farrar
(Arco)

How to Succeed in the Music Business
Allan Dunn and John Underwood
(Music Sales Corp.)

Inner Game of Music
Green & Gallwey
(Doubleday)

Inside Country Music
Larry E. Wacholtz
(Billboard)

Making Money-Making Music
James W. Dearing
(Writer's Digest)

Music in Advertising
Fred Miller
(Amsco)

The Music Record Career Handbook
Joseph Csida
(Billboard)

A Musician's Guide to the Road
Gary Burton
(Billboard)

Rock 'N' Roll is Here to Pay
Steve Chapple and Reebee Garofalo
(Nelson-Hall)

Some Straight Talk About the Music Business
Mona Coxson
(CM Books)

Successful Artist Management
Xavier M. Frascogna and H. Lee Heatherington
(Billboard)

This Business of Music
Shemel and Krasilovsky, eds.
(Billboard)

TECHNICAL

The Complete Guide to MIDI Software
Howard Massey
(Music Sales Corp.)

The Complete Guide to Synthesizers, Sequencers and Drum Machines
Dean Friedman
(Music Sales Corp.)

Customizing Your Electric Guitar
Adrian Legg
(Music Sales Corp.)

Digital Delay Handbook
Craig Anderton
(Music Sales Corp.)

Electronic Drums
Frank Vilardi and Steve Tarshis
(Music Sales Corp.)

Guitar Gadgets
Craig Anderton
(Music Sales Corp.)

MIDI Basics
Akira Otsuka & Okihiko Nakajima
(Music Sales Corp)

MIDI for Guitarists
Marty Cutler and Bob Ward
(Music Sales Corp.)

MIDI for Musicians
Craig Anderton
(Amsco)

MIDI Gadgets
Eric Turkel
(Music Sales Corp.)

MUSIC through MIDI: Using MIDI to Create Your Own Electronic Music System
Michael Bloom
(Microsoft)

The Rock Synthesizer Manual
Geary Yelton
(Music Sales Corp.)

Understanding MIDI
(Gordon V. Thompson)

FOLK

Coast to Coast Fever
Arthur MacGregor
(Ottawa Folklore Centre)

**Come and I will Sing You:
A Newfoundland Songbook**
Genevieve Lehr
(Breakwater Books)

Cross-Cultural Perspectives on Music
Robert Falck and Timothy Rice
(University of Toronto Press)

The Cultural Connection
Bernard Astry
(McClelland & Stewart)

The Emigrant Experience
Margaret MacDonell
(University of Toronto Press)

**The Folk Festival Book:
The Stories of the Winnipeg Folk Festival**
Steve Johnson, Sheldon Oberman and David Landy
(Turnstone)

**For What I Am in This World:
Stories from Mariposa**
Bill Usher and Linda Page-Harpa
(Irwin)

Lumbering Songs from the Northern Woods
Edith Fowke
(NC Press)

Maritime Folk Songs
Helen Creighton
(Breakwater)

La Musique des Inuit du Caribou: Cinq perspectives methodologiques
Ramon Pelinski
(Universite de Montreal)

Music in a New Found Land
Wilfrid Mellers
(Penguin)

Penguin Book of Canadian Folk Songs
Edith Fowke
(Penguin)

Ring Around the Moon
Edith Fowke
(NC Press)

Singing Mennonite: Low German Songs Among the Mennonites
Doreen Helen Klassen
(University of Manitoba Press)

Songs of the Miramichi
Dr. Louise Manny and James Reginald Wilson
(Brunswick)

STYLISTIC

All that Jazz and More
Christy Lane
(McClelland & Stewart)

Alternative Voices: Essay on Contemporary Vocal and Choral Composition
Istvan Inhalt
(University of Toronto Press)

Contemporary Piano Styles
Bill Evans and Tom Glaser
(Music Sales Corp.)

Essai Stylistique Comparee
Elizabeth Morin
(Universite de Montreal)

The Guiness Jazz
Peter Clayton and Peter Gammond
(Guiness)

Heavy Metal
(Sharon Publications)

Jazz
Henri Matisse
(Firefly)

The Jazz Scene
E.J. Hobsbawm
(McClelland & Stewart)

Look at the Record: An Album of Toronto's Lyric Theatres
Joan Parkhill Baillie
(Mosaic)

Making of Jazz
(Doubleday)

Musicanada
Penny Brooks
(Holt Rinehart & Winston of Canada)

Proposal for a Grammar of Melody
Mario Baroni and Carlo Jacobini
(Universite de Montreal)

Talking Jazz
Max Jones
(Penguin)

A Theory for All Music: Problems and Solutions in the Analysis of Non-Western Forms
Jay Rahn
(University of Toronto Press)

AUDIO/VIDEO

Audio Production Techniques for Video
David Miles Huber
(Howard W. Sams & Co.)

Canada's Video Revolution: Pay-TV, Home Video, and Beyond
Peter Lyman
(James Lorimer & Co.)

The Complete Penguin Stereo, Record and Cassette Guide
Edward Greenfield, Robert Layton, Ivan March
(Penguin)

Frame by Frame
Grenda Weston, ed.
(Frame by Frame Publications)

Modern Recording Techniques
Robert E. Rustern
(Howard W. Sams & Co.)

Music Video: A Consumer's Guide
Michael Shore
(Ballantine Books)

New Sound Stereo
Berger and Fontel
(Penguin)

Penguin Guide to Compact Discs
Edward Greenfield, Robert Layton and Ivan March
(Penguin)

Recording Angel
Evan Eisenberg
(Penguin)

Reel West Digest
Martin M. Borycki and Sandy P.G.
Flanagan, eds.
(Reel West Productions)

BOOK PUBLISHERS

Amsco Publications
Music Sales Corporation
24 E. 22 St.
New York, NY 10010
(212) 254-2100

Arco Publications
215 Park Ave. S.
New York, NY 10003

Avondale Press
3490 St. Andrews Ave.
N. Vancouver, BC V7N 1Z9
(604) 980-2653

Ballantine Books
(Random House)
1-800-726-0600

Bantam Books Canada Inc.
105 Bond St.
Toronto, ON M5B 1Y3
(416) 340-0777

Belknap Press of Harvard University Press
Cambridge, MA
(617) 495-2577

Billboard Books
1515 Broadway
New York, NY 10036
(212) 764-7300

The Boston Mills Press
132 Main St.
Erin, ON N0B 1T0
(519) 833-2407

Breakwater Books
277 Duckworth St.
P.O. Box 2188
St. John's, NF A1C 6E6
(709) 722-6680

Brunswick Press
12 Prospect St. W.
P.O. Box 3370
Fredericton, NB E3B 5A2
(506) 452-6671

CM Books
3284 Yonge St.
Toronto, ON M4N 3M7
(416) 485-1049

Canadian Conference of the Arts Publications
126 York St., Suite 400
Ottawa, ON K1N 5T5
(613) 238-3561

Canadian Government
Publishing Services
Ottawa, ON K1A 0S9
(819) 997-2560

Canadian Stage and Arts Publications Ltd.
52 Avenue Rd.
Toronto, ON M5R 2G2
(416) 971-9516

Collier MacMillan Canada
539 Collier MacMillan Dr.
Cambridge, ON N1R 5W9
(519) 740-2222

Core Group Publishers
450-1040 W. Georgia St.
Vancouver, BC V6E 4H1
(604) 688-0382

Dell Publishing Canada
105 Bond St.
Toronto, ON M5B 1Y3
(416) 340-0777

Doubleday Canada Ltd.
105 Bond St.
Toronto, ON M5B 1Y3
(416) 340-7891

Douglas & McIntyre Ltd.
1615 Venables St.
Vancouver, BC V5L 2H1
(604) 254-7191

Facts on File Publications
460 Park Ave. S.
New York, NY 10016
(212) 638-2244

Firefly Books Ltd.
250 Sparks Ave.
Willowdale, ON M2H 2S4
(416) 499-8412

Frame by Frame Publications
92 Sumach St.
Toronto ON M5A 3J9
(416) 862-7766

Frederick Harris Music
529 Speers Rd.
Oakville, ON L6K 2G4
(416) 845-3487

Gordon V. Thompson Music
29 Birch Ave.
Toronto, ON M4V 1E2
(416) 923-7329

Guiness Superlatives Ltd.
35 London Rd.
Enfield, England

Headlands Press
P.O. Box 862
San Francisco, CA 94920

**Holt Rinehart & Winston
of Canada**
55 Horner Ave.
Toronto ON M8Z 4X6
(416) 255-4491

Howard W. Sams & Company
A Division of MacMillan
Publishing Co. Inc.
4300 W. 62 St.
Indianapolis, IN 46268
(317) 298-5400

Irwin Publishing Inc.
180 W. Beaver Creek Rd.
Richmond Hill, ON L4B 1B4
(416) 660-0611

James Lorimer & Co.
35 Britain St.
Toronto, ON M5A 1R7
(416) 362-4762

Jesperson Press
26A Flavin St.
St. John's, NF A1C 3R9
(709) 753-5700 or 753-0633

Lester & Orpen Dennys
78 Sullivan St.
Toronto, ON M5T 1C1
(416) 593-9602

McClelland & Stewart
481 University Ave., Suite 900
Toronto ON M5G 2E9
(416) 598-1114

Microsoft Press
16011 N.E. 36 Way
P.O. Box 97017
Redmond, WA
98073-9717

Mosaic Press
P.O. Box 1032
Oakville, ON L6J 5E9
(416) 825-2130

Music Sales Corporation
225 Park Avenue S.
New York, NY 10003
(212) 254-2100

Musson Book Company
30 Lesmill Rd.
Don Mills, ON M3B 2T6
(416) 445-3333

NC Press Limited
260 Richmond St. W., Suite 401
Toronto, ON M5V 1W5
(416) 593-6284

Nelson-Hall Publishers
111 N. Canal St.
Chicago, IL 60606
(312) 930-9446

New Generation Systems Co.
2153 Golfcourse
Reston, VA
(703) 742-9714

Nightwood Editions
P.O. Box 1426, Stn. A
London, ON N6A 5M2
(519) 433-0382

Ottawa Folklore Centre Publications
744 Bronson Ave.
Ottawa, ON K1S 4G3
(613) 238-7222

Pan Books Ltd.
Cavaye Place
London, England
SW10 9PG

Penguin Books Canada Ltd.
2801 John St.
Markham, ON L3R 1B4
(416) 475-1571

Prentice-Hall Canada Inc.
1870 Birchmount Rd.
Scarborough, ON M1P 2J7
(416) 293-3621

Reel West Productions Inc.
310-811 Beach Ave.
Vancouver, BC V6B 2Z5
(604) 294-4122

Ronald P. Frye and Company
273 King St. E.
Kingston, ON K7L 3B1
(613) 545-1308

Schirmer Books
A Division of MacMillan
Publishing Co. Inc.
866-3 Third Ave.
New York, NY 10022
1-800-265-8672

Sharon Publications
2801 John St.
Markham, ON L3R 1B4
(416) 475-1571

Sound And Vision
359 Riverdale Ave.
Toronto, ON M4J 1A4
(416) 465-8184

Turnstone Press
St. John's College
University of Manitoba
Winnipeg, MB R3T 2M5
(204)474-9860

The University of British Columbia Press
6344 Memorial Rd.
The University of British Columbia
Vancouver, BC V6T 1W5
(604) 228-3259

University of Manitoba Press
106 Curry Place, Suite 244
University of Manitoba
Winnipeg, MB R3T 2N2
(204) 474-9495

Les Presses de l'Universite de Montreal
P.O. Box 6128, Stn. A
Montreal, PQ H3C 3J7
(514) 343-6929

University of Toronto Press
5201 Dufferin St.
Downsview, ON M3H 5T8
(416) 667-7791

Vehicule Press
P.O. Box 125, Place du Parc Stn.
Montreal, PQ H2W 2M9

Vinylvisions Publishing
P.O. Box 335
West Hill, ON M1E 4R8
(416) 266-2152 (evenings)

Waterloo Music
3 Regina St. N.
P.O. Box 250
Waterloo, ON N2J 4A5
(519) 886-4990

Writer's Digest Books
F & W Publications
9933 Alliance Rd.
Cincinnati, OH 45242
(513) 531-2222

W.W. Norton & Company
500-5 Avenue
New York, NY 10110
1-800-233-4830

TWO DECADES OF CANADIAN CHART TOPPERS

The following is a listing of Canadian singles and albums that made it to the year-end best-selling recording charts compiled by music industry trade publications, *RPM* and *The Record*. The information for 1970-1984 was provided by *RPM* from their top 100 listings, and from 1985-1989 it was provided by *The Record*. The charts are based on sales in Canada of all recordings by Canadian and international artists. The numbers on the right of the column represent that title's position on the year-end chart.

1970 SINGLES

1971 SINGLES

1972 SINGLES

1973 SINGLES

1974 SINGLES

1974 ALBUMS

1975 SINGLES

1975 ALBUMS

1976 SINGLES

1976 ALBUMS

1977 SINGLES

1977 ALBUMS

1978 SINGLES

1978 ALBUMS

1979 SINGLES

1979 ALBUMS

1980 SINGLES

1980 ALBUMS

1981 SINGLES

1981 ALBUMS

1982 SINGLES

1982 ALBUMS

1983 SINGLES

1983 ALBUMS

1984 SINGLES

1984 ALBUMS

1970-1984 Top Singles and Top Albums provided by *RPM*.

1985-1989 Top Albums and Top Singles contributed by *The Record*.

(Year-end charts calculated with sales information provided to
THE RECORD on a confidential basis, by the record companies.)

1985 SINGLES

1985 ALBUMS

1986 SINGLES

1986 ALBUMS

1987 SINGLES

1987 ALBUMS

1988 SINGLES

1988 ALBUMS

TWO DECADES OF CANADIAN CHART TOPPERS

TWO DECADES OF CANADIAN CHART TOPPERS

1989 SINGLES

1989 ALBUMS